D0407961

74024

PS 3529 .N5 Z5676 1999b

Black, Stephen A.

Eugene O'Neill

DATE DUE

ILL			
#4270806			
COS			
4-3-03			
GAYLORD			PRINTED IN U.S.A.

Eugene O'Neill

EUGENE O'NEILL

Beyond Mourning and Tragedy

STEPHEN A. BLACK

[YALE UNIVERSITY PRESS   NEW HAVEN AND LONDON]

RED ROCKS
COMMUNITY COLLEGE LIBRARY

#41580494
74024

PS
3529
·N5
Z5676
1999b

Frontispiece: Eugene O'Neill. Sheaffer-O'Neill Collection,
Charles E. Shain Library, Connecticut College.

Published with assistance from the Kingsley Trust Association
Publication Fund established by the Scroll and Key Society of Yale College.

Copyright © 1999 by Yale University. All rights reserved.
This book may not be reproduced, in whole or in part, including illustrations,
in any form (beyond that copying permitted by Sections 107 and 108 of the
U.S. Copyright Law and except by reviewers for the public press),
without written permission from the publishers.

Materials from the Berg Collection of English and American
Literature are reproduced with permission, the New York
Public Library and Astor, Lenox, and Tilden Foundations.

Library of Congress Cataloging-in-Publication Data

Black, Stephen A.
Eugene O'Neill : beyond mourning and tragedy / Stephen A. Black.
p.   cm.
Includes bibliographical references (p.   ) and index.
ISBN 0-300-07676-2
1. O'Neill, Eugene, 1888–1953—Psychology.   2. O'Neill, Eugene,
1888–1953—Mental health.   3. Psychoanalysis and literature—
United States—History—20th century.   4. Dramatists, American—
20th century—Family relationships.   5. Dramatists. American—
20th century—Psychology.   6. Dramatists, American—20th century
Biography.   7. Drama—Psychological aspects.   I. Title.
PS3529.N5Z5676   1999
812'.52—dc21
[B]   99-33897
CIP

Printed in the United States of America.
A catalogue record for this book is available from the British Library.

The paper in this book meets the guidelines
for permanence and durability of the Committee on
Production Guidelines for Book Longevity of the
Council on Library Resources.

10 9 8 7 6 5 4 3 2

RED ROCKS
COMMUNITY COLLEGE LIBRARY

*For Georgina and Gordon
and Lito, Ashley, and Chelsey*

I'm far from being a pessimist. I see life as a gorgeously-ironical, beautifully-indifferent, splendidly-suffering bit of chaos the tragedy of which gives Man a tremendous significance, while without his losing fight with fate he would be a tepid, silly animal. I say "losing fight" only symbolically for the brave individual always wins. Fate can never conquer his—or her—spirit. So you see I'm no pessimist. On the contrary, in spite of my scars, I'm tickled to death with life! I wouldn't "go out" and miss the rest of the play for anything!

—**Eugene O'Neill, in a letter to Mary Ann Clark, August 8, 1923**

Contents

CONTENTS

[x]

A Word to the Reader

The general facts of Eugene O'Neill's life (1888–1953) have been pretty well established since the early 1970s. Amendments of fact offered here tend to be adjustments based on re-examination of evidence. A slightly different date for an event may be given, for example, than has been stated in other works. Frequently, an oft-repeated anecdote or detail is rejected because, when traced backward from biography to biography, it appears to have originated in the imagination of a feature writer or interviewer. What is new in this biography is the interpretations made both of numerous small matters and of the large patterns of O'Neill's life, interpretations that grow partly out of their author's professional training and experience as a literary scholar, a psychoanalytic researcher, and, for a time, a clinician.

O'Neill has been an irresistible subject for biographers since he first received public attention in the early 1920s. At first he was known for being the son of a famous father, educated in good schools, who had gone to sea several times, had many love affairs, known celebrated radicals and bohemians, prospected for gold, and lived the rough life in Honduras, Buenos Aires, New York, and elsewhere. He could claim to know firsthand something about the people he made his characters: sailors, gangsters, down-and-outers, and others whose lives seemed at once exotic and pertinent to playgoers of the time. While America in the 1920s danced, drank, and prospered, O'Neill became famous for dark, serious, tragic plays, plays that ran against the grain, plays that important critics respected and argued about, plays that won frequent literary prizes (and eventually the Nobel Prize). In spite of all this, O'Neill's plays were sometimes immensely popular with more ordinary audiences and readers, and O'Neill himself was among the best-known literary figures in the world. When he went through an ugly divorce in the late 1920s, the scandal made headlines east and west.

After his death he attracted even more biographical attention, largely because of the posthumous publication of *Long Day's Journey into Night,* now his most famous work. It is a work that is explicitly and admittedly autobiographical, as we know from a private dedication written to his widow that she had printed with the text, written to her when he gave her the manuscript. In it he thanked her for the "love and tenderness . . . that enabled me to face my dead at last and write this play . . . with deep pity and understanding and forgiveness for *all* the four haunted Tyrones." Tyrone was the name he gave the O'Neill family. James O'Neill and James O'Neill, Jr. (Jamie), his father and ten-year-older brother, he called James and Jamie Tyrone. Mary Ellen Quinlan O'Neill (called Ella O'Neill) became Mary Tyrone. To himself he gave the name of a third O'Neill son, Edmund, who had died in childhood before the future playwright was born. In the play he told the story of his mother's long struggle with morphine addiction and his father's lost dream of being a great Shakespearean actor (rather than the romantic idol he was), and O'Neill also told something of his and his brother's wild youthful lives. Once he had written the play (in 1940–1941), O'Neill allowed fewer than half a dozen people to read it. He believed it to be his finest work and had every reason to assume that it would bring money and honor. Yet a lifelong passion for privacy led him to conceal the play. With evident ambivalence, he had the manuscript sealed away in the vaults of his publisher, Random House. Notarized and countersigned instructions ensured that it was never to be performed, and not to be published until at least twenty-five years after his death, an instruction he repeated in his will. This, he told various people, was to protect living relatives and safeguard the memory of the O'Neills in the minds of people who might survive him. Eugene O'Neill was at once the most tireless and the most secretive of autobiographers.

O'Neill himself unwittingly prepared the way for a second wave of biographers, beginning in the late 1950s with Doris Alexander and Croswell Bowen, who verified that, in general and with certain exceptions, *Long Day's Journey* was a truthful autobiographical document. Among other things, the biographers, and certain other scholars, including Judith Barlow, Travis Bogard, Virginia Floyd, Michael Manheim, and several others, discovered that not only *Long Day's Journey into Night* but nearly all O'Neill's earlier plays were deeply and deliberately autobiographical, although the family portraits had been so well disguised that almost none of the playwright's contemporaries had recognized them.

The first major biography, *O'Neill,* by Arthur and Barbara Gelb (1962), corrected numerous errors that had been passed on from one biographer to another since the 1920s; they added impressions from interviews with numerous friends of the playwright and included a great deal of information about O'Neill and his times. The Gelbs were the first to present generally accurate details about Ella O'Neill's morphine addiction, and their sense of Eugene's life still seems fundamentally sound.

The late Louis Sheaffer, who began work in the mid-1950s, wrote an outstanding two-volume biography, *O'Neill, Son and Playwright* (1968) and *O'Neill, Son and Artist* (1973). He conducted exhaustive interviews with hundreds of people and formed lifelong friendships with many of O'Neill's relatives and friends. In the process, he corrected errors and uncovered many additional facts; he deepened our knowledge of the playwright. Sheaffer's has been considered a biography that will never be superseded, because of the richness of detail it gives about the man, his friends, and his circumstances. Sheaffer's copious collection of interview notes, photos, personal letters, newspaper clippings, and other documents, filling numerous file boxes, now reposes in the Sheaffer-O'Neill Collection at the Shain Library at Connecticut College in New London, O'Neill's hometown. Exhaustive as his thirteen-hundred-page work was, Sheaffer once noted that his files contained enough information for two more volumes about O'Neill. And now the Gelbs, working with their own sources as well as Sheaffer's, are said to be nearly finished with a three-volume, twenty-four-hundred-page expansion of their biography.

A further commentator on O'Neill's life must be mentioned, the psychoanalyst James W. Hamilton, who published three fine essays in 1975, 1976, and 1979. They are among the very few analytic works before the present biography to approach O'Neill's life from the standpoint of modern psychoanalytic theory.

When work on the present biography began in the mid-1970s, the author was a professor of literature and a research candidate beginning nearly nine years of academic and clinical training in psychoanalysis at the Seattle Psychoanalytic Institute. At the time, a few people who had known O'Neill were still alive (some are still). A decision was made to avoid attempting to interview any of them, on the grounds that personal accounts by witnesses might seem more vivid than the published testimony of the dead and so might bring additional sources of bias to the project. As it happened, Sheaffer passed away in 1993, and his papers, including very extensive interview notes, became available to scholars. On the evidence of his notes, Sheaffer was a remarkably perceptive and empathic interviewer. In nearly all cases where I quote or refer to Sheaffer's published opinions or impressions, I have examined the relevant interview notes and other documents. In some cases I have used material in the notes that did not find its way into his published volumes and have indicated such instances by the parenthetical phrase "(LS papers)." In a certain sense, Sheaffer inevitably became a "character" in this narrative, for the use of his published and unpublished work necessitated examination of his conclusions, impressions, and interactions with witnesses.

At least five friends of the young Eugene died between 1913 and 1919, three (or possibly four) of them by suicide. During this period O'Neill was teaching himself to write plays and was gradually achieving a belated independence from his family. Nothing was harder for him than accepting the losses and mourning his dead. Early difficulties in his life, especially his mother's morphine addiction, greatly affected Eugene's growth toward autonomy and his ability to mourn when death claimed close friends and members of his family.

Just as he had begun to establish his independence, around 1919–1920, a series of new losses beset him. He witnessed his father's prolonged, painful illness and death. Eighteen months later, his mother—youthful-looking and much younger than her husband—who had been free from her morphine addiction for eight years, died of a brain tumor. At once, Jamie O'Neill, Eugene's older brother, determined to drink himself to death, something he managed to do in less than two years. O'Neill lost all the members of his parental family in just over three years. It seems obvious that such a concatenation of losses would greatly affect someone of O'Neill's temperament and background. Yet the losses and their implications have been little noticed and less understood by biographers. The thesis presented in this biography is that O'Neill spent most of his writing life in mourning.

From those terrible days forward, O'Neill was obsessed with his losses, and with the process of mourning. Unable to let the dead remain dead, he showed his preoccupation in everything he did and especially in everything he wrote. He peopled his plays of the 1920s with characters haunted by the dead, like Eben Cabot of *Desire Under the Elms,* who speaks daily to his long-dead mother. Like their creator, Nina Leeds and Charley Marsden of *Strange Interlude* (1926–1927) can neither finish mourning nor cease repeating with others the relationships they had with the dead. The first character O'Neill created who could even attempt to confront her dead was Lavinia Mannon in *Mourning Becomes Electra* (1929–1931). At the very end of the play, Lavinia has herself sealed in the family home, determined to remain there until she has looked her dead in the face and come to know them and her relations with them.

Such is the "work" of mourning, as psychoanalysis calls it, and such is the task O'Neill set for himself. O'Neill had several encounters with psychoanalysts in the 1920s, and in various remarks he made it clear that he thought of his playwriting as a form of self-psychoanalysis. Shortly after creating Lavinia, O'Neill himself turned inward and ceased to write for immediate production or publication. At this time, also, his health started to break down. He began to experience episodes of profound depression that he told his son seemed to him different from the melancholy he had always known. At the same time, a nameless, idiopathic neurological process, which caused a debilitating tremor, increasingly afflicted him. As will be seen later, the depression and the tremor were almost certainly related.

During this time O'Neill also suffered from a succession of more common ailments. Following an ordinary attack of appendicitis in 1937 and an apparently successful appendectomy, he nearly died of peritonitis and was three months in the hospital recovering. He was in bed when the Swedish consul brought him the Nobel Prize medal and read a presentation speech.

The tremor would eventually make impossible the physical act of writing and later affect his ability to walk or speak or swallow. Despite being often sick from various illnesses, he worked from 1935 to 1939 on a vast series of interrelated plays known as the Cycle, in which he set out to give an account of American economic and political history beginning in 1755 and ending in 1932. He evidently completed drafts of as many as six or seven of the plays, only one of which survives in the original form. If the survivor, *More Stately Mansions,* is any indication, the account of American history would have been filled with ghosts of the O'Neills, ghosts studied in almost unbearably intimate detail. Writing *More Stately Mansions* and the others was O'Neill's way of completing the work of mourning.

In 1939, almost casually, O'Neill set aside the Cycle and in the next three years wrote three plays unlike anything he had written before. These were *The Iceman Cometh, Long Day's Journey into Night,* and *Hughie.* There would be two more plays before illness made further writing impossible—a revision of the Cycle play *A Touch of the Poet* and *A Moon for the Misbegotten*. In these plays O'Neill mourned his dead and moved beyond mourning and tragedy to that remote dramatic continent discovered by Sophocles at the end of his working life, when he wrote *Oedipus at Colonos*, or by Shakespeare when he composed *The Winter's Tale*. The growth of O'Neill's artistic powers from the best plays he wrote in the 1920s to the plays of the late 1930s and early 1940s was such that critics and the public only now seem gradually to realize how very remarkable the late achievements are. O'Neill's finest plays were written after he had received the Nobel Prize.

O'Neill fashioned plays from his circumstances that interpreted his own life and the lives of those close to him. Writing plays allowed O'Neill to find in his life an aesthetic coherence resembling that which he gave the materials of his plays. O'Neill probably did not often recognize the internal psychological structures gradually evolving in himself, and he surely had in mind no general aim or plan. But by dint of extraordinary commitment to his work and daily writing stints, he brought himself, little by little, into harmony with events. More than simply developing his talents, O'Neill created a life in which he became congruent with his circumstances.

To put the matter in different terms, the terms of this biography, O'Neill found a way to use the writing of plays as a form of self-psychoanalysis. The analysis was successful to the extent that it allowed him to mourn his dead and to create in his last plays work that must have come very close to fulfilling even so large a talent as his.

It remains to say a little about psychoanalytic object relations theory, the aspect of psychoanalysis most pertinent to understanding mourning. To put it simply, object relations theory has to do with the gradual process by which people grow from a state of almost total dependency in infancy to whatever degree of autonomy they reach in later life. Mourning, from a psychoanalytic point of view, is the process of separating one's mental images of oneself from one's mental representations of the lost person. Because the images referred to are as much unconscious as conscious, the work of separating self-representations from representations of the dead can never be straightforward and always partly escapes intellectual control. The study of such images and their vicissitudes is called object relations theory. The word *object* is taken from traditional philosophical categories, *subject* and *object* distinguishing me from not-me. It is meant neither to imply coldness toward the other nor to reduce the other's personhood. Distinguishing the me from the not-me is one of the necessary achievements of human development in the first twenty or thirty years of life.

In our early lives, our images of ourselves are often fused with our images of our parents; that is, as children we often cannot distinguish our internal, intuitive sense of self from our intuitive interpretations of a parent. Out of these images of self and others, identity forms itself. In optimal circumstances, the representations enlarge and grow more complex with new experiences and impressions of our parents. Each new experience may add something to what we know of the parent and may complicate our sense of who and what the parent may be as a person.

The word *object* does not refer to a person but to an internal representation, a subjective interpretation of a person by a child, a person whose view of the world little resembles an adult's perspective. An infant will not immediately connect various discrete images of nursing with the idea "mother" before having reached a certain developmental stage. In passing through the first years, the child becomes increasingly skilled at assimilating and integrating the various experiences out of which parental images are formed. The child's growing ability to create complex parental images is at the center of development toward autonomy. The more integrated the interpretations, the less the child continues to need its parents, and the closer it is to being ready for unsheltered experience. Anything that inhibits development prolongs the period of dependency.

All kinds of events may inhibit development, with varying consequences. The death of a parent generally has a powerful effect on a dependent child. The child's real experience of the parent ceases with the death, and as a consequence the child cannot continue to modify its internal images of the parent. The child may continue to develop its power to interpret and integrate experience, but it will be partly cut off from its image of the lost parent. The child's internal sense of the relation between itself and the parent is likely to remain unchanged after the loss, at least until the mourner approaches emotional autonomy.

If the unconscious childhood impression of the lost parent is ever to change, and if mourning for the parent is ever to be completed or resolved, the bereaved will probably have to make a conscious and deliberate effort to reconstruct the old relationship. The "work" of mourning is especially complicated when it occurs before one is independent. One must eventually try to reimagine the past from the standpoint of one who is no longer dependent, to allow old images to be seen from a present point of view. One can eventually change one's understanding of the dead: the parent who abandons a needy child becomes a particular person who died leaving a dependent child. To relinquish the old image, one must, among other things, acknowledge one's past and current dependency and understand the particulars of one's needs. The mourner must constantly struggle against the wish to deny the loss and the attendant grief.

The phenomenon of blaming the person who died for abandoning the survivor is a common one. If the bereaved is still arguing with the lost person, he or she in effect denies that the loss has taken place. Fighting with the dead is made simpler when the lost person lives exclusively "in one's head," rather than partly in the outside world. Even so, a death may not be the hardest loss to understand or resolve, simply because it is something we know to be universal and fundamental that forces the separation. Not all losses result from death. One cannot blame death when the lost person remains alive, as in the case of a loss through divorce.

Eugene's problem was still more difficult. He lost his mother when he was fourteen, neither to death nor to a divorce, but to the discovery of her addiction. It reduced and simplified the images he was forming of her. It led him to substitute unspoken code words like *weak* or *fragile* or *ill* or *evil* for the more complex representations of a highly intelligent adolescent struggling toward understanding. The discovery caused him to place his relationship with his mother partly in suspension, for she could not stand the rough and tumble of reciprocity with an adolescent, and he could not stand the guilt of knowing his power to harm her.

The discovery altered Eugene's relations not only with his mother but with the entire environment in which he was trying to grow up. One of the basic necessities for growing up is a sense of safety. A child feels safe when it knows that whatever it does, others in the world will not be permanently harmed, nor will the child have to suffer the worst consequences of its aggression. The sense of safety coexists in uneasy alliance with what is called childhood omnipotence, a subjective belief in the power of one's thoughts to alter the world that expresses itself in, say, a little boy's cockiness or in a teenager's risk-taking. One aspect of the belief in the omnipotence of one's thoughts is that it allows one to acquire gradually, rather than too quickly, the knowledge that reality is largely indifferent to the needs and wishes of a person who (in reality) is small and power-less. Whatever sense of safety Eugene may have felt before he knew of his mother's addiction he lost afterward. There was the realistic concern, any time his mother was free from the morphine, that an upset in the family might send her back to the drug.

An even more profound loss than the loss of the sense of safety oc-curred with the discovery of her addiction, and that was the knowledge that simply by being born he had caused her addiction and permanently changed her life and the lives of his father and brother. There is such a thing as too great a feeling of childhood omnipotence, the consequence of which may be inhibitions, anxiety, and neuroses. Such was Eugene's situation when he learned of his mother's addiction. He lost himself and his parents and then spent the rest of his life recovering them in order to be independent.

The process of transformation that leads from dependency to indi-viduation and autonomy involves a host of issues inescapable in the age of skepticism. The medium of transformation for O'Neill was his writ-ing, the work that occupied most of his time from 1913 until 1943. O'Neill remarked more than once, with as much sincerity as irony, that writing was his vacation from living or that living was something he endured in order to write. It was a complaint about poor health, and it turned post-Puritan and post-Victorian attitudes toward work topsy-turvy. But the remark also implied that the process of working gave the playwright enough satisfaction and happiness to compensate for anything else life might do to him. O'Neill had something like an Aristotelian attitude to-ward happiness, which he thought of not only as moments of pleasure, but as a continual pursuit of *arete,* the complex notion of "excellence," the search for which was assumed to lead to a deeper happiness. (It was arete that Jefferson meant by "the pursuit of happiness.") Whatever happiness O'Neill may have reached, the pursuit gave coherence to his life.

Abbreviations

Sources of quotations from unpublished letters are given thus: (Harvard, EO to AB, Tuesday [January 13, 1920]). That is, the letter is from Eugene O'Neill to his wife Agnes Boulton and is dated "Tuesday night." (Names for which initials are used will be obvious in context.) In this case a further date in square brackets has been supplied by the biographer, who has concluded from details in the letter that the Tuesday in question was January 13, 1920. The word *Harvard* at the beginning of the letter citation refers to the Harvard Theater Collection at Houghton Library, Harvard University, in which the letter is held.

Archives holding letters and documents cited in the biography are as follows:

(Berg): the Berg collection at New York Public Library.

(B.U.): the Department of Special Collections at Boston University Library.

(Harvard): the Theater Collection at Houghton Library, Harvard University.

(Princeton): the manuscript collection at Firestone Library, Princeton University.

(Yale): the O'Neill collection at the Beinecke Rare Book and Manuscript Library at Yale University.

A few sources frequently cited are abbreviated in parentheses, as follows:

CMD: the unpublished diaries of Carlotta Monterey O'Neill, third wife of the playwright, which are at the Beinecke Rare Book and Manuscript Library, Yale University.

Gelbs: Arthur and Barbara Gelb, *O'Neill* (New York: Harper and Row, 1973).

LS1:   Louis Sheaffer, *O'Neill, Son and Playwright* (Boston: Little, Brown, 1968).

LS2:   Louis Sheaffer, *O'Neill, Son and Artist* (Boston: Little, Brown, 1973).

Except as otherwise indicated, citations to the Sheaffer biography in Chapters 1 through 12 refer to the first (1968) volume (LS1); those in Chapters 13 and after refer to the second (1973) volume (LS2).

LS papers: documents in the Louis Sheaffer–Eugene O'Neill Collection at the Charles E. Shain Library, Connecticut College.

Poems: Eugene O'Neill, *Poems, 1912–1944,* Donald Gallup, ed. (New Haven, Conn.: Ticknor and Fields, 1980).

SL: *Selected Letters of Eugene O'Neill,* Travis Bogard and Jackson R. Bryer, eds. (New Haven, Conn.: Yale University Press, 1988).

WD: Eugene O'Neill, *Work Diary, 1924–1943,* preliminary ed. Transcribed by Donald Gallup (New Haven, Conn.: Yale University Library, 1981).

Quotations from O'Neill's plays are based on examination of manuscript material where that is available, of various printed editions, especially those whose publication was supervised by O'Neill himself, and of typeset proofs containing the author's corrections and alterations. For the convenience of the reader, I have given the pages in which the quoted material can be found in the widely available three-volume set issued by the Library of America:

CP1   Eugene O'Neill, *Complete Plays, 1913–1920* (New York: Library of America, 1988).

CP2   Eugene O'Neill, *Complete Plays, 1920–1931* (New York: Library of America, 1988).

CP3   Eugene O'Neill, *Complete Plays, 1932–1943* (New York: Library of America, 1988).

James and Ella
1845–1877

EUGENE GLADSTONE O'NEILL WAS BORN in New York City in the twelfth year of his parents' marriage, on October 16, 1888, in the Barrett House, a residential hotel at Forty-third Street and Broadway. Mary Ellen Quinlan O'Neill had turned thirty-one in August. Ella, as she was called, had been not yet twenty when she married Eugene's father, James O'Neill, a celebrated actor, on June 14, 1877, in St. Ann's Catholic Church in New York City. Bride and groom were both Irish, but they had little else in common at the time of their marriage.

Born in New Haven on August 13, 1857, Ella grew up in Cleveland, where her parents moved while she was still an infant. Thomas Joseph Quinlan, a prosperous entrepreneur and an indulgent father, provided his daughter with a classical education at a fine boarding school; and when she showed a talent for music, he bought her a grand piano.

Ella grew up in privilege, James in slums. Several searches, most recently by Edward Shaughnessy, have revealed no birth information. James O'Neill celebrated his birthday on October 14; he gave his birthplace as Kilkenny, Ireland, and said variously that he had been born in 1844, in 1845, and in 1846. He was the son of Edward and Mary O'Neil (as the family name was then spelled). On his death certificate in 1920 Ella, the official informant, gave the year of his birth as 1845 (Shaughnessy 1991, 20).

James was the third son and sixth child in a family of three sons and six daughters. Fleeing famine, the O'Neils came to a Buffalo slum from Ireland about 1850. Edward O'Neil worked on the docks and drank heavily, and his wife "scrubbed for the Yanks," as her grandson wrote much later, in *Long Day's Journey into Night*. About 1856, Edward had a premonition that he was nearing death, and he decided he wanted to end his days in Ireland. He returned to Kilkenny, where he did die, after someone mistook rat poison for biscuit flour. So went the odd story told afterward by James, who claimed to remember his father only with contempt. The story may have been meant simply to conceal a suicide. Something about the story, perhaps its hint of mysticism and tragic inevitability, led James's son to repeat it in *Long Day's Journey into Night*.

After Edward left, the eldest daughter, Josephine, who had married a saloonkeeper, sent from Cincinnati for her mother, James, and some of the sisters. James, who was about eleven, became an apprentice file maker in a Cincinnati machine shop, and his mother worked in the homes of the well-to-do. But even with fewer children to feed, there was seldom enough to eat. James later remembered that they had twice been evicted from the hovels they were living in. About 1859 or 1860, James went to Norfolk, Virginia, with Josephine and her husband. During the Civil War, he worked in an enterprise that supplied uniforms to the rebels. He may have received some tutoring at that time. He was highly intelligent, a voracious reader all his life. But he was probably his own most constant tutor.

After the war, James returned to Cincinnati with his sister and brother-in-law. As he often told it, a chance event about 1865 led him to be given a role as a supernumerary in a performance at the National Theatre. James took to theatrical life with single-minded dedication and quickly emerged from the ranks. A year after he first walked onstage, he listed himself in the city directory as "actor." By the late 1860s he was playing major roles. Eventually he would be famous throughout the land for a single role, that of Edmond Dantes in a dramatization of *The Count of Monte Cristo;* he played it more than four thousand times over a period of thirty years.

A man of average height and strong build, remarkably handsome, James had modest, warm, and charming manners. He worked hard to train his most noted asset, his beautiful voice. He got rid of his brogue and studied diligently enough that by 1871 he counted fifty roles in his repertoire. He was soon playing with the most prominent actors in the country and attracting their respect.

In the operatic theater of the mid-nineteenth century, voice was nearly everything. People in cities and towns showed up year after year to hear Edwin Forrest or Charlotte Cushman or Junius Brutus Booth (father of Edwin and John Wilkes) rattle the walls, with voices that were compared to trumpets. Local actors stood about the stage in arrangements determined by the visiting idol; otherwise the play had no director and little rehearsal. Sustained interaction between the characters was as ritualized as in Italian opera. Audiences attended to vocal nuance with the same aural sophistication they brought to the opera house. The origins of the theater in bardic storytelling were still perceptible, even if the repertoire ran to melodrama, sentimental fluff, and bowdlerized plays from Shakespeare.

In this world the young James O'Neill caught the notice of visiting actors. Joseph Jefferson, with whom James played in Boucicault's *Rip Van Winkle,* coached him in comedy. The formidable Charlotte Cushman taught him to play Macbeth. He performed *Virginius* with Edwin Forrest. Rheumatic, bitter, and scandal-ridden at the age of sixty, Forrest paid few compliments, but he rumbled to someone that if James O'Neill would get rid of his brogue and work hard he could be an excellent actor. Anecdotes like these told by the Gelbs (23 25) imply that the young James had an unmistakable talent as an actor and that he could charm prominent people and persuade them to take him seriously.

Throughout his long career, James was liked and admired by his colleagues and noted for his kindness to young actors. He helped other actors make the most of their parts, advised them about career decisions, and was lavishly generous with drinks and money. No biographer has found evidence that James was ever otherwise in his professional life. As the Gelbs concluded: "Not an actor, manager or agent ever had anything but glowing praise for his character and generosity, which was remarkable in a profession where petty jealousies and vindictive gossip are so prevalent" (Gelbs, 44). He had everything he needed to earn his rapid rise.

In 1870, the twenty-four-year-old James was hired by John Ellsler to play first or second leads at the Academy of Music in Cleveland. It was a respected theater, and the move was momentous for James in several respects. In Cleveland he played with Forrest, Jefferson, Jean Davenport Lander, and others, and studied Shakespearean roles.

In Cleveland James also met two women who greatly affected his life. The first was a professional actress, Nettie Walsh, with whom James began to live in 1871. The second was Mary Ellen Quinlan, his future wife, then fourteen. Nettie Walsh was said to be fifteen when she and James became lovers, and he was twenty-three. Later, when they were no longer friendly, James swore that he had by no means been Nettie's first or only lover and added that both had known other lovers during their affair.

In 1872 James moved to McVicker's Theatre in Chicago, the leading theater west of New York, where he remained through 1874. It was at McVicker's that James played alongside Edwin Booth in circumstances made famous by James's son Eugene in *Long Day's Journey into Night* (1941). Drawing on conversations with his father in 1919–1920, Eugene showed the character James Tyrone looking back to his youth, when he and Booth alternated in the leading roles, night after night, in *Julius Caesar* and *Othello;* above all, James recalled the artistic idealism that had once guided him. Eugene believed that playing Shakespeare with Booth was the high point of his father's career. In writing *Long Day's Journey into Night,* he has James Tyrone tell his son Edmund:

> I loved Shakespeare. I would have acted in any of his plays
> for nothing, for the joy of being alive in his great poetry.
> And I acted well in him. I felt inspired by him. I could have
> been a great Shakespearean actor, if I'd kept on. I know that!
> In 1874 when Edwin Booth came to the theatre in Chicago
> where I was leading man, I played Cassius to his Brutus one
> night, Brutus to his Cassius the next, Othello to his Iago,
> and so on. The first night I played Othello, he said to our
> manager, "That young man is playing Othello better than I
> ever did!" . . . A few years later my good bad luck made me
> find the big money-maker. . . . And then life had me where
> it wanted me. . . . [*Bitterly.*] What the hell was it I wanted to
> buy, I wonder, that was worth—Well, no matter. It's a late
> day for regrets. [CP3, 809–10]

For James Tyrone as for James O'Neill, Booth's praise had represented the apex of the younger actor's career. In his old age, James seemed to feel that within a few years of that point he had slid into successful mediocrity.

James had in his youth kept his eye on prosperity, it is true, but in 1874 the main chance involved no obvious artistic compromise. After James O'Neill's success with McVicker's, Richard Hooley, J. H. McVicker's chief competitor in Chicago, offered James the chance to form a Shakespearean repertory company that would play in Hooley's Opera House and would also tour. In 1875, when Hooley's company went to San Francisco, James went with them. James's star was still rising, and it continued to do so for several years.

When James moved to Chicago in 1872, Nettie Walsh remained in Cleveland, but she visited James from time to time. In the meantime, James was becoming romantically involved with a respected married actress, Louise Hawthorne, who was noted for performances of great intensity and for a disfiguring scar that marked one side of her face from chin to temple. The scar was popularly believed to intensify the depth of her performances. James brought Louise into the repertory company he formed for Hooley and took her to San Francisco with him.

Before the move west, Nettie Walsh visited James in Chicago for a stormy reunion. As James became involved with Louise Hawthorne, and as his celebrity increased, his patience with Nettie diminished. Problems came to a head in 1874 when she demanded support for her son, whom she called Alfred Hamilton O'Neill. According to Alexander (1962, 7–8) James offered to raise the child himself, if it was his, but on the condition that Nettie renounce any claim to the boy or to him. She refused, and James must have hoped it was the last he would hear of her. She returned to Cleveland, where she was living with a man called Alfred Seaman. At some point she began calling herself Mrs. James O'Neill. In letters she pressed James for money.

In 1875 Louise Hawthorne went to San Francisco with James and the Hooley Shakespearean players, and she remained with him over the next winter. In San Francisco and on tours, James's fame continued to spread; he was now known widely as a leader among his generation of actors. Early in 1876 James was offered the chance to move, in October, to New York, to join A. H. Palmer's respected stock company, which performed at the Union Square Theatre. James's feelings for Louise Hawthorne were apparently cooling, although she remained ardent. She returned to Chicago, while James remained in San Francisco; when James returned to Chicago, she watched him perform on June 27. James, who was staying at the same hotel as Louise, the Tremont House, said later that he had visited Louise in her room that night. He was apparently the last person to see her alive. It has been assumed that at their last meeting he confirmed what she already knew, that he wanted their affair to end. She fell that night from the window of her sixth-floor room, and although her death was ruled accidental, rumor thereafter held that she had killed herself for love of James O'Neill.

Louise Hawthorne's death must have greatly shaken James. Everything we know about him suggests that guilt was for James as deep and inescapable as fear of the poorhouse, and guilt and dread were intertwined: nemesis and retribution. His sense of metaphysical justice told him that Fortune's wheel would reclaim all it had allowed him to gain and would return him to the slums.

Throughout his life, in adversity or public conflict James would deny all and put the best face on things, whether in conversation with intimates or in interviews with the public press. But denial solved a problem only for the moment. James brooded ever after in private. He hid his guilt from others, whether he felt it for real misdeeds or injurious wishes; but he could never rid himself of old remorse. If he could explain to himself that Louise Hawthorne's death was consistent with the pattern of her life, he could probably never fully convince himself.

So it must have been also with Nettie Walsh's demands. Knowing of her other lovers, he would have believed it foolish to acknowledge the boy she said was his. Yet his offer to raise the child implies that he could not feel much conviction in denying her claim. As with most things throughout his offstage life, he did a bit of this and a bit of the other, shifting from remorse to denial to self-justification before finally half doing something impulsive and kind.

In Chicago and San Francisco, James in his late twenties must have felt himself the envy of men: the lover of a celebrated married actress who traveled with him across the continent; pursued by another mistress, who traveled from Cleveland to Chicago for a touch of his hand. Other conquests may have lingered in his memory and fantasies. He was idolized by schoolgirls all over the country; brought from convents to see him perform, the girls waited afterward to hear a word or catch a smile. But he could never escape the sense that nemesis and retribution awaited. With Louise Hawthorne's death Fortune's wheel turned a little.

Such were apparently James's state of mind and circumstances when, in October 1876, he moved to begin his New York engagement at Palmer's Union Square Theatre.

During the time James had lived in Cleveland, he had become friendly with Thomas Quinlan, one of whose enterprises was a tobacco and liquor shop that attracted a theatrical trade. Thomas was about twelve years older than the twenty-four-year-old actor, but both were immigrant Irish and self-made men. James could only admire Thomas as an example of the success he himself sought. Thomas, for his part, liked the young actor well enough to bring him to his home. In the Quinlan household, the children enjoyed a prolonged dependency, a luxury neither Thomas nor James could fully understand, even though each created such conditions for his own children.

If Thomas knew that James was living with a very young actress, probably no hint would have been given to the Quinlan children. James's manners and charm were all that the Quinlan children needed to know of him. They were sheltered but they were not uninformed. They knew that James was an actor, and no further caution would have been needed. Thomas must have prided himself that the prosperity and position he had worked for had brought his family safety and sophistication.

When the Quinlans arrived in Cleveland, they lived over a store on Ontario Street, where Thomas sold books, stationer's supplies, magazines and newspapers, baked goods, and sweets. Bridget Lundigan Quinlan seems to have been several years older than her husband, and an executor of discipline and common sense in the household.[1] William Joseph Dominick Quinlan, Ella's younger brother, was born in 1858, probably after the move to Cleveland. In 1868 Thomas became manager of circulation for the Cleveland *Plain Dealer*. The position, and the profit from his other enterprises, allowed him to move his family into a fine house at 208 Woodland Avenue and furnish it with luxuries that included a library and the piano. In the boom that followed the Civil War he made lucky investments in real estate, and he and a partner opened Quinlan and Spirnaugle, the liquor and tobacco shop through which he met James O'Neill. An open, accessible man who didn't drink at all but enjoyed being with friends who did, Quinlan was popular with church and commercial leaders. He read widely and liked to talk about the books he read. He made friends with many of his customers, and he and the young James O'Neill must have felt they had many things in common. Like Thomas, James was clearly on the path to success. It must have pleased Thomas to bring the unassuming and charming young man to meet the Quinlan family, to see the fine home a hard-working immigrant could make in a baker's dozen of years. The visits probably began in the fall of 1871, because Mary Ellen was apparently fourteen

when she first met James; late that fall she went to South Bend to boarding school.

James must have noticed the young Quinlan daughter. A school
friend, Lillie West, later remembered her as "a tall, superb creature with a
kind of burnt-gold hair in profusion and deep brown eyes" (Alexander
1962, 5). A photograph taken about the time of her marriage shows a slim
girl who looks much younger than her age. She has the dark eyes and
abundant hair that Lillie West mentioned. Something unsettled in the
line of the mouth suggests shyness and the mobile features of one who has
not learned to pose or to hide her feelings. Her face is oval; she has a long
brow and straight nose, high cheekbones, and a short upper lip. The picture hints at an innocent flirtation with the photographer. In *Long Day's
Journey*, Mary Tyrone's husband recalled his wife as a schoolgirl as "a bit
of a rogue and a coquette."

Above all, the picture shows girlishness and immaturity. Lillie West
said that "Ella Quinlan . . . was almost a child when she married O'Neill"
(Alexander 1962, 9). Biographers have found nothing to contradict the
impression. The Gelbs wrote of the young Mary Ellen: "No trace of the
rugged adaptability that had brought her parents from Ireland could be
found in her pliant personality or in her delicate features" (13). Even more
than her beauty, James would have seen and been touched by an innocence that betokened her upbringing in a gentle world in which the young
were not thrust into workhouses but sheltered, a world to which he, like
Thomas, could aspire as a newcomer. The innocence also implied a lack
of internal resources, which made frustrations hard to bear and would
leave her vulnerable, years later, to recurring morphine addiction. But the
dangers of her immaturity would not have been evident to James in 1877
when he married her.

He would have seen in her a child who was incomparably less
worldly than Nettie Walsh. From James's point of view, Ella knew nothing of "reality"—and so much the better! To James, reality was hardship
and the threat of returning to the slums.

For her part, Ella might have said that James knew nothing of reality. That was the force of Ella's repeated complaints throughout her marriage that her husband would not buy the home she wanted and indeed
had no idea what a home was. Her manners and sense of society referred
to a world of family, school, and friends, a reality that pushed James's to
the margins. Ella's middle-class manners and sheltered self-assurance

would not have permitted her to show that she knew James did not understand her world, if she indeed did know it. James surely respected the middle class and aspired to join it, and yet he must simultaneously have thought its assumptions about reality to be those of an inspirational tale for children.

Neither James's nor Ella's version of reality was adequate for living in a time of change; nor was any better theory of the world available to them. The conflicting visions of reality of Mary Ellen Quinlan and James O'Neill came close to typifying the split views of the world that resulted in the political, social, and philosophical revolutions of the nineteenth and twentieth centuries. Their cosmological incompatibility made for an anxious marriage. At the level of dramatic art, their youngest son would make the marriage stand, in *Long Day's Journey into Night,* for the most intense crises of the Age of Anxiety. That was all in the future, however. Meanwhile, James, a guest in the Cleveland home of Thomas Quinlan, gently won Ella with the same charm and kindly condescension that had conquered the theater-going public.

When they first met, Ella lived in her father's house and had not yet begun boarding school. James may have been a frequent visitor in the Quinlan home, but he probably did not see Ella often or converse with her intimately, and he would have been unlikely to consider himself her suitor. Ella would have been an unusual schoolgirl if she had not developed a crush on James, a safe enough attachment, given that he was her father's friend. Not long after the first meeting, Thomas sent Ella to boarding school in South Bend, Indiana, half a day's train trip west of Cleveland.

The renowned St. Mary's Academy was one of the finest convent schools in the Middle West. Not yet accredited as a college, St. Mary's offered higher education for young women when it was still uncommon. Non-Catholic as well as Catholic families, including the parents of Ella's friend Ella Nirdlinger, sent their daughters to South Bend. Ella Nirdlinger's son George Jean Nathan became an important theater critic, one of Eugene O'Neill's first advocates and a lifelong friend, as his mother had been to Ella Quinlan O'Neill. J. H. McVicker had sent his daughter Mary there to school a few years earlier (she would later marry Edwin Booth, go mad, and die young). Lillie West, Ella's seatmate and confidante at Saint Mary's, went on to become, under the pen name of Amy Leslie, a respected theater reviewer for a Chicago newspaper. Ella Quinlan maintained until her death epistolary friendships with Ella Nirdlinger, Lillie West, and several other women she had met at St. Mary's. Although she was not so friendless as Mary Tyrone complains *she* is in *Long Day's Journey into Night,* Ella O'Neill must often have felt very lonely.

Students at St. Mary's in Ella's time received a broad Catholic education ranging from catechism to general history, mental philosophy, trigonometry, French, geology, and astronomy. Ella had a special talent for music (a gift that her son Eugene would inherit), and her father arranged for piano lessons, over and above her regular studies at the conservatory of music. She studied with Mother Elizabeth Lilly, a descendant of George Arnold, who was organist to Elizabeth I. A cultivated and sophisticated English widow, she had converted and come to America, where she founded an instructional program in music that continued at St. Mary's for a century.

Inspired by Mother Elizabeth, Lillie West imagined going on the stage in light opera; Ella Quinlan decided that she would become either a nun or a concert pianist. From the standpoint of talent, Ella's aspiration may not have been unrealistic, for she graduated with the gold medal in music and played a Chopin polonaise at commencement. But her aspiration to be a nun or a professional musician raised other questions, which also intrigued her son.

Throughout *Long Day's Journey into Night* Mary Tyrone speaks with adoration of Mother Elizabeth. Late in act 4 O'Neill has her say, "It may be sinful of me but I love her better than my own mother." *Long Day's Journey* gives us an exceptionally full and complex interpretation of Ella O'Neill, but one of the most striking aspects of the portrait is that it shows Mary Tyrone almost entirely ignoring her mother. If a usual thing is absent, the absence may have meaning. Assuming that O'Neill's representation is accurate, a possible explanation is that Ella had never made a significant differentiation from her mother but remained psychologically identified, herself in a dependent role. The wish to be either a concert pianist or a nun implies that Ella made an adoring identification with Mother Elizabeth. She seems to have abandoned her music after she graduated, and it seems clear that she lacked the single-minded drive and commitment required for a career as a professional musician.

The identification with Mother Elizabeth also implies something unsettled in her feelings toward her own mother, a reluctance to be like her mother, which at the time meant making her own home and having and rearing children. Discomfort at the thought of following in her mother's footsteps implies a struggle to find her own identity. To find it, she would have to separate her self-image from her internal image of her mother and abandon or at least come to terms with a wish never to have to leave the protected state of childhood. It was a change she would have to make in order to become the protector of her own children. The struggle to find oneself is a nearly universal problem for adolescents who have enjoyed a prolonged dependency. The dependency and lack of separation from her mother might eventually have been outgrown in the ordinary course of things. But circumstance interfered with the ordinary.

Ella went to St. Mary's in the fall of 1872 and returned each fall until she graduated in June 1875; she spent summers and holidays at home in Cleveland. Circumstances were not the same when she returned in June 1873. Her father, previously a teetotaler, had begun drinking, and his health had taken a turn for the worse. By the summer or fall of 1873 he probably already had a rapidly developing case of consumption. Ella returned to St. Mary's in September, and on the following May 25, her father, aged forty, suddenly died. She never recovered from the loss.

Ella went home to Cleveland for the funeral and did not return to the convent until fall. Like many a young person overwhelmed by a loss, Ella probably did not often show grief, but there must have been times when denial failed and she felt lost or angry or overwhelmed or all of these at once. School friends may have felt uncomfortable about her loss and confused about how to act with her. Judging by patterns of the next two years, Ella and her mother spent a good deal of money; shopping was a specific against sorrow. A few days after the funeral, the family heard Thomas's will.

Thomas Quinlan had made his will in autumn 1872, just after Ella went off to college. To his son he left his books, and to his daughter the piano. The rest, money and property, was to be his wife's, unless and until she remarried, at which point it would be divided between his children. The will stipulated that the children should have every chance to finish their education, and the wish was observed. In autumn, Ella returned to South Bend for her final year at St. Mary's.

Quinlan added a final statement to his will which indicated his awareness that his children were far less prepared for life than he had been at their ages. He admonished them "that they each of them shall use the talents which they possess and the education which they may acquire to earn for themselves when they arrive at an age proper for them to do so an honest, honorable and independent livelihood, not relying upon their mother nor upon such share of the property as may descend to each after her demise nor before then" (Gelbs, 15). Thomas need not have worried about his son Joseph, who eventually prospered; at his death in 1911 he left his sister a sizable estate.

As for Ella, Thomas may have been so smitten with her musical gifts that he believed she might support herself with a career in music, but it is hard to guess what career she might actually have made. Perhaps he thought she might become a teacher, like Mother Elizabeth, and conceivably one aspect of Ella's wish to be a nun was a desire to teach music. If so, none of her son Eugene's portraits of his mother suggest that she might have expressed such a thought. As for her becoming a concert pianist, Thomas Quinlan, the friend of traveling actors, knew well how rough that life was, and how little his daughter was prepared for so strenuous a career.

Ella must have felt lost indeed when she thought about her father's death. Living without her father's love at the center of her emotional life must have been unimaginable, even without the injunction that she become self-supporting. Among the reactions that were psychologically possible for her, one we might consider was presented dramatically much later by her son in several characters whom biographers and critics believe are based on his mother. Characters such as Emma Crosby in *Diff'rent,* Ella Downey in *All God's Chillun Got Wings,* and Mary Tyrone in *Long Day's Journey into Night* evince a striking ability to alter what they perceive as real when reality is unbearable.

A brief scene in *Long Day's Journey* shows Mary refusing to accept that her son Edmund is seriously ill, and creating alternate realities for herself, changing from moment to moment, to escape what the others consider real. Late in act 2, scene 1, Mary notices a drinking glass near Edmund and asks him sharply:

> Why is that glass there? Did you take a drink? Oh, how can you be such a fool? Don't you know it's the worst thing? (*She turns to Tyrone.*) You're to blame, James. How could you let him? Do you want to kill him? Don't you remember my father? He wouldn't stop after he was stricken. He said doc-

tors were fools! He thought, like you, that whisky is a good tonic. (*A look of terror comes into her eyes and she stammers.*) But, of course, there's no comparison at all. I don't know why I—Forgive me for scolding you, James. One small drink won't hurt Edmund. It might be good for him, if it gives him an appetite. (*She pats Edmund's cheek playfully, the strange detachment again in her manner. He jerks his head away. She seems not to notice, but she moves instinctively away.*)

The behavior attributed to Mary seems so improbable, so self-contradictory, and so specific, that it is hard not to take it seriously as an attempt to represent something the author believed he had seen. It also makes sense, considered psychologically. In this brief episode Mary tries to balance her dread that her youngest son Edmund might have tuberculosis against the need to deny that T.B. killed her father, and more importantly, to deny that her father is dead at all.[2] Such episodes occur throughout the play. Near the end of act 3 Edmund tries to tell his mother that the doctor has confirmed that he does indeed have consumption. Mary rails against doctors, claims that they make you an addict and then force you to beg for the drug or go crazy, and finally scolds Edmund for being melodramatic—all in the service of not letting him say aloud what all the Tyrones already know. In despair he tries to make her listen to him: "People do die of it. Your own father—" Mary interrupts him: "Why do you mention him? There's no comparison at all with you. He had consumption."

It is a shocking moment; in performances, the remark usually stops everything, onstage or in the audience. Nothing that we ever learn about Mary Tyrone or Ella O'Neill suggests that either would consciously or deliberately be so cruel. Mary is certainly not lying or deliberately falsifying. The only remaining explanation is that for the instant she has no idea at all how such a remark might affect Edmund. Apparently, she has no other resource for protecting herself against pain than denial, and because it does not work very well, it forces her to evacuate the world she finds herself in and move to one less painful. When she thinks of her father, she no longer recalls the world in which Edmund can be hurt by casual cruelty.

It does not seem far-fetched to assume that what was the case for the adult was also true when Ella was seventeen. She would not have been unusual for an adolescent if she met painful circumstances with her gift to re-create the world; not merely to deny pain and its cause, but to abolish the whole world in which it existed and substitute a more pleasant one in its place.

In the fall Ella returned to St. Mary's, and her friends record no striking change in her personality such as might reflect a loss she would never get over. She seems to have denied the loss of her father altogether. She graduated with honors the next June, received the gold medal for music, and performed her polonaise. So ended the portion of her life that would ever after be the world to which she retired when the here and now became unbearable.

Little is known of the summer and fall that Ella spent after she returned to Cleveland from the convent. After Thomas died, Bridget Quinlan no longer cared to remain in Cleveland. Ella, away from the ordered life at the convent and separated from the order her father represented, must have felt at loose ends. Up until then her life had been organized around gaining the readily available approval of her father and Mother Elizabeth.

Ella probably continued with her music, but there was no one in particular left to please, and nothing indicates that she sought a teacher who might have prepared her for the concert stage. Unable then as later to set goals of her own, and lacking direction or any real ambition to take up a career, her life would have seemed empty. The family had relatives in the East—in New Haven, New London, and New York. In the fall Bridget and Ella decided to move to New York, and there they went early in 1876. The Gelbs report a series of large checks drawn on the Quinlan estate that testify to the style in which Bridget and Ella established themselves (Gelbs, 16). Bridget now controlled a sizable fortune.

Biographers have written that Ella persuaded her mother to move to New York because James O'Neill had gone there; but in fact, she and her mother were already there when James, who was working in San Francisco, was offered his position with Palmer's repertory company. If they had heard anything of James, it would have been scandalous rumors of the suicide of Louise Hawthorne, or the accusations of Nettie Walsh. In all likelihood they heard nothing at all, occupied as they were by their personal losses and the bustle of settling affairs in Cleveland and moving.

When James arrived the following autumn, Ella remembered him and arranged for someone to take her to his play. Afterward, she had herself escorted to his dressing room, and the two renewed their acquaintance; the former schoolgirl was now a "tall, superb creature," and the former provincial leading man was thirty and a leading man on a New York stage. By all accounts, they fell in love at once and were soon engaged.

The vast differences between the actor and the convent girl were obscured at the renewal of their acquaintance. Circumstances had put each of them in a prime situation to be drawn toward marriage with the other. Ella saw a man handsome, charming, and successful, the idol of a million schoolgirls, and her father's friend. Like her father, James adored her. By marrying James, she could sidestep mourning; she could avoid acknowledging that her father was permanently lost to her, and she could expect to restore to her life the structure and order she had felt in her father's home and then the convent.

James had reasons as compelling as Ella's to be drawn toward marriage now. Strongly sexual and needing more than prostitutes or casual flings, dreading loss and abandonment himself, he had chosen women who were decidedly clinging. Nettie Walsh could not let their affair end but pursued him shamelessly and caused a scandal; and Louise met a terrible death after James ended their affair. James had found women damaged by fate; to his conscience, it must have seemed that though he had not abused them, he had seized the opportunity to play at marriage with them while trying to avoid the full consequences; and he had come away from his ventures full of guilt and chagrin.

To remorse new worries were now added. The New York theater critics did not find him an effective actor. His beauty and voice did not impress them, and they complained that he did not match his style to the parts he played. If he thought he had mastered the art of acting, he had to think again. It was a warning never to take success for granted, and it fit with the need he felt to change the way he lived his life. Ella, daughter of the prosperous and successful Thomas, knew advantages of background unimaginable to Nettie or Louise, which showed in her charming self-assurance. James must have assumed she had inherited the strength and resilience that had carried her parents to success. He must have been certain that marrying Ella would bring him the middle-class stability he envied. He surely expected that with her musical gift and her Irish blood, she could respect his art and survive the rigors of being an actor's wife. In marrying Ella, he must have felt he was bringing his personal life into harmony with the success he was reaching for in his career. With his decision to marry, James prepared himself to enter his prime.

On the whole, *Long Day's Journey into Night* is accurate in matters of fact about the author's parents' lives. Eugene apparently intended to work from the facts as he knew them to discover whatever understanding might emerge from unconscious thoughts and feelings as a consequence of re-creating habitual family patterns. There is, however, a cluster of interesting inconsistencies between facts about the senior O'Neills and dramatic facts about the Tyrones. In act 3 Mary Tyrone tells the servant, Cathleen, of her meeting with James Tyrone. As Mary describes it, she was at the convent when her father wrote to say that he had met the famous James Tyrone, whom all the other girls at the convent used to rave about, and that when she came home from school, her father would take her to meet him. And he did; he took her to a play about the French Revolution; she cried and was afraid her eyes would be red when her father took her backstage to meet the actor.

As we know from a private autobiographical document that O'Neill wrote for his own psychotherapeutic use about 1926, Eugene believed that his mother's father was still alive in the early years of the marriage. Eugene continued in this belief in 1940, when he wrote *Long Day's Journey,* and he apparently never learned that his grandfather had actually died in 1874.

The error is interesting, because until the end of his life Eugene was known for having nearly total recall. One must infer that he frequently heard his mother speak of her father as still alive at the time she married, and never heard any other information about his grandfather's death. The mistaken fact implied an important psychological reality for his mother: that her father had not died before she married but in fact had introduced her to her husband and bought her wedding dress.

Late in act 3 Mary reminds her husband about the wedding and her dress. "My father told me to buy anything I wanted and never mind what it cost. The best is none too good, he said. I'm afraid he spoiled me dreadfully."

Thomas Quinlan might well have indulged his daughter had he still been alive, but it was Bridget Quinlan who wrote a check for a thousand dollars for Ella's trousseau (Gelbs, 38), a sum that in 1877 would have bought a good house. Assuming that Eugene recorded what he had heard, many questions arise, including this one: Did Ella recall the details accurately and yet deliberately tailor them to reflect her adoration of her father and condescension toward her mother? Or did she rearrange unconsciously? Perhaps there was a bit of each. Following this hypothetical line of reasoning, let us assume that, if pressed, Ella could probably have forced herself to remember that her father had actually died three years before she married James O'Neill. But in a certain way, Ella's distortion tells the real truth of her world: that her father never did die, that if her mother wrote the check, it was still her father who had wanted nothing but the best for her and who had earned the money that bought the dress. By marrying James O'Neill, Ella kept Thomas Quinlan eternally alive and postponed forever acknowledging her loss.

2

The Marriage
1877–1884

ALTHOUGH ST. ANN'S ROMAN Catholic Church, where Ella and James were married, was favored by the fashionable and the Catholic elite, the service was virtually private. As the Gelbs write, the wedding was attended only by a handful of Ella's relatives, including her mother, who was matron of honor, her Aunt Elizabeth and Uncle Thomas Brennan, who gave Ella to James, and Ella's brother (Gelbs, 38). The bride's gown was elegant, and the wedding ring had been purchased from Tiffany's. Newspapers described the weather as gloomy and threatening. The marriage lasted more than forty-three years, until James died in 1920. From 1883 to 1913, the *Monte Cristo* years, James traveled almost constantly, hopping about the continent from city to city for short runs. Despite the discomfort of life on the road, which Ella detested, husband and wife seldom let anything but ill health separate them.

By the standard of the times, it was a good marriage. Life brought them immense difficulties that severely tested their fortitude and character, and they did not always pass the tests. Yet after forty-three years of marriage, each remained devoted to the other, perfectly content to pass most hours of every day with the other. No one who knew the senior O'Neills doubted that they loved each other deeply throughout their lives. Ella was cherished, adored, and protected by her husband, who almost never required her to raise a hand to do the least domestic chore. She could tell her daughter-in-law forty years after her marriage that she had never learned to cook, could barely boil an egg. Ella O'Neill could also have said truthfully, as Mary Tyrone assures the "second girl," Cathleen, in *Long Day's Journey into Night,* that there never was a hint of scandal involving James and other women. Life brought Ella and James severe trials, but however harsh they were, the couple survived them without losing their love for each other. If one of their sons failed to reach his potential, another was awarded the Nobel Prize.

Nevertheless, if it was loving and durable, the marriage constantly chafed each partner's greatest vulnerabilities. No one in the family escaped the trials, but the cruelest test was surely suffered by Ella, who endured the twenty-five-year ordeal of morphine addiction that began in 1888. Ella's struggle affected the other O'Neills only slightly less painfully than it did her. Behind her addiction lay an event that impinged on every aspect of her adult life, the cessation of her personal development following the death of her father when she was sixteen. From this point on, the recurring theme in her life was loss or the threat of loss: she dreaded the loss of people on whom she depended, the loss of self-esteem, the loss of money and the particular things money meant to her. Loss was also the principal threat to James, and, like Ella, he experienced and expressed his perception of that menace in the ways he used and thought about money. Whatever the ultimate causes, the problems in the marriage usually centered on money, and they began almost at once.

The wedding had been private for at least two reasons. Everyone believed that a married matinee idol would appeal less to the nation's schoolgirls. Beyond that was a more immediate threat of trouble. James had received letters from Nettie Walsh in Chicago demanding money for herself and for the child she said was James's son. His Chicago friends told James that she was coming to them to demand money, that she was calling herself Mrs. O'Neill, and that she was threatening to sue the actor if he did not pay. James believed that if she heard of the marriage, the news would exacerbate her rage. Shortly after the wedding, a newspaper, the *New York Clipper,* published the rumor that James O'Neill had "deserted" a wife and child in Chicago.

James and Ella had a brief honeymoon, then went to Chicago where James was to act at the Union Square Theatre until Palmer's company began its 1877–78 season in early November. The O'Neills settled into the Clifton House. James's acting won high praise from critics, and the rumors of scandal led to teasing and innuendo in reviewers' stories and sometimes on news pages. James inspired high praise for his *Othello,* the tragedy of one who loved not wisely but too well. The irony did not escape newswriters, but Ella, at first, seems to have paid no attention at all to the Nettie Walsh affair—this according to her former school friend from St. Mary's Lillie West, with whom she spent much of her time. West had become a reporter for a Chicago daily and now took a personal as well as a professional interest in the James O'Neill scandal.

Nettie Walsh sent at least one threatening letter to James at the Clifton House, which he apparently ignored. Nettie would not be ignored. On September 7, she sued James for divorce and now gave the press more than rumors and threats. She displayed to reporters her son Alfred Hamilton O'Neill, and the reporters judged in print that "Little Alfie" looked just like James. The suit accused James of committing adultery with an unnamed actress, now dead, and mentioned, without using the word bigamy, that he had recently married in New York. Nettie asked for alimony and support for her son from James, whom she described as highly paid and, because he was "parsimonious," wealthy, worth at least fifteen thousand dollars.

The effect of the lawsuit on Ella was hard to understand at the time and is so in retrospect. In *Long Day's Journey into Night* Eugene shows the mother as never forgetting, or letting her husband forget, that she innocently began marriage in the midst of a scandal. Her reproachfulness is certainly an understandable response to a real grievance. But at the time of Nettie's lawsuit, Ella apparently showed no reaction at all. Lillie West (under the name Amy Leslie) later wrote: "Ella Quinlan never seemed to know what it [the divorce suit] was all about or worth. She had been my seatmate in college for a year and was almost a child when she married O'Neill, but when, kidlike, I blurted out one day: 'Oh, Ella, what on earth can you do about this woman?' Ella looked a little blank and said, sweetly: 'What woman, honey?' and I had to explain to bring it to her mind. She did not care a rap, and, having myself fallen at the feet of James regularly, I was allowed a matinee" (Chicago *News*, July 10, 1909, quoted in Alexander 1962, 9).

The sangfroid Lillie West attributes to Ella—"She did not care a rap"—seems at first inconsistent with Eugene's portrayal of Mary Tyrone as never letting her husband forget that she began her marriage in the middle of a scandal, and inconsistent, also, with Mary's complaint of being snubbed or pitied by her former friends because of the suit. West does neither, but she tells the story because the bland denial was surprising under the circumstances: How could Ella not know what woman? Ella's denial is more nearly consistent with West's previous remarks: that "Ella Quinlan never seemed to know" what the suit entailed, and that "she was almost a child when she married O'Neill." Ella was not naive, nor was she ignorant of the suit's implications, but she could apparently make it completely disappear from her consciousness. Ella's power of denial is the key to the seeming inconsistencies. At the moment Lillie asked about "that woman," the woman did not exist for Ella, and Lillie needed to remind her of the world of womanizing men, vengeful women, and lawsuits. While the newspapers made hay of the scandal, Lillie and Ella went to see James play Othello.

James countersued, claiming that Nettie was "under the influence of sundry designing persons who sought to ruin" him professionally. He admitted that he had met her on August 1, 1871, in Cleveland, and that they had lived together for about a year, until his move to Chicago in early fall of 1872. Thereafter he saw her only "at wide intervals" and considered that their relationship was "extinguished" by 1875. He said that he had never married Nettie in Cleveland or anyplace else, and that because she had had other lovers, he had no way of knowing whether her child was his (Gelbs, 40). On October 23, after listening to the depositions, Judge Williams asserted that no evidence that a marriage had ever taken place had yet been presented, but he scheduled another hearing for late November and ordered James to pay interim alimony of fifty dollars a months, with a hundred dollars for legal fees. James returned to New York to open in *The Mother's Secret* with Palmer's company on November 13, and in Chicago, his lawyers arranged a settlement. By one account James's lawyers gave Nettie a sum of money, rumored to be five hundred and fifty dollars, in lieu of alimony and in return for her signing an agreement never to trouble James again (Alexander 1962, 68). In December the suit was dismissed for lack of evidence that a marriage had taken place, and probably none ever had; but a circumstantial case can be made that James believed Little Alfie to be his child, and Alfie himself came to believe it. As Alexander has pointed out, the boy Alfie signed no agreement to leave his father alone. Twenty years later the younger man brought another suit; this suit James also settled, after three years of disputation, giving his putative son enough money for the young man to start a career of running successful enterprises (Alexander 1962, 8–10, 68). (Alfred Hamilton O'Neill turned up again in 1922; his lawyer asked Eugene for a portion of James's estate, but this time Alfred got nothing.)

Outwardly, the scandal of 1877 did little harm. James seemed open and forthright in handling publicity about the trial and won the press over to his side. The public generally took James's part also. He was a matinee idol, and because he cut a romantic figure in public as well as on the stage, such scandals seemed inevitable. Nevertheless, the suit and the allegation of paternity cannot fail to have struck him where he was painfully vulnerable. To the extent that he could not definitively deny being the father of Little Alfie, he recognized at least partly consciously that he was abandoning his son, as his father had abandoned him and his mother. It seems likely that he made the two settlements with Nettie and her son in order to avoid hating in himself what he hated in his father. Even more than the threat of financial loss, the suit reminded James of the inescapability of the past.

The suit crystallized a change in James's character that had begun two years earlier. The trouble he had experienced when Nettie Walsh refused to accept his wish to end their affair and when Louise Hawthorne died after he had broken off with her, together with such marks of success as Edwin Booth's praising his Othello to McVicker, had led James to settle down, to marry—and to marry the respectable and middle-class Ella in particular. Marriage was the first step in the gradual process that would eventually lead him to elevate family ideals over artistic ideals.

Like many a man of his time, James came to believe that so long as his family held together, he could stand against the world. Louise Hawthorne's death and Nettie Walsh's suit and accusations probably had something to do with his lifelong fidelity to his marriage vows. The new James would remain the faithful protector of his wife during the dark decades of her addiction and would tolerate their sons when it seemed that they lived only to torment him and when he believed he would have to support both of them all their lives.

Flush with his legal victory, James told everyone he wanted a large family. In spring 1878, after a successful season in New York, Palmer's repertory company traveled to San Francisco. James and Ella, who was now pregnant, went with them.

The Bay Area press had not forgotten James, who had become a favorite adopted son of the city in 1875. With bully boy heartiness, and no regard for Ella's gentility, the papers outdid one another in teasing James about his romantic exploits on and off the stage. He was hailed as a "black-mustached Adonis" who had been "claimed by three or four wives in

Chicago" (Gelbs, 43). Young men, the press reported, took out their turnip watches and timed the kisses James bestowed on his leading ladies. Betting pools were organized over the question of how long the longest of his kisses would last.

James took the teasing well, kidding the reporters in kind. But he also was careful to begin establishing his new bourgeois persona. The papers were informed that the O'Neills lived in a residential hotel, where Mrs. O'Neill was completely free from the least domestic chore. On fine days, the public learned, Mr. O'Neill took his beautiful bride on buggy rides on which the devoted couple saw the most splendid sights nature could offer. Mr. and Mrs. O'Neill, by the way, were anticipating a blessed event in September. On some of their drives about the countryside, the famous actor looked at land investments. Might the city hope that its favorite actor would settle permanently in California? The eye James turned toward land assured the public that beneath the good looks and actor's talent lay something more substantial, the instincts of a man of enterprise. The O'Neills made friends with businesspeople like the family of Henry M. Black, who had founded a carriage-making firm.

On September 10 the O'Neills' anticipation was fulfilled by the birth of James O'Neill, Jr., who would be called Jamie or Jim. In consideration of his son's birth and his wife's increased responsibilities, James senior resigned from Palmer's company and joined Baldwin's Academy of Music as its leading man. For the next two years the couple were free from the constant travel that marked most actors' lives; it was to be the longest such period they would know for nearly forty years. He also went about becoming a man of property.

Knowing little of land values, James had to depend on his judgment of the acquaintances and salesmen who urged this or that investment on him. He soon began acquiring high-risk mining mortgages; he hoped that if some did not pay off, one or two successful mineral finds would put him ahead of the game. Even with the ventures that did not pay off, land was still land and could be resold for some other use. His father-in-law's example shone in the distance, for it was through property speculation in post–Civil War Cleveland that Quinlan had made his fortune. Real estate investments, James hoped, would allow him to give his wife and children the best of everything, just as it had Thomas Quinlan.

Ella was also interested in property, but of a different kind. She wanted then, as she would all her life, a fine house on a fashionable street in New York. Any talk of her husband's getting rich as her father had done was less interesting than re-creating a life with the company of women like herself who lived in homes like her father's. The great gulf between husband and wife widened as she tried to cope with her baby. Nearly everything in her present life, even connections to prominent San Franciscans, served to remind her that life with an actor was nothing at all like life in the vanished familial home in Cleveland.

On days when there was no excursion in a rented buggy, and no meeting with a property agent, James slept late and took an afternoon meal with Ella. Then to the theater to prepare for the evening performance. After the curtain he would go out with friends to drink and talk for hours. If Ella did not go to the theater, she would seldom see him until the small hours, when he came home full of drink and ardor. In later years, according to her younger son, she complained that she felt humiliated that her husband drank heavily and spent so much time in saloons, and she compared him invidiously with her father, who did not drink. Yet it seems clear that her father also led a gentleman's life, as it were, as proprietor of Quinlan and Spirnaugle's, and might be up all hours with theatrical friends after performances. If one tries to understand her unhappiness, one figure seems striking by its absence, her mother. The home Ella longed for was run by her mother as executive for her father. It seems clear that though Ella focused her attention on the loss of her father, his attention, and his home, she missed her mother as much, perhaps without being fully aware that the orderly and stable home she craved was run by her mother. Yet she would not consider living with her mother in New York or New London while her husband traveled. Nor was Ella able in her own marriage to make for herself any such role as that her mother had played in the Quinlan home.

Probably, during Jamie's first months of life Ella began her lifelong effort to persuade her husband to buy a permanent home for the family. A family without a home, or at least a family without the desire for a permanent house, must have been to her unimaginable. But for them to have a home in New York, James would have had to abandon a professional situation in which he was enjoying great respect and success. Undoubtedly James agreed that he would look for a suitable opportunity to return to New York. In the meantime, they lived in a residential hotel, and life went on in a way that to James was pleasant. Ella spent most of her time with the baby, Jamie, and with women friends.

In March 1879, the routine of daily life was upset when James was arrested and put in jail for public blasphemy. It was an event that at first seemed overinflated but then turned ugly. At the time, and for some time after, it seemed serious enough that James believed his career was ruined.

In late autumn, the young David Belasco had decided to produce a version of the Oberammergau Passion play adapted for the North American stage by a visionary called Salmi Morse. James is said to have given up tobacco and alcohol to prepare himself spiritually to impersonate the Christian Savior, and to have permitted his colleagues to indulge in no vices or improper speech backstage—so it was reported on the theatrical pages. At other times the papers incited public outrage by calling the planned performance blasphemous. Salmi Morse announced that the Catholic bishop of California approved of the pageant, but several Protestant clergymen led protests, and when the outcry arose, the Catholic Church declined to speak either for or against. Before the March 3 opening, the cast was threatened with lynching.

The performance succeeded only too well with its audiences. When James O'Neill appeared crowned in thorns, women fainted and both men and women fell to their knees. Some of the audience raged out of the theater and into the streets assaulting Jews and smashing windows in their houses and businesses (Timberlake 1954, 70–74). Publicity against the production was so strong that audiences dwindled despite the success, and the play was withdrawn after a few performances. A few days later, Belasco's courage returned and he brought back the Passion. By now the city was ready with a newly created ordinance. Cast members spent the night in jail, and the next day James paid a fine of fifty dollars. (The actor who played Judas was fined five dollars.)

It seems strange that a man as worldly as James failed to anticipate that San Francisco in the late 1870s would be shocked by a theatrical representation of the Passion. James's failure of judgment probably occurred not because he was naive but because he was genuinely devout. He frequently told reporters that as a youth he had thought of becoming a priest. Much later, a younger colleague, Brandon Tynan, told of regularly celebrating Mass with James when they acted together, and of feeling that James wished his own atheistic and troubled sons were like Tynan (who himself loved James as he would a father). James's authority in the role and his blindness to the circumstances probably derived from the intuitive sense that playing the role of Christ allowed him to unite two powerful currents in his personality, his religious and theatrical impulses. The arrest must have disturbed him in complex ways.

James's career of course survived the scandal. He returned to conventional roles, and the city, recovering its good humor, restored him to his place of favor. James basked in the public good feeling; but Ella, who was intensely private, was ruled by internal demons that doomed her never to forget her husband's shame. James enjoyed success after success in the remainder of 1879 and 1880, and then accepted an invitation to return to New York for the 1880–81 season, to join Booth's Theater. (Booth himself was in England and no longer connected with the theater that bore his name.) The O'Neills returned to New York in the fall, shortly after Jamie's second birthday.

A decline, a loss of professional idealism, a lowering of goals began to appear in the life of James O'Neill. James, now thirty-five, wanted to secure his income and consolidate his reputation as a major theatrical star, and he was losing interest in developing his exceptional gifts as an actor. In 1882 he bought a play called *An American King*, which had been written especially for him. He aimed to make the play perennially popular in countrywide tours (as James Jefferson had done with *Rip Van Winkle*). But people did not like *An American King*, and he gave it up when he was offered the chance to return to Booth's for the 1882–83 season. He and Charles Thorne played in *The Corsican Brothers*, but Thorne fell ill and had to be replaced. James was praised as the younger brother. After *The Corsican Brothers* closed, Booth's had planned to do another "French" melodrama, Charles Fechter's adaptation from Dumas of *The Count of Monte Cristo*, with Thorne. But Thorne died suddenly. James was rushed into the part, and the play opened before its star knew his lines. Although the first night, February 12, 1883, did not go well, the play was soon popular with audiences. This would be the role James had sought to make him a star. James and Ella could not have seen clearly in 1883, or for some time after, the changes *Monte Cristo* would bring to their lives. James could never have imagined that his success in *Monte Cristo* would go on more than a few seasons.

The effects on their lives were indeed considerable. Except for the two years in San Francisco, James had traveled a great deal, as all actors did, going wherever an interesting role or a repertory offer or good money led him. He settled in the new city for several weeks or several months until the next move came. But with his success in *Monte Cristo,* travel became an almost daily event. James now played large towns as well as cities, and travels might take the family anywhere in the United States or Canada. In the spring of 1883, James, Ella, and the five-year-old Jamie began to live out of trunks.

Constant travel was a fact of theatrical life, and a hard life it was. Often, the morning after a late night they would catch an early train and leave before any restaurant was open. Hungry and uncomfortable, they would ride for hours in the noisy, smoky rattler until they reached the next town. At the best of times someone would have gone ahead to arrange for meals, lodging, and publicity. Otherwise James would find the most comfortable place he could for Ella to wait while he and his colleagues sought food and accommodations. When his wife was settled, James had to find the theater and make whatever arrangements he could before the performance would begin. This was their life for weeks at a time, broken by occasional longer stays in larger cities, where they could stay in a residential hotel.

The birth of James's and Ella's second son late that summer, a welcome event to both, compounded the difficulties of the new theatrical venture. Unable to be apart from her husband, unwilling to stay with her mother in New York or New London, Ella set out for St. Louis with five-year-old Jamie and the newborn Edmund shortly after giving birth. James named his second son Edmund Burke O'Neill, after the Dublin-born statesman. (Previous biographers, following a 1940 letter by Eugene, have given Edmund's birthplace as St. Louis, although no birth certificate has yet been found. In a personal communication, Margaret Loftus Ranald told me that the late Myron Matlaw found Edmund's death certificate, which indicated the child's place of birth as New York City.)

The family wandered until the following June. James played *Monte Cristo* from city to city and town to town, lured by the guarantee of earning more than fifty thousand dollars for his first full season. It was a vast sum. But to Ella the cost matched the gain: constant discomfort, little opportunity to see friends, even when the troupe was near someone she knew from school or from Cleveland, and living apart from everything she had been taught to consider civilized. Simply looking her best was hugely complicated: clothes were always wrinkled, and cleaning, pressing and mending were difficult to arrange. Maintaining personal hygiene according to middle-class standards was almost impossible in hotels that were seldom clean and never convenient. And with few other stylish women in sight (except perhaps for an actress or two, women with whom she was uncomfortable), it was hard to avoid the blues. Even with Jamie for company, she must have longed for the simplicity and safety she had experienced in her father's home or the convent.

Given that Jamie had no more possibility of meeting other children than Ella had of meeting other educated women and that James was busy most of the time, mother and son became constant companions. Jamie was of an age to be at the height of the childhood oedipal crisis, an event that (even in pre-Freudian times) called forth from intuitive, empathic parents the best combination of discipline, calm, and tolerance. From the standpoint of a boy's childhood desire, nothing could be more gratifying than to have almost exclusive possession of his mother, especially a mother who gave the constant impression of preferring her young courtier to the self-educated husband who caused her to lead such an inconvenient and uncomfortable life. There grew up between mother and son a society of mutual adoration. He loved her for the charm that she bestowed, and she loved him for his adoring her. It was to be the pattern of their relationship for life. Jamie would never outgrow the childhood form of his attachment to his mother.

In June 1884, after a taxing but financially successful season, the O'Neills retreated to New London, Connecticut, where Bridget Quinlan had settled to be near relatives, especially her sister and brother-in-law, the Brennans. James liked the town, then considered one of the most beautiful port cities in New England, and he had a good friend there, John McGinley, who was starting a newspaper, the New London *Day*. Ella felt uncomfortable in the town and snubbed her cousins, but James attributed her feelings to the difficult year she had had. He set about looking for the home she kept saying she wanted. For her twenty-seventh birthday, on August 14, he made her a gift of the deed to two large, sloping lots on Pequot Avenue in New London, with good southerly views of Long Island Sound and the island. James could imagine sitting on the porch and admiring the square-rigged deepwater sailing ships anchored in the harbor.

The lots were on the edge of a fashionable part of a good street, but the street was not in New York and the house would never be fine in the way that Ella wanted. On one lot James began construction of a pleasant cottage known as the Pink House. On the other lot, at 325 Pequot Avenue, stood several structures, including a disused combination store and residence, and, almost abutting it, an abandoned schoolhouse. The store was well built, with excellent floors and fireplaces and an attractive stairway leading up to four small second-story bedrooms. James got the work started that would join the store to the schoolhouse and remodel the former store. The schoolhouse became the kitchen and pantry for the new house. The house, which James called Monte Cristo Cottage, still stands at 325 Pequot Avenue and is a Registered National Landmark, open to the public when funding permits. A wide, latticed porch runs across the front of the house and partway along the sides, opening down diagonally from the southeast corner in a graceful two-stage stairway to the front walk. The house is protected on the north and east sides by fine maples and pines, still standing, and by elms. Ella found the trees oppressive; it is assumed that her complaints about the trees gave Eugene the germ of a stage design for *Desire Under the Elms*. The new Pink House was built to bring in a little revenue and was usually rented. Monte Cristo Cottage was to be the closest thing to a permanent home that the James O'Neill family would ever know.

The house was undoubtedly far from perfect and far from what she had in mind, but Ella was unhappy with it to a degree that is difficult to understand when one looks at it nowadays. Possibly it reminded her of the residence above a store that she and her parents had occupied in Cleveland before her father's success in real estate. She complained about it to various townspeople whenever she was in New London, and Eugene reproduced her complaints in *Long Day's Journey into Night*. The actress Florence Eldridge, who played Mary Tyrone in the first American production in 1956, wrote of visiting the house along with the director, José Quintero, and the other actors. "I was surprised to find it full of attractive possibilities and charmingly situated looking out on the sound. I decided then that Mary Tyrone was a victim, not only of her life but also of her own inadequacies, and must be played as an immature person." Eldridge's impression of Mary Tyrone was influenced by a conversation with the respected psychoanalyst Marie Nyswander, who was also an expert on drug addiction. Eldridge also met Carlotta Monterey, O'Neill's third wife, who Eldridge and Quintero believed was partly the model for Mary Tyrone. With regard to Mary, Eldridge wrote that Dr. Nyswander concluded that "if O'Neill had accurately observed his mother's behavior, there was pathology involved as well as addiction" (quoted in Floyd 1979, 286).

To Eldridge's impression another may be added. Ella never tired of complaining about Monte Cristo Cottage and never ceased reminding her husband that he didn't know what a real home was and had hurt her irreparably by refusing to get her a proper home. Yet she apparently had the means on two occasions to buy for herself (or for her family) the home she said they needed: in 1887, when she inherited a substantial estate from her mother, and again about 1911, when she inherited her brother's estate. Perhaps she could neither cope with the difficulties of making such a purchase nor stand to turn the problem over to James. Perhaps her concept of a "real home" required that the house be provided for her by her husband, as her first real home, the Woodland Avenue home in Cleveland, had been provided by her father.

Ella's needs dovetailed in a most unfortunate way with James's needs to appease the gods of Fortune. He had something like an Irish peasant's, or an ancient Greek's, pride in austerity and dread of provoking the envy of the gods or other men. James protected and cherished his good-luck talisman, that is, his wife. Ella's complaints about the house, like her complaints about other of James's gifts, reflected her frustration at having no authority or control over the cottage that was nominally hers. She wanted simultaneously to be the protected child of her father and to have the power and authority of the trusted wife of a generous man. James probably wanted her to share his concern about family finances yet could not yield authority to her or anyone else where money was concerned.

The matter of the family home brings to the forefront the issue of how Ella and James used money, and what money meant to each of them. The subject would later preoccupy Eugene, for whom the varieties of financial morbidity were a regular dramatic theme.

As mentioned, Ella twice inherited large amounts of money, from the estates of her mother who died in 1877, and her brother, who died in 1911. Emily Rippin, a New London friend of the O'Neills, told the biographer Louis Sheaffer that about 1913, "Mrs. O'Neill . . . told me she'd gone through two fortunes [presumably the inheritances from her mother and her brother, about whom practically nothing is known], and that was why Mr. O'Neill didn't give her an allowance. He felt that she didn't know how to handle money, that if she had any she'd give it to the boys and they would never work" (LS, 262; the bracketed explanation is

Sheaffer's). What happened to Ella's inheritance is unclear. It did not go to buy a family home. Some of the money from Bridget Quinlan was invested about 1906, on James's recommendation, in a mail order company that prospered for a few years. In a 1909 letter to his parents, Eugene mentions the company and continues, "I suppose when I see you again that Mama will have all her money back" (SL, 18–19). His reference to "her money" makes it clear that Ella kept her money separate from James's money, including the money she allowed him to invest. She bailed out of the mail order company independently of her husband. (James lost heavily when the company went bankrupt in 1912 [LS, 216]). It seems likely that large amounts of Ella's money went to buy fashionable clothes. She also frequently gave money to Jamie and Eugene.

In *Long Day's Journey into Night* Eugene studied the financial ways of all the O'Neills in careful detail. Because finances invaded every corner of the marriage of James and Ella, the issue justifies some discussion, even though historical information is scant and most inferences derive from Eugene's subjective representations of family conversations. Near the end of the play, when she is deeply regressed on morphine, Mary tells her husband that her father

> spoiled me dreadfully. My mother didn't. She was very pious
> and strict. I think she was a little jealous. She didn't approve
> of my marrying—especially an actor. I think she hoped I
> would become a nun. She used to scold my father. She'd
> grumble, "You never tell me, never mind what it costs,
> when I buy anything! You've spoiled that girl so, I pity her
> husband if she ever marries. She'll expect him to give her
> the moon. She'll never make a good wife." (*She laughs affec-*
> *tionately.*) Poor mother! (*She smiles at Tyrone with a strange,*
> *incongruous coquetry.*) But she was mistaken, wasn't she,
> James? I haven't been such a bad wife, have I?
>
> TYRONE (*Huskily, trying to force a smile*): I'm not com-
> plaining, Mary.
>
> MARY (*A shadow of vague guilt crosses her face*): At least, I've
> loved you dearly, and done the best I could—under the cir-
> cumstances. (*The shadow vanishes and her shy, girlish expres-*
> *sion returns.*) That wedding gown was nearly the death of
> me and the dressmaker too! . . . Where is my wedding gown

now, I wonder? I kept it wrapped up in tissue paper in my
trunk. I used to hope I would have a daughter and when it
came time for her to marry—She couldn't have bought a
lovelier gown, and I knew, James, you'd never tell her, never
mind the cost. You'd want her to pick up something at a
bargain. [CP3, 784–85]

In Eugene's interpretation of his parents' marriage, Mary treads on
issues of great sensitivity for herself and for her husband. Mary remembers a conflict between her parents over the use of money. She recalls her
father as generosity itself, telling her to buy anything she wanted, that the
best was none too good. His spoiling her made her adore him. But her
mother was strict; she complained that her husband spoiled their daughter and also complained that he was not as generous to his wife as to his
daughter.

The mother's complaints meant to the daughter that her mother
was "jealous": not envious, but jealous. In a well-spoken person like Mary,
the word is important: jealousy refers to anxiety over the loss of someone's
exclusive love or preference; envy refers to greed for something possessed
by another or an advantage gained by a rival. Using the word "jealous" reveals Mary's belief that she replaced her mother in her father's love and
that the proof of preference was that her father spoiled her.

Such a belief as Mary's is nearly universal at certain stages of childhood development, but often gives way to wry self-awareness in adults.
The word reveals that at least sometimes, decades after the deaths of her
father and mother, this woman of fifty-four understands her parents' marriage as she did when an adolescent.

It seems likely that the Quinlan marriage was more complicated
than Ella remembered it, but in the play Eugene was representing his
mother's memories. It probably was the case that in daily life, Thomas
Quinlan enjoyed the role of spoiling his daughter with grandly generous
gestures. In the politics of the marriage, Bridget fell into the role of disciplinarian and fount of common sense. But we have other evidence of
Thomas's ways with money and discipline. He had the shrewdness and
self-discipline to develop a small business into several successful enterprises. The paragraph in his will that urged his son and daughter to seek
independence and to expect to make their own way in the world rather
than depending on their mother or the estate implies something besides

fond indulgence. Thomas could comfortably play the adoring, spoiling papa only if he was confident that Bridget exercised the control over family spending that he himself required of her. In Eugene's reconstruction, the mother's grumbling seems to have meant not only that she envied her daughter's getting whatever she wanted, but that she was warning her daughter not to expect the world always to treat her as her father did. She and Thomas agreed that the children needed to learn responsibility.

Eugene believed that his mother, like Mary Tyrone, had no sense at all that her parents had a complicated relationship behind the surface they let her see, let alone any understanding of what their relations actually were. An interpreter who asks why or how Mary could have understood so little faces a series of increasingly complicated questions, one of which is this: When Mary speaks of saving her wedding dress to give to her own daughter because Tyrone would never tell his daughter, "Never mind the cost," she plays the parts that each of her parents played, in a compromise version of a family drama. It was Bridget, not Thomas, who actually spent lavishly on Ella O'Neill's trousseau—although Bridget may have grumbled about the expense just as if her husband had still been alive. In her fantasy of providing her daughter's wedding dress, Mary Tyrone seems to play the role Ella's mother played. But in making the grand gesture of the imaginary gift to the daughter she did not have, she acts in the style of her father. Mary Tyrone's monologue re-creates the conditions she remembers from her safe and indulged childhood. (It is assumed that Eugene's supposed "mistake" about who bought the wedding dress, which other biographers have noticed, was not Eugene's but his mother's, and that Eugene reproduced the details of a familiar family scene. Eugene probably did not know who paid for the trousseau, but in any case his concern was to represent his mother's subjective reality.)

Most of the time, in her relationship with her husband, Mary played the daughter; but by frequently mentioning James's penny-pinching, she forced her husband to play the role not of her father but of her mother, the disciplinarian, the voice of frugality and common sense. She may have adored her father and have had trouble with her mother, but in her marriage she expressed through action a need, previously fulfilled by her mother, to have her husband keep domestic finances under control.

Extrapolating from anecdote and from *Long Day's Journey into Night*, one can infer that through reckless spending Ella forced her husband to play the part her mother had played in the Quinlan family. If she could lead her husband to play the role previously played by her mother, she would not have to face the fact that her mother was gone. She showed her discomfort with the idea of becoming an adult woman like her mother through her flights from domestic and maternal responsibility. If she had had to manage a home, she would have had to confront the thing she refused to accept, that her father was dead and the protection gone that had allowed her to know only as much about the world outside her home as she chose. Impulsive spending helped Ella deny loss and indefinitely postpone mourning for both her parents. In this way, each time James showed anxiety about money, it forced Ella to glimpse, and then required her to deny, the loss of her father and the loss of her childhood. Ella would protect herself by gaily confessing (as she had to Emily Rippin) to being a spendthrift.

In fact, for reasons of his own, and in his own way, James O'Neill tried his best to re-create for his wife the sheltered childhood she had lost. With the recollection of his father's mistreatment of his mother, and his mother's slaving in domestic service to support her children, and fully aware how hard was the life he gave Ella, James protected her almost completely from domestic responsibility. He idolized her and considered her a superior creature. Indeed, he boasted to his friend George Tyler of his adoration, his good fortune in having her as his wife, and his protection of her. After James died, when Eugene told Tyler that his mother was showing a flair for straightening out James's tangled real estate holdings, Tyler replied: "It delights me beyond words to hear that she is taking a real interest in things. You see—she never had a chance before—your dear father loved her so much that he couldn't bear to see her be anything else than an ornament" (LS, 40). The tactful phrase "dear father" softens the criticism in Tyler's judgment. Tyler recognized that James went even further than the ordinary run of Victorian men in confining his beloved to a (semi)gilded cage and evidently felt that by restricting her responsibility, James gave her no encouragement to grow or develop. Ella was content to be helpless.

By shunning responsibilities in the marriage—by never learning to cook, by ignoring her children when they were ill—Ella maintained a semblance of the protected childhood she longed to resume, but a caricature that constantly reminded her of the loss of the real thing. Knowledge of loss abraded the chronic underlying anxiety that required Ella to deny her father's death. Her anxiety, in turn, constantly exacerbated James's fundamental anxiety that fate would return him to the slums.

Dread of poverty not only made James vulnerable to the threats of losing self-respect and the respect of others; it also made him crudely manipulative in handling the family finances. Controlling the money meant to James the power to control the members of his family—just as it had to his father-in-law. But whereas Thomas Quinlan controlled his family indirectly through grandly generous gestures, James never tried to conceal that he dreaded the possibility that his family would spend him into the poorhouse. By not concealing his vulnerability, James lost the confidence of the others and made them anxious that home and father gave them no protection against the consequences of their impulses. The anxiety Ella and her sons felt about James's weakness came out in arguments with him, in mockery, and in guilt about their dissatisfaction with a man they generally admired. Eugene points up the ambivalence that his father's stinginess evoked in the funny and painful argument between James and Edmund Tyrone over which sanatorium the son would go to: "You can choose any place you like! Never mind what it costs! Any place I can afford. Any place you like—within reason" (CP3, 808).

His manipulations were so much less subtle than Thomas Quinlan's that Ella saw James's strategies as attacks, and she felt provoked to counterattack by spending recklessly, and by denigrating her husband's acts of generosity. The more Ella defied James's penny-pinching, the more vividly he remembered the horrors of poverty and the more tightly he grasped; and the more he grasped, the more he forced Ella to recall the loss of her father and to deny it—that is, to spend.

In an autobiographical narrative of 1926, and in *Long Day's Journey*, Eugene showed that with the loss of her father fresh in her thoughts, anything Ella said at such times was likely, directly or indirectly, to compare James with her father, always to James's disadvantage. It was a comparison bound to make him uncomfortable. The same habits of mind that made James expect that a turn of Fortune's wheel would reduce him to poverty again made him unable to feel truly confident that he deserved the success he had earned. To be compared with his father-in-law brought near the surface the unconscious idea on which his sense of self rested. It could not fail to remind him that his father had been a drunkard who had deserted his family and possibly committed suicide. It reminded him that he would always be a slum boy and had better not pretend to more, or else he would excite the envy of the gods as well as the contempt of the gentry. It accounted for the qualities his sons would later mock, his crying poverty to salesmen and doctors, his wearing shabby clothes around the house, and his enforcing on everyone penny-foolish economies.

The permanent underlying insecurity that James expressed through his use of money was fundamentally related to his enduring devotion to Ella and his lifelong fidelity to his marriage. James's devotion to Ella matched his dread of losing wealth and class. So long as he kept Ella safe, her presence helped him fend off the destiny that would sooner or later return him to the slums. He might not deserve her for his wife, but he would do anything to avoid showing his unworthiness, and he gladly tolerated any hardship she caused him.

3

The Sons of Monte Cristo
1884–1895

IN THE SUMMER OF 1884, construction began on Monte Cristo Cottage, and the O'Neills faced the daunting prospect of returning to the road with two children in tow. In a private autobiographical narrative written about 1926, Eugene tried to reconstruct his mother's point of view on the great events that he thought had shaped her life. Regarding the circumstances surrounding James's decision to build his future around the *Monte Cristo* tour, Eugene wrote: "Husband now 'on his own' touring nine months place to place, one-nights mostly, no chance to form contacts except for brief summers in N[ew] L[ondon] which M[other] hates." The toddler Edmund, entering his second year, would require constant attention, while the six-year-old Jamie would require an equal amount of attention of a different sort. Everyone thought Jamie extremely bright, and his parents knew the boy needed to begin his education. School would be out of the question on the road, and a tutor would be expensive and complicated when travel, board, and lodgings were taken into account. James could not help hesitating over the expense. For Ella, losing the company of Jamie meant redoubled loneliness and isolation on the road. Evidently the O'Neills could reach no decision about Jamie's schooling. By the end of summer James and Ella were brought to the point of agreeing that for the first time in their seven years of marriage they would somehow endure a prolonged separation. Ella, her mother, and the boys moved to the Richfield, a Manhattan residential hotel. James went alone to begin his second season in *The Count of Monte Cristo*, traveling through New York State and New England. He had time for brief visits to his family during the autumn, and at Christmas he could spend a couple of weeks. For people who had suffered losses as painful as James's and Ella's, separation was intolerable. Early in January when James headed west, Ella went with him.

Late in February, Ella's mother wired from New York that Jamie had measles, and at the end of the month a further telegram told that Edmund had caught the measles from Jamie. On March 4, as Ella packed to return to New York, Edmund died. James's show had to go on, so Ella made the train trip east alone. She and her mother had the dreary task of taking Edmund's body to New London, where they buried him in St. Mary's Catholic Cemetery. Even before the O'Neills ever spent a night in their new home, Monte Cristo Cottage and New London represented to them a loss that compounded older losses still not accepted.

With the death of Edmund began a most difficult period in the marriage, especially for Ella, one that would lead three years later to her addiction. Hard times amid prosperity afflicted all the O'Neills for the better part of three decades—the entire period of James's *Monte Cristo* tour. Then and in later years Ella blamed her husband for forcing her to leave the baby with her mother and accompany him on his travels. That, she said, was the reason Jamie had been able to go into the baby's room and infect him. She apparently believed that if she had stayed with her mother and the children, she could have done what her mother could not, control Jamie every moment. For many years her sons usually took her side in the war against Papa. In the private narrative of 1926 Eugene described the circumstances of his brother's death: "Birth of second child five years after first. While still infant, M[other; that is, Ella] is forced to leave him to travel with husband who is morbidly jealous of her, even her affection for children. Baby is left with mother [that is, Ella's mother], catches measles, through carelessness of mother in allowing older brother who has measles to see baby. Baby dies. M[other] gets back too late—dead— she is prostrated by grief—blames herself—husband for keeping her away, bitterly [angry?] at mother for lack of care—elder boy as direct cause, unconsciously (?)." Later, in writing *Long Day's Journey into Night*, Eugene gave his father's side of the situation, as well as his mother's, and showed both parents as unable to tolerate separation from each other. But in both the document and the play, Eugene emphasized the importance to Ella of the loss of Edmund, a loss that led directly to her downward spiral into despair and drug addiction.

The Denver *Republican* reported the heartbreak of "poor Jim O'Neill" over the loss of his baby in "far distant New York" (LS, 17). The reporter must have had a tip on a story and have sought out James, who habitually grieved in silence. (It is striking that we have no idea when James's beloved mother, Mary O'Neil, died, except that it was sometime after 1866, the last time she is listed in the Cincinnati directory. Evidently James never mentioned to anyone an event that must have affected him greatly.) Stoicism served him well enough. He could immerse himself in work, and the continuing success of *Monte Cristo* brought him a little consolation as he tried to accept the loss. Ella had no work, and no confidence that she might succeed in coming to terms with a great loss. James surely sympathized with Ella, and he may even have understood how the loss was even harder for her than for him. His stoicism was probably the outward part of denial. Her overt expression of grief must have made denial the harder for him to maintain, and in his mind he could not help resenting that Ella's show of grief exacerbated the sorrow he wanted to hide from himself. Where a loss might have brought another couple together, the death of Edmund isolated the O'Neills from each other.

James, who wanted a large family, saw the solution to Ella's grief in having another child to replace the one they had lost. One infers from the five-year gap between the births of Jamie and Edmund that the question whether to have more children was probably an old source of conflict between husband and wife. The intransigent grief that possessed Ella implied that James was unlikely ever to have the large family he wanted, and that Ella's despair would pervade their marriage. In *Long Day's Journey into Night* Eugene dramatized Ella's belief that God had punished her for leaving Edmund in order to be with her husband, and her feeling that it would be defiant or blasphemous for her to have more children. In the 1926 document he wrote that she "evidently shuns idea of another child—guilty about second—husband talks of large family but she knows his stinginess would make this difficult for her."

Eugene then records a statement that, if factual, shows Ella's desperation as extreme. Eugene believed or had heard that in the months between Edmund's death and his own conception his mother underwent a "series of brought-on abortions—(defiance of husband?—how did she justify this with religion (?) did this mark beginning of break with religion which was to leave her eventually entirely without solace?)." There are a few factual errors in the narrative, but these words have the ring of something always known and accepted as true. Perhaps his mother, high on morphine and grasping at any weapon, threw her shame and guilt in his father's face when she needed to show her sons how hard James had made life for her.

The knowledge of the series of pregnancies said to have been aborted between 1885 and 1887 leads one to wonder whether there had been abortions during the five years between Jamie's birth and Edmund's birth. It is not unlikely that she nursed Jamie for two years or more, a circumstance that may have provoked quarrels with James, who wanted more children. Hearing a word or two of such quarrels may have led Eugene to his belief that his father was "morbidly jealous" of Ella's "affection" for their children.

Eugene's question about how his mother reconciled the abortions with her religious belief is pertinent. Another middle-class Catholic woman of the time, more worldly and more comfortable with compromise than Ella, might have found a way to reconcile psychic necessity with conscience and religious doctrine. Nothing we know about Ella suggests that such a compromise was open to her. The sheer logistical problem of arranging abortions, probably without her husband's knowledge, while traveling about the country, would have defeated many people. But with the resourcefulness of the truly desperate, she apparently found ways. Eugene's hunch is plausible. The loss of religious faith must have been the price Ella paid for bowing to psychic necessity. The cost of the abortions to both Ella and James must have been extreme.

Somehow the O'Neills got through these years. In June 1885, they moved into Monte Cristo Cottage. The furniture was makeshift, and little was done to decorate or make the house comfortable. In *Long Day's Journey into Night* Eugene shows the Tyrones employing servants and a cook. But most of the time the O'Neills took their meals in boardinghouses, using the cottage as if it were a hotel. Ella disliked the house and despised the town. Eugene said she hated New London because of "Her feeling [of] superiority to people there. Her poor relatives who live there make this hard. She feels they are obstacles to her socially, make that town impossible" [Autobiographical narrative, third paragraph]. A brownstone in Washington Square would have solved her problems neither with her losses, nor with a husband whom she thought undereducated and miserly and who cared little about associating with the best people.

In any case they were in New London, not New York. Another summer passed without the O'Neills' deciding what to do about Jamie's education. Ella, for whom the boy was increasingly the chief intimate and confidant, still could not bear to part with him, or imagine the tedium of life on the road without him to adore and admire her, and James fretted about the cost of tuition. All three O'Neills resumed the tour in September with the issue of Jamie's education still up in the air.

Probably upon James's insistence, they finally decided late in the fall. In December 1885, James and Ella took the boy to Notre Dame, where Ella herself had gone at fourteen. There Jamie impressed his interviewer, an English teacher named Charles Stoddard, as "pretty" and "wonderfully clever" (Shaughnessy 1991, 43; the details of Jamie's education have been uncovered by Shaughnessy, 36–64). At St. Edward's Hall the nuns of St. Mary's who had taught Ella would look after her son. At an annual tuition of a hundred and twenty-five dollars, including room and board, he was enrolled in the Minim Department of Notre Dame on December 7, 1885, and resided in St. Edward's until 1892, where he maintained an outstanding scholastic and social record for most of his stay. (In 1892 he passed into the division for older boys, who lived in Carroll Hall. His tuition went up to a hundred and fifty dollars.) Ella and James frequently visited Jamie and the nuns. James senior was a great favorite among both the boys and the faculty. He became a friend of two university presidents, attended theatricals, judged elocution contests, donated medals, and gave recitations. Whenever he played South Bend, he brought faculty and students to the theater as his guests.

Jamie was also a favorite at Notre Dame, and his record heartened both his parents. Shaughnessy found that "hundreds of times" during his nine years in Indiana, Jamie's name was published in the list of boys who had, in a certain week, "given entire satisfaction to the faculty." After studying Jamie's school records and surviving writings, Shaughnessy wrote: "Jamie was a boy endowed with precisely the faculties to take full advantage of [the Notre Dame] program. One seldom sees in him the piety and fragility of his mother or younger brother. He was temperamentally more like his father—gregarious, garrulous, and convivial. He knew how to please (a capacity that seemed almost second nature) those whose esteem he craved" (Shaughnessy 1991, 43, 44). From the beginning, Jamie caught the favorable attention of faculty members, including Father Edward Sorin, who had founded Notre Dame in 1842 and who, in his seventies, still was sponsor of the Minims.

From the beginning Jamie was hailed for his performances in school plays, for his skill as an orator, and for his play at shortstop on the baseball team. Out of school, Jamie passed his summers beside his mother, usually at Monte Cristo Cottage, or with the friends he made easily in town. Summers were probably fairly happy times for Ella too, despite her contempt for New London, for at least she was not constantly traveling.

Jamie saw his parents whenever James's tour neared Indiana. Ella and often James visited Jamie, and some of the visits were occasions celebrated in the *Scholastic,* the college paper. James scheduled his tours to arrive in Chicago during the Christmas season, and Jamie was brought to the city to spend holidays with his parents. According to the *Scholastic,* they visited in April and May 1886 and again in May 1887. The late spring visits usually preceded the return to New London for the summer, when the boy could rejoin his mother.

Jamie, however, did not spend the summer of 1887 with his mother but remained at Notre Dame. Hoping to restore his wife's Catholic faith and improve her morale, James took Ella to Lourdes and Oberammergau (LS, 20). The European cure may have helped, because in the following spring, when she once again became pregnant, Ella did not abort the child.

The forces of change and loss did not stop while the O'Neills holidayed at European shrines. When they returned to New York in mid-August, they learned that Bridget Quinlan, aged sixty and suffering a painful bone ailment, had died on July 28, 1887. They were in England at the time awaiting the ship that would bring them home, and they were still there on August 1 when Bridget was buried. If Ella's faith was renewed by the European trip, it does not seem to have helped her accept her losses, mourn them, and make her own life.

Now in suspended grieving for her father, her toddler, and her mother, Ella must have felt driven beyond protest. When she found herself pregnant that winter, she let James persuade her to carry the baby to term. During the summer in New London, both parents came to hope for a girl. Eugene was born the following October.

In September and October 1888, James toured New England in *Monte Cristo*. Jamie, who was beginning his fourth year at Notre Dame, had his tenth birthday on September 10. Ella waited out her term in a Manhattan residential hotel, the Barrett House, which then occupied the northeast corner of Forty-third Street and Broadway. Sixty-five years later, when he himself was waiting to die in the Shelton, in the Back Bay, Boston, Eugene found enough strength to wisecrack, "Born in a goddam hotel room and dying in a hotel room." Between birth and death, he stayed in more hotels than he cared to count, and in several stately mansions that his mother might have envied, but he stayed no place for very long. To be born and to die in hotel rooms suited a life of earthly and psychic wandering.

October 16, 1888, the day Eugene O'Neill was born, was gray and drizzly. James returned to New York in time for his own birthday and for his son's birth two days later, and he remained with Ella for some weeks after. Ella suffered in giving birth because Eugene weighed eleven pounds. Her physical pain and her recovery were complicated by an anxious depression. James was concerned and consulted a doctor, who prescribed morphine for Ella, a standard treatment then as now for acute pain. Almost at once, Ella became addicted to morphine, and she, and the rest of the O'Neills, struggled with the addiction off and on for the next twenty-five years.

James had to return to his *Monte Cristo* tour while Ella was still ill, and neither had any idea when he left, or for some time after, that Ella was addicted or that a new phase in their ordeal had begun. So far as either of them knew, Ella was recovering from childbirth and nursing an irritable but healthy baby when she resumed traveling with her husband. It is now known that morphine passes into a nursing woman's milk. Eugene must therefore have gotten some of his mother's drug. At the least morphine would have made him irritable and affected his appetite. According to family lore, Eugene was a "nervous" baby, taking after his mother, and possibly he would have been so even without secondhand morphine; but the morphine cannot have helped. Whether Eugene ever learned that he had ingested morphine in infancy is unknown. But he sometimes spoke of "having been born without a skin," meaning that he believed he had been hypersensitive from birth, and he must sometimes have wondered if he had not been physiologically affected by the drug.

Either when the O'Neills returned to the road, or soon after, James hired an Irish nanny to help Ella care for Eugene. The nanny apparently traveled with the O'Neills for the rest of the 1888–89 tour, and was released at the end of the season. The *Monte Cristo* tour reached Chicago at the Christmas season. As always when James played Chicago, the O'Neills visited Jamie at school, and when the Christmas holidays began, the boy was brought to Chicago to spend the season with his mother and to meet his new brother. Ella took Jamie back to school in early January. She used the opportunity to visit her former teachers and show off her new baby, "a beautiful child," according to the college *Scholastic* of January 12, who "promise[d] to do honor to his name" (Shaughnessy 1991, 49).

All biographers believe that Eugene's birth was upsetting to Jamie, who had to watch his mother lavish on yet another new brother the attention that had been his alone for his first five years. Nevertheless, if the new rivalry was upsetting, it did not affect Jamie's schoolwork or his behavior at Notre Dame, which continued to be exemplary until Eugene was about four. Ella, for her part, must have found the return to the cloister and the nuns a comforting change from life on the road, but one wonders if she noticed a difference between the reality of the place and the cloisters of her inner world to which she retreated whenever life became too painful. James was concerned about both her and their baby, and he hired Sarah Jane Bucknell Sandy, a formidable Cornishwoman, to be governess to Eugene and companion to Ella; she would be the boy's substitute mother until he was seven.

During Eugene's first seven years, the O'Neills and Sarah Sandy traveled nine months each year and spent the summers in New London. Life on the road was just as hard on Eugene as on his mother. Besides enduring the more ordinary childhood diseases, he nearly died of typhoid fever when he was two. He developed rickets, a disease of malnutrition that left his rib-cage marked with a permanent rachitic "flare." According to a story that became part of family legend, he once developed colic so painful that he cried himself "sort of black in the face," in the words of his father's advance man, George C. Tyler. Ella, fearing that she was going to lose a second baby, sent Tyler out into the snow to find a doctor, who told them that the colic was a routine case.[1] Whereas Jamie was stocky and robust, mischievous, and outgoing, Eugene was lean, less hale and hardy than his brother, and more inward-looking. He took after his mother a bit more than after his father, but did not look much like either. The others knew him from the start as distinctly his own person, with a stubborn streak and the will to get his way.

During the touring season, Eugene's day-to-day life was ruled by Sarah, who took him to zoos, museums, tent-shows, parks, and natural wonders. Whatever sights were to be seen, in the place they happened to be, they saw. Traveling with the O'Neills gave Sarah a chance to see the country, and she took full advantage of it. Eugene was the beneficiary of her curiosity. Plump, blonde, affectionate, and bright, her wide-ranging interests expressed themselves in sight-seeing, omnivorous reading, and a taste for the macabre. She read to Eugene from Dickens, whom she adored, and from the penny-dreadful press that was her daily fare. Jack the Ripper had gone on his surgical spree during the months surrounding Eugene's birth, and the publicity had created an insatiable public craving that lasted several years for tales of hideous crimes. Sarah was an avid consumer and purveyor of such dramas. She loved waxworks exhibits that depicted grisly murders and freaks of nature and missed no chance to see them, with her young charge in tow, and she routinely read to him of the latest ax murderers or poisoners.

Eugene also learned of his nurse's hardships and difficult life. Born in Cornwall to a tin-miner's wife, Sarah had been sent out in her youth across the sea to earn money so that the rest of her family could follow her to America. Like Anna Christie, she had been a "nurse gel" in her teens, and had scrimped to procure for her brother and a sister the education that had been denied to her. She did not conceal from Eugene or anyone else that she felt hard done by, and she blamed on that early deprivation her never having a chance to marry and make a family of her own. Yet she had the independence, strength of character, and guile to survive and make a life for herself. Certain of Sarah's qualities, and a few specifics of her life, would eventually be transformed and find their way into some of Eugene's earthy, maternal characters, from Anna Christie to Sara Melody and Josie Hogan.

Eugene became closer to Sarah than he could consciously know at the time or much later. To the very young Eugene, Papa was a distant, revered figure. Backstage, in costume and makeup, he gave the orders; on-stage, his voice boomed through the hall; in the hotel room he appeared briefly for a few moments of play before disappearing with Mama. If Mama was less commanding, she was no less intriguing; at times she was remote and at others strikingly unpredictable. When other people were

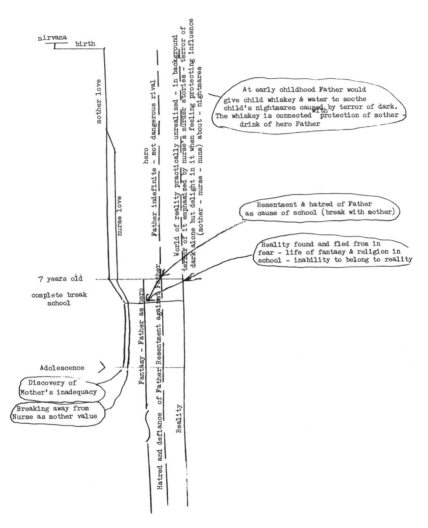

nirvana

birth

mother love

nurse love

Father indefinite – not dangerous rival

hero

World of reality practically unrealized – in background – terror of it emphasized by nurse's murder stories – terror of dark alone but delight in it when feeling protecting influence (mother – nurse – nuns) about – nightmares

At early childhood Father would give child whiskey & water to soothe child's nightmares caused by terror of dark. The whiskey is connected with protection of mother – drink of hero Father

Resentment & hatred of Father as cause of school (break with mother)

Reality found and fled from in fear – life of fantasy & religion in school – inability to belong to reality

7 years old

complete break school

Fantasy – Father as hero

Adolescence

Discovery of Mother's inadequacy

Breaking away from Nurse as mother value

Hatred and defiance of Father Resentment against Father

Reality

Diagram 1. Retyped version of O'Neill's life diagram (see p. 48).

Diagram 2. Detail of O'Neill's diagram (upper half of Diagram 1).

about, she was charmingly shy. But if they were alone, he could not anticipate when she might overwhelm him with affection. When she was ill and in bed, her illness would be explained evasively. Sarah was constant and reliable, however terrifying the tales she told him.

Sarah became the conveniently available figure on whom Eugene could express the ambivalent love and hate which are the normal by-products of a child's relations with parents, some of which was transferred from his feelings about his untouchable mama and papa. It would not be until he was in his teens that Eugene could feel comfortable enough with his father to express directly the full range of his feelings. His mother would always seem too fragile for such give and take, so Papa later bore the brunt of Eugene's ambivalence about Ella as well as the inner conflicts over his own actions.

Much later, Eugene traced out graphically the complexity of his early relations with his mother, father, and governess, and their effect on his understanding of the world. (Diagrams 1 and 2).

Three vertical lines represent development, with "nirvana" and "birth" at the top. The lines stand for mother on the left, Father in the middle, and the World of reality on the right. The left-hand line labeled "mother love" branches near the top, with a diagonal (labeled "meaning") leading to the secondary mother-line, which is labeled "nurse love." The label "meaning" on the diagonal branch implies that what the infant originally took for mother love came from the nurse. Thereafter he was aware that mother and nurse were different people and that there was a difference between "mother love" and "nurse love." The upper middle line is labeled "Father indefinite hero—not dangerous rival." (Anger toward the father appears with adolescence.) The right-hand line is explained: "World of reality practically unrealized—in background."

Just over halfway down, the lines are bisected by a horizontal line labeled "7 years old complete break / school." The mother-line and nurse-line both shift diagonally to the right, then resume the vertical, but they are now closer together. They continue to parallel each other for a short distance, then break off permanently at another horizontal line, "Adolescence." The break with the mother is explained: "Discovery of Mother's inadequacy," suggesting the discovery in Eugene's adolescence not only of Ella's addiction, but of the general fragility that made much of life intolerable to her. The word *inadequacy* is appropriate because it expresses Eugene's feelings about being deprived of her maternal care. The sense of deprivation remains conspicuous throughout Eugene's life.

The explanation of the ending of the nurse-line is less clear: "Breaking away from nurse as mother value." Eugene evidently recognized (long after the fact) that he had transferred some of the ambivalence he felt toward his mother to Sarah. For several years after he began boarding school, when she no longer worked for the O'Neills, Eugene continued to spend holidays with Sarah, and she always gave him small Christmas and birthday gifts. But some of the mixed feelings that Eugene felt were part of the relations between himself and Sarah in their own right.

In particular, he blames Sarah for the unimportance to him, in his first five to seven years, of the "World of reality," which he felt was "practically unrealized—in background." Eugene took for granted the extraordinary amount of sightseeing he had done with Sarah and didn't count it as reality. The reality he referred to in the diagram was whatever caused terror and nightmares. "Terror of it [reality] emphasized by nurse's murder stories—terror of dark alone but delight in it when feeling protecting influence (mother—nurse—nuns) about—nightmares."

None of what Eugene records in these notations seems especially unusual for a child's first seven years, except perhaps the nightmares, which were frequent and intense. The diagram suggests that Eugene thought that the form and imagery of his fantasies, dreams, and nightmares probably derived from Sarah's macabre tales, but the terror (and delight) must have had myriad sources, especially including Eugene's innate sensitivity and intensity of character. His mother's intermittently strange behavior, induced by depression or morphine, and his own identification with Ella probably played a part in the nightmares. Sarah seemed sturdy enough to survive being blamed for his terrors. Her love gave Eugene an advantage over his brother; Jamie never learned to tolerate his own ambivalent feelings toward his mother. Sarah's presence allowed Eugene to preserve, into his early teens, his idealization of his mother.

With regard to the nightmares, Eugene added the note: "At early childhood father would give child whiskey and water to soothe child's nightmares caused by terror of dark. This whiskey is connected with protection of mother—drink of hero Father." The last phrase, "drink of hero Father" seems to mean that in early childhood the son felt he was allowed to partake in some fellowship of heroic elders. But how is the "whiskey connected with protection of mother"? It seems that O'Neill must have meant that his having nightmares terrified his mother, and in soothing the child, the father was protecting his wife. The tone of the note is mythic, almost mystical, implying more strongly even than the phrase *hero Father* the reverence O'Neill recalled feeling in childhood for his father.

From the standpoint of Eugene's emotional development, the most important revelation of the diagram is apparently unconscious, that Eugene took for granted that he was part of a triangle: mother-nurse in one corner, hero-father in another, and himself, the child, in the third. It gave Eugene another advantage that Jamie never knew. Besides being forced to develop a tolerance for ambivalent feelings, Eugene could never deny the importance of Papa in his world, and in his early years he idealized his father as heroic. Idealizing his father gave him a model around which to organize his own developing male identity.

Later on, he came to resent his father for sending him to boarding school and thus separating him from his father, his mother, and Sarah. Later still, Eugene sometimes hated his father and openly defied him. All of the feelings were important, and all were (among other things) by-products of a tumultuous process of emotional development. But the most important thing to Eugene was that he was sufficiently confident that his father could tolerate a son's defiance and hatred that he was able to express the turmoil within him. It gave son and father the possibility of an intimacy that the anger he had to contain could never allow him to have with his mother. He would never be confident that she could survive the violence of his feelings.

Instead of being comfortably intimate with his mother, Eugene came to see her as a person to be studied, approached with great care, and understood through sympathy and empathy. In the autobiographical narrative of 1926, Eugene speculated about his first years, and in particular his mother's state of mind during his infancy.

> E[ugene] born with difficulty—M[other] sick but nurses child—starts treatment with Doc, which eventually winds up in start of nervousness, drinking & drug addiction. No sign of these before.
>
> E spoiled from birth—concentration of all M's love on him in her loneliness—she shares him reluctantly with nurse but makes friend and confidant out of nurse to further compensate for loneliness. Husband very proud of his

birth (confirmed by stories to me)—44 years old at time. She pleads for home in [New York] but he refuses. This was always one of her bitterest resentments against him all her life, that she never had home. M gets rid of one nurse at end of year or so (Irish woman) and gets English woman [actually the Cornish Sarah Sandy]. (Husband hates English intensely. Always hostile to nurse secretly and she to him. Was M actuated by revenge motives on husband in this choice— to get reliable ally in war with husband(?))

Absolute loneliness of M at this time except for nurse & few loyal friends scattered over country—most of whom husband resented as social superiors)—logically points to what must have been her fierce concentration of affection on the child, E[ugene]. This must have been further intensified by the fact that at age of 2 he nearly dies from typhoid.

(This nurse later becomes companion in beer & stout drinking—later still (after E is in school) in whiskey drinking and probably messenger for obtaining drugs(?)).

The picture Eugene gives here of his mother is of a woman desperate and without resources, isolated from her husband of twelve years, and in fact lacking any companion except her baby's nurse. In 1926 when he wrote the narrative, Eugene was struggling with his mourning for his mother, father, and brother, and so he did not seem to notice that to his mother's old grief for her father and her dead baby, a more complicated mourning had just been added, for her own mother, a mother ambivalently loved and resented. Eugene was painfully aware that Ella had been made to bear a child she had wanted to abort. The very fact of his birth was a cause of lifelong guilt. Except that the issue of Ella's drinking is omitted in the play, there is considerable similarity between the pictures of Ella O'Neill in the document and of Mary Tyrone in *Long Day's Journey into Night.*

Although no previous biographer has mentioned that Ella had a drinking problem as well as an addiction to morphine, there seems to be no reason to doubt the veracity of the document in regard to either addiction. Eugene writes of her drinking habits as from a personal memory of seeing her drink with Sarah. Perhaps the drinking began when Sarah or the Irish nurse before her urged on Ella the popular belief that ale and stout enhance a nursing woman's milk. Drink, like morphine, might soften temporarily the edge of desperation. But as with morphine, she must have welcomed the alcohol for the comfort it brought.

Even though it was written from his mother's point of view, the narrative of 1926 was consistent with the diagram in the interpretation it offers of Eugene's early development. Because the boy spent most of every day with Sarah, as well as with his mother, the bond between Ella and Eugene would never be like the tie that bound Ella and Jamie for life. Eugene's testimony (previously quoted) was carefully complex on this point. "E spoiled from birth—concentration of all M's love on him in her loneliness—she shares him reluctantly with nurse but makes friend and confidant out of nurse to further compensate for loneliness." Speaking from his mother's point of view, he depicted the concentration of "all" her love on the baby; next, the reluctant sharing of the baby with the nurse; and finally, her increasingly intimate friendship with the nurse. Although Eugene had many reasons to know that his mother's love for him was equivocal and ambivalent, he shows no signs here of the knowledge. Apparently acting out a need still acute, he wrote that his mother concentrated "all" her love on him; he excluded his father and brother from her attention and took all for himself.

From the beginning, Eugene was involved in a three-party relationship, a triangle that "worked," or at least remained stable, until he was seven. The stability of that triangle made possible another, one that included Eugene, the combined mother-nurse figure, and his father. Eugene shares in his father's glory of middle age: "Husband very proud of his birth (confirmed by stories to me)—44 years old at time. . . . M[other] gets rid of one nurse at end of year or so (Irish woman) and gets English woman [Sarah]. (Husband hates English intensely. Always hostile to nurse secretly and she to him. Was M actuated by revenge motives on husband in this choice—to get reliable ally in war with husband(?))."

Writing from his mother's point of view, O'Neill showed that even when he agreed with her criticisms of Papa, he took it for granted that because he could not really be her ally in the marital wars (as Jamie had been), Mama had to seek an ally in the nurse. Eugene could not be her ally because his grievances against her led him to identify more closely with his father's side of things than with his mother's. The difference between Eugene's relations with his parents and Jamie's paralleled the difference in the later lives of the brothers.

Although Jamie spent his first six years with both his mother and his father, the boy's relationship with his mother tended to exclude the father. Rather than form a triangle, the family at that point consisted of three dyads, two much more prominent than the other. Father and mother had their complex relations, which Jamie understood from a child's point of view. Mother and son looked at the father as the "governor," someone to be pleased and got around, but not someone essential to their lives or fit for their inner circle. (There seems not to have been a strong outward relationship between James and Jamie until much later, when they were forced into partnership in order to care for Ella in her illness.)

For Jamie and Ella, the relationship throughout life was nearly symbiotic. Jamie saw his father almost entirely through his mother's eyes, and in fact, in times of anger or despair, he saw *only* what she saw. Jamie identified so closely with his mother's frustration and anger toward James that he came to hate whatever of himself resembled her persecutor, his father, whose appearance, talents, and voice he had inherited, and with whose maleness he was inescapably identified.

At the time of Eugene's birth, Jamie's difficulties lay far in the future, and his future looked unclouded. Jamie may have been his father's rival, but in 1888 he was not yet in open conflict with James. Like his mother, he was expert at pleasing the Governor, and he easily extended his arts to pleasing the fathers at Notre Dame. Near the end of the 1888–89 school year, when his parents could be present, he received his first communion. On September 30, 1890, Jamie was one of nine "princes" honored with gifts, religious pictures initialed by the Very Reverend Father General Edward Sorin—the "best nine" in the school—the excellence of the boys having been judged at the end of each month of the foregoing school year. Jamie was chosen to represent the "youthful *protégés* of Very Rev. Father General" in a ceremony two weeks later by giving a speech in honor of the founder. Jamie's address, the *Scholastic* reported, "was a beautiful poetic production, and his clear, musical voice added much to the affectionate sentiments it contained." Jamie's marks often placed him at or near the top of his class. He frequently received "gold or silver medals and premiums in elocution, rhetoric, grammar, arithmetic, Christian doctrine, and penmanship" (Shaughnessy 1991, 45–46).

Shaughnessy (1991, 46–47) prints a poem written by Jamie in the fall of 1890 which shows both the gifts and limitations that initially inspired his teachers and later disappointed them. The poem, a tribute to President Walsh of the college, was printed on the front cover of the December 20, 1890, issue of the *Scholastic*. The first stanza shows that the twelve-year-old Jamie had a precocious grasp of poetic technique.

> There are no blossoms in this cold December
>   There are no roses or no violets sweet,—
> The days of summer we can but remember,—
>   The dry grass frosted dies beneath our feet;
> Persephone has fled to realms of night-shade,
>   And Ceres desolate laments her loss,
> But in our hearts there is a constant light made
>   By love's sweet fire that comes from Holy Cross.

After proving to himself that he could control the form, Jamie lost interest and took whatever came closest to hand.

> We're grateful for your care, O Kindly Father,
>   We're grateful for your love, O watchful Friend,
> And when the waves of life may bear us farther
>   Into life's sea, we'll love you to the end.
> [The second excerpt is the beginning of stanza 3.]

The poem revealed both Jamie's exceptional gifts and the pattern of failure that would mark his life. That he could write so well as he did in the first stanza seemed to mean nothing to Jamie. He did not value his gifts or even seem to recognize that he had them, except insofar as the response of others showed that he had won a moment of praise from someone he had decided to flatter. He seemed never to know a moment when he thought of his gifts as a potential end in themselves, nor did he think of making them a part of himself around which he could further his own development—as Eugene would do. It was as if the immediate success he often had with a new challenge instantly proved to him that the task was not worth doing. His success itself trivialized his accomplishment.

In the generous sample of Jamie's school and college papers, essays, and poems appended to his article, Shaughnessy (1991, 72–89) allows the reader to understand both how Jamie maintained his remarkable scholastic record and how it could be that he failed to graduate and was unable ever to make a career for himself after school. The work is literate, fluent, and technically competent; but where one might expect Jamie to rebel against authority and convention, he expresses instead opinions unfailingly ordinary for the time. Even in his satiric verses, the objects of ridicule are safe targets. It seems it would be a mistake to assume that Jamie's rebellion was part of a coherent dissatisfaction with the conventional wisdom of his father and teachers or that he had alternative values to propose or prefer. Jamie's writings show his skill at flattering his teachers, just as the poem written at age twelve shows him to be a competent flatterer of Father Walsh.

Jamie's conventionality is important to note because Eugene, in his adolescence and after, believed Jamie to be a rebel, and he identified his own social, intellectual, and aesthetic rebellions with what he took to be Jamie's values. His misunderstanding of his brother would later make it especially difficult to pass through the stages of mourning when Jamie died; that is, Eugene would have had to know the boy and man his brother had been in order to work through his mourning.

Jamie continued to do well in 1890–91, except for a lapse in March, when his name is missing from the Roll of Honor. At midterm of the next school year Jamie, now thirteen, moved from St. Edward's Hall to Carroll, where the older Minims lived. A year later, he played the young Duke of York in a school production of *Richard III* and won high praise in the *Scholastic*, which called him a well-known young actor who had "inherited the histrionic talent of 'Monte Cristo.' Nothing more piquant or artistic than his mockery of the misshapen Richard," the reviewer went on, "has ever come from a boy who is just on the verge of his teens." Jamie continued to do well the rest of the year.

Jamie's academic facade began to show cracks in autumn 1892, about the time he apparently learned for the first time of his mother's drug addiction. In *Long Day's Journey* Eugene has Jamie Tyrone describe catching his mother "in the act with a hypo" ten years before Edmund found out about her addiction, a discovery that seems to have occurred in 1902. Shaughnessy carefully and correctly points out that other things affected Jamie besides his mother's addiction, including the onset of adolescence, with all its problems and changes. As with most psychological events, Jamie's scholastic problems almost certainly had multiple causes.

The discovery of Ella's addiction and Jamie's entry into adolescence coincided with an economic depression that brought hard times from late 1892 to 1896 and must have affected James O'Neill psychologically as well as financially. If James was more worried, impatient, and irritable than usual, his moods inevitably affected his older son. Jamie's schoolwork deteriorated in October and November of 1892, and during the Christmas holidays he had a serious row with his father.

On January 9, 1893, James confided his concern about his fourteen-year-old son in a letter to President Walsh of Notre Dame. He had warned Jamie, he said, about the consequences of smoking, but he feared that the boy required careful watching. "[I]f he can be kept well in hand for the next two years[,] I am sure he will make a good man[.] [O]n the other hand there is a possible chance of his going to the dogs. During my conversation with him in Chicago I found I was no longer talking to a child[.] He has some very old ideas of *Life* and not the best by any means. I supose [*sic*] he has picked these ideas up from the older Boys with whom he comes in contact in his department" (Shaughnessy 1991, 50).

By "old ideas" James probably meant that Jamie had discovered prostitutes, and he hastened to assure Father Walsh that, gossip about actors and old scandals notwithstanding, the boy had surely not received any such ideas from his father. Then, as was characteristic with James, having denied one form of guilt, he obliquely acknowledged another. "During the next few years I shall write him often, doing all I can to keep him at his work and in the right path" (Shaughnessy 1991, 50). Although he was far from a neglectful father, James was confessing that he felt he had not always given his son enough attention and that he meant to do better.

Back at school in mid-February, Jamie carried on his misbehavior to the point of being one of the boys who inspired a public complaint from an editor of the *Scholastic*. These boys disturbed others by singing intrusively, and by "affectation of fashion or imitations of the Bowery." One boy called by the editor "the elocutionist," sounds very like the son of an actor: "He imagines himself to be King Lear, or Shylock, and he rants and roars until his very voice gives out. Then he lays it 'on Macduff,' but soon changes to the madness of Hamlet. Would that he were mad!" Jamie may also have been the "would-be tough" whose "face wears a natural jeer heightened by a contemptible smile. A cigarette always decorates his mouth, and he walks with a genuine Bowery swagger. A 'dice box,' some ages old, is tipped forward over his forehead, and if he meets you he will put up his dukes and glibly remark: 'I'm a sport, full-blooded, see?'" (Shaughnessy 1991, 51). At any rate, he sound very much like a character from *The Hairy Ape* or *"Anna Christie."*

Jamie recovered himself sufficiently to regain his place on the Roll of Honor, but the difficulties soon resumed. With infinite cheek, the next September, Jamie wrote the new president of the Notre Dame, Father Morrissey: "Mamma has requested me to write to you concerning the opening of school. As we have received no scholastic [*sic*] we are in doubt whether school will open on the first or second Tuesday of the month. Will you kindly let us hear from you at once and oblige" (quoted in Shaughnessy 1991, 63–64).

Despite or because of his behavior, Jamie was chosen by the boys of Carroll Hall to speak for them on Founder's Day in official praise of Father Sorin. Jamie's address, platitudinous and fulsome, but without visible irony, was published in the *Scholastic* of October 14, 1893. It was his father's forty-ninth birthday, and Eugene was about to turn five. Jamie's name continued to appear on the Roll of Honor until late the next January; then his school work fell off. His father blamed the decline on "lack of application" (Shaughnessy 1991, 52).

Jamie intended to return to Notre Dame when he went home for the summer of 1894, but it was a difficult holiday for the O'Neills. At the end of August, his father wrote President Morrissey that Jamie felt dissatisfied "with the result of last year's work," the blame for which, James emphasized, did not lie with the school. Jamie, he continued, "seems to have lost heart [and] appears devoid of ambition. . . . I have talked this matter over with his Mother and after due consideration we have come to the conclusion that a change is absolutely necessary[.] He needs a 'spur to prick the sides of his intent.' On the other hand Mrs. O'Neill's health may not permit her to go west with me[.] She will likely spend most of the winter in New York[.] Under these circumstances we have decided to send James to Georgetown where his mother can run over to see him frequently doing all in her power to keep him on his metal [*sic*]" (quoted in Shaughnessy 1991, 52–53). (Except for the last one, the emendations in this and the preceding quotations are by Shaughnessy.)

James O'Neill spent the summer of 1894 in the midst of a complex crisis involving his wife and older son. Within the near-symbiotic relationship between Ella and Jamie, the troubles of one exacerbated the troubles of the other. Whatever other causes there might have been, Jamie's problems in school were partly related to Ella's addictions to morphine and alcohol. At the time and for long after, alcoholism and especially drug addiction among women were considered vices of the impoverished. For all his seeming precocity and sophistication, Jamie would have found it hard not to assume that (in the words of Jamie Tyrone) only whores took dope. Acknowledging his mother's addiction meant to Jamie losing his mother. Unable to tolerate his own simultaneous love and hatred, he could only alternate between trying to deny that his image of his mother had to change and being furiously contemptuous of her and ashamed of himself for his naive trust. Ella, for her part, could not help feeling responsible and guilty for Jamie's problems in school—when denial did not keep her from thinking about Jamie's problems.

At some point over the summer, Jamie decided he could not face returning to Notre Dame. All this, and much else, led Ella to become truly ill, ill enough to make it impossible for her to go west with her husband. After a decade of the *Monte Cristo* tour, Ella must have felt that she could bear no more of it. Brooding about the travel, and about the town she disdained, and about Jamie's failure in school, and about Jamie's knowing of her morphine addiction, and about her losses—all of it probably led to a prolonged alcoholic or morphine binge, which must have greatly affected Jamie. All James could do was hope that with Jamie in Washington, Ella would be inspired to recover herself and try to help him through his difficulty.

Shaughnessy (1991) shows that at Georgetown in September, Jamie made a strong start. Now going by the name James Henry O'Neill (which he continued to use for several years), he made high midterm marks. But by December and January his grades fell below passing. In February Jamie left Georgetown and joined his father's acting company in Atlanta.

The following fall (1895), the seventeen-year-old Jamie entered the St. John's Preparatory School Division of St. John's College in New York—now Fordham University. At the same time, his seven-year-old brother was enrolled at St. Aloysius Academy for Boys, also in the Bronx.

The World Discovered and Rejected
1895–1902

WHEN HE WAS SENT TO boarding school just after his seventh birthday, Eugene perceived it as a "complete break" with his former life. Whatever the hardships, touring nine months of the year offered the boy a life that was continually exciting—rich, complex, and various. Most evenings he was privy to the backstage secrets of theatrical magic tricks. During the days, Sarah took him sightseeing, told him her stories, or read to him. He caught the knack of reading and entertained himself for hours with books his father gladly provided. As the boss's son, Eugene was petted by the actors, who liked the handsome, quietly observant boy.

He was superficially obedient, and he learned to conceal the curiosity he felt toward everything, a trait that he carried through life. Much later, his third wife told Louis Sheaffer an anecdote that revealed the quality of Eugene's attentiveness. The couple were taking a motor trip in the French countryside when "they saw coffins from an old cemetery being moved to a new site, carried in a religious procession that stopped every few feet for the participants to kneel in prayer. In contrast to his wife, who was stirred, O'Neill seemed indifferent to the spectacle . . . ; months later, however, he alluded to the procession and went on to recall it in minute detail" (LS, 66).

When he began writing plays, he found that he not only understood at the deepest levels practically everything about theatrical illusion but could effortlessly devise whatever new effect he might require. Few people can ever have had a better primary education in the theater or have better learned the lessons. Besides developing his theatrical mind, Eugene saw more of the country during his first seven years than most people see in a lifetime. Except when he was with Sarah, and sometimes his mother, he was usually treated as a young adult by adults who did not spend much time with children.

From a grown-up world of make-believe, he went to an austere world where children were strictly governed by nuns and priests. Backstage, as well as in the intimacy of his family, reality tended to be subjective and idiosyncratic; differences might take one aback, but they were tolerated. Long before he could ever have heard of such an idea, he understood the primacy of psychic reality, and the uniqueness of each person's private world. Long before he could have known in any disciplined way what knowledge is, he had the cast of mind that might suit a future psychoanalyst or a philosophical skeptic or a poet.

Growing up amidst theatrical illusion prepared him in one way—and only one way—for Catholic boarding school: he was used to the idea that reality was never what it seemed. Not that the multiple realities of the theatrical tour would have been tolerated at school. Reality, at school, was not what came with a whim or from psychic necessity, but what came from God and was God. It was a time he recalled, for the rest of his life, with dislike; he thought it a "rigid Christian exile," according to one of his early interviewers, Elizabeth Shepley Sergeant (1927, 88).

On the whole, life at school could hardly have been more different from life in the theater. Except during the summers, he had seldom been around other children, and when he was, he had little understood their ways. His cousin Phil Sheridan complained to Sheaffer, "It was no fun going over to his house. He didn't want to play ball or anything; all he wanted to do was read" (LS, 68). All the summer before and into the fall he pleaded with his father not to send him to boarding school, but this time he did not get his way. Two days after his seventh birthday, on October 18, 1895, he entered St. Aloysius Academy for Boys.

Eugene's attitude toward school is implicit in his life diagram (see Chapter 3). A horizontal line across the middle intersects the descending chronological lines. The horizontal line represents his becoming seven years old, at which point there was a "complete break—school." The two lines representing "mother love" and "nurse love" veer to the right, toward the father-line, then continue down, closer together than before, and closer to the father-line. The father-line is now marked "resentment against father," with the amplification "resentment and hatred of father as cause of school (break with mother)." To the right of the father-line is the reality-line. Like the mother- and nurse-lines, it is blank for the period between age seven and "adolescence." The changed position of the mother- and nurse-lines seems to represent the agreement of his mother and Sarah with his father that the boy should go to school.

A new line appears between the nurse-line and the father-line, below the point where the veering mother and nurse lines right themselves and begin to run vertically again. The new line (interrupted with a narrow S curve set off by breaks above and below) continues to the bottom of the diagram. It is labeled "Fantasy—Father as hero." The new line tells how Eugene believed he survived the six years he spent in Catholic boarding schools.

St. Aloysius stood on a sixty-five-acre campus that overlooked the Hudson in rural Riverdale, a campus it shared with the College of Mount St. Vincent, a fine school for girls comparable to St. Mary's, where Eugene's mother had studied. There were fifteen boys in Eugene's class, most of them brothers of girls who attended Mount St. Vincent. The campus had originally been the estate of the actor Edwin Forrest, who had built a home and gardens for his wife, then separated from her amid scandal before they ever lived in it. In 1856 Forrest sold the estate to the Catholic Sisters of Charity for a hundred thousand dollars. The main building, a turreted stone mansion, had become the girls' school. By the 1890s, the mansion had become the priests' residence, and it later became the library and archives.

The boys lived on the upper floor of a two-story lodge originally intended for a gatekeeper; it was a handsome house, but still without central heating or indoor plumbing in the 1890s. The boys took their meals and had their classes on the lower floor.

Eugene was later remembered by a nun who taught him, and by some of his schoolmates, as a boy who talked little—a good student, even-tempered and very determined. He was quiet and mannerly, always reading or writing, always a little detached from the other boys; he usually went his own way when his cooperation was not required. Sister Mary Florentine assured Sheaffer sixty years later that she remembered him vividly. He had been "different, the quietest of the lot, always reading he was, and I remember he had an occasional twitching of the head." The twitching of the head, and a tremor of the hands, he inherited from his mother. It was Sister Mary Florentine's first teaching assignment and first group of students, and it was a small group of boys, so she remembered them well (LS, 65).

Most of the campus was a working farm that provided the food everyone ate. The boys helped with harvest or planting, fed the chickens, or tended the other animals. Eugene was remembered years later by the supervisor of the farm as the boy who never showed the least interest in the farmwork. But he missed his dog terribly, a foul-smelling creature called Perfumery, which had been left with a New London cousin. Eugene persuaded a priest to build a doghouse at the school so that he could have Perfumery with him; but when he sent for the dog, he learned it had run under a carriage and been killed. The cousin, Josephine Brennan, told the Gelbs that Eugene would not speak to her for two years after the dog's death (Gelbs, 66).

At school, discipline and routine prevailed. The boys were roused at half past six, took the chilly walk to the outhouse, washed in cold water, had a breakfast of hot oatmeal, and commenced their classes, which lasted until half past three. From then until dinner, and after dinner until bedtime, they were free. The boys usually played among themselves or helped on the farm. Eugene read and wrote.

Like many youngsters who have grown up mostly in the company of adults, Eugene tended to think more in the style of an adult than of a child. It gave him what one of his schoolmates described to the Gelbs as an "aura of sophistication that endeared him to the sisters" (Gelbs, 67). He had an advantage in contending with the other boys because he was used to trying to outthink adults; and he had the benefit of advice from his expert older brother. Jamie had used his advantage to outwit and charm schoolmates when he was sent to Notre Dame; Eugene mostly ignored the other boys and spent his lonely days and hours exploring the world that reading, writing, and imagining opened to him.

The immediate aim of Eugene's reading, writing, and imagining was to enable the boy to survive the intense isolation he felt at St. Aloysius. Eugene half-unconsciously created a kind of presence that he "never quite saw. It was a presence felt that made me complete. In my dream I wanted nothing else—I would not have anyone else." He remembered the dream when he began to fall in love with Agnes Boulton in 1917. "I had to dream that I was not alone," he told her. "There was me and one other in this dream. I dreamed it often—and during the day sometimes this other seemed to be with me and then I was a happy little boy." He added, "I would have resented anyone else—this other was so much a part of myself" (Boulton 1958, 62–63). The chief quest of his adult life was to find a mortal who would be as close to him as the phantom of his dream, a person who would become part of himself, who would bring him some of the happiness that he sometimes felt when he was a little boy and the other seemed to be with him.

The psychoanalyst James W. Hamilton, writing in 1977, concludes that throughout his life O'Neill suffered acutely from what analysts call separation anxiety, an anxiety that stems from the fact or expectation of being separated from someone believed necessary to one's survival. Separation anxiety replicates the panic experienced by an infant who feels abandoned and in mortal danger. If a child has frequently felt abandoned, separation anxiety may recur in adult life when something sets off an expectation that the early trauma is about to be repeated. Writing about the boy Eugene's imagined companion and related childhood imaginings of a great estate of which Eugene was sole possessor, Hamilton links the fantasizing to "transitional phenomena"—objects or processes on which one expends narcissistic energy and which give consolation at bedtime and other times of anxiety. Hamilton writes that the childhood fantasy of companionship with an unseen other that made Eugene feel "complete" was the ideal for his marriages. The analyst D. W. Winnicott, who coined the concept of "transitional" objects and phenomena, has often suggested links between such processes and artistic creativity. It seems certain that the playwright's adult writing grew out of and was an extension of the fantasizing, reading, and writing that in childhood helped the boy withstand episodes of acute separation anxiety that threatened to overwhelm him at boarding school, perhaps as often as several times daily.

Several years later, Eugene would discover a gift for friendship, and as an adult he would make close and lifelong friends. But as a boy he had no notion of fellowship with other children, and in fact very little experience of being childlike. He had learned to avoid and survive the kinds of crises that occurred backstage, and the crises between his mother and father. But the ordinary distresses of school life that might erupt in playground squabbles were new to him, and so was the punishment meted out by the nuns. Jamie remembered being whipped by his father, but Eugene was seldom punished before he went to school. The nuns whipped and knuckled and thumped their charges, and the boys tussled with each other. At the age of seven Eugene was confronting for the first time the ordinary jostling that most of his fellows would have known since they were toddlers.

So it was natural for him, in his isolation at St. Aloysius, to think of friends as people one wrote to, as he wrote to his mother, father, brother, and nurse. He wrote frequent letters to a San Francisco girl somewhat older than he, Anita Black, the daughter of friends of his father, a girl who had once played a maternal role when he was sick (LS, 71). He deluged his parents, Jamie, and Sarah with letters, although the last two were both in New York and visited him often. He had learned already to make writing serve as a way to help him create and organize a world apart from the casual accidents of reality, and through voracious reading he continually learned new things he could do by writing. He played with writing the way a child of today might play with a computer—and learned to make it serve him.

His first roommate, Joseph McCarthy, who was two years older, told the Gelbs and Sheaffer that he remembered Eugene constantly reading books that were "beyond his years"—McCarthy mentioned Kipling and Anatole France. Ella, Jamie, and James all had an influence on what Eugene read. McCarthy recalled Eugene as constantly writing letters to his parents and especially to his brother. McCarthy suspected he was writing poems as well. (In fact, Eugene wrote poetry all his life; he believed his fundamental literary impulse was toward poetry, and he lamented his inability ever to write verse of even ordinary schoolboy quality.)

Another schoolmate, Stephen Philbin, told the Gelbs (Gelbs, 68) that at one time the boys at the school were much given to imitation and talk of James O'Neill's stage prowess with a sword (James was famous for his fencing skill). Eugene had taken the boys to a matinee of *The Musketeers,* in which James was playing D'Artagnan, and in his dressing room afterward, James had charmed the boys with his kindness and attention. In 1933 Eugene described to Richard Dana Skinner, one of his early biographers, an incident at school in which the boys were playing swords with tree branches. A nun scolded them and warned of the evils of the theater, all the while glaring at Eugene and clearly implying that his father was to blame for the error into which the boys had fallen. Almost forty years later, Eugene still resented the misguided attack on his father, whom he thought as devout a Catholic as a man might be. It was one of many incidents at the school that made him contemptuous of the Church.

Joseph McCarthy recalled that Eugene seemed bored by the talk of fencing, but he remembered his acting in school plays. If McCarthy's memory is correct, it was one of the few activities in which Eugene joined. Lean, muscular, and athletic, he also swam with the other boys in the school swimming pool. Later he would be known among his friends as fearless and nearly tireless in the water; he would swim a mile or more out into the ocean. But he had none of Jamie's interest in playing baseball or any other team sport. Yet if he seemed a loner, maybe even a little odd, he did not make enemies or have much trouble with the other boys or the nuns.

An incident described by the Gelbs and Sheaffer suggests the extent of Eugene's estrangement from his schoolfellows. Eugene invited Joseph McCarthy to spend the Easter holiday of 1897 with him in New London. He showed Joseph his father's extensive and well-used library and invited him to help himself. From then on, Eugene ignored his guest and spent the vacation reading. Biographers have cited the incident as evidence of Eugene's alienation and oddness. In this case at least, there seem to have been mitigating circumstances.

The visit occurred about three weeks after Nettie Walsh's son had sued James to demand money and acknowledgment. The suit brought up once again the scandal that twenty years before had scarred the O'Neills' honeymoon. Eugene probably knew nothing of the scandal when he invited Joseph home with him, but he could tell that something was wrong once they arrived. Eugene may not have learned exactly what had happened, however, until much later; rather, coping as he usually did when trouble was in the air, he lost himself in books.

Still, even if no external crisis had threatened, Eugene might not have been much more forthcoming, for his cousin, Phil Sheridan, also complained about Eugene's neglectfulness as a youthful host. Circumstances in the O'Neill home were always complicated, partly by Ella's frequent indispositions and partly by the family conspiracy to keep Ella's addictions secret, even from Eugene.

In later life Eugene could sometimes enjoy himself in the company of lively, outgoing people, even after he had stopped drinking and become semireclusive. But someone like Joseph, who was himself shy and thoughtful, could not lead Eugene out of himself. In fact, a visit with Joseph McCarthy in 1931 was similarly silent. McCarthy concluded, "He was always a lone wolf" (LS, 69).

The tone of the two letters Eugene wrote leading up to the 1931 meeting was friendly and animated. Joseph reminded his old roommate that Eugene sometimes used to call him Mowgli (Gelbs, 67). Eugene replied that the mention of Kipling had brought Joseph back to his mind. The image of the person was connected to a literary association. The memory of Joseph brought back in turn schoolboy language: "Do you remember Sister Martha who used to knuckle us on the bean?" Eugene wondered (SL, 370). McCarthy had seen *Strange Interlude* in London. Writing to express his appreciation, he asked Eugene for copies of his other plays. Eugene thanked him, sent an autographed book immediately, and wrote to request his publisher to send others. Not long after, Joseph wrote that during an illness he had read them all. "Pretty gloomy reading for one with a cold," Eugene replied. Joseph was right, he conceded, "in thinking that life at different times has given me 'the works' and that this comes out in my plays" (SL, 378). Eugene could be open because Joseph had also known hardship; he had been orphaned in childhood, and he, like Eugene, had survived a bout with T.B. Eugene's response was forthright, describing the deaths of his mother, father, and brother. He lightened the letter by describing with self-deprecating humor his dreadful acting in his father's company and his youthful drunkenness (without mentioning that he had been dry for more than five years). Finally he invited Joseph to visit. But when the visit took place, it was strained.

Eugene apparently liked Joseph, who was quiet and thoughtful. But the goodwill Eugene felt found no outward personal expression. As in most of his personal relations, however deeply he might feel, he showed almost nothing of what he felt face to face. It is as if the real relationship occurred for Eugene in an internal landscape, where transactions occurred in writing and could be composed and revised. Eugene wrote frequent letters to his lovers and wives when he was apart from them and sometimes even when they were in the same house, and the letters could hardly have been more ardent or intense. Face to face, with his wives as with his friends, he usually said and showed little.

The details of experience, and especially his own feelings and mental images, became most fully real to Eugene when they reached the fluid condition of internal linguistic images capable of transformation and recombination. The life lived in the world where he was creator would always be the most important; it always superseded the accidents of daily life. The quotidian was matter to be transformed, with the transformation taking place in the act of converting sensual experience into words, and then into written language. It seemed to others that in the immediate event Eugene could not make small talk, that he was so absorbed in his private thoughts that he had no attention to spare for anyone else, or that he simply did not care about others. Yet there are stories about his recalling much later every detail of a conversation or some passing event that he had seemed to ignore while it was happening. At such times, his mind must have been racing around the event, like that of a dramatist (or future dramatist), from many perspectives and in different lights; he was so busy understanding the event and the other people in his silent, poker-faced way that the others felt ignored. Others did not sense hostility in his preoccupation. They did not dislike him for it, but they often felt they did not understand him.

For Eugene, life at St. Aloysius never became pleasant or even tolerable; he resisted and hated it until the end. At St. Aloysius, all the boys took turns assisting the priests as altar boys at the six o'clock Sunday morning Mass. James O'Neill must have taken his sons to Mass with him as often as he could while they were traveling and during the summers in New London to St. Joseph's, but his mother almost never attended after she became addicted. Except in New London, Eugene never attended a particular church. The years at St. Aloysius provided his most sustained exposure to Catholicism. In his only "Catholic" play, *Days Without End* (1933), he described the central character's exposure to institutional Catholicism as a shocking change from the notion of Christianity he had formed at home, the "God of Infinite Love" being supplanted at school by "a stern, self-righteous Being Who condemned sinners to torment" (CP3, 128).

God and religion were probably never so simple for Eugene as for John Loving in *Days Without End,* but Eugene served his Sunday morning stint at the altar, just as he complied with the rest of his duties at St. Aloysius. Stephen Philbin and Joseph McCarthy both told Sheaffer that they had observed little interest in religion in Eugene, though they had regularly served with him as altar boys. Sheaffer writes that neither boy "gained an impression of spiritual turmoil or seeking" in Eugene (LS, 69). Joseph remembered being startled once when Eugene told him, "Religion is so cold" (Gelbs, 69). Throughout his adult life, O'Neill showed in his plays a wide-ranging and intense interest in the metaphysical, and he read extensively about ancient and modern religions. One reason for the importance to him in childhood of Catholicism seems to have been that it offered him a connection to his father. In Eugene's later life, Catholicism seems to have been most prominent as an antagonist in a three-way metaphysical conflict with paganism and skepticism. His particular sense of the tragic was the product of the complex metaphysical conflict. In later life he would have deeply understood Stanley Cavell's remark: "Tragedy is an interpretation of what scepticism itself is an interpretation of" (1987, 5–6). Man and boy, Eugene answered skepticism through imaginative creativity. He might have said: As long as I can imagine, I exist.

When Jamie agreed to enter St. John's College Preparatory School in the Bronx in 1895, academic life in New York must have seemed a lesser evil than struggling against his father's authority on the *Monte Cristo* tour. James began to fancy that Jamie might have a career in the law, and Jamie, who had the mind to learn anything, entertained the idea for a time. During the school year 1895–96 he received high marks in trigonometry and grammar and won first prize in English composition, second prize in Greek, Second Distinction in Latin, and Third Distinction in religious instruction. He wrote fluent conventional prose and was an excellent public speaker and debater; these were accomplishments his brother would never share.

After Jamie's first year at St. John's, the O'Neills summered in the Catskills. For the next several years they would spend most summers away from New London. Ella was having an increasingly difficult time, and being near her relatives apparently exacerbated her shame. Shaughnessy states that the following fall, after Jamie's eighteenth birthday, he was promoted to the senior level of St. John's preparatory division, and at midterm, in January, he was moved ahead again to the freshman level at St. John's College. During the next three years he debated and orated, served as an editor and writer for the *Fordham Monthly,* and entertained vague thoughts of becoming a professional journalist. He won numerous scholastic prizes. He made outstanding marks at an excellent college, and was expected to complete with the highest honors a program that demanded of its graduates competence in "Natural, Mental and Moral Philosophy, in Evidence of Religion, in the Philosophy of History, and in Higher Mathematics. [Candidates for the bachelor of arts degree] must also give evidence of having attained a specified standard in Latin and Greek and General Literature," according to the college bulletin (quoted in Shaughnessy 1991, 61).

Jamie began his freshman year in the face of new family difficulties. In early March, Alfred Hamilton O'Neill sued, alleging that twenty years before, James O'Neill had duped Alfred's mother, Nettie Walsh, "by a series of false and plausible promises and also by and through threats of various sorts" against his mother's good name. Through "the most outrageous fraud upon the court," his claim stated, "the defendant, James O'Neill, procured a decree to be entered that no marriage ever existed between Nettie and the defendant." He wanted his mother's good name restored and his own legitimacy acknowledged. The suit did not attract as much publicity as Nettie's original suit, but enough, it seems, for Jamie to learn more about the old scandal than he had previously known, and for Eugene gradually to find out about it. The recurrence of the old scandal probably was enough to make Ella insist on shunning New London for another summer. It could not be pleasant to see pity in the eyes of relatives whom she considered beneath her. James explained to the newspaper that the salt air disagreed with Mrs. O'Neill, but in fact the O'Neills took a beach cabin on Staten Island.

For the next two years, Eugene continued to detest his life at St. Aloysius. At St. John's Jamie maintained an outstanding academic record. But he was also becoming more and more reckless in drinking and womanizing, and more outrageous in the constant battles with his father over his misbehavior. He still showed no serious signs of choosing a vocation.

Jamie had always been a quasi-mythical figure to Eugene. Eugene had heard about his brother's academic and athletic feats since infancy and had seen in his mother's eyes the gleam that Jamie's name evoked, but during the years on the road, he had lived with his brother only during the summers. Jamie was a teenager before Eugene was old enough to hold much of a conversation with him. Now Jamie piled up successes at St. John's College.

As Eugene passed the years in his rural isolation furiously writing his stream of letters to Jamie and the others, he made an increasingly potent figure of his brother, taking Jamie's adolescent adages for common sense and even wisdom. Idolization of Jamie coincided with growing defiance of his father. More and more Eugene consciously resented James for sending him into exile. Eugene began to notice the chinks in his father's heroic armor as the lawsuit with the illegitimate son dragged on. Jamie no doubt gave Eugene his own version of the old scandal and wised him up to the ways of the world and the old man.

Disillusioned with his father, Eugene came to see Jamie as the sanest, most sensible, most reliable person in the family. It was surely Jamie who gave him a plausible explanation for the boarding-school exile: that Papa was jealous of Mama's attention to her sons and got rid of them as soon as he could. It was the old man's randy peasant Irish nature that had got him into trouble with that woman before he got married, and that caused Mama's problems too, because he would never leave her alone, even when she was sick or out of sorts. He had always talked about having many children, even though it was obvious that Mama didn't want any more and was too high strung and fine-grained to put up with a noisy brood of brats. Increasingly, Jamie came to take the place of Papa in Eugene's day-to-day longing for company and advice, although the old heroic image of his father continued to thrive in the boy's imagination. Near the end of act 4 of *Long Day's Journey,* Eugene shows Edmund struggling to understand his own lingering dependency on his brother, and his brother's struggle with ambivalent feelings toward "the kid."

In fall 1899, his senior year, Jamie began to have trouble at St. John's. Shaughnessy found that Jamie's name ceased to be listed among those who had won academic honors. Jamie had been elected editor-in-chief of the *Monthly* and had taken up his duties in September. In December, without explanation, his name was not on the masthead and had been replaced with that of a classmate. The same month, Jamie was expelled, after bringing a prostitute to a school affair and introducing her to college fathers as his sister, a story recounted in *A Moon for the Misbegotten.*

On his papa's insistence, Jamie began after Christmas to look for a career. He tried and failed at several jobs, including newspaper writing, then kept a job for a time as a traveling salesman for a lumber firm. When that ended, his father gave him work playing small roles in the *Monte Cristo* company; he performed passably, the reviewers thought, until he was cast as the son of Edmond Dantes. His father thought he understood Jamie's problem. "We all know," he had written President Morrissey of Notre Dame years before, that "his great fault is lack of application."

But no one could have achieved Jamie's record at Notre Dame and St. John's without application. At each school Jamie had done well until he approached graduation, which portended the loss of the place and circumstances in which he felt secure and had succeeded. He had absorbed his mother's dread of leaving home or convent; Catholic boarding school was his convent. Deliberately or otherwise, Jamie had found a way to return to his mother's side, and to avoid the decisive step toward independence from his father that graduation would have forced him to take. He would continue until death to be financially and emotionally dependent on his father and mother, tied to his father by a bond of conflict that was stronger than friendship.

After Jamie's failure, Eugene began to doubt as well as admire his brother. About the same time, the lawyers were finally settling the lawsuit, and Eugene's idealization of his father was more and more tinged with Jamie's hatred of the old man. Amid all the commotion, and with Mama ill and unpredictable, Eugene entered his final term at St. Aloysius (where boys were taught only until they were twelve). Eugene now for a time made himself embrace his father's belief. His mother had transferred to Eugene her own childhood desire to be a nun; she told him from time to time that she wanted him to take vows. Willing himself to believe that it might help both him and his mother, he cooperated in the preparation for first communion, which he received May 24, 1900. His parents and brother and some Sheridan and Brennan relatives attended, all holding their private feelings.

The O'Neills spent another summer away from New London, and Ella, perhaps inspired by seeing Eugene's first communion, took another cure, which seemed more effective than usual. James, now in his mid-fifties, was to play in New York in a new and lavish *Monte Cristo* produced by George Tyler. For the fall season he and Ella took an apartment at 8 West Sixty-eighth Street, near Central Park. Now that Ella was in better spirits, Eugene would live with his parents once again and attend De La Salle Institute, a few blocks away on Fifty-ninth Street at Sixth Avenue, as a day student.

Sheaffer describes the sharp contrast between the schools. St. Aloysius was feminine and severe. Several of Eugene's classmates expressed to various biographers much later their opinion that discipline had been overly strict. Surrounded by the bustle of midtown Manhattan, De La Salle was heartily masculine and more relaxed (LS, 82). Ella, trying hard to pay attention to Eugene, took him to Yeats's *Land of Heart's Desire* and Browning's *In a Balcony*. After the latter, she led her son backstage to meet Eleanor Robson, who remembered years later how the shy, lanky boy had stared at her while the two women chatted. Miss Robson, later Mrs. August Belmont, found Ella shy and fragile but thought that the two of them had got along surprisingly well, considering Ella's reputation for avoiding theatrical people. Jamie was working as a traveling lumber salesman and was not always around to provoke his father. Ella was behaving normally. But after a few months, Ella began to act strange again, so James enrolled Eugene as a boarding student at De La Salle.

The change was all the more bitter because Ella had been appropriately attentive for several months, and life had gone well for all of them. Eugene still did not know what caused his mother's erratic behavior, but once again, he blamed his father for separating him from his mother. Rather than explain, James put up with his son's angry disapproval.

Trying to patch things up, James gave Eugene a walk-on part in the new *Monte Cristo*. On a tryout in Boston, Eugene made his first appearance on a professional stage, but overcome by stage fright, he blundered into a wall and fled to the wings. Jamie, after failing as a lumber salesman, was given the part of Edmond Dantes's son and tried hard for a time, hoping to win his mother's approval. His performance varied, ranging from "stiff" to fairly effective, according to the reviews, but was so inconsistent from evening to evening that James gave him a lesser part as soon as he could replace him. Eugene, having got over his initial stage fright, was showing a little more promise, but he never grew to like acting.

He was working harder at his studies, hard enough to do well, with high marks in history, English, and religious studies. By the end of his second year at De La Salle, in the spring of 1902, he stood sixth in his class of twenty-two. Now going on fourteen, nearly six feet tall, an outwardly well-behaved boy, he had privately rejected Catholicism—"brushed with" it, as he put it much later in a private chronology he called Cycles. When school was out and the O'Neills retreated for their summer at the shore, the rebellion developing in Eugene came to the surface.

Once again avoiding New London, the O'Neills took a place in the fashionable New Jersey resort community of Asbury Park. There, during the summer, Eugene declared his emancipation from Catholicism and Catholic education. He somehow found a way to persuade his father to allow him to change schools. Instead of agreeing to return to De La Salle, he insisted on switching to Betts Academy, a good secular school in Stamford, Connecticut, near New Haven, which sent many of its graduates to Yale. Under ordinary circumstances it would have taken a tremendous force of will on Eugene's part and entailed a tremendous battle with his father to force the change.

Throughout his life, James O'Neill seemed to those who knew him unambiguous both in his faith and in his wish that his sons should be good Catholics. Yet in the summer of 1902 a boy not yet fourteen compelled his father to accept a change that meant abandoning Catholic education. It seems likely that Eugene had help in the argument, possibly from an external event. It was either in the summer of 1902 or the following summer that Eugene learned of his mother's morphine addiction. If the discovery came in 1902, it would be easier to understand how Eugene persuaded James to accept the change of schools.

In *Long Day's Journey into Night* Mary Tyrone reminds her younger son of a time she had "gone mad" because a doctor had refused to refill her prescription for morphine and had advised her to use her willpower to endure the withdrawal. It was "that time I ran down in my nightdress to throw myself off the dock. You remember that, don't you?" Mary asks her son. The son replies "bitterly": "I remember, all right. It was right after that Papa and Jamie decided they couldn't hide it from me any more. Jamie told me. I called him a liar! I tried to punch him in the nose. But I knew he wasn't lying. (*His voice trembles, his eyes begin to fill with tears.*) God, it made everything in life seem rotten" (CP3, 787).

No historical evidence has been found of an attempt by Ella O'Neill to drown herself. There may have been one or more such episodes during the difficult years following 1893. It seems likely that a crisis of some kind with Ella preceded Eugene's being told of her addiction.

The other circumstances as described in the play seem a plausible account of how Eugene learned of Ella's addiction. James and Jamie decided between them that it was better for Eugene to understand that his mother's despair had an external cause than to assume something else.

James probably convinced himself that the news would be easier to take coming from the idealized twenty-four-year-old brother than from an old man who was no longer worshiped as a hero. Passing the buck to Jamie also allowed Papa to duck some of the uproar and accusations that were sure to follow. Besides hating to hear about his mother's addiction and wanting to find someone to blame it on, Eugene could not have helped feeling outraged that he had been deceived for many years. Nor could he escape the realization that the others irrationally but consciously blamed him for causing his mother's addiction.

Perhaps the most difficult thing for Eugene was that he could not avoid siding with his mother, father, and brother in blaming his own birth for Ella's addiction—and hating himself for existing. It was a guilt he would carry the rest of his life. And yet he was naturally outraged at being blamed for what he could not help. James must have understood at least some of the cataclysm that the news about Ella caused in Eugene's soul. Yet Eugene did not turn all his rage and guilt inward: not all of it. Original sin, an idea that negates any distinction between guilt and responsibility, had come into his life in boarding school. Learning about Ella would have been enough to bring Eugene's apostasy into the open. Changing schools might allow him to separate the fact that his birth had led to his mother's addiction from the guilt he felt for being inseparable from the cause of her affliction.

At such a time James may have been less ready than before to fight to keep his son in a Catholic school. Permitting the change to Betts may have seemed small, compared with the other problems James faced and saw his sons facing. It seems likely that an actor with a feel for tragic drama must surely have understood at least some of the turmoil Eugene now experienced. In an instant Eugene lost both the world he had known and himself as he had believed himself to be. Seen in another frame of reference, Eugene at fourteen was made to understand the problem of responsibility that Sophocles allotted King Oedipus.

Sophocles understood that no matter how reasonably and logically Oedipus might deny responsibility for slaying his father, the cost of denial was greater than the cost of acknowledging responsibility and living with an irrational but inevitable sense of guilt. To deny the unwitting act meant to deny the most important fact about one's self. That is why, at the end of the play, Oedipus insists that he receive the punishment he decreed at the beginning for the killer of Laius. Oedipus rightly says that he could not have done differently than he did; but the statement, once spoken, becomes meaningless, because it is based on a view of the world that the event has made obsolete, a view that people can control destiny and the future.

In a discussion comparing Wittgenstein's philosophical methods with "the progress of psychoanalytic therapy," the philosopher Stanley Cavell writes of what the Greeks called anagnorisis. As in a psychotherapy, philosophical "problems are solved only when they disappear, and answers are arrived at only when there are no longer questions—when, as it were, our accounts have cancelled them." Cavell continues: "The more one learns, so to speak, the hang of one's self, and mounts one's problems, the less one is able to *say* what one has learned; not because you have *forgotten* what it was, but because nothing you said would seem like an answer or a solution: there is no longer any question or problem which your words would match. You have reached conviction, but not about a proposition; and consistency, but not in a theory. You are different, what you recognize as problems are different, your world is different" (1969, 85).

Cavell has in mind someone who, like Wittgenstein, already understands the problem of understanding. Before Wittgenstein or O'Neill might begin to seek, he would discover that he is lost and knows almost nothing. For Eugene, the great discovery of 1902 or 1903 showed him he was lost and always had been. It changed him, his problems, and his world. Reaching conviction and consistency, reaching the point where the problems vanished, would be the aim of a lifetime's work. Eugene's first discovery took him only as far as what Oedipus first learned, that he did not know who he was or how little control people had over their lives. Over the next decade, Eugene O'Neill gradually understood what he had learned on a single day. When he finally found himself, he began to develop himself around a sense of the tragic that would eventually be Sophoclean.

5

Growing Up at School and on the Streets
1902–1907

OVER THE NEXT SEVERAL YEARS, as he attended Betts Academy in Stamford, Connecticut, Eugene did not see his mother at all while he was at school. James visited his son at the Stamford campus as often as he could, several times each term, and became friendly with Billy Betts and several masters. But Ella apparently never set foot on the Betts campus. Where she stayed while her husband visited their son is not known. Possibly she visited her cousins in nearby New London, although she tried to avoid them those summers they all spent in the same town. It is likely that her morphine addiction continued to be particularly severe after her suicide attempt. As long as Eugene had not known about her condition, she had been able to avoid acknowledging it in his presence. Now, within the confines of her family, denial was even more difficult than before. Probably, shame and guilt made her avoid her son now that he knew.

Decades later, several of Eugene's classmates vaguely remembered understanding that Mrs. O'Neill was dead or that there had been a divorce. Their recollections suggest that Eugene himself never mentioned her. If Eugene did not speak of his mother, it was probably not simply because he was ashamed of her condition. It must have been part of an effort to avoid thinking at all about her affliction, and about himself as the cause of it. For her part, Ella retreated further and further into her private world, dreaming perhaps (as Eugene thought) of the convent where she had spent her youth—or perhaps of other retreats. She apparently had several stays, between 1893 and 1911, in sanatoria and convents, where she tried to free herself from her addiction and to recover her faith and her soul. For several years Eugene saw very little of his mother.

With their mother out of sight much of the time, both O'Neill sons turned their frustrations on James. Jamie became an increasingly serious problem for his father, and a growing influence on Eugene. Still hoping that Jamie would straighten himself out, James could not resign himself to detachment at seeing his first-born drink himself out of every job his father got for him. Nor could James learn to avoid quarreling with Jamie, who could be savage when he was drinking. James saw no choice but to employ Jamie in his company, a solution that brought its own nuisances. Audiences and reviewers pointed out that Jamie was visibly drunk onstage. Ladies in the audience and sharp-eyed reviewers complained that they could detect the shape of Jamie's genitals through his costume tights and deduced that he wore no underwear (LS, 96). When his mother accompanied the tour, Jamie tried harder to behave himself, but when Ella was absent, he spent his nights at local brothels and brought painted ladies to a prominent box where they conspicuously admired the performances of father and son. James never complained publicly about Jamie and always praised him to the press, but he must have seethed in private. When James could stand no more, he returned Jamie to New York with enough allowance to let him pursue his true interests. However Job-like James may have seemed to outsiders, he got no credit from Eugene or Ella in these battles. Ella counted Jamie a fellow victim and ally in her war against her husband's parsimony. Out of ordinary adolescent rebelliousness, Eugene counted every criticism of his brother as evidence of Jamie's perfection.

Eugene's former love and hero-worship of his father still flourished, but admiration was increasingly concealed in adolescent ambivalence. In the private autobiographical document of 1926, Eugene revealed the origin for his own sometime contempt for his father: "[Mother] always remembers [her father] in contrast to husband's stinginess—also as 'gentleman,' educated, in contrast to husband who is self-educated peasant. M always a bit of a snob in reaction to world which finally becomes altogether her husband's world since she has little contact with reality except through him."

Eugene began the narrative as an objective record but almost imperceptibly shifted to his mother's point of view. As he began to write about his father's early poverty, his identification with his mother took command, and he consciously and unconsciously adopted and experienced the attitudes toward her husband, his father, that he perceived to be hers. His ambivalence, the simultaneous love, admiration, and contempt for the father, is echoed frequently in plays written over the whole range of Eugene's career, from *The Personal Equation* (1915) to *Long Day's Journey into Night* (1941).

The education James worked so hard to give his sons rebounded against him in the form of his sons' embarrassed contempt for their benefactor's own lack of education. Eugene loved his father and admired James's pride in his peasant roots; he was proud of what his father had accomplished, and frequently took schoolmates to watch his father act. James knew Shakespeare and other great writers of English; but he could not write a letter without making elementary mistakes in spelling, usage, and punctuation. Jamie missed no chance to poke fun at "Sweeney," his ignorance, his peasant ways, his obliviousness to the middle-class values that were life itself to his mother, and he wasted no second thoughts on his father. Eugene often enough joined in the joking; but he was periodically embarrassed to catch himself mouthing middle-class platitudes. Yet another source of anger for him was his half-conscious impression that his mother had caused him to feel contempt for his father. Eugene would take nearly a lifetime to sort it all out.

He and Jamie joined in blaming their father for having no idea what his wife meant in wanting a home and all the middle-class things that went with it in her mind. They internalized her claim that James was thus to blame for her affliction, just as they adopted as their own her belief that dosing the boys with a sip of whiskey when they were young and ailing or had a nightmare caused them later to become alcoholics. Someone had to be blamed. For no one to be blamable implied that no one could improve things, and more, that everything that afflicted them was beyond human control. The sense of helplessness that went along with such a view of things was even less tolerable than the constant quarreling over who was to blame. Mother could not be blamed. The least hint of confrontation had disastrous effects on her. Father was a more solid target. While Mother seemed fragile, James seemed to his sons impervious to recrimination. It was safer to blame everything on James than to show the least doubt of Ella. James, for his part, survived the others' assaults by blandly denying the existence or importance of anything that was not an immediate danger.

Both James and Eugene must have realized, at least sometimes, that Eugene's anger toward Papa was often deflected from its true targets, his mother and himself. James, and perhaps Eugene also, understood that a boy's show of filial contempt didn't mean he really hated and despised his father. The understanding must have made Eugene's provocations just bearable—for both father and son. To make the situation more tolerable, Eugene transferred to Jamie the idealization he had previously conferred on his father.

Eugene increasingly believed Jamie to be the only sane and realistic person in an otherwise crazy family. To Jamie, Papa's refusal to acknowledge and discuss obvious family problems was as crazy as Mama's addiction, and probably caused Mama's despair. Bland Victorian denial was so intensely frustrating to Jamie that he gave James no peace but called him on every hypocrisy, deceit, folly, or mistake. By avoiding confrontations and hoping always for the best, James undoubtedly gave the family its stability. But Jamie believed that his father's impassiveness also prevented problems from ever being solved. Adopting a rationalist's stance, Jamie insisted he believed that progress was possible, but only through confrontation. And so he and his father battled on. James clung to rose-colored spectacles, and Jamie attacked whenever he saw an opening. Eugene increasingly followed his brother.

Of all his boyhood attitudes, Eugene's idealization of Jamie would prove one of the most durable, and one of the most troublesome for him, not just because he misjudged his father and spent years more alienated from the Governor than adolescence made necessary; and not just because he followed his brother's ways with alcohol, to the detriment of his health. The most damaging effect of Eugene's faith in Jamie was the belief that Jamie's analyses of the family's problems were more worldly, more useful than they were. Between his father's denial of what seemed like common sense and his brother's bitter, funny nihilism, Eugene chose the latter, attributing to his brother wisdom and judgment that Jamie never developed, and attributing to his nihilism a coherence it lacked. Eugene was near the end of his life before he could understand that his brother loathed himself more than even Eugene could imagine—and loathed anyone who seemed happier than he. One of the major goals in writing the last plays, four decades later, was to understand Jamie and his influence on Eugene's own development.

In 1901 and 1902 Eugene shot up to nearly his full adult height. He was tall, wiry, and strikingly handsome, with thick black hair, intensely dark eyes, and an unusually penetrating gaze. Coached by Jamie, he was a dandy. Photographers of the playwright in his adulthood were fascinated with the eyes and the handsome, masklike face. Like the sharp clothes, the mask was meant to conceal the discomfort of a shy, self-conscious man, his preoccupation with himself and his inward world, and an exceptional intensity. Malcolm Mollan, city editor of the New London *Telegraph* in 1912 and Eugene's boss, once described the youth's eyes by saying that they were "very big, very dark, and he can do things with them." It seems that some who could withstand the gaze found those eyes expressive. Mollan also described a grin. "Grin is the word . . . . Nobody can grin who hasn't red corpuscles and a throbbing heart inside him. O'Neill used to grin, often at his trying to be a reporter" (Mollan 1922, 3). Eugene's schoolmates must have sometimes seen the grin, and some found the boy no more daunting than Mollan did. Some must have noticed that however poor a reporter Eugene would remain, his eyes and gaze betrayed a curiosity about the world that missed almost nothing.

The view from within was different from what people usually saw from the outside, but it fits with the impression Mollan describes. Eugene perceived himself to be, as he later often said, "a man born without a skin." Growing up as he had, he had always known more about most things he saw than he wanted to know, and had always felt more than he wanted to feel, also. By making a mask of his face, he meant to protect the exposed nerve endings of his sensibility. The schoolboys at Betts Academy, who met Eugene in September 1902, saw the jittery mask, and, from time to time, they also saw traces of the discomfort, the nerviness, the curiosity, and the intensity.

Eugene entered Betts just before his fourteenth birthday and, except for holidays, remained until he graduated in the spring of his eighteenth year, 1906. It would be one of the more pleasant periods of his life.

The previous year, his second at De La Salle, Eugene had not fit in much better than he had as a boarding student at St. Aloysius. He had kept to himself, had taken no pains to make friends, had avoided sports, and had read and written a great deal. He had been more comfortable at

De La Salle than at St. Aloysius, because he had had a little more privacy, but he had detested the hearty athleticism and authoritarian Christianity of De La Salle as much as he had detested the Christianity of the moralizing sisters at St. Aloysius. Either way, the dissatisfaction at school had exacerbated all the guilt, vague or specific, that he carried. Although Eugene had disliked De La Salle, he had made few enemies and was liked by the boys who got to know him. Some who had befriended Eugene were taken to see James play in *Monte Cristo*. One of the boys, Ricardo Amezaga, a Cuban, told Sheaffer that Eugene, who was reading *Don Quixote* at the time, frequently wanted to hear how Spanish names were pronounced (LS, 86–87).

At Betts, boys slept in double rooms. Eugene was free from religious instruction, which was not taken so seriously at Betts as at De la Salle. Betts was known for academic soundness, for vigorous athleticism, for getting a high number of its graduates into Yale, and for succeeding with problem boys. At Betts, boys who had gotten in trouble at home or at other schools learned to get along with masters and other boys. Betts boys called the masters by nicknames, competed with them at sports, tried to outwit them in the dormitory, and learned enough English, mathematics, science, and history to be admitted to good colleges.

At Betts, masters and students competed with and against each other in every sport that Billy Betts knew of. Eugene told schoolgirls he was trying to impress that he was on the football or baseball team, but in fact he was one of the few boys who successfully resisted the push to compete on teams. He would go so far as to enjoy—from the sidelines—the football or baseball match against the Yale freshmen or the boys from Hotchkiss School or Lawrenceville. In later life he avidly followed sports that ranged from six-day bicycle races to baseball, college football, and rowing. At Betts he took his exercise by swimming or rowing. By himself or with one or two other boys, he took long walks. Sometimes he played catch or tennis; one boy remembered that he had a good arm, and a letter from him as an adolescent suggests that he knew how to play tennis. But he never developed the urge to compete in games, perhaps because he had had so little to do with other children until he was seven: he had no experience of cooperative play. Later, growing pains and adolescent neurasthenia may have contributed to Eugene's sitting out games in the Betts grandstand. He may have wished to avoid making enemies. Just as he declined to test his eye and hand against his peers, so he ignored whatever competition for marks existed among the students. All his life he knew what interested him, and he felt that interest without regard for what mattered to others.

Eugene came to enjoy his life at Betts. He confided in a 1923 letter to Billy Betts that he was happier at the school than in most other periods of his early life (LS, 93). In small classes of six or seven, each student received direct and individual attention. The school aimed "to encourage each [student] to proceed at his own rate, and to cultivate in them sound habits of observation and research," according to a brochure that the Gelbs found (Gelbs, 75–76). "In observation work," the brochure went on, "the first task of the student is the inspection of things that are constantly before him, such as plants, animals, the stars, etc. He is thus taught first to *see* and then to *tell* what he *sees* going on around him in nature and in practical life, and is required to record his observations in well-systematized books." It is hard to imagine a better grounding in the disciplines of a writer.

About sixty boys attended Betts when Eugene entered, including several from Latin American countries, whose parents felt that the small classes would improve their sons' ear for English and ease their way to college in America. In theory, Sunday church attendance was required and supervised. In fact, however, little supervision was exercised and, as a master, "Algie" Walters, and several students were to recall, little effort was required to avoid religious services. Walters told a newspaper interviewer in 1936 that Eugene never went to Sunday mass with the other Catholic boys but sometimes asked to go by himself during the week, and permission was always granted (LS, 86–87). Eugene probably meant to commune with a pack of Sweet Caporals or sought some other off-campus pleasure.

At Betts, between the ages of fourteen and nearly eighteen, Eugene gradually came a little way out of his shell. Much later, former students recalled him as well liked among his fellows, if never gregarious. It probably didn't hurt his popularity that his father was a famous actor, that his schoolmates had the chance to meet James during his frequent visits to the school, and that Eugene sometimes took school friends to see his father act. Eugene's pose as the bohemian in the grandstand, aloof from the silliness and hurly-burly of adolescence, was tolerated, perhaps because the boys sensed a touch of decadence that was beyond the experience of most of them.

Eugene earned respect as a dedicated rebel against all authority. He smoked in his room or on the roof of the school building. He was implicated in putting Limburger cheese in the ventilation ducts. He joined other boys on his floor in throwing wet towels and pillows, soap, pails, and wastebaskets out his window, late one fall night, then faked sleepy innocence when Billy Betts rounded on the culprits. With other boys, he would sneak off campus to eat or drink a beer at a café run by the former heavyweight champion Bob Fitzsimmons. One night he helped stack a tower of chamber pots at the top of a stairway, then sent the lot crashing down the stairs in a splendid clamor. Unable to isolate the ring leader, Billy Betts suspected Eugene and predicted that he would die in the electric chair. The Gelbs are probably right to guess that "Eugene was flattered" (Gelbs, 78).

A former roommate recalled with a tinge of envy that Eugene did well in nearly all his classes without apparent effort (Alexander 1962, 93). No wonder. Eugene entered Betts Academy far better read and a far more experienced writer than most people who have graduated from college. Several students recalled Eugene being shouted at in class by masters who thought he was daydreaming: "Wake up, O'Neill!" Usually he could give the correct answer.

Eugene did passably in Latin and French but never took Greek, a choice he regretted in the 1920s when he tried to learn enough of that difficult language to make his way through the plays of Aeschylus and Sophocles. He may have failed mathematics once, possibly because of a struggle of wills with Algie Walters, the math teacher and his housemaster. But Greek and Roman history fascinated him, and he did well in English. In substance and in the intensity of the teaching, Eugene's preparatory school education compares favorably to a baccalaureate program of today at a good American small college. It is a mistake to assume, as many have, that Eugene had little formal education.

A certain peculiarity in Eugene's manner of speaking contributed to the effect he had on others. Throughout his life, except when drinking, he spoke hesitantly, with frequent long pauses between words. He mumbled, swallowed his words, and spoke in a voice so low in both pitch and volume that he was hard to understand. Years later, Bennett Cerf, his publisher at Random House, recalled his first meeting with O'Neill. "I'm very impatient and never let a person finish what he's saying, but I never cut in on O'Neill, even though he talked slowly, very slowly—there'd be long pauses between words." Cerf assured Sheaffer that O'Neill had "the greatest natural dignity of anyone I've ever met," an impression that must have lent the publisher more patience than usual with hesitant speech (LS2, 416). Eugene's fellow Betts students recalled that it was hard to avoid feeling an impatient empathy when one was waiting for Eugene to choose words. The trait was probably related to Eugene's shyness in face-to-face conversation. His letters that survive from this time are fluent or even glib, verbally precocious, sometimes pretentious, and wholly inconsistent with all accounts of his speech; they are also somewhat inconsistent with later letters, in which a hint of a mumble can sometimes be detected.

Apart from the hesitation and the mumble, he spoke with a conspicuous accent that mingled New York and New London phonemes. (The Sterling Library at Yale holds a dictating machine recording made about 1944, in which O'Neill joked with his wife and a friend, sang some sea songs he had learned in his youth, and read speeches from the then unperformed plays *The Iceman Cometh* and *Long Day's Journey into Night*.) The Gelbs wrote of Eugene's speech that he "cherished and never outgrew" the slang and underworld argot of the first decade of the century; for some reason he clung to the old slang long after it grew outmoded, and seemed to ignore changes in colloquial fashion (Gelbs, 87–88).

The hesitant speech and accent seem especially striking in a person from a family like Eugene's. James and Jamie were known for their beautiful natural speaking voices, as well as for their gift of gab and way with words, and both had the trained voices of actors. Ella, like every educated middle-class person of her time, was taught elocution from childhood, and Jamie and Eugene were similarly instructed. Eugene must in some deliberate way have cultivated his mumble, his accent, and his slang, probably borrowed from the street scene of New York and New London that he haunted in his adolescence and after. Perhaps his accent was his equivalent of his father's brogue. It may also have expressed or wish to separate himself from the elocutionary splendor of the other O'Neills and that relieved him of the necessity of competing with his father and brother. Later it contributed to the early myth of O'Neill as an untutored genius who had ascended to Broadway from the ranks of sailors and hoodlums.

As he came out of his shell, his behavior with teachers began to change. Formerly he had been invariably cooperative and exceptionally courteous. He became increasingly contentious, arguing any point that struck him, even after he had been shown to be wrong. When cornered, he would not express anger directly but sulked in sullen withdrawal. The change paralleled a more ominous development. Eugene was beginning to drink heavily. When he drank he often kept drinking until he lost consciousness. As the binges became more frequent, he might resume drinking when he awoke with a hangover. Increasingly, he could not stop until alcoholic gastritis caused him such pain that he could not eat or drink anything.

When he was drinking, his personality changed greatly. He might become garrulous and declaim on any topic that crossed his mind. Occasionally, volubility changed abruptly to violent rage. Drinking afforded a compromise between warring impulses; it allowed him to forget for the moment his anger and guilt and at the same time punished his crimes with illness.

Given that he became more outgoing under the influence of alcohol, it is likely that his friends encouraged Eugene to drink, even knowing that it sometimes made him destructive. Certainly his brother did, even though he realized that Eugene could seldom stop, once he had begun. Eugene was now spending weekends in New York drinking with Jamie, flirting with showgirls and prostitutes. Jamie now took his brother's education in hand. Whenever Eugene could get to Manhattan, Jamie led him on rambles through the dressing rooms of showgirls in Broadway theaters and into brothels. He aimed to wise up "the kid" to the ways of the world, to teach him to understand women as he believed they really were. Jamie had much to do with the aura of decadence that Eugene's Betts schoolmates detected.

One story, the source of which was apparently Carlotta Monterey, Eugene's third wife, ran that the fifteen year-old future playwright was taken by his brother to a particularly rough brothel, where he was introduced to sex in a way that Carlotta said was traumatic for him. Supposedly, this difficult experience affected Eugene for life. It should be kept in mind that Carlotta often created "memories" of events that were illustrative of her interpretations of her husband and that frequently conflicted with one another. It seems hazardous for a biographer to leap from the supposed traumatic event at a brothel to any interpretation at all, let alone to assume that Eugene was scarred sexually for life, as has been written. But it is undoubtedly true that Eugene had far more experience with women of the world than many of his peers.

In adolescence Eugene developed a certain technique with show-girls. Instead of chatting up a woman, he would silently fix his intense, dark gaze on one who caught his attention. Being stared at by Eugene was a disconcerting experience, according to men and women who met him at various periods of his life; it made people feel he "could see right through" to one's soul, as several people told biographers. No doubt the gaze had a powerful effect on showgirls, who knew that the tall, hand-some boy was the son of a famous actor and the brother of a man with a good reputation as a sport.

Eugene at fifteen, sixteen, seventeen, drunk and emulating Jamie, was all fashion, whim, and aggression. He was the devotee of the gods of sex and death he had encountered in Baudelaire, Balzac, Zola, Wilde, Swinburne, and Ibsen. One difference between the brothers was that Eu-gene's intellectual hunger and curiosity had nothing to do with satisfying school authorities or impressing his father or mother. Both brothers were highly intelligent, but for Jamie, it seems, intellect was useful only for out-witting the world and the Governor. There is no sign that Jamie got per-sonal or emotional satisfaction from his reading or his education. One part of Eugene, however, a part that eventually proved to be the core of his adult personality, fed and depended on ideas and thinking. Some of his attempts to copy his brother led to development in Eugene that Jamie would not achieve.

At sixteen Eugene sometimes loved in the style of his later love af-fairs. He lost himself in love for a time with an extremity and intensity his brother thought naive and absurd. In June or July of 1905 Eugene met in New London a girl from Hartford named Marion Welch who was visiting a neighbor of the O'Neills. Marion was a tall, slim, blonde beauty; Eugene called her Boutade, by which he apparently meant whimsical one. In a photo she stands beside a tennis net with a racket in one hand and three balls in the other, looking as if she knew what to do with the racket. They played tennis together, and Eugene taught her to row in a sleek boat his fa-ther had bought him. They took pictures of each other, flirted, gossiped about other people, and fell in love. He tried and failed to seduce her.

In the letters they wrote after she returned to Hartford they talked about the poets, novelists, and philosophers they were reading. They out-did each other to seem esoteric and sure of their taste. When she told him she was reading Darwin with pleasure and counted him a hero, she in-timidated Eugene a little. His reply is striking. "I don't see how anyone can go to Darwin for enjoyment. Alex. Dumas pour le mien. I could read every book in the world and no heroes could ever replace 'D'Artagnan, Athos, Porthos and Aramis,' 'Monte Cristo' and 'Bussy' in my estimation" (SL, 12).

Unable to compete successfully, Eugene replies in something very close to the tone James Tyrone uses in *Long Day's Journey into Night* when his younger son Edmund has revealed his modern, morbid tastes. One assumes that that is the way James O'Neill spoke to the schoolboy Eugene. In the letter, written at a time when Eugene could hardly spend a moment with his father without quarreling, he could nevertheless speak in the voice of the old hero worshiping identification with James, an identification that was probably unconscious at the moment. The identification shows the source of Eugene's ability to have an affair with a young woman that was more complicated than the quick seduction of a showgirl or a transaction with a hooker. That Eugene could be at least partly comfortable with his identification with his father explains why he would eventually develop in a way that Jamie never could.

In a personal chronology called *Cycles* that he made in 1946, Eugene said later that during the summer of 1905, when he met Marion Welch, he "started reporting life." The obscure phrase suggests that he was doing some kind of writing and had conscious ideas about "life." He may have been reflecting on ideas about the world acquired from George Bernard Shaw and the other writers he was reading. Perhaps he was scribbling philosophic speculations. Besides Shaw, he was reading Marx and Engels. He read the poems of Dowson, FitzGerald, Swinburne, Baudelaire, and Wilde. He read Dostoyevsky, Tolstoy, Gorky, Conrad, and London. Probably Conrad or London led him to Melville, decades before the author of *Typee, Omoo,* and *Moby-Dick* would be rediscovered by scholars and publishers. Through Shaw he found Ibsen and heard of Schopenhauer, Nietzsche, and Wagner.

Back at school in the fall, Eugene found his interest in Marion beginning to fade. He was spending his weekends in New York, drinking and carrying on with Jamie. He was caught smoking in his room so often that he was moved to a room across from that of his friendly enemy the math instructor. He decorated his room with publicity pictures of showgirls in tights, as well as actual examples of ladies' undergarments. They were souvenirs of trips with his brother up and down Broadway. The school authorities made him redecorate.

In his third year at Betts, Eugene developed a friendship with another student, a boy named Hans ("Heinie") Schleip, whose father ran Pabst's Café, adjacent to the Majestic Theatre on Columbus Circle. Eugene and Heinie would hang around Broadway theaters whenever they could get to town. One or the other boy's father could usually arrange for tickets to some show. Or the two boys would follow Jamie on his rounds of the women's dressing rooms. One of Alexander's informants remembered that Eugene and Heinie carried on more rambunctiously than most of their schoolmates and were envied for their decadence (Alexander 1962, 94–95). By the time Eugene left Betts, he was an experienced participant in the New York sporting life.

After graduating from Betts in June 1906, Eugene spent an unsupervised summer in New London with Jamie. James and Ella went to England to attend a celebration for Ellen Terry. Jamie spent the summer drinking and whoring, and Eugene followed suit, but he was also reading his seditious authors, who now included Nietzsche. Nietzsche led him to Wagner, the Greeks, and tragedy. At some point Eugene made a decision about college. He would not go to Yale, as most Betts graduates did and as his father hoped he would. Perhaps he had heard enough about Yale from Betts masters to know that he would have had to conform to its standards and would not have had much luck making it adapt to him.

For some reason, he chose Princeton. Perhaps he had heard that change was under way at Nassau. The new president of Princeton, Woodrow Wilson, was trying to enact reforms; he had supplemented the lecture system by hiring young scholars as preceptors to meet in small groups with undergraduates and give them individual attention. Perhaps word of reform led Eugene to believe that at Princeton he might be able to develop further his own interests, regardless of whether they coincided with the curriculum.

At any rate, he entered Princeton in the fall of 1906. It seems that for several years Eugene had some notion of becoming an engineer. Although he had not done especially well in mathematics up until then, he signed up for the science program that required him to pass algebra, physics, spherical trigonometry, and conics, as well as Latin, French, and English, in his first year.

As he had done at Betts, he read and wrote avidly. Early in his career at Princeton he discovered Benjamin Tucker's Unique Book Shop on Sixth Avenue in Manhattan. He made friends with Tucker, a man who had been a regular at Pfaff's café, for years the center of bohemian intellectual life in New York. Tucker had known Walt Whitman when the poet lived in Camden, and had been his advocate when *Leaves of Grass* was banned and condemned. Eugene discovered in *Song of Myself* the most naked expression of modernism, the claim for legitimizing the self not merely as a fitting literary subject but as the principal source for modern poetry.

In a certain way it is hard to imagine a more studious young man than Eugene, although he never became a good university student. Regardless of why he went to Princeton, his behavior there in his first term was much like his behavior at Betts. But he was now drinking more than at Betts, and as he went to New York at every chance, he began to skip classes. Benjamin Tucker introduced him to Emma Goldman, who took to Eugene and remained a friend for many years. (Her nephew, Saxe Commins, would later be Eugene's devoted friend and literary editor for more than thirty-five years.) Tucker also introduced Eugene to Wilde's *Picture of Dorian Gray,* Nietzsche's *Also sprach Zarathustra,* and Max Stirner's *The Ego and His Own: The Case of the Individual Against Authority.*

Whitman, Nietzsche, and Stirner were intellectually of great and permanent importance to Eugene. In 1927 he wrote to his friend Benjamin de Casseres that he had reread *Zarathustra* at least once a year since he had first discovered it at eighteen and was "never disappointed which is more than I can say of almost any other book" (SL, 245–46).

If Whitman showed him that the self should be a legitimate literary subject, Nietzsche and Stirner helped Eugene begin to think about what the self was. Further, they help him develop the beginnings of an alternative to the Christian view of the world that he resisted in his father's home and in all his schools. These three and the other authors his father considered degenerate had made it possible to think about a world organized around "myself," rather than around a monotheistic and omnipotent God. They also made it possible to separate the ideas "good" and "evil" from the absolute of God.

Making good and evil relative had great psychological importance for Eugene in easing a conscience that was rigid beyond the ordinary. In addition to whatever guilt and anxiety would have assailed him simply because he was adolescent, he carried his Sophoclean burden. Besides being simply oedipal in the Freudian sense, he was also like Oedipus, author of crimes he could not knowingly have committed. In Eugene's neurosis he had constantly to defend himself against his own charges that he was responsible for his mother's addiction and for the other family problems that followed from her illness.

Many consequences may ensue from detaching morality from the idea of a deity; it was certainly neither the American way nor the Catholic way, but it must have been comforting to Eugene to learn that there was no such connection in Greek mythology or the literature that grew out of the myths. It gave Eugene a space in which to contemplate responsibility as an idea not always identical with guilt. It must have been at this time that Eugene began consciously to identify with Orestes, the son of Agamemnon and Clytemnestra who is compelled by Mycenean ethics and by the god Apollo to kill his mother and, in consequence, is driven mad by the Furies. Orestes would be the archetype for several characters in O'Neill's plays based mostly on himself, including the son, Orin, in *Mourning Becomes Electra* and Parritt, the young suicide, in *The Iceman Cometh.* Creating a mythico-intellectual structure in which to view his crime and punishment gave Eugene a semblance of objectivity—call it sanity. The view of life that evolved in Eugene owed a debt to Schopenhauer and Nietzsche as well as to Greek mythology and had analogies with psychoanalysis. It is a view that O'Neill called tragic and that stood in his mind in intellectual and emotional opposition to the Christian view of life.

The more he understood the tragic view, the more Christianity came to seem the enemy. He developed a particular resentment toward the requirement that he attend Sunday chapel at Princeton, where students were compelled to listen to Henry van Dyke, a Presbyterian minister and English professor who was known widely as an author and speaker on behalf of the "contagion of virtue" and other inspirational topics, and whose verses on such themes frequently appeared in literary as well as popular magazines. Twenty-five years later, when van Dyke denounced with outrage the award to Sinclair Lewis of the Nobel Prize, Eugene's old irritation at the preacher flared up again, in a letter to George Jean Nathan (LS, 116).

Eugene believed that van Dyke spoke for everything Eugene most detested in the America of his time (as well as in his own father), especially the rejection of reality in favor of bland Christian optimism. He resented the power of American bully Christians to silence the truth-tellers he favored: Shaw, Nietzsche, Swinburne, and the others, and among whom Eugene wanted to count himself. Van Dyke and his son, a Princeton undergraduate who penned inspirational verse for the school literary magazine, reminded Eugene unpleasantly of his alienation from his world.

In response to the social power he thought the van Dykes represented, the disciple of Baudelaire tried to be always drunken, and he recreated in the Princeton dormitory the decor of his Betts room. He draped a piece of fishing net on a wall and hung from it an assortment of actress's slippers, tights, brassieres, stockings, and step-ins, as well as a poker hand, scandalous posters, and publicity pictures of noted chanteuses. The most "gruesome" display, a less worldly classmate told Sheaffer, was several used condoms (LS, 116–17). As he had been at Betts, he was noted among his fellows for his decadence. He boasted that a married woman in New London was in love with him. He was also involved with a woman who lived in a brownstone in the Village. With new friends that he met through Tucker and at Princeton he explored bohemian saloons in Greenwich Village, and homosexual bars in Hell's Kitchen. He described what he saw to those less adventurous Princeton classmates who asked. Sometimes he took his friends to his parents' apartment at the Hotel Lucerne and treated them to the lobster salad.

While at Princeton, Eugene developed a close friendship with a boy about his age, Louis Holladay, whom he met in New York, a friendship that lasted the rest of Louis's life. Louis was a tall, blond, handsome young man, bright and hard-drinking like Eugene, and he was having an even harder time finding himself. The problems among the Holladays rivaled those of the O'Neills, and perhaps exceeded them, for there was no one to hold things together in the Holladay household as James O'Neill held his family together. (James seems to have known Louis's mother, Adele, a sometime actress, who had once had a connection with his friend Otis Skinner.) In 1906–1907 Louis was living with his older sister, Polly, who over the years operated a series of restaurants in Greenwich Village. Polly once told Eugene that she had seduced Louis when he was very young, a story that made Eugene fear and distrust her. Perhaps a shared sense of their history of family difficulties brought Eugene and Louis together. Virtually no details of their early relationship are known, for no letters between the two exist. Apparently Eugene often stayed with Louis during his weekends in the Village.

At Christmas Eugene and his mother traveled by train to San Francisco, where James was trying to establish himself in a new play about John the Baptist, *The Wanderer*. It was another effort to escape from *Monte Cristo*, once again to no avail. John the Baptist failed, and James had to return once more to the Château d'If. Eugene took the chance for some sight-seeing in the city he had often visited in childhood, and he was so impressed by the devastation caused by the earthquake of the previous April that, some time later, he convinced a girl he was trying to impress that he had lived through the event himself.

Eugene's visits to class became ever rarer during his second term, and he was drinking harder. On one occasion, drunk on absinthe, he wrecked his room: he took the radiator apart and smashed furniture. On another, he not only wrecked his room but also several times pulled the trigger of a revolver he was pointing at Louis Holladay. Fortunately, the gun did not fire. He had an affair with a woman in Trenton, ten miles from Princeton, and because she let him sleep over, he was frequently absent from his dormitory during the week, as well as on weekends, when he was in New York.

The most important event of Eugene's second and last term at Princeton occurred when he went to see Alla Nazimova in Ibsen's *Hedda Gabler*. As he described it much later, the event was a revelation to him. Writing in 1938 to the editor of the Norwegian-American newspaper, *Nordisk Tidende,* Eugene said that he remembered "well the impact upon me when I saw an Ibsen play for the first time, a production of *Hedda Gabler* at the old Bijou Theatre in New York—and then went back again and again for ten successive nights. That experience discovered an entire new world of drama for me. It gave me my first conception of a modern theatre where truth might live" (SL, 477).

Why was it so important to him? He must have felt that he had found a writer who knew something true about the world, but he would have already known that about Ibsen from reading his plays and from Shaw's *Quintessence of Ibsenism.* It must have been something more personal that kept him going back to the Bijou night after night. O'Neill makes a mocking allusion to *Hedda Gabler* in an early farce, *Bread and Butter* (1914), and he sometimes called one of his girlfriends "my Hedda Gabler." But these allusions do not indicate any more clearly than the laudatory letter exactly the nature of Eugene's discovery. It is interesting to surmise what it may have meant to him.

Hedda rules those around her through whim, but she in turn is ruled by an imp of self-destructiveness. Possessed by an aestheticism that makes her long to do anything she does in high style, she despises others not for weakness per se, much less for moral insufficiency, but for any lack she detects of fineness, of want of style, of living without flare. Most of all she is unforgiving of herself when she suspects she has done something common. The crisis of the play comes just after she marries a man whom she considers without style and beneath her. In judgment of herself, she first drives a man with whom she identifies to kill himself and then follows him in suicide. Something in the play and the performance doubtless made O'Neill see with a certain objectivity qualities of his own—the qualities he had in common with his mother.

Nothing that Princeton might offer could compare with Eugene's chance discovery of Ibsen. By the middle of the second term, it was apparent that Princeton was wasted on him and vice versa. So much for academics. From the point of view of the registrar, Eugene had been to so few classes, had done so little work, and was passing so few courses that he could not be admitted to the second year. It was a matter of bookkeeping.

In later years, Eugene's hell-raising at Princeton made for lively journalism, and over time the stories were elaborated and embellished. His best-known Princeton caprice was made notorious by George Jean Nathan, who claimed that it caused O'Neill's "expulsion" from college. Repeated in many versions, this anecdote had Eugene, egged on by friends, drunkenly throwing a whiskey bottle through the living room window of the University president, Woodrow Wilson. Actually, Eugene told Hamilton Basso in 1947, "I *liked* Woodrow Wilson. I would never have done a thing like that if I had been swimming around in a lake of vodka." Basso reported that the window belonged to the division superintendent of the Pennsylvania Railroad and that the missile was not a bottle, but an errant rock casually thrown at a barking dog (Basso, February 28, 1948, 45).

Such anecdotes suggest that in his two terms at Princeton Eugene had a splendid time—reading by day, drinking and sporting all night, shunning everything disagreeable. Sheaffer reports that Eugene spent so much time indoors that his usual dark tan faded and revealed "a pinkish tinge in his cheeks" which he feared "might portend tuberculosis. However," Sheaffer continues, "he made no effort to cut down on his smoking and dissipating" (LS, 124). It is remotely possible that, as Eugene later speculated, the tuberculosis diagnosed late in 1911, four and a half years later, had begun in 1907. Whether that was the case or not, his belief that he might be seriously ill is important. As always with Eugene's vices, a Hedda Gabler–like desperation and self-destructiveness were evident. He half believed that he might have consumption, and yet he did nothing to find out about his condition or cease doing what he had reason to guess might aggravate it. He had an expectation of fatal punishment, and a wish to flirt with mortality. In the next few years, Eugene would become far more reckless in challenging his daemon to save him from himself.

For now, however, nothing more serious happened than that he had to leave Princeton. It was not because of the rock thrown at the dog (which led merely to a two-week suspension). He had attended so few classes and done so little of the required work that he chose not to take the few exams he would have been allowed to sit for. In June he was dropped for "poor scholastic standing."

Eugene Adrift
1907–1911

IN 1907, AT SIXTY-TWO, James O'Neill found himself with two grown sons who showed not the least sign of ever being able to support themselves. One had failed so many classes that he couldn't return to college, while the other had been expelled outright. Both were drunks, both were adrift, and both were completely dependent, financially and emotionally, on their father. Angry and uncomfortable in their dependency, and feeling chronically hopeless about their mother, Eugene and Jamie turned their frustration against their father. One must infer that James partly understood their misdirected anger and secretly sympathized with it, for he continued to support sons who showed him little but contempt. Yet James O'Neill also despised the ingratitude he had lived with for years. In the absence of any overt or immediate satisfaction in his family, he turned as always to his life and work in the theater. He dreamed of playing King Lear, a part he had never tried. It seemed the part that destiny had in mind for him.

James had now been playing Edmond Dantes for about twenty-three years and had been thoroughly tired of the part and the play for at least two decades. He was widely liked and respected in the profession and was generally considered one of the more accomplished actors of his generation. By the time he retired from the play in 1914, he had made numerous attempts to put *The Count of Monte Cristo* behind him, but he had become so identified with the part that people would not accept him in another role. As late as 1912, he was called on to make a five-reel movie of *Monte Cristo,* and he did it very creditably, showing youth and vigor that belie both his years and his boredom. Each time he tried to perform a new play anywhere but in the most sophisticated cities, audiences rejected it, and he had to bring back *Monte Cristo* to pay the bills. In 1907, when Eugene left Princeton, James attempted another escape.

James had an idealistic concern for the state of acting in America and thought he knew how to improve things. Concerned that the high Victorian style of performing Shakespeare was vanishing, he decided to establish a repertory company of talented young actors. He would train them to speak dramatic poetry as he believed it should be spoken; his company would perform the Shakespearean tragedies, and other serious plays as well. The group was to start with Knowles's *Virginius* and move to *Julius Caesar* before tackling *Lear.* Jamie was to be a member of the company. Perhaps, as Alexander (1962, 110) suggests, one of James's motives in creating the company was to surround Jamie with seriousness and dedication, in order that the older son might find himself as an actor and a man. If so, paternal concern undermined James's artistic ideals. Jamie performed as poorly with the new company as he usually did when onstage with his father. Worse, correctly gauging the discomfort felt by the young actors for values they thought antique, Jamie carried on his private war by quietly ridiculing to the company his father's idealism. Jamie's subversion surely contributed to the failure of the venture. As always, Jamie's destructiveness eventually hurt him more than it did others; in the long run, each little destructive act added to the list he kept of reasons to despise himself.

James also faced the problems of his younger son's idleness and aimlessness. The former was solved more easily than the latter. James had invested some of Ella's money in the Brittain Supply Company, a mail-order firm that sold goods ranging from costume jewelry to gramophones and Kodagraph home motion picture machines. He arranged for Eugene to become secretary to the president, Henry Brittain. For helping with correspondence and orders, Eugene received twenty-five dollars a week. In fact, Eugene spent much of the workday writing poetry and reading Schopenhauer, whose pessimism afforded Eugene a consolation similar to that which it had given to Wagner and Nietzsche. Away from the office, Eugene was usually wandering the town, drinking with Jamie and other friends, studying the bohemian scene. Among other affairs, he was still carrying on with the married woman from New London.

He made a new friendship, with his father's press secretary, James Findlater Byth or Bythe. An elegant little Cornishman, Byth had cultivated a Scots accent and devised a story full of hints that he had been born in a Scottish country mansion, perhaps a castle, and that he had covered the Boer War for Reuters. Five years later, in 1912, Jimmy Byth would save Eugene's life when O'Neill nearly died from a deliberate overdose of veronal. A year and a half after rescuing Eugene, Byth himself died a suicide. He was the subject of O'Neill's only published short story, "Tomorrow," and the model for Jimmy Tomorrow in *The Iceman Cometh*. Byth and O'Neill occasionally roomed together during the five years after Eugene left Princeton. But for now, Eugene was staying with his parents at the Hotel Lucerne.

Eugene hung around the rehearsals of *Virginius*. He flirted with actresses in his peculiar fashion—with his fixed stare that reminded one woman of the gaze of the god Pan. Sheaffer infers that Eugene observed with silent approval and amusement as Jamie used his lacerating wit to quietly sabotage his father's efforts to educate the young actors (LS, 127). *Virginius* achieved a mild success. James was probably more saddened that Jamie was panned than gratified by praise for his own performance. After rehearsals or performances, Eugene and Jamie went on drinking rambles and pursued swift beauties in the dressing rooms of other theaters.

Despite its mild success in New York, *Virginius* failed on the road. James switched to *Julius Caesar,* but only he among the cast felt any enthusiasm for it. He lamented that the younger actors were too lazy to learn the style, too cynical to try to understand *his* Shakespeare. Before long it was clear that he could not make his idea for a repertory company work, and James had to abandon his reform movement. Not long after, Jamie got the lead in a touring company production of *The Travelling Salesman,* a farce by the Canadian playwright James Forbes. He toured New England as the salesman Watts for two and a half years; it was the nearest he came to a theatrical success, although even then reviewers often complained that he was visibly drunk onstage, and that his drunkenness spoiled the play's humor.

Eugene, fully as rebellious and self-destructive as Jamie, became more reckless than ever in his drinking and womanizing. He seemed to flaunt his dissipation to his father, perhaps because he constantly required reassurance that he was loved. Both sons believed that they were useless and parasitic, and both felt helpless to change. Both Eugene and Jamie assumed that their father was invulnerable, and they assailed any weakness they detected in him, in an attempt to divert to themselves the attention and devotion that they thought James gave only to his work.

In the fall of 1908, when the Brittain mail-order company began to fail, Eugene lost his job and was again dependent on an allowance from his father. Eugene seems to have been rooming with Louis Holladay. Most evenings he spent in the Tenderloin, a neighborhood world famous at the time as a mecca of vice. To locals it was the center of the New York sporting set. The favorite places for Eugene and his friends were Jack's Restaurant, where they watched Tammany Hall politicians; the Hippodrome, where there were the elephants and showgirls; Mouquin's, a good, inexpensive French restaurant; and the Haymarket, a combination dance hall, variety theater, and hangout for hookers, gamblers, and gangsters, about which Eugene wrote a passable sonnet:

> The music blares into a ragtime tune—
> The dancers whirl around the polished floor;
> Each powdered face a set expression wore
> Of dull satiety . . . .
>
> In sleek dress suit an old man sits and leers
> With vulture mouth and blood-shot beady eyes
> At the young girl beside him. Drunken tears
> Fall down her painted face, and choking sighs
> Shake her, as into his familiar ears
> She sobs her sad, sad history—and lies!

Eugene roamed with new friends and old; besides Louis Holladay, they included the painters Edward Keefe, a New Londoner, and his roommate, George Bellows. Keefe later told interviewers that Eugene seemed determined to try everything. When drinking, Eugene could be affable and gregarious or unreasonably contentious, and he could shift from one mood to the other without warning. At times he seemed simply crazy. Raymond Terry, a Princeton friend, described to Sheaffer (LS, 140) an incident in which he invited Eugene to have a drink with him at the bar at Jack's. Without visible provocation, Eugene hit the bartender in the face and was immediately set upon by bouncers and beaten up. His destructiveness, like Jamie's, usually ended up making him his own worst victim.

There were many such incidents, and they apparently made as little sense to Eugene as they did to others. Years later, questioned by his early biographer, Barrett Clark, about the wild episodes, Eugene admitted that when reminded, he remembered carrying on as people said he had, and he sometimes remembered particular impulsive acts. But they seemed to have no meaning or reality to him. "I simply cannot recognize the person in myself, nor understand him, nor his acts as mine . . . although my reason tells me he was undeniably I" (SL, 203). The curious dissociation that Eugene experienced in trying to recall these acts is characteristic of the way many people recall adolescence and suggests that at nineteen and twenty he was going though a stage that many men pass through five years earlier in life. Both the wildness itself and the feeling of detachment from the memories of crazy acts probably indicate that Eugene's adolescence was delayed and protracted. Various circumstances must have been responsible, especially the discovery of his mother's addiction. A kind of amnesia for affects may also have resulted in part from his heavy drinking.

In the fall of 1907, while his father and brother were traveling their separate ways, Eugene lived with his mother at the Lucerne. Eugene and Ella were seldom comfortable with each other, and the discomfort showed with Ella's rare visitors. Ella sometimes saw one of her Brennan cousins, Agnes, who was a few years older than Eugene. Agnes had a musical gift and was studying piano in New York, and she and her friend Sadie Koenig, another music student, were sometimes invited to visit Ella at the Lucerne. Ella charmed them, although at times she repeated herself, seemed drowsy or incoherent, or became lost in her thoughts. Neither visitor had any idea that Ella used morphine. James once explained to them that his wife had taken a drop too much. Both young women were upset when Eugene and his mother quarreled. Sadie thought that at that time in his life Eugene was "a kind of bum." She told the Gelbs that Eugene would sometimes come in while the two girls were there and throw himself on a bed. Ella would ask him, "Are you at it again?" and Eugene would yell back, "You'd be better off if you'd sleep a little more." Mother and son would argue unrelentingly and Eugene mocked his mother "in what seemed, to Sadie, an outrageous fashion." Ella and Eugene would accuse each other of taking "too much," a reference that was unclear to Sadie (Gelbs, 123). Eugene was becoming as provocative as Jamie.

When James returned, he expelled Eugene from the Lucerne. The boy moved in with Ed Keefe and George Bellows in the studio they shared at Broadway and Sixty-sixth with Frank Best, a young advertising man. Eugene later made use of this ménage in an early four-act play, *Bread and Butter* (1914). Trying to get control of his son, James cut Eugene's allowance to a dollar a day. Eugene retaliated. Keefe told several interviewers that in revenge, Eugene picked up the most flamboyantly red-haired prostitute he could find in a Tenderloin brothel and took her to his father's box at the Broadway Theatre (LS, 143).

In January 1909, Eugene led Keefe and Bellows out to an old farm near Zion, New Jersey, that his father had owned for years and that was unoccupied. The three camped out in the unheated house "and damned near froze to death," as Eugene later told his son Shane. Taking pity on the young, James sent several bottles of whiskey and a box of cigars. The bohemians stuck it out for a month then returned to the city. Keefe and Bellows brought back paintings of frigid hillsides; Eugene had a few sonnets written in "bad imitation of Dante Gabriel Rossetti" (SL, 499).

Not long after returning to Manhattan from the farm, Eugene was introduced by Frank Best to Kathleen Jenkins; the two soon became lovers. The affair led to their marriage the following October. Much later, Kathleen told Sheaffer that in the several months of their relationship she never saw Eugene drunk; nor did she even guess at any of the wildness that other people remembered. She tried in a gentle way to be impersonal in her recollections, but she gave Sheaffer the impression that she had been "deeply in love" and that she believed Eugene had felt swept away by the tide of her feelings (LS, 145).

Like Eugene, Kathleen had been born to prominent parents, but hers had arrived earlier than the O'Neills or Quinlans. Her mother's father had held a seat on the New York Stock Exchange, and her father had been an appraiser for Tiffany's and a member of the Larchmont Yacht Club. But Charles Jenkins had a drinking problem. Kate Camblas (or Camblos) endured Charles's waywardness for several years but then parted from him while their only child, Kathleen, was still young. Kathleen and Eugene had in common one urgent thing: both were trying to escape from difficult family circumstances and from an uncomfortable state of dependency. Both seem to have assumed, at least unconsciously, that marriage would automatically make them adults and get them over the hurdle that seemed to stand between adolescent dependency and adult independence.

Whatever drew Kathleen and Eugene together, it had little to do with the people they were or would become. About 1920, when she and Eugene had not seen each other for a decade, and she began to hear about the celebrated young playwright whose name was the same as her first husband's, she could not believe it was the same man. Nothing about the Eugene she had known had left anything of a literary impression in her mind, and when she saw and read some of the plays, she recognized nothing at all in them of the man she had married. She recalled that Eugene had written poems to her, but that was what young men did in those days. Eugene could not have ignored, even in the few months of their affair, the obvious fact that they had practically nothing in common intellectually. Kathleen might take an interest in whatever he said about Nietzsche or Ibsen or Schopenhauer simply because he said it; but it was plain that she could not lose herself in a passion for philosophy or literature.

By September, Kathleen knew she was pregnant. Eugene's reaction to the pregnancy was complicated and suggests how intense was the conflict in his feelings. Instead of denying responsibility or simply walking away, he offered to marry Kathleen, and he cooperated fully in the plans she made for the two of them to elope. Until that point he had said nothing at all about her or the affair to his parents. Now he told some of the story to his father, allowing James to conclude that Eugene was the victim of a schemer, much as James himself had been with Nettie Walsh. Perhaps Eugene partly expected Kathleen to be the gold digger that his father and brother believed any woman was likely to be.

James decided that he must remove his son from harm's reach, and he turned to one of his investments for a solution. He had backed a Portland, Oregon, mining engineer named Earl Stevens, who had graduated from Columbia and was about to go gold prospecting in Honduras. He now arranged for Eugene to join Stevens and his wife, Ann, on their expedition. Eugene would meet the Stevenses in San Francisco and sail with them. Eugene agreed to his father's plan. He may have told Kathleen that he was going to Honduras to seek his fortune, a story her mother later gave out to the newspapers. He said nothing to his father of his plan to marry Kathleen.

On October 2, 1909, Kathleen and Eugene took the ferry to Hoboken and were married there in Trinity Protestant Episcopal Church by the Rev. William Gilpin. On the marriage certificate, Eugene gave his age as twenty-two, his residence as Zion, New Jersey, and his occupation as engineer (Gelbs, 133). He and Kathleen agreed to keep the marriage secret. A few days later, Kathleen and James met for the first time at Grand Central when they put Eugene on the train for San Francisco. Kathleen later told Sheaffer that James was very pleasant to her when they met, but she was sure he would not have been if he had known that she and his son were already married (LS, 149).

Eugene had surely done as close to the right thing for Kathleen as he could, given his own state of dependency, immaturity, and general confusion. Yet what he did was far less than he believed he should have done. For the rest of his life he felt acutely guilty for mistreating Kathleen. His guilt seems to have been more general than specific.

His unwitting role in his mother's addiction tainted all his feelings about women throughout his life. The contamination was too primal for him ever to get over it. But some of his guilt was specific to his feeling that he had mistreated Kathleen. He had made her pregnant and then could not accept the responsibility of being a husband and father, or even face her in the shame that came from discovering the inadequacy. The circumstance brought about a general confrontation with most of the shortcomings of his development, such as it was to that point. It was a confrontation he would never forget. Not long before he died, he told her son, his first son, Eugene Jr., in the presence of his second son, Shane: "Of all the women I treated badly, and there were many, I treated your mother the worst. And she was the one who gave me the least trouble" (Bowen 1959, 322).

In fact, Kathleen seems never to have considered herself mistreated in the affair with Eugene; she believed herself to be as responsible for the situation as he was. When Eugene set off for San Francisco and Honduras, Kathleen returned to her mother and remained with her during the pregnancy. Two years later, when she divorced Eugene, she asked for neither alimony nor support for their son.

There is no sign that Kathleen ever expressed recrimination or blame toward Eugene, or in any way exacerbated the guilt that he carried with him the rest of his life. The guilt was an internal matter, and it had a great and positive importance for Eugene's future development. He was already on the way to becoming the man he would be, intellectually; but emotionally he was still adolescent. From a guilt that apparently arose almost entirely from within himself came the discovery that his actions had consequences. The discovery would eventually lead him out of adolescence. But the change would not begin to be visible for another two years.

He fled from Kathleen, shortly after their secret marriage, never having lived with her. The old jumbled anger toward his mother and women in general drew him often to share his brother's misogyny or his father's Victorian condescension. As time passed, it became clear that Kathleen would never justify any mistrust he may have felt, a fact that brought a new, gradually evolving discovery: that he knew much less about women than he had thought, and that possibly most of what he knew was wrong. He had reason now to mistrust his father and brother as authorities on women. As the difficulties of Eugene's second and third marriages and a series of searching plays about marriage would later testify, he was left to find his way by dead reckoning in the seas of romantic love. In the next several years, there would gradually develop a marked change in his relations with his women.

Eugene spent his twenty-first birthday, October 16, 1909, on the Pacific, sailing a southeasterly course along the coasts of California, Mexico, and Central America. Borne by his natural element, he had leisure to contemplate the varieties of betrayal, guilt, and inadequacy, and to reflect on how little he had learned from his poets and philosophers about the world.

Eugene had been adrift since leaving Betts. Adolescent belief in immortality was affected by his affair with Kathleen and its consequences, which reawakened his guilt and now made him aware of a new sense of inadequacy. He set out on a three-year meander through the Western hemisphere, during which he became increasingly vulnerable to various dangers, psychological and physical, including serious illness.

Two letters to his parents from Honduras, the only letters known from these wander-years, show Eugene's state of mind at the beginning of his adventure. On November 9, after a three-day trip on muleback from the port of Ampala to Tegucigalpa, he was full of enthusiasm. He liked the city, the climate, and the altitude. He was "brown as a native" from the sun and was starting a mustache "in order to look absolutely as shiftless and dirty as the best of them." He advised his father that there "are lots of mining lands down here that can be taken up for a song," and he hoped his mother would recover her money from the Brittain venture. The concerns about his parents' money seems to show a consciousness of what his trouble was costing them and perhaps even a touch of gratitude. He praised Ann Stevens for "bearing up fine under all the hardship—which is more than one woman in a thousand could do" (SL, 18–19).

By Christmas he had begun to discover a different order of hardship, and admiration of Mrs. Stevens had given way to self-pity. He resented like a child the discomforts of the jungle and foreign travel. He hated the fleas, gnats, and mosquitoes: "*I have never been free from bites one day since I arrived in this country*"—he underlined the complaint. The food was "rotten . . . vilely cooked," he complained, and upset his stomach, and he had had a fever off and on. His frustration exploded: "From a two months experience, and after having been in all the different zones of this country, I give it as my candid opinion and fixed belief that God got his inspiration for Hell after creating Honduras. The country as far as climate and natural advantages goes is fine but the natives are the lowest, laziest, most ignorant bunch of brainless bipeds that ever polluted a land . . . . Until some just Fate grows weary of watching the gropings in the dark of these human maggots and exterminates them, until the Universe shakes these human lice from its sides, Honduras has no future" (SL, 19–20).

The invective seems to stem from an experience in which he and the Stevenses were led through some "unexplored" country on a promise of gold that did not pan out. Eugene himself seems to have been taken by himself to a place where the jungle was impenetrable and where he felt lost and panicky. His first reaction was the rage expressed in the letter toward the natives who had toyed with him. Much later he gave his panic to the Emperor Jones, whom he caused to become lost in a similar jungle.

Eugene ends his letter: "Cannot tell how much I miss you both. I never realized how much home and Father & Mother meant until I got so far away from them. Lots of love to you both" (SL, 20). The last line may have given a bit of hope to James and Ella that perhaps Eugene might have a future different from Jamie's present. But there would not be many encouraging signs for several years.

Eugene stuck it out in Honduras into the new year, 1910. He had been having afternoon attacks of fever since December, and by February he was too sick with malaria to continue. He made it back to Tegucigalpa, where he found all the hotels full for a fiesta. According to an oft-repeated story, the consulate had too few blankets to keep him warm during attacks of chills and fever, and so he was wrapped in old American flags until, as Eugene later said, he "looked like George M. Cohan" (Basso, February 28, 1948, p. 36). The consul found him a doctor and, three weeks later, when he could travel, sent him back to New York. There he knew that he would find waiting for him Kathleen, who was about to have their baby, and his father, who had been furious to learn through the newspapers that his son had lied to him and married the girl.

No one met his ship. When Eugene reached his parents' suite in the Lucerne, he was drunk, and no one was home. He set out to unpack his trunk. Sheaffer suggests that it was finding in his trunk a machete he had used in Honduras that set him off. Perhaps it was just that no one was there. He went amok as he had done at Princeton, hacking at things all over the apartment, cutting off the legs of tables and chairs. His mother found him amid the wreckage, asleep on the floor.

James created a job for Eugene as "assistant company manager" for the touring company of a production of a sententious and sentimental Catholic play, *The White Sister,* in which James had taken a supporting role. Eugene hated seeing his father relegated to minor roles and hated the play for itself. They toured New England through April. At the Mystic Wharf in Boston, he saw a Norwegian square-rigger, the *Charles Racine,* which was outfitting to sail for Buenos Aires (LS, 158). The image of the beautiful, tall-masted bark stayed in his thoughts when he returned to New York.

There he found newspaper headlines awaiting him that broadcast his shame and guilt to the world. Kathleen gave birth to Eugene Gladstone O'Neill on May 4, 1910. (The date is sometimes given as May 6 or 10.) Later he would be called Eugene Jr. by his father. Newspapers announced that the son of James O'Neill, who was off in a mine in Honduras, might not know for weeks that his bride of last July had given birth to a ten-and-a-half-pound son. So ran the story in the *New York World,* the source of which was Kathleen's mother (Gelbs, 139).

Eugene's mother was astonished and upset. James had learned of the marriage over the winter but had persuaded Mrs. Jenkins to keep it secret for Ella's sake (LS, 158). Within a day or so it was known that instead of being in Central America, Eugene was in New York, where he had been seen lunching at the Green Room Club with his father; and furthermore he had not yet seen Kathleen or his baby. Mrs. Jenkins, making the best of the embarrassing situation, told the *World* she could not believe the story, but if Eugene were in New York, he must know that he could come and live with her and his wife and child in her home. "There would be no 'mother-in-law' about it, either, and he knew that," Kate Jenkins assured him through the press (Gelbs, 140). She blamed someone besides her son-in-law for Eugene's behavior; she would not say whom. Acting on James's orders, the O'Neills made no response and avoided Kathleen and her mother. Eugene may have once visited Kathleen—there are conflicting reports—and he may or may not have seen the baby. If he did go to Mrs. Jenkins's apartment, it must have been a brief, tense, and silent visit. Eventually, the O'Neills won the war of nerves, if that is what it was. Kathleen and her mother took no action against Eugene or his family, and later Mrs. Jenkins would pay for Kathleen's divorce.

Once again James urged flight and Eugene fled. At a cost of seventy-five dollars, James arranged for Eugene to sail as a working passenger on the *Charles Racine*. A steel-hulled three-master, two hundred feet long, the *Charles Racine* was one of the last commercial sailing vessels built. Captain Gustave Waage sometimes supplemented the thirty-five-man crew with two or three quasi passengers, like Eugene, who would have duties of a less hazardous sort than the regular crew. Eugene must have been glad at the chance for a taste of Melvillean labor on the windjammer. Among other things it would ease his conscience a little about once more evading his responsibilities toward Kathleen and once again having to endure the condescending lectures that accompanied his father's charity.

On the voyage south Eugene began to be conscious of a nature mysticism, actually an oceanic mysticism, within himself. It would become increasingly prominent in the way he thought about the world and himself. It was something he had previously taken for granted and that seemed to him innate. Since childhood he had loved water, swimming, and boats. As an adult he would swim often when he was near water, sometimes braving winter storms or icy water. He would swim far out into the ocean, beyond sight of land. There is no reason to doubt that on the voyage to Buenos Aires Eugene had some such experience as the one Edmund Tyrone describes to his father in act 4 of *Long Day's Journey into Night*:

> When I was on the Squarehead square rigger, bound for
> Buenos Aires. Full moon in the Trades. The old hooker
> driving fourteen knots. I lay on the bowsprit, facing astern,
> with the water foaming into spume under me, the masts
> with every sail white in the moonlight, towering high above
> me. I became drunk with the beauty and singing rhythm

of it, and for a moment I lost myself—actually lost my life.
I was set free! I dissolved in the sea, became white sails and
flying spray, became beauty and rhythm, became moon-
light and the ship and the high dim-starred sky! I belonged,
without past or future, within peace and unity and a wild
joy, within something greater than my own life, or the life
of Man, to Life itself. To God, if you want to put it that way.
(CP3, 811–12)

We cannot know when Eugene became conscious that his experience of
dissolving into the ship and sea implied a meeting with life itself and with
God. He might have seen it in the instant, or the understanding may have
crystallized later or developed over years. But the other part of the experience, of losing himself, of "actually" losing his life, would have been apparent at once.

It marked the beginning of a long downward spiral toward the bottom of the maelstrom. If Eugene had been flirting for years with self-
destruction, the flirtation was over; he now embraced it. But the experience, like the mystical metaphor that describes it, points two ways at once.
From the standpoint of psychological development, it was simultaneously a time of great danger for him and a time that might lead to a consolidation of the ways in which he had grown and of his sense of self.

Eugene sailed from New York on June 9, 1910 and, as he later said,
was out of sight of land for two months. Hamilton Basso wrote that on
the voyage Eugene "scrubbed decks, climbed riggings, spliced ropes,
[and] ate dried codfish and hardtack" (February 28, 1948, p. 36). The hard
work agreed with him.

In some sense, by the end of the voyage he was a different person
from the youth who had embarked; and in the seven months he spent in
the Argentine capital, he would become more different still. In O'Neill's
own descriptions of this period to several interviewers, his accounts are
generally consistent. This is not to say that they exactly jibe with other evidence. Eugene claimed several times not to have seen land for "sixty-five
days" at a stretch; Louis Sheaffer (LS, 171–87), who compiled the most
detailed account of the Argentine episode, writes that Captain Waage reported in his log a fifty-seven-day trip from New York. Eugene does not
mention having a companion on the voyage, but two former sailors interviewed by Sheaffer, faintly remembered that Eugene was accompanied

by another youth, vaguely recalled as tall and blond. As Sheaffer points out, the description fits Louis Holladay. That Louis accompanied Eugene is plausible. If, as Agnes Boulton believed, Louis's mother, Adele, had known James O'Neill in the theater, James may well have known Louis from his youth and have sent him on the voyage with Eugene.

Eugene also told many people that he had taken a two-months' voyage on a cattle boat to Durban, South Africa, and back. After a thorough search of records, Sheaffer concluded that O'Neill made no such trip. During seven months away from the States, Eugene drifted further from the mainstream than he had been before. If the hard work at sea on the voyage south had improved his health, he wasted no time in dissipating its good effect.

For the first several weeks in Buenos Aires, while the *Charles Racine* refitted in port, Eugene could sleep in his cabin and take an occasional meal in the galley. He quickly spent the sixty dollars' wages that he had received on landing. To get money for drink and women, he worked briefly as a draftsman for Westinghouse Electric and did odd jobs at the Singer Sewing Machine Company; he cleaned hides at the Swift meat-packing plant in La Plata and worked at various other jobs when he could find them. During cold weather he roomed with at least two casual friends. Eventually he wound up "on the beach," the phrase the European community of Buenos Aires applied to its down-and-out. As the weather grew milder during the southern summer of 1910–1911, he slept on park benches and, as Basso puts it, "hung around the dives along the Buenos Aires waterfront with outcasts (from whom he was indistinguishable)" (February 28, 1948).

Between stints of hired labor, Eugene carried out the main work of his time in Argentina, the search for rock bottom. On September 26 the *Charles Racine* sailed for Nova Scotia, and Eugene lost most of the friends he had made among the sailors, as well as his cabin and the galley. He got to know the sailors' underworld of Buenos Aires, a world he described in some detail to the journalist Louis Kalonyme (Louis Kantor) in 1924. He frequented a large café known as the Sailor's Opera, where sailors drank, told tales, met women, played cards, and fought. He was seen from time to time bloodied, with bruises and torn clothes, and he was usually drunk. At the Sailor's Opera, a fellow might be asked to sing for his supper. "If your voice cracked," Eugene told Kalonyme, "your head usually did too" (Estrin 1990, 65). He found a friend who shared his taste for the rough life, and the two explored the Barracas and its brothels. The Barracas, a waterfront suburb, was full of pornographic shows and movies; prostitutes trailed through the audience during shows and did business as they went, two pesos a job. Eugene told Kalonyme: "Those moving pictures in Barracas were mighty rough stuff. . . . Every form of perversity was enacted" (Estrin 1990, 67).

An unnamed American who caroused with Eugene in Buenos Aires described to Sheaffer an incident in one of the brothels he and Eugene frequented. Four or five young men went into a place on Junin Street but found no one to entertain them, not even the madam. "The place had a revolving round table" the man said, "on which the girls sometimes posed as living statues, in the nude of course, while another pushed the wheel around. Since no one was there to entertain us, we took turns in taking a ride, striking all kinds of poses. But when Gene's turn came, he gave the floor a good wetting—said he didn't know where the toilet was." Before he was finished, the madam emerged and called the police, who threw them all out. Eugene's friend mused to Sheaffer, "Gene had been drinking, but what made him do things like that?" The bewildered question implies that the friend, like most who drank with him, could not fully realize the extreme disorder that alcohol created in Eugene's brain. Eugene became involved for a while with an Argentine girl from one of the brothels (most of the prostitutes were European). One day when the American friend saw the girl alone, she reacted angrily at the mention of Eugene's name. He had insulted her while they were making love, she said, and "left her feeling 'humiliated'" (LS, 176).

For a time Eugene was friendly with a hard-drinking young Englishman who had fled some kind of scandal at home involving his fiancée. Kalonyme wrote that the roommate reminded Eugene of Oscar Wilde's Dorian Gray: young, "extraordinarily handsome, blond, almost too beautiful." By O'Neill's account, this man "was the younger son of a traditionally noble British family. He had been through the English public schools, had acquired a university accent, and, finally down in London for good, became one of its lordly young men. He became, for example, an officer in a crack British regiment and joined the usual clubs. Then suddenly," Kalonyme quoted Eugene as saying, "he messed up his life—pretty conspicuously. Though he didn't have to leave England, he couldn't face his life there" (Estrin 1990, 66). In this wise he wound up, like Eugene, on the beach in Buenos Aires. The Englishman seems to have been the model for the character Smitty in O'Neill's one-act play *In the Zone* (1917).

During the last months of his stay in the Argentine, Eugene either did or did not make the trip to Durban, South Africa. He spent a few days sorting raw hides at the Swift plant, labor he detested. In 1947, recalling the episode for Basso, he still felt revolted at the remembered stench of the hides, which got into his clothes and his very pores. The plant burned down about this time. In another interview he wisecracked to Kyle Crichton, "I didn't do it, but it was a good idea" (Estrin 1990, 192). About this time, another down-and-outer suggested that Eugene help him rob an agency that exchanged foreign currency. Eugene declined because, as he told Basso, he felt certain they would be caught. It wasn't a moral issue, under the circumstances, "since you aren't given to taking a very moral view of things when you are sleeping on park benches and haven't a dime to your name" (Basso, March 13, 1948, p. 37).

Bad as things were for Eugene in Buenos Aires, it was also a time of growth, though it was almost imperceptible. One of Sheaffer's informants, Charles Ashleigh, reported meeting Eugene from time to time. Ashleigh, a freelance reporter and would-be poet, recalled meeting Eugene in a bar and eventually beginning a conversation, which quickly turned literary. That evening found the two comparing the poems they were writing. Ashleigh told Sheaffer that even if he had never heard of Eugene O'Neill the famous playwright, he would never have forgotten the literary nights so unexpectedly spent in the stews of Buenos Aires (LS, 182–83). Evidently Eugene wrote a good deal of poetry. Another Argentine acquaintance, Fred Hettman, recalled to Sheaffer that a poem of O'Neill's about "a prostitute under a street lamp slipping money into the bosom of her dress went on to compare her favorably with women who sell themselves in loveless marriage for financial security" (174). Even if the poetry was not very good, it continued the practice Eugene had begun at St. Aloysius of using the process of writing to create and give structure to the interior self. Writing gave him a pinch of objectivity to leaven the intense self-absorption that attended his lonely exile.

O'Neill's constant drinking and sleeping in parks took its toll. The malarial fever he had developed in Honduras recurred and scared him into returning home. On March 20, 1911, he signed on as an ordinary seaman aboard a British tramp steamer, *Ikala*. The steamer, rather than the square-rigged *Charles Racine,* was the one Eugene wrote about in his plays of the sea. While aboard the *Charles Racine* Eugene had caught a glimpse of integration and coherence, and of the world lost because of technocracy. The *Ikala* was a ship for alienated times, with its crew of simple, lonely men. Along with stories that he would later integrate into plays, Eugene brought back from his voyage homeward the memory of terrible food. "British food isn't too good even when it's good," O'Neill told Crichton, "and on that ship it wasn't even eaten by the British. They served something called 'preserved' potatoes; preserved how, for God's sake; I *never* found out. The crew could do a lot of things, but it couldn't eat preserved potatoes. We lived on hardtack and marmalade. I never felt better in my life; weighed a hundred and sixty-five" (Estrin 1990, 193).

As an adult, drinking or sober, Eugene struggled to maintain a weight even as high as a hundred forty-five pounds, and that only by dint of regular and strenuous exercise: swimming, punching a light bag, and walking or running on the beach. Shipboard work and fare must have pacified whatever kept him gaunt, whether the cause was psychic or endocrinal.

In other respects, too, the Eugene who returned to New York on the *Ikala* on April 15, 1911, was a different person from the youth who had sailed on the *Charles Racine.* He had not fit in comfortably with his family since he learned about his mother's addiction, but things were far more awkward now. He had found a niche among the sailors, petty criminals, and beach rats he had lived with for nearly a year. It must have seemed hardly possible that circumstances could be the same with his mother, father, and brother, when everything about himself seemed different.

For a few weeks after he returned to New York, he tried to live with the other O'Neills. Back in New London, he watched the old patterns and quarrels. Jamie was living off the old man again after two years of touring in *The Travelling Salesman;* he and his father alternately quarreled and worried about Ella's condition. James, just concluding a long run in *The White Sister,* worried that his career was ending and that he would never play another leading role. He was looking for something new that he could develop himself. He settled on trying to construct an entertainment from episodes of Tennyson's poem *The Lady of Shalott.* Jamie and Eugene resumed drinking in New London's sportier establishments, and Eugene resumed old friendships with Art and Tom McGinley, longstanding pals of the O'Neill brothers. Art was now a reporter for the New

London *Telegraph.* Eugene spent some time with Frederick P. Latimer, the paper's editor. The *Telegraph* began to publish occasional poems or prose observations by Eugene, most of them unsigned or pseudonymous. Art McGinley wrote a fanciful account of Eugene's wanderings for the *Telegraph.*

According to the *Telegraph,* James, Ella, and Jamie left on a vaudeville tour, in which James and Viola Allen performed scenes from the Tennyson entertainment. Declining to join them, Eugene returned to New York. He made a sudden visit to Kathleen and saw his son, now a year old—the last time he would see the boy for a decade, and the last time he ever saw Kathleen. He drifted to the place he now felt at home, the waterfront slums. Somehow James remained patient. He settled on Eugene a weekly allowance of seven dollars. While James was traveling, he insisted that Eugene present himself weekly at the offices of Liebler and Company, where George Tyler paid him his pittance and could certify to James that his son was still alive.

The seven dollars would, if carefully managed, suffice for food, drink, and lodging. After a chance meeting with his former roommate Jimmy Byth, Eugene found a room he could afford where Byth was staying at 252 Fulton Street. It was a flophouse above a saloon known as Jimmy the Priest's. (Later it would be one of the models for the saloon in *"Anna Christie"* and for Harry Hope's saloon in *The Iceman Cometh.*) James J. Condon, the proprietor, described by Eugene and others as cynical, callous, and hard as nails but tolerant of the helpless and hopeless, got his nickname for his austere manner and his charity. His saloon thrived on the lunchtime and after-work rush of sailors and workers on the docks and at the Washington Market across the street. It was the kind of place where if someone were careless enough to show that he had money, he might be rolled outside. But Jimmy allowed no fights or other rough stuff on the premises.

At Jimmy the Priest's, Eugene made no more effort to manage his money than usual. Like his father, he was generosity itself in a barroom. He gave what he had to whoever asked, and soon he was also asking. He continued his womanizing. A fellow denizen of Jimmy the Priest's recalled to the Gelbs decades later that Eugene was involved with several women, including a prostitute called Maude who lived on West Forty-seventh Street and who said she was in love with him (Gelbs, 163). Between women, booze, and handouts, he had plenty of uses for his seven dollars a week. A few hours or days after getting his allowance, he was living on the free lunch, usually a hearty soup, that Condon put out for his lodgers and regulars. Eugene told Mary B. Mullett, a decade later, that he occasionally got casual work cleaning, painting, or scrubbing the decks of ships that were loading or unloading at the docks (Estrin 1990, 30). In 1947 he told Hamilton Basso that he sometimes got work loading and unloading the mailboats that plied the coast.

At Jimmy the Priest's, Eugene made friends with several sailors, including a Liverpool Irishman of legendary strength named Driscoll, Chris Christopherson, the model for Anna Christie's father, and certain others who were models or partial models for characters in the sea plays. In July, Driscoll and another lodger at Jimmy the Priest's, James Quigley, signed aboard the American Line's luxury liner SS *New York,* bound for Southampton and Cherbourg. Sheaffer learned that O'Neill also signed on, as an ordinary seaman (LS, 194).

If Eugene was seeking mystical experiences like those he had had aboard the *Charles Racine,* he was quickly disillusioned. "There was about as much 'sea glamour' in working aboard a passenger steamship as there would have been in working in a summer hotel," Eugene told Mary Mullett. "I washed enough deck area to cover a good-sized town" (Estrin 1990, 30).

In the Mullett interview and in numerous others, including the conversations that led to the Barrett Clark and Hamilton Basso biographies, what Eugene did not mention seems at least as important as what he did. In the summer of 1911 Eugene was approaching a great psychological crisis, and it is readily understandable that years later he would choose not to reveal the crisis or events associated with it. He said nothing of having witnessed a famous historical event, the so-called Great General Strike of 1911 that paralyzed Britain for several days. Because Eugene's developing crisis seems unrelated to that upheaval, it is difficult to guess why nothing is said of the strike in interviews, especially given O'Neill's use of the subject in an early (unproduced) play *The Personal Equation* and allusions to a similar event in *The Hairy Ape.* (As will be seen, voices and images from the trip to Southampton found their way into several O'Neill plays, early and late.)

Eugene had been friendly with Greenwich Village radicals for about five years. He had read Shaw and Marx and Engels, he knew the relation of labor to capital, he usually sympathized and often identified with people at the lower end, and at the moment felt more comfortable living among them than he had residing with his parents or in the Princeton dormitory. Many a middle-class radical has found the makings of a lifetime vocation, even the makings of a self, in the experience of watching some great political event like that Eugene was to witness, yet nothing of that kind happened with him. He may not yet have known it, but the core of his developing self had begun to form long before, around the continual writing efforts made since the first days at boarding school. Great events might be for one person the occasion for action. To Eugene events were something to be watched and experienced from many points of view, and perhaps to be examined for possible use in a poem or letter. (As far as we know, Eugene did not yet think of himself as a playwright.)

He spent his trip to Southampton scrubbing the deck. He resented the condescension of passengers when they could not avoid noticing him. Although deckhands and stokers were usually as clannish as were passengers or sailors, he got to know the furnace-room gang through his friend Driscoll. "He was a giant of a man," O'Neill told Louis Kalonyme, "and absurdly strong. . . . He thought a whole lot of himself, and was a determined individualist. He was very proud of his strength, his capacity for gruelling work. It seemed to give him mental poise to be able to dominate the stokehole, do more work than any of his mates" (Estrin 1990, 67). The alienated Eugene was absorbed by the puzzle of Driscoll's mental poise.

They arrived in Southampton a day late because of engine-room trouble, and after the brief run to Cherbourg, the ship went into drydock, in Southampton, for repairs. Eugene got a taste of British waterfront life. He found the stews and dives and saw drunken sailors crimped or shanghaied onto bad ships.[1] James Quigley, the other sailor from Jimmy the Priest's who had made the trip, told the Gelbs years later that his most vivid recollection from the stay in Southampton was the effect Eugene had on the women they met in bars. "Gene was so handsome. . . . He didn't have to look for women. They'd come over to his table and ask for the privilege of sitting down with him." He was taken by a woman he insisted on calling Cecilia, although that was not her name. "'My heart has dreamed dreams I might never have known—a beautiful whore!'" he said to his Cecilia. Quigley said she was delighted. Quigley found an excuse to fondle her ankle under the table. "She withdrew indignantly and returned to her dreamy contemplation of O'Neill," the Gelbs report. Another night, in defense of his lady's good name, Eugene started a brawl that led to black eyes for him and Quigley both (Gelbs, 168).

Eugene heard strike talk and was still in Southampton in mid-August when the strike occurred, spreading out from Liverpool and paralyzing the nation. The railroads stopped running, ships stood in port, food became scarce, commerce and communication were crippled. Then the strike was settled, and in a few days things were back to normal. The most debilitating long-term effect was probably the dread inspired in ordinary people by the threat of disruption of daily life. Having witnessed the general strike from Southampton, which was less affected than most port cities, Eugene was left with the sense that his neutrality toward politics and political solutions was the most sensible course for him. However sympathetic he was with workers, he could find no reason to believe that strikes, unions, movements, or other actions or institutions could do anything but change for a little while the names of those with power.

After the strike, the SS *New York* being still in drydock, Eugene and Quigley returned with Driscoll to the States on a sister ship, SS *Philadelphia*. After all the events, great and small, the most important to a biographer seems so trivial that its significance must be explained. On the return voyage, Eugene was promoted from ordinary seaman to able-bodied seaman. This was the first outward indication in five years that Eugene might ever have the least success in the world or might someday be self-supporting. He apparently understood what his promotion implied. He kept all his life the certificate that showed his "A-B" rating, and he also kept a black uniform jersey embroidered with the legend "American Line." Sheaffer reports that Eugene's third wife, Carlotta, had the moth-eaten sweater mended; when she gave it to him, the gift left him speechless with pleasure (LS, 197).

Returning to New York in September 1911, he visited his family in New London and, while there, met his old partner in misery Ed Keefe, with whom he had spent the cold January of 1908 on his father's New Jersey farm. Keefe had given up painting, had left George Bellow in sole possession of the studio at Sixty-sixth and Broadway, and was now studying architecture.

Eugene resumed living on Fulton Street, where he roomed with Driscoll. Mostly, that fall, he drank and whored. But when his father's producer, George Tyler, brought the players of the Abbey Theatre from Dublin for their first American tour, Eugene had a resurgence of interest in the theater like that of 1907 when he had gone ten times to see *Hedda Gabler*. It is not unlikely that he was already thinking about writing plays. Using his paternal connection, Eugene, along with Jimmy Byth, saw every one of the Abbey productions—plays by J. M. Synge, William Butler Yeats, Lady Gregory, T. C. Murray. Humorless New York Irishmen repeated the Dublin riots when the Abbey performed *The Playboy of the Western World*. As George Tyler explained in his memoirs, it was a riot of Irishmen interrupting Irish actors performing an Irish play, who were arrested by Irish cops and sentenced by an Irish judge. In bitter delight, Eugene laughed at the Irish who could not laugh at themselves. But the plays and the actors made a great impression, especially Murray's *Birthright* and Synge's *Riders to the Sea*. In later years Eugene compared the Kamerny Art Theatre, which he admired, to the Abbey players, and he found the Russians wanting. Apart from superb unmannered acting that became his standard for the art, O'Neill found something like his own sense of the tragic in Murray and Synge. He long remembered the old woman in *Riders* and once, in an anxious time, compared himself to her, feeling he had "gotten to that stage now where nothing can hurt or anger me" (SL, 114).

A Stroll on the Bottom
of the Sea
1912

SEEING THE ABBEY THEATRE AND its plays impressed and exhilarated Eugene. In some way the experience may have contributed to the crisis that now unfolded. Every high experience with admired poets and philosophers, with great playwrights and fine acting, reminded him of the vast gulf that separated the life he could sometimes imagine from the life he was making for himself. The life he saw on the stage or on the page was heightened, intensified, rich in meanings; life in the world was sometimes exalting and intense, but randomly so, and its meaning seemed more often banal than enriching. He trusted his power of perception and knew that occasionally in a poem or letter he approached saying what he sensed and what he found in a few writers. The occasional success must have been more depressing than otherwise, for it seemed chancy and beyond his power to control. He never expected to find the words or syntax or images; mumbling, as Edmund Tyrone said, was his native eloquence.

Around the time he saw the Abbey players, Eugene learned that Kathleen was going to divorce him. Through her mother's lawyer he and his father were told that Kathleen sought neither alimony nor child support. James's cautious relief can be imagined. Eugene's reaction was much more complex. As with certain large events in his later life, including the deaths of his mother and brother, he showed little of what he was feeling. He agreed to cooperate with the lawyer's single request, that he furnish proof of adultery to satisfy New York law. He arranged to be seen in bed with a prostitute hired for the purpose. On December 29 he presented himself at a Times Square brothel at 148 West Forty-fifth Street. There, in the company of his father's lawyer and a lawyer friend of the Jenkinses named Warren, he chose a woman to take to a room. Warren testified at the divorce trial that "this Eugene O'Neill and this woman [were] in bed together; O'Neill at the time was undressed," and so was the woman. Warren added that he and O'Neill left the brothel together at six the next morning (Gelbs, 173).

Eugene may have gone on a brief binge—accounts are contradictory. He may have wound up in a gambling joint with a friend and may have won two hundred dollars at faro, a story he told in part to various people. Or the binge and the gambling win may have been wholly contrived, to conceal an incident kept largely private throughout his lifetime. The incident was a nearly successful attempt to kill himself.

Not long after the official act of adultery, when Eugene was sober, he went to several pharmacies and bought from each a quantity of the narcotic veronal, which could be purchased in moderate amounts without prescription. When he had enough, he returned to Jimmy the Priest's. Saying nothing to anyone, he went up to his room, hooked the door, swallowed the veronal, and reclined on his cot to await oblivion. About 1919, he told Agnes Boulton, his second wife, that he "passed out without even having time, first, to experience that glimpse of eternity or nothingness which he had expected and was waiting for." Agnes's account continues: "'I must have been there twenty-four hours, maybe longer,' Gene told me. 'I vaguely remembered coming to, hearing a knocking on the door, then silence. . . . Perhaps I didn't think at all, just felt resentful that the veronal hadn't yet completely put me out and that I could hear the knocks'" (Boulton 1958, 185). Agnes reported Eugene's describing his thoughts in language that sounds a little like one of Edmund Tyrone's soliloquies in act 4 of *Long Day's Journey into Night*, a play that had just come out when Agnes began her memoir.

The language she recalls also reminds one of Nietzsche's paradox of eternal recurrence: "'Then a horrible thought came to me,'" he told her. "'I was dead, of course, *and death was nothing but a continuation of life as it had been when one left it!* A wheel that turned endlessly round and round back to the same old situation! This was what purgatory was—or was it hell itself? My body was dead, but *I* was there too. Frozen in a sort of motionless unbearable horror, I went into a stupor, hardly conscious—at least that was an escape from purgatory, or hell, whichever it was. . . . At last—how long I don't know—the knocking came again'" (Boulton 1958, 185–86).

Finally, the rescuers, led by Jimmy Byth, succeeded, after several hours of occasionally trying to rouse Eugene. Someone pushed the door open and they found the pill bottles; so he had to tell them what he had done. The friends went downstairs to celebrate his "return to life," but Eugene was too wobbly to get to his feet (Boulton 1958, 186). Jimmy the Priest, probably worried that Eugene would die at his place, insisted he be taken to Bellevue Hospital.

In stories told to Agnes and to two or three other people, Eugene made light of what followed. His friends got a taxi, which took them all not to the emergency room but to the alcoholic ward. Eugene once wise-cracked that as he was the only sober person there, he was released while his friends were kept overnight to dry out. In several casual accounts that Eugene gave to interviewers—who thought he was describing a pro-longed binge rather than a suicide attempt—he wound up drunk on a train for New Orleans and arrived there only to discover that by coinci-dence his father was about to arrive there also with a vaudeville version of *Monte Cristo*. In the interviews, Eugene passed over the entire circum-stances of the winter of 1911–1912 as simply another episode of early dis-sipation, saying nothing of his first marriage and divorce, and nothing of the suicide attempt.[1]

Sometime in the 1920s, Eugene gave an account of the suicide at-tempt to his friend George Jean Nathan. As with Agnes's version, it is not always possible to know which details come from Eugene and which from the reteller. Nathan makes the suicide attempt seem half-hearted and on the whole makes light of it, but one detail stands out. In Nathan's ver-sion, Eugene says that he was unconscious for some time while his stom-ach was being pumped and other treatment given, and that he was finally revived, to the great relief of his friends. This sounds like a medically se-rious situation, and the description would fit the ingestion of a large amount of veronal. It seems unlikely that the son of a famous father would be released immediately after such treatment, even from a busy Manhat-tan hospital. Evidently Eugene received treatment and had a stay in the hospital for some length of time.

As Sheaffer worked things out (LS, 210–15), Eugene's poisoning was taken very seriously. James was in Memphis. Someone, probably George Tyler, told the actor what had happened, and that Eugene had survived. A member of the company told Sheaffer that the even-tempered James became suddenly upset and the mood backstage turned very quiet and serious. It was rumored that some "misfortune" was afflicting Eugene. After several days, James wired money in response to a telegram from his son that supposedly began, "To eat or not to eat, that is the question" (LS, 215). When Eugene met his family in New Orleans, no one but the O'Neills saw him for several days, and no one was joking.

Eugene had been heading toward the suicide attempt for a decade, since the discovery of Ella's addiction and her apparent suicide attempt. Shortly after he learned of her situation, he began drinking (as Jamie had done shortly after *he* learned of his mother's addiction). With both sons, the addictive drinking expressed (among other things) identification with both Ella and James. James drank heavily but showed few signs of addiction, and liquor appears never to have affected his long and healthy life for the worse. Eugene had to prove over and over that when it came to drinking, he was not the man his father was; he proved again and again that when it came to intoxication he was his mother's son. The suicide attempt was, in part, an extension of Eugene's identification with his mother and with her drinking and morphine use.

The suicide attempt was the culmination of the multiple problems Eugene had in his various conscious and unconscious identifications with his mother. For Eugene the discovery of Ella's drug use and drinking carried the special burden of his knowing he had been the cause of them. His drinking had a more obviously self-punitive purpose than Jamie's. Jamie, like his father, seldom showed his liquor unless he wanted to, and seemed not to suffer physically from his drinking until late in his life. Eugene's personality changed when he was drinking (to the point where he sometimes seemed psychotic); he had dreadful hangovers that led to more drinking; and if he kept on drinking, he eventually suffered excruciating cramps. Through the decade 1902 to 1912, except for his reading and letter writing, and the attempts at poetry, there are very few signs that Eugene might find anything within himself that he could value, or that he would ever learn to live in ways that would allow him to develop his gifts.

Yet, on close examination, a few hints of growth can be found, hints that, in retrospect, seem to foretell the man he was to become; and the hints come a little more frequently as the decade nears an end. In

1906–7 Eugene had gone to see *Hedda Gabler* ten times. He had spent more and more time writing poems. It matters little that the poems were poor; in fact, it is the more impressive that he continued even though he knew he was not a very good poet. His goal must have been not to become a competent maker of verse (his brother had been that at twelve), but to find something within himself in the only way he could, by spinning out language to see what kind of web it made.

He found that he not only loved being at sea but felt something transcendent there; at sea, something briefly emerged from the inner self besides appetites and guilt. On the American Line ships, he followed orders well enough to get promoted to able-bodied seaman. He found something exhilarating in Synge, Murray, and the Abbey players. He felt whatever he felt toward Kathleen that let him know he ought to treat her honorably, even if he could not be a husband and father. Ironically, the signs of progress in Eugene were more the cause of his trying to kill himself than was his waywardness. Signs of what he might become made him increasingly intolerant of what he was.

When Kathleen began divorce proceedings it crystallized all the guilt he felt toward her, and that in turn made him face all the guilt he felt toward his mother, which lay at the core of his sense of who he was. In his own eyes, the essential Eugene was the person whose birth had caused his mother's addiction. That Eugene expressed itself in every act of self-indulgence, in every sin or folly or disobedience of parental injunction, and in the extremities of wildness that emerged when he was drunkest. If he thought of himself in the words of his Christian parents and teachers, he had to see himself as fundamentally "evil," and evil in a way that could not be meaningfully confessed or absolved. Within the Christian worldview he stood somewhere outside nature, beyond ordinary human depravity. Discovering the tragic sense of life not long after he learned the nature of his essential self gave him fleeting, occasional alternatives to self-hatred.

If he thought like Schopenhauer and Nietzsche and Ibsen and Synge, the word for his essential self was not *evil* but *destructive*, in the sense that fire and flood and earthquake can be casually destructive. For that reason tragic, so-called pessimistic writers had an exhilarating, liberating effect on Eugene. They allowed him to acknowledge what he knew existed in his essential self and still find that he was not beyond the pale of the natural order. To Eugene, Christianity did not imply the possibility of infinite mercy, forgiveness, and redemption, but only eternal guilt, moral damnation for what he could not have controlled, and lifelong self-loathing. When he said of himself, "Once a Catholic, always a Catholic," he must have had in mind the inescapable conscience that he identified with the dogma of sin and guilt. The tragic writers did not offer absolution or redemption, but they allowed him to be as he knew he was and not to seem to himself outside of nature.

In January 1912, when he tried to kill himself, Eugene had only an inkling of how the tragic sense of life offered consolation for his being who he was. Deepening and enlarging the understanding would take the rest of his life. But when reading certain philosophers and poets, he felt a liberation take place within; that is why he returned to them over and over.

According to the tragic sense of life, death is the point of orientation, the great constant, the only universal. They who forget death lose the reason to value life. Philosophers and poets may sometimes offer a glimpse of life's splendor in the guise of a glance at death and a clue to the nature of things. To know oneself a being in nature is to know that one is mortal.

Freud believed that few people ever subjectively understand or accept their own mortality. It is axiomatic that young people believe themselves immortal, and not many of their elders acknowledge their own mortality except as an intellectual truism. Some people who have faced imminent death and somehow survived may be exceptions. In surviving his veronal poisoning, Eugene became one who was aware of his own mortality. That dawning awareness marked the beginning of a reversal in the way he lived his life. He would spend the rest of his life trying to understand and express the way the world looked when one subjectively accepted mortality, and he would eventually create numerous characters who take themselves to the brink of death and then react to what they have seen. They include a youth who regards his nearly successful suicide as an "Exorcism"; Lazarus, who loses his orientation when Christ brings him back from the dead; and Edmund Tyrone, who has survived suicide and now faces consumption.

In writing act 4 of *Long Day's Journey into Night,* O'Neill created a conversation between a father and son in which the son tries to talk to his father about his attempted suicide. James Tyrone compares his own hard early life to his son's "being homeless and penniless in a foreign land" and adds: "But it was a game of romance and adventure to you. It was play."

EDMUND (*dully sarcastic*): Yes, particularly the time I tried to commit suicide at Jimmy the Priest's, and almost did.

TYRONE: You weren't in your right mind. No son of mine would ever—You were drunk.

EDMUND: I was stone cold sober. That was the trouble. I'd stopped to think too long. [CP3, 807]

Tyrone continues to deny his son's version of his own experience, but then he reveals the effect the story has had on him: his rambling thoughts lead him to his own father's possibly accidental death by rat poison after he went home to Ireland to die. "My bet is," Edmund remarks, "it wasn't by mistake." Eugene O'Neill could claim to know a thing or two about self-poisonings. It may even have given him a moment of feeling that he recognized the grandfather he had never known.

Let it be assumed that when Eugene arrived in New Orleans, he did not enjoy rich and satisfying conversations with his father and mother about the tragic sense of life, or the consolations of Schopenhauer, or the exhilaration that can come from having survived opiate poisoning. When the run in New Orleans finished, Eugene was still an unseen presence and remained so during a long train ride from Louisiana to Ogden, Utah.

In Ogden, Eugene was put onstage and given dialogue to learn. In the forty-minute vaudeville abridgment of the three-hour *Monte Cristo,* Eugene played a prison guard who uttered the words "Is he . . . ?" to another guard who was to reply, "Yes, he's dead." Eugene had acute stage fright and worried that if he sneezed, his false mustache would fly off, and he and the other guard sometimes made mistakes that created gales of unexpected laughter. After Ogden, the Orpheum tour went to Salt Lake City and Denver and ended at last in St. Paul.

Early in March the O'Neills were back in New York, where they remained a few weeks before proceeding to New London. Now sixty-six, the man who might once have succeeded Edwin Booth as America's leading actor had been reduced to a doing a forty-minute stint on a vaudeville bill, enacting fragments of a melodrama so drastically cut that the plot made no sense. James boasted to an interviewer that the Orpheum tour would bring him earnings "well up in four figures," but Sheaffer learned that he actually made only twelve hundred and fifty dollars, out of which he had to pay all the expenses and salaries of the members of his company (LS, 217).

The decline in earnings was offset by better news. James sold a piece of real estate at a profit and settled into town life in New London, that is, drinking and talking with cronies. Kathleen Jenkins, true to her word, filed for divorce and asked for nothing from Eugene. (The petition was heard in White Plains in June, and an interlocutory decree was granted.) The senior O'Neills put Kathleen and the child permanently out of their minds, and Eugene tried to do the same but, as always, could not escape his conscience.

A project arose for James to make a movie of *Monte Cristo*—there was talk of filming it in Bermuda and of hiring well-known supporting actors. In the end it was filmed in ten days in New York, and the cast included Jamie, but no established actors except James. James's contract called for 20 percent of the royalties, which provided income until he died—eventually about four thousand dollars, less than James had hoped.

The change in Eugene after his suicide attempt was not immediately obvious. Back in New London, he settled with relish into local sporting life. He and Jamie caroused with old friends: Art and Tom McGinley, Ed Keefe, "Hutch" Collins, "Ice" Casey, and Doc Joe Ganey. But Eugene was writing more than ever. Sheaffer learned that by the fall of 1912 O'Neill had "a bureau-drawer full" of poems and prose sketches, and some of the sketches extended to great length. One informant thought some of them were written "with the theatre in mind" (LS, 225), although Eugene always gave the following spring as the point at which he began writing plays.

In August, at Eugene's request, James arranged with "Judge" Frederick Latimer, the editor of the New London *Telegraph,* for Eugene to work as a reporter, with James secretly subsidizing his ten-dollar-a-week salary. Eugene found the experience interesting, although he had no instinct for straight reporting. Later, when he had become famous, former colleagues from the *Telegraph* wrote comic accounts of the playwright's incompetence as a news-gatherer. In his 1922 article, Malcolm Mollan, city editor of the *Telegraph* in 1912, remembered being quite severe with Eugene's mistakes, but he said he found something substantial in the youth. In later years Eugene cheerfully agreed that he had been "a bum reporter." Yet he was apparently conscientious about the job. The paper's publication of a number of poems and "mood" pieces, in its department "Laconics," was no doubt prompted by the respect that Latimer had formed for James O'Neill's unconventional second son. The judge developed something more than a fondness for Eugene, who in later years said that Latimer had been the first person "who really thought I had something to say, and believed I could say it" (Clark [1926] 1967, 18).

In an article called "Eugene Is Beyond Us" (New London *Day*, February 15, 1928), Latimer gave a vivid picture of his relationship with Eugene in 1912. Eugene was hypersensitive and at the least criticism would sulk or withdraw. Yet he flaunted his unorthodoxy and seemed to invite disapproval. "When we sailed with him on the river or talked with him of moonlit nights or in the shadows of a smelly back room, he used to often make us choke with wrath at the queer wildness of his ideas," Latimer wrote. Eugene must naturally have known that the tragic sense of life would not mix smoothly with Latimer's practical Jeffersonian idealism (LS, 229).

It cannot have been approval for his views that he sought; he must have been looking in these conversations for some sign that the thinking he was trying to do had some coherence to it, was something to be taken seriously. It was. Latimer believed that he had read virtually everything that Eugene wrote for the next three years. Eugene at the time, Latimer later said, had that "innate nobility which inspires and drives a man against whatever hindrance to be himself, however Heaven or Hell conspires to rob him of that birthright" (LS, 229). The word "hindrance" may imply that Latimer knew or guessed at problems in the O'Neill family. (Many New Londoners suspected that Ella was seriously affected by some secret illness, and a few nurses had noticed needle scars on her arms; the doctors who gave her prescriptions, of course, knew her state, and some Brennan and Sheridan relatives apparently knew of or guessed at her addiction.)

More important, Latimer appreciated the qualities that had allowed Eugene to survive his passage through the Strindbergian inferno of the past decade, the traits that kept him on his own course and enabled him to listen to hints from that within him which sought to be developed. "From flashes in the quality of the stuff he gave the paper, and the poems and play manuscripts he showed me, I was so struck that I told his father

Eugene did not have merely talent, but a very high order of genius" (LS, 229). Eugene agreed. He told several New Londoners that summer that in the future James O'Neill would be best known as the father of Eugene O'Neill. In October the paper raised Eugene's weekly salary to twelve dollars.

Late that summer, Eugene, by now almost twenty-four, fell in love with an eighteen-year-old neighbor, Maibelle Scott, the daughter of a prosperous grocer, and the niece of Captain Thomas A. Scott. Like Ella during her Cleveland girlhood, Maibelle enjoyed a sheltered life amid family and school friends, whose parties and weddings she attended. Like Marion Welch and Kathleen Jenkins before her, Maibelle must have appealed to some desire in Eugene to understand "normal" life, or at least a life lived differently from the O'Neills' and especially his own. Judging by the young women that attracted him at this time, his notion of ordinary life probably derived from his mother's tales of her Quinlan childhood. Maibelle was tall and beautiful, according to the reminiscences collected by the Gelbs. She was still a beauty when the Gelbs and Sheaffer interviewed her much later.

Eugene was assigned to cover for the *Telegraph* a wedding in which Maibelle was an attendant. Knowing she was to be there, Eugene borrowed an opera cape from his father and introduced himself dramatically, the cape draped over his arm. Much too late that night he called her home to ask for a date. From that day on, both the senior Scotts wanted to shoot Eugene, and the senior O'Neills worried either that he might create a scandal with a respectable family or that he might marry the daughter of a Protestant grocer. For the next two months, to the discomfort of everyone but the lovers, he and Maibelle saw each other every day. The romance flourished despite all obstacles, but it was not easy for the couple to avoid watchful parental eyes.

Eugene put Maibelle on an intensive course of remedial education, starting with *Zarathustra*, his first gift. She became a willing fellow disciple, who felt a burden lifted by Nietzsche's assault on those "cradle gifts" of Christian moralizing, Good and Evil. Soon she was arguing with her strict parents as fervently as Eugene did with his. On Eugene's urging, she read Schopenhauer, whose atheism infuriated her father, and Wilde, who had been convicted of perversion. James O'Neill warned Mr. Scott that Eugene was "a no good drunken loafer" and Maibelle was too good for him; it only made Maibelle take Eugene's side and wonder at a father who would speak so of his son (Gelbs, 208). She told biographers that she never saw Eugene anything but sober and gentle, and several girls her age took her side, helped her contrive to meet him, and remembered Eugene later with fondness. It seems that after his suicide attempt, Eugene reduced the frequency of his binges and on the whole drank much less.

Eugene told Maibelle at the beginning about Kathleen and his son, and that he was still legally married (the final divorce decree did not come until October 11—Gelbs, 208). Even though they met every day, they wrote several letters a day; the two used friends and even neighborhood children to carry mail. Maibelle later told the Gelbs that when she and Eugene formally ended their love affair in August 1914, she destroyed about two hundred of his letters. In many letters they argued the meaning of difficult philosophic passages. Braving the wrath of both the O'Neills and the Scotts, Judge Latimer invited the couple for dinner several times. Eugene and Maibelle seldom quarreled, and it seems to have been a happy time for both, despite their problems with parents.

By October they were talking about marriage, although Maibelle felt that Eugene's salary was insufficient for them to marry immediately. But she enrolled in a secretarial course, she told the Gelbs, in order to be able to rise in the middle of the night and take down the words of her genius husband should inspiration awaken him. Twenty years later he would celebrate the affair, and much else about that summer, in *Ah, Wilderness!* (Judge Latimer was the model for the father of the adolescent hero.) Eugene at twenty-four was entering the ordinary stage of late adolescence that circumstances had made impossible when he was sixteen.

James O'Neill, in the meantime, continued to watch the decline of his career. He waited through the spring, summer, and fall for offers of work that did not come. After nearly thirty summers in the Pequot Avenue cottage, he installed a furnace and winterized the house in other ways. He worried about his wife, despaired over Jamie, and fretted about money. He and Eugene had been getting along better for a time, but the affair with Maibelle greatly upset both Ella and James, and he and Eugene were again bickering frequently. One visitor heard Eugene scornfully refer to his father as "the Irish peasant" (LS, 241). Jamie obsessively studied the ups and downs of his mother's morphine use, argued with his father, and sought lethe in booze and brothels.

As he often did when troubles closed in, James bought property. He bought a run-down farm occupied by one John "Dirty" Dolan, adjacent to the estate of Edward Crowninshield Hammond. When he was fifty-five, Eugene would use this farm as the setting for *A Moon for the Misbegotten,* the last play he would finish; Dolan and Hammond are said to be partial models for the characters Phil Hogan and T. Stedman Harder. Sheaffer points out a belated irony, that in the 1960s, the former Hammond estate became the site of the Eugene O'Neill Memorial Theater. Eugene would have grinned ironically, as he would have on learning that, after considerable controversy, Main Street in New London had been renamed Eugene O'Neill Drive.

Late in October, while Eugene reveled in intellectual union with Maibelle and in their mutual adoration, he developed a troublesome cough. By early November it was clear that he had more than a cold. This is the moment in dramatic time when the action of *Long Day's Journey into Night* occurs, just before the younger son's consumption is diagnosed. Eugene, eager to keep working at the *Telegraph,* and dreading the worst, at first insisted that he was suffering a recurrence of malarial fever.

The family physicians, Daniel Sullivan and Harold Heyer (both were respected, and neither resembled the Doc Hardy of *Long Day's Journey into Night*), tentatively diagnosed pleurisy. The diagnoses greatly alarmed Ella and set her into an agitated depression. Her reaction to an excess of morphine was an atypical one, the so-called cat response. When she took too much, instead of becoming dreamy and lethargic, she got jumpy, her thoughts came in a jumbled rush, and she rode an emotional roller coaster (Eldridge 1979; Freedman 1980).

The nurse who was called in told Sheaffer much later about a nightmarish day and night she had spent with the family. When she arrived, the three O'Neill men were having a shouting match around the dining table. Ella paced the floor upstairs and moaned, "My son, my son," her long white hair wildly undone, her dark eyes enormous and unfocused. After pacing for a time, she would collapse and rock back and forth, clutching her knees to her breast or wringing her hands, and grieving for her son. The nurse told Sheaffer (LS, 236–37) that when Ella moaned "My son, my son," she sometimes meant Eugene and sometimes meant the baby, Edmund, who had died twenty-eight years before. The nurse could offer only comforting words and an alcohol rub, which were briefly soothing. While giving the massage, the nurse noticed the needle marks on Ella's arms, but as she told Sheaffer, she did not guess that Ella might be an addict. She had been told only that Mrs. O'Neill had a nervous condition. While Ella whimpered, the shouting continued downstairs, and at three in the morning the house was still in an uproar. The day and evening were so upsetting to the nurse that she refused to go back.

When Eugene was diagnosed with tuberculosis a few days later, Ella became quiet and withdrawn. A more experienced nurse, Olive Evans, hired to look after Eugene, said she sometimes heard Ella crying softly "like a kitten," but she was told in very specific terms that she must never go to Ella unless invited. Presumably, Ella had got her dosage under control, and the family could simply close the blinds against the snooping world.

On finding a drawerful of manuscripts, Olive asked if she could read what Eugene was writing. What she read seemed immoral, and she complained. Not immoral, "unmoral," Eugene told her—and added that that was what he was, too. The nurse, who remained with the O'Neills for about a month, until early December, found herself liking Eugene, despite her disapproval. She detested Jamie, but she found James courteous and kind. She silently objected when Eugene would ask, "Has the Irish peasant gone to mass yet?" (LS, 241). Although she saw little of Ella, she noticed that whenever James had gone out, and it was nearing the time for him to return, Ella would stand at the window watching for him and could hardly contain her anticipation. Olive said that each time this happened, when James saw her in the window, he would break into a run, greet his wife with open arms, and hold her tenderly.

Olive said she believed neither was "acting"; indeed, she was convinced that they were in love in the way of new lovers, after thirty-five years of marriage (LS, 241). Olive's judgment echoed that of many other people who knew the O'Neills over the decades of their unusual marriage. Without in the least doubting James and Ella's devotion, one might say that there was a theatrical quality to their display of it, and the sons must frequently have been the audience. The senior O'Neills' intimacy excluded their sons and created internalized images of marriage that each son struggled with in his own way. Jamie through lifelong scornful doubt denied the reality of his parents' devotion to each other. Eugene fell wildly in love with Maibelle, and with a succession of other young women over the next several years, in reckless emulation of what he understood of his parents' example, and in a driven effort to seize for himself what the Irish peasant had and he lacked.

Her afternoons being free, Olive was pressed into service by Eugene to carry letters to and from Maibelle. With both sets of parents trying to suppress the affair, Olive had to work cautiously through third parties. Ella, who once caught her and told her to stop, brushed aside Olive's denial and coldly informed her, "I know what's been happening." Olive told Sheaffer that Ella had said, "We don't want this affair to go on, and religion is the principal reason" (LS, 240). Nevertheless, whenever he felt up to it, Eugene sneaked out and met Maibelle, who had not the least fear of contagion from the white plague.

Not so his mother. Throughout his life sweet and childlike in illness, Eugene longed for his mother, who would seldom come near his room but would instead brood downstairs. Olive said that from time to time Ella would fix him eggnog—one of the few foods she could prepare—and bring it halfway up the stairs. Olive would fetch it the rest of the way to Eugene's room near the head of the stairs. Sheaffer believes that Ella dreaded becoming infected if she got any closer (LS, 241). The sight of Eugene ill probably increased her old terror of bereavement by bringing to mind the loss of her second son and her father's death of tuberculosis nearly forty years before. For the rest of his life Eugene would try to understand why his mother could not be maternal when he was ill. Sooner or later he came to realize that the old wound of her father's sudden illness and death was still open. In writing *Long Day's Journey into Night*, Eugene dramatized his understanding by showing Mary Tyrone repeatedly associating and confusing Edmund's illness with her father's, to the point that it sometimes seemed she did not know which of them she meant.

One night in late November or early December, Eugene sneaked out, supposedly to meet Maibelle, and had not returned by late that night. Someone told the worried James that Eugene was drinking at the Crocker House, and James arranged for him to be brought home. When Eugene got home he was very drunk and went on one of his rampages, wrecking some furniture. What set him off is not clear: a quarrel with his parents, frustration with Maibelle's chastity, worry about his illness, or perhaps all three.

In early December, Olive was left in Monte Cristo Cottage with Ella and Eugene while James was in New York to try to land a part in a new play, *Joseph and His Brethren*. Jamie, meanwhile, vanished for about a week. When James returned, he arranged for Eugene to be sent to the Fairfield County State Sanatorium in Shelton. Sheaffer, who believes that Eugene is unfair to his father in *Long Day's Journey into Night*, reports that well-off New Londoners, including Ed Keefe's older brother, were patients there at the time of Eugene's illness (LS, 242).

The threat of loss represented by Eugene's illness had all the O'Neills acting oddly. Olive Evans told the Gelbs that just before Eugene was taken to the state sanatorium, James took him to the best tailor in town, Charles Perkins, and had a fine suit made for him. Olive, who was present at a fitting, remembered Eugene as being very particular about the fit. After Eugene was released from the sanatorium the following June, James bought him a secondhand powerboat, an eighteen-foot Atlantic dory. The boat cost James $200. Eugene's stay in Gaylord Farm, the semiprivate sanatorium where he spent more than five months, had cost $167.35. Whatever lay behind James's erratic spending, Eugene never forgot nor entirely forgave what he took to be a shameful economy.

Olive accompanied Eugene part of the way to Shelton. On the way they saw several coffins being transferred from another train to theirs. The sight set off in Eugene grim thoughts about what awaited him. His father met the train before it reached Shelton and was with Eugene on December 9 when he checked into the sanatorium (LS, 244).

Two days later, he checked himself out and got on a train for New York, where his father had gone. Eugene had remained at Shelton just long enough to get a thorough examination and a favorable prognosis; he had a "good" chance for recovery with proper rest, food, and treatment. At this point, Eugene must have confronted his father in something like the way he shows in act 4 of *Long Day's Journey into Night*, when Edmund Tyrone confronts his father and forces the old man to agree, "You can choose. . . . any place you like—within reason" (CP3, 808).

The most striking aspect of the scene, Edmund's most severe criticism of his father, calls for some comment because of what it shows about Eugene's understanding of the son and his feelings for his father. Edmund is given a building diatribe that ends: "This last stunt of yours is too much! It makes me want to puke! Not because of the rotten way you're treating me. To hell with that! I've treated you rottenly, in my way, more than once. But to think when it's a question of your son having consumption, you can show yourself up before the whole town as such a stinking old tightwad! Don't you know [Dr.] Hardy will talk and the whole damned town will know! Jesus, Papa, haven't you any pride or shame?" (CP3, 805).

Edmund's criticism is not what one expects, and it is too complex for most audiences and readers to grasp at once. He can stand having his father treat him rottenly as part of their warfare. What he can't stand is his father's revealing himself to other people as a tightwad and a man without pride or shame. Edmund shows an impressive confidence in his ability to force his father to give him what he wants, and then to survive the disease. Beyond this, the son's words imply a deep love of the father, a confidence in the father's love of him, and a confidence in the father's willingness, beneath the surface of his behavior, to do anything to save his son. Edmund feels outraged that his father's nervous anxiety about money will make him seem to others a father who does not love his son enough to protect him. In addition to wanting his father's love, Edmund needs to be proud of his father. He wants his father not to act like the Irish peasant that, in Edmund's thinking, he must seem to outsiders. At a much deeper level, Edmund knows he needs to feel fully confident that through identifying with his father he can grow up to be as strong as James, a man who commands the respect of the community.

Eugene may have understood some or all of these implications consciously either when he wrote the play or—though this seems less likely—when some argument like the one in act 4 took place between him and his father in 1912. His conscious reason at the time for wanting his father to behave with pride is not important. What is important is the evidence it offers that Eugene has escaped the downward spiral of his life as he has lived it for a decade. The former self-destructiveness is reversed, and he acts to preserve his health and to promote his psychological growth.

In any case, the outcome of the argument was that James sent Eugene to two nationally known New York T.B. specialists, Livingston Ferrand and James Alexander Miller. On December 19, Dr. Miller arranged for Eugene to be admitted to an excellent private sanatorium, Gaylord Farm Sanatorium in Wallingford, Connecticut. Eugene checked in on Christmas Eve.

8

A Tragic Playwright in the Making
1913–1914

OUTWARDLY, THE SIXTEEN MONTHS FROM the beginning of 1913 through the summer of 1914 were less eventful and more ordinary for Eugene than most of his life had been so far. Beneath the surface, however, it was a time of great change. He recovered from tuberculosis, he seems to have nearly stopped drinking, and he began writing plays. Thinking of himself as a playwright brought about a change in his feelings toward his father and toward his own health. In the first year of playwriting, he completed at least a dozen plays, one of which is still frequently performed. Writing plays became for him both a means of examining his life and a means for making increasingly coherent the philosophical ideas that had preoccupied him for a decade.

The circumstances in which Eugene reached Gaylord Farm Sanatorium, including his arrival on Christmas Eve, were more dramatic than any outward event in his five-month stay as a T.B. patient. His case was very mild and had been caught so early that he was able to make a full recovery. Later he would say he had had so light a case that he hardly knew he was ill. At the time, however, anxiety left no room for doubt. He was a model patient who fully cooperated in his treatment. He weighed 146 pounds when he entered. Five months later, at his discharge on June 3, 1913, he weighed 162, nearly as much as he would ever weigh. Throughout his stay, and for some time after he was discharged, he showed little sign of the self-destructiveness that had ruled him for a decade. Another Eugene was beginning to emerge.

In the sanatorium, Eugene began to take much better care of himself than in the past. He became a favorite with David Lyman, the superintendent of the sanatorium, and with the nursing staff, and he corresponded with Dr. Lyman and several nurses for years after his discharge. He carried on a flirtation with a wistful young patient named Kitty McKay, who died of tuberculosis a couple of years later. (She inspired the central character in a little-known play, *The Straw,* which O'Neill wrote in 1918–1919.) But above all things, in the enforced quiet of hospital routine he found his vocation and in some secret way committed himself to spending the rest of his life making the best writer he could of himself.

The emerging commitment to writing plays showed most clearly in the reading he did at Gaylord Farm. Forced to spend most of his time in bed, Eugene read almost constantly. He mentioned Dostoyevsky's *Idiot* as one of his most important discoveries of the time, and he read many other novels as well. But especially, he read plays. In later years he would say that the discovery of August Strindberg led him to start writing plays—Strindberg's *Dance of Death* had just been published in English, along with *By the Open Sea, Son of a Servant, The Red Room,* and *Zones of the Spirit.* He also read Synge, Murray, Yeats, and Lady Gregory, as well as Frank Wedekind, Eugène Brieux, Gerhart Hauptmann, Clyde Fitch, and William Vaughan Moody. Toward the end of his stay, he may have begun to sketch out ideas for plays. By the end of 1913 he had made a serious vocational commitment, although it would not be apparent to others until a little later.

In 1906, apparently fascinated with Ibsen's celebration of eccentricity in *Hedda Gabler,* Eugene had kept returning to the play because he believed it depicted emotional truths he knew intimately, in a setting different from the parlor of Monte Cristo Cottage. In the newly translated Strindberg he found another voice that spoke of Eugene's world with tortuous, madly comic accounts of domestic horror. Strindberg, with flights into the metaphysical, became a new feature of Eugene's literary landscape and took a place alongside Ibsen, Nietzsche, Schopenhauer, Whitman, the Irish playwrights, the decadent French and English poets, the naturalistic novelists, and Shakespeare. As a sense of the world gradually became clearer to Eugene, he began to find within it a place for himself.

Strindberg and many of the other moderns whom Eugene admired had in common a belief that the central literary object for the modern world should be the self. Whereas earlier poets had put God or nature at the center of the poetic world, the revolutionary poets of the late nineteenth century believed that the self might lead to discovering God and nature—though such a view of God and nature still seemed heretical in Eugene's day.

As he discovered his literary self, Eugene was also finding a new tranquillity in his personal life. His passion for Maibelle, so intense for a few months, had begun to wane after he had gone to Shelton. Maibelle's parents took her with them for a winter in Florida. Eugene wrote almost daily progress reports to Maibelle but he also wrote frequently to Olive Evans, his former nurse, and to several other New London girls. Once away from Eugene and New London, Maibelle's passion changed to interested friendship. Eugene probably detected the change in Maibelle even before she did, but he continued to write frequently. The daily routine at Gaylord Farms emphasized rest, the avoidance of worry or excitement, and a positive, active attitude toward fighting the disease. The routine encouraged a self-preoccupation that came easily to Eugene. The enforced discipline and his desire to recover allowed him to hold in suspension any anxiety he might have felt about his future with Maibelle. His feelings for her, too, were relaxing into simple friendship.

Late in May, Eugene wrote his father to say that he had been judged in "A-1 shape" and was about to be discharged. James wrote Dr. Lyman hinting that his wife's condition was delicate; he worried that Eugene might infect her. Dr. Lyman reported that the disease had almost certainly never reached the stage in Eugene where it was contagious. Reassured, James arranged for Eugene to return to New London.

Back in New London, Eugene spent the summer taking long walks with Maibelle, during which they talked at length of Strindberg and of Paul Verlaine, whom they had added to the list of authors they were trying to understand. Maibelle later told Sheaffer that Eugene began also to talk with her then about plays he wanted to write. Both Maibelle and Eugene were dating other people and, since talk of marriage had stopped, the Scotts opposed Maibelle's unconventional friendship less stiffly.

Other changes were visible in Eugene. Gradually he came to believe that in the lottery of fathers he had not drawn so badly as he might have. Probably in response to the détente, as well as in relief at Eugene's recovery, James bought a high-sided powerboat, in which Eugene sunbathed naked in the sound, sometimes to the alarm of ferryboat passengers when the dory drifted near enough to the ferry lanes for him to be seen. In good times, James was openhanded with his money; in bad, he grasped and schemed. Good times were not measured in dollars by James, although his responses to good and bad times often were. Money was more the medium through which he expressed anxiety than the source of anxiety.

James had now to determine how Eugene's recovery might best be completed. He himself had to meet the cast of *Joseph and His Brothers* in New York, where they would begin a road tour in late summer, and Ella and Jamie were to go with him. Given Dr. Lyman's prohibition against alcohol and high living, it probably seemed best to keep Eugene away from New York and the theatrical tour.

Over the summer the O'Neills had gotten to know the Rippin family, who lived across and up the street in the Packard, a boardinghouse at 416 Pequot Avenue. James liked the Rippins and felt a certain confidence in leaving his youngest in their charge. Usually, the Rippins accepted boarders only during the summer, but Mrs. Rippin liked Eugene and the other O'Neills. For twelve dollars a week, Eugene would have an upstairs bedroom and three healthy meals a day. James threw in an extra dollar to be doled out to his son each week for spending money. As things worked out, Eugene earned a little additional money by writing occasional items for Judge Latimer's paper.

This would be the first time in his life when Eugene would know firsthand the life that most Americans of his time considered ordinary. Twenty years later Eugene wrote *Ah, Wilderness!*, a sunny, nostalgic comedy about a youth growing up in a stable small-town family. He once said that in it he imagined the kind of family life he wished he had known. In fact in 1913–1914 with the Rippins he did experience several months of life in such a family. The time he spent among them was important for his development, probably more important than he could have known. Among the more subtle lessons was one he never fully accepted, that family intimacy did not always lead to desperation and extremity as it did with the O'Neills. Later he would recall (as he wrote Dolly Rippin when they were both middle-aged) a "deep warm sense of gratitude" toward the family for that year (SL, 364). Warmth and gratitude he certainly felt, but that does not mean that his behavior became more conventional, or that he learned to fit comfortably into a family.

The O'Neills had gotten to know the Rippins in the summer of 1913 because, as usual when they were in in New London, they took their meals in a boardinghouse, and that summer they boarded with the Rippins. The Rippins had enjoyed a simpler experience as immigrants than the O'Neills. They had come to New London from the rural west of England, near Wales, about ten years before, and during the summers they served meals to vacationing boarders. James Rippin, a quiet man, worked at various outdoors chores and jobs, and he and his sons disapproved of liberal American ways. His wife, Helen Maude Rippin, quietly accepted people as they were, and it was she who made a success of the boardinghouse. She and her daughters were happy and high-spirited. James O'Neill and Mrs. Rippin found each other congenial. James was known to utter Shakespearean lines in the kitchen to which Mrs. Rippin would remember or improvise responses. They undoubtedly entertained each other, the other guests, and the Rippin daughters.

The Rippins sensed that things were not altogether right with Mrs. O'Neill. Ella had taken a liking to Emily Rippin, an outgoing, friendly girl who seemed to invite confidences, and would take her riding in the car, where Ella would ramble on about family matters or whatever else came to her mind. Possibly in a mild state of morphine-euphoria, Ella once went so far as to coyly tell Emily that her husband never trusted her with money because she had "gone through two fortunes," and still worried that if she had any money she would give it to her spendthrift sons (Gelbs, 224). From other details of Emily's and Jessica's recollections, it seems clear that Ella was using morphine that summer, although the Rippins did not suspect that that was the cause of her odd behavior. Often that summer Ella ate nothing, although she usually sat through meals with her husband and sons. Once Emily saw Ella sweep her arm mechanically across the table, pushing food and other items on the floor. Except for James's brief apology to Emily, sons and husband went on eating as if nothing had happened. Seemingly by design, the O'Neills usually arrived for meals after other boarders had finished.

The male Rippins were not happy when Eugene moved in, with his reputation for decadence. His outspoken defiance of convention offended Rippin and his sons. But as Mrs. Rippin liked Eugene and saw no harm in him, the opposition gradually subsided. After a decade of the loosest living, Eugene now began to live a life that seems to have been largely chaste and sober. With the change of habits, he was now rediscovering the person he had been when he learned of his mother's addiction more than a decade before, and in the process, he was rediscovering the world he had rejected while at Princeton.

During his year in New London, Eugene seems to have stayed at Monte Cristo Cottage the first several weeks, but when cold weather set in, he moved into the upstairs room in the Packard, bringing a few personal articles, his clothes, and some books. There he spent much of each day writing. At night he followed the practice at the sanatorium of sleeping on an unheated downstairs porch with only screens on the windows. A pet cat often slept with him and sometimes startled him with the gift of a rat. With the waters of Long Island Sound only a few feet away, he would lie facing the sound of water. Eugene became especially friendly with the two youngest Rippin daughters, Emily and Dolly (christened Grace), who still lived at home. Like the other Rippins, they were bright and literate. Eugene flirted with both younger girls, and with their older sister Jessica, who worked as a dietitian in Philadelphia, and he kept up a friendly correspondence with them in later life.

When Eugene first moved in with the Rippins, his hands trembled so at breakfast that he spilled things. The tremor upset the girls, and his self-consciousness and anxiety increased. Mrs. Rippin gently suggested that he might enjoy sleeping in, and for a time he breakfasted alone. After a few months, the tremor was better, and he took his meals with the family. He could not trust the simple intimacy he saw in their lives and kept attacking it as if to see whether it could withstand such challenges to intimacy as were given among the O'Neills. Such seems to have been the motive behind a test he once devised for Jessica. "My wife and I will live on a barge," he told her. "I'll live at one end and she'll live at the other, and we'll never see each other except when the urge strikes us" (Gelbs, 246). Jessica failed the test. The idea seemed to her simply repulsive and animal. To Eugene, it seemed an attractive alternative to the politics of intimacy that bound the O'Neills in loving, deadly war. Perhaps Eugene was trying to let Jessica know how different from hers was his experience of family life.

As with most of his friends at the time, Eugene felt he had to create common ground on which friendship might grow. With the Rippins, Eugene immediately set out to correct the education of Emily and Dolly. He advocated socialism, free love, and liberal authors and criticized all established powers. He got them reading *The Decameron,* an act of sedition that annoyed their father, but he could not convince them that the rewards of Strindberg and Nietzsche outweighed the difficulties and unpleasantness. Jessica once asked Eugene to recommend something to read and he carefully wrote out the title, " *Three Plays by Gerhardt Hauptman* [sic]" and the names of the plays: "Drayman Henschel," "Rose Berndt," and "The Rats" (B.U.). He seemed to take anyone's conventional views as an affront and as an opportunity to test the power of his contrary ideas.

He used himself and his own disreputable history as tokens in his war against the conventional worldview and often made his past sound even more lurid than it actually had been. He told his former nurse Olive Evans that the son he had abandoned in 1909 was "just an accident of nature" (LS, 263), as if neither the baby, its mother, or the event mattered in the least to him. No one would have guessed from that that guilt over Kathleen and Eugene Jr. had driven him to try to kill himself. Probably he was trying to deny to himself that he ever had been so affected by guilt. In the same mood he told the Rippin girls that he had abandoned Kathleen when he learned she was pregnant, not mentioning that his conscience had driven him to marry her against the wishes of his parents and against his own instinct merely to flee.

Jessica Rippin told the Gelbs that Eugene talked in detail about his sexual adventures, spoke "of girls as 'pigs,'" and "was always trying to 'make' us." The girls disapproved of his words but felt no fear of him; they rather liked him, and they sensed the shadows behind his seemingly hard surface. "Gene was not a rapist," Emily told the Gelbs; "You were safe with him as long as you wanted to be safe." Emily had once gone as far as "an experimental kiss"; she decided that was enough—and found that Eugene accepted rejection without its affecting their friendly relations (Gelbs, 246–47).

The male Rippins tolerated Eugene, but just barely. James Rippin, Jr., believed that his sisters were in danger and sought to protect them, but neither they nor his mother shared his concern. James may have been a little jealous of his sisters' friendship with Eugene, and he was also annoyed at the interest that his bride, Jane, felt toward the fledgling playwright. Jane Deeter of Philadelphia, who later became national director of the Girl Scouts, was a member of a family with serious artistic interests; her brother Jasper would act in several of Eugene's plays as a member of the Provincetown Players (he played the Cockney trader in *The Emperor Jones*), and he later founded the Hedgerow Theatre of Philadelphia.

James Rippin, Jr., and Jane Deeter were in the Rippin family parlor one winter night when Eugene read aloud, until four in the morning, several short plays he had written, acting every part. James and Jane told Sheaffer that Eugene usually mumbled "as though he had a cigarette in his mouth," but that night he spoke clearly. "After that night," James Rippin complained to Sheaffer, "I could hardly have Jane to myself—he was always hanging around her" (LS, 266).

Eugene's flirtations with the Rippin women were playful and oddly innocent. To Dolly he once wrote the following doggerel (B.U.):

> She is there with the jest and the jolly
> She's a pure peacherino, a pippin!
> And a foe to all blue melancholy,
> > by golly!
> There isn't a name for the folly
> > That I wouldn't do
> > For a sweet smile or two
> From
> > Always imperious
> > > Rather mysterious
> > > > Never quite serious
> > > > > Dolly

At the holiday season he enjoyed the first conventional Christmas of his life. He helped Helen conceal from her daughters the dresses she was making for them, but it never occurred to him that he would be included in the gift-giving. When the day came, he found that he was offered small thoughtful gifts by Helen and the girls. The gifts so embarrassed him, and a simple family Christmas made him so ill at ease, that he excused himself and went to the empty Monte Cristo Cottage. Later he was seen by startled townspeople swimming in the frigid waters of the sound, breasting nature in splendid isolation. Late that evening he returned to the Rippins and presented Helen and her daughters with boxes of chocolates. He told them he had sold a screen play for fifty dollars, but none of them believed him. He had probably borrowed money for the chocolates from Judge Latimer, or perhaps he had wired his father; the dollar a week allowance James gave him would have left nothing for Christmas gifts.

Life with the Rippins evolved into a comfortable routine, which the Rippin daughters described to Sheaffer. Eugene wrote in the morning, then took a long swim. He wrote in the afternoon and would meet Maibelle or perhaps another girl for a long walk and talk, or perhaps a row on the sound. Sometimes he would write at night after seeing his girl or another friend (LS, 264–65). The routine, together with the fear of tuberculosis, helped him mostly avoid alcohol during the year in New London, and the following year too. He maintained variations on this routine throughout much of his later life.

Along with plays and poems, he devised scenarios for movies, amusing himself with fantasies of immediate wealth. The fantasies reflected the new drive to find freedom from his father's purse strings. Throughout his life Eugene enjoyed unusual creative fecundity, ideas for new plays coming to him almost constantly. Notebook sketches that survive from a few years later probably resemble the ideas he fired off to the pictures. "Honor Among the Bradleys" begins with a drawing of a stage set, notes on the scenes and characters, and a few thoughts on plot. Here are two more:

> Long play—man of 45—most popular doctor in small
> town—a personage. His wife, 40, with a life of her own in
> social activities—a leader. They started out with romantic
> illusions—married when he had still been medical student,
> she a college girl. The little things of their small town life
> have erected a wall between them. They feel they have lost
> youth. It is the doctor's 45th birthday. [Floyd 1981, 30]

> Long Play—abandonment of the T.B. sailor by whaling
> captain in the Marquesas—his care by natives and restoration to comparative health while the Islanders are scourged
> by his disease—the coming of the missionaries, etc.—His
> fight against them, preaching the real gospel of Christ—etc.
> [Floyd 1981, 30]

Composing at the typewriter and typing as fast as he could, he wrote numerous sketches for movies, perhaps several a day. (Typing was a mode of composition he could never use at all with work he took seriously.) He sent out his "photo-plays" and told everyone that a writer had to live, implying that he was an old hand at artistic compromise—something he never learned to accept easily, in actuality. He mocked his fantasy that writing would soon make him wealthy. He once wrote the following undated note to Dolly (B.U.):

> Dolly dearest! You will bring me good luck "por cierto" if you mail this for me. Please put a stamp on the envelope inside the outer envelope in case of rejection. Then seal and mail. Caesar and his fortunes are inside so be careful!
>
> Thanking you again and a-gain, pledging my oath that you are as good as you are adorable, and assuring you I am the fond slave of your every whim, I remain
>
> Yours in perpetual adoration.

He never sold a photo-play but showed no discouragement at the stream of rejections. His self-esteem was never much affected by how others judged his work, either at the beginning or later in life. He took for granted that he would often make mistakes, but he also believed in his gift and felt certain he would get better.

He kept on working. By the end of 1913 Eugene had completed at least four one-act plays as well as numerous movie scenarios, and by late the following summer he had finished at least ten plays, including two long ones. Most of them deserve little attention from anyone but a biographer, but one was *Children of the Sea,* written around March 1914. With a little revision it became *Bound East for Cardiff,* the first written of the four sea plays set on the SS *Glencairn.* It would be the first O'Neill play to be performed and remains one of the most frequently revived.

The earliest and slightest of Eugene's plays express either predictable personal themes or favorite philosophical ideas. The very first, *A Wife for a Life,* shows a young man Eugene's age and his partner, an older man, mining gold in Arizona. The young man confides that for years he has nourished a secret love for a married woman whose husband has abandoned her after making her life miserable by dragging her around to mining camps with him. Now the wife has gotten a divorce and the young man is free to marry her. Certain details, including the husband's forcing on his wife a rough itinerant life, suggest that the author had his parents' marriage in mind—as he saw the marriage at that moment. The woman the protagonist loves is of course the wife of his partner and best friend, who lets him go off to claim his bride without letting on that he is the former husband.

Probably O'Neill meant the sketch to illustrate the inexplicable workings of fate or coincidence, à la Stephen Crane or Gerhart Hauptmann. A later twentieth-century reader cannot help noticing the oedipal triangle and the protective attitude of the older miner toward his young friend, even after he knows the whole situation. At the time, James and Eugene were enjoying a rapprochement, in which Eugene was comfortable with his need for and love of his father. Exactly when Eugene learned about Freud's Oedipus complex, and whether he meant to show any such thing in the sketch, is unclear. Freud and his ideas began gradually to be widely known in America following his 1911 lectures at Clark University.

In his own development, Eugene seems to have been going through the sort of resumption of intense oedipal conflicts that occurs in early adolescence, after the first resolution that usually occurs between the ages of five and seven. O'Neill's personal conflicts are much more fully expressed in the melodrama *Recklessness,* the manuscript of which he dated November 25, 1913. Mildred Baldwin is married to Arthur and lives in his remote mountain fastness with various maids and with the chauffeur, Fred. The story is about the reckless affair of Mildred and Fred, and Arthur's revenge. The affair ends with Fred's death in an auto crash and Mildred's suicide.

Eugene gave detailed sketches of the Baldwins and of Fred, the chauffeur, Mildred's lover. Mildred is "a tall strikingly voluptuous-looking woman of about twenty-eight" (CP1, 55). Her husband, Arthur, "a stocky undersized man of about fifty. His face is puffy and marked by dissipation and his thick-lipped mouth seems perpetually curled in a smile of cynical scorn" (59). She wears "a low-cut evening gown of a grey that matches her eye" (55). Arthur is "foppishly dressed in a perfectly fitting dark grey suit of extreme cut" (59). The sketches suggests a perverse sexuality oriented around Arthur's possession of and dominance over Mildred. The model for such dominance and possession is an oedipal child's interpretation of the relationship of parents.

Fred resembles the author in appearance: a "tall, clean-shaven, dark-complected young fellow of twenty-five or so with clear-cut, regular features, big brown eyes and black curly hair" (CP1, 56). (A photo of Eugene taken not long after the play was written shows him clean shaven and otherwise resembling the sketch of Fred.) The point of view of the playwright seems to coincide with that of Fred, who is offstage after the first scene and who is given even less development than Arthur and Mildred. Perhaps O'Neill, who hated being onstage, imagined playing the part himself.

In Fred's only scene, at the beginning, he and Mildred furtively embrace; at any moment they expect Arthur to return from a trip. She wants them to run away together immediately. She loathes Arthur; she is his sexual toy; he uses his money and her lack of it to control her; she can't bear his touch; she feels she could kill him. Fred counsels patience. They will have to wait because he doesn't yet have money or a profession. Soon he will take his engineering exams. "I won't be anybody's servant then," he says (CP1, 57). Mildred offers to take money from Arthur to finance their elopement, and when Fred protests, she offers to sell her jewels. But Fred refuses to be indebted to Arthur in any way. He conveniently overlooks his benefactor's support of both him and his mistress.

Fred continues to resemble his creator, a young man struggling to be free of dependencies, who has his eye on a distant goal. As with Eugene, there is a distinct ambivalence in his struggle to be free. His wish that he and Mildred remain in Arthur's home until he has a profession and an income shows a certain common sense. But Fred feels content that Mildred remain with her husband and that he continue to share her with Arthur. If Fred hesitates, perhaps he feels himself not yet ready to renounce paternal support. Or if, despite his passion, he seems a little reluctant, perhaps it is because he notices and fears that if they run away on Arthur's money, Mildred will then control the money and also control him. He may become dependent on her in the same way she now is on Arthur and risk becoming the sexual accessory.

Although Eugene developed none of these possibilities in the play, he knew well from family life the breadwinner's manipulation of his wife and sons, and the reverse, along with subtler persuasions. By frequently giving money to her sons, Ella O'Neill infuriated their father on several grounds, one of which was that she lessened the control he held over Jamie and Eugene by weakening his power to withhold. Doling out funds was a strategy in the warfare of husband and wife as well as a way to maintain favor with the sons. *Recklessness* seems to hint that Eugene sensed the complexities of unacknowledgeable bargains between his mother and her sons, but it would be many years before he felt able to explore them.

The fledgling playwright got a little further with Mildred and

Arthur than with Fred. He created in Mildred someone who sounded newly enlightened by feminism, a set of ideas that seemed intermittently attractive to Eugene. The strongest appeal came from Eugene's identification with the plight of women trapped by their dependency on husbands. To him it seemed little different from his situation of dependency on his father. Beyond this, there was a stronger threat than financial dependency, one that disturbed Eugene more deeply than his dependency on his father. His passion for Maibelle had taught him how deeply vulnerable he might be to the whims of his beloved. However strong the need for his father, the threat was greater that in loving a woman his self would be absorbed into a sea of need for maternal love. Feminism seemed to insist on a certain distance in the relations between men and women, a distance that appealed to a young man who lost himself when he fell in love. That reason lay behind the ideal of marriage-on-a-barge that Eugene tried to sell to Jessica Rippin: temptation was kept at arm's reach, to allay the dread of absorption. Mildred was one of the first of numerous O'Neill women characters who stood, among other things, for aspects of the author.

Like her author, Mildred sometimes seems wholly absorbed by love but otherwise seems coldly detached. One moment she tells Fred, "I'd rather die of starvation with you than live the way I'm living now" (CP1, 57). But her plan to elope using money she will get from her husband puts Fred into the position she is herself trying to escape, of depending on the one with the money. Consciously or otherwise, she seeks to assume her husband's position. When Fred counsels patience, she coolly reflects on the exact degree of Arthur's meanness to her. In fact, she decides, "in his way" he has been quite kind: "He has looked upon me as a slave to his pleasure, a pretty toy to be exhibited that others might envy him his ownership. . . . but he's been a very considerate 'owner'" (58). Why does she hate him then, she asks herself. "Well, I simply don't love him—there's an end to it. And so—being his wife—I hate him!" To her it seems obvious and logical, as if one takes for granted that love is all or nothing. Moments later, recalling that Arthur will soon be home, Mildred thinks of how he will "claim me—force his loathsome kisses on me" (59).

To a psychoanalytically minded reader, nearly everything in the play seems to express the problems of dependency that Mildred and Fred speak of in the first scene. Like his creator, Fred is a young man struggling to escape from and to cling to adults who support him and who constitute a kind of family. Arthur and Mildred seem most meaningful not as representations of James and Ella O'Neill but as distorted, generalized parental figures who represent sexual and economic power—as understood by one who is young. The play expresses a fantasy of being seduced by an older woman in a conspiracy to outwit her husband. The game of betrayal seems intended to give the woman revenge on her husband for possessing her and enlists the young man's cooperation by seeming to offer, with no consequences to him, the enjoyment of what the older man possesses.

But the fantasy also expresses the younger man's fear of the consequence of winning his game—that if he should win, he might find himself in the same position with his mistress that she previously complained about as wife of the one with the money: if the younger man runs off with the wife, he might wind up as no more than a sexual accessory, an accessory that might be cast off when a less familiar trinket appears. Thus Eugene shows Fred acting cagy when the wife offers to finance their elopement with money taken from her husband.

The relationship that Eugene depicts between Arthur and Mildred hints at some of the fantasies and simplifications through which the oedipal lover interprets the politics of his parents' marriage.

Arthur enters, observes his wife's décolletage, and compliments her appearance. "Is it to welcome the prodigal bridegroom?" he sneers. She forces a smile: "Of course!" He continues to sneer: "And how has the fairest of the fair been while her lord has been on the broad highway?" (CP1, 59). After some exposition, she leads the conversation back to the topic of her appearance and excuses herself to change into something more comfortable. He assures her that he appreciates the trouble she takes, that she looks "more than charming" (61).

The plot's pivotal character now appears, Mildred's personal maid, who is named Gene. This woman, whose name is spelled as the author spelled his own, comes to Arthur and proceeds to tattle on Fred and Mildred, her motive being, she tells Arthur, her jealousy over losing the affection of her lover Fred (CP1, 61). "I shall have to chide him," Arthur says; "his morals are really too corrupt for his station in life" (62). When Arthur finally understands from Gene's hints that his wife is Fred's lover, he becomes enraged, nearly chokes Gene, and insists that she produce evidence. This she does, in the form of a love note from Mildred that Gene has filched from Fred's closet.

Why does Eugene create this character and then give her his own name? Unconsciously, at least, he seems to mean her to represent the homosexual aspect of the normal oedipal lover, who loves his father possessively, is jealous of the father's lover (his mother), and wants to do away with her. (Fred represents the heterosexual aspect.) In an adolescent, the sexual origin of the wish to possess is often unconscious, repressed in the resolution of the first oedipal crisis, but the wish to possess may be conscious. This part of Eugene leads him to make Arthur the most interesting aspect of *Recklessness*.

Arthur is less a realistic character than a compendium of characteristics, interestingly chosen. His "thick lips" are mentioned twice, and his joy is twice described as "savage." His jealousy is volcanic. Without a hint of remorse he nearly strangles Gene when she hints that Fred's lover is Mildred. He plots Fred's destruction without remorse and shows no qualm when he learns of Fred's death or when the body is brought to the house. He tortures Mildred mercilessly, reveling in the shame he sees when he confronts her with the details of her adultery. When a gunshot sounds at the end, Arthur is startled, but steels himself to calmness and tells a maid that Mildred has shot herself and a doctor should be called.

Normand Berlin, in *O'Neill's Shakespeare* (1993), identifies many traces of *Othello* he finds in O'Neill's work. It is one of the several Shakespeare plays that Eugene carried whole within him: it had been burned into his sensibility by his frequent imagining of his hero-father playing the Moor—one of James O'Neill's best roles. In one attempt to tell the story of his parents' marriage, *All God's Chillun Got Wings*, Eugene portrayed his father as the black Jim Harris and his mother as the white Ella Downey, black and white standing for peasant and lace-curtain Irish.

Recklessness is Eugene's earliest redaction of *Othello*, with improvements. Gene O'Neill, in the guise of Gene the maid, plays the role of Iago, covert lover of the Moor called Thick Lips (CP1, 66) and destroyer of his rival, Desdemona (now Mildred). The scene in which Othello is aroused to jealousy, in O'Neill as in Shakespeare, comes to its climax when the husband nearly strangles the informer. In *Othello,* the scene ends with Iago pledging to the Moor, "I am your own for ever." No need for Eugene to have Gene make such a pledge; for the moment, Iago and the playwright are one.

As playwright, Eugene can make changes. Shakespeare's Desdemona was pure as snow, despite an artful wit and tongue. Eugene's Desdemona is far from pure; and whatever her intent, she is as destructive to her lover as she is faithless to her husband. Now Desdemona's guilt is not in doubt; Gene the maid comes forearmed with the proof that Iago had to cook up. O'Neill's Othello devises his own plot for revenge, reserving for himself the pleasure that Shakespeare gives Iago. In Eugene's version, Desdemona, not Othello, knows shame and dies by suicide. This Othello has no reason to know himself mistaken, to be shamed, or to kill himself. The last we see of Arthur is of a man coldly self-righteous. *Recklessness* ends with all forces turned against the faithless wife and mistress, and with an affirmation of rough, natural justice, as many would have seen it at the time. Beyond that, the play constitutes a gift from son to father, the gift of a conspicuous part for a leading melodramatic actor.

In years to come, the motive of writing parts for his father to play often seems to figure prominently in the background of Eugene's creative drive. James seems to have recognized the gift as such; he offered to perform the role of the older miner in *A Wife for a Life* if a backer could be found, and for a later play he helped his son rehearse a cast. He was increasingly impressed as Eugene gained skill, though he was still troubled by his son's modern ideas and his pessimism. A few years later, when Eugene had his first major success, James was observed to leave the theater with tears of pride in his eyes.

In Eugene O'Neill's case, the weaker plays usually reveal their author more directly than the good plays. Even among the early plays, few are as bad—or reveal as much—as *Recklessness.* The play makes clear something that is usually hard to detect in Eugene: that however much he might sympathize with his mother's illness, anger and even dread outweighed his love for Ella O'Neill. He identified with her in many ways and knew that he took after her in his acute sensitivity and in numerous other qualities. He often shared her scorn and condescension toward his father, but far more often, and probably with some consciousness, Eugene hated and feared his need for his mother. The negative feelings were expressed in the improbable suicide Eugene imposed on Mildred. The anger is also expressed in, and comes at the expense of, several other women characters in the earliest plays.

Eugene may not have been conscious of all the implications here construed from *Recklessness,* but he perhaps understood many of them. Both he and his father probably recognized that Arthur was a better part than his father was otherwise being offered in the twilight of his career. James appreciated his son's gift. In March 1914, he arranged to pay three hundred dollars to the Gorham Press of Boston to publish five plays, *Thirst, The Web, Warnings, Fog,* and *Recklessness.* The book, which came out the following August, was called *Thirst and Other One Act Plays* and was printed in an edition of a thousand copies. It sold only a few and received hardly any reviews.

Of the five plays, James would have found *Recklessness* the most conventional and theatrical. Arthur's villainy and Mildred's voluptuousness could make for an entertaining theatrical hour, and the play would offend almost no one. *Warnings* would also have seemed conventional to James. Its first scene is interesting to a biographer because it shows a beleaguered, impoverished mother of several children keeping peace among her brood through empathic, well-timed responses to their complaints. Eugene had learned something from watching Helen Rippin manage her family; he named one daughter Dolly. Otherwise, the play takes the father's side in the O'Neill family melodrama that arose from the father's never being able to quit his tedious, urgent work because poverty had so haunted him.

The tone of the play shifts abruptly when the father enters. A ship radio operator, James Knapp knows he is going deaf and should quit, but worry about his family and his wife's need for more money so affect him that he postpones resigning until after one more voyage. The last voyage ends in shipwreck when he fails to hear a warning. At the end Knapp kills himself out of guilt over his mistake.

James O'Neill would have seen in *Warnings* a play about that prime Victorian virtue, duty. The play warns that a man must provide well enough for his family that his professional duty is not affected by the dependency of a wife and children. The most affecting scene shows the misery of Knapp's marital life: the children whine, the wife nags, and the husband feels guilty. In retrospect it is clear that what interested Eugene in the story was the web of circumstance that leads inexorably from marital misery to the shipwreck. To Eugene, Knapp's guilt over his wife's unhappiness is a fact of life, like her complaining. The Knapps can no more change their marriage than he can change his deafness. But this is not what an audience would have understood. If the play had been performed, an audience would have seen only a man weak enough to be upset by a nagging wife and would have had little sympathy for Knapp's sensitivity. The play would have seemed a conventional warning not to give in to softness or guilt. James would probably have considered the play a vindication of himself as a man who had provided well for his family and who resisted his wife's demands for luxuries beyond his means; but he might have suspected that his son had sniffed out the sensitivity James tried to hide, and the pain he felt over the contempt of his wife and sons. Eugene was reaching not for conventional wisdom but for the vein of tragedy exposed by Conrad, Crane, Dostoyevsky, Strindberg, and the other authors he valued. In Eugene's eyes, tragedy centered around the illusion people cherish that they can master nature and control their destinies, an illusion that is repeatedly exposed when people find they have done the very things they tried to avoid doing.

Eugene was years away from being able to express convincingly the tragic sense that had driven him to pore over Nietzsche and Schopenhauer and Baudelaire, that had helped him discover what he thought of himself, the world, and the way he existed in the world. But in most of the early plays, one can see him reaching.

Eugene called *The Web* his first play—he considered *A Wife for a Life* a vaudeville sketch, not a play. He probably wrote *The Web* in September 1913. As Margaret Loftus Ranald suggests, it was based on Hauptmann's *The Weavers*. (In 1916 when *The Weavers* was performed in New York, he saw it six times.) Crude in dialogue, awkward in plot, *The Web* tells the story of Rose, a consumptive hooker. Her cough infuriates her boyfriend, Steve, who threatens her. A neighbor, Tim, comes to the rescue and drives out the cowardly Steve. When Steve ambushes Tim, Rose, caught in a web of circumstance, is arrested for the murder. However weak is the play up to this point, the ending has a certain force. "Gawd! Gawd!" Rose mournfully cries as the police lead her away. "Why d'yuh hate me so?" (CP1, 28). The blasphemy shocks the policeman, and his shock makes the reader see what the author has wanted to do.

In *Long Day's Journey into Night* the long conversation in act 4 between James Tyrone and his younger son centers on the different views the two have of the world. Tyrone ostensibly believes that a man is the master of his fate and captain of his soul. Edmund sees his father driven to his eccentricities by forces in his past and his temperament that control him and sees his mother time after time driven back to her drug, apparently against her will, although she seems to hate herself when she lapses. It seems funny and unspeakably sad to him that his father claims never to waver in his optimism and Christian faith, although neither prayer nor positive thinking helps his mother conquer her addiction.

When Tyrone has told Edmund about his artistic idealism and his guilt over betraying it, Edmund is deeply moved; but he expresses his emotion through laughter. "What the devil are you laughing at," his father demands. "Not at you, Papa. At life. It's so damn crazy" (CP3, 810).

The idea that life is crazy, with its implication that life itself is what drives one to betray one's ideals, is even less tolerable to James than his guilt. "More of your morbidness," he growls. "There's nothing wrong with life. It's we who— 'The fault, dear Brutus, is not in our stars, but in ourselves that we are underlings'" (CP3, 810–11). Better to think ourselves a failure than admit the possibility that we have much less control over ourselves and our world than we want to believe. To Eugene, the tragic sense arises from the human desire to believe that people control their lives and from the refusal to remember the repeated lessons of existence that the belief is mistaken.

Edmund insists on imagining the world to be a place that holds a human being in no more special regard than it does a seagull or a fish. He has enjoyed walking in the fog, where "everything looked and sounded unreal. Nothing was what it is. That's what I wanted—to be alone with myself in another world where the truth is untrue and life can hide from itself. Out beyond the harbor, where the road runs along the beach, I even lost the feeling of being on land. The fog and the sea seemed part of each other. It was like walking on the bottom of the sea. As if I had drowned long ago. As if I was a ghost belonging to the fog, and the fog was the ghost of the sea. It felt damned peaceful to be nothing more than a ghost within a ghost" (CP3, 796). In Edmund's fog-vision, the distinction between fog and sea is lost. One might call it a molecular view of nature. The difference between fog and sea consists in the presence or absence of certain molecules and the molecular density that results.

Life seen at the molecular level gives one a different orientation from James Tyrone's. At the molecular level no one can imagine that it matters to nature or life that people can breathe in fog but drown in water. One cannot easily personify nature or life when thinking about molecules. James resists Edmund's fog-vision by calling it morbid pessimism, and he offers an antidote. "Why can't you remember your Shakespeare and forget the third-raters. You'll find what you're trying to say in him—as you'll find everything else worth saying. [*He quotes, using his fine voice.*] 'We are such stuff as dreams are made on, and our little life is rounded with a sleep'" (CP3, 796). In James's interpretation, Prospero offers consolation to the young that soothes away knowledge of death and doubts of human significance. Sleep may not be permanent, and if it come to us, perchance eternity may be passed a-dreaming.

Edmund refuses Shakespeare's consolation, not merely to provoke his father, and not merely to resist his father's effort to change him. The vision he is striving for is subtle and may easily be obscured by the official optimism to which his father pays lip service. "Fine," says Edmund. "That's beautiful. But I wasn't trying to say that. We are such stuff as manure is made on, so let's drink up and forget it" (CP3, 796). Although he passes it off as a wisecrack, Edmund is serious, and his idea is more complex than first appears. He finds no consolation in hedging on death's permanence; instead he finds relief in embracing the knowledge that he will eventually be manure. His words call to mind Walt Whitman's theory of the wondrous compost that takes the leavings of death and disease and transforms them into the new grass. "Now I am terrified of the Earth!" Whitman says; not because it is harmful to him or other people but because of its sheer power.

> It grows such sweet things out of such corruptions,
> It turns harmless and stainless on its axis, with such endless
>   successions of diseased corpses,
> It distils such exquisite winds out of such infused fetor,
> It renews, with such unwitting looks, its prodigal, annual,
>   sumptuous crops,
> It gives such divine materials to men, and accepts such
>   leavings from them at last. [*Leaves of Grass,* 1860 ed.,
>   210–11.]

Edmund's fog-vision, like Whitman's vision of compost, gives a glimpse into nature according to the scientific paradigm. The vision of human unimportance need not mortify us, and it may even offer a paradoxical consolation. What importance can one's own guilt or narcissism or shortcomings have when one has glimpsed life's fundamental processes?

Whether or not Eugene and James O'Neill ever spoke the words exchanged between Edmund and James Tyrone, the argument from *Long Day's Journey* reflects the sense of purpose driving Eugene's unconventionality. Conventionality was itself the problem, because it prevented people from seeing the world in any light besides the official one. In person Eugene defied convention. In trying to write, he reached for tragedy. A notion of Eugene's developing sense of the tragic illuminates his intent in his early plays (an intent one can acknowledge without making any claim for their quality).

Thirst (dated in the typescript fall 1913) puts a dandified gentleman and a bedraggled blonde dancer into a lifeboat with a mulatto West Indian sailor and lets thirst, starvation, and fear of the circling sharks take their course. At first the three talk philosophically about their fate. The dancer tells of watching the captain shoot himself out of guilt over losing his ship. Before long, the woman goes mad and dies. The gentleman, while trying to prevent the sailor from eating her body, causes them all to fall overboard, where all three bodies are devoured by sharks. Nature has no interest in talk of fate—or of nature.

Nor is Nature interested in humanism. *Fog* is also set in a lifeboat. A silent Polish peasant woman and her dead infant, a businessman, and a poet drift in a fog off the Grand Banks of Newfoundland. The poet expounds on what he calls "humanism," while the businessman tries to be hopeful. The poet says he had been planning to commit suicide when the ship was wrecked, and then he thought he could conceal his suicide as part of the shipwreck; but somehow he wound up in the lifeboat with the businessman. As a steamer seems about to rescue them, they drift against an iceberg. The poet believes that if they shout, they may lure the steamer to its destruction. The two men quarrel, and the poet stifles the businessman's call for help. Nevertheless, they soon hear a boat rowing toward them. The officer tells them they owe their lives to the child whose crying led the rescuing rowboat directly to the lifeboat. Both men swear that the child died the day before, and they find that the woman, too, is now dead. The officer thinks both men have gone mad, and the poet and businessman find the officer's story unaccountable. The poet decides to remain in the lifeboat with the dead woman and child while it is towed to the ship, to contemplate what he does not understand, a decision the officer calls morbid. Humanism has led the poet to feel suicidal, but a brush with death leads to the recognition of one's ignorance and restores one's sense of the ordinary.

Calamity and death fill Eugene's early plays. There are at least a dozen deaths, including four suicides, in the first nine plays. They undoubtedly reflect Eugene's brush with tuberculosis, and the suicides reflect Eugene's suicide attempt and perhaps even more the death of Jimmy

Byth, who killed himself about the time Eugene came home from Gaylord Farm. Eugene's father may have grumbled about his son's morbidity and wondered aloud if he was sick in the head. But Eugene, like the poet in *Fog*, explores ignorance, his own as well as the general human ignorance, about death.

Can that be anything but morbid or even pathological? Possibly. If one cannot believe conventional affirmations or accept religious faith, if one distrusts all conventional human ways of knowing, if one distrusts even language itself with its assumption of various givens, if, in short, one has been a philosophical skeptic long before knowing what skepticism was, and if one then learned that philosophers have always seen reason to doubt that people can know anything about the world in a way that makes sense philosophically, then one is left with one great and indisputable fact, that of death.

The optimistic Walt Whitman found in death (among other things) powerful evidence of the Dionysian life force. For Eugene, thinking about death served the philosophical skeptic as a point of orientation; death was a polestar in a world where everything else was changeable and obscure. Staying attentive to death might help a wanderer find his way through a world where all other signposts mislead.

In this way Eugene lived with the Rippins in relative happiness and comfort. Free from the chronic tension that haunted the O'Neills, having his romances, swimming, rowing his boat he wrote play after play filled with dread and death. He did not want Helen Rippin to read his plays, but her daughters or sons evidently described them to her, and she worried about his not letting his plays end happily. "Life doesn't give us happy endings," he told her (LS, 264). It was the happiness of the ordinary during his months with the Rippins that allowed him to explore in increasingly coherent form his sense of the world. A few years later he wrote Jessica Rippin: "I've never worked harder or with pleasanter surroundings than I did those *cold* months in the Packard [House]. Your family gave me the most real touch of a home life I had had up to then—quite a happy, new experience for an actor's son! I've never forgotten to be grateful to all of you for it—above all, to your mother" (letter of February 4, 1919; SL, 84). The letter closed with a warm greeting to Jessica's mother and the other Rippins. And in 1941, the Gelbs report, Eugene wrote to Helen Rippin just before her death that "living in her home had helped him become the playwright he was" (Gelbs, 243).

As for Eugene's own mother, a momentous change apparently occurred in the spring of 1914. Sometime before early May, Eugene did a most uncharacteristic thing: he mentioned to Emily Rippin that Ella had been away in a sanatorium. Emily told the Gelbs that he said: "My mother was ill, but now she's better" (Gelbs, 248). On May 5 Eugene unexpectedly and abruptly ended his stay with the Rippins and went to prepare Monte Cristo Cottage for his family's arrival for the summer. Evidently the family was returning before he expected them.

Sheaffer has worked out a circumstantial but persuasive case that between late March and late May, Ella went into a hospital, sanatorium, or convent, and there she went through another of her periodic cures for morphine addiction. He speculates that it was a convent in Brooklyn, and he believes that a return to her childhood religious faith enabled the cure to succeed and helped her remain healthy.

Unlike the many previous cures, this one worked; she remained free of the drug until her death in 1922, not even resuming her habit after she had major surgery in April 1919, when morphine would surely have been prescribed for postsurgical pain. Furthermore, the surgery was a mastectomy for breast cancer. The shock of disfigurement would have tested the character of someone far stronger than Ella. It seems especially remarkable that she would not return to the comfort of her old enemy after the mastectomy. The critical change, it seems, was that for the first time in the quarter-century since Eugene's birth, Ella was daily attending Mass, beginning in June 1914. Sheaffer finds no other public change in her behavior; Ella seemed to visitors as shy and retiring as always.

Sheaffer is undoubtedly right about the importance of Ella's resuming her religious faith, but she had often tried and failed. Some change must have enabled her to recover her faith. One of the most important differences was that James made only a few more road tours. He continued to act when he could get a part, but usually in New York. Ella was now free from the constant travel she loathed. She didn't have the fine town house in New York she had always said she wanted, but at least she was living comfortably in the city she preferred. James and Ella now made their residence in the Prince George Hotel on East Twenty-eighth Street near Fifth Avenue and returned to Monte Cristo Cottage only during the summers.

Another possible factor in Ella's recovery was that at fifty-five, she would have been completing menopause and thus have been free of any worry about pregnancy. Her dread of pregnancy dated back at least to the years before Eugene was born, when the baby Edmund died. Freedom from that concern would surely have affected all aspects of her life. In *Long Day's Journey into Night* Eugene O'Neill shows Mary Tyrone moving out of the marital bed when she was using morphine and into the spare room. One can perhaps infer that Ella O'Neill found it easier to let morphine speak than to say no to her husband. Menopause may have relieved one source of chronic anxiety.

Finally, there is the ambiguous issue of the Harrison Narcotic Act of 1914, which made it much more difficult than before to obtain all opiates. Ella had always obtained the drug through doctors' prescriptions and thus would probably not have been directly affected. Nevertheless, the act nudged users of restricted drugs toward classification as criminals, and that might have offended Ella's upper-middle-class sensibility.

The O'Neill men could not have known for some time that this cure would last longer than the others, let alone know that it would be permanent. Yet they would have noticed that Mama seemed different, and her going to Mass would have seemed a notable change. Jamie and his mother grew ever closer, once her attention to him was no longer distracted by morphine. James continued to grumble at his dependent elder son and to play pater familias, to the amusement of Jamie and Ella. As for Eugene, he had other things on his mind.

9

Among God's Fools:
In Love in New London and Cambridge
1914–1915

IN MAY 1914, EUGENE STARTED to date Beatrice Ashe. She was nineteen and, like his mother and Maibelle Scott, was the pampered only daughter of well-to-do parents. Her father was superintendent of the New London trolley company. Beatrice was tall, full-figured, and considered very pretty. She had an independent streak that concerned her mother a little, but Mrs. Ashe need not have worried. Bee, as she called herself, would marry a naval officer (he rose to become vice admiral) and would live to tell the Gelbs and Sheaffer of her youthful adventure with a playwright. She had a dramatic flair, expressed in the clothes she wore, and a pleasant soprano voice. She sang at church socials and in amateur theatricals and acted in school plays. A good deal is known about the friendship she and Eugene had in 1914–1915, because nearly eighty of his letters to her survive.[1]

The amour closely resembles the playwright's future affair with Agnes Boulton, Eugene's second wife. Although we have fewer details about the friendship with Maibelle Scott, and about others yet to come, the one with Bee seems to follow a pattern that prevails in Eugene's relations with the women in his life who were important to him.

The affair did not take off immediately. Eugene was dating other women and Bee was dating other men, but they had noticed each other, and Eugene contrived a meeting. For Eugene, things were not quite finished with Maibelle, although he had lost the idealism of new love and they did not see each other as often as before. Maibelle was getting serious about a Coast Guard Academy cadet she was now dating. Eugene, now in a flurry of writing, was beginning to expect success.

He was finishing up his first long play, *Bread and Butter*, which he built around two issues that would be prominent in his life for the next several years, financial dependency and certain ideals concerning marriage. John Brown loves Maude Steele (whose name alliterates with Maibelle Scott's). He wants to be a serious painter and talks his father into paying for his studies in New York, where he lives with other artists in the sort of studio Eugene once shared with Ed Keefe and George Bellows. His father, a self-made businessman who has no truck with the fine arts, hopes that John will use his talent for commercial art. After a confrontation, Brown cuts off John's allowance and tuition. Full of misgivings about Maude, but starving and drinking too much to be able to paint, he convinces himself he loves her, takes a job working for her father, and marries her. They are soon locked in a marriage based on need and contempt for each other. After several miserable years, a particularly terrible fight ends with John's killing himself. Curtain.

The characters and ideas were beyond his powers at this point, but there are occasional moments that remind a reader of moments in his mature plays. The character of the cynical older brother resembled Jamie, and from time to time, a few lines of dialogue prefigure, for later readers, passages in *Long Day's Journey into Night*. John's artistic idealism was certainly Eugene's. In writing the play, the author neglected to mention that he (if not his alter ego) had acquired his artistic ideals in identification with his father's. Probably Eugene did not recognize its source at the time.

One of Eugene's motives for writing the play was probably to complain about the allowance of a dollar a week that James gave his son. Shortly after Eugene began the play, James stole some of his son's wind by offering to subsidize the publication of *Thirst*. Eugene changed direction at once to explore the consequence of letting love lead him into marriage with a woman he now believed too hopelessly bourgeoise for his tastes. Thoughts of Maibelle still preoccupied him. Writing the play seems to have been partly aimed at exorcizing Maibelle's power and his love of her power, and also at exorcizing his memories of his marriage to Kathleen.

That spring, Jessica Rippin introduced Eugene to Clayton Hamilton, a young man with prematurely gray hair and an avuncular manner who was making a name for himself as a drama critic; he was book review editor of the *Bookman* and *Vogue* and lectured on the drama at Columbia. Hamilton had sometimes stayed with the Rippins, and Jessica admired him; now he had rented a beach cottage for his honeymoon and was boarding at the Rippins. Eugene at first found his manner "patronizing" but slowly warmed to him. About April O'Neill asked Hamilton to read some plays, and the critic encouraged him. Inspired by Hamilton's attention, Eugene experienced a spurt of creativity. In April he finished the four-act *Bread and Butter* (copyright May 2), which he had begun in December or January; immediately after, in early May, he wrote his first good play, *Children of the Sea* (copyright May 14); then, hardly pausing, he wrote *Abortion* (copyright May 19). He completed *The Movie Man* before the end of June (copyright July 1).

Hamilton's friendly interest did not end with reading the plays and encouraging their author. In July he suggested that Eugene apply to George Pierce Baker for admission to English 47, a postgraduate course on playwriting that Baker had been teaching at Harvard for a decade. When *Thirst and Other One Act Plays* came out in August, Hamilton reviewed it for the *Bookman* and the *Nation*—the only two reviews the book received aside from puffs in the New London *Telegraph*. Hamilton was probably the first reader of *Children of the Sea* (better known in its revised version as *Bound East for Cardiff*).

Those who have written about *Children of the Sea* have noticed its "poetic" quality; its style could not be more different from the conventional stagy dialogue of most of Eugene's early plays. It is unconventional for the time, proceeding by rhythmic movement rather than by plot. George Pierce Baker would later say that it was not a play at all (Clark 1967, 28). Among plays in English of the time, it seems to resemble most nearly Synge's *Riders to the Sea,* which works by the gradual unfolding of the effect of loss upon an old woman; learning of the deaths of her two sons is subordinate for the audience to feeling the effect on her of the news. O'Neill's particular genius, when he finally settles into it, is to express the meaning of feeling. That is the way *Long Day's Journey into Night* works, and the same can be said of most of O'Neill's good plays, even as early as *Children of the Sea.*

Set in the forecastle of an unnamed British tramp steamer—later called *S.S. Glencairn*—it quietly presents the dying of Yank, a merchant sailor. Yank talks with his friend Driscoll about dying. The conversation is interspersed with Yank's episodes of pain and with anecdotes told to avoid thinking about Yank's coming death.

It was just a meaningless, careless mistake. While letting himself down into the hold to chip rust, Yank has missed the ladder and fallen; now he is dying without much complaint, but he dreads being left alone before he goes. When the watch changes, his mates go on deck, and Yank has a moment of terror. "Don't leave me, Drisc. I'm dying, I tell yuh. I won't stay here alone with everyone snorin'. I'll go out on deck." When he finds himself too weak to move, he pleads again, "Don't leave me, Drisc!" (Atkinson 1972, 95).

Yank's friend Driscoll arranges to switch his watch, and for the rest of the play the two talk of five years spent together on bad ships and in rough ports. Some of the anecdotes can be recognized as Eugene's own adventures. Yank says he is not frightened to know he is dying, yet the word is not easy for him to say. But he does say it. He tries to face his circumstances as bravely as he can, and he finds he can face death pretty well as long as he has someone to talk to. The play is not about courage but about how it feels to understand that one is dying.

The death is harder for Driscoll to watch than it is for Yank to experience. It is Yank who consoles Driscoll: "You mustn't take it so hard, Drisc. I was just thinkin' it ain't so bad as people think—dyin'. . . . Whatever it is what comes after it can't be no worse than this. I don't like to leave you Drisc, but—that's all. (Driscoll groans and rocks from side to side on the bench.) This sailor life ain't much to cry about leavin'" (Atkinson 1972, 100).

When Yank throws up blood, Driscoll decides he should go for the captain, but Yank begs him to stay; they both know that the captain can't do anything, and Yank can't stand to be left alone. Driscoll screws up his courage and stays. Yank wonders about the fog he sees in the forecastle and they both realize the end is very near. Yank remembers wild times in Buenos Aires and a fight on the docks at Cape Town in which he killed a man who tried to murder him. If there is a God, he asks Driscoll, do you think He'll know it was self-defense? A little while later Yank realizes that because they're a week from Cardiff, he will be buried at sea. Maybe it wouldn't be so bad on land, he thinks. He wills his pay to Driscoll "to divvy up with the rest of the boys"; then he remembers a bar maid in Cardiff who has been kind to him. "Buy her the biggest box of candy yuh c'n find in Cardiff before yuh divvy up my pay." Says Driscoll, "A gallon of gin wud be more welcome." At the end the pain grows, and Yank has a vision of "a pretty lady dressed in black"—perhaps an allusion to Synge's "black hags that do be flying on the sea" to keen dead sailors. When Yank is gone, Driscoll tries repeatedly to remember a prayer but succeeds in recalling no more than "Our Father Who arrt in hivin" (Atkison 1972, 105).

Children of the Sea offers its audience a glimpse of what its author knows about the reality of death. A biographer cannot read the play without being reminded of Eugene's account of half waking up from his suicide attempt and feeling somehow changed. Each anecdote, each moment of conversation between Yank and Driscoll, takes us deeper into how it feels to die or to watch a friend die. The play, which works like music or a poem, is not in the least discursive; nor can the way it works be fully revealed by discursive analysis; it has to be experienced. But it may help to notice the author trying to find something authentic behind the sentimentalities and conventional usages of people caught in the act of meeting the absolute; little by little, the sentimental and conventional drop away, leaving only the people and mortality. As in his later work, Eugene makes habits of stage speech serve as musical elements. As Eugene much later told a friend, "in [*Children of the Sea*] can be seen—or felt—the germ . . . of all my more important future work" (SL, 438).

Eugene undoubtedly knew at once that he had written his best play when he finished *Children of the Sea*. But he could not recapture its style at will, and the other plays he wrote that spring and summer seem by contrast even more conventional and shallow than they would otherwise. *Abortion* is another one-act play about death. A girl from the town dies after an abortion arranged by a Princeton baseball hero. Jack kills himself out of guilt over the abortion and its consequences. On P-Rade day, in the midst of family and school celebration, he is confronted by his girl's tubercular brother, who tells him his sister has died. Face to face with his class assumptions, Jack suddenly sees himself as the brother and the girl have seen him; overwhelmed at the recognition, he shoots himself. So outlined, the play shows a potential that goes unrealized. *Children of the Sea* works because Eugene lets himself feel from moment to moment what Driscoll and Yank are feeling. But he cannot get close enough to Jack's feelings to find out what they mean. Whatever Eugene has learned from his brush with death, whatever he may know about his guilt concerning Kathleen Jenkins and his abandoned son, he allows nothing of it to develop in *Abortion*.

Earlier in the spring, on a visit to New York, Eugene had met the radical journalist John Reed, who would become a close friend in 1916 and later. The two men hit it off almost immediately; Reed was living nearly as wild a life as O'Neill had lived. Jack Reed was about to return to Mexico, where he had been witnessing and writing about Pancho Villa's revolution, and he apparently talked Eugene into going with him. According to the Gelbs, Jack persuaded his magazine, the *Metropolitan*, to advance an extra three hundred dollars for Eugene's expenses (Gelbs, 262–63). Apparently, Eugene did not go; at any rate, the Rippins and others remember no long absence that spring, and much of his time can be accounted for by tracing the dates of his writings and other known events.

Instead of joining Jack Reed, he imagined the Mexican revolution. From his conversations with Jack he devised a farcical play, *The Movie Man*, about the manipulation of the revolution to suit the needs of some movie makers who are trying to film it. Broadway wise guys both, the movie men bribe General Pancho Gomez to fight a crucial battle in daylight, when it can be photographed, rather than at night, when it would make sense to launch a guerrilla action; the movie man's right to dictate military strategy is covered in a contract. Gomez needs money for ammunition even more than he needs a victory, and he agrees. The movie man also buys the favors of a girl whose father is in danger, and at the end looks forward to collecting from her. Anyone who has felt the magic of *Hughie* (1941) can perhaps look with a little indulgence on the wise guys in *The Movie Man* as early explorations of street characters.

Eugene finished *The Movie Man* in late June. July was a busy month for him; he was making plans that would take him away from New London for the next year. On July 16, Eugene wrote to George Pierce Baker about taking the play-writing course at Harvard that Clayton Hamilton had mentioned. Without waiting for Baker's reply, Eugene went sailing with friends on a trip that lasted nearly a week and took him to New Haven, then to Block Island, and finally back to New London. When he got home, he found a letter from Harvard. Baker asked to see his work, and on July 29 Eugene sent two plays he said he had just completed, one of which was *Children of the Sea*.

We know about the sailing trip because of several long letters to Bee

Ashe, written on the boat and in hotels, describing his doings. The letters show that matters between Eugene and Bee had developed to the point where he was experiencing moments of acute loneliness in her absence, even though he was surrounded by merrymaking. Still, he had not forgotten several other New London girls, including Maibelle. In mid-August, when his book *Thirst and Other One Act Plays* came out, he gave her a copy inscribed "To Scotty," with an affectionate poem, and signed with his name as it appeared on the title page, Eugene G. O'Neill. The book was a parting gift. Maibelle had decided to marry her Coast Guard cadet and asked Eugene to return her letters, which he did. She told the Gelbs that she, in turn, burned more than two hundred of his letters, saving only the poems (Gelbs, 266).

In August, Judge Latimer celebrated the publication of the book of plays with a puff for *Thirst* in the *Telegraph,* together with a summary of its contents. The notice mentioned that two of the plays, *The Web* and *Recklessness,* would be performed by the actor Holbrook Blinn (LS, 290). No performance took place. James O'Neill, in New York, deplored his son's pessimism but nevertheless persuaded several theater colleagues to talk to Eugene about the plays. Late in August, Judge Latimer happily recorded the news that Harvard had accepted Eugene. James was more anxious than ever about money now that his career was winding down, but his relations with Eugene were still passable. Pleased that one of his sons was finding himself, James agreed to pay tuition and living expenses in Cambridge. He was preparing for what would be his last road tour, on which he was playing two short patriarchal roles in *Joseph and His Brethren.*

In August and September Eugene and Beatrice became increasingly close. They spent long afternoons or evenings on walks, swimming, rowing, or cruising on the sound in Eugene's boat. Eugene found a secluded beach on the Hammond estate where, after dodging security guards, he found privacy and did not have to share Bee with her other admirers. On the beach, on their walks, and in the boat he tried, as he had with other young women, to interest her in the authors he admired, reading to her from Strindberg, Ibsen, Wilde, and Nietzsche. He may have had less success with Bee than with some others; she told Sheaffer that she remembered none of Eugene's books except Wilde's *Salome,* and that for the Aubrey Beardsley drawings. Eugene's letters to her are less full of literary talk than one might expect, but he does frequently discuss his own writing. He was working in August on a three-act play, *Servitude,* and said he expected that one of his long plays, either *Servitude* or *Bread and Butter,* would soon be produced in New York.

Almost as soon as he finished *Servitude,* he went to New York, where his father had arranged several meetings, including one with George Tyler, who was now a producer. Times could not have been worse for a young man of anti-establishment tendencies to try to make a name on Broadway. America had suffered a series of economic crises since the onset of the European war that affected the commercial theater, as they did most peacetime industries. Liebler and Company, James's producers, with whom Tyler worked, was only months from bankruptcy. Out of kindness, Tyler encouraged Eugene to leave his plays, but no one read either one. Around Christmastime, when the agency declared bankruptcy, Eugene got his plays back with the original wrapping undisturbed. So much for connections, as Eugene told a young writer, much later.

On August 27 he went to Cambridge, where he stayed in the Brewster Hotel for a couple of days, registered at Harvard, and looked for a furnished room. He found a room in a suite rented by Mennonite students. Bartley Ebel, a professor at a Mennonite institution in Hillsboro, Kansas, was studying Greek at Harvard and had brought his family to Cambridge with him. He lived with his wife, Katherine, and two sons, in a ground-floor suite at 1105 Massachusetts Avenue. To help support his studies, he preached in a Baptist church. In the other ground-floor suite in the house lived Bartley's brother August, who was studying art, and Katherine's brother Daniel Hiebert, a medical student at Boston University. Eugene paid thirty dollars a month for meals and a pleasant corner room in the suite with August and Dan. Katherine took care of her sons, kept house, and cooked. For his keep, Eugene bowed his head in prayer. James sent ten dollars a week. After the thirty-dollar bill for room and board was paid, a little was left for books and dissipation.

The Ebels told Sheaffer that Eugene was often absent on weekends—his classes met on Wednesdays and Thursdays—and they took it for granted that he was carousing. In fact, in September and October, Eugene took the train to New London three or more weekends to visit Bee, and on several other weekends wrote her long letters complaining about Sunday blues. Throughout his life, Eugene did most of his reading and writing while lying on his bed. The Ebels assumed that he was lazy and doing little studying. In fact, he worked very hard that year, among other things spending an hour a day each to improve his French and to begin learning German in order to read a little of playwrights whose work was not being translated. He worked hard enough on his German that during the winter he boasted of reading *Also sprach Zarathustra* with the help of a dictionary (LS, 303–4).

Various of O'Neill's fellow students in Baker's class told the Gelbs, Sheaffer, and other biographers tales of Eugene's decadence during those months in Cambridge. (Sheaffer's notes express skepticism about some of these accounts.) Eugene's letters to Bee give a diary-like record of his daily activities. Between language study, his voracious reading of modern, Greek, and Elizabethan plays, a series of lingering colds and episodes of tonsillitis that put him into the infirmary, swimming in the YMCA pool when he was healthy, long hours drafting and revising scenarios and plays, composing poems to Beatrice, writing meditative prose poems, which often found their way into letters, and drafting, revising, and then recopying the letters themselves, which are often long, he would seem to have been too busy for much dissipation. Because we know that Eugene tended to keep drinking for several days once he started and that few days are unaccounted for, it seems unlikely that he drank much that year. It is possible that he lies in his letters to Bee, but over his lifetime, Eugene's lies are usually those of omission. His letters reassure her several times of his continuing temperance and fidelity.

Even before he settled in with the Ebels, Eugene had made plans to return to New London to visit Bee, and on the first Friday, he returned, persuading her to meet him at the train station. The following Tuesday he wrote that all he could think of was being together the night before, which left him feeling "abysmal aloneness." Without further warning, the next paragraph plunges into the state of Eugene's psyche in his current circumstance, in love and separated from his beloved. "Life has become for me a phantom show in which there are but two realities—you and my love for you. All else is misty shadow of illusion, vain fretting most valueless. I exist as I am reflected in you. I can only endure myself when I see my image in your eyes—in their gray pool does this Narcissus see himself, and admire, and feel so proud to be there" (SL, 28–29).

This prose poem seems to say that he doesn't know he exists, except as he sees himself reflected in her eyes. Agnes Boulton wrote that O'Neill repeatedly stared at himself in mirrors; to someone who once asked about it, O'Neill said he was looking to make sure he was alive. The anecdote catches a basic paradox of narcissism, that Narcissus treats his body as if it were a beloved other person and he cannot love—indeed, may hate to the point of loathing—his own self.

Eugene seemingly records in this letter an adult recapitulation of an infantile experience assumed to be universal, in which an infant sees itself reflected in its mother's loving gaze. Making no distinction between mother and self, it learns to love itself. If something interferes with the mother-infant bond, the infant cannot fully develop the self-love that precedes and makes possible love of another. Now, as an adult, Eugene tries to recapitulate an early developmental process that has turned out badly and so pass beyond the childhood need that still drives him.

In the poems to Beatrice, Eugene often writes of her breasts in ways that suggest a suckling infant, and he sometimes quotes fragments of the poems in his letters. On October 7, he closed a letter by musing: "And oh, that time, that golden time-to-be, when dream and desire come true, when my glad, mad heart shall beat against your own, when 'My lips sleep on your bare soft breast, / The beating of your heart their lullaby'" (SL, 29–30). It is less a fantasy of adult sexual possession than of the satisfaction that permits an infant to sleep after nursing.

In an imitation of Whitman called "Upon Our Beach," he catalogues his memories of being with Bee, and of her beauties: "Your limbs are beautiful, your breasts are beautiful—my lips yearn for them" (*Poems,* 52). In a poem called "A Dream of Last Night," one stanza reads:

> I remember your breast,
> And a purple stain
> Where my lips had rest.—
> Your Beloved Best!—
> I remember your breast.
> I torture my brain.
>
> (*Poems,* 63)

In "Lament for Beatrice," he writes:

> To hear within your swelling breast
> Your heart beat underneath my head;
> To lie within your arms and rest
> With sleepy kisses on your breast.
>
> (*Poems,* 64)

Time after time, in many poems and letters, Eugene associates his lady's breasts with sleep and rest. Creating the images perhaps allows Eugene to feel that he can undo the interference, caused directly and indirectly by morphine, in his original attempts to nurse at his mother's breast.

One short poem, "Triolet of my Flower," consists entirely in two variations on the image:

> Sleep on her breast
> Rose of my heart!
> Flower so blest,
> Sleep on her breast;
> I crave thy rest,
> Alone, apart!
> Sleep on her breast,
> Rose of my heart.
>
> (*Poems,* 70)

Still another poem called "Just Me N' You" [*sic*] is subtitled "(From a child to a child)."

Psychoanalysis posits stages of human development along various lines. The line known as psychosexual development calls the beginning phase of life the oral stage, so-called because the mouth is the main source of pleasure and the center of experience (Rycroft 1968, 108). It appears certain that Ella O'Neill's addiction to morphine, beginning in the first days of Eugene's life, must have led to recurrent experiences of oral frustration greater than an infant can ordinarily tolerate. Morphine passed on to Eugene through Ella's milk would have been toxic to him in various ways, affecting especially his digestion, and would also have contributed to lowering his tolerance for frustration. When frustrations accumulate in infancy they can affect all aspects of future development. At the very least, such a beginning would probably lead to a person's being intensely vulnerable to separation anxiety, a condition very apparent in Eugene's unchanging, five-year-long resentment at being sent to boarding school when he was seven. While at Harvard in 1914, he feels in the keenest way every separation from Bee, especially when they are newly parted after each of his frequent visits to her in New London.

Separation from Bee brings back the early need with seemingly primal intensity. Eugene cannot prevent himself from spending most of his time alone obsessively evoking for himself thoughts of what he feels he has lost. Writing to her of his obsession seems partly intended to persuade himself that the loss can be undone or the feelings at least mastered. On October 8, he wrote, in part:

> I have done little but dream, pondering over the harshness of a fate which condemns us to languish apart from each other. Life, so I deem, is a bitter concoction at best but our cup seems to be unnecessarily dosed with wormwood. Things might be worse, of course,—I might lose a leg or something—but when I am not with you my optimism sort of bogs down and I see existence "as through a glass, darkly." It seems such a sorry shame that our dreams cannot be grasped and turned into realities, that we should ever be rainbow chasing after "Tomorrows" while the sun-kissed hours of Youth die swiftly one by one, never to be lived over though the heavens crack with our clamorous supplications.
>
> I have gone over all the days of our summer together, all our wonderful hours, and I am sad this evening; sad with the knowledge that all of it is "put behind me, long ago and far away." I am sad with the oppression of fall, time of dead leaves and withered things. There is a feeling in the air of inevitable loss: of the death of warm days and caressing sunlight, of the passing of hot sand and wave-swept beaches. I want to live it all over again, every hour of it with you, and I know this is impossible. The meaninglessness of the windings of this great river of chance and change goads me into wailings of fretful impotence. I would like to "pull the pillars of my life upon me" were it not for the great certainty which rises beautiful out of the chaos and ruin—Our Love.
>
> What a chance it offers for me to throw off my load of bitterness and take up life again as one who is reborn into a fairer greener world. To live in you, for you, by you—it is an immortality springing from the grave of my dead life. You are my happiness; I know it. I feel you calling to something in me which has never been touched before, something finer, way down in the depths of being, perhaps a soul. All of the sordid values the world has rubbed into me lose their cruel validity before your love. When I look into your eyes I

1. Ella O'Neill about the time of her marriage. Museum of the City of New York.

James O'Neill about the time of his marriage in 1877. Sheaffer-O'Neill Collection, Charles E. Shain Library, Connecticut College.

3. James O'Neill, Jr., aged about six, in costume. Billy Rose Theatre Collection, the New York Public Library for the Performing Arts Astor, Lenox and Tilden Foundations.

4. Eugene in infancy. Eugene O'Neill Collection, Collection of American Literature, Beinecke Rare Book and Manuscript Library, Yale University.

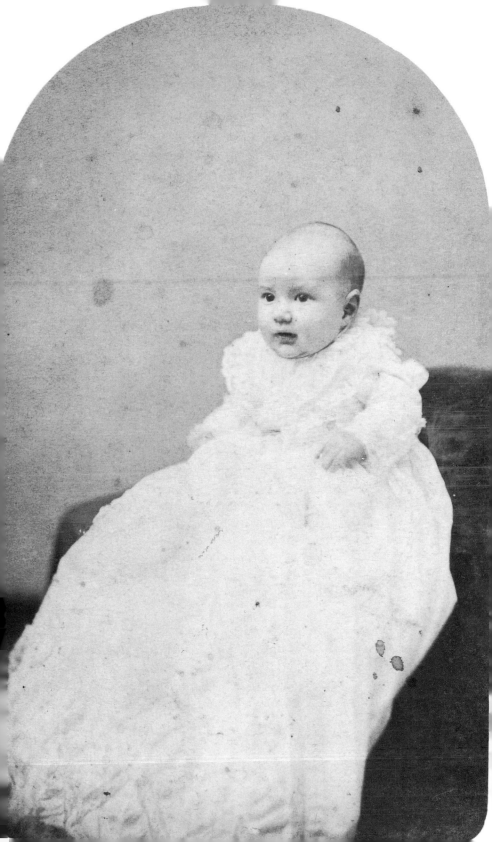

5. Eugene with a puppy. Eugene O'Neill Collection, Collection of American Literature, Beinecke Rare Book and Manuscript Library, Yale University.

6. Eugene at St. Aloysius, perhaps at the time of his first Communion. Sheaffer-O'Neill Collection, Charles E. Shain Library, Connecticut College.

7. Eugene reading, Jamie biding his time, James waiting it out—on the porch at Monte Cristo Cottage. Eugene O'Neill Collection, Collection of American Literature, Beinecke Rare Book and Manuscript Library, Yale University.

8. Able-Bodied Seaman O'Neill in 1911. He kept the certificate and the American Line sweater all his life. Eugene O'Neill Collection, Collection of American Literature, Beinecke Rare Book and Manuscript Library, Yale University.

9. Eugene O'Neill, Jr., and his mother, Kathleen Jenkins O'Neill, in 1911. Sheaffer-O'Neill Collection, Charles E. Shain Library, Connecticut College.

10. At Harvard, apart from his beloved, Eugene sent Bee this phot probably taken by one of his roommates, an art student. Sheaff O'Neill Collection, Charles E. Sha Library, Connecticut College.

11. James O'Neill, about 1915. The Hampden-Booth Theatre Library at The Players.

12. Agnes Boulton, photographed by Nikolas Muray about 1920. Courtesy
Nikolas Muray Photo Archive.

13. Aggie and Gene, photographed by Edward Steichen in the early 1920s.
Reprinted with permission of Joanna T. Steichen (courtesy Carousel Research).

14. O'Neill in Provincetown. This photo by Nikolas Muray was printed in 1923 and again in March 1999 by *Vanity Fair*. Courtesy Nikolas Muray Photo Archive.

15. The playwright in the role of Poseidon at Peaked Hill Bars. Sheaffer-O'Neill Collection, Charles E. Shain Library, Connecticut College.

16. The playwright in a moment of illumination. Eugene O'Neill Collection, Collection of American Literature, Beinecke Rare Book and Manuscript Library, Yale University.

17. Hands all around. Sheaffer-O'Neill Collection, Charles E. Shain Library,
Connecticut College.

18. Mrs. Clark adored Shane, whom she cared for from birth. Her death in 1929, just after Agnes had gone to Reno, greatly affected Shane. Sheaffer-O'Neill Collection, Charles E. Shain Library, Connecticut College.

19. In the lee of a dune—Shane and Agnes. Sheaffer-O'Neill Collection,
Charles E. Shain Library, Connecticut College.

feel a sense of deep shame; I want to cry out and ask your forgiveness for being what I have been, to crave your indulgence for the grimy smears on my life, to pray your pity for the tattered wings of my spirit stained with the muck of the long road. I long for some clear well of the spirit wherein I could cleanse and purify my rag of life. I would like to stand beside you with some faint hope that I was not so utterly unworthy.

Alas, I need you so much! It is you alone who can give me back the Joy of Living, who can justify my existence to myself. To make you happy, to fill your life with tender care, to call you to my aid where the ways are rough, not to shelter you—you are no Doll Girl nor shall our house be a Doll's House—but to give you a part in all my life and make my life worthy for you to take part in. All this is my ambition, my Highest Hope which must be kept holy.

And to be foiled in this great purpose by bread and butter, to be held at bay by a theory of Economics—ah, the irony of it! Alas, I need you so much! I am weary of the hopelessness of the past and I turn to My Beatrice beseechingly for—

"There is no resting place for tired head / Like her soft breasts, there is no love like hers."

Good night. I love you! [SL, 30–31]

The last line of the letter tries to undo the separation by pretending that he can speak to her and she can hear. Throughout, he tries to use rhetoric to control and give form to the sense of loss and need; he feels driven to cling to his regained idealism, which he believes protects him from the old bitterness that ruled his life for a decade, and which threatens to possess him again.

In letter after letter to Bee, thrusting his trust on her as an analysand does with the analyst, Eugene speaks of his most intimate fears and desires. He tries to make her play the consistently nurturing and adoring mother that his own mother could not be. In some way he believes that believing in love can help him remake his life; that he can learn to love himself by identifying with Bee's love for him.

The return to life is O'Neill's constant theme in the letters of the next several months. "Out of the chaos and ruin" of his past life rises "our love." He feels himself reborn. In the letter just quoted, Eugene writes: "What a chance it offers for me to throw off my load of bitterness and take up life again as one who is reborn into a fairer greener world. To live in you, for you, by you—it is an immortality springing from the grave of my dead life." His desire for rebirth seems oriented less toward the idea of Christian salvation than toward Bee as the specific person Eugene needs her to be: one who will allow him to nurse at her beast, to be as infantile as he needs for as long as he needs, and who will not resent his demands. He wants literally to live in her—in her arms, at her breast, in her womb: "To live in you, for you, by you," that is his chance of rebirth.

Believing that he can be reborn makes all that he did in his years of wandering seem disgusting. "When I look into your eyes I feel a sense of deep shame; I want to cry out and ask your forgiveness for being what I have been." Yet he cannot deny or forget the past; it must be justified to the present. That is what being with her means to him. "It is you alone who can give me back the Joy of Living, who can justify my existence to myself." The goal that now justifies existence is to "make my life worthy for you to take part in," if she will marry him (SL, 30). Almost from the beginning Eugene has spoken of marriage and called her "My Own Wife," "Own Little Wife," "Bee O'Neill," and other such love-names. Marriage is the ideal around which he builds his "reformation"; marriage is the ideal that will help him keep the unspecified "promise" to her, evidently a promise to avoid binges, and the dissoluteness that went with them. Marriage implies the constancy and lifelong commitment he needs someone to make to him that will bring the lifelong love he requires as a foundation on which to rebuild himself.

In these letters and later ones, Eugene explores an ideal that was as unfashionable in 1914 as it is now, an ideal that he made the subject of the three-act play *Servitude,* written in August and September while he was falling in love with Bee. The play idealizes service as espoused by medieval knights and troubadours. It entails giving oneself—one's body, soul, and life itself—to serve one's lord in war and one's lady in love, and finding in service the deepest happiness. The ideal is complementary to the Nietzschean idea of the superman, and Eugene may have learned of it from Nietzsche's remarks about *Tristan und Isolde.* To present it in another context, growth through service is analogous to the psychoanalytic idea that one grows to autonomy through identification with a parent whom one imagines to be omnipotent.

In *Servitude* David Roylston, a playwright-novelist who seems modeled on Shaw or Ibsen, attracts disciples with his liberated views of female independence. Mrs. Frazer, a Fabian in all but name, arrives on the master's doorstep late one night. She says she wants to thank him for liberating her from the ideal of serving her husband that she had been bred and trained for. Reading Roylston's books has led her to study her husband's business life; she has found him venal and unworthy of her goal of service and has left him. She has renounced his and her father's wealth and begun a new life working at different jobs, each of which has failed to "justify" her need for an ideal in which to lose herself. She demands of Roylston: "Restore my peace of mind by justifying me to myself" (CP1, 249).

The conversation of Mrs. Frazer and David Roylston becomes decidedly flirtatious. She discovers that she has missed the last train back to the city, and he insists she must stay in the guest room. But your wife? She will never know; she is in the city with the children. He starts to ask; she asks him to stop, then reveals that she knew she had taken the last train. It is a test of him. Which he passes. By showing his attraction to her and yet restraining himself, he has proved himself a "real man." Real men are "the greatest sinners," he says. "But they protect the helpless," she smiles, and goes to bed. "Damnation!" he says, putting on his hat and coat, and leaves the house to go to a hotel (CP1, 254–55).

Act 1 is amusing, and the dialogue is fairly crisp; act 2 wanders when Mrs. Frazer meets Mrs. Roylston, a character beyond the young Eugene's capabilities as a playwright. He wants to create a woman strong enough to show a convincing alternative to Shaw's or Ibsen's Fabian ideals. A quarter-century later O'Neill would finally succeed, with Nora Melody in *A Touch of the Poet,* a woman who convinces the audience that she finds a deep, quasi-religious happiness in serving a man, who is usually shallow and undeserving. Nora is a great dramatic part, as Geraldine Fitzgerald and Vanessa Redgrave have proved.

In 1914 Eugene is so little able to create such a character that all he can do is have Roylston and Mrs. Frazer describe her. In act 3 Mrs. Frazer forces Roylston to recognize how remarkable a person his wife is and to confront his narcissism: "Mr. Narcissus," Mrs. Frazer says, "I would only be your reflection" (CP1, 275). When he can finally see his wife and realizes that he was about to desert her, he despises himself and vows to free his wife from his own egotism.

The idea of happiness in servitude had deep roots for O'Neill, and it came up repeatedly when he tried to write about love and marriage. In 1914 he was discovering, though, that servitude to his art might lead to the deepest happiness he had yet known; giving everything to learning to write might free him from his chronic attacks of self-loathing. At the same time, he was trying to make real in life an idealized love in which each lover offered absolute servitude to the other.

The affair with Bee refused to conform to his medieval ideals for it. On Saturday, October 10, Eugene complained that he lacked train fare to New London and so had to spend a dreary weekend in Cambridge, but he vowed to come the weekend of his birthday. On Sunday he wrote of feeling "desolate today—always do on the without youless Sabbath" (*sic*) and begged Bee to meet his train the following Friday (SL, 32). After their weekend together, the weekend of his twenty-sixth birthday, Eugene plunged into the deepest suffering.

He felt that life extracted a "damned unfair payment" from him in return for the ecstasy of being with her. Evidently, while he was in New London, she fixed a meal for him ("You and I play at husband and wife"), but he had no appetite and was getting a bad cold. While they were together, he miserably anticipated their coming separation. The more intense his love became, the more he thought about it in all-or-nothing terms. In the same letter of October 19, he told Bee that while with her he could not bear to imagine being without her and he got sick and sullen when he thought about going back to Cambridge on Monday. Once he was back there, all he could think and write about was his misery, even though he knew that such letters upset her. Medieval troubadours lamented the suffering that accompanied exaltation in the madness men call love and the loss thereof. As Eugene reveled and suffered in his case of it, he sounded sometimes like Hamlet and sometimes, with his winds and waters, like Cleopatra (Berg, EO to BA [October 19, 1914]).

Being in love brings out the worst in Eugene as well as the best. It makes him childlike and sometimes passive-aggressive, and it affects his resistance to minor illnesses. That is only part of the story, but it is a significant part. He can't sleep, he complains, because of the medicine he has taken for his cold. He seems to blame her for his being ill because she is the object of the adoration that ails him. In the letter of October 19 he writes: "I was sorely tempted to seek a little oblivion from the flowing bowl last night—but I didn't. Dear One, please, believe in the sincerity of my resolve to try, and become worthy of you! You do, Sweetheart, don't you? I need you so much!" (Berg, EO to BA [October 19, 1914]). Here Eugene virtually threatens Bee because of some implicit failure he attributes to her. In the context of the letter it must be that she is not present when he needs her.

Perhaps Bee has frustrated him by resisting his seductions; or perhaps something else between them accounts for some of the aggression in this letter. But there is almost certainly an element of transference; that is, Eugene assails Bee as if she were someone else, presumably his mother. At the same time he implores (like a normal five-year-old or adolescent) that she ignore his tantrum and love him constantly and unconditionally. From Bee's standpoint, demands like this must have been trying, although she seems to have adjusted to them somewhat, and as the months go on, she becomes a little more tolerant of Eugene's moods and whims. From Eugene's standpoint, he is driven by everything within that needs to grow; he needs to repair the failures of earlier efforts to grow. Just as he makes his writing serve development, so he seeks to grow through his love affairs and marriages—and, indeed, most other aspects of his life. O'Neill's relationship with Bee resembles that of a person in psychoanalysis with the analyst. As the months of letter writing go on, Eugene becomes increasingly aware of the effect his irrationalities have on her and is often able to be considerate. But he demands exceptional tolerance.

Beatrice apparently reacts strongly to the letter of October 19 and complains that he imposes himself by writing too often and too urgently; such can be inferred from his next surviving letter (postmarked October 22), which mentions a one-letter-a-week limit Eugene has imposed on himself—which he is breaking. Presumably, he has meant to prevent himself getting so lost in his longing and regression. He goes to New London the next weekend and lasts only one day back in Cambridge before writing again. The letters suggest that writing her has a compulsive urgency for him.

He writes again on October 29 in a mood of "Stygian gloom." He apologizes; "I hate to wail life's discord into your ears and make you a sacrifice to my moods; but I have to tell someone how I feel, and I depend on your love, dear, to forgive me my childishness." He feels so out of harmony with himself that he can't write creatively: "My brain is fallow and barren" (Berg, EO to BA [October 29, 1914]). On October 31 he reports that his muse has returned, but he now has a bad cold and sore throat.

On Sunday, always a bad day for him, he writes a long letter that begins with an account of Strindberg's *Married.* These stories, he says, show that the curse of young lovers and youthful marriage is lack of money, an idea he thinks profound. He works himself into a state worthy of Young Werther, full of bittersweet memories of past happiness with her, until finally "tears, real tears" have risen in his eyes. He now blames himself entirely for their quarrel and swears there will never be "another day or night spoilt by me." In a postscript he adds a self-criticism: "This is more of a *real* letter than I've written in some time. It's written with my blood" (SL, 35). Along with the melodramatics and vanity, the comment shows a grain of self-scrutiny that alleviates the self-indulgence a little. He hopes to come to visit her soon. This she evidently forbids, insisting that he remain in Cambridge until Thanksgiving.

In Baker's class, Eugene immediately found himself studying the professor's "fascinating personality," he told Bee (SL, 28). Student and teacher had little in common, but Baker turned brilliant sarcasm against certain literary sentimentalities that Eugene despised. Baker was interested in Ibsen and other European playwrights and was more open to the modern than Eugene had expected. Impatient with the clichés of New York theater fare, Baker aimed for reform by teaching principles of sound playwriting to young writers through various exercises. A competent critic, Baker could explain very precisely how Yeats or Synge used the speech rhythms of the Irish counties to create a character. Baker taught a certain kind of discipline in writing. He insisted that students sketch out a detailed scenario before they began writing dialogue, and Eugene learned to use the writing of the scenario as a trial run for the creative process itself. It was a practice he usually followed from then on.

Baker's first assignment was to adapt a magazine story into a one-act play or skit suitable for a vaudeville bill. Having been handed a story, the student had to write a scenario, which was read and criticized, and then, when the scenario was approved, to write the play. Eugene's effort was called "The Dear Doctor" (or "Dear Doctor"—the text has not survived), and it was praised by Baker in class and admired by the other students as amusing. Baker encouraged Eugene to explore selling it to a vaudeville circuit, but on checking, Eugene learned that the story Baker had picked had itself been adapted from a vaudeville skit.

Between writing and typing "The Dear Doctor" Eugene wrote an original one-act play, *The Sniper*, probably the best thing he did that year, and one of his two works written for Baker's class that survive. Set in the Belgian countryside, it presents Rougon, a peasant whose wife, son, and son's fiancée have been killed by German soldiers. The father can accept the death of his son who was a soldier; but the other losses madden him, and he, a noncombatant, begins shooting at the soldiers in the fields around his house. A civilized, educated German officer is required by the rules of war to execute Rougon. A priest looks on, but the grieving father rejects the comfort of religion. The audience is asked to sympathize with both the priest and the officer, both shown as decent men, and to see how weak they and the institutions they represent are in the face of the force of nature that Rougon and his grief represent. The play reaches for more than it achieves, but it lingers in a reader's memory. Baker admired it and said so in class. But later in the year, when it was proposed for performance by the Harvard Dramatic Society, he vetoed it, on the grounds that a war play would be "injudicious" in the midst of national debate over whether America should enter the war.

Eugene developed friendly relations with Baker and a few of his fellow students who tried to get to know him. One was William Lawrence, future science editor of the *New York Times*, a Latvian Jew and a fellow Nietzschean, who told the Gelbs that he got Eugene started reading Andreyev, Gorky, and Chekhov and also persuaded him to reread the Greek dramatists (Gelbs, 277). Two other friends, whom he saw occasionally in later life, were wealthy and generous students, Colin Ford from Cincinnati and Felton Elkins from San Francisco, both married. They entertained him in their homes in Boston and at expensive restaurants. Sheaffer turned up testimony that Eugene supplemented his allowance by revising the work of fellow students before it was submitted. One such projects, the script of which is lost, was a poetic epic in seven acts called "Belshazzar," a collaborative effort apparently proposed by Colin Ford but written mostly by Eugene. Eugene told Bee he hoped that it might be produced in New York with Ford as backer, but it was not (LS, 302).

Hard work made Eugene less vulnerable to the "blue devils" that plagued him when he thought about Bee. Bee apparently wrote more frequently and ardently, and she sent Eugene keepsakes from time to time—bits of underwear, an imprint of her lip rouge—and on the whole his letters in November seemed less despondent and showed much more confidence that his love was returned. He wrote extensively about working on his plays—he had now begun a scenario for a long play about abortion. On November 7 he ardently defended his love for her, physical as well as spiritual, and paraphrased Nietzsche in support of it (SL, 23). He had been rereading *Zarathustra* in November and felt spurred to work harder on his German. He delighted in reporting his sexual dreams of her, sparing her most of the details, at least in the letters. In letters he often spoke of being a slave to her, of serving her, of kissing his fetters. "I never knew true Liberty until I wore them," he wrote on November 12 (Berg).

Both Bee and Eugene dated other people while apart, and they described their dates in detail to make each other jealous and thereby provoke a sign of the other's attachment. Eugene noticed his own "childishness" but showed an increasing ability to tolerate seeing it. He recognized that it seemed to be part of being in love—and of being creative. The letters often reveal an impressive power to think about what he was doing and feeling and saying while he was acting, surely an essential quality for a writer. During Thanksgiving break in New London Eugene and Bee evidently argued about sex. She had decided, she wrote, that he was "'the Original Quick Lunch Kid'" a phrase he quoted back to her in his letter of December 7 (Berg, EO to BA, Monday [December 7, 1914]). Not so, he protested; he was a "great barren-of-restraint-person." She thought him a quick-lunch-kid only because of her "super-cool collectedness." "However," he went on, "I detect that same unsatisfied message in your flushed face and the languorous expression in your eyes. Next time I promise to be most calculating" (Berg, EO to BA, Monday [December 7, 1914]). His letter of December 9 was almost entirely devoted to sexual entreaty. He counted the days until he would be home for Christmas. This time no quarrel would mar the beginning of a holiday.

In his December 12 letter he showed an important aspect of his fantasy about marriage and his idealized future life: "Will'st play Little Wife in earnest this time? Will'st become my banker—for the good of my soul? Will'st let me place all my shining sequins and sesterces and rubles in your hands and then deal them out to me grudgingly, questioningly, as becometh a true wife? Honest, it sure would be a relief to me if you would. Where money is concerned I am totally irresponsible, it burns holes in my pockets, I am absolutely uneasy until it is gone. So become my banker, do! Don't shirk your just duties! Or I will be destitute before half the vacation is over—and nothing to be hoped for" (SL, 43).

It was a striking request. For years, Eugene and his father had fought over his fiscal irresponsibility. James had made dependency as unpleasant for his sons as he possibly could, and Jamie and Eugene were accustomed to turn to Ella, who usually gave them what they wanted. The letter implied that Eugene wanted Bee to become a combination of father and mother: she would have the money and question him about how he wanted to spend it, but she would be nicer about it than Papa. In refusing to take control of and responsibility for his money and insisting that doing so would be his wife's role, Eugene seemed to ask to continue the state of dependency that had been so irksome most of his life. Among other things, the description of feeling "absolutely uneasy" when he had money referred to the anxiety that arose at the threat he unconsciously sensed of losing his father, the person who in good times and bad had been his rock and safe harbor. Remaining irresponsible seemed to pacify Eugene's unconscious dread of loss. In fact, he would be about forty before he began to take effective control over his money.

Giving control of his money to Bee seemed evidence of a triumph over the "Gene O'Neill of the past," who would have drunk away all his allowance within days. "I am born again—your very own child" (SL, 44). The theme of being reborn and the Christian-sounding talk of a reformation apparently referred to a lapse over the Christmas holidays. Emily Rippin told the Gelbs that Eugene and a girl she didn't know had come into a jewelry store where she worked over Christmas, and that he was drunk (Gelbs, 279); Emily said that it was the first time she had seen him so. Eugene, in his subsequent letter, begged forgiveness. "Someone said, 'We are as God made us, God help us.'" Usually, O'Neill pointedly referred to the idea of deity in the plural, but here he made concessions to Bee's Christian beliefs. The long letter of January 6 contains an analysis of what Eugene calls his "depression":

> I open my eyes and see nothing but this dreary room, and a horrible despair grips my soul.

Sweetheart, I love you so, I want you so, I need you so!!!

Beneath all this depression is a feeling of pride, pride in myself, in you, in Us, for my triumph of yesterday afternoon (or rather *your* triumph). Now indeed do you possess all my soul. You have routed the Gene O'Neill of the past. I am born again—your very own child. Your influence in my life has ever been of the sweetest and finest. You have inspired my manhood with a great desire to be clean, and faithful to your trust in me. Your clear girlhood or womanhood has put my unwholesome cynicism to shame, has called out all the best that is in me. When I think of all the wonder which is you a sense of my own unworthiness saddens me—*but I do love you so!* At least my love is worthy. No one could love you more.

Be assured that, although you are far away, your influence is with me always. I will do nothing that I cannot look in your eyes and tell you about, without sorrow to you or shame to myself. I will make my life as you would have it— for, after all, it is *your* life.

Do you, for your part, remember my many weaknesses. I am far from strong, and if I should do this thing or that, say this thing or that which hurts you, tell me about it, and I will try to never do or say it again. Thus will my sins become fewer and fewer against you and finally, please the Gods, they will vanish completely. Whatever slips I may make, please attribute them to carelessness and not to intent, and out of the charity of your great little heart—pardon me for them. (When I say slips don't think I am referring to my promise. Nothing like that can occur. I mean minor slips in everyday matters.)

In all humbleness of spirit I lay my life at your feet—a poor gift but my best. In all gratitude of soul I thank you for your love which is making so much finer a man of me. Dear Little Wife! Sweet Woman of Mine! We shall, we must live our lives in happiness—together!

He ends by eschewing pessimism: "I am as you made me, God bless you" (SL, 44).

No summary of these letters suffices; only the language itself conveys the emotional urgency that drove Eugene in the first months of the affair.

After being with Beatrice at Christmas, the loneliness back in Cambridge was overpowering. He tried to find ease, as always, in writing: re-creating in words the oceanic engulfment he felt in loss, adoration, loss of self, finding himself anew, remembering happiness. "All our 'foolishness' comes back to me," he writes. "How delightful it is to be numbered among God's fools!" (SL, 45). In poems, prose meditations, and letter after letter he celebrates folly. After his friend Elkins's wife praised his Belgian play, he gloated to Bee: "You can imagine how I returned home all puffed out like a pouter-pigeon and did strut before the glass twirling my mustache with gusto and exclaiming with admiring satisfaction: 'Aha. Perhaps they were not kidding me. You may, with luck, escape hanging yet'" (SL, 49). And he enclosed more poems for her.

On January 29, he had a long evening chat with Baker, at the latter's Brattle Street home; good talk was accompanied by Baker's gold-tipped cigarettes. On Baker's encouragement Eugene told "with plainest frankness" some of the story of his "life and adventures on the Ragged Edge." The taciturn Eugene did most of the talking. "I held his interest all right for it is almost unprecedented for him to give up a whole evening to one student" (SL, 51).

For several weeks, Bee's letters came less frequently and seemed distant. The least change in her mood set all his antennae aquiver. Late in February all became clear. She had been seeing a former suitor, who had renewed his interest and forgave her infatuation with the ne'er-do-well younger O'Neill. He had asked her to marry him in May. She still loved Eugene, she wrote, and felt very confused and upset. Immediately Eugene replied that he had intuitively known what she concealed; it was well to make the matter clear. He told her she must choose. He made the strongest case he could for his own suit, he reiterated that he had long since rid himself of all old ties, and told her again how deeply he loved her. If she loved him, she could not love the other man; he, Eugene, loved her completely, with no reservations. She must write "whatever-his-name-is and tell him in such a way that he cannot doubt, that he is out of your life forever." Or, "If you love him and do not love me, why marry him in May, as he suggests." What the other offered her, Eugene said, amounted to no more than "a platter of bread & butter," alluding to his play of that name and the practical concerns that caused its artist-hero to marry the wrong woman. Rising to his full height (in his prose) Eugene told her that if she could allow this fellow's Canadian lodge and his castle in Liberia to distract her from anything as absolute as the love of Bee and Gene then "I urge you as my greatest revenge to marry him in May! I shall take great delight in watching life punish you for being untrue to your own soul. . . . If you, confessing that you love me, were to marry him, you would be in my eyes such a mean and pitiful caricature of my ideal of you, that only hate and disgust would remain of my love." He still loved her, he insisted, but pointedly hesitated to call her "my own" and ended the letter by insisting that she choose; he prayed she would choose him. Immediately after writing the letter, he begged or borrowed train fare and went to New London for a long weekend (SL, 57–59).

The most striking feature of the letter is the absence of the childlike qualities in which Eugene so often reveled. There was no pouting or sullen withdrawal, but instead a strong, reasoned, and unambiguous declaration of love and intent, and an arguing of his case. He wanted to marry her and did not have the least doubt about it. But he could not solve the main problem, his lack of money.

For ten days Bee did not reply, and he fell into the deepest gloom, which finally overflowed into an uncharacteristic and uncontrollable prolonged fit of weeping. The next day, March 2, he learned that she had proclaimed to several people, including the other suitor, that Eugene was her "husband-to-be." "Our Spring is at hand," he replied (SL, 60). For a month things between them were sunny. Then once again she began to have doubts. Matters went back and forth. No letters survive for the period between March 31 and May 12. During this time Bee was recovering from a case of rheumatic fever, and Eugene was working on his most ambitious play to date, *The Personal Equation*. Baker selected Eugene as one of four students to invite back for a second year—the others were all Radcliffe women. Eugene felt honored and accepted immediately. One more letter, written May 12, which seems to follow a visit to New London, thanked Bee for a sweet letter. He seemed happy and fully expecting to marry her.

School recessed and he went home to New London for the summer. Malcolm Morley, a young English actor who had been in the *Joseph* cast and then had joined Eugene in Baker's class, visited the O'Neills for several days. He was one of the very few houseguests received at Monte Cristo

Cottage since Eugene's birth, and his presence implied that Ella was free from morphine. He told Sheaffer that Ella was gracious but mostly silent during his visit. He remembered swimming with Eugene in the sound. A strong swimmer himself, he found himself greatly outdistanced by his host. Eugene "was a magnificent swimmer," he reported (LS, 316). On July 5 Eugene published a poem in "Conning Tower," a celebrated column of notable miscellany in the *New York Tribune* selected by Franklin P. Adams. The poem, slangy and sometimes funny, he called "Speaking, to the Shade of Dante, of Beatrices." Eugene was not yet Dante, but he thought he might open a conversation.

He and the other O'Neills lived at Monte Cristo Cottage and the family again took their meals with the Rippins. Beatrice had not fully recovered from her bout of rheumatic fever and spent most of the summer at home, resting. Eugene was apparently not allowed to visit her often or long, and he spent a good deal of time hanging around Clayton Hamilton's cottage. There he met a young woman, Nina Jones, who was spending the summer studying playwriting with Hamilton. When she developed "a romantic interest" in Eugene, he "did nothing to discourage it," Sheaffer reports, but exploited Nina's interest to make Bee jealous. At least once during the summer, Eugene's frustration with Bee erupted. She told Sheaffer that he threatened that "unless she loved him, unless she would marry him, he would return to his old life of hard drinking and other excesses" (LS, 323). He probably wrote her letters and poems, as he had done when forbidden to see Maibelle. Almost certainly, he expected things to work out in the long run.

Eugene seemed to be busy and happy. He was in a mood for comedy that summer. He flirted with Emily Rippin. When Emily announced her engagement, Eugene earnestly told her he wanted to be the father of her second child (Gelbs, 280). The outrageous joke must have left even the quick-witted Emily speechless. He wrote a one-act comedy, "A Knock on the Door," later destroyed, and scenarios for three more comedies.

As late as Tuesday, September 21, he expected to return to Harvard. He wrote to Dan Hiebert on that date for help in finding a room and said he would see him the following Monday about 2:15. Between Tuesday and Monday something happened. Eugene did not return to Harvard but instead went to New York and fell back into his old ways, staying drunk for days and weeks at a time, hanging out with Greenwich Village bohemians, living on a dollar-a-day allowance from his father, writing nothing, carrying on brief flings and occasional longer affairs with a series of women, several of whom he asked to marry him.

Years later he apologized to Baker for failing to return for his second year. He had wanted to, he wrote, but "didn't have the money and couldn't get it" (SL, 89). The Gelbs found it "inconceivable" that he could have thought he had the money on Tuesday, "only to have it withdrawn by his father" a few days later, but they saw no alternative explanation (Gelbs, 281). Margaret Loftus Ranald points out that James actually was having financial problems at the time, but she does not appear to consider the problem a sufficient explanation for the change of plan (private communication with the author, spring 1998). Sheaffer speculates that Eugene did or said something that so enraged his father that James cut him off (LS, 319).

A careful reading of the letters that Eugene wrote to Bee in 1914 and 1915 suggests that the change in plans in late September involved Beatrice. As the time drew near to be separated again, perhaps Eugene demanded that she marry him at once and come with him to Cambridge. She would have refused, saying once again that he had no money. The argument escalated. She revoked her proclamation that Eugene was her "husband-to-be." He left in a rage, got drunk, went home, and insulted his father or worse, insulted his mother, as he did from time to time, when drunk. Perhaps he made some cardinal insult that his father heard. It seems to have been easier for James to forgive insults to himself than those to Ella.

In 1918 Beatrice married a navy officer. She told Sheaffer that she had not married Eugene because "he was always talking about having his head on my breast. . . . I felt that he wanted someone to baby him, that he needed to belong to somebody. But I also felt that he would have wanted to possess me, that he wouldn't have let me belong to myself. When I met the man I later married, one of the first things he said was that he wanted to be the father of my children. Eugene would never have said anything like that" (LS, 308). She was almost certainly right in her judgment, and she apparently made the right decision for herself. Eugene would never find fatherhood easy, and his progress toward the sort of maturity Beatrice wanted in a husband came slowly.

Eugene's regressions undoubtedly troubled Beatrice. Eugene often wrote that he wanted to be her child, to put his head on her breast, to exalt in his dependency on her. He understood the changes going on in himself well enough to explain to her that the man he was also was the child he once had been and that his love for her was the love of the child as well as that of the man. Bee, neither naive nor a prude, enjoyed being numbered in the company of God's fools, running in the snow and catching snowflakes in her mouth. To some considerable extent she understood Eugene's point about his regressions, and she realized that with some effort he could draw out of them at will. She probably understood that adoring and idealizing her was an antidote for the distrust of women he had formerly cultivated, and that it marked his return to the civilized world. Eugene himself could not know that in the natural course of development he might pass beyond idealizing her, when idealization had served its developmental purpose, and might love her in more complex ways than he could understand at present. Neither could Beatrice, for that matter, yet fully understand such a thing, although she knew what she wanted when her future husband told her that he wanted to be the father of her children.

Still in all, in the year he lived with the Rippins and in the year he had been in love with Beatrice, Eugene made far more progress toward emotional emancipation than he had in the dozen previous years. During these two years he got control of his alcoholism, and that step allowed him to progress in many other ways. If he had not resumed the debilitating binges, it is likely that the rate of his progress might have continued. It seems that he was facing in his mid-twenties the adolescent developmental processes leading to emotional emancipation that had aborted when he learned of his mother's addiction in 1902. In his letters to Bee, he showed the emotional ups and downs one sees in a difficult adolescence.

That is what Bee objected to in his possessiveness, his need to belong to her, his longing to rest his head on her breast. At least partly, she understood, as we all do, that he had to re-experience childhood needs in order for them to become less urgent, and she was often patient with his ups and downs and his demands. The psychoanalyst James Hamilton (1979) has written persuasively of the oral possessiveness and rage that marked the letters Eugene wrote to Bee while he was at Harvard.

The psychoanalytic phrase *oral rage* refers to the all-or-nothing rage of an infant so overstimulated by hunger that the world seems about to end; and to the recurrence of such desperation in an older person who feels the presence of something that symbolizes the original threat. Oral rage is conspicuous in the patterns of O'Neill's drinking. It seems likely that more than any other single thing, it was the loss of Bee that plunged him back into heavy drinking.

IO

The Road to Provincetown
September 1915 – January 1918

NO MATTER WHAT THE DETAILS of the parting, the rejection by Bee must have been largely responsible for the return to destructive old ways Eugene had escaped after he had begun writing plays. Bee's rejection repeated for him both the loss of his mother when he discovered her addiction and the previous loss of her at his birth. He would undergo more losses in the next year and a half, and more love affairs as he sought to fill an inner emptiness he had known most of his life.

Almost as soon as he reached New York, he must have learned that his admired friend Driscoll, with whom he had shipped to Southampton and back, had died at sea, a suicide. A few weeks earlier, on August 12, Driscoll had gone over the railing of his ship, the SS *St. Louis*, and was dead by the time he could be hauled into a lifeboat (LS, 335). Just after Eugene had been discharged from the sanatorium, Jimmy Byth—Jimmy Tomorrow—had killed himself at Jimmy the Priest's, and now another old friend from that Bottom-of-the-Sea Rathskeller, as Eugene once called it, had swallowed the anchor.

As with Jimmy Byth's death, the news greatly affected Eugene; he spent years trying to understand it. He had made Driscoll, under his own name, the friend of the dying man in *Children of the Sea*, and, as Sheaffer suggests, Driscoll was probably also the model for the dying Yank in that play (SL, 196). After Driscoll's death, Eugene made him a character under his own name in three other one-act sea plays, and he also made him a character, Lyons the stoker, in the short story "Tomorrow" that he wrote to commemorate Jimmy Byth. In 1918,

Eugene wrote directly about Driscoll and his suicide in a lost short story, "The Hairy Ape," which he tried and failed to publish. In 1920, he created the character Mat Burke in *"Anna Christie"* around Driscoll, and the following year he made another attempt at understanding, by writing *The Hairy Ape,* one of his finest plays. Three years later, Driscoll came up in a conversation with a *New York Times* reporter. Looking back more than a dozen years, Eugene remembered that to a youth prone to hero worship, Driscoll had seemed a Nietzschean superman. "Driscoll's curious death puzzled me. I concluded something must have shaken his hard-boiled poise" (Kantor 1924, 68).

The end of the affair with Beatrice, the renewed difficulty with his parents, and Driscoll's suicide gave Eugene several reasons to drink. He drifted back into street life and saloon life, and took to sleeping wherever he could find a bed. He ate little and irregularly, and friends who had seen him in the last two years thought he looked ill. In later years he frequently said that he never could write in New York. Through the fall and winter of 1915 he apparently wrote only a few poems and some letters to Beatrice.

When he first went to New York, he and Jamie stayed at the seedy, bustling Garden Hotel, a few blocks' walk from the luxurious Prince George Hotel, where his parents stayed. But he soon moved south to the Village, where his old friend Louis Holladay had started a restaurant. For a few weeks he apparently stayed with Louis, an arrangement that ended when Louis was found to be serving liquor without a license, an offense that cost him a jail sentence.

Tall, blond, literate, and good looking, Louis was trying to recover from even more difficult problems than Eugene's, including heroin addiction. Louis had attracted the interest of a young divorced woman of good family, Louise Norton, who believed she could rescue him from alcohol and heroin. She arranged for Louis to go to Oregon when he got out of jail. There he would manage an apple orchard for a year. He told friends that he thought if he could stay sober for a year, Louise would marry him.

When Louis went to jail, Eugene fell in with a friend of the Holladays, Terry Carlin, a sixty-year-old anarchist who was widely respected among Village radicals, who had known and been admired by the likes of Theodore Dreiser and Jack London. That fall and winter, Eugene and Terry intermittently roomed together, if that is the word for it. They would stay in an abandoned loft or building, and when the cold came, they would try to find an unoccupied apartment and stay there until other tenants or a landlord made them leave. In these months Eugene became involved with several people on whom he would later model characters in *The Iceman Cometh*. Terry was the model for Larry Slade.

For food, when they were sober enough to know they were hungry, there were at least three places Eugene and Terry could usually get a free meal. There was a café operated by Polly Holladay, Louis's sister, whose cook and lover was Hippolyte Havel, the model for Hugo the anarchist in *The Iceman Cometh*. There was a place called Romany Marie's, run by a flamboyant Rumanian woman who liked to pretend she was a gypsy and whose husband did the cooking. But their favorite was Louis's old place, now run by Christine Ell. She had cooked for Louis and had taken the restaurant over when he had gone to jail.

A generous, talented woman, famed among Villagers as a mimic, Christine was admired by Dreiser, whom she imitated famously. Later Charlie Chaplin was delighted by her impressions of Hippolyte Havel, Dreiser, and others. Sheaffer was told that in imitating Dreiser she would draw herself up, "and taking on a heavy Germanic look, she would finally say, her eyes snapping with disapproval, 'Everything is crap!'" (LS, 331). She acted in some of Eugene's early plays. She was married and had many affairs, to the distress of her husband, including flings with both O'Neill brothers. About six feet tall, with a beautifully voluptuous body, long legs, and gorgeous red hair, she had a face described by friends who loved her as ugly—"the ugliest face ever seen on a woman," wrote Agnes Boulton, one of those who loved her (Boulton 1958, 16). She chose to play the clown. She is believed to have been a partial model for several characters, including Anna Christie, Cybel—Mother Earth—in *The Great God Brown*, and Josie Hogan in *A Moon for the Misbegotten*.

Eugene and Terry and Christine and Polly and Hippolyte and many other friends, even sometimes Jamie—all drank at a bar known as the Hell Hole (the sign at Sixth Avenue and Fourth Street read "The Golden Swan"). It was one of three places that O'Neill had in mind in creating the setting of *The Iceman Cometh* (the others being the bar at the Garden Hotel and Jimmy the Priest's). From time to time, Eugene had a room upstairs above the barroom of the Hell Hole. At those three places Eugene met most of the people he would sketch in *The Iceman Cometh*. He based Harry Hope partly on Tom Wallace, the Hell Hole proprietor, who had ties with Tammany Hall and spent his days with cronies in an upstairs room while Lefty Louie (just Lefty to regulars) served his patrons in the barroom. Lefty was probably the model for the bartender Rocky in *The Iceman Cometh.*

At the Hell Hole Eugene became acquainted with members of a notoriously violent Irish waterfront gang, the Hudson Dusters. The members of the gang took to Eugene, perhaps because he was Irish and had a famous father. At least twice, people saw Eugene bawling out gang members, once because some of them had gone into Romany Marie's restaurant and frightened Marie and her husband. The Dusters took Eugene's criticism. The Gelbs report that later, one of them offered to boost a new winter coat for him, noticing that he didn't seem to have one. He declined, with thanks (Gelbs, 301).

At times he seemed lost once again, cut off from his parents, seldom seeing Jamie, and living on next to nothing. His father left a dollar a day for him with the desk clerk of the Prince George; but when drinking heavily, Eugene was physically unable to make the long trek up to Twenty-eighth Street to get whatever cash had accumulated. Sometimes Jamie, worried that he had not seen his brother for a while, brought the allowance to him. Sometimes lack of funds or too prolonged a binge led to a terrible sobering-up, with excruciating abdominal cramps. Sober, Eugene and Terry Carlin would make their way uptown to collect so that they could resume drinking. Eugene must have been attracted to Terry as a substitute father, something Terry declined to be. Nevertheless, Terry was one of several people Eugene credited with helping him stay alive that winter of 1915–1916, along with a black gambler, Joe Smith, who sometimes took him into his home, fed him, and gave him a bed. O'Neill based Joe Mott in *The Iceman Cometh* on Joe Smith. Christine Ell, and Polly Holladay, and Romany Marie often forgot to bring a bill for a meal. Later, when he had some money, Eugene supported Terry and helped Joe Smith from time to time when they were down on their luck. He eventually buried Terry, when the old anarchist died in 1934.

Sometime in early 1916, Eugene began hanging around with the radicals who were publishing the anarchist weekly *Revolt,* which published a few of his poems. He later wrote Bee Ashe that he helped get out the paper, and perhaps he did do a little something. In such company he met Jack Reed again.

Jack, who had recently been in Europe having a stormy affair with

Mabel Dodge and writing about the war, now lived with a striking woman from Portland, Oregon, Louise Bryant, described by several people as an "Irish" beauty, with reddish brown hair and blue gray eyes. Jack had met Louise when he went home to Portland on family matters; Louise had left her husband, a dentist, to follow Jack to New York after he returned east. Eugene felt a renewed liking for Jack, but he complicated the friendship by falling in love with Louise. For a time, however, Eugene and Louise ignored each other.

When spring finally came, Eugene began to yearn to get out of New York, where he could not write, and get back to work. On hearing Jack and Louise talk of their plan to go to Provincetown for the summer, Eugene and Terry decided to go too. As biographers say, it was a fateful decision. A few days after they arrived, Terry met his old friend Susan Glaspell, who asked him whether he had any plays lying about. No, he said: he was a talker, not a writer, but young O'Neill had a trunk full of plays—actually a small wooden box labeled Magic Yeast. When told that he had been invited to read his plays at a certain cabin, Eugene hesitantly agreed. He arrived at nine with the manuscript of *Children of the Sea*. Too shy to read the play himself, and full of mixed feelings about getting involved with theatrical amateurs, the son of Monte Cristo stood out of sight in the kitchen while an actor named Frederick Burt, one of the few professionals in the group, read the play to the others. Writing about that night years later, Susan Glaspell described her feeling when they had heard the play through to Yank's dying words. "Then we knew what we were for," she wrote (1927, 248).

"We" included Susan, her husband, George Cram Cook, known to everyone as Jig; Jack and Louise; Hutchins Hapgood and his wife, Neith Boyce; Teddy and Stella Ballantine; Robert Edmond (Bobby) Jones, a theater director and designer and a protégé of Mabel Dodge, who had a place on Cape Cod; Wilbur Daniel Steele and his wife, Margaret; Mary Heaton Vorse, a writer who owned a ramshackle warehouse on a wharf; and others. Inspired by the idealism of Jig Cook, they had begun the previous summer to present their own plays in make-do spaces. Jig wanted to create a new art theater that would be completely independent of the established professional theater. He and many others believed that the reason no American dramatists could rival American novelists and poets lay in the nature of the professional theatrical establishment. They started calling themselves The Provincetown Players—the P.P.

Jig and Susan and some of the others had been involved with the Washington Square Players, one of the first art theater groups in the country, which had formed about 1912. But Jig, having more on his mind than mere theatrical reform or literary nationalism, had broken away. He aimed for nothing less than a theater that would save the American soul. A man possessed by the conviction that under the skin he was an ancient Greek, Jig hoped to reestablish the theater as a temple of Dionysos and so reawaken the Glory of Classical Athens in an America in which the word *vision* usually referred to capitalist enterprise or mechanical ingenuity. By restoring to the theater its ancient function of mediating between the everyday world and the world of the gods, the Players might foster the growth of the materialistic, utilitarian American soul to Olympian height. In 1916 Eugene was too cynical to listen to such claptrap, but over the next decades it would sink in and he would adapt Jig's ideals to his own spirit.

The previous summer, an audience sitting in the front room of the Hapgoods' bayfront cottage had watched through the windows as actors on the veranda performed a play called *Constancy,* a one-act comedy by Neith Boyce about the romance, just ended, between Mabel Dodge and Jack Reed. The play had been staged by Bobby Jones. When *Constancy* was over, Jones had the audience move their chairs out to the veranda and watch the actors inside perform the other part of the bill, a spoof on Freudian psychology by Susan Glaspell and Jig Cook called *Suppressed Desires,* one of Glaspell's several plays that is still a favorite with little theaters.

Jig and Susan and others persuaded Mary Heaton Vorse to allow the weather-beaten warehouse on the wharf to be converted into a summer theater, and they sold subscriptions, $2.50 for a pair of season tickets. They raised enough money to install electricity and make benches. They had a theater and an audience, but no new plays had emerged that the Players especially liked—thus Susan's question to Terry when she first saw him, had he written any plays? They would begin with a revival of *Suppressed Desires.* After hearing *Children of the Sea,* the Provincetown Players put it on their second bill and soon scheduled *Thirst* for late August.

Eugene, meanwhile, had started writing again when he arrived in Provincetown. He set to work on a three-act farce. *Now I Ask You* begins ends with a joke about *Hedda Gabler.* In between, two young couples experiment with free love, only to find themselves as possessive as the bourgeoisie they despise. Some of the couples surrounding Eugene were finding that free love might lead to as much domestic misery as marriage, and no couple was more convenient for observation than Jack and Louise, whose noisy quarrels were audible to Eugene and Terry from their nearby apartment in a block of flats over John Francis's store, where some of the Players were also staying. The flats offered a fine view of the bay. Eugene also revised *Children of the Sea* into *Bound East for Cardiff,* after some tightening and trimming. The longest single cut was of an anecdote in which Driscoll describes murdering at sea a brutal mate who forced the crew to eat maggoty food. Eugene may have cut it because he believed that the story might be true.

Just before *Suppressed Desires* was to open, a fire broke out at the theater. The blaze scorched the inner walls of the warehouse but left the building repairable. With everyone working frantically, the second season opened on time to a friendly and appreciative audience. In late July, Eugene wrote Beatrice to try to persuade her to come to Provincetown and see his play performed. He told her that he was busy directing the production. He didn't mention that he played the smallest role in the play, that of the second mate who appears momentarily, to speak one line. Jig Cook played the dying sailor, Yank, and Frederick Burt played Driscoll. Eugene had set the play on a fogbound ship whose fog whistle sounded about once a minute. Susan Glaspell reported that the night of the first performance was foggy, and a fog bell in the harbor sounded throughout the play. "The tide was in," she wrote, "and it washed under us and around, spraying through the holes in the floor, giving us the rhythm and flavor of the sea while the big dying sailor talked to his friend Drisc of the life he had always wanted deep in the land, where you'd never see a ship or smell the sea" (Glaspell 1927, 254). Susan reported that the audience was thrilled.

In the letter to Beatrice Ashe written on July 25, Eugene made little fuss over the first-ever opening of one of his plays, probably because he could not yet take the amateur group seriously. He was more concerned about giving the advice Bee had requested on strategy for making a break with her family and moving to New York to establish a career as a singer, model, and actress. The brotherly tone of the letter seemed aimed at convincing her that he had escaped his former enslavement to her. With a certain world-weariness, he promised to tell her in a future letter of the scandalous lives of those who surrounded him, and he also promised that, if she came, she could stay, chaperoned, with his friends Jack Reed "and his wife" (SL, 73).

It was a complex invitation. Not only were Jack and Louise not yet planning marriage; Eugene felt greatly attracted to Louise, and she showed interest in him. Having Bee in the house with Louise would complicate in interesting ways the already complex situation of Eugene, Jack, and Louise. If Louise could play at having two men, then he could do the same with two women. Yet he also seemed to long for the more straightforward situation of earlier days, when he was simply in love with Bee. The last line of the letter had a ring of sincerity heard nowhere else in it, when he confessed that his love was "ten times more poignant than of old" (SL, 74). Perhaps in a way it was. In part he longed for the idealism he had felt a year before when he expected to marry Bee, when he was not drinking heavily and had cast off his old cynicism. It seems that he wanted or hoped to be in love with Bee again because it would be simpler than being in love with Louise, a woman much more complicated and unpredictable than Bee, and feeling disloyal to Jack.

The state of affairs between Eugene, Jack, and Louise was approximately as follows. Since coming east, Louise had often been uncomfortable. She had moved in with Jack, but he was away much of the time on journalistic assignments, and she (and most other people) assumed that he seldom slept alone. Large and ruggedly handsome, openhearted and generous of spirit, Jack had infinite charm. In New York, where Jack seemed to know everyone, Louise knew no one, and she had nothing to say to Jack's brilliant, politically and artistically sophisticated friends. Although Jack encouraged her efforts at journalistic writing, she had little success, and, in Barbara Gelb's judgment, she lacked the nose for a story that makes a journalist. His friends were standoffish because she was beautiful and Jack was fickle. When she and Jack were together, they wrangled noisily. Louise felt drawn to the one person who was as obviously alienated as she among the fluent strangers in Jack's radical crowd, the silent, dark-eyed poet, Eugene. After they all moved to Provincetown, Eugene and Terry spent many evenings with Jack and Louise in their neighboring flat.

On one such evening, Louise lent Eugene a book of poems with a note in it, "Dark Eyes, What do you mean?" Soon there was another note: "I must see you alone. I have to explain something, for my sake and Jack's. You have to understand." All accounts of this love affair include the following story of Louise's seduction of Eugene: Louise wanted to explain that because of a serious kidney condition, Jack could not have sex, and she and he lived together in chastity (Boulton 1958, 105–6). The kidney ailment was real, but the rest was imaginary. Eugene chose to believe her. Soon after, he told Terry, "When that girl touches me with the tip of her finger, it's like a flame" (LS, 350).

It seems that one of the conditions necessary for Eugene to write was that he be in love. For the next year and some months, Louise was his muse. While entangled with Louise, in the summer of 1916, Eugene finished the three-act farce *Now I Ask You* and also wrote a madly comic Strindbergian monologue. Modeled on Strindberg's *The Stronger, Before Breakfast* is a two-character play in which only one character speaks or is seen. A wife nags her silent husband, who is mostly offstage, until finally he cuts his throat with his razor, moaning as he dies (his only line). Much better when acted than when read, the play keeps an audience chuckling, makes the nagging wife sympathetic, and makes light of the husband's end.

The other play written in 1916, *Now I Ask You,* shows that Eugene had few illusions about his companions from the Village, and only the most tenuous bonds with them. The same was true for the P.P. He kept nearly everyone at arm's length except Jig and Susan and Jack and Louise. That summer he also wrote his short story about Jimmy Byth, "Tomorrow," and a short story version of *The Movie Man.* Louise cannot be blamed for the slight success of the work she inspired, but the affair with her did not bring forth Eugene's best work.

A lesser work, *Thirst,* also succeeded with its Provincetown audience. Again Eugene directed. Jig played the gentleman, and Louise played the dancer who tries to seduce the sailor, goes mad, and dies, indirectly precipitating the fall of all three into the mouths of the waiting sharks. The part of the cannibalistic mulatto sailor was played by Eugene, so dark from his daily swims that he needed no makeup. The Players probably mused at how the triangle in *Thirst* reflected the triangles in their midst, and they may have wondered if some of their number might founder in the seas of love. On the whole, the group believed that the discovery of a playwright they considered possessed of genius justified their endeavor.

In September, after a season that seemed to please everyone in Provincetown, the Players moved back to Greenwich Village, their idealism at flood tide. On the way to New York from Provincetown, Eugene visited his parents in New London to introduce his new love, Louise. Jessica Rippin told Sheaffer that Louise appeared a day or so after Eugene arrived, and that she stayed at Monte Cristo Cottage. It must have been an awkward visit. Jessica said Louise walked about the neighborhood wearing a pair of Eugene's trousers, her hair loose and unkempt. She did not seem to Jessica the beauty that Eugene had described. "She was a mess," Jessica said; "she looked like a Greenwich Village character who could stand a bath" (LS, 360). The visit could not have improved relations among the O'Neills. Whether Eugene meant to be provocative or whether in the bliss of love he believed his parents would admire Louise as he did can hardly be guessed.

Back in New York, Eugene, warming a little to the group, joined the Provincetown Players in establishing the Playwrights' Theatre. Acting on the principle expressed by Hutchins Hapgood that "organization is death," the Playwrights' Theatre formed itself around two deliberately loose and vague ideas: that they would do only a play they thought interesting, regardless of whether it might please the masses; and that "the author should produce the play without hindrance, according to his own ideas" (LS, 358–59). Eugene may have hoped that it would give him the same chance to develop that the Intimate Theatre of Stockholm had given Strindberg, but O'Neill cannot have had much faith in the amateur actors, and he did little to help out. The group set out to establish itself in New York; Eugene went along for the ride.

Jig almost immediately found the group's "theater"—that is, he rented the parlor floor of an old brownstone house at 139 MacDougal Street, next door to Christine Ell's restaurant, the Liberal Club, and Frank Shay's Washington Square Book Shop. Under Jig's and Bobby Jones's direction, and with the benevolent approval of the owner, alterations were made to create an acting space ten and a half by fourteen feet, with room for 140 people to sit and watch. The first play on the first bill was *Bound East for Cardiff*, and if Eugene had not taken seriously the amateur performance in Provincetown, he certainly took New York seriously. His main effort in preparing for the P.P.'s New York opening was to direct his play. He had never directed before, except in Provincetown a few weeks earlier, and it is not known whether he worked with someone else. In between stints of carpentering, making costumes, improvising lighting, and fitting out a small closet as a changing room, the Players and their friends sold subscriptions.

Eugene ignored everything that did not concern him directly. But he did draw people into the group who made significant contributions over the years. He made friends with Frank Shay, who later published in a series of booklets some plays performed by the Provincetown Players. Shay printed *Bound East for Cardiff* in December. Eugene's Village colleagues now included Hutch Collins, an old friend from New London, who joined the Players and became one of the more reliable actors. Eugene recruited another old drinking friend and former sailor, Scotty Stuart, to play the role of Driscoll.

Largely because of Jack Reed's efforts, about four hundred season tickets were sold, so several bills could be mounted in some security. The first opening succeeded with the audience, but only Stephen Rathbun gave it any public notice, panning Louise's play *The Game* as "amateurish" but praising *Bound East for Cardiff* as "real" and "subtly tense." It "avoided a dozen pitfalls that might have made it 'the regular thing'" (LS, 363). The last point is significant for Eugene's early plays. Often what is most remarkable about them is the temptation Eugene silently avoids to include something that would make them ordinary. The second bill was more popular because of Susan Glaspell's *Suppressed Desires* and *Enemies* by Neith Boyce and Hutchins Hapgood, who enacted the feuding wife and husband. A few professional critics attended the first two bills, and one, Heywood Broun, continued to come and eventually wrote a review when Frank Shay published the first of a series of Provincetown plays as pamphlets, praising Susan for *Suppressed Desires* and *Trifles,* and Eugene for *Bound East for Cardiff.*

The first New York opening of an O'Neill play broke the ice between Eugene and his father. James attended and was impressed by what he saw. He invited the author to come and live at the Prince George with his parents. Eugene declined because he had a room in a boardinghouse in Washington Square near the theater, a few doors from the apartment of Jack and Louise. But he invited James to rehearsals of the play that would open in the third bill on December 1, *Before Breakfast,* and asked for his father's advice about staging the play. No reviews of the third bill are known, and it was unpopular with the P.P.'s audience, but some of the Players recalled Mary Pyne, hiding her red hair and her beauty, and playing the frustrated wife effectively. The two-week run of *Before Breakfast* marked Eugene's last appearance on a stage, or rather that of his "sensitive hand" with slender, trembling fingers, seen by the audience reaching through the bedroom door for a bowl of water for shaving. Presumably Eugene also provided the husband's dying groan.

Outside the Playwrights' Theatre during November and December, a private drama unfolded. Jack Reed's nephritis had reached the point where he had to go to Johns Hopkins Hospital to have a kidney removed. A few days before he went into the hospital, he and Louise got married. Louise went to Baltimore with him to see her husband through surgery. Jack remained in the hospital for several weeks to recover, and Louise hurried back to New York to Eugene, who, being forty-six dollars in debt to his landlady, with no income in sight, had had to vacate his boardinghouse. The Playwrights' Theatre paid no royalties. With Eugene homeless and Jack out of town, it seemed natural for Eugene to move in with Louise; the marriage did not end the affair. When Jack got out of the hospital in mid-December, Eugene moved in with Jamie at the Garden Hotel. Perhaps Sheaffer is right in believing that Jack so loved Louise that he refused to know about the affair. More likely Jack found some complex way for his admiration for Eugene to coexist with jealousy, for he apparently did know. In November he bought a house in Croton-on-Hudson, to which he and Louise moved shortly after his return from the hospital. He and Louise saw less of the Players, and Eugene saw less of Louise.

In the absence of Jack's tactful leadership, Jig increasingly lost control of the anarchic P.P. group, whose members now seemed to go in all directions at once. According to various accounts, the acting was often terrible and the staging worse, with actors bumping into scenery and one another, forgetting their lines or speaking them to the wrong character, or even vanishing altogether just before a performance. The fifth bill was not saved by Eugene's other lifeboat play, *Fog*.

In retrospect, it is a wonder the Provincetown Players survived their first New York season. Probably they would have perished, if it had not been for the arrival of Nina Moise from California. She had graduated from Stanford and had acted and directed with stock companies in California, and she now wanted to act in New York. Instead, because she could direct, Jig drafted her to chair the production committee. Later he hired her for fifteen dollars a week as a permanent director of plays. For the seventh bill, opening February 16, 1917, she directed Eugene's *Sniper*, a popular play with subscribers. Calm, pleasant, and tactful, Nina brought order and quiet competence to the Players' productions and to the group. From that point on, instead of writers' automatically directing their own plays, the task was shared by the professionals in the group— Margaret Wycherly, Frederick Burt, Teddy Ballantine, and Nina Moise. Their first joint bill earned a favorable review from Heywood Broun. As a further step toward professional competence, Jig hired Louis Ell, Christine's husband, as stage manager.

Separated from Louise, Eugene felt lost and spent most of his time drinking in the Hell Hole. In March he decided he needed to get away from New York to write. He persuaded a drinking friend, the freelance writer Harold DePolo, to go to Provincetown with him; once there, they both settled down to work, staying in the Atlantic Hotel and taking long walks on the dunes between writing stints. On March 28 they were involved in one of the oddest events of Eugene's life. Both men were arrested at pistol point by Constable Kelley, who believed he had caught two German spies. There was, in fact, offshore German submarine activity. Cape Codders were alert to their situation and ready to lynch spies and saboteurs. A complaint about prowlers from a government radio monitoring station in nearby North Truro had set the constable to looking for enemy agents, and he settled on the two strangers who had recently come to town, one of whom had been seen fiddling with a black box out on the dunes. Eugene and Harold spent a night in jail, while Secret Service Agent Weyand spent the night in his car driving to interrogate them. As it turned out, the black box was a typewriter, and the agent learned that Eugene could give as a local reference the name of John Francis, his landlord the previous summer and a respected man in Provincetown, and his father's famous name as well. The next morning Weyand recommended that the charges be dismissed, and they were. But both Eugene and Harold were badly shaken by the experience.

According to Harold DePolo, Eugene had already written a play called *In the Zone* before the arrest took place (LS, 381). In later years Eugene dismissed the play as "a conventional construction," which it is; because of a sentimentality that O'Neill avoids in the other plays, it is certainly the slightest and least poetic of the four *S.S. Glencairn* plays. But the circumstances of its writing, if it was really written before Eugene was arrested, are odd. In the play, a mournful, aloof young Englishman, Smitty, is suspected by his shipmates of secreting a code device in a black box, which he keeps under his bunk, and is accused of being a spy for the Germans—falsely, it turns out, for the black box holds love letters from his fiancée, who has rejected him because of his drinking. The disclosure embarrasses the sailors and humiliates Smitty. It would have been natural enough for Eugene to express his feelings about the arrest in a play, and that has been the general assumption about the origin of *In the Zone,* but, as Sheaffer points out, Harold DePolo and Eugene were consistent in claiming that the play was written first.

Event followed event. On March 26 Eugene had sent his story "Tomorrow" to the magazine the *Seven Arts.* It was accepted almost by return mail. Three days after his arrest, Eugene wrote to Waldo Frank, the editor, about changes in the text. He learned he would be paid fifty dollars when it came out, a significant and highly encouraging sum. On April 2, President Wilson addressed Congress to prepare the country to enter the European war. A draft was organized, although public opinion remained deeply divided about joining the war. At some point in the spring or summer Eugene wrote Dr. Lyman to inquire about an exemption from the draft because of his susceptibility to tuberculosis and the danger of reinfection he had heard was associated with life in camps and in the trenches. He insisted that he was not trying to dodge service and said that he had tried to enlist in the navy and been turned down for "minor defects." Perhaps he had tried to enlist. He did not lack physical courage, and he loved being at sea. But, he added in regard to the army, "it seems silly to commit suicide" for one's country (SL, 80). Certainly he felt no sympathy for the war.

Eugene kept on writing. He wrote *Ile,* a strong, grim one-act play about an obsessed whaling captain who takes his wife on a whaling voyage, where she goes mad and the crew is about to mutiny because the captain persists in his quest, even after polar ice surrounds the ship. As Sheaffer and Michael Manheim suggest, the story seems to refer to James O'Neill, carrying his wife around the country in his monomaniacal quest for theatrical whale oil, with a dash of Captain Ahab added (LS, 382–83; Manheim 1982, 16). Usually Eugene believed that his mother went willingly on tour because she was unable to stand being separated from her husband. The play can be taken as a hint either at some general alienation that Eugene felt from his father after the year at Harvard or at a specific disagreement.

Eugene next wrote the other two one-act *Glencairn* plays, *The Long Voyage Home* and *The Moon of the Caribbees*. *The Long Voyage Home* resembled *Bound East for Cardiff* in that it generated its momentum from the accumulation of meaning and significance, rather than from the novelty of its ideas or some twist of plot. In a London waterfront dive, the sailor Olson promises himself that this time in port he will not get drunk as he usually does but will instead save his money for passage home to Sweden. Just one drink, his friends say. He agrees. Before long he is too besotted with a bar woman to notice that he is being drugged. Soon he has been shanghaied aboard a bad ship, and another long voyage away from home has begun.

Eugene completely avoids sentimentalizing Olson. The key to the play is not its realism or its naturalism, but instead what Keats called negative capability. Referring to Shakespeare, Keats had in mind the gift of being able to write from a position of empathic neutrality toward all the characters and their circumstances and the other material of the play. It is comparable to the quality that Freud said was essential for persons wishing to practice psychoanalysis, the ability to maintain "evenly suspended attention" in which they consider everything, look for nothing in particular, see what is there, and can notice what is not there (Freud 1912, 111–12). Analyst and analysand are at once participants in and observers of the analysis. A playwright's negative capability allows what is significant in the material to reveal itself without manipulation or contrivance. At the end, the writer may be lucky enough to find that something real has been allowed to emerge, possibly something the playwright has not expected.

The fourth play Eugene wrote in the spring of 1917 represented what he considered a great breakthrough. Writing to Barrett Clark later, he called *The Moon of the Caribbees* "my favorite," and "distinctly my own." The play began and ended with the motions of the sea. Completely plotless, it is set on a ship at anchor. Women in bumboats bring rum and themselves to sell; gaiety is followed by a fight, and then life quietly reverts to its original state. It was in writing this play that Eugene felt he had first stepped completely out of the conventional and begun to work in the world of his own imagination. "The spirit of the sea" he told Clark, "is the hero." Comparing the character Smitty in *In the Zone* to the same character in *The Moon of the Caribbees*, Eugene continued:

"In *The Moon*, posed against a background of [the sea's] beauty, sad because it is eternal, which is one of the revealing moods of the sea's truth, [Smitty's] silhouetted gestures of self-pity are reduced to their proper insignificance, his thin whine of weakness is lost in the silence which it was mean enough to disturb; we get the perspective to judge him—and the others—and we find his sentimental posing much more out of harmony with truth, much less in tune with beauty, than the honest vulgarity of his mates" (SL, 87).

O'Neill increasingly saw the world coherently, and as he did, it became apparent that he believed that individuals were driven less by the values of society than by nature and its rhythms. Eugene was developing a profoundly antihumanistic viewpoint and rejected the general trend in the Western tradition of placing people at the center of the universe and acclaiming them masters of the world. Eugene's sense of the tragic caused him to take people seriously but question the fundamental humanistic belief that human intelligence granted people control over the world or themselves. Beauty and truth were manifest in the sea. Silhouetted against, and driven by, rhythms that are eternal, humanity is simply part of the picture. His tragic vision was neither pessimistic nor optimistic, but in it, the power of nature took precedence over the power of human beings; this fundamental point it shared with Greek tragedy, with Shakespearean comedy and tragedy, and with certain other modern comedy and tragedy. The neutrality of the tragic vision balanced O'Neill's personal vulnerability to depression and pessimism. When he could maintain the balance, his plays were truly tragic, yet not necessarily pessimistic, depressing, or sad.

His art aside, the powers driving Eugene in 1917 were essentially negative. His lifelong dread of losing himself if he merged with a group was so strong that a sign of conventional behavior in a person he cared for might bring forth, at the least, a lecture on Nietzsche or something even more formidable. His dread of groups matched his dread of loneliness. He simply could not bear to be alone. The two fears together produced a third necessity, a drive to find a particular woman with whom he could completely merge so that both would lose their identity and become part of a new entity that combined their two selves. The idea was no fancy of the moment but had been basic to the idea of rebirth of which Eugene had repeatedly spoken in his letters to Beatrice Ashe, and it would be the main subject of a play, *Welded*, which he wrote several years later. Given such conditions, Beatrice had declined to marry him. He had had several brief affairs during the fall and winter of 1916–1917, including flings with Peggy Baird (later Mrs. Malcolm Cowley) and Becky Edelson, who had made headlines for going on a hunger strike in prison, following a labor protest. He had also had other affairs, about which little is known. Louise Bryant had so far not decided to leave her husband and come to Eugene. Late in the spring of 1917 Harold DePolo returned to his family in New York. Unable to be alone, Eugene wrote for Terry Carlin to come to Provincetown.

Eugene and Terry moved into one of John Francis's flats where they had spent the previous summer. Terry brought with him the news that Louise and Jack had separated, apparently over Jack's involvement with another woman. Eugene had written to Louise frequently since going to Provincetown in March, but she had not told him about leaving Jack. Terry reported that Louise had an assignment to write about the war and was going alone to Paris. Having longed for her to decide that it was really he whom she loved, and believing that it would happen because he wanted it so much, Eugene was unprepared for the news. Only now did he begin to realize that whatever Louise felt for him was not reciprocal with his need for her. Eugene and Terry got drunk and stayed that way for a time.

Eugene had to go to New London to register for the draft on June 5, an experience that led him to write an antiwar poem, "Fratricide." He and his father argued over the United States' entry into the war, and the war fervor in New London disgusted Eugene. Depressed about Louise and the war, Eugene got drunk and insulted his father. James persuaded Eugene's friend Art McGinley to go with him to Provincetown in the hope that his son would recover himself. McGinley told Sheaffer that when they arrived, Eugene was on one of the prolonged binges during which he could not stop drinking until so ill with gastritis that he could not continue. Probably the motive for the binge was not so much the war as the rejection by Louise.

Eugene's story "Tomorrow" appeared in the *Seven Arts* in June, and the magazine further accepted *In the Zone*. The *Seven Arts* failed before *In the Zone* could be published, but Eugene got fifty dollars, nevertheless. The money allowed Eugene to pay in advance the season's rent of forty dollars, and the surplus, together with the eight dollars a week that James was sending for meals, allowed Art, Terry, and Eugene to keep on drinking.

There was still more good news. Late in May, Eugene had sent three plays to H. L. Mencken, coeditor with George Jean Nathan of the *Smart Set,* a magazine that at that time had a status comparable to that of the *New Yorker* in later decades. Mencken wrote back that he was turning over the plays to Nathan, who already had a reputation as a drama critic. Nathan soon wrote accepting *Ile, The Long Voyage Home,* and *The Moon of the Caribbees.* The earliest letters between O'Neill and Nathan have not survived, but one of them may well have mentioned that in the 1870s their mothers had been close friends at St. Mary's College in Indiana. (Nathan and O'Neill would themselves eventually become good friends and remain so for three decades, but they did not meet face to face until two years later.)

In July Eugene heard from Louise that she had returned to New York—she had given up being a war correspondent without ever filing a story—and she and Jack were together again. In late August, Louise wrote to Eugene that she and Jack were going to Russia to observe and write about the revolution they anticipated. With America now in the war, mainstream newspapers and magazines turned to the right. Although Jack had been for several years a highly respected and busy political journalist, he had now become so ardent a communist that his old connections, including the *Metropolitan,* would no longer publish his work. The man who was soon to write *Ten Days that Shook the World* went to Russia representing only the *Masses.* Jack and Louise reached Petrograd in late September, and she remained until January. Eugene never saw her again.

In an attempt to understand the affair between her and O'Neill, Sheaffer interviewed William C. Bullitt, the diplomat who later married Louise. Bullitt told Sheaffer that she had once asked him to read a thick sheaf of letters from Eugene, which she then burned. Bullitt said he believed the letters were sincere and that they showed a man "violently in love with her. [Eugene's] letters to Louise were wails of despairing, unrequited love." He added, "So far as I know, Louise was never in love with O'Neill," but she admired his talent and wanted to help him through "his frequent fits of drunkenness and his suicidal inclinations" (LS, 383). Probably the letters resembled those Eugene had written to Bee Ashe, except that they were more "violent" and despairing because he was drinking; and with Bee, he had been confident that at times she returned his love.

Louise Bryant had an extraordinary effect on men, including Bullitt. A man of wealth and substance, Bullitt was the first American ambassador to the Soviet Union; while he was ambassador to France during the late 1930s, he and Princess Marie Bonaparte helped Freud and his family escape the Nazis. He married Louise in 1923, and they had a daughter. But Louise drank so heavily that after a few more years of marriage Bullitt divorced her, retaining custody of their daughter. By all accounts, Jack Reed was as desperately in love with her as Eugene. His biographers Granville Hicks (1936) and Barbara Gelb (1973) report that Reed told several people that Louise was "the first person I ever loved without reservation" (Gelb 1973, 205). What she inspired in others is perhaps what she wanted to feel or achieve herself yet could not: apparently she could love someone else greatly only by identifying with that person's love of her, and that only for a while. After her divorce from Bullitt she drifted back to Greenwich Village, drank more heavily, and became impoverished and increasingly alone and alienated. She went to Paris, apparently began using drugs, and was living in a tawdry hotel when she died suddenly in 1936.

The men who became involved with her could neither forget Louise nor easily come to terms with the memory she left of excitement, loss, and frustration. Accepting the loss of her from his life affected Eugene in something like the way that letting go of Maibelle Scott had affected him, two years earlier. The affair with Maibelle had led him to write *Bread and Butter* and *Before Breakfast*, both plays with axes to grind about conventional women marrying and trying to change artistic husbands. For Eugene, writing to argue a point, illustrate a theme, or get even with someone led to artistic failure. Trying to forget Louise, Eugene wrote a satire, "The 'G.A.N.,'" about the Industrial Workers of the World (IWW), and then a "novelette" that he called "S.O.S." on a "sea-theme," and another story. Eugene destroyed the three works he wrote that summer, probably because they fell far short of the achievement of *The Moon of the Caribbees*. Almost all that is known of these destroyed works is their names and themes, which were recorded in a catalogue that Eugene made much later of his writings.

The fourth work of the summer, a lost story called "The Hairy Ape," was about the stoker Driscoll's suicide. Apparently Eugene tried directly to understand what the man was looking for and couldn't find and who on that account killed himself. On Jack Reed's advice, he sent the story to the *Metropolitan*. Carl Hovey, the editor, praised it but remarked that it was too long and also that the ending, in which the protagonist joined the IWW, "seemed unfinished, or not just the right turn" (LS, 389).

Eugene later said that the story contained merely the germ of the idea that he developed in the play of the same title, which he wrote in 1921. Probably the earlier story was about the man Driscoll, as "Tomorrow" was about the man Jimmy Byth; while in the play *The Hairy Ape* the character Yank represents the situation of Anyman in what O'Neill subtitled "A Comedy of Ancient and Modern Life."

Returning to New York in September, Eugene immediately began preparing three plays that were to open in the fall, *In the Zone, The Long Voyage Home,* and *Ile.* Having accepted that he had misunderstood Louise and her feelings for him, he seems to have been lonely but not particularly depressed. He set out to find a new girlfriend and began wooing Nina Moise. In directing *The Sniper* the previous February, she had given considerable effort because she respected the play. From the beginning, his practice had been to ignore a director, avoid rehearsals, and not attend the opening. O'Neill had a lifelong aversion to seeing his work onstage, because of the shock consequent upon finding that it existed outside his imagination and control. Perhaps he half-consciously blamed actors and directors for taking his plays away from him. Nina, knowing nothing of such feelings, saw his rudeness and disliked him, while continuing to admire his plays. Now he wanted her to like him, and she did—that is how she described the start of the friendship that developed. "When he smiled . . . it was like the sun coming out," she told Sheaffer (LS, 378). Before long Eugene asked her to marry him. She declined, and they never became sexual lovers, but their friendship deepened and lasted many years. The need Nina sensed when he proposed was very powerful. Often, in this period, Eugene seemed terrified of being alone for even a few hours.

Without giving up on Nina, he drifted into a deep friendship with Dorothy Day, whom he met at the Hell Hole. Then a journalist of twenty-one, she was a tall, very striking woman. Brought up a Republican and an Episcopalian, she would later found the Catholic Workers movement. For several weeks Dorothy and Eugene were inseparable; he needed her by his side at every moment. They wandered the waterfront for hours at night, accompanied and protected by Hudson Dusters; sometimes they rode the El for hours at a time (LS, 403). She, in love with his mind and his plays, believed him a genius, and was very attracted to him, though not sexually. She told her biographer William Miller of taking Eugene to her apartment at night when he was very drunk, putting him in her bed, and holding him so that he could sleep, while gently declining his gentlemanly proposals to end her virginity (Miller 1982, 110–11). Miller believed that Dorothy told him the story to let him know that she considered herself the model for Josie Hogan in *A Moon for the Misbegotten*, the woman who holds Jim Tyrone in her arms all night to chase away his devils, "a virgin who bears a dead child in the night, and the dawn finds her still a virgin" (CP3, 936).

Eugene lived with Dorothy in this way for a few weeks. When he awoke late in the morning, he would immediately call her at work to come home to him. Once he formed an attachment to a woman, all barriers dropped and he became wholly dependent on her for a time. He could not stand finding Dorothy absent. Yet she did not resent his demands, because she so valued the attention and empathy he gave her and other people. "One of the fine things about Gene is that he took people seriously," she told Sheaffer (LS, 404).

At times the two could be weirdly bacchic. Dorothy was famous for knowing a great many bawdy verses of "Frankie and Johnny," which she might suddenly begin to sing in, say, the Hell Hole, in an odd staccato style. Everyone would stop talking to listen. For his part, Eugene sometimes recited Francis Thompson's apocalyptic Catholic poem *The Hound of Heaven* in its entirety. Probably he had had to learn it while he was a boarding student at St. Aloysius. Once she heard him do so with several of the Hudson Dusters hanging on every word.

Although his love life was in a state of barely controlled chaos, a certain order began to appear in his professional life. The Washington Square Players, forerunners of the Theatre Guild, accepted *In the Zone* and gave it an effective performance, with Frederick Roland playing Smitty. Although Eugene despised the play as trite and sentimental, it was (and is) effective onstage. Later, when he sold it to the Orpheum Vaudeville Circuit, it gave him his first steady income from writing.

Two days after *In the Zone* opened, the Provincetown Players started their season with *The Long Voyage Home*. The production was apparently not reviewed, and one can only guess at its success; but O'Neill was beginning to be known. The Players' second bill, which opened November 30, featured the third new O'Neill play of the season, *Ile*, which Nina Moise directed, with Hutch Collins playing the obsessed whaling captain, and Clara Savage the wife who goes mad. In a fifteen-month period,

Eugene had thus seen seven of his plays open in New York. The name O'Neill was beginning to make theater people think of someone besides James O'Neill.

The lovelorn emerging playwright drank through September, October, and November, spending most nights in the Hell Hole with a growing circle of companions. In November he met Agnes Boulton there, a friend of Christine Ell and Mary Pyne. In the memoir she wrote about 1957, after Eugene was dead and *Long Day's Journey into Night* had just appeared, Agnes described a strong and immediate attraction. She had gone into the Hell Hole early one evening looking for Christine. The bar was very dark and nearly empty and she had seen Eugene, almost invisible in a dark corner, staring fixedly at her in a way that was "startling" and seemed "at the same time both sad and cruel." Somehow he did not make her uneasy. He appeared shy and reticent and seemed to want to "absorb himself into the . . . room's dark shadows" (Boulton 1958, 15).

Later that night, she sat at a table in the Hell Hole with Christine, Eugene, and Jamie. Jamie, complaining that any woman who saw Eugene first paid no attention to him, flirted amusingly with both women. Eventually Eugene walked Agnes to her hotel and left her at the door, proclaiming "I want to spend every night of my life from now on with you. . . . I mean this. *Every night of my life*" (Boulton 1958, 20). From the start they seem to have had an exceptional affinity, thanks to which they felt they knew the feelings and sometimes the thoughts of the other. Reading letters written by the two of them a couple of years later, one is startled at how often crossing letters mention the same matter in similar words. Yet in important ways they also remained unknown to each other.

Friends thought Agnes looked a little like Louise, although they believed that Agnes was much prettier, and indeed certain photographs suggest a slight resemblance. Her features were small and regular, her nose straight, her lips full and attractive, her face oval, and her chin graceful. A studio picture taken about this time shows her with long chestnut hair, and a hint of smiling playfulness. The picture does not show that her hair trailed clear to her ankles. Her eyes, like Louise's, were blue gray. She was tall, and so thin that various people, then and later, worried about her health.

A few days after the first meeting, which had ended with Eugene's saying he wanted to spend every night of his life with Agnes, they saw each other again at a party on MacDougal Street. Eugene pointedly ignored her, argued with Playhouse friends, and sat at the feet of Nina Moise, who studied the spectacle with amusement. Agnes watched, feeling blue, and went back to her hotel.

Some days later, they walked around the Village together, and at a certain point where a narrowly triangular building commanded the space up two converging streets, Eugene described his battle plan for the revolution, shooting with machine guns from the upper windows in the Flatiron Building at the militia that would eventually kill him. It seems to a reader that he was making it up as he went along, inventing a character and creating a play around the character. As a fellow writer, Agnes thought him "a strange, mad, great person" (Boulton 1958, 44). Another time they met to drink coffee in a dark room with candles on the tables and he did not take his eyes off her face. Eugene was tapering off in his drinking.

One night, though, after drinking a good deal, they went to someone's apartment with Hutch Collins and were joined by Scotty Stuart, who had a possessive attachment to Eugene and instantly disliked Agnes, seeing her as a rival. In a gentlemanly attempt to balance things, Hutch paid Agnes a little attention, sitting on a bed with her and talking for a time. After a long, difficult evening, Eugene went to bed very drunk and called Agnes to come to him. He lay rigid, facing the wall, and she, for warmth on a bitter night, huddled against his back, the two of them partly covered by his overcoat. The next morning while he still seemed asleep, she got up and dressed and was about to leave when he suddenly confronted her. For several minutes (as it seemed to her) he poured out a tirade of insulting words. She watched him speaking, watched herself remain somehow untouched by the flood, and left. Several hours later, she decided she couldn't stand any more, either of being ignored or of being abused; she was about to check out of her hotel when the clerk gave her a large envelope from Eugene. It contained *The Moon of the Caribbees*. She went back to her room and read the play, then went to find him at the Hell Hole. He started a guilty apology but she did not let him speak and said only that he had to get out of New York so that he could keep on writing. Eugene replied that he could not go anyplace without her.

They talked about what had happened the night before to cause his rage that morning. She remarked that he seemed jealous, that she thought he wasn't sure of himself, and that he ought to have seen that she had been chasing him ever since she'd met him. Various friends of the playwright have mentioned to biographers that it seemed, in his many affairs, that he was usually the seduced, not the seducer. Agnes sensed this without fully understanding the guilt that lay behind his seeming passivity. He admitted that he was jealous, not of Hutch for talking to her, or of anyone else at the party, but of her daughter. Eugene's rage, it seems, had arisen after she had shown him the newspaper story about her being a widow with a young child. She wrote that he insisted: "'I wanted you alone'—a pause—'in an aloneness broken by nothing. Not even by children of our own'" (Boulton 1958, 63). All evidence confirms that that was the principle, accepted by both, on which their love and their marriage was to rest. He spoke at length of his absorption in her since their first meeting and continued his former thread: "I want it to be not you and me but *us, one being not two*"(65). He would go back to Provincetown after Christmas, he said; would it be possible for her to go with him? Yes, she answered immediately.

Agnes moved into rooms on Waverly Place, where, rather against her wishes, she was joined by Dorothy Day. Her biographer concludes that Dorothy wanted to keep an eye on Eugene, even though she denied a sexual attachment. Eugene kept his room above the Hell Hole but spent much of his time with Agnes and Dorothy at Waverly Place.

Sometime in late fall, possibly as late as Christmastime, Eugene learned of the death of a former roommate at Jimmy the Priest's, Chris Christopherson, whom he had known since 1911. Chris, with his streak of mystical love and hatred for the sea, would be the model for Anna Christie's father. Whether by accident or intent, Chris had drowned near his barge late the night of October 15–16, after a bout of heavy drinking at Jimmy the Priest's. His body was found by harbor police eight days later, and he was buried in the same Brooklyn cemetery where Jimmy Byth had been buried in 1913. Counting Driscoll, three of the people Eugene had known well had died hard deaths in three and a half years, and there was about to be a fourth.

In mid-January the return of Louis Holladay to New York was awaited with interest by Eugene and Agnes, by Polly and Adele Holladay, and by many others who counted Louis a friend. During his year of managing the apple orchard, Louis had stayed clear of alcohol and heroin and was returning to his friends, and especially to Louise Norton, who had arranged his cure and who he now hoped would marry him. He arrived

January 22 and would die early the next morning at Romany Marie's restaurant, from what the coroner called chronic endocarditis.

As Sheaffer points out, there are many conflicts in accounts of that night. Most accounts suggest that Louis had sustained himself while in Oregon with idealizing reveries of marriage to Louise. Louis may or may not have met Louise that night. Louise Norton told Sheaffer she never saw Louis after he returned from Oregon (LS, 410). She had written Louis, she said, to tell him she had fallen in love with the avant-garde composer Edgar Varèse, whom she planned to marry. (She worked tirelessly throughout Varèse's life to get a hearing for her husband's rhythmically brilliant, unconventional music.)

Agnes believed that Louise had met Louis on his last night. In her memoir, Agnes wrote that she saw Louise come to the Hell Hole after midnight. (For Agnes's account of the event, see Boulton 1958, 79–85.) She said she remembered watching Louise and Louis sit together for some time talking before she, Agnes, went home exhausted, leaving Gene there with other friends, including Dorothy Day, Christine Ell, the painter Charles Demuth, and another painter, Eddie Fiske (who would later marry Agnes's sister, Cecil). Terry Carlin was there, and also a friend of Eugene's whom Agnes called P——. P—— was probably Robert A. Parker, whom Sheaffer later interviewed and who had known Eugene since about 1908.

At some point that night, after Agnes had left, Louis obtained a quantity of heroin. The Gelbs (367) wrote that Terry Carlin had gotten it for Louis, but Robert Parker denied to Sheaffer "that Terry had any hand in the matter," adding that he, Parker, and Charles Demuth had taken some of the heroin with Louis (LS, 410). Sheaffer writes that as soon as O'Neill saw the heroin, he became "immediately angry . . . and told his friend he was being foolish and reckless, then hurried out into the night." Sometime after Eugene left, Louis inhaled a large enough quantity of the drug to cause a heart attack. Louis's friends, including Eugene and Agnes, considered the death a suicide.

Eugene had returned to Agnes, saying nothing to her about Louis. He seemed in great distress, turned out the light, and got into bed with her. He buried his face in her shoulder and clung silently to her. They held each other for some time. That is how Dorothy found the two of them a little later. Louis had died in her arms shortly after Eugene had left, Dorothy told them. She said that they had to return with her to Romany Marie's to talk to the police. Dorothy showed them the container of heroin, which she had pocketed before the police arrived.

Dorothy, Eugene, and Agnes started out to return with her to Romany Marie's, but on the way Eugene veered off, saying he was going back to the Hell Hole. Agnes and Dorothy returned to the restaurant clutching each other and answered a few questions from the police, while Agnes kept looking at Louis's body until the reality of his death began to sink in. Polly Holladay told the police and coroner that her brother had a history of heart trouble. Eugene had known Louis was going to kill himself, accepted it as done, and immediately felt the reality of the death. His own suicide attempt and the deaths of Jimmy Byth, Driscoll, and Chris in the past three years had made death all too real to him.

After leaving Romany Marie's, Agnes found Eugene in the Hell Hole, drinking and still unable to talk. Agnes believed that Louis's suicide affected Eugene more deeply than she could fully comprehend; it seemed to her to bring to the surface "something violent and destructive," which he controlled with his "unnatural quiet" (84). After a few days, Eugene left the Hell Hole and stayed with Jamie at the Garden Hotel. There he gradually tapered off in his drinking, became "gentler" and more calm, and could go to Agnes at Waverly Place. He suggested that they arrange to get married. Agnes felt they should postpone marriage until they were both more serene. He got their tickets for the Fall River Line boat that would carry them toward Provincetown, and they packed and left New York.

Gene 'n' Aggie
1918–1919

WHEN EUGENE ELOPED WITH AGNES to Provincetown in late January 1918, he was fleeing Louis Holladay's suicide and all the things the suicide meant to him. Like his mother, Eugene felt every new loss reawaken the early compound loss: in his case, of his mother to her addiction at his birth, of his sense of self when he discovered himself to be the cause of her addiction, and of his idealized image of her when he learned that she was a dope fiend. But his later losses were also of persons in their own right. Louis had been a close friend intermittently for a dozen years.

Besides causing Eugene to grieve for Louis himself, Louis's suicide by heroin reminded Eugene of his own near-suicide from veronal, as we know from a one-act play written a year and a half later, in the summer of 1919, called "Exorcism." O'Neill destroyed the play, but not until it had been performed a few times. From a review we know that it described a young man's suicide attempt. The story closely corresponded to the description of Eugene's account to Agnes of his own suicide attempt. Eugene incorporated into the play at least one detail from Louis's story: the main character, contemplating his descent into the depths of despair, recalls being offered a chance to rehabilitate himself by going out west to work on a farm. Unlike Louis, Eugene's character declines the chance.

The list of losses that Eugene was trying to repair by eloping with Agnes must include the several women he had fallen in love with in the preceding five years who had rejected his proposals of marriage, especially Bee Ashe. Eugene had experienced enough losses in recent years to seriously affect someone less sensitive than he by temperament, and he had been further sensitized by his childhood losses.

From a psychoanalytic point of view, a loss affects someone not only as an external separation from an actual person but also as a rending or splitting within the self. The split threatens the integrity and survival of the sense of self. To the extent that the lost person is part of one's self, as a parent or close friend is by definition part of one's ego, the loss seems to be a tearing away of a part of oneself. So it is that one's first reaction to a death or other loss is often to deny that it has taken place. To try to maintain the denial, many seek some new person to fill and soothe the hurt, torn place in the soul.

Nor was eloping the only way that Eugene sought to ease his injured soul. In childhood, when exiled in boarding school, Eugene retreated in his mind to a private estate where, behind walled gardens, he was king, with no other clearly imagined people except vague others who would wait on him and come and go at his bidding. By constant reading, he enlarged and complicated the imaginary world to which he retreated. He also wrote his many letters to his parents and brother, hoping to restore the former life of traveling with his idealized father, who commanded life backstage and was idolized by audiences. Thus he rejected the day-to-day life of boarding school.

Eventually Eugene tried to use poetry to repair the loss. In two important books, *Loss and Symbolic Repair* (1977) and *Creativity as Repair* (1982), Andrew Brink has traveled to the deep sources of lyric poetry in poets who have suffered early losses. Quoting Yeats, Brink reminds us that rhetoric arises from quarrels with others, "poetry out of quarrels with ourselves" (1982, 1). Transferring Yeats's perception to the world assumed by psychoanalytic object relations theory, Brink studies the rending of the self that feels like a quarrel with oneself. "My assumption," he writes, "was that, whenever possible, human beings seek to enhance, or to restore if lost, the integrity of the personality, creativity in the gifted individual being a principal means to this end" (1). Brink then examines the theoretical basis for the claim that "symbolic repair of lost ego integrity is a major mode of creative behaviour" (2), an attempt to "elucidate the meaning of imaginative ego repair and to get at the essence of imagination itself" (3). The lyric poet, Brink asserts, "communicates most directly with the inner self, whose communications from the unconscious are least confused by the need for conventional discourse in clichéd-language."

Eugene wrote lyric poetry all his life and always wanted to be a good poet, but some inhibition made him mock himself when he tried to write in his own person and often spoiled his poems with "conventional discourse in clichéd-language." So eventually he became a playwright. Only when disguised as a character in a play could he allow the communication with the inner self to take place that made for the poetic. He created characters with a touch of the poet. His plays have seemed to many people "poetic" even when they lack the eloquence and exquisite flexibility of language that he sought and seldom found. Cut off from poetic language, he found in his soul musical gifts that he translated into such formal elements as dialogue or setting, or the crescendo and decrescendo of mood and intensity.

To repair the losses his soul had sustained, he wrote plays. We happen to know some details about the way Eugene approached his writing after Louis Holladay's death, including information that connects his work with his reaction to the loss. For several months Eugene had been contemplating a new play, the idea of which began with the title, *Beyond the Horizon*. At first he thought of the horizon chiefly in geographical terms.

In November, before Louis's suicide and possibly before he had learned of Chris's death, Eugene had asked Agnes to go away with him to Provincetown because he wanted to start work on a long play, a *Peer Gynt*-like chronicle of a "Royal Tramp," who left home and family to roam the world. By late January when he actually got to Provincetown, he set to work on the play almost at once, but he soon found the idea going out of focus. When he got it in sight again, it had markedly changed. The horizon no longer referred to global travel. The central character was no longer a rover but instead the consumptive, poetic Robert Mayo, who stayed home, impulsively married a passive, unhappy woman, and devoted his life to traveling beyond the horizons of the imagination.

The two major changes seem clearly a response to the playwright's long list of losses, and particularly to the death of Louis Holladay. Having his character abandon all ties must have seemed too desperate a risk for Eugene to imagine when he had newly experienced a loss and been reminded anew of death's finality. In a gesture of reparation, Eugene had Robert, who has planned to leave the next day on a years-long sailing voyage around the world, discover at the last moment that he and his brother's fiancée love each other and want to marry. Elated to find himself loved, he forgets that he has longed all his life to leave the farm and decides to try to learn to be a farmer. While Eugene imagined Robert Mayo's impulsive marriage, he contemplated his own elopement.

John Francis, Eugene's former landlord, met Eugene and Agnes when their train arrived in Provincetown in late January. Eugene had written for a room without mentioning that he was bringing a woman with him. After taking a moment to think and inspect Agnes, Francis led them to a block of studio apartments that he owned in the middle of town. He installed Eugene in one studio and explained that, it being a slack season, there would be no charge for Agnes's identical studio next door. Each studio consisted of one large room with a sink, a couch and table, a woodstove, a small kerosene cookstove, and a balcony loft with a bed. Eugene paid for rent and food out of fifteen dollars a week that James O'Neill sent. Agnes later recalled that she may have brought to the venture a little money left from the sale of a story.

Preoccupied with his "Royal Tramp" play, Eugene had already begun to drink less heavily on the way to Provincetown. According to Agnes, Eugene had been consuming about a quart a day since they had met in November (Boulton 1958). To taper off, he took precisely measured and timed doses from a pint he had bought for the purpose before they boarded the Fall River steamer. In a few days he had stopped; he would remain dry until May. For the next several years, his drinking was to follow this off-and-on pattern.

The new-found sobriety did not, however, enable him to get the new play in focus. In a letter later written to the *New York Times* (published on April 11, 1920), he explained that before he could find "some fixed outline" for the Royal Tramp story, a new plotline, according to which Robert Mayo stays at home and marries Ruth, came to him in what he called an "unexplainable flash" (LS, 416, 417). He then set out to develop the flash into a scenario. Thus was the sickly, bookish, mystical Robert Mayo born.

Robert, the second son of the Mayos, lacks his father's gift for growing things. The father, James, runs the successful family farm with his first son, Andy, Robert's robust older brother. Andy is to marry Ruth, the daughter of the widow who owns the adjacent farm. As a character, Robert's mother is hardly developed at all. Robert has somehow survived a very serious lung disease, and although he hasn't a trace of the farmer in him, and although the others do not understand him and have no interest in the poets he constantly reads, they love and admire him for the "touch of the poet" he possesses. Having recovered, he feels driven to see what lies beyond the horizon. Robert prepares to set out on the sailing voyage with his uncle, the captain of a bark.

With the vastness of the world before him and the loss of his place and family imminent, Robert gives in to panic on the eve of his departure: this is the interpretation Eugene gave of his character in the letter to the *Times*. Robert's instinct to experience the world was "too conscious, intellectually diluted into a vague, intangible, romantic wanderlust. His powers of resistance, both moral and physical, would also probably be correspondingly watered. He would throw away his instinctive dream and accept the thralldom of the farm for—why almost any nice little poetical craving—the romance of sex, say" (LS, 417).

Robert has secretly loved Ruth. The last night before he is to sail, Ruth confesses to him that it is he rather than Andy whom she loves, and she cannot bear to think of his no longer being part of the only world she has ever known. Robert cannot tell Ruth, as O'Neill's less diluted man might, Yes, but you and I will both adjust to the changes that adult life brings. Instead, Robert decides that rather than allow either of them to lose the world of their childhood, they must marry, and he will stay on the farm and learn to be a farmer. Thus they pretend that they can escape adulthood and the sorrows and losses they know will come. The rest of the play develops the consequences of Robert's choice. Such was the stuff from which O'Neill created the first play written in North America that deserves to be thought of as a tragedy in the tradition of the Greeks.

Before Eugene could get very far with the writing, however, a new complication distracted him. Louise Bryant, who had gone to Russia with Jack Reed, returned alone after four months. Back in Greenwich Village, she very quickly wrote her impressions of the revolution in *Six Red Months in Russia*. In a series of letters to Eugene she demanded that he return to her, she begged forgiveness for the misunderstanding she had created by running off with her husband, and she said that she loved both men but now realized that Eugene needed her more than Jack did, and Jack agreed with her decision. Agnes recalled her letters coming daily, sometimes two a day.

Eugene immediately became gloomy, and Agnes decided that "he liked to suffer" (Boulton 1958, 103), an impression that to her mind accounted not only for his infatuation with Louise but also for his admiration of Strindberg and that has been amplified by several writers. The matter of Eugene's depressions is complicated and discussion of it will be deferred to a later chapter. As for his reaction to Louise's letters, a more conservative interpretation may answer.

It seems likely that the letters made Eugene feel guilty and also intensified whatever doubts he had about eloping with Agnes. Any woman that he cared for could tweak his ancient maternal guilt, sometimes without trying. Louise's complaints had the effect of reminding him that he had not been perfectly constant either, as was proved by his running off with Agnes. Along with making him feel guilty, the letters may have deflected his concentration from the long play.

Agnes's memoir suggests that once Eugene heard from Louise, he did little but mope, but other evidence suggests that it might be closer to the case to say that he did little but write. He set aside the long play and in a few days wrote another play on similar themes, greed and prodigal sons. The one-act play *The Rope* was written to fill the P.P.'s last bill of the season. The story depicts a crazy old farmer whose favorite son has run off to sea but now returns to his family. While the old man spouts quotations from the biblical story of the prodigal son, the son plots to steal his father's hoard of gold. When *The Rope* was finished on March 18, O'Neill sent it to Jig Cook, who immediately scheduled it for the season's final bill. It opened April 26. The play is rough, but it can be effective when well acted, as in the 1989 television production with Elizabeth Ashley, José Ferrer, and Len Cariou. It is important as a first sketch for *Desire Under the Elms* (written in 1923–1924).

Once he finished *The Rope,* Eugene returned to his other prodigal sons, Robert and Andy Mayo. When Robert suddenly announces that he will stay home and marry Ruth, Andy is stunned. Having decided that he cannot remain to witness his girl's betrayal with his brother, he goes off on his uncle's bark. At this his enraged father disowns Andy and dies shortly thereafter. The running of the two farms is left to the inept Robert. Andy settles in Argentina, grows rich playing the stock market, loses all his money, and finally decides that nothing in the world holds any interest, including money or romance.

Love turns to ashes. Robert and Ruth grow to hate each other, and only Robert cares for their sickly daughter. He does what he can on the farms, but his health is failing, and his mind is always on the poets, to whom he turns every moment when he is not in the fields. The child dies, leaving Robert with only his books. As he grows increasingly ill, he and Ruth pass beyond hatred to a kind of reconciliation based on the insight that both have finally gained into the arrogance that led them to their dreadful pass.

From the reconciliation Eugene created a subtle and complex ending. When Robert is about to die, Andy comes home with a plan to save the farm. But Robert is more concerned about saving his brother's soul. Eugene had the dying Robert insist that Andy marry Ruth, not to support and take care of her, but so that Andy could awaken from the sleep in which he has led his life. He is a man who, like America itself, has been given every natural endowment, who was born into his natural, instinctive place in the world and, but for Robert and Ruth's mistake, would have lived out his days in it. Yet, like America, he did not know what he had, did not value it, and threw it away. (Thus O'Neill described his nation in 1916.) Robert insists that Ruth teach Andy what she and Robert have learned about their own arrogance and help him survive the suffering that will come when he awakens.

By the time of his death, Robert has earned a prophetic authority and dies mystically calling to the sun. Eugene invests in him some of the same odd authority Sophocles gives the old Oedipus, who goes to die at Colonos. The mood of O'Neill's play is somber, yet as tragic plays often do, *Beyond the Horizon* leaves one feeling thoughtful rather than depressed, and also, perhaps, elated in a way that is hard to account for.

In less than two months, working long shifts and writing at the speed of light, Eugene completed a very long draft of this strongly developed, deeply thought-out play. All the while he continued to receive letters from Louise Bryant, each of which, Agnes said, he answered.

Louise was not the only distraction. Eugene was offered the chance to sell rights for *In the Zone* to agents for the Orpheum Vaudeville Circuit. The production developed by the Washington Square Players would tour the country with a guaranteed income (variously given as anywhere between seventy and a hundred dollars a week) to be split by the author and the Players. After first rejecting the offer on principle—that he was above vaudeville—Eugene decided that the money would be welcome. To this point James had generously supported Eugene and Agnes in Provincetown. Perhaps Eugene accepted because it struck him that he was asking his father and Agnes to pay for his principles. It was a decision in favor of financial independence, a recognition that he would eventually have to stop depending on his father's allowance. He got an advance of two hundred dollars, with an additional fifty dollars a week, which continued until after the war ended the following November. As a further distraction, George Jean Nathan had persuaded an important new theatrical producer, John D. Williams, to read and see several O'Neill plays, and Williams was interested in meeting Eugene.

The income seems to have spurred the couple's plans to marry, whatever Eugene's misgivings. Meanwhile, various people in Provincetown were concerned about getting Eugene and Agnes respectably wedded. Partitions between the studios were so thin that a spoken word might be understood two rooms away. The other tenant in the studios, an artist named Lytton Beuhler, called and diffidently told them that he had not been able to avoid overhearing them say that they wanted to marry but did not know how to go about it, given that the town had no justice of the peace who was licensed to perform marriages. Beuhler explained that they should see the druggist, John Adams, who would get them a marriage license. Alice Woods Ullman, a writer who had befriended Agnes, told them of a Methodist minister, Mr. Johnson, who would be glad to marry them in his parlor. Eugene and Agnes married on April 12, 1918. To Nina Moise, Eugene wrote:

> We were married two evenings ago—in the best parlor of a
> parsonage by the most delightful, feeble-minded, Godhel-
> pus, mincing Methodist minister that ever prayed through
> his nose. I don't mean to sneer, really. The worthy divine
> is an utterly lovable old idiot, and the ceremony gained a
> strange, unique simplicity from his sweet, childlike sincer-
> ity. I caught myself wishing I could believe in the same gen-
> tle God he seemed so sure of. This sounds like sentimental-
> ity but it isn't. It's hard to describe—the wedding of two
> serious children he made out of it; but it was startlingly im-
> pressive. The meaning behind the lines "got across with the
> punch" to both of us. (And just think we were intending to
> have a Justice perform but, luckily, there isn't one in town
> with the requisite authority.) [LS, 416]

Two serious children. "Babes in the woods," Agnes wrote. Indeed. They thought of their marriage as if it had no context outside itself. No, they insisted on that. That is the theory behind the pact they made and remade, never to let any considerations of family, children, or anything else interfere in their perfect intimacy. They ordained that marriage must isolate them from their families, and from all consequences of their actions. One likely consequence of their marriage they dealt with by denial. "As for having any children of our own," Agnes wrote in her memoir, "I am sure we never thought of it. A strange attitude," she comments, "for people getting married, but then Gene was an unusual man, and so, perhaps, at that time, was I." She continues: "No—to be alone with me was what he wanted; we had everything—work, love and companionship. Never, *never* let anything interfere with work or love" (Boulton 1958, 156). That Agnes had a daughter, Barbara, seems never to have occurred to either, nor did the thought that Barbara might live anywhere but with her Boulton grandparents.

Agnes thought of herself as unconventional and came from a family of freethinkers. She had been born on September 19, 1893, in London, where her parents were staying with her grandparents, and had been educated mostly by her parents, and for a time at a convent near Philadelphia. She grew up in various places in rural New Jersey, Pennsylvania, Connecticut, and New York.

She was the oldest of four daughters of Edward and Cecil Boulton. A respected portrait painter, Teddy Boulton had been a protégé of Thomas Eakins and had been chosen to help Eakins take the famous death mask of Walt Whitman. Agnes described her father as a gentle, lovable, unworldly soul with little interest in practical affairs. He had resisted pressure to enter the family shipping business but did not break with his family. He married a girl from London, Cecil Williams, whose father, Robert Williams, had been a Greek scholar at Christ Church and Merton College, Oxford, and had known Lady Wilde and her circle, the Russells, Swinburne, the Rossettis, and other prominent people. Grandmother Williams had trained as a librarian and had become a freethinker. She was one of the educated, thoughtful women to whom Shaw addressed his guides to socialism, and who were celebrated by Forster.

In middle age she had converted to Catholicism, and Agnes's mother, then seventeen, also converted. Grandmother Williams later became a devotee of Mme. Blavatsky and Mr. Sinnet, and a subscriber to the Oriental Esoteric Society. Agnes grew up reading difficult books—

she writes that she attempted Kant's *Critique of Pure Reason* when she was fourteen. She found the substantial publications of the Esoteric Society ordered by her grandmother more manageable, including the Upanishads, various guides to Buddhism, and books on yoga. In her early teens she worked for some time to become an adept, rising at three in the morning to meditate and study. Through much of Agnes's adolescence, the Boultons lived on a farm near West Point Pleasant, New Jersey, in a large old house belonging to Teddy's aunt Agnes Boulton, for whom Agnes was named. The farm passed into the possession of the second Agnes Boulton, and she kept it all her life. This was the farm where Agnes and Eugene spent their second winter together.

At the time of her marriage, Agnes's younger sisters were still at home with the Boultons, along with Agnes's daughter Barbara Burton. Agnes in her memoir quotes the heading of a news story about herself that described her as a "young widow" who had been supporting her parents and daughter by dairy farming and who had now come to New York to make her living as a writer (Boulton 1958, 62). Probably the story was written by someone Agnes knew through her connections with pulp magazine publishers, with the aim of making her better known as a writer.

To what extent Agnes supported her parents, sisters, and daughter, and to what extent the family got along on Teddy's small commissions and on contributions from Grannie Williams, is not known. The Boultons had few expenses, because they lived on various properties belonging to Teddy's family, grew much of their food, and educated the children mostly at home. Cecil governed her four daughters strictly. In talking with Sheaffer, Agnes mentioned painful recollections of being disciplined by severe whipping with a belt (LS papers).

Agnes's daughter, Barbara, was about two when Agnes went to New York to try to become a full-time writer. From the few brief references to her daughter in her memoir, it is hard to form much of an impression of the bond between Agnes and Barbara. Nothing is known about Mr. Burton or about Agnes's first marriage, except that it may have taken place in London, and Burton may have died in the war. Various researchers have found no record of the marriage at Somerset House in London or in New Jersey, New York, or Connecticut.

At the time she met Eugene, she was twenty-four and had been selling romance fiction to pulp magazines since she was seventeen. She was intelligent and widely read, and she had a good literary education. She did not aim to write literary work, but she took her work seriously and understood the craft of writing popular fiction. In 1944 she published a novel, *The Road Before Us,* which earned favorable reviews, and her memoir of her marriage to Eugene, *Part of a Long Story* (Boulton 1958), shows a spirit able to step beyond self-interest.

Eugene wrote to his parents, who were touring with *The Wanderer,* to tell them of Agnes and his marriage. Agnes remembered the letter as being very complimentary to her. But she did not meet the senior O'Neills until late the following fall. She wrote to her parents that she had married, but Eugene did not want to meet his in-laws and would not do so for some time. In fact, he became resentful when Agnes got letters from her mother, especially if they contained no worse news than ordinary troubles in the family.

The matter of Louise Bryant remained unsettled after the marriage. As before, the sequence of events is unclear. But it seems that around the time of the marriage, and possibly in response to news of the marriage, Louise redoubled her efforts to summon Eugene to New York. Her book came out, and several articles giving her impressions of the Revolution were also published. She was soon known as an authority on the new Russia and would testify about the Revolution to congressional committees. Despite her new fame, she wrote, it was Eugene she wanted. "Page after page of passionate declaration of their love," Agnes recalled, "of hers, which would never change; of his, which she knew would never change. . . . It was all a misunderstanding and *her* fault for leaving him, for going to Russia with Jack" (Boulton 1958, 103).

Agnes remembered being patient at first, but she scoffed at the story of Louise and Jack's not being sexual lovers. Don't go to New York, she insisted. Once back there, you may start drinking again, she warned. Think about your play. Don't you see that all Louise wants is to show everyone in the Village that if she beckons, Gene will come? When she thought he had decided to go, Agnes summoned her self-control, stopped arguing, and proposed the Fall River compromise. She told him to go to Fall River and meet Louise at the steamer terminal. They could talk things over and decide what to do. She would await his decision in Provincetown.

Finally, Eugene wrote and rewrote a long letter to Louise reviewing the history of their affair and proposing the compromise, which he gave Agnes to read. She described it as a beautiful letter that seemed perfectly spontaneous and unrevised. Agnes reported that on reading it, Louise was enraged; she belittled Agnes, denounced Eugene. The letters dwindled to a trickle and eventually stopped. Various sources report that Louise, who had not drunk at all when Eugene had known her, now drank heavily. In a further twist, disputed by Barbara Gelb (1973, 190), Agnes claimed that Louise later spread rumors that Eugene had come to her and that she had turned him away and had found him drunk on her doorstep after she rejected him. Barbara Gelb and other writers agree that Eugene never saw Louise again after he married Agnes.

Neither of the two serious children had much of a feel for the practical aspects of life, especially married life. From her description of a few meals, it sounds as if Agnes knew a thing or two about cooking, but Eugene was helpless in the kitchen, and neither took pleasure in it. All biographers concur that such housekeeping as they did at all was done casually.

Money was a particular problem for both of them. In 1915, about to go home for Christmas break from Harvard with some money from his father, Eugene had confessed to Bee Ashe that "Where money is concerned I am totally irresponsible, it burns holes in my pockets, I am absolutely uneasy until it is gone" (SL, 43). Little had changed by 1918. As soon as he and Agnes got to Provincetown, Eugene insisted that Agnes be his banker and financial keeper, much to her discomfort. Agnes's own financial affairs were tangled. She had some mortgaged property and the residue of a small trust from her great-aunt Agnes, but she owed money on a series of notes, which had been passed from one insolvent person to another. When she married, all of them descended on her. Neither she nor Eugene could determine what she owed or to whom. Although Eugene had a substantial income after 1920, his financial affairs remained tangled throughout his marriage to Agnes.

Eugene began to earn money almost as soon as he had married. When he finished his draft of *Beyond the Horizon,* he sent copies to Nathan and to the producer John D. Williams. Almost immediately, Williams sent Eugene a check for the impressive sum of five hundred dollars for an option to produce it. At the time the money and the option seemed a gift from heaven. In fact, it turned out to be a curse. It gave Williams sole rights to *Beyond the Horizon* and also to any other long plays Eugene might write, and it did not compel Williams to act promptly.

Agnes says not a word about how they spent the money. Another couple might have thought of using it to buy a house. (A few months later Eugene persuaded his father to buy him a house near the outer tip of Cape Cod that cost a thousand dollars.) But most of the advance from Williams seems to have gone on a trip of several weeks that they immediately took to New York. Probably Eugene repaid numerous small debts of money, drink, and hospitality that he had run up in the last two or three years. More went on hotels and clothing.

Eugene was elated that at last one of his long plays would be produced. He and Agnes went to New York partly to meet Williams and partly to see *The Rope,* which Nina Moise was directing. Williams and O'Neill formed good first impressions of each other. Eugene believed that Williams genuinely admired *Beyond the Horizon,* and was convinced that he would give it a serious production. Heywood Broun's praise for *The Rope* probably led to an immediate revival by the Washington Square Players that opened on May 13. Several reviewers saw it in the revival and praised its strength, and *Theatre Magazine* found "real literary worth" in O'Neill's script (LS, 423). Eugene and Agnes remained in town several weeks and saw much of Jamie. Eugene had arranged for John Francis to move their belongings to his bayside apartment block known as the Flats, which had excellent views of the water. But Eugene started drinking with Jamie and some old friends, and another week passed before Agnes could get all of them on a train. Jamie had found a mangy dog somewhere and argued with the conductor, before being made to deposit it in the baggage car. Both brothers were talking about having the d.t.'s on the train.

John Francis put Jamie into the flat next to the one he had reserved for Agnes and Eugene. Jamie and Eugene continued drinking. Agnes found that Jamie was quiet, thoughtful, and gentle with the two of them, a very different man from the witty bon vivant she had always seen in the Village. Eugene, she said, relaxed around Jamie as he did with no other person. Nevertheless, Eugene and Agnes found it wearing to share their solitude with even Jamie.

Before long, Provincetown was full of their friends from the Village—the Cooks, Wilbur Daniel Steele and Margaret Steele, Mary Vorse, Terry Carlin, Harold DePolo and his wife, Saxe Commins, the sculptor William Zorach, and the painter Charles Demuth. Someone told Sheaffer that Zorach and Demuth were the only people besides Eugene who really seemed to work during the summer. And Christine Ell, who came for the summer, opened a restaurant, so everyone ate well and cheaply.

Eugene continued drinking for a while after returning from New York, then gradually stopped and resumed writing. It was a fertile summer for his imagination, even for O'Neill. He started two long plays that he would not finish until the following spring, one about his dead friend Chris Christopherson, and one called *The Straw,* about a girl dying in a T.B. sanatorium. He began cutting and revising *Beyond the Horizon* and obtained a second copyright in early August for the revised version. He discovered James Joyce and read *Dubliners* and *A Portrait of the Artist.*

O'Neill wrote at least four more short plays that spring and summer, trying to give Jig and Susan something to open the season. These include *Shell Shock, Where the Cross Is Made,* the destroyed "Till We Meet" (of which nothing is known), and *The Dreamy Kid. The Dreamy Kid,* about a young black who murders a white man, grew out of a story told Eugene by his old friend from the Hell Hole, the gambler Joe Smith, whom he had seen in May. At first the Cooks were enthusiastic about the play, particularly as Eugene wanted the black roles to be played by black actors. The Players decided to defer *The Dreamy Kid;* the production, with a black cast, would open the first bill of the 1919–20 season a year later and run two weeks. Meanwhile, the Players needed a play for the first bill of 1918, so Eugene turned to another idea. He had outlined a third long play the previous summer but had not yet begun to write it— the play that later became the melodrama *Gold,* a play whose story came from one of Agnes's unpublished stories called "The Captain's Walk." Eugene decided he could make a one-act play of the last act, and he called it *Where the Cross Is Made.* The Players took it and opened with it on November 22.

Shell Shock, which may have been written as early as February, deserves a word of mention because it shows Eugene's interest in the phenomenon of war neurosis. Traumatic neuroses interested Freud because they seemed to run counter to his theory of neurosis; that is, they did not seem to arise from an internal, sexual etiology. A severe external shock could create debilitating symptoms that resembled neurotic symptoms but could often be permanently relieved by verbal catharsis or might otherwise simply vanish; or they might last a lifetime. The play gives a clinically accurate, convincing account of a soldier's symptomatic behavior suggesting that O'Neill had read about the topic and recognized something that he himself knew about repetitive neurotic behavior. The soldier had a symptomatic ritual in which he compulsively begged cigarettes from other people, took a few puffs, put the cigarettes out, and saved the butts in his pocket, all the while reliving in his thoughts an act of his in battle that he considered selfish and disgusting.

The soldier's achievement of insight in conversation with a friend has an authentic ring that convinces one that Eugene knew something about both traumatic neurosis and, more important, the achievement of insight. Further, the addictive quality of the smoking is so strikingly presented that one can speculate that Eugene was thinking about his own drinking. The traumatic event in Eugene's life is evident. It was the time his mother tried to kill herself when she had run out of morphine, the time when Eugene learned that she was an addict and he was the cause of her addiction. At this point he began addictive drinking. The pattern of his drinking is something that Eugene studied from time to time.

Through the summer and early fall, Eugene and Agnes wrote, loved, swam in the ocean, and rambled about the end of the cape. Not far from the tip they found the house they decided should be theirs. It was a former Coast Guard station called Peaked Hill Bars, which had been abandoned because the ever-changing shoreline made it likely that before long the building would slide into the sea. The financier Sam Lewisohn had bought it from the Coast Guard several years before. Mabel Dodge had decorated it in strong quiet style, and she and Lewisohn had used it as a retreat for a time but had grown tired of it a couple of years earlier. By now the drifting sand had piled clear to the eaves, so one could scramble up the dune and onto the roof. Eugene and Agnes imagined living in the house and found that John Francis was trying to sell it for Lewisohn.

Meanwhile, Eugene waited to hear from John D. Williams about *Beyond the Horizon,* which he expected to open in the fall. Williams said he expected to sign John and Lionel Barrymore to play the Mayo brothers. Jig and Susan and the other Players returned to New York and set about moving the theater from 139 to 133 MacDougal Street. The magazine *Current Opinion* published a shortened version of *In the Zone,* praised its author, and passed on the rumor that O'Neill's first long play "would be presented in New York this season" (LS, 439). Eugene learned that John Barrymore would act in Tolstoy's *Redemption* and waited weeks without hearing from Williams. Word came that Williams was doing Oscar Wilde's *An Ideal Husband* and another comedy. In fact, Williams was to produce *The Jest* instead of the Wilde play. Eugene decided that he needed to be closer to New York for the winter to keep after Williams, yet he knew that if he lived in the city he would start drinking again and would write nothing. He and Agnes decided to move to the farm she had inherited from her aunt Agnes in West Point Pleasant, New Jersey, a comfortable two-hour train ride from the city.

The worldwide epidemic of Spanish flu sickened huge numbers of people, many of whom died. Eugene and Agnes in Provincetown learned from Jamie that Ella was stricken, though fortunately her case was a light one. Provincetown also was affected by the epidemic, but it seemed a better place to be than New York. They read daily news of the war, which was ending. People in New York were enraged as its toll became increasingly evident, the news aggravated by revelations of political and economic interests that had seemingly contrived and benefited from the slaughter of youth. Ella had recovered from the flu but in late October was diagnosed with breast cancer. She had to go through a mastectomy. Eugene and Agnes finally visited his parents to console Ella while she recuperated.

The deep oedipal ambivalence Eugene felt toward his mother, awakened by her dangerous and disfiguring illness and surgery, erupted the night before he was to introduce his wife to his parents. Eugene got drunk at a party given in his honor as a homecoming by P.P. friends. Agnes seemed to him to be flirting with Teddy Ballantine, who was acting with Barrymore in *Redemption*. According to Agnes's account, Eugene shoved her, then slapped her "as hard as possible with the back of his hand" (LS, 440). Stella Ballantine bawled out Eugene and took Agnes home, counseling her all the while that the slap meant nothing; it was simply something that went along with genius, and it meant only that Gene had resented the attention she was getting from Teddy. Much later, guilty and ashamed, Eugene returned to their hotel, but he could not face his parents in the morning and had Agnes call to make excuses. The meeting was deferred until evening, after dinner.

When they did meet, James was gracious and courtly and Ella charmed Agnes with her beauty and an aura "of serenity and goodness." The meeting must have greatly impressed Agnes, who gave a very detailed account. Agnes, who may have been a little taller, remembered Ella as being small and elegant, her white hair beautifully waved, her speech precise; Agnes recalled Ella wearing a black silk dress with fine lace at the collar and wrists, and exquisite shoes. Leaning over to speak to Eugene, Ella put her hand on Agnes's hand, and Agnes noticed a faint, "elusive" perfume. Ella took Agnes to her closet and showed her a full length Persian lamb coat and seemed about to give her a mink scarf, then thought better of it. From later conversation, Agnes got the impression that the gift of the scarf had been discussed and had been vetoed by James. Conversation was very polite until Jamie entered, very potted, announcing himself with the call: "*What ho! The prodigal returns.*" Jamie, James, Ella, and Eugene commenced to argue in a style that, in Agnes's account, sounds very like a scene from *Long Day's Journey into Night* (Boulton 1958, 213–14).

Before they went on to West Point Pleasant, Eugene tried to see Williams but had to settle for John D.'s brother Joe, who was worried and put Eugene in a gloomy mood. Eugene also met with Jimmy Light about the production of *Where the Cross Is Made* that was to open the Provincetown season on November 22. While Eugene talked about plays, Agnes discovered a problem with their plan to move to the West Point Pleasant farmhouse, the problem being that her parents, grandmother, sisters, and daughter were living there and had no idea that Aggie and Gene were on the way. Perhaps her mother had not mentioned that they were going to move there from Connecticut, or perhaps Agnes had known and forgotten. A farce was now enacted, complete with a character who meets relatives without recognizing them, and a character who has no idea about things everyone else knows.

Agnes wrote to her mother that her genius-husband simply could not stand the least distraction when writing. It simply would not be possible for them all to be there together. The Boultons were well settled in the house, with Teddy Boulton working on a series of watercolor landscapes in his studio. For reasons that are not clear—perhaps because Agnes owned the house—her parents moved out on almost no notice into a house that they rented nearby. Teddy Boulton abandoned his landscapes and took a ten-hour-a-day, ten-dollar-a-week job at the local hardware store to pay the rent. Possibly because she was ashamed of the situation she felt she had caused and believed that Eugene did not want to know anything about her family, Agnes said nothing of all these arrangements. Once Eugene bought something at the hardware store from his father-in-law without knowing who the man was. When letters for Agnes came in envelopes from the hardware store, Eugene suspected her of having an old lover there, particularly because she seemed to find awkward excuses for frequent visits to the store. Agnes and the Boultons, particularly Agnes's younger sisters, found the situation amusing and joked about the lion to be bearded that ruled their sister's pride.

The situation caused resentment rather than amusement among local people, who thought it unnatural for a daughter to throw her parents out of a house they had occupied (off and on) since before her birth. The mailman and the jitney driver who took them shopping to town showed their disapproval. Such resentment may have been the cause of an ugly incident that winter. Eugene had adopted a large white dog he called Brooklyn Boy, with which he walked alone or with Agnes in the woods near the farmhouse. One morning they found the dog's body in front of the house, his throat cut. Some time later, a country woman asked Agnes if her husband used drugs, having decided that no normal man would walk by himself in the woods and having heard that he did not drink. In local lore Eugene was held to blame for the expulsion of the Boultons.

Sometime later, Eugene accidentally learned that the Boultons lived nearby and complained to Agnes about her secret. Before long, Eugene had met all the members of her family, starting with her grandmother, who had met the Russells, Swinburne, the Rossettis, and other people Eugene had long admired. When the two middle sisters dropped by to look at him, he hid in a closet, for some reason unable or unwilling to face them; the sisters giggled silently, understanding what he had done, but tried to avoid further embarrassing him. But as he met the Boultons little by little, he found he liked them all. As Agnes says, Eugene remained on good terms with all the Boultons throughout the marriage. He occasionally contributed to their finances, supported Agnes's daughter Barbara, and apparently paid more attention to Barbara during her summer visits with the O'Neills than Agnes did. On the whole, by Agnes's and others' testimony, Eugene was not an intolerable son-in-law and usually managed to be a decent if eccentric member of the family.

Agnes's account of the move to the farmhouse is very odd; the Gelbs call the incident "typical of the scatterbrained arrangements O'Neill and Agnes were inclined to make," surely a mild and reasonable judgment (Gelbs, 386). But it is interesting to try to understand how the problem might have arisen. One of the things Agnes must have felt she could contribute to the marriage was the various properties she owned. Having promised them a place to live, perhaps she simply could not stand the shame of going back on her word or explaining her mistake, and so she persuaded her mother to help her save face. Perhaps, too, she overestimated Eugene's reluctance to be acquainted with her family. Eugene no doubt grumbled about meeting his in-laws, but when in fact he did meet them, things went well. Agnes perhaps took the grumbling for something worse and acted accordingly. The odd event points to something that had not yet developed and never did during their marriage, the gift for mutual empathy that allows lovers or mates to know each other intuitively. From time to time they experienced an intense merging of souls, especially when they were physically separated; but they could not know each other's thoughts and feelings while retaining a sense of the boundary between their separate selves. They seem not to have enjoyed the relaxed day-to-day intuitive connection many couples know.

In fact, Eugene was always hard to read. Throughout his life he appeared to ignore things going on around him or things others told him. His third wife, Carlotta Monterey, told Sheaffer about getting used to the idea that even when he seemed to be lost in his own thoughts, he missed virtually nothing. Eugene's friends somehow learned to take for granted his poker face and his concealed alertness. Agnes apparently never did.

Instead, she resorted to guessing at what might please him. Eugene seemed to her mostly to want her attention and admiration, and much of the time that may have been what she most wanted to give. She was fascinated with the creative process, which she (and he) thought of as mystical. He reciprocated her attention. According to her account, he strongly encouraged her writing and shared her interest in tracing how ideas arose and where they might come from. She believed him to be a genius and felt deeply rewarded by participation in his creative life. For her it was a continuation of a mystical interest that had begun in her adolescence and had probably had to do with watching her father paint. In writing her memoir, Agnes gives an account of Eugene's asking her to watch him exercise with a ball that she connects by association with her grandparents' illustrious literary associates, and her father's affiliation with Thomas Eakins (Boulton 1958, 259–61). In so doing, she does not appear to be name-dropping, or even remarking on her husband's childlike desire to be watched. Instead, she seems to regard with wonder such lives caught up in the whirlpool of creativity, a maelstrom that banished all illusions that one controls very much of one's life.

Eugene, for his part, must have realized the effect his silences had on her, but he did not or could not become more open. From childhood he had been taciturn. When the ardor of their love was at the flood they could express it with their bodies; when it ebbed they grew silent and still. Both were believers in the mystical rhythms of love. Unable to find ordinary conversation, they were helpless when the mystical tides inscrutably drew them together and then left them to drift amid tense silences and guesswork. Neither could find a basic trust in the constancy of their bond that might have eased the ebb and flow of intimacy.

Testy about Williams's procrastination and about finding a place to write in a strange house, Eugene gradually settled down to work on *The Straw* and *Chris Christophersen,* but his work was often interrupted by letters to and from the Players about the production of *Where the Cross Is Made* and by worries about the delay of *Beyond the Horizon.* He made several trips to town to help with rehearsals of *Where the Cross Is Made* and to try to confront Williams. The main problem with the one-acter was that ghosts were supposed to be visible to the audience and one member of the cast but not to the rest of the cast. In the tiny theater, the illusion did not work—that is, the three men representing the ghosts simply looked like three men trying to act like ghosts. Heywood Broun praised the play, and Nathan once classed it among O'Neill's better works, but Eugene disliked it from the first, considering it interesting only as an experiment in trying to persuade the audience to doubt its sanity in the matter of seeing ghosts. Like several plays written in 1917–1919, *Where the Cross Is Made* was written because the Players needed a play and because Eugene needed to be working constantly.

In New York, Eugene saw a good deal of his father. James had been struck by a car, and although he did not appear seriously injured and seemed to recover quickly and fully, his spirit was somehow affected, and he ceased to seem much younger than his age—then about seventy-four. A new phase now began in their relationship. James was increasingly respectful of Eugene's plays, even when he found them upsetting or pessimistic, and was growing to think of his younger son as an adult colleague. Around Christmastime, hearing of the house at Peaked Hill Bars, James bought it for Eugene as a wedding present. While James negotiated the price of the old lifesaving station, *The Moon of the Caribbees* was rehearsing at the Playwrights' Theatre, directed by default by the very young actor Thomas Mitchell. With a novice director, a complicated set, and a large cast (not many of whom attended rehearsals), the play disappointed everyone, especially the playwright, who would always consider it one of his favorites.

Eugene and Agnes settled into a satisfactory working routine: writing every morning until midday, having a silent lunch—both still absorbed in the work to which they would return after eating—and calling it quits in the afternoon. Then for Eugene might follow a half-hour workout with a punching bag, or an hour of chopping wood for the various stoves that heated the house. Finally, they would take a long walk with a dog, perhaps to the shore, half a mile away. In the evening after supper, they read or wrote letters.

The Moon of the Caribbees failed at its premiere. Reviewers considered it not a play at all but simply an interlude, an impression still held by people who believe that O'Neill is primarily a naturalistic or realistic playwright. Yet at least one of his early fans saw what Eugene was aiming for. After watching the disappointing performance, Richard J. Madden introduced himself to the author. A partner of Elizabeth Marbury in the American Play Company, theatrical agents, Madden had carefully followed O'Neill's career before seeking him out. Sheaffer describes Madden as "a gentleman in a hyperthyroid business . . . an agent of taste and integrity who handled only writers he respected." The two men went upstairs to Christine's restaurant and talked for hours. Madden wrote to his wife that he found the playwright "so intelligent," but also "vulnerable," impressions also held by several of Eugene's closest friends (LS, 448–49). Like Saxe Commins and several other friends, Madden instinctively took a protective attitude toward O'Neill.

With only a handshake for a contract, Madden became Eugene's agent and friend. The relationship lasted until Madden died. Madden's first task was to try to persuade Williams to mount *Beyond the Horizon* or release it to another producer. Eddie Goodman had heard about *Beyond the Horizon* and was interested in producing it with the Washington Square Players, who had succeeded with *In the Zone*. Eugene was also worried about *The Straw*, almost completed, which was bound to Williams by the option on *Beyond the Horizon*.

Good news and bad news came together. In January 1919, the adventurous publishing house of Boni and Liveright, publishers of the Modern Library, of Ernest Hemingway, Theodore Dreiser, T. S. Eliot,

Sherwood Anderson, e. e. cummings, Ezra Pound, Robinson Jeffers, Hart Crane, and William Faulkner, offered to publish a group of seven one-act sea plays, including the four *Glencairn* plays, and *Ile, The Rope,* and *Where the Cross Is Made.* It was a momentous occasion, at least as notable a sign of recognition as the New York production of *Beyond the Horizon* would be.

The end of the same month brought Eugene yet another shocking loss. Hutch Collins, a friend from New London since their adolescence, caught the flu and then pneumonia. Jamie wrote to Eugene that Collins had died within a few days. Sheaffer quotes from a letter to Susan Glaspell that Eugene wrote on January 29: "[Hutch] possessed, above all other men . . . such a pronounced delight in living. . . . In New London days we were thrown into the closest intimacy by the very narrowness of our environment. . . . You can imagine, then, my sense of deep personal loss, of abiding sorrow" (LS, 448). Through January, Eugene had labored to finish *The Straw.* After Hutch died, Eugene buried himself in his other long play, *Chris Christophersen.*

Hutch's death was followed by news of yet another important Event—the word was always capitalized in Eugene's letters. In March or April Agnes discovered herself to be pregnant. From her account it sounds as if she had not considered such a thing possible and was quite uncertain how or when it could have happened. So uncertain was she, she writes, that she gave the family doctor incorrect information, from which he calculated a parturition in late September. (The baby would actually be born October 30.) She felt she could not tell her husband about the pregnancy. As often, she felt she could not read him at all. To her surprise, when she hesitantly told Eugene the news, after choosing her time carefully, he already seemed to know. Yet she continued to feel apprehensive. "I could not tell what he was thinking about. I was miserable imagining what he *might* be thinking about. He was withdrawn, deep in himself, not hostile, not even perturbed, so far as I could see. But there was no contact between us." While she worried about his response, one of the cats chose the moment to have kittens and insisted that Eugene, as Agnes puts it, be present to hold her paw. Eugene became very enthusiastic about his midwife role and sang sailors' work songs in his cracked baritone, which he insisted soothed the cat in her labors. Eugene named the kittens Whiskey, Blow, and Drumstick (Boulton 1958, 275–77). Despite Agnes's misgivings, Eugene was quietly happy and proud that he was to be a father.

Eugene's prospects continued to shine. Williams liked *The Straw* and wanted to place it under option. Eugene at first agreed, then, perhaps after conferring with Madden, changed his mind before signing a contract. Williams wanted a long-term option on future work, without being willing to give any assurance of speedy production. When Eugene refused the option, Williams released the play, and it was sold instead to James O'Neill's old friend George Tyler. It began to seem that whatever the delay, further productions of the plays would take place. Letters arrived from strangers who wanted to produce this or that one-act play by O'Neill.

In early May, furthermore, Eugene had a letter from a respected theater critic, Barrett Clark, who wanted information about the author for a review he was writing of *The Moon of the Caribbees and Six Other One Act Plays of the Sea,* the Boni and Liveright volume. Along with the letter, Clark sent Eugene a copy of his anthology *European Theories of the Drama,* which had come out the previous fall. Also in May, Eugene finally met George Jean Nathan. Nathan later recorded his first impressions of O'Neill: "extremely shy" but with "vast confidence in himself . . . a deep-running personality—the most ambitious mind I have encountered among American dramatists" (LS, 452). Eugene now resumed his relationship with Baker, sending him the Boni and Liveright volume and telling of the long plays he had written. Baker, Nathan, and Clark would all become members of the small circle to whom Eugene occasionally showed unpublished, unproduced work. The sea plays received uniformly favorable reviews when they came out.

As Eugene began to gain success and recognition, no one was prouder or happier for him than his father. The two grew increasingly close. Eugene's frequent visits to New York, often in the company of Agnes, usually ended in a long evening with his father and mother. Both were completely delighted that they were to be grandparents, and James was happy that when the younger couple went to Cape Cod at the end of May, it was to the house he had bought for Eugene.

When Eugene finished *Chris* in early May, he sent it to Tyler, who liked the play but had doubts about the last act. For the next year and a half Eugene would tinker constantly with the material, eventually changing every aspect of the play—the plot, the setting, and all the characters except Chris himself. He would work for weeks, believe he had solved the problems, send it to Tyler, then decide that the problems remained or that he saw new problems, and set to work again. In the meantime, he tried to persuade Tyler to produce *The Straw,* but everyone who looked at it thought that because of the recent flu epidemic, a drama set in a T.B. sanatorium would play to empty theaters. Tyler eventually read the play and pronounced it "wonderful," but he declined to say yes or no.

In addition to revising *Chris,* Eugene wrote three one-act plays over the summer, "Exorcism," "Honor Among the Bradleys," and "The Trumpet," all three of which he destroyed—although "Exorcism" was not destroyed until after it had been performed. But on the whole, Eugene was losing interest in short plays. While he struggled with *Chris,* he seethed at seeing Williams's production of *The Jest* with the Barrymore brothers thrive. It ran until late spring, closed temporarily for the summer, but would reopen in October and was expected to run through the next season. Its success implied further delays for *Beyond the Horizon.* As for *The Straw,* Eugene now looked for hope in a new direction. The Washington Square Players had collapsed in the spring, but from their ashes rose a new organization, the Theatre Guild, led by Lawrence Langner, Philip Moeller, and Helen Westley.

In late May or early June, Eugene and Agnes had moved into the house at Peaked Hill Bars after some days of shoveling away the drifted sand that had blocked the doors and windows for a couple of years. The windows had been scoured to opacity by wind and sand and had to be replaced every year. Inside the couple found treasure after treasure among Mabel Dodge's furnishings, made or purchased for the house and sold with it. According to Agnes, they found copper cooking pots and skillets hung on the walls, a fine willowware dinner service, platters, a tureen, sets of glassware—"everything beautiful, unusual and useful," Agnes wrote (Boulton 1958, 284). The floors, with seven coats of a deep but not dark blue paint, seemed lacquered, as did the walls and ceilings, which were white, and all the surfaces seemed luminous, even in the dark, so deep was the light held by the layers of pigment. Agnes said that she tried several times in later years to reproduce the blue of the floors, without success. Eugene loved the house, and Agnes thought he was always happy there. Over the summer they followed their routine: writing in the mornings, swimming and walking the beach in the afternoons; they read at night. Once a week they trudged over the sands to Provincetown to visit Jig and Susan, the Hutchins Hapgoods, the Ballantines, Terry Carlin, or Mary

Vorse. In the afternoon they returned to their isolated station in a horse-drawn wagon, bearing provisions.

In September, still acting on her original miscalculation, Agnes arranged for her mother and one of her sisters to come the first of September and stay with her for the birth of the baby. Eugene, Mrs. Boulton, and Margery got along splendidly. The trek to town from the station became too much for Agnes, and with encouragement from her doctor, Eugene's old Harvard roommate Dan Hiebert, they arranged with John Francis to rent a cottage called Happy Home. As things worked out, Agnes and her mother instead moved in with Stella Ballantine, who would not hear of the two women's staying in an empty cottage at such a time. For several days Eugene remained at Peaked Hill Bars to finish yet another stage in the revision of *Chris* and wait for the Event. Eugene and Agnes hired Fifine Clark to be a nurse to the baby. Mrs. Clark, who was about fifty-six at the time, would stay with the O'Neills for a decade. Terry Carlin and Susan Glaspell visited frequently, to encourage the parents and witness the Event. Through the neighboring Coast Guard, which made daily trips to town in a wagon, Eugene sent Agnes a prose love poem. September passed with the baby still unborn, and Mrs. Boulton had to return to her family. Eugene closed the station and came to town, working in Happy Home during the day and staying with Agnes at night at the Ballantines, across the street. Through October they waited, both for the baby and for news about *Beyond the Horizon* or *Chris Christophersen*.

Agnes ends her memoir with a powerful account of the birth, which gives a sense of the mysticism that she shared with Eugene and that bound them in their love. In the evening, they had seen a rare display of the aurora, and both of them "felt" in their bodies what Eugene thought was an effect of "the electrical storm—the northern lights." She describes giving herself up later that night entirely to the labor, to the pain, to the swings of love and hatred, to the animal self that emerged in fierce concentration of rhythms, moving flesh, and lapping waters within her. She also writes of feeling, with part of herself, the calmness of Eugene and Dan Hiebert soothing her, then holding upside down "a dark, long, angry ten-pound boy" for her to see and admire, who screamed and kicked in his father's arms while the doctor finished his work: the baby was another black Irishman, whom Eugene at once named Shane the Loud, a quibble on the name of a supposed O'Neill ancestor, Shane the Proud. Eugene would boast that Shane had inherited his grandfather's famous voice. He told Agnes, as he gave her the baby to nurse, "It'll be *us* still, from now on. Us—alone—but the three of us." In the last words of her book Agnes tells of seeing a "real tenderness in his eyes" as Eugene enlarged the limits of their marriage contract.

12

Beyond the Horizon
1919–1920

LATE IN NOVEMBER 1919, THE O'Neills had little in the treasury, and the family had expanded to four, for Fifine Clark, as nurse to Shane and general helper for Agnes, took her meals with them. Eugene went to New York to try to force a showdown with Williams and to try to hurry Tyler with *Chris* and *The Straw*. He stayed at the Prince George and played cards with his parents by night, drank little, and talked during the day to his agent, Dick Madden, and to Williams and Tyler.

His father and mother, he wrote to Agnes on December 1, were "full of thous. questions concerning the baby and crazy to see him." His mother took Eugene to Lord and Taylor's for a new tweed suit, an overcoat, some shirts, and some collars. "Mama knows everyone there," he told Agnes (SL, 98). He and his parents had long sober nights of rummy and conversation. James had felt ill for some time and had nearly stopped drinking even before prohibition had passed. He had begun to believe as early as a year before that his time was coming. He had sold Monte Cristo Cottage and the adjacent properties and had transferred other property into Ella's name.

Apart from spending every night with his mother and father, Eugene had almost no social life. Prohibition had sufficiently taken effect for booze to be hard to find anywhere in town. He made one visit to the Hell Hole, where he and other regulars were reduced to drinking sherry, until he bought a single very expensive bottle of bootlegged bonded, which provided a couple of shots for everyone. Lefty the bartender and Joe Smith seemed as delighted as his parents to hear of Shane's birth. That night Eugene learned that Lefty was the author of the song he had given Chris in the play, "My Yosephine." Eugene said Lefty was pleased to learn that his song might be famous if the play ever went on.

Tyler remained vague about a production of *Chris;* Williams insisted convincingly that he admired *Beyond the Horizon,* but he became evasive when asked to set a date for an opening. No suitable theater was available, he said, because the season had proved unexpectedly successful. But he would keep trying. He was enjoying a successful production of an Elmer Rice play, *For the Defense,* with Richard Bennett. Bennett was eager to direct *Beyond the Horizon* and play Robert Mayo when the Rice play closed, but no one could predict when that would be. He had gone over the script and suggested many changes and cuts, and Williams had also gone over it and suggested cuts.

In Provincetown and New York, respectively, Agnes and Eugene tried to cope with the separation. Throughout their marriage, whenever they were parted, both felt an intense and acute loneliness; the word *emptiness* recurs in their letters. In these periods, their moods became volatile, sometimes swinging to so deep a despondency that they felt abandoned and doubted whether they could survive. In the affair with Bee Ashe, Eugene's mood swings had been as deep, but she had maintained an even keel. Agnes was as lost without Eugene as he was without her.

Within minutes of his boarding the train to Fall River, where he and Jig Cook would catch a boat to New York, Eugene and Agnes had both begun letters to each other. Eugene wrote: "I already feel that pang of great emptiness which always gnaws way down at the roots of my soul as soon as I become sickeningly aware of the vacant spot by my side where you should be" (SL, 97). He contrived to have the letter mailed before the train left Massachusetts, so that Agnes might get it the next day. "The feeling of emptiness you speak of almost drove me crazy this afternoon," Agnes replied, "until I got your letter." The letters make the emptiness seem physical, palpable. Such is the experience that analysts represent by metaphors for "internal" objects that seem to be part of the self. Agnes added: "The first hours after you left were simply torture" (Harvard, AB to EO, Tuesday noon [December 2, 1919]). The letters are full of gratitude for each other's love, and guilt at insufficiently appreciating the other until the two were separated.

As Agnes was dreading "something frightful" to come, Susan told of her own fears for Jig. Ida Rauh, a director and actor with the Players, had invited Jig to stay and write in her apartment while he was in town; Jig had written to Susan to say he didn't know what to do. Agnes stops short of saying she worries that Eugene will be similarly seduced, but she indignantly sympathizes with Susan and rails at Ida as vehemently as if she were the offended one (Harvard, AB to EO, Tuesday [evening December 2, 1919]).

Agnes and Mrs. Clark were having trouble with Shane. Fifine Clark had no children of her own and had never cared for a child before, and Agnes was no more comfortable with children than was Eugene. Since mid-November, Shane had had three-month colic, and with his extremely loud voice he had become the dominant force in the household and perhaps the neighborhood. Although she was not completely new at being a mother, Agnes reacted in the way typical of an anxious, inexperienced mother, by trying to comfort the baby by nursing him whenever he cried, thereby giving his uncooperative digestion yet more food that he couldn't manage. Mrs. Clark also favored feeding Shane whenever he cried and felt as frustrated as Agnes at his persistent discomfort. In her helplessness, she extended her sphere of influence to incorporate Agnes as well as the baby. Agnes frequently sought solitude to escape Mrs. Clark's ministrations as well as the intensely distressing sound of poor Shane's discomfort. She would take the latest letter upstairs to Eugene's bed, where she would read it over and over and try to imagine her way into the circumstances it described in New York.

With mingled gratitude and annoyance, she wrote to Eugene that Mrs. Clark, having decided that Agnes was unhealthily thin, fed her custards, soups, and cornbread and made her eat hearty meals at regular times. Sounding as if she was trying hard to be a doting mother, Agnes wrote of her delight that Shane had smiled three times today; she hoped that he had his father's smile. She could not wait for Eugene to return.

He returned at the weekend with no firm news about either play, but the meetings with Madden had stiffened his resolve. They had decided to try to force Williams to give Eugene a more favorable contract and either to produce *Beyond the Horizon* at once or to relinquish it. To distract himself from his New York worries and from Shane's discomfort, Eugene worked a little on *Gold* over the holidays.

Christmas and New Year passed without news of a production, but there was other news. James Condon—Jimmy the Priest—and his bartender were arrested for homicide. Several men, some of them lodgers, some casual drinkers, had died from drinking poisonous booze while in the barroom or in upstairs rooms. Condon, believing he had been established so long that nothing could damage his place in the waterfront community, was said to have refused to deal with a particular bootlegger. The prosecution case fell apart in court—all the victims had been drinking elsewhere before they drank anything at Jimmy the Priest's on the day they died. But the saloon was ruined, and it closed immediately after the trial. Eugene would have read the story in the New York papers about December 29. Memories of rooming at the flophouse with Jimmy Byth and Driscoll and drinking with Chris Christopherson would have set off his annual holiday melancholy, had he escaped it thus far. The first scene of *Chris* was set in the flophouse bar, like the story "Tomorrow" and the one-act play "Exorcism."

Early in the new year he got a telegram from Tyler saying that there was a possibility of a production of *Chris* with the noted English actor Godfrey Tearle. Tyler wanted Eugene to come to New York to meet with Tearle, and to help with casting, sets, and rehearsals. Tyler wanted four or five weeks of rehearsal, to allow for making changes in a script that still did not satisfy either author or producer. He had engaged Frederick Stanhope to direct.

Before going to New York, Eugene wrote a "firebrand letter" to Williams, and when he reached the Prince George on January 12, a messenger boy brought word from the producer. Eugene and Madden met Williams on the next two days, a "terrific battle" ensued, and Eugene's old contract was torn up, Williams agreeing in principle to "a new one, more fair to me," Eugene wrote to Agnes on January 13 (SL, 101-2). Also, Williams set a firm date and place for *Beyond the Horizon* to open: the Morosco on February 3, after one out-of-town performance. It would run as a matinee using actors from the cast of *For the Defense,* and when the Rice play closed, it would take over the theater in the evenings with a slightly different cast. Less than three weeks was left for casting and learning lines, for costumes, sets, and rehearsal. Eugene was to have approval over all aspects of the production, and he also had to go over the two sets of changes proposed by Williams and Bennett to get a script for the actors to learn and rehearse.

There were further developments with Tyler. He wanted his new prodigy, the nineteen-year-old Helen Hayes, to try out in *The Straw* in

Boston in the spring, a suggestion that alarmed Eugene. He believed that the part of Eileen Carmody in *The Straw* required an experienced and highly competent actress, and although he had not yet seen Helen Hayes, he thought that someone so young could not get the part right. He worried now and later whether Tyler understood that the play was about Eileen, rather than the male lead, Stephen.

As for *Chris,* Tyler had happier news to relay. Godfrey Tearle had played to excellent reviews in a poor play, and he wanted to remain in America a bit longer if he could find a play he liked. Tyler told Eugene that Tearle had read fifty scripts but found nothing. He had booked passage home, but then he had read *Chris* and had canceled the booking. Tall and handsome, a leading man, he wanted to play a character part but was not sure he could do it. He went so far as to arrange a private tryout to see if he could bring it off, and when he reluctantly decided he could not, he came to Eugene, rather than Tyler, to explain his decision. Tearle's courtesy greatly impressed Eugene and encouraged him about his chances. Tyler fell back on his original idea of casting the excellent character actor Emmett Corrigan in the role of Chris.

Elated by the progress and encouragement and stunned by the amount of work he faced, Eugene felt psychically and physically overwhelmed. With a lifetime of backstage experience, he saw no chance at all of creating a credible production of *Beyond the Horizon* in less than three weeks, even with a cast of experienced professionals. To add to his mix of woe and wonder, the weather was foul, and a new flu epidemic was developing. People were staying off the streets and away from crowds to try to escape it. Theater attendance was immediately affected, and Eugene felt certain that no one would come to see his play. Dr. John Aspell, who had operated on Ella in the fall and who now attended James at the Prince George, was concerned about Eugene, whom he pronounced "Keyed up tight as a string." Eugene wrote to his wife that the doctor, worried lest his patient snap, was urging him, "Let down! Don't worry! Forget your work and rest!" (SL, 103). Eugene couldn't imagine how he could follow the advice, but the doctor inspired his confidence; after submitting to a longer examination on Saturday, Eugene agreed to stay inside the hotel and rest for several days, as long as the weather was foul and the flu remained a danger.

For several days he worked far into the night going over the script and felt alternately "keyed up" or blue and listless. One night he stayed up with Bennett at the actor's home, drinking absinthe and going over changes. Bennett said that he and Jack Barrymore had the only absinthe in the country. Impressed by the absinthe and Bennett's home, Eugene convinced himself that the actor understood the play and the part. He let go of the script and drifted into a sense of passive helplessness, losing confidence in his sense of the play. He believed the performance would be terrible and he felt incapable of improving it; he simply wished it were over. Using the doctor's orders as an alibi, he shunned rehearsals, for he dreaded to see what might be going on. After several days inside the hotel he went to the Village and drank enough bad red wine with Christine and Louis Ell to have a hangover.

When he finally saw a rehearsal, he found his worst fears confirmed and again felt a helpless sinking back into his blues. He couldn't fall asleep at night, and when he did get to sleep he had nightmares. Because of the flu epidemic, the city passed a regulation on theater opening hours. Eugene wrote to Agnes that he felt "the Curse of the Red Hand of Ulster" which, "after minor victories, through no fault of their own, always smites the O'Neills at the wrong moment" (SL, 108). On January 27, with only four days until the tryout in Yonkers, Eugene went to a rehearsal, a "massacre," where the "characters don't seem to hang together." The actors "appealed to me to dope out for them the real meaning of what they were trying to do. I tried my best, [but] I'm no director, God knows, and whether my talking will result in any improvement I don't know" (Harvard, EO to AB, January 27, 1920).

The next day he had a "stormy session" with Bennett. The two "'went to the mat' with a loud bang," Eugene insisting that his directions for reading the lines be observed. Bennett tried to instruct Eugene about "the true nature of the hero in tragedy." It was a serious mistake with Eugene, "because I know more about that than he ever dreamed." Bennett must have confused Eugene's hesitant, halting speech with timidity or ignorance. After a dispute watched with interest by the actors, Eugene agreed to take over as director, accepting responsibility for a production that Bennett said would be a failure. No, an "artistic success" Eugene insisted. Bennett, to his credit, played Robert as Eugene asked. When this happened, the other characters also fell into place. With the play now feeling right, the actors became confident in it. Even the author began to feel mildly optimistic about the cast, although some of them still barely knew lines. "So it all ended in the most friendly manner," Eugene wrote Agnes.

Bennett is "sincerely fighting for the play as much as I am" (SL, 108–9). Afterward, Eugene mentioned several times that the experience of working with the actors in the production was one of the most valuable things he had ever done in learning his craft.

Through Eugene's almost daily letters, Agnes had been following the events in New York as she struggled with her feelings about being away from her husband. Indeed, with Eugene absent, Agnes was living through his letters, reading them over and over, trying to imagine the details of his daily life, trying to put herself next to him as he went through the struggles at the theater. She had many sources of frustration in her separation from Eugene, but above all, Agnes felt isolated from the thing that had become most important in her life, more important even than Shane. Identifying with Eugene to the point where she seemed to have nearly lost her self, she focused her entire attention and energy on the premiere of *Beyond the Horizon*. Agnes's letters written between January 11 and early March show her going through a prolonged crisis in which she was often in a dreamy state, projecting herself into the Morosco Theatre, where great events were in the making. A long separation made it clear that the ideal of the two as being one in soul and body meant that for Agnes the world was largely defined as Eugene's world.

The problem with Shane's colic continued, causing intense anxiety and frustration for both Agnes and Mrs. Clark. Both continued to react by over-feeding Shane, but Agnes skipped her own meals when she was anxious or blue, and she was even thinner than she had been before her pregnancy. Mrs. Clark thought she looked unwell. Adoring Eugene, Mrs. Clark rapidly became attached to Shane, and an implicit rivalry developed between the two women that Agnes still felt years after Eugene had died. Agnes reported that Mrs. Clark said she would never have allowed so swell-looking a husband to travel alone, and she would have made him wear a wedding ring.

However annoyed Agnes may have felt, she was grateful for Mrs. Clark's help with Shane and the household. When she wasn't dreaming of rehearsals at the Morosco, she worked on a story for which, with Eugene's encouragement, she was aiming for other than a pulp magazine audience. She was taking a month instead of an evening to write it. Also with his encouragement, she was rewriting Eugene's farce *Now I Ask You* and, in so doing, trying to feel her way into playwriting and develop her gift for comedy. Their letters contain frequent allusions to bits of dialogue in the farce. Probably Eugene wanted her to understand his world better and form a clearer appreciation of the particularities of his writing. But he also deeply believed that people with talent needed to aim as high as they could in order to fulfill themselves, and he believed Agnes to have much more talent than she was calling on.

When Eugene had first gone to New York, Agnes had been afflicted by a "dreadful sense of emptiness" (Harvard, AB to EO, January 11–12, 1920) and often had no appetite. Mrs. Clark continued her campaign to induce Agnes to feel healthier, by setting out a schedule for every activity—working, running errands, even playing with the baby or drinking malted milk. Agnes reported that she did indeed have more energy, and she urged Eugene to try malted milk. Eugene evidently agreed that Agnes was too thin, but he stayed out of her struggle with Mrs. Clark.

As the separation continued, Agnes became painfully dependent on the mail service that brought Eugene's almost daily letters. She resented almost any other social encounter and felt dislike for herself and the other person afterwards, even if it was Susan Glaspell, who was her closest confidante in Provincetown. Terry Carlin, who had remained in Provincetown in the fall, was supposed to go to New York with Eugene and stay there. Instead, he had changed his mind about going and had taken to dropping in to visit almost every day. Agnes complained that he read whatever newspaper or magazine had come, even if she had not yet read it; sometimes he surprised her by playing with the baby; sometimes he made one-sided conversation. After several complaints, Eugene encouraged her to tell him that he must respect her privacy or to show Terry a strong paragraph in one of Eugene's letters that made the point. Both were sympathetic with the old man, who was increasingly organizing his life around Eugene's life, but Terry and Agnes did not especially like each other.

Usually Agnes struggled to avoid revealing her various discomforts in her letters, and she succeeded as long as she got a letter every day from Eugene. But once when a letter went astray and she went three days without hearing from him, her doubts erupted. Failing to hear from him, she said, made it seem that "I have no control of my 'inward' feelings at all. . . . I do actually get sick—a feeling as if my backbone had been removed, a deadly depression, combined with a nervous sensitiveness that becomes perfect torture. I cannot eat and can hardly sleep." With that warning, she launched into several paragraphs of severe scolding of Eugene, who had mentioned his visit to drink red wine with Christine and Louis Ell. Agnes ended by begging him to consider that she was stuck with the baby and isolated from everything that was important: "Your letters are absolutely the only connection I have with any of it—and I can keep up the bluff to myself that I don't care—as long as *they* come" (Harvard, AB to EO, January 21, 1920).

The next day the missing letter arrived, but there were ripples for days from the scolding. "You never used to be a moralist," he wrote, "and I've never in my life stood for that stuff, even from my Mother. . . . [Not] even Christ or Buddha should tell the lowest slave what he should do. That slave has something actuating him that they can never understand." In any case there had been only one day he had not written and he had been feeling punk (Harvard, EO to AB, January 22, 1920). He seems also to have written a harsher letter than this one, and Agnes a harsh reply, both of which were apparently destroyed. From this point on, her letters show how greatly the vagaries of the mails affected her moods. Whenever Eugene's letters were late, her letters gave the impression that within her mind everything in the marriage has been lost.

The separation made them examine the forces that drove their marriage. In a letter of January 25, 1920, Eugene went on at great length in sentences that read in part: "If you and I, who love each other so much, . . . at this so crucial moment of our union, we cannot keep petty hate from creeping into our souls like the condemned couples in a Strindberg play; if our letters are to become an added torture to our hearts already tortured by separation and by the mishaps of outside shame; . . . then we are lost; and my only remaining hope is that the 'Flu', or some other material cause, will speedily save me the decision which would inevitably have to come at my own instance. If you and I are but another dream that passes, then I desire nothing further from the Great Sickness but release" (SL, 108). Constructing these exalted sentences was apparently Eugene's strategy for coping with the despair that he felt at the moment. He could not bear to imagine going through all that he was suffering, without the knowledge that Agnes loved him and was waiting for him in a place he considered a haven from the creative theatrical chaos at the Morosco.

Agnes, for her part, believed she was going crazy in quiet Provincetown and felt she simply *had* to travel to New York. She urged Eugene to look for rooms that they could rent where Mrs. Clark and Shane could stay with them. Eugene reported that his mother and some of her friends had looked, but apartments were very expensive and required a lease through the summer. The flu epidemic was still in the headlines; convinced that he could return to Provincetown within days, Eugene felt that it made no sense to risk bringing the baby to town. Dr. Hiebert also dissuaded Agnes, and she tried to resign herself to being alone a little longer. Late in January, right on schedule, Shane's colic ended and he became a happy, smiling, chuckling baby, so Agnes began to feel less guilty and anxious about him and could enjoy his company. Most of Agnes's letters from this point on mention how happy and good-natured Shane was.

Eugene was busy with *Beyond the Horizon* and also with *Chris,* which he was revising and discussing with Tyler and Stanhope, the director. He was also deeply worried about his father. James's continuing illness was serious enough, as Eugene had written Agnes, that his mother had once thought to call for a priest and her sons. James was in so much discomfort that old friends had started dropping by in the evenings to visit. One night George Tyler and Will Connor contrived and performed for Eugene and James an amusement in which the two theater veterans argued at length whether *Ile* or *The Rope* was the "best one act play ever written" (Harvard, EO to AB, January 14, 1920). Eugene was too flattered to entirely ignore the blarney. A tribute to James in the *Morning Telegraph* of January 14, 1920, announced that he was failing and called him a "noble veteran" and "a brilliant actor" (LS, 471).

The nightly talks with his father were very important to Eugene— he described them in detail nearly a year later in a letter to Tyler. As the letter to Tyler shows, the talks became the basis for the conversation between James and Edmund Tyrone in act 4 of *Long Day's Journey into Night* (1941). Driven by his illness, James reflected on his life and career and remembered his youthful dreams of becoming a great Shakespearean actor; he dwelt on the lingering disappointment of seeing his talent serve *Monte Cristo* and what he now regarded as his desperate grasping after money.

Even though talking with his father of such matters was deeply satisfying to Eugene, it made demands on a sensibility already strung tight as a violin string, as Dr. Aspell had suggested. Eugene continued to expect to go home to Provincetown as soon as the premiere was over. The wait was even harder on Agnes. On learning that Eugene felt unwell, Agnes became desperate, fearing he might catch the flu and die almost overnight, as Hutch Collins had exactly a year before. She agreed that the city was no place for Shane, and now that he was happy, she tried to cultivate patience, for it seemed Eugene would be home in a few days.

Tyler had arranged a March 8 tryout of *Chris* in Atlantic City. On January 26 the cast assembled for a first reading, which Eugene skipped. He planned to go to a few rehearsals the following week but said he was confident that the director could handle the play on his own. Even if Eugene's help was needed later, he would return to Provincetown. Agnes was consoled. She resumed work on her story and finished it, and she even encouraged him not to come to Provincetown if he had the least chance of catching the flu while traveling. But now that she would not be going to New York, she began to wonder if she would ever see *Beyond the Horizon* onstage; she tried to master every detail of the situation that Eugene faced with Williams and the actors. Learning of the struggle with Bennett and of Eugene's taking over the direction of *Beyond the Horizon,* she demanded to know in detail why the play was opening as a matinee with actors who would not necessarily carry over to the evening performances later.

Her letters continued to show the strain she was under. In many of her letters, such habitual matters for a professional writer as syntax, capitalizing names and first words, punctuation and spelling, and even her handwriting itself deteriorated, perhaps because she was drinking quite a lot, and she flew into rages that she seemed unable to control. Williams had decided to give *Beyond the Horizon* very little publicity but to rely on word of mouth to bring in an audience, a strategy that proved sound. Hearing of his decision she wrote, "I'd like to have him here. I'd tear him limb from limb! What an idiot, and fool he must be! Not even an *announcement.* . . . Who does he think will go to see "*Beyond*"—a lot of actors and actresses, who aren't playing on those days? Why, it just seems to me that everything is being done by him to make the play a failure" (Harvard, AB to EO, January 29, 1920). The rest of the letter is in the same tone. The rage is a sign that to protect herself against her loneliness, she identified so deeply with Eugene that she ferociously protected their interests in a situation she knew only at second hand; the identification temporarily helped her deny the separation, while the rage expressed her frustration over being apart from him.

Adopting the theory of the Curse of the Red Hand of Ulster she wrote: "Sometimes I have a dreadful feeling that when the inevitable success does come there will be something to spoil it all for us" (Harvard, January 31, 1920). Eugene makes no comment at all when Agnes seems to lose herself in these rages. Usually, all Agnes needed to restore her good humor was a letter or two in the next mail delivery. Eugene seldom missed a day, and he carefully explained if he did. In a happier moment she sent a parcel of roasted chicken and other foods, which were appreciated by Mama and Papa as well as by Eugene, who passed on the thanks of all. Both he and Agnes were sexually hungry and made intermittent allusions to the frustrations of "Mr. N[ightingale]" and "Miss "P[ussy]."

With the serious intention of developing an audience for *Beyond the Horizon* by word of mouth, Williams tactfully asked Eugene to find out if he might use the Provincetown Players' subscriber list. Eugene passed on the request to Agnes and asked her to mention the delicate problem to Susan. Agnes succeeded; Susan agreed that Eugene had a right to the list, although people expressed concern that the friends of the Players might be alienated or that Williams might use the list on some other occasion without permission or authority. Eventually a solution was found that satisfied everyone.

The dress rehearsal for *Beyond the Horizon* was awful, and Eugene decided to skip the tryout in Yonkers. He probably would have slipped out of the opening at the Morosco, which began at three on Tuesday afternoon. At three in Provincetown, Agnes went upstairs to Eugene's room and lay on the bed, staring at the wallpaper and thinking about what was happening at the theater. That night she reflected: "If a year ago, when we were down in Pt P. some one had told me I'd be in that room—in Provincetown—alone and you, and Beyond in N.Y.—I suppose I should have rebelled! Certainly I'd never have believed it—I'd have said—'I'll get there *somehow!*'" (Harvard, February 3, 1920). Writing to Agnes of the premiere, Eugene said that Williams had given him no chance to escape but, grasping him firmly, had propelled him to a seat in the middle of the theater and kept him there during intermissions.

The performance lasted until nearly six, despite Eugene's having cut thirty minutes of dialogue. The problem lay in slow set changes between the five scenes, from an interior to an exterior (the two scenes of act 1 having been compressed into one to reduce the number of changes). The audience was quiet throughout and Eugene was intensely conscious of every fault of memory, intonation, or movement. He wrote to Agnes that he left the theater "convinced that *Beyond* was a flivver artistically and every other way" (SL, 112). He felt so depressed that he couldn't stand to write her or send a telegram, and he dreaded seeing the morning papers. Knowing nothing of his dread, Agnes was crushed to hear nothing that night. Next morning, when Eugene did see the notices, he immediately wired her: "BEYOND IS A TRIUMPH ALL I EXPECTED." The reviews were favorable, without exception, and new reviews kept appearing in national magazines as well as newspapers. He was compared to Ibsen and Hardy, and one reviewer prophesied that *Beyond the Horizon* was probably too great a work to be popular with the public.

The letters Eugene wrote to Agnes in the next several days were full of the ardor and chattiness missing from those leading up to the premiere, and he was once again able to empathize with her feeling of alienation. He took pains to reassure her of his fidelity and devotion. "Only one night . . . have I been out since my arrival. I'm getting to be a 'rummy' fiend. Mama, Papa and I play every night"—except the previous night, when he and his mother had gone to see Helen Hayes close in *Clarence* (SL, 112). Tyler still wanted to try her in *The Straw* in Boston. In Provincetown, Agnes was in despair: no mail was reaching her, because a blizzard had interrupted service. "What I feel about you, all I want to tell you now that you have your great success—*our* great success!—should be told close, *close* to one another—hardly in words at all. . . . Then a curious rage—resentment . . . made me tremble. . . . Against all the circumstances that keep us apart, just when we should be together. . . . So forgive my stiff letters," she concluded, then caught herself being stiff again: "THERE—do you see how I blunder! . . . I'll be offering you 'cordial congratulations' next!" (Harvard, AB to EO [February 6, 1920]). They plotted ways to get Shane and Mrs. Clark out of the house and keep Terry away so that Mr. N. and Miss P. could spend some time together. Conscious of the delays caused by the weather, Eugene anticipated how bad she would feel at receiving no word from him about the day's events.

By Tuesday, February 9, the strain and the long days had caught up with Eugene; he came down with the flu, caught, he believed, from his mother, who had gotten sick a few days after their night out together to see Helen Hayes. Agnes immediately fell into panic and could not stop thinking of Hutch Collins's sudden death. Eugene was quite sick through the rest of the month, unable to eat, unable even to drag himself from his room on the fifth floor to his parents' room on the eighth. By the middle of the month he thought he looked "like a medical student's chart, every muscle outlined and every bone and bit of sinew" (SL, 114). He estimated that he weighed about 125 pounds. Now resigned to having to stay in New York through March because of *Chris Christophersen,* he tried to get a room for Agnes and the baby at the Prince George, only to be told that there would be a wait of at least two weeks; nor could he find any other place for them that was suitable or did not require a long lease.

On Friday the 13th, Agnes wrote him three letters, in which she tried to get beyond sounding "hysterical and silly"; in the last she regretted that she had mailed the first two, which have apparently since been destroyed (Harvard, AB to EO, Friday [February 6, 1920]). In thrall to "the green-eyed demon," Agnes imagined "blonde beauties" perched on Eugene's sickbed. She developed a headache that laid her low for two days (Harvard, February 15, 1920). Then she went through a dental nightmare, the drilling out of a broken tooth without anesthesia. But nothing prevented her from keeping abreast of all the news of *Beyond the Horizon.* She also wrote regularly to her mother and to Ella with news of Shane, and she encouraged Ella and Eugene to get well. February 20 was the first time in nearly two weeks that Eugene's temperature was normal; at last, he started to feel a little better.

Rehearsals for *Chris* had been going on for two weeks, and Eugene had seen none of them. As yet, no New York date or theater was scheduled. Eugene had developed bronchitis as a complication of the flu. He had a constant racking cough and still could not leave the hotel. He endured interviews with reporters from the *Tribune* and *Theatre Magazine.* To the *Theatre Magazine* interviewer he gave "as bitter and poisonous" a blast of his "philosophy of life" as he could and won from her a flirtatious exit line (Harvard, February 21, 1920). He was asked for a picture to accompany interviews and decided he must have a studio portrait done. Early the morning of February 16, Eugene had felt intense chest pains "just over my heart. I thought first: 'this is cases,' and afterwards 'it's pleurisy.'" It was the worst pain he had ever felt, he told Agnes. The doctor diagnosed a neuralgia. "I've gotten . . . like the Old Woman in *Riders to the Sea.* I feel I've won that spent calm where neither joy nor sorrow over anything exist." Finally, on the night of the 26th, he went to the Hell Hole, where he ran into a crowd of "rough necks," probably Hudson Dusters, among others. There he got "pickled" on rotgut whiskey, lost his neuralgia and his cough, and returned to the hotel "100% better . . . after all medicines had failed. Alcoholic Christian Science is my only dope!" (SL, 114).

Eugene did not write the following day, February 27, because the neuralgic pain returned; meanwhile, Agnes, who had heard about his neuralgia, snapped. She decided he had been hearing from Louise Bryant. "It is very obvious," she wrote, "that your feeling toward me has changed. I was reading over some of your old letters last night, and comparing them to the ones you write now. *Quite* a difference. Well I knew success would do *something!* Your sickness, if you really cared, would make you need and want me more, instead [of] less. Well don't bother—I certainly don't intend to hang round your neck" (Harvard, February 26, 1920). Whether she mailed this letter is unclear, for no reply to it is known, and she does not refer to it in later letters. Agnes, too, developed neuralgic pains and flulike symptoms. She felt nauseous and evidently had a migraine, for Dr. Hiebert gave her ergot.

If she did mail that letter, Eugene would probably have received it on Saturday, February 28, or Monday, March 1. Her letter of February 27 makes no reference to the despair of the previous day. Agnes reports on her illness, which the doctor now believed might be a light attack of flu, with "nerve-pains" in her arms and legs but not in her joints. Dr. Hiebert also advised her on filling out her income tax: 1920 was the first year of the national income tax, and Eugene had left the matter to her to cope with. Her extreme despair of the preceding day, it seems, may have been set off by her frustration over the income tax form. Both Agnes and Eugene showed the greatest resistance to being made to think about money. She blamed the income tax and having to explain to him the state of their budget for making her "feel too blue" to write the "nice" letter she had intended. "Any man who goes off and leaves the income tax to his poor wife" gives her "good grounds for divorce." She still felt "rocky" from the migraine. She also continued to feel alienated because she did not know when or even whether she would see *Beyond the Horizon*. "Anyhow," she continues, "I wouldn't want to see *Beyond* even if I were in town" (Harvard, AB to EO, February 24, 1920). It made her furious to read in a review that Robert Mayo's final speech had been deleted. She would be content with seeing the book, which would be dedicated to her. In this sentiment she echoed Eugene's preference, expressed throughout his life, for the printed versions of his plays over most of the performed versions. Adopting his point of view seemed to help Agnes control her changes in mood (Harvard, Saturday night [February 28, 1920]).

Circumstances intervened to avert another Strindbergian quarrel.

On February 28, James O'Neill had a stroke and nearly died. As James lay unconscious, with Ella and Eugene nursing him, "watching his every movement," Dr. Aspell told them that he had diagnosed a tumor in James's intestines and that even if the old actor recovered from the stroke, the cancer was inoperable, and he would die soon. Eugene wired to Agnes at once and then tried to write, but he could hardly finish the letter he started on March 1. "To have this happen just at the time when the Old Man and I were getting to be such good pals! . . . I'm all broken up and begin to cry every time the meaning of it all dawns on me" (SL, 117–18). "Papa is all gone," he wrote two days later. "It's horrible to see him fade from day to day. . . . Of course he has a chance of living quite a while yet— to die by inches and in pain all the time" (Harvard, EO to AB, March 3, 1920). Now began the long ordeal of loss.

Eugene's letters of January and February referred only once to Jamie, and when Agnes asked if he was in New York, Eugene did not answer (LS, 5; all citations from Sheaffer from this point on are to LS2, unless otherwise noted). Perhaps Eugene did not see his brother during the time he was preparing for the opening of *Beyond the Horizon* or possibly there was some dispute between them that Eugene did not feel like describing to Agnes. Sheaffer writes that Jamie did not see *Beyond the Horizon* until several weeks after it had opened (LS, 6). Probably Eugene's hat size was temporarily enlarged, what with the attention from so many prominent people, and Jamie found the change unbearable. More important, Jamie felt unexpectedly distressed by his father's illness (as we know from a letter written in May). He may have stayed away from the Prince George for some time, unable to tolerate the love and pity that James's illness evoked in him: intimacy was easier for Jamie if it could be mediated through irony or anger.

James's stroke affected Eugene by robbing him of the energy to think or work. Even though *Chris* was to open in a few days, he excused himself to Tyler on the grounds that both he and Agnes were ill (they were better by that time) and went back to Provincetown. When *Chris* did open, the reviews were not as bad as Eugene had feared, but they were mixed at best. No one seemed to know what to make of the old salt's mysticism, which for Eugene was the heart of the play. Producer and author exchanged suggestions about the ending, but Eugene still pleaded illness and said he could not give it due attention. He answered letters of congratulations for *Beyond the Horizon* from George Jean Nathan, Barrett Clark, and others, but his replies were skimpy and full of apologies.

Eugene readily took the blame for *Chris's* failure. No play that he had written so far, and few he would write in the future, gave him as much trouble as this one. Sometimes he destroyed plays that failed, and usually he could think of them as lessons from which he had learned. With *Chris Christophersen,* he could neither let the play go nor feel satisfied with his effort. As March wore on, Tyler continued to send suggestions. Through March Eugene thought about revisions, suggested changes to Tyler, and sounded out possibilities in frequent letters to the producer. As the text of various drafts and the letters to Tyler reveal, the reasons for his problems lay in the play's presentation of relations between parents and children, problems that he was trying to solve in life as well as in drama. As the possibility of losing his father became more real to him, the problems of separation and autonomy continually changed form in his mind.

Chris Christophersen was O'Neill's second attempt to write a play that combined his efforts to understand his relationship with his father and his mystical feelings about the sea. While at Harvard, he had written *The Personal Equation* (also known as "The Second Engineer"). The earlier play was about a motherless, thoroughly spoiled young man, Tom, who sneers contemptuously at his father for having given his life to a shipping company, and for seeming to love his ship's engines more than anything else in life. In a scene where the father and son appear together, O'Neill shows the father doting on his son to the point of folly and hoping against reason that the son will eventually grow enough to return his love. To win the favor of a radical young woman, Olga, Tom agrees to sabotage the engines on his father's ship and is accidentally shot when his father tries to defend them. As the play ends, the father and the fiancée, who is pregnant, join in a vow to care for Tom, whose mind has been permanently damaged by his head wound.

In that earlier play Eugene tried to understand his father's lifelong commitment to the theater, a commitment he was now beginning to understand a little. Seeing something of himself as he looked to his father had been so humiliating that, to punish himself, Eugene imagined almost killing off his old self but leaving open the possibility that he might be reborn as the child that Olga carries. The pregnancy implies a second chance for the repentant prodigal son. The baby will grow up with its mother and

Tom's father. In his letters to Bee Ashe while he was writing *The Personal Equation,* Eugene frequently spoke of feeling "reborn" in her love, of getting a second chance to grow up. The play seems to mark a point when he almost killed off the "old Gene O'Neill" by attempting suicide. Having survived, he came to see himself reborn.

In *Chris Christophersen,* Eugene returned to the same pattern and similar themes but altered the characters. He split Tom, the prodigal son of the earlier play, into two characters, a daughter and the daughter's lover. The father became the mystical old salt, Chris. Instead of love for the ship's engines, Chris feels a love and hatred of the sea, which he knows to be sentient and malignant toward humanity. Chris, formerly a bosun on square-riggers, has lost most of the members of his family to the sea—the men drowned or injured on ships, the women abandoned ashore to sicken and die of loneliness and neglect. When the play opens, Chris operates a barge, towed between New York and Boston.

Chris's daughter, born in Sweden, was educated by relatives in England after her mother died. She has come to New York seeking a job and meets her father for the first time since childhood. Superficially emancipated, she has been trained to accept humane, rationalist values. She smiles at her father's quaint superstitions when he tries to teach her to fear the sea. Delighted to find himself the father of a tall, bright, well-spoken daughter, he encourages her without resentment when she corrects his Swedish pronunciation of English words. Rationalist though she is, Anna feels romantically drawn to the sea and perversely refuses to blame it for drowning her two brothers and causing her mother to die of loneliness.

In a dense fog, a British steamer strikes Chris's barge. The steamer, which is bound for Buenos Aires, rescues Chris and Anna and takes them along. Anna falls in love with Paul Andersen, the steamer's mannerly second mate, who proposes marriage. Out of jealousy and envy, Chris opposes the match and even tries feebly to kill Paul. Anna, for her own reasons, rejects the proposal; as he has admitted to her, Paul has avoided responsibility and led the life of a wastrel.

In his effort to understand Anna and old Chris, Paul gradually faces up to his own weakness. He has criticized Chris for succumbing to his fear of the sea; but Paul admits to his own fear of responsibility. He decides he is ready to accept the burden and declares himself a changed man. He will take the examination to become a first mate. He again proposes marriage to Anna, and, with some ambivalence, she agrees. The ship captain offers Chris the job of bosun on the steamer, and the play ends with the old Swede shaking his fist at the sea for its latest dirty trick, a trick that draws him back to the life he has tried to escape and that leaves Anna vulnerable to the sea's whims because of its hold on her men. He firmly expects that in the end the sea will destroy his whole family. Nevertheless, Chris settles into more ordinary complaints about the job and sings his mournfully cheery song, "My Yosephine," the song of Lefty Louis, the bartender at the Hell Hole. This was as far as O'Neill could go with the material in early 1920.

George Tyler took the play as a conventional love story and could see no point in Chris's mysticism, which he advised cutting. To Tyler, it was more important to make Paul's change of heart convincing. Eugene agreed that both elements needed more work. For reasons he could not fully explain, he regarded Chris's mysticism as the real heart of the play; the love story he saw as banal. The mysticism amounted to a declaration of his intent to abandon modern humanism and rationalism and accept a much older notion of the way the world worked. Probably Eugene himself was not fully aware that through old Chris he was making a serious declaration of faith in the tragic sense of fate.

Eugene divulged an important aspect of himself in Anna as well as in Chris. Although she is too well-bred to call her father an Irish peasant, her elocution lesson conveys that judgment as surely as did the insults that the O'Neill sons hurled at James. Her attraction to the sea supplants her earlier rationalism. She tells her father, "When the fog swept over us . . . I began to feel . . . it." She reflects: "It seemed to come over me suddenly—while we were drifting in that fog with that queer silence all about." Anna's discovery of the sea seems to her nothing less than a rebirth. "As if you'd come home after being away a long, long time; as if everything had changed, and nothing could ever be the same again; as if everything you'd lived through before was small—and wrong—and could never mean anything to you again" (CP1, 855-56).

When Anna accepts the primacy of fate, her decision seems to render meaningless her search for independence. In both word and deed, she drifts into a regressive, dreamy dependency on her father and on the sea. But sex attracts along different axes. When Anna finds herself drawn to Paul, the impulse toward self-rule reasserts itself. Neither her lover nor her father is allowed to tell her what to do, or to claim possession of her will. Eugene recognized on reading reviews of the Atlantic City tryout that the ending of the play left the relation between the two themes muddled.

On March 14, Eugene wrote to Tyler that he had firmly decided that the ending of *Chris* had to be "radically rewritten." He wanted to undercut any hint that the play was a conventional love story with a conventional happy ending. He proposed to have Anna show her doubts about Paul's vows to reform by asking him for promises and then asking her father whether she had done the right thing. Chris would warn her that he had promised not to abandon Anna's mother for the sea, and would remind her that even now he was agreeing to accept the job of bosun. Anna insists to Chris that "Andersen is different. . . . He *will* become a captain and take her with him all over the world. . . . Chris sees [that his opposition] is no use. He turns to the sea, gives his last speech—and curtain" (Princeton, EO to GT, March 14, 1920). Eugene meant for the audience to leave the theater musing that the more we try to avoid fate, the more we become tangled in its web.

As March wore on, Eugene continued to think about *Chris,* and in several letters to Tyler suggested further changes. Their letters turned angry. Tyler accused Eugene of leaving him dangling with *Chris* and of turning his attention to *Gold.* Eugene replied that he had not touched *Gold* since early January but said he did in fact plan to resume work on it, because he felt too muddled about *Chris.* He accepted responsibility for problems with the writing in *Chris* but blamed the production and acting for other problems. Tyler complained about the investment he had made in the play; Eugene implied a lofty unconcern for the money and promised Tyler he would do no less than write a whole new play on the "Chris" idea. But Tyler would have to wait until he, Eugene, recovered his objectivity about the story.

The dispute sounds very much like one that Eugene might have once had with his father over money and undoubtedly shows the effect on both him and Tyler of their impending loss of the dying James O'Neill. His father's mortal illness caused a regression in Eugene that did not allow him to think constructively about the problem of a young man who is trying to become independent.

The letter of March 14 reveals Eugene's state of mind about his father's illness. Eugene tells Tyler that Jamie or Ella has written that X rays are being taken to "decide whether an operation will be imperative or not." Imperative? Surely the question must have been whether an operation would be possible or useful. The inapt word implies that Eugene must have been intermittently denying how serious James's condition was. "This sickness of the Governor's is really hell to me," he wrote Tyler. "The thought that there is a chance of losing him just at the time when he and I, after many years of misunderstanding, have begun to be real pals—well, you can imagine" (Princeton). The issue of loss pervades *Chris Christophersen:* Chris's and Anna's losses of her brothers and mother and Chris's new loss of Anna, just when she has been found, and hers of him. No wonder Eugene could not work effectively on the play with his father dying.

On March 26, the Provincetown Players opened the one-act play Eugene had written the previous fall, "Exorcism," which described the nearly successful suicide attempt of one Ned Malloy. In order to get a divorce, Ned had to be seen in bed with a prostitute. A young man of good family, he had scraped bottom and was further depressed by the charade of adultery. After declining an offer to work on a farm out west, where he may have a chance to change his life, Ned decided to end it all by taking an overdose of morphine. He was roused twenty-four hours later by a character called Jimmy, said to have resembled Jimmy Tomorrow in *The Iceman Cometh.* When awakened, Ned discovered that his accidental survival, after he had been certain he was about to die, made it seem he had a new start. He felt that the demons driving him had been exorcized, and he turned to the world with renewed interest. Now he was ready to go out west to the farm.

When "Exorcism" opened, it received at least one favorable review (from Alexander Woolcott in the *Times*) and would probably have continued to run to the end of the bill. Eugene, however, caused the performance to be canceled, collected all copies of the script, and destroyed them. (All that is known about the play is based on reviews or on interviews by Sheaffer of Jasper Deeter, who played Ned, and Alan MacAteer, who played Jimmy [LS, 210].) Biographers have guessed that Eugene destroyed the play either because he had decided that it was poor or, more likely, because once he saw it onstage, he found it too revealing of something he wanted to conceal.

Both explanations may be true, but more obvious possibilities must be considered: that seeing the play when his father was dying must have made it seem a different work to him from the one he had given the Players before he knew of his father's illness. Also, it exposed a family problem in a way that was bound to distress his mother and father. He must have thought about their reaction to seeing it, whether they did or not. He may have enticed his mother to see the play without telling her its subject. The mere reference to morphine in a review would have greatly upset his father and mother. Possibly his parents complained to him after hearing about the play, and the complaint led him to see it from his family's point of view and he withdrew it. Thoughts about any of the many reasons the play might offend his family probably led him to destroy it. From that time on, Eugene's autobiographical themes were usually so well disguised that they were seldom suspected to be that, even by close friends.

Late in March, still dissatisfied by his grasp of the problems of *Chris Christophersen* and too confused to try to solve them at once, Eugene turned to *Gold,* which Williams agreed to consider as soon as it was finished. Probably he started working on *Gold* not because it especially interested him but because he could not stand to be idle when his thoughts tended to turn to his father. The result was a strained, hoarse play that seemed thinner than the one-act play composed from the same material, *Where the Cross Is Made,* the old tale of greed and hidden treasure. As Sheaffer points out, *Gold* frequently echoes *Monte Cristo* and clearly demonstrates that Eugene's thoughts were full of his father.

One seeks an unconscious motive in the interest O'Neill took in material that seems simplistic for a writer who had already achieved so much more. It is remarkable that later in the year he told Nina Moise and George Jean Nathan that he valued *Gold* more highly than he did *Beyond the Horizon.* The role of Captain Bartlett would have suited his father well. Writing a play for the old actor served both as an unconscious way for him to deny that he was about to lose his father and also as a parting gift.

In late April, while Eugene was typing the finished script of *Gold,* Agnes took Shane to New York and New Jersey to visit the senior O'Neills and her parents, and she was finally able to see *Beyond the Horizon.* After the show and a few drinks, she wrote a furious private review of the performance to her husband, lambasting nearly every actor in the replacement cast. (Eugene later told Nina Moise that he liked the second cast better than the first.) When he finished typing *Gold,* Eugene met Agnes in New York, where they remained several days, visiting his father and mother.

In late May James nearly died and was taken to the hospital in excruciating pain. Jamie sat by his bed for a time and wrote Eugene a sorrowful letter, describing how James's pain had ceased for a few days, a phenomenon no one could explain. With heavy irony, Jamie recommended hospitals to Eugene as a suitable place to observe human weakness, especially cupidity. Papa "won't have to linger a hell of a while to leave Mama on the rocks for cash," Jamie wrote. Jamie felt torn between pity and laughter, while "Mama was on the verge of a breakdown, staying up purely on her nerve" (LS, 20). On June 10, James was moved to the Lawrence and Memorial Associated Hospitals in New London. Even with Monte Cristo Cottage sold, he wanted to return to the seaside town where he had spent most of the previous thirty-five summers.

The argument between Eugene and George Tyler smoldered through May and flared up in early June. Jamie had written to Eugene saying he had heard Tyler describe *The Straw* to their papa as a Romeo and Juliet play with coughing and spitting, and that Tyler planned to omit the T.B. parts. Eugene reiterated that the play was about Eileen, that Murray was an incidental character; therefore, it was not a love story; furthermore, the sanatorium and the material on the therapeutic regime was essential to the action and meanings. He continued that, as he was now convinced that the producer could not produce the play as written, he saw no choice but to repay the advance and make other arrangements—although, he assured Tyler, no one else had shown interest in it. Tyler replied by return mail that he was by no means the "idiot manager" of Eugene's "youthful impression" (SL, 128). The quarrel sputtered out without being resolved.

In late June, Eugene found himself the topic of a thoughtful appraisal by Nathan in *Smart Set,* which called him the one American playwright "who gives promise of achieving a sound position for himself" (SL, 129). Nevertheless, Nathan predicted that within ten years O'Neill would have written himself out. In a private letter, Eugene replied that he hoped to prove the critic wrong. "God stiffen it, I *am* young yet and I mean to grow!" (130).

A day or two after writing to Nathan, Eugene was notified that he had been awarded the Pulitzer Prize for *Beyond the Horizon.* The Pulitzer had been established several years before but was still so obscure that Eugene had never heard of it. He assumed that he would have to attend a ceremony in order to collect a medal, and he was about to decline the honor when he learned that he need do nothing but accept an award of a thousand dollars. He was to receive the award twice more in the 1920s and a fourth time, posthumously in 1956, for *Long Day's Journey into Night*. Eugene was grateful not only for the money but, even more, for something that brought pleasure and pride to his father.

James lingered through the next weeks. Late in July the call to Provincetown finally came, and Eugene went to New London. "The situation is frightful!" Eugene wrote to Agnes while sitting at his father's bedside. "Papa is alive when he ought to be dead. The disease has eaten through his bowels. Internal decomposition has set in—while he is still living! There is a horrible nauseating smell in the room. . . . He is unspeakably thin and wasted. Only his eyes are alive—and the light that glimmers through their glaze is remote and alien. He suffers incredible tortures—in spite of their dope" (SL, 131). In lucid moments James begged God to take him.

"Surely he is a fine man as men go," Eugene wrote. "I don't believe he has ever hurt a living thing intentionally. And he has certainly been a husband to marvel at, and a good father, according to his lights. . . . At any rate, looking at it dispassionately, he seems to me a *good* man—in the best sense of the word—and about the only one I have ever known." James awoke while Eugene was writing and called his son closer. "'Glad to go, boy. . . . This sort of life—froth!—rotten!—all of it—no good.'" It consoled Eugene to see that his father truly believed in a "'better sort'" of life "'somewhere.'" It surprised him, Eugene told Agnes, not to hear his father mention God in these late words, and said his "somewhere" didn't sound like a Catholic heaven. It seemed "like a dying dialogue in a play I might have written. Yet I swear I am quoting verbatim" (SL, 131–32).

Eugene wrote three more long letters before Agnes came to New London. Eugene and Ella were staying with Ella's Sheridan cousins; the cousins had finally become friends, and Mary Sheridan told everyone she had adopted Ella. Later Eugene wrote that he and Agnes hoped she would adopt them too, and he thanked her most warmly for her kindness to all of them. James lived until a few hours past midnight of August 10. When he was gone, Eugene and Jamie went off for a private wake to escape the considerable crowd that had gathered at the Sheridans', where James's body lay in state.

13

After Papa Died
1920–1922

EUGENE REACTED TO HIS FATHER'S death with a creative upwelling. A day or two after James's official wake, Eugene returned to the play he had struggled with for the past two years, *Chris Christophersen*. From time to time since its failure in Atlantic City in March, he had toyed with ideas for revision. Now in about a month he created a new play, which retained only some of the opening scene, a few elements of plot and setting, and the old mariner. The difference between the two plays tells much about the developments taking place in Eugene's inner life, especially his reaction to his father's death.

O'Neill still intended to emphasize Chris's mysticism, but as he later explained, the new character of Anna forced herself on him. The British Anna of *Chris* had as a child lost her mother and had been educated away from home according to conventional values. These and a few other traits she shared with Eugene, that is, with the conventional, mannerly boy that Eugene had seemed to his classmates at St. Aloysius and De La Salle. In revising the play into its final version, *"Anna Christie,"* Eugene changed Anna into a young woman who represented the parts of himself that had violently rebelled after the second loss of his mother when he learned that she was an addict.

The well-spoken, British Anna disappeared from the new play, to be replaced by a cynical, desperate ex-hooker from Minnesota who has been sent to a hospital when police closed the brothel. Still ill from a lung ailment, she comes to New York to seek from her father the childhood she never had. Instead of the pallid, educated Paul Andersen of *Chris,* she would meet Mat Burke, a black Irishman modeled on Driscoll. Whatever the shortcomings of the play, it would offer wonderful parts for a succession of fine actors, including Frank Shannon, Charles Bickford, Liam Neeson, Pauline Lord, Greta Garbo, Ingrid Bergman, and Natasha Richardson.

O'Neill changed the plot and setting almost completely. Mat Burke nearly drowns in a shipwreck and is saved by Chris and Anna. Mat falls in love with Anna at first sight and spends half the play persuading her to marry him, while Chris, his mysticism still sounding merely eccentric and irrelevant to the dominant plot, grumbles about the latest dirty trick of the sea that would steal his newly found daughter. Anna finally forces herself to tell Mat she has been a prostitute in a brothel, certain that she will never see him again. In the commotion that follows, she forces both her father and Mat to see who and what she has been and how she got that way. Eventually, Mat decides he still wants to marry her, and her father accepts his prodigal daughter—as James O'Neill, the Irish peasant, repeatedly accepted and forgave his prodigal sons. In these circumstances, Anna agrees to marry Mat and keep a home ashore, and her husband and father will sail out as shipmates.

The play, when it finally went on, was hugely popular with audiences, and most critics liked it too and voted it another Pulitzer Prize. The ending satisfied everyone but the author and a few critics, the latter carping that O'Neill had compromised his tragic sense by giving the audience a conventional happy ending. These were the critics who interested O'Neill, and he tried to respond to them in a letter to the *New York Times.*

Eugene denied the charge but accepted responsibility for somehow failing to write the ending in a way that would make the audience and critics take seriously Chris's last words, "dat ole davil sea—she knows!" (CPI, 1027), as an assertion of what the play is really all about.

The playwright fell a little short, in that he could not prevent the lovers' taking over Chris's play. He failed because his immediate personal concerns overbalanced his philosophical aims. When he wrote the first version of *Chris Christophersen* in the summer of 1918, he was reaching a state of reconciliation with his father. He and Agnes were newly married, he had a substantial income from the vaudeville *In the Zone,* he had written more than thirty plays, including *Beyond the Horizon,* and he had seen several of them produced in New York. He was beginning to feel secure enough in his independence to imagine himself his father's colleague. He had every reason to be proud of his accomplishments, not least his accomplishment in at last getting past his adolescence.

The story of reconciliation between a father and child asserted itself, however strong O'Neill's intent to write about the peasant father's mystical attunement to the sea. Eugene was too preoccupied with himself and his growth to be able to give as much dramatic attention to the father as he tried and intended to do; and he was not conscious enough of his preoccupation to be able to prevent it from affecting what he wrote. "Anna forced herself on me," Eugene told George Jean Nathan a few months later (SL, 148). When Eugene returned to Chris's story after James O'Neill had died, he approached the problem of family reconciliation differently from the way he had when he wrote *Chris Christophersen,* but his most prominent driving idea was still largely unconscious.

The new Anna resembled the self-destructive Eugene. In her rough life, she has been sexually precocious, she drinks too much, and she has had a serious lung ailment. Like Eugene and like the earlier Anna, she has fallen in love with being on the sea and lost in the fog. But now the young person's story is no longer one of becoming an adult. Whereas the British Anna had only a mild grievance against her absent father, Anna Christie blames her many woes on men in general, and on Chris in particular for abandoning her. In her genuine loss, her anger, her self-pity, and her sadness, she represents Eugene's feelings during his long intermittent war with his father.

The new Anna's reconciliation with her father does not so much create a new relationship—as in *Chris Christophersen.* Instead, it rectifies an old loss, one that has been deeply felt and resented. The reconciliation is doubly asserted in the new play. O'Neill ended it with Anna about to set up a home for her husband and father; Mat and Chris are about to ship out together, bound as father- and son-in-law. O'Neill laments the loss of his father in the new version of Chris's play and twice denies the loss—through Chris and Anna's reconciliation and Mat and Chris's bond as shipmates.

Eugene wrote *"Anna Christie"* as both an act of mourning for his father and a denial of death and loss. That O'Neill felt in doubt over the resolution was evident in his various defenses of the ending against complaints about an unjustified "happy" ending. It shouldn't be seen as an ending at all, Eugene told Nathan. "In fact, I once thought of calling the play "Comma," he wrote, and elaborated on the ending's "false definiteness," which he called "misleading" (SL, 148). Indeed, he wanted there to be no ending.

Loss inspired O'Neill to creative acts of repair—the losses of Jimmy Byth, Driscoll, Chris, Louis Holladay, and Hutch Collins, the loss of his father, loosed a torrent. Almost immediately after finishing the new play about Anna on September 18, he began another new play, *The Emperor Jones,* which he finished October 4. Like *Gold,* it was written around a magnificent part for a romantic actor. The complexities of mourning would thenceforth dominate the playwright's creative life.

The same day he finished *The Emperor Jones,* Eugene wrote to his father's old friend George Tyler "to apologize for the overstrained letters I wrote you" last spring. "Those letters," he continued,

> were written during a period of great worry and nervous tension when I was scarcely responsible. They sadly misrepresented my true feelings where you are concerned. They were merely childish outbursts of which I am now heartily ashamed. That I should seriously quarrel with so old and dear a friend of my father's is absurdly wrong. If he were alive, he would be the first one to tell me how damn wrong I was. However, I know it without being told. My letters were ridiculous, unwarranted, peevish—and silly! I have always regarded you as a friend and always will. So, if you have not already laughed those stupid letters into the oblivion they deserve, please do so now—and give me another chance. [Princeton, EO to GT, October 4, 1920]

This previously unpublished letter acknowledged the grief that Eugene had felt as he watched his father dying. The apology ignored the question of why Eugene had been so irritable toward Tyler. In some intuitive way both men probably understood that Eugene had transferred his anger at losing his father to his father's old friend, a man he had known all his life. The apology assured Tyler that the father's attempts to teach Eugene a sense of responsibility had not been in vain. At the same time, he reassured himself of the continuing presence of his father's spirit within: I know what to do without having my father here to tell me.

The urge to repair the loss continued to drive him. A few days after finishing *The Emperor Jones* in early October he began another new play, the underrated and interesting *Diff'rent*, based on the tale of a Provincetown woman told to him by Fifine Clark. He finished it October 19. In act 1, set in 1890, the twenty-year-old Emma Crosby, possessed by her sense of being "diff'rent" from the rest of the villagers, settles on Caleb to be her husband because she believed him to be "diff'rent" too—a chaste whaling captain. When she learns his chastity had not been perfect, she calls off their marriage, not because of moral rigidity per se but because her sense of her uniqueness has to be validated by a unique husband. In act 2, thirty years later, Emma, now a boozy, overage flapper, is having a sordid affair with Caleb's worthless young nephew. When she sees herself through Caleb's eyes, she hangs herself, and Caleb kills himself out of grief for her.

Performed in tandem with *The Emperor Jones, Diff'rent* ran a hundred performances that winter, in spite of a shaky cast. Sheaffer and Manheim have argued that Emma resembles Mary Tyrone and Ella O'Neill in various ways, and a number of other O'Neill women as well. Emma also resembles Hedda Gabler. Eugene seems especially interested in the phenomenon of her narcissistic obsession with being unique. Perhaps he also takes his father's side in the old family quarrel that centered on the paternity suit against James just after he and Ella married. Although James was ever a model of fidelity, Ella when under the influence of morphine would always hark back to the old scandal.

Evidently Eugene first offered *The Emperor Jones* to the Theatre Guild, which turned it down at once, possibly in a dispute over casting. He then turned it over to the P.P., which immediately set about putting on a production. O'Neill and most of the P.P. believed that Jones should be played by a black actor. Jasper Deeter remembered seeing Charles Gilpin give a remarkable performance as the slave in *Abraham Lincoln*. Gilpin was tracked down at Macy's, where he was operating an elevator. He was interviewed on the job and came to MacDougal Street to read the part for O'Neill. He is said to have been the first black actor ever hired to play a leading part in a white American production. He also became the first actor to get a substantial salary from the P.P.—fifty dollars a week, once the play's success was established. Deeter, playing the trader Smithers, received thirty dollars a week, and several other actors were paid as well. Jig Cook was the nominal director, but O'Neill was the last one to leave nearly every night of rehearsal; he worked with Gilpin after everyone else had gone.

The Emperor Jones opened in the Playwrights' Theatre on November 1. Poetic, tragic, swift-moving, and expressionistic, the play caught some critics by surprise and suggested that there might be more to O'Neill than mere realism. Conservative critics had a reservation or two about what they called a "trick" in the accelerating drumbeats that accompanied the action—as if music were not a legitimate dramatic idea. But nearly all reviews were entirely favorable. In 1946 O'Neill named Charles Gilpin as one of three actors who had fully realized one of his characters. *The Emperor Jones* was a sensation from the first performance, and for two months, the little theater was full nearly every night. On December 27, it moved uptown to the Selwyn and was replaced on MacDougal Street by *Diff'rent*. On January 21, *Diff'rent* moved to the Selwyn to run with *The Emperor Jones*. The publication on January 23 in *Theatre Arts* magazine of the text of *The Emperor Jones* gave the production another boost. The bill ran for another hundred performances and began touring as soon as it closed in New York.

For the first time Eugene asked for and received royalties from the Players for one of his plays. He wrote to a friend that he did so reluctantly and only because he was in serious need of money, a problem he mentioned to other correspondents as well. He and Agnes had gone through the royalties from *Beyond the Horizon* and also the thousand dollars from the Pulitzer.

Eugene pressed Tyler to decide about *"Anna Christie"* and *The Straw*. Tyler offered to relinquish both options because he could not find a theater and knew Eugene needed money. When the playwright's need eased, thanks to royalties from *The Emperor Jones* and *Diff'rent,* Eugene was still determined to have the other two plays go on while his name was before the public with *The Emperor Jones*. With a success in hand, he was in a position to insist. In any case, Tyler's option on *"Anna Christie"* would expire in early March. Eugene was buttressed by Nathan's assurance that the new version was an improvement, and Eugene asked George Jean to mention that impression to his friend the producer-director Arthur Hopkins. Nathan did so, but *"Anna Christie"* still had to wait until the fall for its moment. Eugene also nagged Williams, who continued to delay the production of *Gold* after rushing Eugene to finish it.

Meanwhile, Tyler had another brainstorm: he wanted Eugene to write a new version of *Monte Cristo* to be put on in honor of his father. In reply Eugene went so far as to toy with the notion of starting completely from scratch with the old warhorse, but then he went off in a tirade against the play and its contribution to his father's loss of artistic idealism. Eugene's reply also carried the news that, to everyone's surprise, Ella was proving a competent manager of her husband's estate—selling off weak investments, getting Jamie to force tenants to make long-overdue rent payments, and generally taking things in hand. She and Jamie now spent most of every day together, and Jamie handled Ella's correspondence with lawyers. Jamie had completely stopped drinking for the first time since adolescence. Apparently the emptiness he had tried to fill with liquor was appeased by having his mother to himself. A bitterness that had been increasingly noticeable in his behavior for several years seemed to vanish at his father's death. Letters to his friend Frank Dart during this period show Jamie to be courteous, gentle, urbane.

Eugene wrote nothing for several months after finishing *Diff'rent*. Throughout the 1920s and 1930s, he was driven to write constantly, even at times when none of his continually emerging ideas were ripe for picking. Writing, he sometimes said, was his vacation from living, but at present he was looking for escape from mourning.

He turned to an idea he had entertained for some time for a play about an anthropologist named Jayson who roams the world in search of a modern golden fleece, the earliest human remains. This Royal Tramp has a wife who accompanies him on his travels and sacrifices everything to his goal.

O'Neill's bereavement intruded on whatever plot idea he originally had, and the play came to center on the couple's unending grief over the death of their young daughters, years before. In the action, the Jaysons are about to set out on an expedition, but Martha finds herself pregnant again and is afraid to tell her husband, because it violates their agreement never to have any more children that they might lose. She dies in childbirth, and Jayson gives his son to an aunt to raise for him while he sets off on his quest. "I'll come back," he tells his aunt at the very end. "When he's old enough, I'll teach him to know and love a big free life" (CP2, 116). It is perhaps the best moment in a tedious and implausible play about small-town pettiness and gossip.

Besides his bereavement, the growing distance between the O'Neills interfered with whatever he might have done with the Jason myth. As he and Agnes drifted apart, O'Neill imagined the dying Martha even more perfectly subservient to his needs than Agnes had been—and killed her off. The theme of the play seems related to Ella O'Neill's refusal to go through with several pregnancies after the death of her second son, Edmund. It seems that Eugene's reluctance to become a father may have been partly the result of identification with his mother's inability to tolerate the possible loss of another child after the baby Edmund died. Jayson seeks immortality in anthropology rather than fatherhood, and Eugene sought it in play-writing.

The ideal of marriage presented in the play had its origin in the marriage of his parents, in which his mother had followed his hero-father all over the continent (in his quest for the golden fleece of Monte Cristo). O'Neill had been writing about his ideals for marriage since his first plays—in *A Wife for a Life,* and in *Servitude, Bread and Butter,* and *Beyond the Horizon,* among others. In several other plays about marriage Eugene would express his deep identification with his father. Misbegotten though it was as drama, *The First Man* showed Eugene making normal progress through the process of mourning, drawing from conscious and unconscious sources prominent issues and personal themes that arose from the identifications that formed his childhood self, and trying to make sense of them from an adult perspective.

On March 18, O'Neill wrote to the critic and producer Kenneth Macgowan that he had finished a draft of *The First Man* and half-acknowledged to himself that it needed more time to "smoulder . . . in the subconscious" (SL, 150). Unable to tolerate inactivity, O'Neill was preparing to plunge into his next project, "my Fountain of Youth play," and he asked for advice on books to read about the theme besides Frazer's *Golden Bough,* a request he had also put to Bobby Jones, with whom he was increasingly friendly. Eugene intended *The Fountain* to be a modern Faust play, expressionistic in style, epic in conception. It was an early stab at a theme that would preoccupy O'Neill the rest of his life, the squandering of America's resources by the European colonizers, a theme that would eventually lead him to the multiplay Cycle of the 1930s. *The Fountain* was to be written in verse. Although Eugene had rejected Tyler's idea for a new play about the Count of Monte Cristo, the idea of a romantic play on a grand theme appealed to him. Part of the attraction must have been the theme itself. The fountain of youth implied the denial of death. In this respect, the play served his need to continue denying the loss of his father.

When *The Emperor Jones* moved to Times Square, Charles Gilpin began drinking heavily and started changing lines. Eugene was so exasperated with him that he said he would have Gilpin fired if he didn't play the role as written, and, when that didn't work, O'Neill said he wanted to beat him up. Backstage, Gilpin sometimes was so disoriented that he had to ask, "What's the scene?" before he went on (LS, 35). Gilpin was justly singled out for recognition the next year by the New York Drama League, but the honor was tained by a rump campaign to exclude a man of color from a dinner of white folks, and the affront could not be fully undone even when O'Neill and others publicized the scandal and the dinner went off as originally planned. As Sheaffer tells the sad story, Gilpin's great theatrical success apparently destroyed his life. When *The Emperor Jones* closed, he took the money he had saved and bought a chicken farm in New Jersey. He could not return to menial work or to playing lesser roles, and he was drinking so heavily that despite his great gifts, he could not get leading parts. His son got into trouble, and extricating him cost Gilpin most of his money. He died in 1930 in poverty on his farm, all but forgotten (LS, 34–39). Jimmy Light told Sheaffer he thought Gilpin had deliberately drunk himself to death.

Gilpin was only one victim of *The Emperor Jones's* success. The production sowed discontent among the regular P.P. actors, stagehands, and directors about money and billing in a way that differences of opinion over artistic ideals had never done. When *The Emperor Jones* finally closed in New York, it immediately went on the road. Further success created a new split in the Players, some of them becoming part of a glamorous touring company, which was to go to London in July, the others staying home to look for unknown worthy plays and plan for the next year's activities. The Players would never again be as willing as before to work for nothing and sometimes subordinate themselves to Jig's ideals or their own. Jig himself had worked day and night to ensure the success of *The Emperor Jones*, even sleeping in the theater to save costs. The theater survived for seven years after that and had further triumphs, but Jig was becoming increasingly envious of Eugene's success, especially when his own plays found no favor with critics nor popularity with the public. Eugene, who had never shared the ideal of amateurism, was not much affected by the change, but he increasingly turned to friends like Saxe Commins and the critics Nathan and Kenneth Macgowan as readers of his manuscripts and as a sounding board for his ideas.

In the spring, as Eugene was at work on *The Fountain*, he learned that, without telling O'Neill what he was up to, Williams had tried to sell *Gold* to the movies and was also trying to sell stage rights to the Theatre Guild. The news reached Eugene in Rochester, where Saxe Commins was doing some serious and painful dental work on his friend. Eugene exploded in a letter to Agnes at the deficiencies of the actor Willard Mack, whom Williams wanted to play the captain. Williams partly pacified Eugene a few weeks later, but in late May when *Gold* was about to open, Eugene found that Mack had still not learned his lines. Eugene despaired of the play, tried to ignore the production, and felt justified in his pessimism when it closed after thirteen performances.

All summer the O'Neills had visitors at Peaked Hill Bars, chief among them Jamie, who stayed for a couple of weeks and quietly charmed local girls. Ella probably came with Jamie, but the recollections of Agnes and others with whom Sheaffer spoke were hazy on the point. Bobby Jones visited, and Kenneth and Edna Macgowan and their children. Saxe, who refused to send a bill for more than a week's strenuous dental work, labor that pained him as much as his patient, visited at the end of the summer. Through it all, Eugene put in long stints on *The Fountain*, isolating himself so much of the time that his guests sometimes worried that they were intruding on his creative privacy. As during his school days, he had very little aptitude for being a host, and Agnes apparently had little more.

During Jamie's visit, Eugene did a little drinking and, it seemed to Agnes, he relaxed. But for much of the summer he was remote and appeared to be under considerable strain. Young Agnes Carr, who looked after Shane that summer, told Sheaffer much later that when she first saw O'Neill, he looked so sad she wanted to cry. She said that Mrs. Clark explained to her that his sadness was the consequence of his birth's having caused his mother's sickness. Apparently, Eugene had made of Fifine Clark a deep confidante.

About August 14, Eugene wrote to Agnes, who was visiting her parents at the Connecticut farm, that he was suffering "my regular attack of August melancholy" (Harvard, EO to AB, Sunday [August 14, 1921]), an anniversary reaction that had probably begun with his mother's attempted suicide in August 1902 and his awakening to her addiction and his responsibility for it. To these old sources of grief he had added his father's death the previous August.

His letters show he was aware that his enormous efforts on *The*

Fountain were not paying off. In the afternoons, instead of being sociable with guests, he would punch a punching bag until he tired of it, then take his kayak far out to sea or go off for a solitary walk. He developed a bad cold during Saxe's visit that hung on long after Saxe returned to Rochester. Saxe saw so little of Eugene while at Peaked Hill Bars that he wrote when he got home to ask if he had somehow offended. Eugene reassured him, but he did not explain about his melancholy or his problems with *The Fountain*. Only with Jamie, that summer, had Eugene been able to relax.

In September, the good news came that Arthur Hopkins, who was about to begin rehearsals of *"Anna Christie,"* had taken an option on *The Fountain*. To celebrate, the O'Neills gave a party, and Eugene got drunk. Piecing together several reports, Sheaffer has reconstructed the end of the evening. After the party, Eugene's Irish terrier, Mat Burke, attacked their cat, Anna Christie, and Agnes grabbed a poker and hit the dog. Eugene, furious, warned her not to hit *his* dog again or he would kill her; blazing back, she hit him with the poker, and Eugene grabbed Agnes by her long hair and began dragging her off toward the beach. Agnes Carr tried to separate them, but Fifine Clark placidly told the girl, "This has happened before." Agnes Carr then went to fetch Terry Carlin and Louis Kalonyme from the beach, and eventually peace was restored. Next morning, Eugene was remorseful, but Agnes Carr had seen enough and quit (LS, 63–64). Soon after, Eugene and Agnes went to New York to watch the rehearsals of *"Anna Christie,"* and they stayed with Bobby Jones.

While staying at Jones's apartment, Eugene made the acquaintance of his first son. During the spring, Kathleen Jenkins had written to Eugene (through her lawyer) with news of Eugene Jr. In 1915 she had married George Pitt-Smith, a divorced office manager, and had renamed the boy Richard Pitt-Smith. Until the marriage, Kathleen and Eugene Jr. had lived with Kathleen's mother, and Eugene Jr. had become very attached to his grandmother. Eugene Jr. was about five when his mother remarried; he lost the daily contact with his grandmother and had some difficulty adjusting to having a stepfather and to a stepbrother, George Jr., who lived with his father half of each year. Eugene Jr. was sent to board at military school, which he hated; he ran away several times. To complicate matters further, Mr. Pitt-Smith had become an invalid not long after he married Kathleen.

Much later, Kathleen told interviewers that in 1920, when she first began to hear the name of the dramatist, she made no connection between it and her first husband. Only gradually did she realize that it was he; they had known each other so little that she had not thought of him as being literary. Since the Pitt-Smiths were having financial problems, Kathleen decided to write to her son's father and ask for help in paying for the boy's education. Eugene agreed immediately to pay his son's tuition at Horace Mann School, and in September he arranged to have the boy visit him in Manhattan.

Eugene Sr. was so nervous about the meeting that he begged Kenneth Macgowan to be present for moral support. The fears turned out to be groundless. The visit went well, father and son talking easily about baseball and school. At eleven, Eugene Jr. learned who his father was and what his own name had originally been. After he met his father that afternoon in Manhattan, he resumed using his original name. Kathleen told Sheaffer that the visit had gone so well that after the visit she felt "peculiar": "They hit it off so well that [I felt] I'm losing my son" (LS, 67). In fact, changing schools and meeting his real father seemed to help the boy, who began to do superior academic work, and he became friendly with his stepfather, whom he began to call Uncle George. He also developed a lasting closeness with his stepbrother. From that point on, Eugene Jr. had an increasingly solid place in his father's life.

In addition to welcoming his firstborn into his life, Eugene spent October attending rehearsals for *"Anna Christie"* and *The Straw.* He found Arthur Hopkins eliciting much better performances from the cast of *"Anna Christie"* than he had expected and, not long after the opening, wrote to his New London friend Ed Keefe that, leaving aside the quality of the play itself, he thought *"Anna Christie"* "one of the best acted I have ever seen, and the best set" (SL, 156). He and Hopkins, both quiet, empathic men, got along well, mostly in comfortable silence. The opening on November 2 was very successful. Macgowan, in the *Globe,* declared the play more fully realized than *Beyond the Horizon,* and he had nothing but praise for the actors. George Marion as Chris was "merely perfect," and Pauline Lord's performance was "minute, exact, and subtle" (November 3, 1921). To praise Frank Shannon as Mat Burke, it was enough to call him a match for Pauline Lord. Even critics who found fault with O'Neill's ending or his ear for dialogue agreed about the performance. The play stimulated reviewers to deeper, subtler consideration than is usually possible under pressure of deadlines. The play would run 177 performances.

With "*Anna Christie*" going better than he had expected, after so long a delay, Eugene gave short shrift to *The Straw* when it opened on November 10. He rated Otto Kruger an improvement over Tyler's original choice of John Westley for the role of Murray. But in the main role of Eileen Carmody, Margalo Gilmore was "beyond her depth," as Alexander Woolcott wrote, in "a role which seems to ask more than she yet knows how to give" (in Cargill 1961, 155). Spotty as it was, the performance gave critics a glimpse of the author's ambitions aims. Woolcott described it as "O'Neill's study of hope," and Robert Allerton Parker, who enjoyed a longer deadline for the *Weekly Review*, carried the point further. Eileen reaches "the belated realization that she may vanquish death because she must live to save the life of her lover." Not that she will live very long. But "it seems to be Mr. O'Neill's great and thrilling point that [her decision to live] does come: and that with this decision his heroine lives, lives intensely, triumphantly, if only for a few days or a few moments" (quoted in Miller 1965, 30). *The Straw* lasted for only twenty performances. Eugene himself never saw the play.

By the end of November when *The Straw* closed, memories of Driscoll were returning to the surface of Eugene's imagination. He now found the form he had sought for several years through which he could explore Driscoll's death. By December 10 he had begun his sixth new play since his father's stroke, *The Hairy Ape*. He finished the play less than two weeks later.

From the start, he envisioned Louis Wolheim in the role of Yank, and when he turned the play over to the P.P. to produce, he asked that they cast Wolheim in the part. O'Neill wanted no royalties unless the show moved uptown. Jig Cook was to direct, with help from Arthur Hopkins. Cleon Throckmorton would design the sets and Blanche Hays the costumes, with help from Bobby Jones if he recovered soon enough from a breakdown. Wolheim would turn out to be as effective in the role of Yank as Gilpin had been as Jones. The first production ran 127 performances, and over the years the play would be revived almost as often as *The Emperor Jones*.

When the year had begun, Eugene had needed money. By the end of it, he could look back on the successful production of *The Emperor Jones* and *Diff'rent*, the beginning of a long run of "*Anna Christie*," and the openings of *The Straw* and *The First Man* as well. Counting the publication of various plays in magazines and books, and royalties for revivals, he had earned about fifteen thousand dollars. Eugene and Agnes were now prosperous.

In the fourth year of the marriage, Eugene and Agnes were clearly drifting apart. Agnes increasingly complained that their sex life had become routine, and Eugene thought that his success was bringing out the social climber in her. Agnes had begun looking for a house in Connecticut suitable to their new status. Eugene, meanwhile, thought about little except his writing, but work on *The Fountain* was still going badly. Many of his letters that year begin with apologies for his belated replies. When he was not writing, he fell into deep depression or drank heavily. When he and Agnes were both drinking, they sometimes had spectacular fights. While in New York for rehearsals, Eugene met the analyst Smith Eli Jelliffe, who was treating Bobby Jones and Arthur Hopkins. Sheaffer believes that it was the drinking and his outbursts of anger toward Agnes that led Eugene to see Jelliffe several times (LS, 82). Given his prolonged depressions and the problems in the marriage, O'Neill had plenty to talk about. In retrospect, it seems that his spirit was ruled by his alternation between denial and acceptance of his father's death.

On the surface, Jamie and Ella seemed less affected than Eugene by the loss. Since James's death, Ella and Jamie had settled into a life that satisfied both of them, spending most of every day together from morning to night. Ella had persuaded Jamie to stop drinking shortly after her husband died, and by the end of 1921 he had gone nearly a year and a half without a lapse. He had evidently given up his women as well and told several friends that he had become impotent. For years he had predicted he would become impotent when he was forty, an age he had reached in 1918, and perhaps the wish behind the prophecy fulfilled itself.

Eugene told Harold DePolo that Jamie had developed a system for betting on horses, which allowed him to "create quite a small bankroll in reserve" (SL, 162). In early January, Jamie and Ella boarded a train for New Orleans, where Jamie meant to watch the horses for a week. Then they would proceed to Los Angeles, where Ella wanted to sell a piece of property that James had once bought in nearby Glendale.

Eugene and Agnes meant to visit Ella and Jamie before they left New York, but they were delayed leaving Provincetown until late in January, just before *The Hairy Ape* and *The First Man* began rehearsal. Planning to be in New York only briefly, they left Shane with Mrs. Clark in

Provincetown. Agnes fell ill with the flu almost as soon as they arrived in town. Early in February, Eugene got a wire from Jamie in Los Angeles saying that Ella had had a stroke and was in a coma. She had suffered from severe headaches for several months, and it was assumed that the headaches were related to the stroke. Jamie immediately resumed drinking when his mother was stricken, and in his loneliness he fell in with a woman he had known in New London.

Ella regained consciousness but was partly paralyzed by the stroke or by the brain tumor that was diagnosed. Eugene received a series of contradictory telegrams. Jamie said that Ella's condition was less serious than it had at first seemed. A few days later Jamie begged Eugene to come to Los Angeles; Ella was in coma again and unlikely to awaken. Eugene consulted Dr. Jelliffe about his own condition and his mother's. The case sounded hopeless from reports, but Jelliffe gave Eugene the name of a Los Angeles neurologist, Samuel Ingham, for a second opinion, which Eugene passed on to Jamie. Pleading nervous exhaustion, Eugene wired that his doctor had warned him against the consequences for his health if he went. Even if he went, he added, his mother would be unconscious and would not know him.

Eugene faced crises on three fronts: his mother appeared to be dying, he had two plays in rehearsal, *The First Man* and *The Hairy Ape*, and the Players, as a group, seemed on the verge of falling apart. O'Neill chose to focus exclusively on the one crisis in which he thought something he could do might be effective. *The First Man* seemed beyond hope, with its bungled script and casting problems. He focused all his interest and spent most of his waking hours in the Playwrights' Theatre.

Staging *The Hairy Ape* on the tiny stage at MacDougal Street, with no overhead "flies" and hardly any space backstage, presented formidable problems. Sets had to be brought up from the basement through holes in the stage. Even more complex problems developed in the directorate of the Players. Once again a play by O'Neill appeared headed for critical and commercial success. At a time of general discouragement caused by the failure of his own plays, Jig came to believe that Eugene had intentionally sabotaged the amateur spirit of the group by taking *The Emperor Jones* uptown and thus making money a topic of contention among the group. Jig felt himself and his spirit of dedicated amateurism being driven out of the company he had created. He criticized O'Neill for using the P.P. to try out plays that he feared he could not get directly into uptown theaters. The charge was true as far as it went: O'Neill had never concealed his hopes that the company would gradually become more competent, more professional, and more international in its outlook. He had explicitly offered them *The Hairy Ape* with the hope that, like *The Emperor Jones*, it would move uptown, a hope most of the company shared, and they had accepted the terms. The clash in ideals was real, although Eugene had no interest in controlling the group and was personally upset that Jig contemplated abandoning his offspring.

In fact, Jig blamed not only Eugene but most of the other members of the group for betraying the founding ideals, and finally he decided that he was simply out of step with the ideals and values of his time. Feeling deeply alienated, not only from the Players, but from the modern world as a whole, Jig convinced Susan that the time had come for a sabbatical in Delphi, where they would live as shepherds on the slopes around the ancient temple.

The Gelbs describe an argument between Jig and Eugene the day of a farewell party for Jig and Susan. Supposedly, Jig accused Eugene of vanity: "You can't pass a mirror without staring at yourself." To which Eugene replied, "I'm just looking to see if I'm alive" (Gelbs, 493). The farewell party for the Cooks probably took place on February 28—they left on March 1 for Greece. February 28 began for Eugene with the arrival of a telegram telling him that Ella had died in Los Angeles. The anecdote about the mirror, if the details are correct, suggests that something was at work besides Eugene's vanity. The response, spoken by a man who deeply identified with his newly dead mother, might mean literally that he was looking to see whether he himself was still alive.

After Jig's abdication, Eugene took over direction of *The Hairy Ape*. He was assisted by Arthur Hopkins, who quietly observed. In the program, Jimmy Light was given credit as the director. Throwing himself completely into the production of the play, which would always be one of his favorites, Eugene worked late into the night with Louis Wolheim. Later he would list Wolheim among the three actors who fully realized the character he imagined. A strong, intelligent man with a face scarred by football and boxing at Cornell and drunken brawling with police in barrooms, Wolheim had degrees in math and Romance languages and a background in teaching and engineering. In Mexico he had participated in Pancho Villa's revolution. Wolheim had drifted into acting after being an extra in a movie being filmed in Ithaca. (After his great success in *The Hairy Ape* he had another success in *What Price Glory?* and then major roles in several movies, including *All Quiet on the Western Front.*)

On February 28, 1922, Ella had died. She was sixty-four. Being extremely busy with two productions probably helped Eugene stay sober and numb to his mother's death for several days. Sheaffer found a detailed eye-witness account by a friend of Ella's, her hairdresser Libby Drummer, of doings in Los Angeles that Mrs. Drummer considered tawdry and chaotic (LS, 82–85). The deed for the Glendale property disappeared for a time and then turned up. Ella's jewelry disappeared and was never recovered. When Ella had a second stroke, Jamie resumed drinking and was drunk most days. Mrs. Drummer reported that Jamie's woman friend, Marion Reed, used her power over Jamie to manipulate his mother's attempts to make a will. Somehow Mrs. Reed had herself named executrix.

At first, Jamie persuaded his mother to give him the most valuable property in the estate, a property at 53 Columbus Avenue in Manhattan. Sick as she was, Ella found the strength to insist that all the property in the estate be divided equally between the brothers except the Glendale property, which she gave to Jamie. Mrs. Drummer came to the apartment as often as she could trying to ensure that Ella's wishes were followed in the will, and she largely succeeded. Sheaffer reports that a lawyer friend of Mrs. Reed drafted the will and guided Ella's hand to make an X on the document (LS, 83). When Ella died, Jamie was not capable of arranging for her body to return to New York. Ella's friend, scandalized by the scene and having done what she could to preserve order, wrote a detailed account to another friend of Ella in New York with hints that she pass on the letter to Eugene. Mercifully, Eugene did not hear the full story until late in March. (Libby Drummer's letter is given in full in the next chapter.)

On February 28, drunk and overwhelmed by grief, Jamie wrote to Frank Dart in New London, "My dear friend, my mother died this morning. I know your devotion to yours so you can appreciate the awful desolation that has come into my life" (LS, 83). Someone, possibly the Los Angeles lawyer, arranged for Ella's body to be taken by an undertaker and then carried to Union Station for the long trip to New York. Jamie tried to decide whether to remain in Los Angeles with Mrs. Reed, who seldom let him out of her sight, or to return to New York. Mrs. Drummer told the undertaker to put the body on the train and make sure that Jamie was also on the train, and this he did.

In New York on March 4 Eugene listlessly attended the opening of *The First Man,* hardly caring that it was as weak as he had feared. The train bearing Jamie and Ella's body arrived in New York on the evening of the ninth, the night that *The Hairy Ape* opened. Sheaffer's notes and various biographies and other published documents carry differing reports of the events that evening. The following draws on published and unpublished accounts.

One of Sheaffer's chief informants was Frank Wilder, a nephew of James O'Neill's old friend and colleague Will Connor. Wilder had known Eugene when he himself was about seven and Eugene about fifteen, and he remembered Eugene's tormenting him, which made him detest Eugene ever after. Wilder told Sheaffer that Eugene had asked Will Connor to go with him to meet Jamie and his mother's body, for he was afraid he might not be able to face the task alone. Eugene must have longed for his father's help at that moment and transferred the need to Connor.

Following Wilder, Sheaffer concludes that Eugene's nerve completely failed him shortly before he was to meet Connor—O'Neill called to beg off. The stern Connor refused to be understanding with a man he had long considered a spoiled and willful boy, and when Connor spoke of duty, he set off in Eugene the sort of stubbornness that Eugene had formerly exhibited when angry with his father. Sheaffer believes that Eugene remained in the hotel with his demons, while his duty was done by Connor and his nephew. Wilder told Sheaffer that he and his uncle had arranged for Ella's coffin to be moved to a funeral home, but that they had not been able to find Jamie. Finally, after a search of the train, they found him half-conscious amid the empty bottles in his compartment. Jamie had passed the unendurable trip drunk with a woman. Connor transported Jamie in a taxi to a Times Square hotel.

Sheaffer's published biography blends Wilder's account with a narrative that Saxe Commins sometime later wrote for his private use and that was eventually published by Saxe's wife in a collection of correspondence between Saxe and Eugene. It should be noted that there are several mistakes of fact in Saxe's narrative.

Saxe wrote that he used Eugene's ticket to accompany Agnes to the opening of *The Hairy Ape,* while Eugene went to meet Jamie's train at the station. At the Playwrights' Theatre, Agnes and Saxe were greatly impressed with Eugene's new play, but, worried about Eugene and his dreary task, they listened with mixed feelings to the hearty applause and calls for the author. When they returned to the hotel where Eugene was to meet them, he told them briefly about Jamie's condition.

Saxe described Eugene as looking "ashen"; his lips were blue, and "he seemed to have lost control of his hands" (Commins 1986, 22). Commins thought that Eugene greatly needed company and led his friend on a long walk in Central Park. Nervous and filled with compassion, Saxe rattled on—about Wolheim, the play, and the audience's enthusiasm—meanwhile ignoring Eugene's insistence that he did not want to hear about the play. After a silence, Eugene began describing his mother's life. Saxe thus became one of the few outsiders, along with Harold DePolo and Mrs. Clark, to hear Ella's dreadful story. According to Saxe's memoir, Eugene blamed *Monte Cristo* for his mother's addiction and showed empathy, compassion, and sardonic exasperation toward his mother, who had been removed from her natural surroundings and transplanted into the theatrical world. No wonder, Saxe wrote, "she had to seek another [world] in a faraway narcotic dream" (22). In telling this painful history, Eugene spoke clearly and more fluently than Saxe had ever heard him do.

As Saxe remembered it, Eugene saved his bitterest denunciation for Jamie, especially for wasting his talents for being "natural and easy and pleasant" with people and his gifts for graceful speaking and writing, all gifts that in Eugene were inhibited and that he envied (Commins 1986, 25). Probably Eugene's envy of his brother's verbal ease was mingled with the image of Jamie drunk with a hooker on the train bearing Ella's body, which he did not mention to Saxe but which he wrote about two decades later in *A Moon for the Misbegotten*. To Commins, it seemed to annoy Eugene most that Jamie valued none of his gifts at all.

When told of Wilder's and Saxe's accounts, Agnes made certain corrections. She told Sheaffer that Saxe did not go with her to see *The Hairy Ape,* and that no one searched through Grand Central for Ella's coffin, but that arrangements had already been made to send it on to New London. She said that she met Gene at their hotel after the play and went with him to Grand Central to meet Jamie but that they couldn't find him until they finally searched the train. Jamie was nearly unconscious with alcohol. They took him to a hotel, and on the way he told them about spending every night on the train trip with a prostitute to help him forget his dead mother in the baggage car.

Returning to Saxe's account, the long confession, which must have been exhausting for Commins, seemed to help O'Neill. The next morning, he was able to attend Ella's funeral at St. Leo's Church, where his mother had regularly gone the last several years for morning Mass. Jamie did not go. Wilder told Sheaffer that he and his mother, Will Connor's sister, went to Jamie's hotel to try to take him to the funeral, but Jamie refused, saying he was "too broken up" (LS, 87).

By chance, the priest who officiated at the funeral had been a boy at St. Aloysius with Eugene. Agnes said that Eugene saw Sarah Sandy, who tried to speak to him, but he avoided meeting her, perhaps because at that moment she stood in Eugene's mind for Ella's inability to care for him. Or perhaps Eugene felt he might be overwhelmed with a tide of old dependency. He never saw Sarah again. Ella was buried in New London at St. Mary's Catholic Cemetery next to her husband, her mother, and her son Edmund. Her image remained in Eugene's mind as an object of obsessive reflection and compulsive writing for the next two decades.

14

Eugene in Mourning
1923

WHEN HIS FATHER DIED, EUGENE reacted in a way that, psychoanalytically speaking, was sublimatory and reparative. After sitting by his father's bedside to see him to his grave, he went on a creative spree that yielded six plays in less than eighteen months. Through much of this time Eugene was sober, and he worked effectively not only at writing but at getting his work produced and published.

When his mother died, Eugene's reaction was very different, even before he knew the outward circumstances of her death. He could not bring himself to go to California to ease her dying or accompany her body home. After three years in which he had greatly moderated his drinking, his alcoholism intensified after her death. He drank heavily, in prolonged binges that made writing impossible, and several times when drunk he reached a state in which he seemed psychotic.

The difference in his reactions to his parents' deaths probably has many causes. His relations with his father were simpler and more straightforward, and generally friendlier, than those with his mother. As an adult he tried to cultivate and enhance many of the traits in himself that he identified with his father. But the traits he identified with his mother, including his depression, his hypersensitivity, and his alcoholism, he usually despised. His love of his mother was colored by the belief that she could not return his love unconditionally, and he resented to the point of hatred her inability to care for him in infancy or care for him when he was sick.

Jamie's feelings about Ella's death were much more straightforward than Eugene's. Jamie was now drinking much more heavily than ever in the past, and he told several people that he intended to drink himself to death as quickly as he could. At first his friends were greatly concerned for his health and state of mind. Jamie's friend Frank Dart, the lawyer administering the O'Neill estate, wrote to Eugene in late March urging him to try to get medical help for Jamie. Jamie stopped eating, his weight dropped to 150 pounds, and he had acute attacks of gastritis, apparently the result of his drinking. Eugene called a doctor, but neither he nor Eugene could deflect Jamie's determination to die as he wished. Jamie's mood became so savage that his oldest friends often found him unbearable.

Eugene felt deeply ambivalent about his mother's death, and his confusion was compounded by a growing sense that he had not known his brother: that he was a different person from the man Eugene thought he had known. Although the brothers seemed to get along during a visit Jamie paid to Eugene and Agnes in the summer of 1922, after Ella died, Jamie and Eugene became increasingly estranged, partly because Eugene believed that Jamie had tried to cheat him out of an even share in their mother's property. Jamie told friends that he believed Agnes was bitter about the Glendale property and had poisoned Eugene's mind. In fact, a friend of Ella's in New York had given Eugene the long letter from Ella's friend Libby Drummer, who had tried to protect Ella in Los Angeles. The letter, which detailed Jamie's behavior during Ella's illness, gave Eugene reason to wonder whether he had ever known the real Jamie. Ella's death thus marked for Eugene the beginning of his mourning not only for his mother but for his brother as well. Not only was Jamie dying in body and spirit, but Eugene's internal images of his brother were shaken and upset by what he was learning. Old idealizations that he had maintained almost unchanged since adolescence were proving false, and it was as difficult for Eugene to give them up as to lose his brother in life. His mourning for Jamie, like that for his mother, would go on for the next two decades and would supply the themes and moods that would fill his remaining plays. Indeed, Ella's death and his disillusionment with Jamie sent Eugene into a self-psychoanalysis that lasted the rest of his writing life.

A letter of April 3 to Frank Dart shows Eugene caught in intense ambivalence about Jamie. He was deeply worried about Jamie's health and state of mind, but his hero worship faced a severe test. Eugene sent Dart a copy he had typed out of Libby Drummer's letter describing the details of Ella's illness in Los Angeles and the making of her will. Eugene's copy of Mrs. Drummer's letter (in the Sheaffer-O'Neill Collection) reads as follows:

Your nice letter received and so pleased to hear from you, and would have answered sooner only I have not been so well myself since Mrs. O'Neill died but I am now feeling better. I am so glad you told me about the funeral. I was so worried. I did not know if Jamie would ever reach New York alive. He was in a dreadful condition, I understand, when he left. The nurse called me up and told me and later came in the store to see me and told me everything.

Well, dear, the whole thing is *very sad,* and it will take me a long, long time to get over it, if ever. I am going to tell you just what happened and you can place yourself in my position. It was dreadful. You remember I told you that the first I received a card from Mrs. O'Neill that she was in town and would love to see me. Well I answered and went out to call on her. She had rented a furnished apt. of four rooms at 115 a month. Well when she answered the door and I saw her I felt very bad. She dragged one foot when she walked and her mouth was a little crooked. I spent the evening with her. Jamie was to the pictures show. She spoke of a Mrs. Reed and said that this Mrs. Reed's husband was a friend of Mr. O'Neill's. Before I left Jamie came in. He was not drinking at that time and I invited them both to dinner the following Sunday.

Well, they accepted my invitation and Jamie saw me to the car. He seemed very much worried and wanted to know what I thought about his Mother. I told him to see a doctor at once. Well, I did not see her again until the follow-ing Sunday when they came to dinner. I will never forget Mrs. O'Neill was dressed lovely and her whole face was all to one side. It was a most pitiful sight. I felt more like crying every time I looked at her. She wanted to stay with me the worst way but I didn't have room for them. If she had been alone I would have kept her right with us but I had no room for Jamie. She never mentioned her condition and you know me I would not speak of it, only I told them to see a doctor and where he was. He was an electric doctor and I thought he could help her.

Well, then I did not see them again until the following Thursday. Jamie came up to the store and said that his Mother had another stroke and would I come out there as she wished to see me. I went out and oh what a sight. All of her right side was dead from head to toe. And Mrs Reed and some gentleman friend of her's was there, also a trained nurse by the name of Griffith. This Reed woman was running everything. She is with the Movies. She is married and has two little sons. She did not like it one bit that I was there and let me see it, but I stayed for a few hours as Mrs. O'Neill wished me to. I think that was the day that Jamie started drinking. He is very weak. This Mrs. Reed had him over to her home day and night. I did not like her and could see through her from the first moment I met her. I went to see Mrs. O'Neill every other day and she was waiting for me and I kept praying and hoping that she would get better. She asked me to get her two silk night dresses and I did. Well I took them to her and she was so pleased with them but did not mention to pay for them. I did not say anything and the next time I went to see her she was breathing hard and could hardly talk. All this time the nurse was telling me that Jamie spent the most time with Mrs. Reed and at her house.

Then Jamie came to the store and asked me to come out that night as his mother was going to make her will and he wanted me for his witness. So Min and I went and when we got near the house at the corner we met Jamie and he said a new complication had set in. His mother's jewelry, her deed to the Glendale Property, and the return tickets were missing. While we were talking to him this Mrs. Reed came along and she had a grip with her with a typewriter in it and she asked Jamie where he was going and he said to have something to eat, and she went with him and Min and I went to the house. The nurse let us in and I spoke to Mrs. O'Neill. She was breathing hard and sort of snoring. I spoke to her and kissed her but she never moved, and I felt very bad. I thought she was gone.

Along about eight o'clock they came back and the lawyer came. He was a friend of Mrs. Reed's and from what I understand they—Jamie and this Reed woman—were at the lawyers all afternoon. They introduced him to us and Jamie went outdoors. The lawyer went in to Mrs. O'Neill and roused her, told her that he was the lawyer, and had come to draw her will, and she seemed to understand but could hardly speak. It was very hard for her. I spoke to her and she knew me and called me by name and was so glad that I was with her. She gave equal division to Jamie and Eugene to everything except the Glendale property. Her mind was made up and seemed very clear. Jamie wanted the New York property [by far the most valuable property in the estate] but she wanted Eugene to have half. The Glendale property is worth twenty thousand. The nurse said that she intended giving Jamie the New York property but changed her mind that morning and nothing could change her. They made Mrs. Reed executrix and Jamie power of attorney. It was the saddest thing that I have ever witnessed. She seemed to be quieter after and I went to her and held her hand and asked her if she was satisfied with what she had done. She said yes, and I said now you will rest better and she said yes. Then she started breathing hard again and seemed to be asleep.

Well, she seemed to get worse every day and Jamie kept drinking harder all the time and the worst part of it is I think she knew he was drinking before she died and realized everything and was helpless. I tell you it was dreadful. It just nearly killed me. I wanted to stay with her until the end but I was hardly able. You have no idea how it affected me.

Then she passed away the following Tuesday morning. The nurse phoned me just as soon as it was over. The next day she phoned me and wanted me to come out to the house to see if I could do anything with Jamie as he was drinking so hard. Well, Min and I went and oh, my dear, it was pitiful. The two nurses were there with him and his condition was dreadful between dope and drink and his mother at the undertakers, and he wanted to ship her home to Eugene as this Mrs. Reed wanted him to remain here. He was a little afraid of me and when he mentioned it I said by no means, you are going back with your mother or I wire Eugene. Then the next day I went to the undertakers and had a talk with them. He had left the whole thing to them, even to buying his ticket. I told them not to let the body go back without him and explained it to them and they saw that he left. The nurse came the next day and said that she and this Mrs. Reed and her gentleman friend had seen him off and that he had ten bottles of whiskey with him and that he had a compartment. You can imagine what a condition he was in when they arrived. The nurse said he had found the tickets and the deed but no jewelry. They were in the trunk and only three people had been in it—Mrs. Reed, Jamie and Mrs. Reed's friend so it must be one or the other that took it. I did not know that she had any jewelry as I had never seen any on her but her wedding ring. The nurse said that she told her that she had left her rings in New York.

Jamie gave each of the nurses a dress and a pair of Mrs. O'Neill's shoes. Mrs. Reed got her silk stockings and he gave her a check for 150 dollars and no doubt she took other things. What she wanted was the fur coat. They had a quarrel over it, the nurse said before Mrs. O'Neill died and he wouldn't give it to her. He didn't give me a thing and I sure didn't want anything. I would have liked a little picture of her. I don't know when I felt so bad for anyone as I did about Mrs. O'Neill. It was the saddest closing chapter of any story I have ever read in any book.

From what I understand Jamie intended coming out here again. It would be better for Eugene to keep him there as all this Mrs. Reed wants him for is his money.

Typing this detailed account of greed, weakness, and pity must have been affecting indeed for Eugene. As he wrote Dart on April 3, he considered Mrs. Drummer trustworthy. She had described in what Eugene called "the minutest detail" Jamie's attempts to persuade his mother to give him and not Eugene the most valuable portions of her estate (Sheaffer-O'Neill Collection). Even more damning was her portrayal of Jamie as unable to protect their mother from apparent opportunists when she was nearly helpless. Mrs. Drummer's letter initiated the collapse of Eugene's old idealization of Jamie.

The letter had a further effect. Learning that Jamie had meant to do him out of the lion's share of their parents' estate, the New York property, awakened in Eugene an awareness of his own greed. From that point on, greed would be an increasingly prominent theme in the plays.

Eugene must have been deeply moved by the circumstances of his mother's death. Nevertheless, in the April 3 letter to Frank Dart, Eugene for the most part concealed his feelings about Jamie and even spoke moderately of Mrs. Reed. He shared Dart's concern for Jamie's health and despaired of making Jamie stop drinking or take care of himself. Jamie "promised to return with me here [to Provincetown] when I come up for good . . . but I doubt very much if he will when the time comes," he wrote. Only at the end, in a postscript, did Eugene show some of his feelings. Reading Mrs. Drummer's "letter has made me pretty sore at Jim. Can you blame me?" (Sheaffer-O'Neill Collection). That was all he exposed of a great change in progress.

When trying to separate himself from an internal object fused with himself, O'Neill habitually made a dramatic character of the object. It is striking that O'Neill created no characters around this time who closely resemble Jamie, and in fact there would be no very full or accurate (disguised) portraits of his brother for some years. But it was not for want of trying. About 1920 O'Neill had sketched an idea for a "long play—Jim [that is, Jamie] and self—showing influence of elder on younger brother" (Floyd 1981, 32). Sometime in 1922, undoubtedly after Ella had died and he had seen Mrs. Drummer's letter, he conceived *The Great God Brown*, a play in which the characters Dion Anthony and William Brown are compilations of Jamie's traits as internalized by Eugene. The extreme expressionistic style he adopted for *Brown* worked against making either characterization, Dion or Brown, full enough or human enough to clarify the "influence of elder on younger brother." In fact, it would not be until the late 1930s that O'Neill could think sufficiently clearly about Jamie to model complex characters on him that could help him understand his brother and their relationship.

From a psychoanalytic viewpoint, it seems that circumstances in Jamie's first seven years conjoined to make irreconcilable the ordinary internal conflicts that Jamie experienced over having to share his mother with his father, and also about having to share his father with his mother. The conflicts were to go permanently unresolved and in fact were never allowed to develop fully. Had they developed, Jamie might eventually have learned to be comfortable in identifying with his father, instead of despising every aspect of himself that reminded him of the old man. A feeling of comfort with himself might have enabled Jamie to make some kind of life apart from his mother in which he could use his many talents. He never did.

Circumstances, in the form of James's constant travel and Ella's misery and loneliness, led Ella to charm away the outward sign of her son's oedipal crisis. She made life on the road tolerable by making Jamie her constant courtier. From this point on, Jamie went through life convinced that his mother preferred him to his father, that he had "won" a contest never waged. To maintain belief in his victory, Jamie had to deny that his mother chose to remain with his father and even chose to tolerate the discomforts of the road rather than be separated from her husband. If Jamie had not been able to convince himself that his mother was the prisoner of a tyrant's monstrous demands, he might have seen himself as a pawn in a marital dispute. Apparently he never did, at least not consciously. Confidence in his victory over his father gave Jamie the self-assurance he would need to succeed in school. Yet the prospect of going out into the world alone was too much to face. When he approached graduation, he caused himself to fail, thus ensuring that he would never have to leave the oedipal triangle and his imagined victory. To put it another way, Jamie's unconscious identification with his mother's dependency on his father became the core around which he would live his life.

Meanwhile, Eugene had to consider that he had known Jamie but little. In his present mood he could only doubt that Jamie had ever been worthy of his kid brother's hero worship. Yet Eugene did not immediately cut off contact. He tried to persuade Jamie to moderate his drinking or go into a sanatorium, as a doctor had recommended. Staying in his mother's apartment on Thirty-fifth Street, Jamie was now drinking much more heavily than before his father's death. At times he still seemed sufficiently his old self to deal effectively with problems. In March Mrs. Reed wrote Jamie asking for any of Ella's clothes and bath powders that had not been given to Agnes. Under pressure from Frank Dart and Eugene, Jamie succeeded in persuading Mrs. Reed to resign her appointment as executrix of his mother's estate. But such moments of competence were increasingly rare for Jamie.

Drinking had previously not seemed to affect his health. Now, however, he had stopped eating and soon drank himself into a condition that sounds like acute alcoholic gastritis. On May 20, he wrote to Frank Dart, who had himself recently been mortally ill: "The fact is my dear friend, I have been as near to taking the last hurdle as you yourself since my arrival here." And in the same letter: "For five days and nights I threw up and threw up—while the pains in my stomach kept forcing me to ineffectual efforts in the toilet. I could neither eat nor sleep. . . . You would not know me," he wrote. "I weigh less than 150 pounds and resemble the Gov. [his father] as he lay in bed during his last illness" (LS papers; see also LS, 95). Eugene, for one, took seriously his brother's insistence that he meant to kill himself with drink. Jamie's "kid brother" went into a state of despair over him, in the belief that the outcome was inevitable.

Life went on. Eugene had to deal with his Brennan and Sheridan relatives, who complained that there had been no funeral service for Ella in New London but only the burial. Old friends of his parents complained that they had not known of Ella's death or funeral, and Eugene had to reply that he and Will Connor had tried to get hold of everyone they could think of, but sometimes they could not locate people after several tries. He added, disingenuously, that they had had no control over when Ella's body would arrive from Los Angeles and therefore could not know exactly when the funeral would be held. Eugene and Agnes moved about from New London to Boston to New York taking care of details. After the burial they went to Provincetown to make the house livable for the summer and to escape memories of the funeral in New York and the burial in New London.

Affairs on Broadway kept Eugene busy. *The Hairy Ape* moved uptown to the Plymouth Theatre on April 17 and ran for 127 performances. Wolheim continued as Yank, but Mary Blair as the heiress was replaced by Carlotta Monterey. Eugene saw Carlotta in rehearsal and was unimpressed with her as an actress, but he thought she looked the part more than Mary Blair. Carlotta later told Sheaffer that she had had a brief meeting with the playwright and thought he showed no gratitude for her stepping into the part on short notice. Preoccupied with his mother, Jamie, and the funeral, he was probably seldom cordial to anyone in those months. Having missed the premiere in the Village, he bought his first dinner jacket to attend the opening at the Plymouth, taking with him a group of roughs and racketeers he knew from the Hell Hole.

Despite the failures of *The Straw* and *The First Man,* Eugene had two successful plays on uptown stages. Perhaps it was a mark of O'Neill's growing fame that the police tried to close *The Hairy Ape* when it moved uptown, on a complaint about "indecent, obscene and impure" language, a complaint that a magistrate immediately dismissed without comment when he read the play. Eugene became involved in the reorganization of the Provincetown Players, who, after hesitant steps in various directions, decided to continue under Jimmy Light's direction for the year Jig and Susan planned to be in Greece.

In May *"Anna Christie"* was awarded the Pulitzer Prize. Writing a friend, Eugene noted that editorials by the IWW paper, *Solidarity,* and by the *Tribune* had praised the play, "both for something I didn't mean," a situation which seemed to him to prove that "it is possible to fool [all the people] all the time" (SL, 168). *"Anna Christie"*'s success and the Pulitzer probably triggered the sale of the play to the movies, a transaction that brought Eugene twenty-five thousand dollars. (O'Neill liked the 1923 film that First National made of the play and was impressed with Blanche Sweet, who played Anna.)

The sale of *"Anna Christie"* allowed the O'Neills to begin to live in higher style. Eugene had never shown much interest in automobiles but now bought a custom-made roadster, and he and Agnes began to search in earnest for a permanent home in southwestern Connecticut. Jamie, bringing with him Terry Carlin and Louis Kalonyme, came in June to Provincetown, where Louis and Terry set up housekeeping in separate beach shacks on the town side of the Peaked Hill Bars station. There they could give early warning of celebrity-hunting strangers.

The O'Neills' marriage had been, almost from the beginning, one in which brief episodes of intense closeness ended with some pushing apart, often a sharp quarrel. Between the episodes of closeness were longish periods in which they seemed almost to ignore each other, and during which Agnes felt, as she suggests in her memoir, almost completely isolated. During the summer of 1922 Jamie and Eugene drank a good deal together, and Agnes felt ignored by Gene and snubbed by Jamie, Louis, and Terry, who considered her a social climber. Years later, Harold De-

Polo told Sheaffer that Jamie had hated Agnes more intensely than he had ever seen anyone hate anyone. Up until that point, Jamie had concealed his antipathy, but apparently he began to let it show that summer, and Eugene did little to salve Agnes's feelings. Agnes's daughter Barbara arrived to visit but went largely ignored by everyone. Her Aunt Margery, Agnes's sister, also visited but spent much of her time typing letters for Eugene. She also typed the manuscript of *The Fountain,* which Eugene expected to be produced by Hopkins in September. Bobby Jones, who was supposed to design the production, stayed briefly; he wrote to his friend Mabel Dodge in Taos: "I worship the O'Neills. They are the noblest spirits there are here, and they know nothing about anything except suffering and hell generally" (LS, 97). The remark was perhaps generally true of Eugene and Agnes, but never more relevant than at the present. Eugene wrote almost nothing; nor was he especially friendly to the various houseguests who came and went.

When Eugene Jr. came in August, his father was proud of his tall, handsome boy and paid him more attention than he did some other guests. Shy and gentle Barbara Burton much later recalled that she had immediately developed a crush on Eugene Jr., and that he had been kind and attentive to her and Shane (LS, 98).

Sheaffer reports several episodes that summer of Eugene's running amok—there are no other words for it. He arranged for a bootlegger to get him a hundred dollars' worth of good liquor, and then he and Frank Shay wrecked Shay's house—smashing all the glassware and china and breaking or overturning the furniture. On another night, Sheaffer reports, "He urinated into a half-empty bottle of whiskey, then drank from it" (LS, 96). At the Artists' Association Ball, wearing nothing but a red clown's fright wig and a leopard-skin loincloth, he frightened a woman reporter who was behaving intrusively. Later that evening, he verbally attacked Agnes for wearing a lace mantilla that had been his mother's. He tore the mantilla from her head and told her, "Go back to the gutter you came from" (LS, 97). After the ball, he and Agnes fought again, and he pulled her by her long hair several steps toward their house.

Such episodes of craziness had apparently not taken place for some time. They were almost certainly a response to Ella's death. When his father had been dying, Eugene had been irritable and had sometimes snapped out at innocent friends. But when he did, he seems to have been aware that he was displacing his sorrow and frustration about the coming loss and transferring his anger to innocent parties, and the eruptions were much less violent than those which followed his mother's death. While the old man was unconscious and barely alive, Eugene had felt his sorrow directly and had sat at his father's bedside. The traumas reawakened by his mother's death seem almost to have preceded language, and he could not react to them with words but had to strike out.

When he and Agnes were separated for ten days in early August, he wrote to her every day and dutifully reported that he missed her, but his complaints of loneliness lacked their former unbearable intensity. Excuses were ready to hand: he was drinking, and he was with Jamie and other friends. But the fact is that the time of greatest intimacy in the marriage had been from 1919–1920, while Agnes was carrying Shane, through the production period of *Beyond the Horizon*.

The letters written in January to March 1920, while Eugene was in New York and Agnes was in Provincetown with Shane and Fifine Clark, reveal that Agnes and Eugene were both liable to powerful, lasting changes of mood provoked merely by whether the mail went through on schedule. If intensity and idealism wane in most marriages and partners discover they are separate people, it may be that often some balance of qualities allows a sense of confidence and permanence to replace changed ideals. Agnes and Eugene found no such balance. Each needed another who could appreciate the problems and achievements of an artist's life. But each also needed someone who could face the quotidian with assurance and competence. Neither could do much to make daily life smooth for the O'Neill household; to a large extent, that was left to Mrs. Clark. Yet Agnes understandably resented Mrs. Clark's adoration of Eugene, and what she saw as the nursemaid's usurpation of her own place, and she could not be comfortable giving Mrs. Clark enough authority to run things as well as she might have. (Agnes's ambivalence toward Fifine Clark was still noticeable in her conversations with Sheaffer nearly forty years later [LS papers].) So matters in the O'Neill household bumped along in a state of such disorganization as one might expect to find with a couple who had no fixed schedules and who were drinking a good deal.

When Eugene's chronic melancholy deepened with his mother's death and his disenchantment with Jamie, he withdrew from Agnes even further than was usual during the nonmerging phases of their cycle. He could not put into words his feelings about his mother, and Agnes, judging by both her memoirs and Sheaffer's very extensive interview notes recording their conversations over several years, seems to have had no sense of the struggle Eugene was engaged in with mourning denied. Both O'Neills were given to all-or-nothing thinking about their relations, and Agnes simply felt Eugene's withdrawal as the end of everything and retreated into her own needs.

The occasional violent fights, like the one at the Artists' Association Ball, had their consequences, especially for Eugene, who felt intensely ashamed and guilty afterwards. Eugene once wrote that he considered them "evil" and felt they brought out the very worst in him. But the fights seem to prove to both that the marriage was still alive; they were accepted by both as a necessary part of the rhythm of closeness and distance. Agnes made many complaints to Sheaffer about how Eugene was growing distant from her, losing sexual interest in her, losing his fire as a playwright, and becoming "boring" when he stopped drinking, but Sheaffer did not record any complaints at all from Agnes about the fighting.

Thoughts about the marriage came to preoccupy Eugene. Over the summer he revised *The Fountain*, but in early September, with no performance in sight, O'Neill began a Strindbergian comedy, *Welded*, about a couple that every biographer has noticed closely resembles Gene and Aggie. Indeed, the process of the play closely corresponds to most inferences one can draw about the process of the marriage, including inferences based on the O'Neills' correspondence. Further, it resembles the process of Eugene's correspondence with his earlier love, Beatrice Ashe, and of what can be inferred about his relations with Louise Bryant.

Welded anatomizes the process of the marriage of Michael and Eleanor Cape, he a playwright, she an actor who acts in his plays. In act 1, the process begins with a reunion after a separation; it moves toward intimacy, then a psychic merging in which each loses ego boundaries. Next, when the threat of loss of self becomes unbearable, they flee from each other.

At the climactic moment of act 1, Michael tries to lead Eleanor upstairs to bed, all the while talking about the world's first cell and about enacting sacraments at an altar, not a kitchen range. Their lovemaking must celebrate the severity of his mystic ideals for the marriage, which include the complete submersion of the self in the other. At this point Eleanor nearly swoons—that is the word for her bewildered ecstasy. Neither character shows the least objectivity or self-awareness at playing out parts in a process. Eleanor revels in the "beautiful madness" she feels when she begins "living in you. I wanted to die and become you" (CP2, 239). But as Michael urges her upstairs, the intensity becomes too much for her, and when a distraction comes, a knock on the door, she escapes from him and herself to answer it. It maddens him.

To him, the disruption violates everything that has gone before, and it denies all his ideals for their marriage. In an instant they pass from Liebestod to mortal combat. He accuses her of torturing him by making him jealous of their friend and colleague John, the visitor, and she replies that while Michael was away, John was her lover and that she loves him. Michael rages at her, "You actress, you barren soul" and storms out, announcing that he will kill their love, drag his ideals through the "vilest depths," and hinting that he is going to find a prostitute (CP2, 251). At first she is shocked and tries to stop him; then, once he is gone, she decides she will leave also. Throughout act 1, both seem to seek the transcendent which they find when they sense themselves driven by powers that they feel they cannot control, a description that applies to the fight as well as to the loving.

Act 2 consists of two brief vignettes, which are presented sequentially but which occur simultaneously. In scene 1, Eleanor goes to John, tries to persuade herself to go to bed with him, but feels herself constrained by something she sees at the head of the stairs, which she at first announces is Michael and then an angel. John's feelings for Eleanor are presented as selfless. He will not persuade her, insists she make up her mind about becoming his lover, eventually decides he is better off not getting what he wants, and drives her home. He complains that she has "treated my love with the most humiliating contempt," and she goes through the motions of apologizing, but it is clear that John's feelings exist in her mind only as a theory (CP2, 258–59).

At the same time, Michael, in a room with a hooker, carries on metaphysically about debasing his ideals before deciding he cannot go through with the betrayal. He so infuriates the woman that she refuses his money and tries to throw him out. He is sufficiently embarrassed to beg on his knees that she take the money, and both pretend to part friends. The vignette leaves the audience with the impression that Michael, like Eleanor in her scene with John, is oblivious to the feelings of anyone else.

Like act 1, act 3 begins with reunion after a separation. Eleanor briefly lets Michael think that she has slept with John, but then confesses that she has always been faithful. For a moment she stands exposed and vulnerable. Michael lets her think he has taken the prostitute, then speaks of a "revelation" he has had of his transcendent love, which drove him back to their apartment. She offers him out of love a separation that will leave him free to write in peace without their quarrels, and she will continue to love him. He perceives the offer as a threat of abandonment but steels himself and says: "Go . . . be strong! Be free! I—I can't" (CP2, 274).

At this moment they are one in mutual feeling of goodwill toward each other. As she prepares to leave, the mutuality of feeling floods them, and they sense approaching transcendence. He speaks of the unity of all life and encourages her to have faith in oneness and their love. Once again they start up the stairs, she leading. She stands at the top of the stairs looking down at him, making a cross with her arms as he ascends, an actor's gesture proclaiming that she offers her whole self, soul and sex, in sacrifice to their love. He rises and merges with her in the cross, each agreeing to sacrifice the self to the transcendent moment, each oblivious to the possibility that they seem merely sanctimonious in their show of devotion to the gods of love.

At the end, the audience sees that it has now witnessed one completed cycle of the process of the marriage. For all the uproar, for all the involvement of other people, nothing has changed between them. In fact, it seems the uproar and the audience of witnesses are aspects necessary to helping the Capes reach the moments of mutuality that lead to the transcendence they seek. But the theater audience should also see at the end something external to the closed world of the Capes: that is, they should see the playwright's scalpel precisely dissecting the anatomy of his lovers' narcissism. Indeed, by having the lovers in their self-importance heedlessly mock the Christian Passion, the playwright seems to invite the audience to join him in laughter at ostentatious romantic ideals.

Brief and swift-paced, *Welded*, like *Before Breakfast, The Straw,* and *Diff'rent,* may be a much better play than is commonly thought. It seems a greatly more complex and interesting play once one becomes aware that the playwright stands beside the audience and observes, even as he experiences his own folly. Producers or actors who have seen in the play only the playwright's troubadourean ideals of love and marriage may not have allowed the play to be viewed in its entirety.

A biography is not the place to develop an assessment of *Welded*, except to note that sometimes a little biographical knowledge in a critic may obscure more than clarify a playwright's purposes. To a psychoanalytic biographer, the importance of *Welded* lies in the evidence it contains that for a moment, O'Neill had become very analytical about qualities in his marriage and within himself and Agnes that seemed self-defeating. He seems to have maintained his marital and metaphysical ideals, while at the same time analyzing them more deeply than he could have done from any outside point of view.

Eugene began *Welded* in September 1922, but his work on it was soon interrupted when he and Agnes found an estate called Brook Farm near Ridgefield, Connecticut. For $32,500 they bought thirty acres of good farmland with a fifteen-room house. They hired servants to help with the house and farm. Agnes and Fifine Clark continued their erratic pattern of supervising the household without coordinating their spheres and periods of influence, except that Agnes took over the fields and orchards, which she managed competently and energetically.

Usually when writing, Agnes told Sheaffer, Eugene was "at peace with himself." But while writing *Welded,* he was "in a vale of despair" much of the time and sometimes drank heavily, a thing he almost never did while writing (LS, 107). While writing *Welded,* Eugene was almost constantly afflicted with obsessive jealous thoughts about Agnes. Once while Agnes was in New York, Eugene became convinced she was visiting a lover, and in revenge he kicked a hole in one of her most cherished possessions, a portrait of her father by Thomas Eakins; he then cut up with scissors every photograph of Agnes he could find in the house. When she returned, he demanded that she tell him her lover's name.

While they were still moving and getting settled at Brook Farm, news came from a New London lawyer that Jamie was heavily involved with gamblers. The lawyer was afraid that the gamblers might swindle Jamie of four thousand dollars that he was about to receive from the sale of the Glendale property. Torn between anger at Jamie and pity, mired in his own deep depression, Eugene eventually replied that he believed he could do nothing to deflect Jamie from the self-destructive process he had set in motion (LS, 105). As Sheaffer suggests, Eugene must have entertained the notion of having Jamie live with him, at least for a while. But he would have had to reject it. With Jamie around and drinking, it would have been almost impossible for Eugene to stay sober or work on *Welded* at all. Further, Jamie had become vicious toward Agnes, and occasionally toward Eugene.

About December, Harold DePolo and his wife, who now lived in Darien, Connecticut, invited Jamie to stay with them indefinitely. Even though Jamie brought with him the four thousand dollars he had just received from the Glendale sale and paid nearly all expenses during his stay, his hosts almost immediately regretted their hospitality. At one point Jamie set fire to his mattress while smoking in bed, and Helen DePolo had to carry the mattress outside. Jamie was too drunk to help, and his ankles were so swollen that he had difficulty walking, even when sober.

When awake and not yet fully drunk, Jamie would stare at his image in a mirror and heap upon it savage verbal assaults. When a little drunker, he would assault others who were within earshot, anyone at all, with a wit described as brilliant and ruthless. He would seize upon any weakness he found and ride it mercilessly. The next morning he would not remember much of what he had done the previous night, but he would be full of contrition and vague apologies—until he started anew. "I can't get over the spirit of the perverse," Jamie once told Harold (LS papers, 8).

Eugene went months without seeing Jamie, until mid-February, when Jamie erupted in a theater. It seems that the DePolos, Jamie, and another friend had gone together to see a road production of *"Anna Christie"* in Stamford. At a certain point, Jamie interrupted the performers to roar in his actor's voice, "Why shouldn't my brother, the author, know all about whores?" and then elucidated with what Sheaffer calls "scurrilous references" to Helen DePolo and Agnes (LS, 107). Harold rushed Jamie out of the theater and called Eugene, who apparently came and conducted Jamie to New London. There Eugene instructed the lawyers to confine his brother if necessary, not to let him leave town, and especially not to let him go back to Stamford, where charges might be brought against him.

Back at Brook Farm, Eugene continued to make erratic progress on *Welded,* which he finished in late April or early May. Soon after he began an eight-act version of the play that became *Marco Millions.* Between drinking bouts, he worked on *Marco Millions* through the summer. In June, after moving to Provincetown, Eugene learned from the lawyers that Jamie had been taken in restraints to a New Jersey sanatorium. By now his hair had turned white, he was nearly blind, and at the end he was disoriented and raving wildly. After several days, when he had recovered a little, he was moved to Riverlawn Sanatorium in Paterson. There he found ways to have liquor brought to him and resumed drinking.

Harold DePolo told Sheaffer he believed that the *"Anna Christie"* incident in Stamford was the last straw for Agnes, that after Jamie's eruption, she was indeed able to turn Eugene against Jamie (LS papers). With Eugene already smoldering about Jamie's trying to do him out of their mother's estate, it would not have taken much persuasion. Eugene refused to visit Jamie in the sanatorium; he communicated with him only when necessary, to settle the estate, and that through lawyers. It seems that the Stamford scene marked a complete break between the brothers.

In Provincetown in September Eugene began another drama about marriage, *All God's Chillun Got Wings,* which he initially meant to be a one-act play. It was written at the request of George Jean Nathan, who wanted something for *American Mercury,* the new magazine he was starting with H. L. Mencken. Later that month, Jamie had a stroke. Eugene worked on *All God's Chillun* between drinking bouts. On November 8, after lying unconscious for several days, Jamie died in Paterson, aged forty-five years and two months. Eugene had not seen Jamie since March and would have nothing to do with the burial. Agnes had to make the funeral arrangements, with the help of her sister Margery. The women arranged two funerals for him, in New York and New London, but Eugene refused to attend either. In the long run, it would be at least as hard for him to come to terms with his brother's ghost as with his mother's.

O'Neill's Analysis
1923–1924

IN AUTUMN 1923, WHILE JAMIE lay dying, Eugene had gone so far in search of forgetfulness as to involve himself in reorganizing the Provincetown Players, a labor he would otherwise have ignored. After Jamie died, Eugene busied himself with almost constant writing. So driven was he that, during and after the Christmas doldrums of 1923, he took the uncharacteristic step of adapting and producing works by others.

He was in flight from obsessive thoughts of his parents and brother. His diaries, letters, and dramatic writing show that flight brought little relief. Everything he wrote and everything he did with the Players showed his preoccupation. There is no historical evidence to support Alexander's recent assertion that O'Neill became suicidal as he had in 1912 (1992, 2). But his drinking again began to disrupt his writing, to a degree it had not since his marriage. When his drunkenness allowed him to write, he fashioned image after image of his dead. He created a series of bereaved characters who, like their author, could neither mourn nor free themselves from their ghosts.

Eugene's prolonged binges and general depression compounded the problems with the marriage that in 1921–1922 had sent him to the analyst Smith Eli Jelliffe in search of advice. It appears from anecdotes told by the Gelbs that he continued to see Jelliffe sporadically until 1925 (Gelbs, 565, 572). Throughout those years, the marriage continued to deteriorate. In an effort to save it, and to save himself, Eugene made several other approaches to psychotherapy, culminating, in early 1926, in some weeks of treatment with another analyst, Gilbert V. Hamilton. Afterward, O'Neill sometimes referred to his treatment as "my analysis."

The psychoanalysis of today that typically goes on for several years was nearly unknown in Freud's lifetime (and O'Neill's), when a lengthy analysis might last a few months. One thing that remains constant, then and now, is that psychoanalysis examines the analysand's transferences onto the imagined person of the analyst. There is considerable evidence that throughout his life O'Neill formed almost immediate positive transferences to medical people, and what little is known about his treatment with Dr. Jelliffe and Dr. Hamilton suggests that an initial positive transference took place with both analysts. How much analysis of the transference took place we cannot know, but it is quite likely that Dr. Hamilton gave few verbal interpretations. Dr. Hamilton told Kenneth Macgowan that he was concerned not to tinker with what might be the sources of O'Neill's creativity.

Nevertheless, we know that O'Neill got a grasp of the phenomena of transference and countertransference from a note about an idea for a play in which the protagonist was to be a "psycho-therapeutist" who becomes entangled in a countertransference to a patient (Floyd 1981, 214). The idea, recorded about 1929, must have arisen from his several flings with analysts. For O'Neill, as for many a writer, the imagined reader or audience is something like the silent, unseen analyst whose responses to things said and felt are imagined by an analysand. The process of construing another person, analyst or reader, helps a writer or analysand "see" from a different point of view from the one that has become habitual. From the new perspective one may seem to know subjective thoughts differently; one may seem to know the familiar with objectivity and see it as if it were new. Coming for Eugene at the end of a decade and more of self-scrutiny, scrutiny that had been especially unrelenting and merciless since his mother had died, the several weeks of therapy apparently served as a formal beginning to a rigorous process of self-analysis that would continue for another decade and more into the future.

As in an analysis with an analyst, O'Neill struggled mightily and with some success against the urge to disown knowledge and memory. For a person in analysis, from beginning to end, a major labor of analysis is analyzing one's own resistance. All one's accommodations to circumstance resist analysis of the resistance. So it is for anyone seeking insight; so it was for O'Neill. Forcing himself to face his dead required him constantly to find strategies that offered a compromise between looking directly at the sun and seeing no light at all. In the 1920s, the compromises occasionally allowed him to construct coherent plays, but more often the result was erratic and inconsistent. The struggle against resistance was to be a major theme for the rest of his working life.

In the fall of 1923, while trying to ignore Jamie, who lay dying in New Jersey, Eugene worked in Ridgefield on *All God's Chillun Got Wings*. When he finished the play in late November, he immediately sent it to Nathan, who published it in the February issue of *American Mercury*. Boni and Liveright published it April 14, 1924, in a volume with *Welded*. Publication brought nationwide infamy before the premiere because the play presented an interracial marriage and required a white woman, the actor Mary Blair, to kiss the hand of the black actor Paul Robeson, who was announced for the role of Jim Harris. As the Gelbs and others have written, the scandal that arose when the play was published and while it was in rehearsal obscured the autobiographical aspects of the story. The distraction was sufficient to keep them hidden until 1962, when the Gelbs pointed out that the husband and wife in the play, Jim and Ella, bore the same names as the author's parents. Although O'Neill repeatedly said that the play had very little to do with race and advocated no position on anything, he was criticized by both black and white community leaders. (Adam Clayton Powell, Sr., led one line of attack when he complained that the play lent credibility to the white fear that education and equality would lead black men to seek white wives.) Well-publicized threats were made that the play would be banned by the Society for the Suppression of Vice; the mayor's office tried to close it, and the Ku Klux Klan sent signed threats against the lives of the author, his family, and the actors. Jimmy Light told Sheaffer that O'Neill scrawled, "Go fuck yourself" on the bottom of a threat to kill him and his family and returned it to the sender, a Klan leader. No one in the audience noticed or cared that behind all the clamor, O'Neill was carrying on his private self-examination.

Welded had behind it two antithetical myths of the self, the one embodied in the ancient myth of Narcissus and the other expressed in the medieval myth of Tristan, the one of self-love that precludes love of another, the other of selfless love that seeks the fiery purification conferred by love of another unto death. In *Welded*, O'Neill had composed an irreverent comedy of the self-absorbed lovers who make a cross of themselves. In *All God's Chillun Got Wings*, using the same myths and some others, he reached for tragedy and came close enough to it to temporarily convert at least one anti-O'Neill critic, Ludwig Lewisohn. The play tells the story of a studious black man, Jim Harris, who has worked all his adult life to pass the bar exam and repeatedly fails, and of his marriage to a white slum girl, Ella Downey, whom he sometimes protected when the two were children growing up on the edge of the slum. Besides the examination, Jim's cross is Ella's madness, in which she often doesn't know him and assaults him without warning or provocation, verbally and physically. Jim proudly persists in his efforts to pass the bar and to maintain an unfailing love for Ella. Lewisohn wrote in the *Nation* (1924, 664), "I have seen nothing that so deeply gave me an emotion comparable to what the Greeks must have felt at the dark and dreadful actions set forth by the older Attic dramatists."

Calling on the myths gave Eugene a modicum of objectivity and let him look at his dead with sufficient indirectness to glimpse the forbidden. The tale of miscegenation both concealed and represented a private source of guilt far more fearful to Eugene: his fear and hatred of and enthrallment to his mother. Biographers and critics, following the lead of the Gelbs, have remarked on similarities that link Ella Harris to Mary Tyrone and, by inference, to Ella O'Neill—and also the less obvious resemblance of Jim Harris to James Tyrone and, by inference, to James O'Neill. Besides the names, Ella Harris in her madness, it has also been said, resembles Mary Tyrone (and presumably Ella O'Neill) high on her dope. Black and white have seemed to some to stand for peasant and genteel Irish. Some have remembered that Jamie Tyrone in *Long Day's Journey* says that before he "caught [Mama] in the act with a hypo," he had "never dreamed that any women but whores took dope" [CP3, 818]) and seen a link between that and Ella Harris's brush with prostitution. Ella Harris often speaks a kind of "baby talk," longs to be childlike, and begs Jim to be a child again with her; Mary Tyrone longs for her protected life in her convent and often speaks in a childlike, dissociative manner.

To a psychoanalytic biographer, the most striking similarity between Ella Harris and Mary Tyrone is the rapid shifts from one psychic reality to another that occur in both characters in moments of extremity.

The process depicted in these plays appears to derive from careful observation of some actual person with an unstable sense of reality.

In an episode previously mentioned, from act 2, scene 1 of *Long Day's Journey into Night* (CP3, 753), Mary Tyrone sees an empty glass near Edmund and immediately strikes out at him: "Did you take a drink? Oh, how can you be such a fool? Don't you know it's the worst thing." She then turns on her husband: "You're to blame, James. . . . Do you want to kill him? Don't you remember my father? . . . He thought, like you, that whiskey is a good tonic!" As she realizes she is on the verge of knowing that her father died of consumption and that Edmund probably has it, she shifts to another view of the world: "But, of course, there's no comparison at all. I don't know why I—Forgive me for scolding you, James." To ensure continuing denial of loss, she speaks James's very words with his heartiness: "One small drink won't hurt Edmund. It might be good for him, if it gives him an appetite."

Here, and at numerous other moments in *Long Day's Journey*, Mary's versions of reality seem only sometimes to coincide with what the others consider reality. She shifts from identifying with one person's point of view to identifying with another's, according to which promises ease from the terror that grips her at that particular moment.

By 1940, when he was writing *Long Day's Journey*, Eugene could go much deeper into Mary Tyrone's inner world than he could, in 1923, into Ella Harris's world. But the flight from threats of loss and the resort to rapidly shifting versions of reality are similar in both characters. In act 2, scene 2, the dramatic climax of *All God's Chillun*, Jim is studying his law books when he hears a noise behind him and turns to see Ella stalking him with a carving knife. He catches her wrist and asks if she wanted to murder him. "They kept calling me names," Ella replies, "I can't tell you what, Jim—and then I was grabbing a knife" (CP2, 310–11).

At one moment Jim seems one of the name-callers she has to destroy, one of the blacks who scorned her as poor white trash when she was a slum child. A moment later she can confide to him the insult to her honor. For an instant she identifies with him sufficiently to see herself as he sees her, and looks at the knife in her hand with fear. Then she becomes a little girl waking from a nightmare: "Don't ever leave me alone! I have such terrible dreams, Jim—promise you'll never go away." In dread of losing her or failing her, he makes the promise, and it leads to another shift of her reality. She becomes the child of slaveholders faithfully served by doting black folks who think themselves members of the family: "I'll be a little girl—and you'll be Old Uncle Jim who's been with us for years and years—Will you play that?" He somehow agrees and coaxes her to go back to bed. There is another transformation: her face "*grows mean, vicious, full of jealous hatred. She cannot contain herself but breaks out harshly with a cruel, venomous grin:* You dirty nigger!" Jim reacts "*as if he'd been shot,*" and his voice or movement or words telling her to go to bed causes another shift in her world; she doesn't know what she's just said and done but thinks she's asked if he was studying hard and wonders why he's mad at her. Like a little girl, she obediently starts off for bed but undergoes another change going offstage, utters the word "Nigger!" and disappears, while Jim sits with his devastation (CP2, 310–11).

Ella Harris has in common with Mary Tyrone and with Ella O'Neill a dread of loss that is the fundamental force in her world. The possibility that Jim might succeed in the profession that establishes and enforces white superiority terrifies her with its complex implication that success may erase whatever folly makes Jim love a thing as worthless as she believes herself to be. If she should lose him, she would face her alienation alone. Killing an uppity nigger who doesn't need her, or being a child in the care of a devoted slave, either fantasy seems in a desperate moment to offer an end to terror. The process resembles Mary Tyrone's alternating desperate need and love for her husband and her condescension toward his lack of education and childhood poverty. Working out the metaphor that conceals and expresses his mother's dread must have brought O'Neill more consciousness of her world than he had had and let him feel justified within himself in retaining the names Jim and Ella for his characters.

All God's Chillun gives a glimpse of one of O'Neill's most prominent traits, the quality that in characters like Robert Mayo and Anna Christie he calls romanticism, the seeking for a Tristan-like love, a love that offers an alternative to the sterility and isolation of narcissism. In search of the Other, the Not Me, he gives himself over to the romantic ideal that seems to have driven his love affairs after 1913 and determined the central dynamics of his marriage to Agnes. The clue comes in the portrait of Jim Harris and his one point of similarity to James Tyrone and James O'Neill.

At the start of work, O'Neill probably modeled Jim Harris on Joe Smith, his gambler friend from the Village who was married to a white woman, and he may also have had in mind Paul Robeson, who had made a futile attempt to be accepted at the Wall Street law firm that had hired him out of Columbia (and that Robeson soon rejected). In their histories and personalities Jim and Ella Harris do not much resemble the senior O'Neills, except in the psychological dynamics of their marriage. Two O'Neills and two Tyrones called Jim worshiped and adored wife and mother, an adoration Eugene himself could not fully share. It was the process of the marriage, rather than the details of the characterizations, that O'Neill borrowed from his family. Jim Harris and the two James O'Neills had been nearly perfect in the faith, love, and devotion they gave to a troubled wife and mother in a difficult marriage. Eugene must have grown up wondering how anyone could be so selfless and seem so contented in love, and he sought to become the ideal lover in affair after affair, each time finding himself inadequate.

The extreme, idealized portrait of Jim Harris's fidelity expressed an important ego ideal for its author, an ego ideal that had determined the character and quality of the love affairs he had with Maibelle Scott, Bee Ashe, Louise Bryant, and others. In these he made so great an issue of his belief in the merging of lovers, and the sacrifice of self for the sake of love, that until Agnes, each of Eugene's women felt smothered, driven to clear a space for herself, to assert her individuality by going out with other suitors or by directly telling him that she felt suffocated. Eugene seems to have sought relationships in which he might taste the trials his father had known throughout his marriage, and in the process to leave himself vulnerable each time to betrayal or disappointment. Each time he found himself wanting, lacking whatever it was that allowed his father to remain constant and loving in the face of pain, condescension, and outright insults when Ella was on morphine. Writing *All God's Chillun Got Wings,* creating Jim Harris, gave Eugene a chance to explore what might inspire and enable a man to be as good and as faithful as his father seemed. The characterization of Harris does not suggest that O'Neill had as yet made much headway toward understanding his father's and brother's devotion to their Ella, but it shows that at the time when he felt that his marriage was disintegrating, he particularly grasped at his ideal of constant love that conferred nobility on the lover.

Long before, in writing *The Personal Equation,* Eugene had portrayed a father who doted on an insolent, thankless son to the point of giving up everything in his life for the boy. It must have been an effort to understand how James could continue to support his ungrateful sons, in spite of everything. Now O'Neill tried to understand his father in the role of husband to an immature and addicted wife. Just as he had wondered how his father could be forbearing with his sons, Eugene must have grown up wondering how anyone could be so selfless and seem so contented in love.

No sooner had O'Neill sent *All God's Chillun* off to Nathan in early December than he turned to two projects involving works by others. The first of these was a production of Strindberg's *Ghost Sonata,* a most significant choice. The play presents Strindberg's obsessive theme, the unmasking of the soul after death. O'Neill decided to make the idea of masks tangible; that is, to have the actors wear actual masks, a device he had first used in *The Emperor Jones.* O'Neill could not properly mourn his dead, because he did not know them; he needed to unmask his dead in order to think about the relation of their selves to their bodies and their ordinary behavior. His reflections on *The Ghost Sonata* would lead him in April to the idea for *The Great God Brown,* and to other stage experiments. In early January when the Strindberg opened he went to New York for a week, and he expressed his satisfaction with it by arranging for Eugene Jr. to see the play.

Meanwhile, in December, after sketching his ideas for the Strindberg production, Eugene had begun another adaptation, this one of Coleridge's *Ancient Mariner.* In his Village days he had sometimes drunkenly recited the whole poem, as he also used to do with *The Hound of Heaven.* Now he arranged for the stage the prophetic narrative of a man like Eugene himself who cannot stop trying to tell his tale, perhaps in the hope that eventually he himself might hear his own words. Like Eugene, the mariner seeks a place in the world from which he was alienated. O'Neill's efforts in behalf of Coleridge were largely directed at creating settings and movement that expressed the hope of Christian redemption on which the poem rests. Eugene seemed to entertain, for the moment at least, notions of meeting his dead on their own Christian terms.

To a psychoanalytic biographer, O'Neill's work on the adaptations seems in large part to have been a means of avoiding what he considered the main task, for he had already decided on his next play, which at first he called "Under the Elms." In early November 1923, around the time Jamie died, he had told Malcolm Cowley that it would be set on a New

England farm and hinted that it took as its basic theme a mother's seduction of her son. He could hardly develop such material without painful confrontations with his own oedipal conflicts, that is to say, with powerfully ambivalent feelings about his recently dead mother. As he prepared to start work, Eugene must have begun to think of Jamie's intimacy with their mother in the eighteen months after his father died, and of Jamie's behavior when Ella was dying. He added the word *Desire* to the title in early January and must have been thinking of the related but separate meanings of the word, those of sexual desire and greed, which became the interwoven themes of the play.

On January 15 he began writing *Desire Under the Elms* and by the 29th had finished a scenario and a draft of part 1. O'Neill's mourning for his dead parents, a hidden force behind the writing of *All God's Chillun,* became an explicit theme in *Desire.* Eben Cabot, twenty-five, the central character, resembled Robert Mayo of *Beyond the Horizon* and also the author. Eben lost his mother while he was a boy, and he still mourns her so intensely that he sees her everywhere: in the landscape of the farm, in the farmhouse where he daily converses with her, and in the towering elm trees described by O'Neill as a brooding, sinister, maternal presence. The play shows from start to finish its author's preoccupation with the difficulty of being free of one's dead, and the theme would be explicit in nearly all the plays O'Neill would write in the future. The psychoanalyst Philip Weissman, who had little interest in mourning per se, wrote about the play in 1962. He was particularly interested in the set description, which follows the list of characters and describes the weeping, brooding, maternal elms that hang over the house. The depiction of the elms led Weissman to guess that its author had been in "the most intense mourning for his mother," a speculation he said he could not confirm (1962, 139).

The famous description of the elms expresses a sense that a maternal presence watches over the farm, inescapable and overpowering; O'Neill's language is more complex than at first appears. The description reads in part: "[The elms] appear to protect and at the same time subdue. There is a sinister maternity in their aspect, a crushing, jealous absorption. . . . They are like exhausted women resting their sagging breasts and hands and hair on its roof, and when it rains, their tears trickle down monotonously and rot on the shingles" (CP2, 318). *To subdue* means to conquer and bring under control and is related to the Latin *seducere,* to seduce. It implies a mother protective, domineering, seductive, and jealously absorptive and leaves readers and actors to ask, Jealous of whom over what? It must refer to those she protects and subdues, a group that at the least includes her children.

The language of the set description carries the germ of the process of the play. As we know, the play centers around two women, one long dead, represented in the elms, in the land of the farm, and in the spirit presence that haunts the parlor of the farmhouse. As the farm, she is the object of desire of the Cabot men and of Ephraim Cabot's third wife, Abbie, who seduces her stepson and later smothers her baby to prove that she truly loves her lover. The oedipal themes are as explicit as can be, and they are inseparable from the themes of loss and endless mourning. Trying to face them all at once in writing *Desire* was like trying to finish one's analysis in the first session.

The difficulty Eugene had getting started is evident in his behavior in early January. After getting the idea for the play mentioned in his first *Work Diary* entry for 1924, he started drinking at Brook Farm on January 2 and went to New York to see the production of Strindberg's *Ghost Sonata* that he had designed. He continued drinking through the 11th and stopped, to work not on *Desire* but on yet another adaptation. Yet he could not escape the obsessive theme of mourning. The adaptation was of the Book of Revelation, with its account of the harrowing of Hell and the dead rising from the ground. (This work was never performed and is lost.) He finished a draft of the adaptation of Revelation and the next day, the 15th, began the scenario for *Desire*. The idea for part 1 had become so clear that he finished the four scenes of part 1 in nine days of writing. The draft required very little revision. These scenes show Eben Cabot proposing to buy out his half-brothers' claims to the farm with money stolen from his father's hoard, and old Ephraim's return to the farm with his new young wife, Abbie. At the end of scene 4, the brothers leave for California with their gold, abandoning Ephraim, Abbie, and Eben to compete for the farm. Without stopping, O'Neill wrote a scenario for part 2, in the four scenes of which Abbie persuades Ephraim to will the farm to her if she bears him a son and Eben and Abbie become sexual lovers in his Maw's parlor. By the end of part 2, Abbie tells Eben she has taken his Maw's place, and the two are showing signs of falling in love.

At this point, O'Neill stopped writing for most of the next four months, during much of which he was drinking. Although he could usually ignore distractions when trying to write, this time his resistance to facing the material of the play was greater than the drive to get it written, and he let himself be distracted by circumstances. These included the scandal over miscegenation in *All God's Chillun* that erupted with publication of the text in *American Mercury* on January 22. O'Neill was involved in rehearsals of the play, and also of a revival of *The Emperor Jones* with Paul Robeson, who was rehearsing *All God's Chillun* by day. (When the play opened in mid-May, none of the expected trouble occurred, except that the city succeeded in banning the child actors who were to play in the first scene. Instead, someone read the scene to the audience. Most reviewers wrote about what had not happened, rather than the play itself. O'Neill, who attended the opening, noted that the play seemed to go over well with the audience.)

O'Neill was also worried about *Welded*, which he considered mis-cast and misdirected. A widely known account of the production from a 1957 article by Stark Young, the director, reported that Eugene and Agnes sat in rehearsals and nodded with recognition and approval as they saw their marital madness enacted onstage, and that article also had Macgowan and Jones casting Doris Keane as the wife and O'Neill begging Young, a reviewer who had never directed a play before, to direct. Sheaffer [1983] learned that the account was wrong in these particulars and believed that it was largely fabricated and unreliable. According to the *Work Diary*, Eugene saw no rehearsals of *Welded* until March 4, after an out-of-town opening in Baltimore, when he noted in his diary that it was "rotten!" He began attending rehearsals to try to bring the performance together but considered the production hopeless in all respects. When it opened, he sounded almost triumphant in proclaiming it "A Flop!"—as if his expectations had been fulfilled.

He attended many rehearsals of his adaptation of *The Ancient Mariner*, and, given that he could barely claim any part of the work as his, it seems likely that he was escaping into the work of rehearsal. He and Agnes were back and forth from New York to Ridgefield several times, and, through much of February, he drank heavily.

One of the many reasons for his drinking was that in late January, probably around the time he stopped working on *Desire*, he got the sad news that Jig Cook had died unexpectedly and painfully in Greece. In Delphi Jig had almost immediately become a popular figure, Kyrios Kouk, speaking Greek with growing competence, spending his days with Susan on the steep slopes with their flock, and drinking retsina with the men in cafés at evening. Susan, who had a heart condition and might have been expected to suffer from the strenuous life, had thrived, and so had Jig, until he caught glanders from a pet dog. His Olympian gods are said to be fond of a joke, and perhaps Jig would have laughed and asked for no other death. Susan returned to New York understandably distraught. Nevertheless, as soon as she arrived, her friends involved her in bickering over the reorganization of the Players that had obsessed them since the fall.

For reasons he could not fully explain to himself, Eugene could not make himself visit Susan, even though he felt guilty over his neglect of an old friend. No doubt part of it was that he felt he and Jig had unfinished business because they had quarreled at their last meeting—the night Eugene learned of his mother's death—when Jig blamed Eugene for driving him out of his own theater company. But a more general and more obscure reason must have been that he had simply had to cope with too many deaths; when not drunk, Eugene could not think without thinking of the dead, and he could not determine whom to mourn first. He drank through most of April and all of May.

Finally at the end of May he wrote Susan to explain why he had avoided her and to apologize for the squabble with Jig. Writing to her seemed to release the inhibitions that had kept him from completing *Desire,* for he stopped drinking and in ten days finished the draft of the play.

When he resumed work on *Desire,* thoughts of Jamie became discernible in the characterization of Eben. As O'Neill described him in the stage directions, Eben physically resembled himself, Eugene, and also Robert Mayo of *Beyond the Horizon. Desire* was in part a continuation of *Beyond the Horizon,* with the sexual tensions of the earlier play made explicit. Certain details pertinent to Jamie found their way into Eben's character. He maintains that he has not the least drop of his father's blood and is entirely his mother's son, but the older brothers call him the "dead spit 'n' image" of Paw. Eben contrives to squeeze his brothers out of a share in their father's estate, although he is straightforward in his negotiations with them. Eugene transformed Jamie's conscious sensual fantasies about his mother, along with a big brother's tales of rapturous sexual conquests (as told to the youthful Eugene), into Eben's near-incestuous affair with Abbie, the young stepmother. Eben came to be not so much a portrait of Jamie as an expression of Eugene's identifications with his brother, particularly his identification with Jamie's oedipal war with their father.

Apart from the text of the play itself, we know how strongly O'Neill was obsessed with oedipal themes from an anecdote published much later, by the critic Malcolm Cowley. In early November 1923, the young Cowley visited the O'Neills at Brook Farm, and in 1957 he described an incident that had stuck with him. O'Neill, he said, showed him a book he was reading, "one of [the psychoanalyst] Wilhelm Stekel's treatises on sexual aberrations—perhaps *The Disguises of Love*. There are enough case histories in the book, Gene says, to furnish plots to all the playwrights who ever lived. He turns the pages and shows me the clinical record of a mother who had seduced her only son and drove him insane" (quoted in Cargill 1961, 45). Cowley added that O'Neill had mentioned that he was working on a play set in New England but had given no other details. Cowley left the reader to infer that the play was *Desire* and that the initial idea of the plot came from Stekel. It seems likely.

If O'Neill meant to write about incest and its consequences, the play as he worked it out after the four-month hiatus largely sidestepped those issues and put the murder of the baby at the center. Sheaffer and others have said that the *Hippolytus* of Euripides was O'Neill's model for the play. If so, it merged with *Medea*. And yet Abbie is no Medea, either, murdering her children to spite their faithless father. Instead, she is a woman to be pitied as much as condemned, one in the grip of a love so intense that she smothers her beloved infant to prove her loyalty to her lover. These characters might be tragic versions of the narcissistic Capes of *Welded*; they might even be Gene and Aggie—with the letter *g* of their names changed to *b*,—whose passion excluded all else, including their children, and finally left only its own ashes.

From the moment late in part 1 when Eben meets Abbie, his new step-Maw, he feels an intense sexual attraction to her, the source of which, in her or in himself, he cannot tell. During the first two months of Abbie's presence on the farm, their mutual attraction at first takes the form of a deadly competition for power over the farm and over old Cabot. The audience probably feels before the lovers do the attraction underlying their rivalry. The sexual scene begins with the lovers separated by a thin wall, she in Ephraim's bedroom and Eben next door in his, so intensely attuned to each other that they read each other's thoughts and nearly come before they ever touch. Here O'Neill seems to draw on his experience with several women, including Agnes, of psychic sexual interpenetration.

Part 2, scene 2, in which the lovers are separated by the wall, ends with Ephraim's leaving the house and Abbie's going to Eben's room, where he insists he hates her, even as they kiss. As with the couple in *Welded,* and as we see in the letters between Eugene and Agnes, anger serves as a separator when lovers are afraid, in merging with another, to lose their separate selves. As they nearly fight, Abbie teases Eben, by saying she is going downstairs to the parlor, a room never entered except by Eben until Abbie's arrival. Abbie says she senses Maw's spirit and tells Eben that his mother accepts their love. Eben feels overwhelmed by what the stage directions call "a horribly frank mixture of lust and mother love" (CP2, 354).

The next morning the lovers seem changed: relaxed, playful, languorous. Except that Abbie is his stepmother, Eben seems a man instead of a rebellious boy. Here O'Neill probably represented in Eben Jamie's contentment, when his father had died, at having his mother to himself; at last he could stop drinking and otherwise behaving self-destructively. The author's situation was more complex. Eugene tried to contemplate and simultaneously to avoid the reality of the sexual wish for one's mother. He substituted his brother for himself, yet he could hardly have escaped scot-free. In expressing fantasies of Jamie's and Ella's intimacy, Eugene must have known the most intense jealousy and envy, emotions that could not have made him an easy marital partner. Throughout 1924 O'Neill was obsessed with the belief that Agnes had a lover whom she visited whenever they were parted, an obsession that led to several explosions.

Aside from the near-incestuous lovers, and the wild, mystical, indomitable old man, the most prominent element in *Desire* is the theme of bereavement and the refusal to let the dead rest in peace. Eben at twenty-five seems as haunted by his dead mother as a child would be. He talks to and clings to her spirit to keep her alive in his mind, and only when Abbie has convinced him that his Maw approves of their love does he feel a little relief from her presence. In part 2, scene 2 he tells Abbie, "Maw's gone back t' her grave" (CP2, 356). Yet the relief is short-lived and ends when he and Abbie quarrel over her loyalty to him. Convinced that Abbie has seduced him in order to lay claim to the farm, he wishes the child dead; he vows to leave Abbie and threatens that his Maw will take her vengeance on Abbie, Paw, and the child. It is a child's wish, My Maw can lick you, and shows how childlike Eben's doubt of Abbie, and his love of her as well, make him. In play after play over the next several years

O'Neill would show bereaved characters as unable as he himself was to face their dead and let them be dead.

Fulfilling the artistic potential of *Desire* does not require O'Neill to work through his own or his characters' mourning or to show characters becoming independent, as they must to mourn. Instead it requires the working out of the lovers' situation. O'Neill finds what is perhaps the only way to do so convincingly. To prove her loyalty to Eben, Abbie smothers her baby. Biographers have noted in this context O'Neill's reluctance to be a father and his (and Agnes's) sometime ambivalence toward Shane's intrusion on their intimacy. O'Neill's conscious response toward such a fantasy, which he must have recognized as his own, is expressed in Eben's horror at what Abbie has done in the name of love. Eben calls the sheriff and the three wait for the law to take Abbie away. At the end Eben finds the courage to tells the sheriff that he is as much to blame as Abbie and both should be hanged. Even his father is impressed. "Purty good—fur yew!" (CP2, 377), says the old man before going to round up the cows.

Shortly after he finished *Desire* in mid-June, O'Neill began an outline for *The Great God Brown*. Writing the outline set him off on a drunk that lasted until the end of the month. Throughout 1925, while composing the play, O'Neill would have to struggle to stay sober enough to write.

In July the family drove to Provincetown, where the playwright immediately set to work cutting and revising several plays that Boni was to publish in a collected works edition. That summer his friend the bookseller Frank Shay mounted a successful Provincetown production of *Before Breakfast*. Next, Shay combined the four short sea plays, *The Moon of the Caribbees, Bound East for Cardiff, The Long Voyage Home,* and *In the Zone* into a production he called *S.S. Glencairn*. The combination surprised O'Neill with its coherence, and it has since often succeeded in amateur and professional productions. In November, a week before *Desire* was to open at the Greenwich Village Theatre, the *Glencairn* production opened on MacDougal Street, where it was very well received by the critics and public.

In mid-July, O'Neill set to work on an eight-act version of *Marco Millions*, which occupied him until late September. He told Macgowan that he was delighted with its progress and that he frequently laughed out loud as he worked. It made him hope the public would take to it also. In August, the O'Neills had several houseguests, but Eugene kept on working and avoided drinking. The idea for *Lazarus Laughed* came to him, but he returned to *Marco Millions* the same day and worked every day until August 27, when he and Agnes went to Nantucket to visit Wilbur Daniel Steele and his wife. The Steeles had recently returned from Bermuda and raved about it so that Eugene, already sorry that he had bought Brook Farm and reluctant to face another New England winter, decided on the spot to go to the island after *Desire* opened in November.

The O'Neills were having serious financial problems. In the past two years Eugene had earned about eighty thousand dollars, nearly all of which they had spent. In buying Brook Farm they had acquired new obligations, for they needed a couple to work full-time to keep the place going, so, besides Mrs. Clark, they now supported the Bedini family. Moreover, the house required expensive renovation, including a new copper roof. O'Neill continued paying for Eugene Jr.'s and Barbara Burton's tuition in private schools, and he made occasional contributions to Agnes's parents and sisters, as well as to various friends who were down on their luck. Regular expenses more than doubled during much of the spring, while the O'Neills were in New York. At a time when their expenses were mounting, Eugene's income for 1924 dropped to about ten thousand dollars.

Eugene hoped eventually to have an income from Jamie's and his parents' estates, but for the time being he could get nothing. He planned to sell all but two of the twenty New London properties. He hoped to receive, from the New York property and some others, a steady income of about five thousand a year once the estate was settled. But the estate, which Eugene now thought to be worth about $125,000, was bogged down in a Dickensian limbo. As O'Neill described the situation to Macgowan on September 4, administrative fees amounting to about $15,000 were owing for probate, which he hoped to pay from the sale of New London property. Nothing was selling, however, partly because the market was flat and partly, Sheaffer learned, because nearly all the property was so run down it could be neither rented nor sold (LS, 149). Meanwhile, the fees kept accumulating interest and charges so inexorably that, Eugene predicted, by the end of the decade everything in the estate would have defaulted to the lawyers (Bryer and Alvarez 1982, 58).

The O'Neills had other problems besides money. Agnes felt increasingly unimportant in the home. Shane considered Mrs. Clark to be virtually his mother—and in fact, Mrs. Clark took almost exclusive care of him. Eugene, uncommunicative under the best of circumstances, had withdrawn further from Agnes in response to his losses, which intensified his chronic emotional needs. Those needs were filled in part by Mrs. Clark's idolization of him, whereas Agnes seemed to Eugene less interested in him than in climbing socially—so he sometimes complained (LS, 145–46). Agnes told Sheaffer that Eugene's sexual interest in her declined during this period (LS papers). She, in turn, became flirtatious with other men, a reaction that infuriated Eugene and sometimes led to ferocious battles, if he was drinking, after which they would be close for a time. A chronic problem that had recently become acute was that Agnes always felt uncomfortable around theater people and Eugene now spent more time with Jones and Macgowan and Light than in the past.

Perhaps with all these matters on his mind, and deciding that Agnes needed a project, he dug into his notebooks of play ideas and came up with an eighteen-page scenario for a potboiler that he had sketched out in late summer 1917, which he had called "The Reckoning." Over the summer and fall and into the new year, Agnes worked on developing the scenario into a four-act play, *The Guilty One.* Certainly the selection of that particular project said much about Eugene's marital discontent.

In the scenario, a woman has forced the man who has made her pregnant to marry her, and she continues to force him to do her will throughout a long, hate-filled marriage. At the end, husband and wife are unconvincingly reconciled and united by patriotic fervor as their son goes off to war. While Eugene revised *Marco Millions,* Agnes converted "The Reckoning" into *The Guilty One,* which she copyrighted under the pseudonym Elinor Rand. (The text is reprinted in Bogard, *The Unknown O'Neill.*) To Floyd (1981, xxiv), the scenario is "obviously a veiled version of *Long Day's Journey into Night,*" given that it focuses on "the sins of the parents against each other," and especially the sins of the mother, "a fiend of a woman," as the husband describes his wife, "a wicked woman, hard and cruel," as the son describes his mother. It is easy to imagine that while Agnes worked, she took an ironic satisfaction in elaborating her husband's misogyny. Agnes had her own mysogynistic grievances, against a mother who had repeatedly humiliated her by strapping her severely with a belt.

By the time of the visit to Nantucket, Agnes knew that she was pregnant again. In 1959–1960 Agnes spoke at length to Sheaffer about her pregnancy with Oona (LS papers). She conceded that she had been at a loss to cope with her first two pregnancies and had done less than she would have wished with Barbara and Shane. But she insisted that she regarded the situation very differently by 1924 and wanted things to be different with her third child. Indeed, it appears that some change was taking place in Agnes. Among other things, she seemed to be growing a bit more independent.

If Eugene's complaints are to be believed, Agnes was becoming less interested in her husband's art, more middle-class, and less extreme in her dependency on Eugene, and so she was drifting away from him. Always uncomfortable with theater people, Agnes deplored Eugene's increased involvement with the Players and their problems. She convinced herself that Eugene was becoming less committed as an artist and too concerned about theatrical practicalities—probably because of the adaptations he had undertaken in December and January and his extended interruption of work on *Desire*. She increasingly made other plans when Eugene was involved in rehearsals and in conferences with Macgowan, Jones, and others; and she started seeking friends of her own. Such small steps toward independence, if that is what Agnes was after, were certain to have a bad effect on the marriage. Little had changed in Eugene's mind about the need for them to be everything to each other, even though he could make fun of the idea in *Welded*.

It seems clear that the marriage was steadily deteriorating, perhaps partly because Agnes was changing, but it also seems clear that neither of them was thinking about its breaking up or was even chronically unhappy. In daily life things went along quietly. Eugene almost certainly got some of what he needed emotionally from Mrs. Clark's devotion and loyalty and her tacit belief that Agnes did not sufficiently appreciate her husband.

The O'Neills passed the summer and early fall in Provincetown. Eugene revised plays about to be published, and worked with *Marco Millions* until a few days before his thirty-sixth birthday, October 16, when he went to New York for rehearsals of *S.S. Glencairn* and *Desire,* both of which were to succeed with New York audiences. Rehearsals of *Desire* gave O'Neill a pleasant surprise. He thought Walter Huston outstanding as Ephraim Cabot. Decades later, O'Neill would remember Huston as one of three actors, along with Gilpin and Wolheim, who had most nearly captured his ideas for characters. *Desire* had a "fine reception," O'Neill noted in his diary, when it opened November 11. Critics, then as now, had mixed reactions. Some found the play disagreeable, unpleasant, and morally objectionable, some showed embarrassment at its intensity, some offered high praise, and almost all acknowledged O'Neill's seriousness of purpose and design.

Desire moved on January 2, 1925, to the Earl Carroll Theater, and soon it was doing well. A few days later, *S.S. Glencairn* moved from the Village uptown to the Princess Theater, where it would also prosper. District Attorney Banton, still smarting from his failure the previous year to close *All God's Chillun,* was now trying to shut down *Desire* and two other plays on grounds of general immorality. After a month of intense newspaper coverage, a nonjudicial forum was convened in lieu of a court trial. The "play jury" found *Desire* and the other plays acceptable for public performance. The renewed publicity brought playgoers out in droves. *Desire* grossed $9,000, $10,000, finally $13,500 a week, while the District Attorney made threats. O'Neill was glad for the numbers and the royalties—he earned almost $8,000 in February and March alone.

But he rightly expected that the play would not be seen on its own terms, and that its future reputation would be damaged by the scandal. In fact, the play still carries a reputation of striving for sensation at a cost to "art." Arrangements for a 1925 performance in London were blocked by a "permanent" ban by the Lord Chamberlain's Office, which was eventually evaded in 1931, by a so-called private performance at a theater club. In fact, the first public performance in London was not until 1940.

Writing in the *Nation,* Joseph Wood Krutch reviewed the reactions as well as the play. He discussed the tendency of the age to "intellectualize" art, to seek in works of art solutions to problems in society, and then to find them lacking if the solutions envisioned by the critics seemed unclear or unattractive. Such an approach, Krutch wrote, denied or diluted the principal achievement of O'Neill's work, the development of situations and characters to a point of almost unbearable emotional intensity. Krutch hinted that critics and audiences should try to bear the experience, and the play's long run of 208 performances suggests that the public had more success at coping with the play's emotional demands than did many of the critics. Krutch conceded to one possible criticism of the play: an excessive number of incidents, emotional extremity piled upon extremity. Nearly all critics praised Walter Huston as Ephraim and Mary Morris, who played Abbie, as well as Bobby Jones's sets and direction.

The play continues to be considered one of O'Neill's finest. Frequent comparisons of the play to a Greek tragedy have been strongly defended (see, for example, Bogard 1972, 213–18; Ranald 1984, 174–77). To a psychoanalytic biographer's mind, the play constitutes a providential compromise that O'Neill happened on in his struggle to acquire and disown his personal oedipal knowledge. In *Desire,* O'Neill gave the theater one of his most successful early plays. "With this play," Ranald writes, "O'Neill establishes himself as a playwright of genius." As she points out, *Desire* gives the lie to the axiom "that tragedy is impossible of achievement by modern playwrights" (174).

Two days after *Desire* opened, Eugene and Agnes went to Ridgefield to prepare for a winter in Bermuda. They sailed on November 29. After a few days in a hotel, they found a property called Campsea, thirty acres of wooded hillside in Paget Parish running down to a long private beach. Oona would be born there on May 14, 1925. The O'Neills and Mrs. Clark lived in a cottage on the property, along with a huge Irish wolfhound, Finn MacCool, that Eugene acquired when they bought Ridgefield; a beast that was sweet-tempered with people but unmanageable and that harbored lethal designs on the neighbors' pets and livestock. Agnes's pregnancy with Oona was beginning to show. The family lived in Campsea, Finn MacCool roamed the woods, and in another cottage on the property, Eugene wrote in the mornings before descending the hill to swim the warm seas.

Further Analysis
1925

EUGENE GOT DRUNK WHEN *Desire* opened in November 1924 and kept drinking for two months. On New Year's Day 1925 he began tapering off and started exercising. He had two jobs in mind: to revise *Marco Millions* and to write *The Great God Brown*. His unrevised diary for 1925 (the only original diary of his that is known) records his depression, his shakes, his insomnia, and his general state of illbeing. He kept track of withdrawal symptoms because of a renewed resolve to end his drinking. Jamie's death had convinced Eugene that he had to stop or he would not be able to continue writing and would probably die as his brother had died. He increasingly looked to doctors for a solution to his drinking problem.

Since 1920, he had discussed with several friends, including Bobby Jones, Kenneth Macgowan, and Jimmy Light, their experiences in analysis. As it happened, the O'Neills' place in Bermuda was close to the home of Maude Bisch, a kindly, friendly woman whose husband, Dr. Louis Bisch, had a New York psychiatric practice. Maude was to become a good friend to Eugene and Agnes. She had several children herself, and as she had once worked as a nurse, she would help Agnes in her pregnancy. (Louis Bisch would later write a popular book, *Be Glad You're Neurotic.*)

Eugene had talked about his alcoholism and his desire to stop drinking with Dr. Bisch, whom he had apparently met during a Christmas holiday visit. Bisch, who had himself written a play, chatted with O'Neill about the creative process, which he also discussed in a radio talk, "The Psychology of Playwriting," broadcast on WOR, New York, in March. The O'Neills were among the listeners in Bermuda. Reception was poor, and Eugene could make out little except his own name repeated from time to time, but he felt flattered at hearing himself discussed. It was an unusual reaction for a man who fiercely guarded his privacy. The reaction suggests that O'Neill had made a rapid friendly transference to Bisch.

As in 1924, O'Neill kept count of his days sober or drunk: January 10 was his first nondrinking day. Two days after he stopped drinking, he quit smoking also, and stepped up a regimen of exercise begun a week earlier. The diary is full of notes on developing new swimming strokes and breathing rhythms, as he built up endurance, speed, and distance. He lifted weights and measured himself as if he were a prize fighter, recording his dimensions in his diary: chest 40″, waist 30 ½″, biceps 13 ¼″, and so on. A month later he noted that he had added half an inch to his biceps.

He began swimming every day with a young neighbor, Alice Cuthbert, whom he thought attractive and unspoiled. Agnes became very angry about the friendship, and during a fight, Eugene or Agnes stabbed a decorative screen. The fight was made up in the evening, and Eugene began swimming with Agnes as well as with Alice. The O'Neills started taking long evening walks with the dog. They continued to see Alice almost daily, for she was staying with her older sister, Charlotte Barbour, a neighbor of the O'Neills who became a close friend. The falling out had deeper causes than Agnes's jealousy of Alice; Eugene and Agnes continued to drift apart. From the point when Eugene tried to stop drinking, Agnes, who did not want to stop, felt abandoned or rejected. Sheaffer believed that there was no sexual affair between Eugene and Alice. Sexual or no, though, the flirtation would cause further spats between Eugene and Agnes.

Preoccupied with the struggle to stop drinking and save his health and his mind, thinking about two writing projects, and above all ambivalent about having another child when he was increasingly doubtful about Agnes and the marriage, Eugene was more withdrawn and undemonstrative than ever. Agnes, by contrast, who felt more positive about having this child than she had with her first two, was constantly affected by her husband's seeming indifference as well as by his increased self-preoccupation as he tried to quit drinking. Decades later she still re-

20. O'Neill, about 1926. Sheaffer-O'Neill Collection, Charles E. Shain
Library, Connecticut College.

21. Fifine Clark and Oona. Sheaffer-O'Neill Collection, Charles E. Shain
Library, Connecticut College.

22. Eugene Jr. and his father at Belgrade Lakes, Maine, 1926. Sheaffer-O'Neill Collection, Charles E. Shain Library, Connecticut College.

23. O'Neill, photographed by Nikolas Muray, about 1926. Courtesy Nikolas Muray Photo Archive.

24. O'Neill and a friend on guard at Spithead. Sheaffer-O'Neill Collection,
Charles E. Shain Library, Connecticut College.

25. Eugene and Agnes at Spithead, shortly before he went to New York and Carlotta and France. Sheaffer-O'Neill Collection, Charles E. Shain Library, Connecticut College.

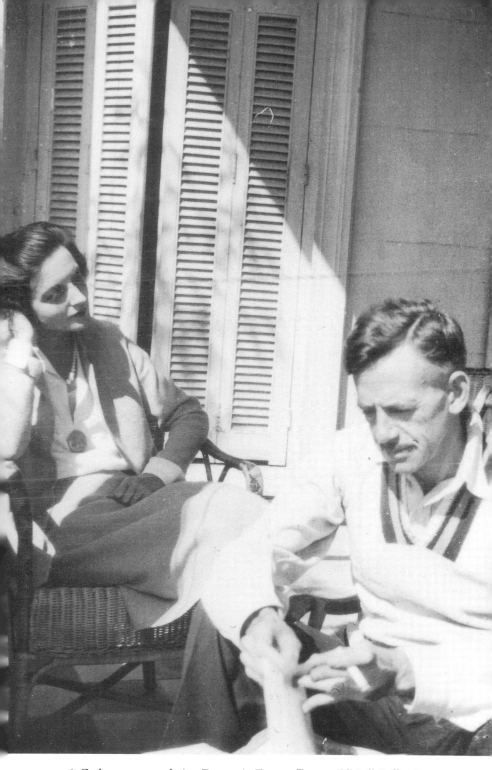

26. Carlotta contemplating Eugene in France. Eugene O'Neill Collection, Collection of American Literature, Beinecke Rare Book and Manuscript Library, Yale University.

27. A moment of closeness. Eugene O'Neill Collection, Collection of
American Literature, Beinecke Rare Book and Manuscript Library,
Yale University.

28. Eugene and his Bugatti. O'Neill told friends that he would drive his racing car as much as a hundred miles an hour on country roads and afterward come home feeling relaxed.

29. In 1931, O'Neill wrote on his anniversary gift: "To my Love and my Life, Carlotta, who sometimes thinks this infant never grew up." At the time of the gift and the rueful remark, he was beginning to make progress. Eugene O'Neill Collection, Collection of American Literature, Beinecke Rare Book and Manuscript Library, Yale University.

30. Shane, about 1934–1935. Sheaffer-O'Neill Collection, Charles E. Shain
Library, Connecticut College, with the permission of the children
of Shane O'Neill.

31. Oona at fourteen with her father at Tao House in 1939. Eugene O'Neill
Collection, Collection of American Literature, Beinecke Rare Book and
Manuscript Library, Yale University.

32. O'Neill about the time he wrote *The Iceman Cometh* and *Long Day's Journey into Night*. Eugene O'Neill Collection, Collection of American Literature, Beinecke Rare Book and Manuscript Library, Yale University.

33. O'Neill at Marblehead Neck, about 1949. Eugene O'Neill Collection, Collection of American Literature, Beinecke Rare Book and Manuscript Library, Yale University.

34. Eugene Jr. not long before his death. Sheaffer-O'Neill Collection, Charles E. Shain Library, Connecticut College.

35. O'Neill in mourning. Eugene O'Neill Collection, Collection of American Literature, Beinecke Rare Book and Manuscript Library, Yale University.

membered feeling betrayed by the change in him and complained to Sheaffer that when they had married, Eugene had been "a bohemian" and "more interesting" but that he had become "dull" by 1925 (LS papers).

Once sober, Eugene resumed work. David Belasco was interested in *Marco Millions* if it could be cut, and Eugene, setting about to extract a play of ordinary length from his eight-act draft, worked up to ten hours a day. He finished on January 22 and mailed the script to Dick Madden the next day. In the meantime, he met a Dr. Wilkinson: "Queer interesting body," O'Neill noted. "Like him" (WD, 474). Evidently he sometimes talked about his alcoholism with Dr. Wilkinson over the next several months.

At this point he was reading Freud's *Beyond the Pleasure Principle*, a difficult work, which Eugene found "dully written—or translated" (WD, 474). By far Freud's most pessimistic book, and turgidly written, as if Freud were reluctant to proceed to his inevitable conclusions, it proposed the theory of a human psychological instinct opposing the sexual instinct, an instinct leading toward death and degradation. For a reader trying to cope with too many deaths, it was a work both dreadful and apt. O'Neill read it to the end, and soon after he read the more lucid and less pessimistic *Group Psychology and the Analysis of the Ego,* a work that takes the situation of the individual within a group as a context for examining the ego and its relation to ego ideals. (The concept ego ideal is a precursor to the later idea of the superego.) Reading *Beyond the Pleasure Principle* and *Group Psychology* would directly influence *The Great God Brown,* which Eugene was about to begin.

As he set to work cutting *Marco Millions,* Eugene began reading a special issue on alcoholism of a British medical journal, *The Practitioner,* probably borrowed from Dr. Wilkinson. He finished it up over the next several days. "Very interesting," Eugene noted, "and applicable to me" (WD, 475). One article in the journal, discussing the use of morphine to end alcohol addiction, must have made Eugene wonder about the relation of his mother's drinking to her morphine addiction. He continued to read books about psychology. Attracted by the title, he picked up *Unmasking Our Minds* by Dr. David Seabury but found the book naive and dropped it. On February 5, in answer to a question in a fan letter, he responded: "Playwrights are either intuitively keen analytical psychologists—or they aren't good playwrights. I'm trying to be one. To me, Freud only means uncertain conjectures and explanations about truths of the emotional past of mankind that every dramatist has clearly sensed since real drama began. I respect Freud's work tremendously—but I'm not an addict! Whatever of Freudianism is in *Desire* must have walked right in 'through my unconscious'" (SL, 192). The Malcolm Cowley anecdote about Stekel's treatise on sexual aberrations implies that the letter disingenuously conceals O'Neill's psychoanalytic readings and interest in personal treatment.

In spite of his sobriety, Eugene took to Bermuda society with more delight than one might have expected. The diary records excursions and visits paid or received almost every day. O'Neill worked in the morning on *Brown*, which was taking a different form from the one he had sketched the previous year. He worked into February on the scenario, noting several times in his diary his surprise at the way the story was working out. When they had no visitors in the evening, he wrote many letters or read.

As he worked on *Brown*, O'Neill continued to read widely about psychology, anthropology, social history, and ancient religions. The god Pan came particularly to his attention while Eugene was still working on *Marco Millions*, because he was reading Anatole France's *Revolt of Angels*. In *Group Psychology*, he ran across more references to the god in a discussion of the group phenomenon panic, which Freud saw as simultaneously expressing and denying a sexual impulse. Freud does not need to explain to a classically educated audience that *Panik* combines the idea of the god's sexual power with that of mortals' dread of encountering a god, but the notion may have startled O'Neill. Meeting Pan twice in one month must have led O'Neill to merge him with Dionysos in the figure of Dion Anthony. Pan was a suitable embodiment of the outbursts of denied sexuality that drive the play.

While he was thinking about the figure who combines Pan with St. Anthony, he fortuitously received a letter from a nun who suggested that he read the lives of the saints for material for future plays. The coincidence startled him enough that he mentioned it in his diary. Reading Freud and the works on old religions and cultures reawakened his interest in Nietzsche and the Greeks, and he read *Joyful Wisdom, The Birth of Tragedy,* and Walter Pater's *Greek Portraits*. Of *The Birth of Tragedy* he wrote: "Most stimulating book on drama ever written" (WD, 486). When Eugene Jr. visited in the spring, the playwright fired his fifteen-year-old son with his enthusiasm and set in motion the process that would lead the youth later to study classics at Yale.

The initial scheme for *Brown* was for a self-divided character, Dion Anthony, to represent in his person the opposite types: Dionysos, god of wine and sexual excitement, and the ascetic St. Anthony, one of Eugene's schoolboy heroes. The physical description of Dion resembles those of characters like Robert Mayo, Eben Cabot, and others taken to be self-portraits, so we can guess that O'Neill originally meant Dion to represent some version of himself. As Manheim has noticed, however (48), the character that emerges seems less like himself than like his brother. This must have been one of the changes O'Neill discovered as he worked out the scenario.

Thoreau required of any writer a simple and sincere account of his life, and no doubt if O'Neill had been able to write straightforwardly of his or his brother's or his mother's life, *Brown* and his other plays of the 1920s would not have been written or would have been very different. How little able O'Neill was to give a simple account of his life is evident in the extreme fragmentation of all the characters in *Brown*. From a biographical viewpoint, Dion Anthony and Billy Brown consist of clusters of O'Neill's internal images of his brother and himself, especially those aspects of himself that are the product of his identifications with Jamie.

If O'Neill had been able to write simply about his brother and mother and his love of them, then his mourning for them could have moved ahead as it had with his father. But problems in accepting the deaths of Ella and Jamie had forced Eugene to delve into his internal images of the two and had reawakened old conflicts with his father as well. What he found he presented in *Brown*. Fragmented internal images of Jamie mingled with fragmented internal images of both parents and of himself. He presented the internal images in the way they may occur in dreams, in parapraxes (that is, slips of the tongue, mistakes of action, or misperceptions), or in the associations of a person in analysis.

O'Neill began thinking about *The Great God Brown* shortly after his mother died, when Jamie was beginning to disintegrate. He returned to the idea after Jamie died, so he had that death as well as his mother's on his mind. He was also thinking about the need he felt to quit drinking, a renunciation that would entail other changes of behavior and would as a consequence affect him like another loss.

In setting down the death of Dion Anthony in Billy Brown's study (act 2, scene 2) O'Neill expressed the cluster of losses: the loss of his mother, his disillusionment with his brother, the latter's death, and the end of his drinking self. What would be left when he stopped drinking, he feared, would be an untalented technician like Brown, a theatrical draftsman with all the genius and madness gone. The fear of discovering himself to be a mere plodder drove O'Neill to challenge himself in every play to exceed anything he had done before. As a result, failure was as common as success for the next few years. He saw himself as being in a double bind: if he did not quit drinking, he would cease to be able to write; but sober, he might lose the inner fire.

Beneath the fear is an oedipal conflict. When Brown usurps Dion's mask, he shows that he believes himself to be a poor thing. Not only does he lack Dion's artistic potency, but he can only imitate the one he thinks a better man in order to appropriate the other's woman. He has failed to penetrate further than skin deep with Dion's whore Cybel; and Dion's wife, Margaret, hardly notices the difference when Brown takes on Dion's mask. Worst of all, Brown loses his ego ideal—his notion of himself as he wished to be, which he has called Dion—and he fears his customers will leave him if his construction firm loses Dion's creative genius.

Brown, like O'Neill's other plays of the time, is overtly and explicitly about death and mourning. At the end of act 1, when drunk in Cybel's parlor, Dion gives obituaries for his parents that seem to reflect the parental images dominant in O'Neill's mind at the moment. Dion's father once employed Brown's father in the firm of builders that Billy Brown took over. Dion sentimentally longs to "sit where [my father] spun what I have spent." Embarrassed at exposing his still-active dependency, he blusters: "What aliens we were to each other! When he lay dead, his face looked so familiar that I wondered where I had met that man before. Only at the second of my conception. After that, we grew hostile with concealed shame" (CP2, 495–96). The realization apparently reflects O'Neill's reconstruction of Jamie's feelings about their father—or perhaps it was even something Jamie said.

As for his dead mother, Dion uncovers an image that must have been central to Eugene's reminiscences about Ella, as he viewed her partly from his own childhood point of view and partly through identification with Jamie. In part he perhaps imagines his mother as his brother must have seen her when he did not have to share her:

> I remember a sweet, strange girl, with affectionate eyes as if
> God had locked her in a dark closet without any explana-

tion. I was the sole doll our ogre, her husband, allowed her and she played mother and child with me for many years in that house until at last through two tears I watched her die with the shy pride of one who has lengthened her dress and put up her hair. And I felt like a forsaken toy and cried to be buried with her because her hands alone had caressed without clawing. She lived long and aged greatly in the two days before they closed her coffin. The last time I looked, her purity had forgotten me, she was stainless and imperishable, and I knew my sobs were ugly and meaningless to her virginity; so I shrank away, back into life, with naked nerves jumping like fleas. [CP 2, 496]

The elegy for Dion's mother (and for Ella O'Neill) should be placed alongside Jim Tyrone's elegy for his mother in *A Moon for the Misbegotten*. Dion's elegy is O'Neill's prose poetry at its best, but it obscures both the speaker and his subject; by contrast, Jim Tyrone's elegy for his mother, written nearly two decades later, allows the listener to know both speaker and subject. O'Neill had far to go before he could let either rest in peace.

When Dion himself dies, the focus of the play becomes Brown's usurpation of Dion's identity by taking up his mask and then taking his wife. When Brown himself dies at the end of the play, it is as if Dion has died twice: first as "himself" in Brown's study, second after Brown has been possessed by the daemon of Dion's mask. Writing the play allowed Eugene to recover and examine some fragmented images of his brother and of his own identifications with Jamie and to experiment with the idea of losing his brother. When Dion dies, Brown remarks: "So that's the poor weakling you really were! No wonder you hid! And I've always been afraid of you—yes, I'll confess it now, in awe of you" (CP2, 511). Here Eugene seems to speak his recognition that his brother was a different person from the idealized figure imagined by himself as a needy youngster. At the same time, the elegy denies the importance of the loss, and so denies the loss itself. *Brown* shows Eugene's mourning, like an analysis, beginning in denial and resistance.

The disillusionment expressed in the phrase "poor weakling" shows Eugene trying to let go of his old idealization of Jamie and of his childhood identification with a brother who appeared uninhibited. Dion is the daredevil schoolboy whom Eugene idolized, the Jamie of unlimited talent who played shortstop, acted well in school plays, and could begin well a poem in a difficult form. But the older, disillusioned Eugene might remember that Jamie would let the poem limp to its end in clichés, had squandered remarkable gifts, and could never grow emotionally much beyond adolescence. Dion represents the parts of the author that arose from identification with Jamie, especially Eugene's wild, rebellious, and self-destructive traits. O'Neill also expresses certain self-images in the form of Billy Brown: the Eugene who envied his brother his obvious gifts and also envied his mother's preference. Through envious identification with Jamie Eugene sees himself as stealing the talents and qualities of his brother that he feels he himself lacks.

To the extent that Dion represents Jamie the whole person, the disillusionment Brown undergoes is that of an idealizing younger brother who finally sees that his idol is no god. By killing off Dion, Eugene experiments with giving up the part of himself that drinks. He wonders what if anything of himself will remain if he can no longer look forward to the relief of the next binge. By trying to examine the images, and by acknowledging his disillusionment, Eugene begins separating the internal image of himself from his internal images of Jamie.

Studying *The Great God Brown* is rather like analyzing a very complex Cubist painting—say, Picasso's well-known *Girl Before a Mirror,* in which one constantly searches for the relation of fragments to each other and guesses at the prevailing point of view and meaning in any particular fragment. The process seems as incapable of completion as the psychoanalytic process. Working out fragments of various aspects of oedipal conflict and of mourning probably had some beneficial effect for O'Neill, who ever after called the play one of his favorites. It is interesting as a sort of staged Cubist painting of oedipal complications.

From a psychoanalytic point of view, Brown's adaptation of Dion's persona expresses a positive, integrating process arising in the playwright. If we recognize that the issue is making the self whole, then we must recognize that when he has Brown seize Dion's mask, O'Neill acknowledges an old mistake, and an old division in himself. To put the matter crudely, since adolescence, since discovering his mother's addiction, Eugene had coped with knowledge of his crime of mother-murder by splitting himself between his Dion self and his Billy self. The real-life splits were not as complete or as drastic as the differences between the two characters seem to be in the play, but they were noticeable to other people. Speaking to

biographers, old friends of the playwright marveled at the difference between Eugene's usual self and his behavior during his occasional explosions of violence or self-destructiveness; as Agnes's sister Cecil once told
Sheaffer, Gene when drinking could seem "a fiend" (LS, 187).

By writing about splitting, O'Neill made it accessible to his scrutiny.
This and other discoveries made while writing *Brown* and other plays of
the 1920s led to deeper insights later. By killing off the drunkard Dion
and having him survive in modified form as the Dion-masked Brown,
O'Neill experimented with temperance to see how it might feel. The feeling of fragmentation evoked through the separate characters he now com-
pounds when Brown begins hopping back and forth between his Dion
self and his Billy self. At this point in the play, audiences may begin to lose
the thread of the overt allegories about artistic creativity and modern sexual ideas. For O'Neill, though, the more important issue throughout has
been, Can he survive without drinking? Brown regresses increasingly to
childlike helplessness. But the artist in O'Neill can make gentle fun of
Dion and Billy and so separate himself from their fates. Writing *Brown*
led to eventual sobriety. For Eugene, writing the play served one function
of psychotherapy or Alcoholics Anonymous, for it gave him some of the
objectivity he needed to make the change.

One of the allegories of *The Great God Brown* offers a critique of
modern sexuality. The god Dionysos, best known to moderns as the central figure of Euripides' *Bakkhai,* represents in *Brown* not only wine but
the polymorphous sexual drive that Freud describes. Pan embodies the
heedlessly procreative masculine animal drive, mocked in the person of
the sterile, Babbitty Brown. O'Neill's modernization of Cybele, Cybel,
one of the names for the great triple god who preceded the Olympian
gods, is the earth itself, casually fecund, prolifically bent on filling all space
with her creatures; but like Brown, O'Neill's Cybel is sterile.

Like other modernists, O'Neill laments that life has isolated sexuality from its place in nature. Cybel's sterility belies the charade of sexuality that the prostitute enacts with her customers. Brown, one of her regulars, represents modern male sexuality, phallic but sterile. He would be
predatory if he didn't worry so about consequences and duty. In her modern narcissistic incarnation, Cybel makes her match with the modern
Dionysos: that is, the two pass the time at double solitaire. They require
some cuddling but shun deeper intimacy. Cybel represents a flight from

fecundity, and Dion flees from his wife and son into a show of the phallic. Like Dion the artist, Dion the lover is all impulse, which he cannot carry out. Following Nietzsche's now familiar indictment, O'Neill condemns Christianity, represented in the play by Dion Anthony's second name, and the self-alienation engendered by modern commercial and industrial life for the crime of trivializing human sexuality.

Eugene was preoccupied by thoughts of sexual dissatisfaction while he was writing *The Great God Brown*—partly because the episodes of estrangement between him and Agnes were getting longer, while the periods of emotional need and sexual urgency that brought them back together were becoming rarer and less intense. To a biographer, it seems that more and more, Eugene's needs were met by Fifine Clark's maternal adoration, giving him an implicit alternative to Agnes—so it seems from a study of Sheaffer's interviews with Agnes. Some of the ambivalence toward Shane is explainable by Eugene's tacit competition with his son for the attention of Fifine Clark. Their need for Mrs. Clark made Agnes less important for Shane and Eugene. O'Neill quietly endorsed Fifine in tacit censure of Agnes for failing to appreciate her husband sufficiently. Such seems to be one source for the triangle in *Brown* of Dion, his wife Margaret, and Cybel (and Dion's sexless relationship with Cybel).

The figure in the play who is not sterile is Margaret. With his wife Dion has become St. Anthony, so distant and so furtive in his sexuality that he is the opposite to the goat god who prances and capers with nymphs on woodland hills, and who formerly impregnated Margaret. The "good, unimaginative" Margaret derives, O'Neill wrote in a note for a playbill, from the "eternal girl-woman," Gretchen in Goethe's *Faust*. O'Neill also told Agnes that the character was modeled on her (LS, 170–71). It seems we must infer that the character partly arose from O'Neill's feelings about his wife at the time he was writing.

The preoccupation with sterility in *Brown* appears to express a wish to undo something that was about to happen. As O'Neill was writing, Agnes drew nearer to delivering her baby, and her pregnancy became ever more conspicuous. As with the birth of Shane, Eugene had mixed feelings. He was hoping for a girl. He told Magowan jokingly, as Agnes's belly grew larger, that he expected "twin girls." The unedited diary shows no references to Agnes's pregnancy from January until May, not even on the date when he notes the seventh anniversary of the marriage. Oona's birth earns three exclamation marks in a line of vital statistics, but the only other references to her in 1925 are a comment on June 27 that Oona had been "all right" during a ship's passage to New York, and the word *baby* in a list of people who made a September drive to Ridgefield.

O'Neill finished his draft of *The Great God Brown* on March 22 "in tears! Couldn't control myself!" he wrote in his diary. He immediately wrote to Macgowan and Nathan to crow about a work he thought his "ceiling," "grand stuff," "much deeper & more poetical" than anything he'd previously written (LS, 167). After going over the play and having it typed, he repeated in his diary his high opinion of his new child, and he would maintain the opinion to the end. A few days after finishing *Brown*, after eighty-three days of sobriety and eighty-one days without smoking, he got drunk, limiting himself to German beer and British ale at first, and resumed smoking cigarettes. Agnes too was drinking heavily; perhaps his own resumption eased the tension between them. With the play finished and the strain of temperance forgotten, tensions eased somewhat between the O'Neills, even though Eugene was not sleeping well and had gone into the usual post-partum depression that followed his completion of a play. The depression was to continue off and on the rest of the year.

Eugene Jr. arrived for a week's visit near the end of March, and his father took him to Hamilton to buy him British tweeds. At fifteen, the boy was nearly as tall as his father, and O'Neill was proud of his fine-looking son. Kathleen Jenkins told Sheaffer that her son looked forward for months to his visits with his father. O'Neill rented a sailboat one day and took Eugene and Agnes and four other friends to picnic on another island.

Not long after Eugene Jr. returned home, when Agnes was nearing her term, O'Neill moved his family out of Campsea with its leaking roof and drafty walls and into a large house, Southcote. He was now drinking very heavily again. Agnes told Sheaffer that one morning before breakfast, according to her count, he had taken three drinks of whiskey. Jimmy Light made a brief visit in April and left on the 25th. The Lights told Sheaffer they didn't see Agnes the first day of their visit because she was drunk in her room (LS papers). From April 25 to June 6, when Jones and Macgowan arrived for a visit, O'Neill made only two diary entries, one of which, on May 14, recorded the birth of Oona. The gap probably indicates O'Neill's state of mind and his drunkenness.

Agnes had an easy pregnancy and delivery. After allowing her mother to raise her first daughter, and after experiencing pronounced ambivalence about the birth of Shane and allowing him to be brought up mainly by Mrs. Clark, Agnes had decided that her second daughter would be her child. Pictures shown to Sheaffer reveal Oona at birth as "a beautiful child with dark hair and large dark eyes that, slanting upward, gave her a charming, faintly oriental look." This child, Agnes promised herself, "is going to be mine!" (LS, 179). Agnes and Eugene picked the name from a list made for them by the Irish poet James Stephens. O'Neill told people that Oona was an Irish form of Agnes. He cabled the news, "It's a goil!" to numerous friends before falling back into hard drinking. He seemed to Agnes to turn his back on the new development in his family. She told Sheaffer that she was deeply disappointed by her husband's inability to share her new attitude toward a child of theirs.

Yet, as always, he was ambivalent. Mostly he concealed his feeling that she was a beautiful child and that he often found himself thinking of her. As with his feelings about Agnes, he could not express them simply and directly but had to write them. During a brief separation in late July he wrote to Agnes: "Every second I spend in the room I miss you like the devil—and I miss Oona over on the couch. I really love her! Never thought I could a baby! And I love you, my dear wife and pal, more than I have power to say" (SL, 196).

Before Oona was two weeks old, Dr. Bisch arrived from New York to visit his family. His arrival was the occasion of the only other diary entry of May 1925. O'Neill was evidently anticipating the visit, for Sheaffer learned that O'Neill was embarrassed for Bisch to see him drinking and tapered off several days before the doctor arrived, hoping to be sober. In fact, he was still drinking when he met the doctor, and he excused himself with the explanation that he usually became depressed after finishing a play (LS, 179–80). O'Neill's reaction to an anticipated visit from a virtual stranger is very striking, very uncharacteristic. It is evidence of the positive transference that O'Neill had formed to the psychiatrist, whom he saw as a father who might hold him accountable for his drinking. In part the transference testifies to the need he was feeling in his despondency for his dead father. But also, at another level of consciousness, he evidently had made up his mind that salvation lay with psychiatry, and that a play-writing psychiatrist must have been sent to him by the gods. "Doctor Bisch arrived," he wrote in the diary on May 28. "They came up in eve. Like him very much." Bisch's visit was brief, but before he left,

Eugene had made an appointment to see him when he got to New York in late June.

Once again, Eugene stopped drinking. He managed to stay dry during a brief visit by Jones and Macgowan, with whom he swam and to whom he read *Brown*. Both were "much impressed," he noted with satisfaction. When they left, he began working on another play idea and in four days wrote a scenario for *Strange Interlude*. On June 27, ensconced in fine ship cabins, the O'Neills returned to New York with their two children and Mrs. Clark. Arriving two days later, they were met by Kenneth Macgowan and Dick Madden. That afternoon, as Eugene noted in his diary on June 29, he went to see Dr. Bisch "to start treatment."

How many times O'Neill saw Bisch is unclear. He made only one diary entry during the next three weeks, to record Agnes's departure for Nantucket, where the family was to spend August and September. On July 17, after forty-eight days without drinking, O'Neill wrote in the diary: "To Harlem with Paul [Robeson] and Harold McGee. Up all night. Disaster." He drank heavily through the rest of July while in New York, catching up with old friends, including his cousin from New London, Phil Sheridan, who came down to visit and stayed overnight. To sober up, he went to visit the Macgowans, who put him to bed for a couple of days. With Kenneth, still drinking a little, Eugene drove up to Ridgefield, which was rented to tenants for the summer, to look the place over and simply roam about the countryside. Back in New York on July 25, Eugene found he could not sleep. Bisch took him veronal at his hotel, which seemed to put him in a stuporous state but did not bring him sleep. For two days he went to bed early to catch up.

Eugene returned from Bermuda not only to see Bisch but to try to help the production of *The Fountain*. After several attempts to find an actor to play Ponce de Leon, the 1921–22 play was finally limping toward a production with Walter Huston—who had been fine in *Desire*—miscast as the explorer. Having been greatly impressed by a notable production of *Hamlet* and believing that John Barrymore was the best young actor in the country, O'Neill had tried to interest him in the part. Barrymore might have saved *The Fountain,* but as it was, the opening in December pleased almost no one, and the play closed after twenty-five performances. Ponce was a part James O'Neill might have played.

O'Neill did not wait for *The Fountain* to open but went to Nantucket to meet his family. There he found that Agnes had taken a house that he immediately disliked because it was right on the street. He began drinking again, continued through August, and stopped on the 25th. After a week he began a scenario for *Lazarus Laughed,* his ultimate exploration of the denial of death. As Manheim (1982) has argued, the model for Lazarus was once again Jamie. Eugene worked steadily on the scenario through September 9, gradually cutting down on his smoking as he worked. On the 19th he had a cable from London announcing the triumphant opening there of *The Emperor Jones,* starring Robeson.

On August 25 he began another forty-day run of nondrinking days, along with a swimming and exercise program. When the time came to return to New York from Nantucket, he began smoking again as well as drinking. He spent two days in New London, looking at property from the estate; he visited Monte Cristo Cottage and felt sad to find it fallen into decay and ruin. In the evenings, he drank with such old friends as Doc Ganey and Ed Keefe and quarreled with Agnes. So went the rest of the year.

At Brook Farm in early October, he began another temperance campaign and health regimen and, as he tried to begin writing *Lazarus Laughed,* gradually got into the rhythm of the new play. He tried to revise *The Fountain* to improve its chances in the theater, but he was more concerned with its publication as a book, which was to occur before the December opening. On O'Neill's thirty-seventh birthday Dr. Bisch came up from New York. "Much talk about divorce," O'Neill noted: both men were contemplating it (WD, 492). It seems O'Neill was changing his mind about Dr. Bisch, for he apparently did not see him again.

O'Neill's temperance lasted until November 22. While in New York to work on rehearsals of *The Fountain* and the casting of *Brown,* he got drunk with Edmund Wilson, Mary Blair, and others while on an all-night tour of jazz clubs. Back in Ridgefield he tried to cut down in order to resume work on *Lazarus Laughed* and worked in the woods for several days to distract himself from thoughts of booze. But the farm oppressed him, and after a few sober days, he got drunk, blaming boredom. "No home for me! Dull as hell."

After Christmas, Macgowan came to Ridgefield to talk about casting *Brown.* O'Neill, tapering off again, was physically ill and deeply melancholic. Macgowan made appointments for Eugene and Agnes to meet Gilbert V. Hamilton, an analyst who was conducting a study of sex in marriage. O'Neill greeted news of the appointment with Dr. Hamilton as "a ray of hope amid general sick despair." On New Year's Eve he noted (WD, 495): "On wagon. Good'bye [*sic*]—without regret—1925 (except for few mos. in Bermuda"). This time, after his several false starts in 1925, he would get his drinking under control. For the rest of his life, O'Neill had only a few more of the drunken binges that had plagued him for so long.

Changes
1925–1927

THE WINTER OF 1925–1926 AT Brook Farm convinced the O'Neills that their future should be lived in Bermuda. Although they had made expensive improvements, they had spent very little time at the estate and now decided to put it on the market and rent it out until it sold. Indeed, they spent about as many nights that winter in New York hotels as at Ridgefield.

Eugene's unsuccessful attempts in 1925 to stop drinking and smoking had added to the strains already affecting the marriage. The rigid self-discipline required to maintain both forms of abstinence made Eugene more self-absorbed than ever, and he felt increasingly distant from Agnes; she continued to drink as before and to complain that he paid her little attention. His dissatisfactions with the marriage were also apparent. More than ever, he wanted a mate who would be an indivisible part of his psyche, who could share the enterprise to fulfill his talent and make it possible for him to write the best plays he could find in his soul. So he and Agnes had agreed when they had eloped and married, and so he still wanted it.

But, as she told Sheaffer much later, Agnes grew less interested in Eugene's work after *Beyond the Horizon* (LS papers). To some extent, her opinion of his plays may have been influenced by the growing coolness in the marriage. If any development had taken place in the emotional needs Eugene sought to fulfill through marriage, the progress was concealed by the regressions of mourning. Sheaffer's extensive notes on his many long conversations with Agnes, and his many letters from her, show no hint that she understood at all the cumulative effect on Eugene of all the deaths.

While Eugene was stuck in his mourning, Agnes was growing. With the birth of Oona a change had crystallized in her ideals. Much later she told Sheaffer that while pregnant she had determined to make Oona her child, to not allow her maternal position to be usurped, as Agnes felt she had allowed Fifine Clark to do with Shane (LS papers). Agnes was delighted to be in Bermuda. She sometimes felt like the odd one out in the family—uncomfortable with Shane, who was more attached to Mrs. Clark than to her; condescended to by Fifine, who felt protected by her adoration of Eugene and Shane; and increasingly isolated from Eugene, who was obsessed with his losses, his health, and his work in progress. Agnes apparently transferred to Oona the need she had formerly had for Eugene's constant regard and formed with her daughter the bond she had not been able to make with Shane.

Such were the circumstances when Kenneth Macgowan approached the O'Neills about participating in a scientific research project on marriage being conducted in New York by the analyst Dr. Gilbert Hamilton. The Macgowans were participating along with a good many other members of the Village artistic and intellectual community. Macgowan respected Hamilton and would write with him a popular account of the results of the study. (Hamilton's work itself was to be acknowledged with respect in the Kinsey report decades later.) Macgowan told Sheaffer that he believed Hamilton might help the O'Neills with their drinking problems and improve the state of the marriage (LS, 188). The O'Neills were looking forward to the opening of *The Great God Brown* on January 23, and Eugene was back and forth between Ridgefield and New York several times a week, so it was not difficult to arrange appointments with Hamilton.

Like other participants, the O'Neills were asked to respond to a long series of questions. Sitting in a chair that faced away from the doctor, participants were silently handed a card with a question on it to which they were to respond as fully or briefly as they wished without intervention from Hamilton. Hamilton used a modification of the basic process of psychoanalysis: asking subjects to associate aloud, if they could, to his questions about sex and sexuality.

O'Neill immediately liked the paternal-looking, unobtrusive Dr. Hamilton and according to the Gelbs was one of six people who continued to see Hamilton after the completion of the survey. Kenneth Macgowan told Sheaffer he believed Agnes also saw Hamilton for treatment. If so, almost nothing is known of her therapy except that she had some correspondence with Hamilton later, in which he suggested that she and Eugene might find interesting the newly published *Collected Papers* of Freud.

If Dr. Hamilton's subjects (many of them were in analysis or therapy), did not already know something of the logic of free associations, they might have learned its dynamics as they listened to themselves in the silent consulting room. O'Neill apparently got far enough to have the experience of watching thoughts or feelings or memories emerge from repression. So one must infer, because a couple of weeks after his treatment ended, when he was back in Bermuda and hard at work on *Lazarus Laughed,* he wrote in his work diary on March 13, "New ideas on everything crowding up—think I've got hold of *the* right method for doing *Strange Interlude* when I come to it" (WD, 23). He apparently meant the idea for having characters reveal themselves by free-associating aloud to the audience. He had been using psychoanalytic ideas and themes for his plays and now began applying the methods and processes of the discipline.

What transpired in conversations between O'Neill and Dr. Hamilton is of course unknown. Macgowan reported to Sheaffer that Dr. Hamilton "told me that Gene was able to stop drinking after he discovered that he had an Oedipus complex" (LS papers). Sheaffer writes that Macgowan and Jimmy Light privately disagreed with the claim because O'Neill himself told them that anyone who wanted to know that he had oedipal conflicts had merely to read his plays (LS, 190). They understood the wisecrack to mean that O'Neill already knew he had oedipal conflicts and that they were obvious in his plays, and that is probably what O'Neill meant. But O'Neill also knew better than most people that insight, recognition, and anagnorisis are tricky.

Not only analysts and analysands know that recognition grows gradually and develops unpredictably. The process of attaining insight, after all, is the main dramatic process of *Oedipus the King,* in which Oedipus spends the whole play denying, and simultaneously accumulating knowledge of, his old crime, knowledge he has always possessed but steadfastly disowns until the critical moment when the world and his own identity change. Although cataclysmic knowledge began for O'Neill with discovering himself the cause of his mother's addiction, it continued to expand and deepen as he lived and wrote. Dr. Hamilton probably avoided intrusive interpretations and took care to speak to matters already at the surface of O'Neill's thoughts, matters that would not threaten to disturb the playwright's defenses. When Eugene and Agnes were ready to return to Bermuda in late February 1922, Hamilton probably encouraged no longer analysis, wished the couple well, and assured them he would be available if one or both wished to resume treatment. Whether or not the treatment directly affected O'Neill's drinking—and it may have had some effect—it surely advanced a process of self-analysis that had been visibly at work in the playwright since 1913.

People entering analysis typically hope to rid themselves of debilitating symptoms or to change habitual patterns of reactions and behavior; perhaps they hope to change their temperament or very self. As analysis progresses, it often becomes clear that change will be lesser, greater, and different than anticipated. Stanley Cavell's (1969) remarks on psychoanalytic changes, mentioned in Chapter Four, are pertinent to the changes in O'Neill's life in the late 1920s. It is not that one gets the answers to questions one has asked all one's life. It is that the questions one has always asked cease to exist. Or rather, the world in which the questions arose ceases to exist and is superseded by a different world or a different paradigm of the world. The change is both psychological and philosophical, both personal and global.

In the case of a person as driven and as introspective as O'Neill, by nature psychologically minded, one who had been using his writing to objectify aspects of himself for well over a decade, even a period of therapy as brief as that which O'Neill had undergone might have some effect. At the least it probably precipitated some changes in O'Neill's conscious view of himself and his life. In the mid-1920s, before ego psychology and object relations theory had developed, practicing psychoanalysts theorized in terms of oral, anal, oedipal, and genital stages of human psychosexual development. O'Neill could not have avoided becoming more aware than before of unfulfilled oral needs (such needs for maternal nurture as dominate the first months of life). From his work with Gilbert Hamilton, O'Neill probably came away feeling a little less guilty about the anger toward his mother, partly suppressed but consciously felt throughout his life. Probably the anger itself would not have abated much for some time. As O'Neill's awareness of certain archaic needs increased, he probably became less tolerant of dissatisfactions in his marriage. At any rate, his feelings about the marriage, though still ambivalent, began to change.

Besides helping Eugene get control of his drinking, analysis and self-analysis led to changes, though not to the sort that people entering analysis hope to make. No large change of personality is discernible, nor much abatement in the basic needs that derive from the early loss of maternal nurture. One does not even find conspicuous changes in symptoms. But whereas mourning for his mother and brother had previously been impossible, slight, slow progress now began to be perceptible.

A slight easing of O'Neill's guilt made mourning a little more tolerable. The plays he would now write show him more able than before to confront directly both mourning as a general process and the specifics of his mourning for his particular dead. By the end of the 1920s he would make visible progress in his grieving, although it would continue for another decade.

Along with progress in mourning would come modifications in his theory of the world, in which residual teen-age skepticism had always alternated with a sort of Whitmanesque nature mysticism. Nietzsche's *Zarathustra* had given O'Neill a taste of relief from chronic guilt through the rejection of the absolutes good and evil. Guided by Nietzsche's *Birth of Tragedy*, Eugene reread Greek tragedy more deeply than before, and he also read scholarly works on pre-Pythagorean philosophy and ancient cultures. His old skepticism increasingly gave way to a religious view of the world. For the next several years he would wobble between a Greco-Nietzschean metaphysic and that of a lapsed Catholic who sometimes clung for stability to the Christian absolutes of good and evil.

The Great God Brown opened to respectful, often puzzled reviews and proved unexpectedly popular with the public. It ran for 283 performances, and the published text sold well. The O'Neills remained in New York until February 24, when they sailed for Bermuda. There they rented a fine old estate called Bellevue in Paget East—twenty-five acres with a sizable house and a private beach.

While Agnes and Oona and Shane and Fifine Clark settled in, Eugene immediately resumed work on *Lazarus Laughed*. Mourning led him to obsess about abstract issues of death and loss: the fear of death and loss, the attraction of death, and the denial of its permanence and importance. Having survived his own near-death by suicide, Eugene might be forgiven for thinking himself an authority on how it might feel to lose one's fear of death. At the same time, having lost several friends to suicide or sudden death, and having lost the other O'Neills, the playwright was equally interested in the effect of the death and resurrection on the risen man's kin.

The start on *Lazarus Laughed* that he had made the previous year now seemed hurried and shallow. He strove to make Lazarus a Zarathustran figure whose survival of death placed him psychologically beyond good and evil and made him heedless of the destructive power he held over the mortals around him. Preoccupied with the magnitude of the task, O'Neill worked long hours every day to rewrite the scenes previously drafted.

The play is effective enough that in reading it, one may wish that it could be transformed into an epic Russian film, and its labored dialogue retranslated into the terse English of subtitles. As it stands, the lines seem impossible for an actor to speak without sounding self-consciously weighty. Seduced by the grandeur of his subject, O'Neill echoed the style of *Thus Spake Zarathustra* in the Thomas Common translation he had read and reread. With its masked choruses and actors, and choric speech and movement, the play would strike potential producers as more pageant than drama. Despite the problem of the play's language, O'Neill succeeded in giving Lazarus something close to the stature of the gods and heroes as Nietzsche conceptualizes them in *The Birth of Tragedy*. That O'Neill well knew how turgid the dialogue of the play might sound on stage is revealed in a particular recurrent idea he had for casting the play. For decades, even long after the singer was dead, O'Neill told people he wanted Lazarus played in Russian by the great basso Fyodor Chaliapin (who spoke little English). No one else, O'Neill thought, could sound the laughter or convey the largeness of the role and the idea.

The creative impulse carried him along. Working every day, O'Neill finished a draft of *Lazarus Laughed* in early May and almost immediately began working double shifts, "scheming out" *Strange Interlude* by day and revising *Lazarus Laughed* by lamplight. Weeks earlier, having recently read the Arthur Symons translation of Hofmannsthal's *Electra,* he had got the "idea [to] use Greek Tragedy plot in modern setting" (WD, 25). Evidently, this was the starting point for O'Neill's version of Aeschylus' *Oresteia.* The creative upwelling seems to have come partly from his commitment to renounce alcohol and partly from the self-analytic process encouraged by his sessions with Dr. Hamilton—specifically, by O'Neill's fascination with the process and insights derived from free association. Writing *Strange Interlude* would take him deeper than ever into mourning; mourning preoccupies the main characters of the play. O'Neill worked on *Strange Interlude* until mid-June when the family returned to the States.

While he was writing, he also continued reading serious writers on a variety of topics from psychoanalysis to studies of ancient cultures and religions. Along with reading scholarly works on early Greek philosophy, on the Talmud and the Koran, and on the new sociology, he began studying Attic Greek and told a friend that he wanted to learn enough to get a sense of the spirit behind the classic tragedies. The intellectual work combined with the self-analytic work to lay the foundation for a great change in O'Neill's mind, his sense of himself, and his sense of the world. It was the consolidation of a change from the virtual nihilism of his youth to the unfocused rejection of pessimism that had marked his better moments since he began to find his stride as a dramatist.

A few years later in "Memoranda on Masks" O'Neill would describe the position he sought to create for the theater in the modern world. Echoing Nietzsche's *Birth of Tragedy,* O'Neill decried the loss to the modern world of the sacred role of the theater. In plays like *Electra,* he aimed to restore to the theater its function as a temple where starving human souls might renew themselves in celebration and worship of Dionysos. Adopting as his own the contempt for later Greek tragedy that Nietzsche considered decadent (the work of Sophocles and especially Euripides), O'Neill tried to make Aeschylus his model. In fact, however, his plays would almost always resemble those of Sophocles more nearly than they would those of Aeschylus or Euripides. O'Neill now substituted a quasi–Attic Greek view of the world for the pessimism and nihilism of his earlier life. He pointed himself toward the future with more evident optimism than he had previously known. The emerging worldview would be visible in the next two plays he would write, *Strange Interlude* and *Dynamo.*

The O'Neills liked their rented house, Bellevue, very well and were about to sign a long lease. But before they could complete the contract, they found the shell of a large early eighteenth-century house on a property called Spithead, set in a private harbor. It had been built as a base for privateers. They found the setting and the story irresistible. For seventeen thousand dollars they bought Spithead. The house had long stood empty and would eventually cost another twenty thousand in extensive rebuilding and remodeling that would take years (LS, 238). Most of the inner structure of the house was beyond repair and had to be replaced. A second house on the Spithead property also needed repair but was more nearly habitable. There the O'Neills settled in December, while a builder worked on the main house. They planned to pay for the remodeling from the sale of Brook Farm.

In March Eugene had been invited by Yale to accept an honorary doctorate. After initially declining, he changed his mind, and one of the first things he did on returning to the States in mid-June was to proceed to New Haven for the ceremony. Afterward, he decided that he was glad he had done it, and he claimed to feel changed inside. The acceptance suggests a new tolerance on O'Neill's part for social institutions, with all their faults and impingements on the freedom of the spirit, a shift hardly predictable even a year earlier. On future occasions O'Neill would sometimes watch a Yale football game from President Angell's box.

The fact is that, like it or not, O'Neill was now a public person. He was nearly as famous a writer as his father had been an actor, and his reputation was growing. From the mid-1920s on, O'Neill would be as renowned and admired a figure as Dreiser or Joyce was or as the young Hemingway would become, and he would be regularly mentioned in connection with the Nobel Prize. Despite being a reluctant (though polite) interview subject, he had become an object of considerable biographical interest. Numerous brief biographies had appeared in newspapers, but he was now the object of more extensive attention. His return to New York in June 1926 prompted several requests for interviews.

One of these was from Elizabeth Shepley Sergeant, who was interviewing a series of notable Americans for the *New Republic;* he had admired her portrait of Bobby Jones. She was invited to spend a couple of days at the O'Neills, Eugene found the interview pleasant, and a few months later wrote to her that he thought her essay "the best thing ever done about me" (LS, 213). Sergeant became a steadfast friend.

O'Neill was less enthusiastic about the book-length work, part biography and part commentary on the plays, being written about him by a theater reviewer, Barrett Clark. The playwright cooperated to the extent of agreeing to read the proofs and correct any errors of fact that he noticed. In a letter to Clark that spring, O'Neill mentioned his own involvement in correcting the long biographical chapter and making changes, even changes in individual words, and recommending numerous cuts. The autobiographical impulse was so strong that he could not help taking over the task, even when someone else was writing the work!

Trying to stand back, he commented on the strange experience of reading Clark's description of himself. It "is legend. It isn't really true," he wrote. "It isn't I. And the truth would make such a much more interesting—and incredible—legend." He muses about "shaming the devil" and mustering "the nerve" to write his own version of the story. His own version would be justified because there was no living person a biographer might consult who had known him "intimately in more than one phase of a life that has passed through many entirely distinct periods" (SL, 203).

As he thought about writing an autobiography, O'Neill wondered whether he could do it at all; "for when memory brings back this picture or episode . . . I simply cannot recognize that person in myself nor understand him nor his acts as mine (although objectively I can) although my reason tells me he was undeniably I" (SL, 203). The contorted and uncorrected sentences show O'Neill discovering a dissociation between knowledge of events in the past and the feelings that originally accompanied them; the dissociation makes the past seem unreal when he reads it in prose, especially that of someone else who could not know the feelings. It further suggests why O'Neill had to express his autobiographical impulse indirectly, through fictive characters and events. Dramatic structures allowed him to represent the complex of feelings and thoughts that he experienced in reality but could not evoke in narrative prose.

With his newly won sobriety in mind, O'Neill decided not to challenge temptation by spending the summer in Provincetown with old drinking friends. He had not enjoyed Nantucket the previous summer, and this time he asked his agent, Dick Madden, to suggest something else. Madden's partner Bess Marbury was about to leave for Belgrade Lakes in Maine and recommended the area to the O'Neills, who made reservations. After the trip to New Haven and a stay in New London to watch the boat races, they went to Maine.

The cabin they were assigned was called Loon Lodge. In July O'Neill confided to Macgowan that what with their recent stays in both Bellevue and Loon Lodge, he suspected God of "becoming a symbolist" (SL, 206). This was not all that the Fates had up their sleeves. Soon after arriving in Maine, the O'Neills went to call on Bess Marbury, whose suggestion had brought them to the lakes. At Bess's cottage O'Neill encountered Carlotta Monterey, who had acted in the uptown production of *The Hairy Ape* and whom O'Neill had previously met just after his mother's death. She was to become O'Neill's third wife, and he her fourth husband. In the summer of 1926, Carlotta seemed to many people to be making a play for Eugene's attention. She went so far as to invite herself along on some of his daily canoe tours of the lake, although she could not swim and was afraid of water. O'Neill's attention was firmly fixed on his play in progress, *Strange Interlude,* and for the time being, Carlotta was a mild distraction.

Despite the afternoons with Carlotta, the distracting presence of biographers, and the closer-than-usual proximity of his children and their noise, O'Neill tried to focus as well as he could that summer on loss and reparation. Without alcohol, nothing buffered the morbidity of his mood or the swings in his feelings about the marriage. He wrote long letters to Macgowan complaining about the lack of "real" friends who might serve, as alcohol formerly had, to ease tension, both the tension within himself and the usually silent strain between him and Agnes.

Indeed, giving up alcohol was in itself as real and complex a loss as the deaths of people. "I rather feel the void," he wrote to Macgowan on August 7, "left by those companionable or (even when most horrible) intensely dramatic phantoms and obsessions, which, with caressing claws in my heart and brain, used to lead me for weeks at a time, otherwise lonely, down the ever-changing vistas of that No-Mans-Land lying between the D.T.s and Reality as we suppose it." At thirty-seven, he was looking back on about twenty-two years of hard drinking off and on and felt an inner "maladjustment" to this new "cleaner, greener land." The change made him imagine "getting over leprosy." He added, "One feels so normal with so little to be normal about. One misses playing solitaire with one's scales" (SL, 210).

All the thoughts and feelings about losses were being concentrated in the act of reparation that was the writing of *Strange Interlude*. Mourning inhibited permeates the play from the very first words until the last. When Charlie Marsden enters at the opening curtain, his first set of associations leads him to think of his father's dying when Charlie was a boy, a death he still mourns. As he thinks about his father, he becomes again, according to the stage directions, the "adolescent boy he had been at the time of his father's death" (CP2, 634). Charlie's associations lead him immediately to another death, that of his host's wife, the mother of the other main character, Nina Leeds, who died when Nina was fourteen. Charlie has little to say about Mrs. Leeds, and throughout the play, Nina herself says nothing of the loss of her mother. Yet an audience attentive to the theme of mourning inhibited must infer that Nina's obsession with the loss of her lover, Gordon, and her acute sensitivity to subsequent losses must ultimately derive from her loss at fourteen of her mother—a circumstance she shares with her creator.

Whether or not he understood it as a general psychoanalytic idea, O'Neill intuitively grasped that people who themselves are still dependent cannot complete the process of mourning. The losses in adolescence suffered by Charlie and Nina must reflect O'Neill's understanding of the effects on him of the losses he experienced at fourteen.

The theme of unmourned losses continues to develop in the first moments of the play before Professor Leeds enters. Charlie thinks about the dead Gordon Shaw, who had had a brief, intense romance with Nina just before going off to war, where he was killed. Now, a few months after the armistice, Professor Leeds thinks of little but his daughter's grief and his own guilt over having prevented Nina's marriage to Gordon. Nina is herself full of guilt for having withheld herself from Gordon, and in her intense grief for him she focuses on a longing for him and for the child of his she might have now if she had not obeyed her father. The main overt theme in her relationship with her father is her struggle to become independent of him, a struggle that is not helped by his wish to keep her with him as an unmarried housekeeper.

She has decided that the way she can atone for withholding herself from Gordon is to become a volunteer nurse in a hospital for wounded veterans, and soon this decision leads to her giving herself sexually to virtually any wounded soldier who wants her. It is worth mentioning that, clinically speaking, promiscuity in adolescent daughters is typically associated with their attempts to separate their self-image from the internal image of the mother. Whether or not O'Neill intuitively understood such a process in adolescent girls, he may have recognized it as an aspect of his own adolescent drinking and sexual promiscuity; and however he understood it consciously, his writer's intuition led him to present Nina's behavior in a way that is psychologically authentic and that coheres with the theme of the play. Nina's promiscuity, like her inhibited mourning, is connected at many points with her battle to become independent of her father. If Nina were a real person instead of a dramatic character, one might speculate that behind her problem with her father lies a more obscure difficulty in separating herself from her lingering image of her (dead) mother. Such is the play's wealth of detail in matters of dependency and mourning, and in the clinical authenticity of the character portrait, that a psychologically minded reader is led to speculate beyond the borders of the text.

When Professor Leeds dies (before the beginning of act 2), Nina, who is still obsessed with the death of Gordon, consciously feels nothing about her father's death; she seems so numbed that Charlie decides working in the hospital has "killed her soul" (CP2, 656). Charlie understands the distortions in Nina's mourning no better than he understands his own, but O'Neill now introduces another point of view, that of Dr. Edmund Darrell, a neurologist who thinks of Nina as an experimental psychologist might, and who tries to explain to Charlie that Nina's lack of feeling is a sign of her being on the verge of psychological collapse. Believing that the cure is to transfer her dependency to a husband, the doctor has picked out the boyish Sam Evans as one who will not demand much of her.

Soon Nina is married to Sam, and shortly after she is pregnant. At this point the plot is weakest. O'Neill has Mrs. Evans, Sam's mother, who appears only in this scene, approach Nina with a long and improbable-sounding narrative. We learn that Sam has grown up in boarding schools, completely isolated from his parents, not even seeing them in summers—all of this arranged by his mother to keep him from discovering that his father is insane, and that insanity affects most other members of the Evans family. She is obsessed by the belief that Sam may become insane, but she believes that if he does not know about the hereditary condition, he may escape it. Having guessed that Nina is pregnant, Mrs. Evans insists that she must abort the child and never have another with Sam for fear that it would be affected by the hereditary Evans insanity. She counsels Nina to find a healthy lover if she must have a child.

A director looking to shorten this extremely long play could probably eliminate the character Mrs. Evans and most of the material about the hereditary insanity, and so remove the most conspicuous distraction from the plot's coherence. But a biographer notes the distraction with interest. The details in this material all seem to refer to prominent events in the life of the author and his family. Eugene told his wives that before he knew of her addiction, he believed his mother was insane and that he was likely to become insane also; he also could trace his alcoholism, which made him at times delusional and otherwise deranged, back to both grandfathers. Eugene spent his years in boarding schools feeling that he had been cast out by his family, and for several years he apparently seldom saw his mother. Act 3 of *Strange Interlude* suggests that he believed in retrospect that his father had put him into boarding school to prevent him from learning about his mother's drug addiction. He also believed that his mother had aborted several pregnancies and that the abortions had greatly affected her. O'Neill probably means to refer also in that act to his mother's loss of her second son. The same associative process that O'Neill was using to develop the characters and themes of the play probably also led him to include personal material connected with his own difficulties in growing up, which must have seemed related but which he could not integrate well with the rest of the material in the play.

The abortion represents the next loss in a growing list of losses that Nina suffers in the play. Before long Nina has made Ned Darrell her lover, partly in order to replace her lost child, and partly so that she can transfer to him the old dependency on her father that she had previously transferred to Sam. This is the pattern for dealing with losses that will prevail throughout the play. Each time there is a loss, the bereaved person denies feelings of grief by substituting a new person for the lost one. The process allows avoidance of the pain of fully feeling a loss but eliminates the possibility of ever outgrowing the original state of dependency.

From the standpoint of object relations theory, the lost object is replaced, not by a new mental structure that permits growth and development, but by a person who is incorporated into the old mental image of the original lost person. For Nina it seems that the original loss was the death of her mother; the internal image of the mother was then enlarged to incorporate that of her father, on whom she became dependent thereafter. When her father died, she transferred the dependency to her husband, and when she found him fragile, she transferred it to Darrell and later to her son with Darrell, Gordon.

The lost lover, Gordon Shaw, serves as a representation of the accumulating mass of losses. As in life, the process works fairly well. If Nina can never grow to psychic autonomy, if she is always sharply limited in the interpersonal relationships she can have, she nevertheless proves surprisingly strong, surviving a long list of losses. At the end, having lost Ned Darrell and her husband, and finally her son (to his wife), she is ready to grow old with Marsden, who has known her since she was born. She adapts to losses by finding people who will serve functions similar to intrapsychic structures she cannot develop.

O'Neill creates in Charlie Marsden a character who parallels Nina in his reaction to losses and in his psychological development. When his mother eventually dies, he at first transfers his dependency to his sister, who moves in with him and takes his mother's place. When the sister also dies, Charlie again defers mourning when he finds Nina available and in need of someone like himself. Both Nina and Charlie have always seemed fragile to themselves and to others. Each loss takes them to the brink of collapse, and neither ever accepts or works through mourning for any of the lost people. Yet in the end, by one means or another, they survive.

Such survival was on O'Neill's own mind at the time he was writing *Strange Interlude*. By mid-October, the time of his thirty-eighth birthday, he had drafted the first four acts and moved with his family back to New York. Agnes took the children to visit her parents in New Jersey, and Eugene stayed at the Harvard Club for a few days before moving to the Wentworth. He saw Carlotta several times while he remained in the City to work with a new production of *Beyond the Horizon* being done by the Actors' Theatre, the latest descendant of the Provincetown Players. Agnes took the children to Brook Farm to close the house for the winter, and Eugene remained in New York. Sheaffer reports that the playwright consulted Dr. Hamilton about some of the psychological ideas in *Strange Interlude* (LS, 233). But O'Neill must have also had other matters on his mind: it was apparently about this time that Eugene and Carlotta became lovers. Sheaffer is certain that despite many temptations and opportunities, O'Neill had never before been unfaithful to Agnes.

Eugene was now more aware of dissatisfactions in his marriage, and the dissatisfactions seemed greater than they had previously. Nevertheless, the marriage did not seem to either husband or wife to be at a crossroads. Rather, relations between them seemed static and distant. Eugene had had the flirtation with a neighbor in Bermuda; and (from Sheaffer's interview notes) it seems that Agnes had had love affairs in Bermuda of some sort and that she told Eugene about them. She seemed not to be troubled by his interest in Carlotta, whom she considered too inferior intellectually to be a real challenge. Eugene himself seems to have had no clear idea what he wanted or what he was doing with Carlotta when the affair started. At some level he may have been contemplating the sort of change in his life that he was writing about in *Strange Interlude,* in which old dependencies would be transferred to a new person. The play, for all its public notoriety about broken taboos, conveys no sense that its characters were libertine or even that any of them found joy in sex; sex in the play seems mainly a means to express and gratify lingering needs related to dependency.

If the play expressed O'Neill's state at the time, it suggested mainly that his inhibited grieving left him often feeling emotionally stifled and subject to unpredictable outbursts. If he tried to awaken Agnes to his needs or to revive the former intensity between them, he found her involved with their baby daughter or her social life. Agnes believed that Eugene sometimes resented Oona, as he had sometimes resented Shane.

That is how matters stood when he turned to Carlotta, with her genius for domestic management. Several of O'Neill's longtime friends told Sheaffer that later, at the time of the breakup, they assumed that the playwright had grown tired of the chaos of home life with Agnes and wanted someone who could manage his home in a way that would let him devote all his attention to writing. Several of Carlotta's early gifts to Eugene were ordinary articles of clothing of the sort a wife might buy a husband: underwear, shirts, and the like.

A remarkable person, Carlotta has inspired and so far defeated several attempts at a full biography. The following sketch derives from published accounts by the Gelbs, Louis Sheaffer, and José Quintero, all of whom got to know her in her old age while they worked on biographies of O'Neill; and especially from Margaret Loftus Ranald's account in *The Eugene O'Neill Companion,* probably the fullest existing biography of Carlotta. The sketch is also influenced by oral anecdotes told by José Quintero and personal communications from Margaret Loftus Ranald. Carlotta's accounts to biographers and others of her life with O'Neill tended to be marked by self-contradictory details and generalizations, by extremes of feeling and judgment, and by the greatest impatience with disagreement. Her voluminous revised diaries for the years 1928–1943 are at the Beinecke at Yale, as is some of her correspondence. The Huntington Library also holds some of her letters and papers. The diaries provide a revised and rewritten day-to-day account of her impressions and feelings about her world.

Carlotta was born in northern California, probably on December 28, 1888, ten weeks after Eugene's birth. Her name was originally Hazel Tharsing. She was born to Nellie Gotchett Tharsing, who had been eighteen when she married Christian Nielson Tharsing, a Danish sailor of about forty who had left the sea and was working an orchard. Nellie hailed from a mixed European background that included German, French Swiss, and New York Dutch. She married Christian at the strong urging of her mother, not long before she gave birth to Hazel. The couple remained together for a few years; then Nellie left, handing Hazel over to a married sister, Mrs. John Shay, who raised the girl along with her own two sons.

Nellie went on to become a notable person in the Bay Area, a woman who carried on serial affairs, often with prominent and wealthy men. For a time it was her business to acquire run-down boardinghouses, which, with a domestic genius that Hazel would inherit, she would clean up, tastefully remodel, make profitable, and sell for a profit, some of which she invested in the next project. She had solid friendships with her lovers that tended to last long after the affairs were over. She was respected as a formidable poker player.

Brought up as a daughter in her aunt's family, Hazel was a beautiful child, as surviving pictures show. She probably attended public schools in Oakland, and her aunt, a strict Baptist, undoubtedly sent her to church and Sunday school. The aunt also arranged for elocution lessons. From 1902 to 1905, while Eugene was at Betts, Hazel attended St. Gertrude's Academy, a Catholic boarding school in Rio Vista, California. There she was remembered as a loner who made occasional dramatic gestures, such as describing in grisly, improbable detail an eye operation she apparently underwent.

In 1906, at seventeen, she was sent or taken to Europe for further education. She studied French in Paris for a time, and in London she enrolled in Sir Herbert Beerbohm Tree's Academy of the Dramatic Arts. She had a short, sturdy figure, but a face of exceptional beauty and a long neck, which made her seem elegant. Much later Lynn Fontanne described Carlotta's voice as "deep," and "rasping, husky," a startling voice, given her "divine face" (LS, 283). In 1907 Nellie Tharsing sent a photograph of Hazel to a beauty contest sponsored by one of her poker-playing friends, the editor of an Oakland newspaper. She was named Miss California and was automatically entered in a national contest. She returned to the States briefly for the contest, in which she was named runner-up.

Having developed a faintly Latin look as she matured, Hazel devised for herself a suitable stage name, Carlotta Monterey, spelled like the name of the dramatically beautiful California peninsula. In the 'teens and 1920s she was known as one of the most beautiful women in the world, and as a poor and exceptionally nervous actor. She often said that she hated acting and the stage.

While living in Europe she met a Scottish lawyer, John Moffatt, a member of the family that made Coates thread. The couple went to New York and married in 1911. They remained married until 1914, by which time Moffatt had suffered several financial reversals. They divorced amicably but remained friendly; in old age, after O'Neill was dead, they corresponded frequently. Carlotta resumed her acting career when she and Moffatt separated.

In 1916, now twenty-seven, Carlotta acted with Lou Tellegen in a touring company production of *The Bird of Paradise* that went to the Bay Area. According to Carlotta, Tellegen told her she would never mature as an actress until she had given birth; so she decided to marry again. While visiting her mother in Oakland, she met Nellie's current friend, Melvin Chapman, and his son. She soon married Melvin Jr., a twenty-year-old law student, and in August 1917, gave birth to Cynthia Jane Chapman. Cynthia was a pretty child, born with a slight facial imperfection that Carlotta could not accept, and although the imperfection was easily corrected, Carlotta never formed any bond with her daughter. As Cynthia later saw it, her mother never forgave her for being the person she was born to be. Shortly after Cynthia was born, Carlotta and Chapman separated. As Nellie had once given Hazel to someone else to raise, Carlotta gave the baby to Nellie and returned to acting. She and Chapman divorced in 1923.

About 1920 Carlotta became the mistress of an elderly New York investment banker and philanthropist, James Speyer, a childless widower. The relationship went on more than six years, until Carlotta had become involved with O'Neill. Speyer and Carlotta never lived together, but for a time he provided her with a fine apartment, and before they parted he gave her a lifetime annuity that brought her an income averaging about fourteen thousand dollars a year. Further, he taught her how to invest her money, knowledge she would pass on to Eugene.

In 1923, while she continued her friendship with James Speyer, Carlotta began to live with the famous caricaturist Ralph Barton, a bon vivant and a dandy as dramatically handsome as Carlotta herself. He was an early member of the *New Yorker* group, a close friend of Charlie Chaplin, and, like Chaplin in those days, an energetic womanizer. Barton apparently never knew about Speyer. In her memoir *Past Imperfect,* the actress Ilka Chase described Carlotta's superb management of her and Barton's domestic life and their entertainment of the celebrated and interesting, as well as the intensity of ardor and hatred that marked the relationship (1942, 61–62). Barton is said to have suffered from manic-depressive illness, and Carlotta, at the least, tended toward extremes of feeling and intermittent explosions. No one who knew either of them predicted long life for the relationship. It blew up early in 1926 when she found him with another woman. Barton and Carlotta were assumed to have married about 1923, but in fact, as Sheaffer discovered (but did not publish), they married hastily in 1926 just before Carlotta filed for divorce. (I am indebted to Margaret Loftus Ranald for informing me of the details of Carlotta's marriage to Barton.)

At some point, Carlotta entered into a relationship with Elizabeth Marbury, the partner of O'Neill's literary agent, a person with connections in the highest artistic and financial circles on both sides of the Atlantic. Bess Marbury had for decades been inseparable from the celebrated decorator Elsie de Wolfe, and she seems to have planned for Carlotta to take Elsie's place. After the breakup with Barton, Carlotta took over the management of Marbury's home and kitchen with a style and efficiency that prompted the actress Florence Reed to tell Sheaffer, "[Carlotta] had, I am not exaggerating, a genius for it" (LS, 229). Bess Marbury decided to adopt Carlotta legally in order to make her her heir and, apparently with Carlotta's consent, informed Nellie Tharsing of her intention. In the summer of 1926, Carlotta went with Bess to Belgrade Lakes in Maine, where she met O'Neill. The following fall they became lovers.

18

Gene and Carlotta Abroad
1927–1931

THE AFFAIR WITH CARLOTTA, WHICH began when Eugene saw her a few times in October or November 1926, was at first probably more the result of Carlotta's determination than of Eugene's attraction. He was undoubtedly vulnerable. Apart from the deterioration in his marriage, he felt, both consciously and unconsciously, a constant sense of deprivation from giving up alcohol. The offer of a beautiful woman's admiration must have seemed at the least a distraction from the void within.

Late that November the O'Neills returned to Bermuda and moved into the gatehouse at Spithead. While builders restored the main house, Eugene revised *Marco Millions* and *Lazarus Laughed* and drafted *Strange Interlude*. On March 4 he wrote Carlotta with the news that he had finished the draft, and the next day he thanked her for a portrait she had sent of herself. The O'Neills moved into the main house, while work continued around them. They began to entertain a stream of visitors.

Almost immediately he set to work on *Dynamo,* a play idea for which he had high hopes. In it he would test metaphysical ideas deriving from Nietzsche and his reading in ancient religions. It would be the first of what he would privately call his God Is Dead trilogy, or, more formally, Myth Plays for the God-Forsaken. In them he meant to explore the effect on humanity's soul of the substitution of scientific rationalism and materialism for religious faith.

The germ of *Dynamo* was an idea for a play he called "Billionaire," which O'Neill derived from the ancient myth of Midas. The billionaire eventually kills himself in a replica of the Taj Mahal that he has built to honor the god who gave Midas his gift (Floyd 1981, 168). When O'Neill recalled that the god was Dionysos, the possibilities for ironic tragedy must have seemed irresistible—to have his modern materialist build a Taj Mahal to the god who was also the patron of Greek tragedy! Little wonder that O'Neill had such hopes for the material that he would work on it in *Dynamo* and later in *Days Without End,* and later still in the Cycle, until illness finally made him stop writing. The thesis of *Dynamo* was that people deprived of God or gods will make gods of scientific icons. Reuben Light, the apostate son of a preacher and a convert to science and electricity, makes of the whirring hydroelectric dynamo a mother-god something like the pre-Olympian Gaia or Cybele. In an ecstatic state, he embraces the copper skin of the dynamo's vast body and, seizing the carbon brushes, immolates himself by electrocution.

O'Neill worked daily on the scenario and was about half through when word came that the Theatre Guild wanted to produce *Marco Millions* and was seeking an option to produce *Strange Interlude* and three future plays. He set aside the *Dynamo* scenario and began revising *Strange Interlude;* he also began cutting *Marco Millions.*

In April, Agnes went to Connecticut to visit her father, who was dying of tuberculosis and had gone into the same sanatorium, now updated, that Eugene had entered in 1912. In one of his better moments, Eugene composed an encouraging letter to Teddy Boulton, but his mood was often grim. As of old, Eugene felt acute anxiety the moment Agnes left. Within hours of the ship's departure he wrote her of "a fit of hysterical crying" on the bed; "my whole control seems gone" (SL, 238). The next day, a little more serene, he began a letter musing about her "dear, familiar, beautiful face" as he had seen it disappear aboard the departing ship (SL, 239).

Later in the same letter he begged her not to think of the Carlotta "incident," as if it were a finished event. Evidently referring to a recent fight with Agnes, he asked forgiveness for his "utter lack of a sense of humor at that time" and his "childish vanity" and begged her to believe that he "was never in love with" Carlotta, no matter what he said in the heat of battle. The tone of the letter, exceptionally strained throughout, is reminiscent of the mannered posing of Con Melody in *A Touch of the Poet.* It is a tone that O'Neill seldom shows in his letters, although Agnes once told Sheaffer that if he wanted to know what O'Neill sounded like in daily life he could find it in Con Melody's speeches to his mirror (LS papers). He believes all his vanity and "inner secrets" have been exposed by his revealing too many doubts and confusions that came to the surface when he spoke to her of the incident. He protests that he writes at such length of the "C." episode only to "relieve" Agnes's mind of "the slightest consideration of it" (SL, 240).

Among many things, the letter reflects one side of an intense ambivalence O'Neill felt about the possibility of leaving Agnes and going to Carlotta. A month after Agnes's trip, O'Neill went to New York, where he stayed with Lawrence Langner to work out a contract and discuss cuts in *Marco Millions* aimed at reducing the Guild's production costs. He saw Carlotta six times during the week he was there and presumably was glad to be with her. But shortly after his return to Bermuda, he wrote to Macgowan (who knew about the affair and sympathized) how good it felt to be with Agnes and the children. Through the rest of the summer he revised *Strange Interlude* and worked on the proofs of *Lazarus Laughed* and an introduction, which he eventually abandoned. During this time he seldom corresponded with Carlotta, and when he did, he found himself unable to explain why it was hard to write to her (SL, 248).

It was most uncharacteristic of O'Neill to tolerate in silence any separation from a lover. The pattern of constant letter writing to the beloved harked back to the stream of letters he had composed to family and friends from his exile at boarding school, and that habit was very marked in the affairs he had had from 1913 on. Apparently, being married and being with his family eased the driving separation anxiety that had characterized his unmarried days and his separations from Agnes. When he was away from Agnes and his family, being with Carlotta did not altogether prevent attacks of intense separation anxiety. Away from Carlotta, with Agnes and his family, he felt little of the old urgent need to write constantly. He had not yet formed the bond of oneness with Carlotta that he had with most of the women he had been close to. Lacking that inner bond, he reacted simply as other people might in the circumstances. The weighting of his ambivalence did not at present favor making a change in his circumstances.

Life went on in Bermuda. Eugene and Agnes tried to speed up the renovation of Spithead. The cost of the work made money tight, for

Brook Farm had not sold, and no funds were forthcoming from productions or publications. While Eugene was in bed much of July with the flu, he decided that Bermuda was too hot and boring in the summer. Much of the time he and Agnes were feeling distant from each other, but at moments they were intensely close.

In late August, feeling ill, restless, and in need of a change, Eugene decided to go to New York to see his doctor, to push the sale of Brook Farm, and to hasten the publication of *Lazarus Laughed*. He begged Agnes to go with him to New York, but she protested that moving the children was too complicated. He accused her of having a lover she did not want to leave. She insisted that they could not afford for both of them to go, and that one of them needed to supervise the builders. So he went alone. He saw several doctors and complained to them of general fatigue. Sheaffer reports that he weighed 137 pounds in his clothes (LS, 262). The doctors found nothing amiss except nervous tension, but eventually they began treatment for a thyroid deficiency and a prostate problem, neither confirmed.

As soon as he boarded the ship, Eugene began a letter to Agnes, and he thereafter wrote daily about missing her and the children and wanting to improve things between them. He pretended to be understanding about her supposed lover, but the tone of the letter was generally contentious. In words that might apply to both of them, she retaliated: "You love me & need me now, yes, because you're bored and lonely—but that love speedily deteriorates into an intense irritation as soon as we've been together two weeks." She felt so frustrated, she wrote, that she was tempted to end it all with her "little pistol." She continued, "Bermuda is so empty & lonely, and then on top of that, one hears again the old mistrust." She offered Carlotta the job of running Spithead; she was "much more beautiful than" Agnes herself. He complained that Agnes seemed not to care about him or the marriage and Carlotta treated him more kindly than his wife did (LS, 264–65).

Carlotta summered in Baden-Baden but returned to New York on September 9, nearly two weeks after Eugene had arrived. From then until he returned to Bermuda on October 19, they saw each other most days. The fall of 1927 was decisive for the pair; she sought and received permission from James Speyer to discontinue their relationship, on the grounds that O'Neill wanted her to marry him so that he could escape a disruptive marriage that had broken down and that he needed her to make a home for him (Gelbs, 635). Speyer agreed and met O'Neill, who took to the older man with a warmth unusual for him; they saw each other several times over the fall and winter. Sheaffer learned that until the 1940s O'Neill believed that Speyer had simply looked at Carlotta as the daughter he had never had (LS, 532). Sheaffer points out that when O'Neill returned to Spithead for a month and then departed again for New York in late November, he brought none of his diaries, private papers, or manuscripts, thereby implying that he fully expected to return to Bermuda (LS, 277).

Probably on Carlotta's advice, he wrote in December to ask that Agnes send his manuscripts and other documents, on the pretext of a possible sale to an autograph dealer. Trying to be high-minded, he wrote of his concern that Agnes have a chance for "any happiness you can get" (SL, 269). At other times he betrayed a stronger feeling, a resentment that she did not care about his work, whereas Carlotta cared passionately about it.

In December, Brook Farm sold at a loss of about ten thousand dollars, and Agnes, leaving the children with Mrs. Clark, traveled to New York. Finally taking the affair seriously, Agnes came to New York and checked into the Wentworth, where Eugene and Carlotta had rooms on separate floors. Knowing full well the intensity of Eugene's need for her, Agnes felt certain she could save the marriage if she tried. But Agnes told Sheaffer that except for one amorous evening, things between the couple wavered between uneasy harmony and Strindbergian quarrels (LS, 280). By day, Eugene attended rehearsals of *Marco Millions* and *Strange Interlude*.

While Agnes and Eugene bickered, Carlotta learned that Agnes was present in the hotel and demanded that Eugene force his wife to leave. Although Eugene did not want Agnes at the hotel either, he did not take well to Carlotta's decree. She became so insistent about it that he walked out, declaring that he was finished with her, and turned his attention to the settlement with Agnes (LS, 280).

Eugene now decided that regardless of what happened with Carlotta, the marriage with Agnes could not be saved. With the guidance of his lawyer, Harry Weinberger, he began negotiations with Agnes over a property division and settlement and a support plan for her and the children. A plan was proposed that would give Agnes six thousand to ten thousand dollars a year, depending on Eugene's income, and life control over Spithead, including the right to rent it out. Ownership of the property was to pass to the children after her death.

Agnes agreed to the proposal before she returned to Bermuda, but later she began to ask for more. Negotiations would continue for two years and become hopelessly bitter. Eventually she agreed to the original terms, but by then the bitterness had permanently divided Agnes and Eugene. Sheaffer believes that it contributed heavily to the estrangement of Eugene from his younger children, especially Oona, who barely knew her father when her parents separated. As for Shane, he suffered a double loss, because the previous fall Mrs. Clark had returned to the States. She told Shane and others that she wanted to escape the muggy Bermuda climate; but she left after a row with Agnes, shortly after the separation. In several conversations with Sheaffer decades later, Agnes seemed defensive about Mrs. Clark's estrangement, a circumstance that permanently affected Shane (LS papers).

Whatever chance Shane might have had for ordinary development was probably impaired by the double loss of his adored father and his adoring Gaga. He was to flunk out of several schools, drift into heroin and other drug addictions, and eventually die a suicide. It is noteworthy, and perhaps it was inevitable, that Eugene, who had himself suffered so greatly from the effective loss of his parents when he was sent to boarding school at seven, should repeat his own early trauma with his seven-year-old son. From a psychoanalytic viewpoint, abandoning Shane seems to have been an unconscious acting-out of what O'Neill felt had been done to him at Shane's age. Perhaps if Eugene had been able to make more rapid progress through his mourning, he might have been more attentive to the effect on Shane of his departure. Whether that would have saved Shane or the marriage of Eugene and Agnes is less clear.

Once Agnes had agreed to the proposed settlement, a few days after *Marco Millions* opened in mid-January, she returned to Bermuda, and soon after, Carlotta and Eugene reconciled. *Strange Interlude* opened January 30, 1928, for a long run. The play brought O'Neill a third Pulitzer Prize. Eventually O'Neill earned about a quarter of a million dollars from productions and from sales of the published text, about a third of his life income. By now, news of the separation was in the press, and Eugene was convinced he could find nowhere in America the peace of mind he needed to write.

On February 10, Eugene and Carlotta secretly boarded the SS *Berengaria,* bound for London; they would not return to the United States for more than three years. After a week they went to Paris, where Carlotta bought an elegant Renault and hired a chauffeur; from Paris they traveled by car to Biarritz. After a few days, they rented Villa Marguerite in the town of Guéthary, France, where they lived until fall. When O'Neill sailed, the press picked up the story, and when his whereabouts could not be ascertained, the elopement and "disappearance" became front-page news. For the next year and a half, Eugene and Carlotta used a forwarding address and persuaded the few confidential friends who knew where they were to keep their secret.

Before the departure, Eugene wrote friendly, often disingenuous letters to Agnes, and he also wrote gently and fairly often to the children. But the tone of the letters to Agnes changed when it became clear to him that Agnes did not mean to act according to the agreement made between her lawyers and Harry Weinberger. It seemed to Eugene that she had reverted to thinking that he was in the grip of a transitory infatuation and that she could wait it out. Before he left for Europe, she invited him to come to Bermuda for a week. He declined, asking her to kiss the children for him, and closed with protestations of his loving friendship. Relations between the O'Neills grew steadily worse. Someone apparently wrote to Eugene suggesting that Agnes was becoming "promiscuous," sometimes in public, and he passed on the report to her in a letter, with a recommendation that she be careful about what the children saw.

For some months, he believed that in the long run Agnes would see that it would be in her and the children's interest if he and she could remain friendly. But later in the spring, her letters to Weinberger convinced Eugene that Agnes intended to make him so poor he would have to return to her. Her words on the subject to Sheaffer, thirty years later, were often ambiguous and contradictory, but Sheaffer's notes reveal that even decades afterward, she could not accept the reality of the break. As *Dynamo* was to show, Eugene's declaration was true that without a certain peace of mind he could not write well; and if he could not write, there would be little or no money for her and their children's support. Agnes acted as if she believed that pursuing her claims as doggedly as possible would close the rift.

The threat of poverty affected Eugene more than it might have years before. Part of the financial pressure O'Neill felt stemmed from his conviction that he needed to be free from immediate financial worry in order to write as well as he could. He had not forgotten the conditions in which he had composed his plays earlier in his career, but he could no longer tolerate the rough life he had once led. A further pressure came from worries that he would not be able to keep up with Carlotta financially. She had as much money as he did or more, and she knew much better how to use it. He would not accept money from her then or later. Throughout their years together, Eugene and Carlotta contributed equally to their living expenses.

Although Carlotta had spent much of her life in the public spotlight, she was extremely sensitive to the growing public scandal, and she pressed Eugene to try to stifle it. Possibly she feared that, egged on by Agnes, some reporter might discover her relationship with and indebtedness to Speyer, a discovery that would have given the lie to the story she had told Eugene and might have led Speyer's relatives to contest the annuity that he had settled on her.

Many of O'Neill's letters to Harry Weinberger show him powerfully affected by Carlotta's concern over the scandal, which would probably have bothered him less if it had not been for her distress. Most of the time in the early days of the elopement he felt squeezed between Carlotta's demands that they normalize their relations and Agnes's refusal to go ahead with the divorce. Though he sometimes pretended to Agnes that he did not care when, if ever, they obtained a divorce, he raged at Weinberger to try to hasten the process.

Agnes escalated the conflict by encouraging a tabloid journalist with whom she was now involved to present her case to the public. James Speyer, in the letters he sent to Carlotta several times a week, tried to assure both of them that the newspapers' interest would soon blow over, but Carlotta and Eugene, each for different reasons, seethed at every public reference to their situation.

Both the delays in the divorce and the publicity were the more intolerable because relations between Carlotta and Eugene, two tempestuous personalities, were often stormy. O'Neill's letters to Harry Weinberger sometimes rant so uncontrollably and at such length that the impression they give is of a man maddened; and in O'Neill's expectation that his lawyer will solve insoluble problems, one detects paternal transference.

Almost as soon as the couple rented Villa Marguerite, Eugene set to work on *Dynamo*. He finished a draft of the play by mid-August, but work on it did not go smoothly or well. Living under Carlotta's domestic sway took some getting used to. Although Eugene was personally neat and tidy, he had probably never in his life been asked to dress for dinner at home, and he had certainly never lived in a private home so finely decorated and expensively furnished. Except at his detested first boarding school, he had never lived in a home efficiently managed and shaped by a feminine sensibility, nor in one intended to manifest a sense of high style to the world. Nor had anyone previously tried to control his life as thoroughly as Carlotta now did. Sheaffer reports that she offered to type his correspondence for him, a practice that she maintained until the early 1940s. She used the opportunity to edit and censor his mail. Believing that most of O'Neill's old friends sided with Agnes against her, she took pains to control what reached him and some of what he sent (LS, 329).

O'Neill did not suspect the censorship until much later, but he saw and resisted other attempts to rule him. The extent of his discomfort emerged when an old drinking friend, the reporter Louis Kalonyme, came to Guéthary to visit and (according to Carlotta) to borrow money. Carlotta's diary for mid-May expressed shock at the roughness of Eugene's friend, and later at her lover's behavior in rough company. Already enraged at Agnes, O'Neill seized the excuse of company to get drunk. He behaved insultingly toward Carlotta and made a mess of a room with blue satin wall coverings. Once more, Eugene had ravaged a room, though the destruction was less thorough than in earlier such episodes. When he continued drinking the next day, Carlotta left but then changed her mind and returned, confiding at length in her diary her shock over Gene's becoming "a different person" under the influence of alcohol. Carlotta blamed Agnes for causing O'Neill's relapse and blamed him for doing what Agnes wanted.

Not neglecting a future audience of biographers, in the revised diary that she gave to Yale with the other O'Neill papers, Carlotta wrote of her shock: Eugene "has killed everything in me that spells love, loyalty, devotion and decency" (CM diary, May 15, 1928). The entries for the next several days mingle fact and fantasy to assure the reader of Carlotta's "strict" and protected upbringing and patrician family; on May 23 she describes the sailor father she barely knew as "a brilliant Dane, educated in Denmark, France, Germany, & China." Despite her years in the theater, her sheltered background, she implied, gave her no resources for coping with such insults as the drunken Eugene inflicted on her. No one could object to her resentment at being insulted; but it is remarkable that she felt the need to justify her outrage by confabulation.

Carlotta obtained bromide and other drugs to help Eugene recover from his hangover and drunkenness and despair. Whether the bromide was her idea or his is not known, but Carlotta's diary records that from this point on he took various drugs prescribed for her, often bromide, to cope with the vicissitudes of life and their relationship. As time passed, the diary increasingly came to read like a medical chart, recording their physical and mental ups and downs. A drive into Biarritz might exhaust both of them so greatly that they would both go immediately to bed on returning and not be able to rise readily the next morning. Probably both were still recovering from the relocation to Europe and from the upset of Eugene's drunken lapse. But the reports in Carlotta's diary that they were "exhausted" frequently, and often for little apparent cause, may imply that both were taking too much bromide; overreliance on the drug would later become a serious problem for both.

For three weeks, Eugene did not write. He returned to *Dynamo* in June but stopped again immediately. The couple set off in her Renault on a trip through southern France, from which they returned at the end of the month. They began planning a cruise of the Orient that would begin in October. Eugene had longed to take such a trip since his sailor days.

In late June, Eugene heard from his old friend Saxe Commins, who had come to Paris with his bride. Saxe had given up a successful dental practice to write novels while Dorothy Berliner, a classical pianist, prepared for a concert career. Saxe almost immediately visited Eugene in Guéthary and read the work on *Dynamo,* which greatly impressed him. He offered to type the manuscript for Eugene. For the next three months, much of Saxe's time was spent typing drafts and revisions. While acting as a volunteer typist for Eugene, Saxe decided he could not write fiction that stood up to his own standards; at the same time he found his true vocation, working with the manuscripts of others. His art and gift let him enter empathically into the spirit of another writer's work. The same gift made him the most loyal, selfless, and enduring friend Eugene would have for the rest of his life. Eventually Saxe would become one of the most respected editors in American publishing; in a career spanning thirty years, he worked with manuscripts by O'Neill, William Faulkner, Sinclair Lewis, Robinson Jeffers, and many other notable writers.

Saxe's interest got Eugene going again on *Dynamo,* and he rushed through the rest of the play, the draft of which he finished by August 21. Since his plays had begun to be performed, O'Neill had habitually kept a manuscript for some time, usually months, after completing work on it; then he would go over it again to make revisions and sometimes write further drafts before declaring it truly finished. This time, after only the briefest revisions, he rushed *Dynamo* off to the Guild, before he and Carlotta embarked for Asian ports. To his eventual regret, the play was immediately accepted and put into production.

Off they went. In early October they took separate cabins aboard the SS *André Lebon*. Through the first weeks, Eugene worked most mornings in his cabin at developing several new play ideas. Accompanied by a combination maid, masseuse, and companion, Mrs. Tuve Drew, Carlotta spent the day on deck, where she was joined by Eugene after lunch. So things went until they reached Singapore. Instead of enjoying their leisure, isolated from letters and other news of the divorce, Eugene worked on "It Cannot Be Mad," a sketch for a continuation of *Dynamo* that would eventually lead him into the Cycle that he would work on in the 1930s.

On board the ship, although things were peaceable between the two, Carlotta frequently reported in her diary a sense of foreboding: "Something awful is going to happen—*I know it!*" she wrote in her diary on October 14. She slept badly and reported a nightmare in which Eugene lost his manuscript "and I had a baby!!!?!!" She continued to worry, felt blue, but was cheered when they reached Colombo to retrieve a cable from Speyer—"Pappa" as she always called him. "Thank God he still thinks of us," she wrote on October 16, Eugene's fortieth birthday.

Still nothing happened to justify her continued foreboding and depression. As was usual when he was writing, Eugene was preoccupied, absentminded, emotionally distant, and sometimes unpredictable. The explanation for her foreboding appears to lie in the following entry for October 20: "Feel low and depressed. Gene insists I am necessary to him—to live! I can't see *how!* But, I'll continue *trying!*"

All in all, even allowing for a good deal of calculation in the revision to the diary (much later), it appears that with no house to run and no way to keep busy, and with O'Neill buried in his new play idea, Carlotta felt useless and unnecessary. Her self-esteem, like Eugene's, required her to be ever doing something worthwhile, such as running or building or remodeling a home or planning and arranging a trip. In part, she seemed to identify with Eugene, who could have been setting off on this great adventure unhampered by an unnecessary and depressed companion. Her feelings drove her to confide her foreboding, and he reassured her that she was necessary to him, "to live!" (October 20). But she did not believe him and continued to worry.

In Singapore on October 28 she reported that Gene had gone swimming in water that she believed was "sewer infestered" (*sic*), as if his behavior justified her foreboding. This long entry she heavily underscored throughout and wrote with heavy pressure on her pen. The next day she reported that he was ill from a touch of sun in the extreme equatorial heat, and he felt "not well from sun" for the next day or so. But he showed no sign then or later of any bacterial infection from foul water. Again in Saigon he went swimming, again in water of which she most strongly disapproved. Again he escaped unscathed. Her upset about his seeming carelessness reflects her extreme unease in Asia. Asia proved for her very far from her expectations: filthy, noisy, crowded, and above all, flagrant in its immorality. Only her cables from Pappa made her feel "still in touch with decency and stability" (CMD, October 30, 1928). The next day, after a drive to a roadhouse, she noted feeling "certain we are en route to hell!" Neither his diary nor hers mentioned a new vice that Eugene acquired in Saigon. At a casino, as he wrote Harold DePolo, the roulette wheel "got" him and he lost substantially. Carlotta scolded him severely, and in rebellion he stormed out, returned to the wheel, and lost a great deal more. They both came down with the flu prevalent in equatorial Asia at the time.

Apparently the two quarreled on the way to Hong Kong and Shanghai. At Shanghai they left the SS *André Lebon,* with the intention of getting medical attention for Eugene's flu. They checked into the Palace Hotel, where a physician attended him, with Carlotta nursing him day and night, and shopping between the stints at his bedside. Once Eugene was up and about, a reporter, Alfred Batson, recognized O'Neill and politely requested an interview. Batson agreed to Eugene's terms and stuck to them; among other things, he gave no hint that O'Neill was not traveling alone. The two men went out to take in the night life, and Eugene returned to Carlotta late, drunk and angry. The lovers fought, and he hit her. She immediately moved to another hotel, but through Mrs. Drew she kept tabs on Eugene's activities. He kept on drinking for two more days, until he went into "a coma or some such," Carlotta wrote. He wound up in County Hospital. Meanwhile, Carlotta also became ill and took to her bed for several days. "I will never feel for him as I have. I do not trust him!" (CMD, November 25, 1928).

Nevertheless, gradually and grudgingly, she forgave her Genie a little and arranged for the two of them to return to Europe aboard the SS *Coblenz,* bound for Manila. Their problems were far from over. Carlotta's diary reports on December 11 that Gene was taking "too much" bromide: "I can see the danger signals." Once prescribed for headache, neuralgia, and neurasthenia, bromide was known as early as the nineteenth century to have serious, long-lasting side effects that included lethargy, depression, and psychotic symptoms. The next day, Carlotta wrote that Eugene had taken too much calomel, a cathartic, apparently because the bromide had made him constipated.

In Manila the reporters caught up with Eugene, despite his attempt to disguise himself as a priest. Sometime after the ship sailed, probably in mid-December, Eugene began drinking with an American newspaper executive, F. Theo Rogers, whose cabin was next to Carlotta's, and the noise they made kept Carlotta awake at night. No doubt she could hear Eugene grumbling drunkenly about her. On Christmas Eve Carlotta complained in her diary about Rogers's noise and drinking and asserted that she despised him as "shanty Irish," but she says nothing that day about Eugene, who was with him. Rogers, for his part, told Sheaffer that he had offered O'Neill sanctuary from Carlotta's "domineering" and nagging (SL, 320). O'Neill refused to give her birthday greetings, and they bickered that day and the next. The fight came to a head when he demanded that Mrs. Drew give him some liquor that Carlotta kept for guests. On New Year's Day, 1929, without telling Eugene what she was up to, Carlotta slipped off the ship when it docked at Colombo; she left Eugene and gave Mrs. Drew instructions to report on Eugene's behavior.

Now began the craziest part of the sad and funny trip. Eugene continued aboard the *Coblenz* bound for Aden and the Red Sea under Mrs. Drew's observation; meanwhile, Carlotta had boarded the *President Monroe,* sailing some leagues ahead on a similar course. For the next two weeks a stream of radio messages passed between Carlotta and Mrs. Drew discussing Eugene's sobriety and his remorse. Carlotta sought out the *Monroe's* radio operator, curious to know the man who transmitted and received the intensely personal messages, and so did Sheaffer, decades later.

By the time both ships reached Port Said, Eugene was judged redeemable, and after a stormy reunion, he was allowed to change his passage to the *Monroe*. "Carlotta again!—and happiness!" O'Neill wrote in his diary on January 15. At Genoa their chauffeur met them with the Renault and they motored back to France.

In Cap d'Ail, they rented Villa les Mimosas, where they lived until June. In late May they learned that a woman, claiming that O'Neill had taken the topic of eugenics from her privately published novel and used it in *Strange Interlude*, was suing him for plagiarism. (The suit eventually went to trial in 1931. Judge John Woolsey ruled that it was "wholly preposterous" and ordered the woman to pay O'Neill's costs of $7,500; O'Neill could not collect because she had little money and indeed had declared bankruptcy [LS, 369]).

No sooner had Eugene and Carlotta settled into Villa les Mimosas than O'Neill reread *Dynamo*. "Not good!" he noted on February 4. "Not anything like what it ought to be—would like to rewrite entirely but too late now—opens 11th." Through February and into March he worked on the scenario for "It Cannot Be Mad," the name of which he changed to "On to Betelgeuse," and wrote a draft of act 1. When the proofs of *Dynamo* arrived, he began cutting and revising, hoping to correct the play's problems for readers if not for the opening audience. But as he had noted, he would have had to start over from scratch to make the play coherent. At this point he hoped to salvage the material by making a trilogy, with *Dynamo* the first play, "On to Betelgeuse" the second, and a play not yet conceived the concluding work (it would be *Days Without End*). In the end, "On to Betelgeuse" progressed no further than the scenario and draft of act 1. Revising *Dynamo* and thinking about the trilogy occupied O'Neill through early April. Later that month, he and Carlotta decided to lease a château, Le Plessis, for three years, not far from Tours, near Saint Antoine du Rocher.

For about twelve hundred American dollars a year they had a thirty-five room château without electricity or indoor plumbing but with extensive, beautiful grounds and wonderful potential. Carlotta put in wiring and a bathroom, and directed a thorough cleaning—it had been unoccupied for years. The O'Neills built a large concrete swimming pool fed by a natural stream. Sheaffer reports that the couple spent about six thousand dollars on repairs and improvements (LS, 330). They moved into Le Plessis in early June.

In early July of 1929, to the great relief of Eugene and Carlotta, Agnes obtained her divorce in Reno. She agreed to a settlement almost identical to that agreed on a year and a half earlier. On July 13, Eugene learned that Fifine Clark had died on the 6th at the age of sixty-six, shortly after Agnes had returned to New Jersey from Reno. A few weeks earlier, Agnes had brought her to West Point Pleasant from Provincetown, to stay with the children for six weeks while she was in Reno. Eugene wrote in his diary that he felt "deeply grieved" at her death, that she was the "real mother to Shane and Oona" (July 13, 1929). Shane, who had become largely uncontrollable when his Gaga had left the previous fall, was greatly affected by the death. Eugene could not write for several days. He and Carlotta began making plans for their marriage, and on July 21 they went to Paris, where they were married the next day in a private ceremony. Carlotta's diary for July reports them both feeling great relief to be free of Agnes's control over their lives and feelings. She mentions one night when they held each other and other times when they felt close, but she gives little hint that she felt anything other than great relief that their union could now be legal. After the ceremony, she writes, "Our knees shook for an hour." After that, they went to the American consulate and to her bank to change her name on her passport and accounts (CMD, July 22, 1929). Later, Carlotta told Sheaffer, they went out for dinner—Eugene reluctantly—and then returned to their separate hotel rooms exhausted: "and that was my wedding night" (LS, 332). Neither's diary alludes to any passionate feelings for the other that might have crystallized during the nuptials. As with most intimate matters between the couple, there is little evidence.

They returned to Le Plessis, and Eugene resumed work. In late April he had begun taking notes on the characters and drawing sketches of sets for *Mourning Becomes Electra*. Through the summer and into the fall he worked on a scenario. The diary records his methodical, slow, daily progress. The diary mentions the death of a dog, trips to the dentist, the purchase of a new Bugatti racing car, and Shane's birthday. Carlotta's diary refers several times to the stock market crash in late October. Thanks to advice from Carlotta and Speyer, O'Neill had made conservative investments and came through the storm in fairly good shape.

O'Neill never mentions the crash in the diary. Most of his attention goes to *Mourning Becomes Electra*, a large, three-play structure whose overall story derives from the myths behind three plays of the *Oresteia* by Aeschylus. (O'Neill's third play, *The Haunted,* bears almost no resemblance to Aeschylus' *Eumenides.*) For all his admiration of Aeschylus, his versions of the story most closely resemble the *Electra* of Sophocles.

Still ashamed of his haste with *Dynamo,* O'Neill determined to redeem himself in his own eyes in this new work, to think and plan as carefully as he could. From that point on, with two exceptions, the rest of his plays would come to completion slowly, and all would be put aside and thoroughly scrutinized before he let anyone else see the result. Through the spring he tried out various speech styles and rhythms. For a time he planned to use masks, as he had in *Brown* and *Lazarus Laughed,* but he came to believe that masks would lead the audience to expect a poetic style of speech that, as experience in writing *The Fountain* and *Lazarus Laughed* had shown him, he could not sustain. He had stopped trying to reach beyond himself. From early spring 1929 and until early fall 1931, O'Neill worked with few interruptions on *Mourning Becomes Electra.* The work would consolidate his public reputation and demonstrably enhance his personal development.

Like *Strange Interlude* and *Dynamo, Mourning Becomes Electra* would be about the effects of losses on its primary characters. In *Dynamo* O'Neill had intended (as he explained to Robert Sisk, a friend at the Guild) to portray "the psychological mess a boy [Reuben Light] got into because he suddenly felt the whole world had turned against him and betrayed him into cowardice. Most of all his mother, whose betrayal really smashes him." In the play, the mother's first betrayal, which seems to arise from sexual jealousy, is to side with his father against Reuben when he wants to marry the neighbor's daughter. But her second and greater betrayal is dying. O'Neill told Sisk: "Psychologically, the interest in the play for me—was how he works it out so that he electrocutes his bullying [preacher] father's [Christian] God, [and] finds his dead mother again in the dynamo," which O'Neill represents as an amalgam of pagan and pseudoscientific godness (LS, 325).

In short, O'Neill meant to show the undoing of loss, the restoration of a union with one now dead, which in the play he effected at the cost of the young man's life: Reuben Light electrocutes himself at the end by embracing the goddess of the dynamo. At the level that most interested O'Neill, he showed that the consequence of loss was the death of the bereaved. In *Strange Interlude,* he had portrayed the consequence of unresolvable mourning as the endless repetition of crisis following loss, and the denial of loss through the repeated merging with another, as practiced by Nina and by Charlie Marsden. In *Dynamo,* despite the play's artistic failure, O'Neill made personal progress by dramatizing for himself the unconscious assumption of many bereaved persons that to accept as permanent the loss of the dead is to die oneself. The dramatization marked visible progress toward reaching the end of the first stage of mourning: accepting the reality of the losses.

Now, in *Mourning Becomes Electra,* O'Neill progressed further. As in *Strange Interlude,* he conceived two bereaved characters, male and female, who would suffer the loss of their parents. In Aeschylus' *Oresteia,* Electra appears only in *The Libation Bearers,* where she joins with her brother Orestes in belated mourning for their dead father, who has been assassinated by their mother. Orestes, the primary human character in the second and third parts of the trilogy, is compelled by the god Apollo and by the ethos of his people to avenge his father's murder by killing his mother, and he is made mad in consequence. Orestes carries out the killing of his mother in a warlike but not a cruel or crazy way. His heroic stature derives from his refusal to pity himself for his appalling destiny. Orestes' fate made him a most likely figure of identification for O'Neill among the Greek mythic characters.

O'Neill's Orestes, Orin Mannon, is neurotic—that is, chronically conflicted within himself—an affliction that Aeschylus allows his character to suffer for no more than a single moment, when he once asks his friend for advice. O'Neill's aim is different. In creating Orin, O'Neill seeks to understand with more objectivity than he can direct toward himself a young man devastated by a seductive mother who, Orin feels, has sexually betrayed him, a young man devastated by his own act of revenge on his mother's lover and by the death of his mother, for which he partly blames himself.

Like Edmund Tyrone in *Long Day's Journey into Night,* Orin is a young man too well acquainted with the gods of sex and death. Orin feels himself to be in a perfect double bind (Bateson 1956), as O'Neill himself has felt himself to be since learning of his mother's addiction: the enemy of his mother is his enemy, and is himself. Orin is so disordered by his experiences in the Civil War that he nearly lets himself be seduced by his

mother, and later, after witnessing his sister Lavinia's affair with an is-
lander in Tahiti, he becomes sexually obsessed with her. Everything to him
is at once too real and not real at all. The war has made him see life and
death as the embodiment of Nietzsche's eternal recurrence:

> I was always volunteering for extra danger. I was so scared
> anyone would guess I was afraid! There was a thick mist
> and it was so still you could hear the fog seeping into the
> ground. I met a Reb crawling toward our lines. His face
> drifted out of the mist toward mine. I shortened my sword
> and let him have the point under the ear. He stared at me
> with an idiotic look as if he'd sat on a tack—and his eyes
> dimmed and went out. . . .
> Before I'd gotten back I had to kill another in the
> same way. It was like murdering the same man twice. I had
> a queer feeling that war meant murdering the same man
> over and over, and that in the end I would discover the man
> was myself! Their faces keep coming back in dreams—and
> they change to Father's face—or to mine. [CP2, 976–77]

The knowledge leaves him an empty shell and then destroys him.
O'Neill's question, for himself and for his character, is, How does one resolve, after the death of the mother, all the resulting neurotic conflicts that
arise in the son? By way of answer, O'Neill creates Lavinia Mannon, his
Electra, his female self.

Lavinia has a psychological rigor that eludes her brother. She plans
the murder of her mother's lover, Brant, and then, using only words,
forces her mother to shoot herself. For some time, Lavinia denies all feelings about the deaths of her father and mother and her part in the murder of Brant. But when her brother unravels and is about to expose the
family shame, she persuades him to kill himself to save the family, and he
does. Shortly after, Lavinia's denial and rationalization fail, and she begins to accept that she must finally face her dead. In the last moments of
the last play she goes into the Mannon home, orders herself locked in, and
vows to remain there until she has come to terms with her dead.

Whereas the story might have led O'Neill to melodrama a year or
so earlier, its careful working out now led him to the tragic. One might
expect a character in such a situation as Lavinia's to kill herself—as one
might expect Oedipus to kill himself after learning who he is and what he

has done. But Lavinia, like Oedipus, wills herself to remain alive, to contemplate who she is, what she has done, and what fate may require of her. She accepts the finality of death. That psychological act, the acceptance of death's reality, links tragedy to psychoanalysis. In psychoanalytic terms, Lavinia reaches the point of being ready to begin the "working-through" stage of grieving. She is the first character O'Neill creates who reaches this stage. In creating her, O'Neill shows he is ready to begin the minute work that will eventually allow him to pass beyond the obsession with his dead that has possessed him for a decade.

Working through the play took O'Neill two and a half years and five drafts, and each revision took him closer to the understanding he eventually reached. In the second draft he tried and later discarded associative "thought asides" like those used in *Strange Interlude* and elsewhere in his plays. In their place he tried what he called stylized soliloquies but also disposed of these. After completing the third draft, he scrapped the idea of the masks and decided that instead of employing an elevated style, which was not working, he would rewrite all the dialogue in plain speech. Between drafts, he and Carlotta traveled a little, to Spain, to the Canaries, to a Grand Prix auto race, to Paris (where he had dental work done). George Jean Nathan and Lillian Gish visited, and so did Eugene Jr., who was about to graduate from Yale with a degree in classics.

In May 1931 the O'Neills returned to New York. The Theatre Guild was in the preliminary stages of casting and planning the production of *Mourning Becomes Electra*, which would open on October 26. O'Neill saw a few old friends, endured dental work, bought a secondhand V-12 Cadillac (which he never drove), and settled into a suite at the Madison. Eugene Jr. brought Elizabeth Greene, whom he wanted to marry, to meet them. The young couple eloped on June 15, about the time Eugene and Carlotta moved to a rented home in Northport, Long Island. Shane visited for five days in August. One day Carlotta gave Shane dancing lessons in her room while his father worked on the galleys of *Mourning Becomes Electra*. In late August they returned to New York to prepare for rehearsals, which began September 7. O'Neill revised and cut as he watched the actors. The day before the opening, he noted: "*Farewell (for me) to the Mannons!*" (October 26). The plays were received with great acclaim and ran for 150 performances.

O'Neill was not wholly satisfied with the cast, but the strong public reception greatly pleased him, and he noted in his diary, "Carlotta and I overjoyed!" (October 27). His usual reaction set in, however, in the aftermath of the first performances. The next day, he lamented: "Reaction—sunk—worn out—depressed—sad that the Mannons exist no more—for me" (October 28). The detail of the diary entry makes it clear that O'Neill experienced the opening as a loss like a death: the Mannons died for him the moment they moved from the world of his imagination to the public stage. By elaborating his sense of the loss, he made it clear how well he now knew that mourning was the great theme of his life.

Among the many events of these years that culminated in the opening of *Mourning Becomes Electra,* several have essential importance. Eugene and Agnes separated, and Eugene eloped to France with Carlotta. Almost at once, he wrote *Dynamo,* a play that, although it everywhere showed promise, was conceived and dashed off so hurriedly that it came out fundamentally incoherent. O'Neill rushed its writing; the feverish pace of work allowed him to deny misgivings about his separation and his hasty commitment to a new wife. The failure of *Dynamo* deeply embarrassed the playwright, who had believed himself incorruptible in his fidelity to his art.

The incoherent play stood as evidence that he had sacrificed viable ideas to spare himself the discomfort of acknowledging the various disturbances in his life, especially his renunciation of alcohol, his stalled mourning of his dead, and his abandonment of his children and their mother. So he was led to the third important event of these years, the slow, careful composition of *Mourning Becomes Electra,* the play that probably led to the award of the Nobel Prize in 1936, and on which his reputation largely rested until a decade and more after his death. In the future he would be very cautious not to let work out of his hands before he was certain that he had done his best with it. As it turned out, writing *Mourning Becomes Electra* also allowed him to make substantial progress with his own mourning—and finally to proceed beyond the first stage of it.

On July 17, 1931, O'Neill conceived a new play idea, which he described and underlined in his diary: "*house-with-the-masked-dead and two living intruding strangers.*" In his notebook he sketched an elderly couple, a man and his wife or mistress, who live in a "Greek" house (like the Mannons' house) haunted by two masked ghosts, male and female. The elderly man and woman want to die before some criminal secret from their past comes out. A younger man and woman come to the house when their car breaks down and become involved in complex interaction with the old couple and the ghosts, which O'Neill described as "eternal conflict and mental plottings and torturing between them . . . climax reacting of the different scenes the old drama might have taken 'if'—always ending in impasse" (Floyd 1981, 226). Floyd reasons that James and Ella O'Neill would have been elderly if they had still been alive in 1931 and shrewdly surmises that O'Neill must have been imagining a version of the story that became *Long Day's Journey into Night,* with its constant second guessing that always leads to impasse.

In fact, O'Neill was nearly a decade away from being able to face directly the ghosts of the dead O'Neills. But it is interesting that he seems to have wanted to write about them in 1931. The Greek house detail, a set idea borrowed from *Mourning Becomes Electra,* links the ghost play idea to the trilogy and suggests how writing *Electra* led to progress in O'Neill's personal mourning. The playwright can show Lavinia abandoning her intellectualizing defenses and giving herself over to mourning because he himself has finally reached the point of knowing that he needs to dwell among the dead before he can return to life.

19

O'Neill's Breakdown
1931–1934

THE SPLENDID RECEPTION NEW YORK gave *Mourning Becomes Electra* delighted O'Neill, and for a few weeks he and Carlotta resumed ordinary life. The O'Neills took a three-year lease on an apartment at 1095 Park Avenue. Sheaffer writes that Carlotta, who had grown bored living in seclusion in France and on Long Island, had a yen for New York social life (LS, 383–84). In late August she began to decorate the eight-room flat in fine Oriental style. Probably at her instigation, the O'Neills became close to Carl Van Vechten and his wife, Fania Marinoff, whom Carlotta had known during her days with Ralph Barton. Van Vechten told Sheaffer that Carlotta seemed to become fully alive in the process of creating a home, as her husband did in creating a play. Carlotta arranged for the couple to entertain various prominent people, and they also saw a few close friends, including Saxe and Dorothy Commins. They frequently saw James Speyer at his estate. Carlotta reports that Eugene had several long conversations with Speyer about the stock market and finance. Probably the conversations were prompted by O'Neill's concern about the continuing depressed market, his own losses in the face of continuing alimony and support payments, and his reduced income from writing.

After the initial pleasure over the success of *Mourning Becomes Electra,* Eugene fell into a deep depression, compounded by November gloom and the overstimulation of being in New York. As always when in the city, he felt he could not write at all. The O'Neills hired a chauffeur and drove south, to a new resort at Sea Island, Georgia. Feeling cheerier at once in the mild southern winter, Eugene's creative powers returned and he sketched out several ideas for plays. Soon they began to talk of living on the South Georgia coast and were ensnared by a young man Eugene sometimes called the demon realtor, George Boll. The O'Neills fell in love with Sea Island and decided to build a home there. Boll, the agent for the Sea Island Company, sold the O'Neills a group of five adjacent waterfront lots for $12,600. Before they left, Carlotta had found an architect and begun making detailed plans for a twenty-room tile-roofed stucco house, a casa in the Mediterranean style. Her meticulous planning was sufficiently detailed that she could specify to an eighth of an inch the precise depth of drawers she wanted built into the walls.

They returned to New York to find that the market had declined ominously. Boll called to offer the O'Neills a privately owned adjacent block of Sea Island lots as large as the parcel they already held. To ensure their privacy Eugene paid five thousand dollars for the block. Construction soon began on the new house, and they sought a way to end their lease or to sublet the Park Avenue apartment. The depressed economy took its toll, requiring them to sublet at a loss of a thousand dollars a year for three years.

In early January, Oona visited her father for the first time since he and Agnes had separated, along with Shane. O'Neill had arranged for Shane to enter the Lawrenceville School despite a poor scholastic record, hoping (like his father before him) that a first-rate education would bring out Shane's latent talents. Indeed, it had worked for Eugene Jr. Shane was now twelve and Oona six. Decades later, Oona told Sheaffer that during the visit, after a lunch of unfamiliar food, she threw up in the car on her stepmother and father and was loudly scolded. Carlotta mentioned in her diary Shane's coming for lunch but didn't mention Oona at all.

Shortly before the O'Neill children visited, Carlotta had heard from her mother that Cynthia, now fourteen and in boarding school, had become rebellious, and Nellie Tharsing wanted to wash her hands of the girl. Looking forward to staying with Carlotta, to meeting her new son-in-law at last, and to enjoying a leisurely stay in the city, Nellie was on the train to New York, along with Cynthia, when Carlotta received her mother's letter. Nellie's visit was brief and cool. Sheaffer, who spoke at length to Carlotta about her mother and daughter, and who also became lifelong friends with Cynthia and her husband, Roy Stram, gave a substantially different account of their relations than exists in Carlotta's diaries. The following is mostly based on Sheaffer's published account, and on his notes and correspondence with the Strams.

Sheaffer came to believe that (contrary to the impression she gives in her diary) Carlotta openly disliked both her mother and her daughter (LS, 393). When they arrived, Carlotta put them in a hotel, but she brought them to the apartment for tea and dinner most evenings of their stay. Eugene immediately liked his salty, shrewd mother-in-law, and they found they could talk easily. Sheaffer believed that Carlotta was afraid Eugene would learn details of his wife's past, which differed in Nellie's memories from Carlotta's stories of a refined, patrician upbringing. (Eugene already had his doubts.) Carlotta hustled Nellie back to California on the sixth day of her visit.

Eugene also immediately took to Cynthia, who reciprocated his liking. Cynthia told Sheaffer that Eugene won her trust by sympathizing with her hatred of boarding school. During her week in New York, Cynthia met Shane and Oona when all the children were taken to the Museum of Natural History. Carlotta arranged for Cynthia to enroll in a Connecticut boarding school, to which she and Eugene drove her. During the ride, Cynthia and her mother said little, but Eugene uncharacteristically kept up a running line of chatter about sights Cynthia was seeing for the first time. Cynthia, who felt unwanted by her mother, father, and grandmother, had three more visits with her mother during her semester in Connecticut: a long weekend in February, a week at Easter, and a week in March after some trouble at school.

Meanwhile, through the late winter and early spring, Eugene worked on several play ideas, especially one for a play about Benedict Arnold, which led him to read American history. (The idea and the reading would later express themselves in the Cycle plays.) By mid-February he was well into *Days Without End,* and he continued into March. He had several medical and dental appointments, in anticipation of the move to Georgia. Before Cynthia's term was over, the O'Neills had returned to Georgia, where they stayed in a cottage rented from Boll, while Carlotta supervised work on the house. Cynthia was to return to California; Carlotta sent the girl directions, and a train ticket. While Cynthia rode the rails, Carlotta was crawling under the house to check on details of construction and scolding workmen whose work was not up to her standards.

O'Neill bought a Gar Wood speedboat and arranged for it to be delivered to Jacksonville. After three weeks of work on *Days Without End,* O'Neill felt stuck again and, after a few days, began a third plot. The many notes and plot ideas for this play show O'Neill at the constant mercy of contradictory impulses over whether the play would end in defiance or affirmation. John Loving has betrayed his wife, Elsa, who has then fallen mortally ill; he believes that whether she dies or lives depends on whether he maintains his defiance of the Catholic faith of his boyhood or returns to the fold. The last scene was conceived early in the composition process as taking place in a church, where John makes his final act of defiance or contrition.

Although the play is of average length, he worked on it for more than two years, from late 1931 until early 1934; he completed seven drafts, each of which expressed a changed idea for the plot, the characters, the ending, or the intended meaning. How much it cost O'Neill in health and peace of mind to write the play can be guessed from his and Carlotta's diaries and other evidence. He and Carlotta both believed that writing *Days Without End* coincided with and contributed to a general breakdown in his physical and emotional health. When he finished the play his doctors warned him he was on the verge of a collapse, and demanded that he rest for at least six months.

The strain of writing the play was evident in various contradictions that marked O'Neill's outward behavior. Having taken heavy losses in the market, he was very worried about money, and his income was down. He had always found it impossible to write in New York. Yet he had let Carlotta persuade him to agree to a three-year lease on the New York apartment. (Within three months he knew again that he could not bear living in town.) The Sea Island house and the several lots, when finished in June, would cost the O'Neills about a hundred thousand dollars, probably not counting the high cost of a good deal of work on the house which had to be redone. (A leaky roof was a recurrent problem throughout their years in Georgia; the central heating worked badly when it worked at all, and it resisted several attempts at repair.) Within two years they were both tired of Georgia and considering other places to live that would be less unbearably hot in the summer and less plagued by mosquitoes.

Further, as Sheaffer reports, O'Neill never drove a car after he and Carlotta returned to the States in 1931. In France, he had owned at least three cars, including a Bugatti and a Mercedes. Cars were very much on his mind. Hardly had they arrived in Georgia in their Cadillac than he arranged to buy a Ford V-8 sedan to spare the Cadillac, he noted in his diary, presumably from wear and tear on the rural roads (WD, May 10, 1932). Before long, he sold the Cadillac and bought a new Lincoln, which he had decided was superior. He picked up the Gar Wood speedboat in Jacksonville and piloted it up the coast to Sea Island. But by the time he arrived, he found that he could no longer adapt easily to a boat's roll, and so he hastily sold the boat. Recalling that the O'Neills had had the first Packard in New London, O'Neill told Brooks Atkinson, the New York theater critic, that he took after his father in his taste for fine cars and boats (SL, 392). His contradictory behavior with regard to cars and real estate expressed his identification with his father's compulsive buying of property when he was worried about money or loss.

Every day through May and June, while Carlotta supervised last-minute work on the new house and prepared for the move, Eugene worked many hours on *Days Without End.* Sometimes he felt satisfied, more often frustrated, but he was determined to push on regardless. He and Carlotta moved in on June 22 and a few days later gave the house the name Casa Genotta (a combination of *Gene* and *Carlotta*). The move threw him off his resolve to work through his confusion about the play, and when Shane and Eugene Jr. came for visits in early July, he stopped working and walked and fished and swam with his sons and George Boll.

When his sons departed in mid-July, Eugene resumed work on *Days Without End* and kept at it into mid-August, but he had to stop to work on a project suggested by George Jean Nathan. Nathan had asked to use O'Neill's name on the editorial board of a new magazine, *American Spectator,* and had requested a prose contribution. O'Neill felt he could not refuse. The result was the reflective three-part sketch, "Memoranda on Masks" (which Nathan published in November, December, and January). In these brief notes O'Neill harked back to the idealism of his old friend Jig Cook to issue his own declaration that he hoped to restore the theater of Dionysos to its rightful place as a temple where poets interpret and celebrate life. Once "Memoranda" was in the mail, O'Neill doggedly resumed work on *Days Without End.*

Five days later, on September 1, O'Neill awoke with a completely new play in mind, fully formed and ready to be written. The play was the nostalgic comedy *Ah, Wilderness!*—a charming fable about the adolescent Richard Miller, who has caught a touch of Swinburnian decadence while growing up in a small town like New London in 1906. In 1947 O'Neill told Hamilton Basso that he wished he had had such a youth as that he invented for Richard Miller. O'Neill set the play in a home like the Rippins' in New London, where he had stayed after leaving the sanitorium in 1913. Sheaffer believes that O'Neill had modeled the editor-father on his onetime boss, Frederick Latimer, editor of the New London *Telegraph*, who in 1912–1913 took seriously Eugene's confused efforts to find himself. The play shows parents and children who basically trust and like each other, in spite of the difference in generations. Nat and Essie Miller instinctively and tactfully restrict or encourage their children in their encounters with the world. Decades later the British child analyst D. W. Winnicott would call such parenting as theirs *good enough*, a phrase precise in its homeliness. It is striking that O'Neill could imagine such parenting and such a home, and his ability to do so is surely a tribute to Mrs. Rippin and her daughters.

Working methodically every day, Eugene finished the draft before the end of September and, after a few days of polishing, called it "done for present" (WD, October 3, 1932). He felt great affection for the play, even while he doubted his judgment of it. It was, he wrote Saxe later, "untried ground for me." Writing with a light touch, O'Neill avoided mocking the foibles of the era and instead tried to understand what he called "its contrasting virtues" (Commins 1986, 140). The comedy arose out of sympathy rather than irony. After several months and a little more tinkering, he let three friends read it, including Saxe, who typed it twice, before and after minor revisions. Nathan convinced him that it should be produced, and O'Neill dedicated the play to him:

TO GEORGE JEAN NATHAN
Who also, once upon a time, in peg-top trousers
went the pace that kills along the road to ruin.

The *Work Diary* for September shows O'Neill in apparent good spirits, unpreoccupied with poor health and unafflicted by the gloomy, pessimistic moods that accompanied his labor on *Days Without End*. From a biographer's point of view, the most important aspect of the composition of *Ah, Wilderness!* is that O'Neill could write it at all, especially at a time when writing *Days Without End* immersed him in unpleasant aspects of his relations with his mother and his wives. That it could spring fully formed from a night's sleep implies that in fundamental ways he understood the family relations that allow the young to grow into their various selves and emerge from dependency.

The day after he finished *Ah, Wilderness!* O'Neill returned to the narcissistic world of *Days Without End.* On that day he decided that he might get the effect he wanted in the play by using masks, one of the subjects of the "Memoranda" he had written for Nathan in August. As in *The Great God Brown,* the main character of *Days Without End,* John Loving, was split into two selves, one polite and hollow, the other bitter and narcissistic. O'Neill did not make use of the idea immediately; at this stage of composition, the style of the play was basically realistic. It seems clear that, both in this play and in *Brown,* the idea of splitting the character is related to the lack of psychological integration in himself that was so marked until he was past thirty.

As work on *Days Without End* progressed, the play grew increasingly impressionistic and surreal. It seems that O'Neill deliberately tried to isolate the narcissistic, fragmented aspects of himself from which the play arose from the more integrated person he was becoming (and had apparently been when writing *Ah, Wilderness!*). Making *Days Without End* less and less realistic must have seemed the best way to try to get control of material that he felt was out of his control most of the time he was working on the play.

In late November, he finished a second draft and the next day methodically began notes for a third. He continued work into 1933, except when interrupted by illness, the occasional visitor, or an intermittent urge to abandon the play altogether; for a few weeks in January and February he worked on another idea until he got stuck on that, too. Working on a fourth draft of *Days Without End,* he bogged down on the ending: "Again reach same old impasse—play always goes dead on me here where it needs to be most alive—or I go dead on it—something fundamentally wrong" (WD, March 2, 1933).

To understand the difficulty O'Neill experienced in conceiving *Days Without End,* it is worth considering how different is the world of a play oriented toward Christianity from the world of a play oriented toward an Athenian sense of tragedy, an aesthetic to which O'Neill had committed himself in the preceding twenty years of playwriting. Ideas of Christian love, forgiveness, and reconciliation are intellectually incompatible with O'Neill's sense of the tragic, according to which death is assumed to be permanent, and the gods are defined by the power to create and destroy; in Greek mythology godly power has almost nothing to do with human ethical or moral qualities. Christianity, which defines God as selfless love, is a completely different idea with different consequences, which assume ideas of absolute good and evil that are incompatible with the tragic sense.

From time to time in O'Neill's life he clearly denied, or at least refused to accept, the intellectual incompatibility of the tragic sense and Christianity and instead tried to bring about some synthesis. The attempt at synthesis seemed to inhibit him from fully realizing the tragic potential of most of his plays of the 1920s. For someone to whom ideas were as real as they were to O'Neill, fully accepting the tragic view meant fully accepting the losses that he still partly denied, and the unaltered mental images from childhood to which he still clung. It is important that O'Neill mentioned in the *Work Diary* that he sensed "something fundamentally wrong" in his conception of *Days Without End.* The remark shows that the underlying incompatibility of tragic and Christian ideas lay close enough to the surface of his mind and of the play to trouble him greatly. The incongruity inhibited his writing of the play, but his recognition of it was a sign of movement in the work of mourning.

On March 3, 1933, hoping to escape the problem, he abandoned the fourth draft and started a fifth, using the mask idea from the previous September, and the next day he vowed to "rewrite every word this time" (WD, 155). He finished the fifth draft at the end of March, and after some revision, sent it to Saxe Commins to type. The persistent problem with the ending showed the degree to which O'Neill felt that his attempts to control his material were driven off course more than usual by unconscious conflicts. Apparently, the conflicts persisted in expressing themselves when he tried to write the play's ending and were as disrupting to his playwriting efforts as they were to his peace of mind. In a general sense, the Christian point of view was the view of his parents. Cutting himself completely free of it meant declaring full emotional autonomy. His prolonged mourning showed him still not able to go so far.

In early spring, while the playwright worked on the fifth draft of *Days Without End,* his publisher, Boni and Liveright, was failing. Saxe, who had become an editor with Liveright in 1929, was very concerned, not so much because he himself would soon be out of a job, but rather because the publisher owed O'Neill a good deal of money in royalties from *Mourning Becomes Electra* and other books. In a private memo, Saxe told of calling a meeting of major stockholders and forcing them to authorize immediate payment of the royalties (Commins 1986, 149). As soon as he had a certified check in hand, Saxe went to Sea Island to give Eugene his royalties, and to discuss the matter of choosing a new publisher from the several who had offered contracts. O'Neill chose Bennett Cerf, once a vice president of Boni and Liveright, who had bought Modern Library from the company when he left and made it the backbone of his new firm, Random House. When Cerf came wooing, O'Neill made it a condition of his contract that Saxe be hired as editor; Saxe continued with Random House until his death in 1958.

Meanwhile, Eugene persevered with the intransigent *Days Without End*. In the fifth draft he had introduced the element of the mask for the character Loving, who was now separate from John. (When Loving spoke, the other characters reacted as if John had spoken.) In this version, O'Neill had eliminated the element of Catholicism, which he had put in and taken out in different drafts (while the play remained Christian in all the drafts). In describing the sixth draft, O'Neill explained to Lawrence Langner that he conceived *Days Without End* as an interpretation of Goethe's *Faust*, in which Mephistopheles would wear a mask of Faust, indicating that both "Mephistopheles and Faust are one and the same—*are* Faust" (Floyd 1981, 162). During the June visit with Nathan, O'Neill described *Days Without End* to him, expecting Nathan to hate it simply because of its Christian theme. He was somewhat heartened that Nathan was not automatically put off. Possibly because of Nathan's response, O'Neill decided he could safely restore the Catholic element. In another letter to Langner he emphasized how important it was to him to bend over backward to be fair to Catholicism, to give it the best breaks possible in the play's production, because in writing it, he was "paying an old debt" (SL, 424). He apparently meant an old debt to his parents, especially his quietly devout father.

Through the increasingly abstract character of John Loving, O'Neill sets out to explore in greater depth both his narcissism and his attachment to and identification with his mother. From its first conception, *Days Without End* was a play about a man whose mother had died when he was still dependent on her and whose loss he had never finished mourning. O'Neill expressed the extreme ambivalence he had felt about the Church as a child, when he blamed it for failing to save his mother from her addiction and loss of faith. The waxing and waning of his anger at his mother can be traced in the revised endings that marked each draft, changes that determined whether the husband accepted or defied the church and thus determined whether his wife died or was saved by a miracle.

Floyd's study of the play (1981, 149–67) shows that O'Neill was conscious from the beginning that he was dealing with a son's obsessive feelings about his mother. In notes dated May 9, 1932, just before he began the first draft, O'Neill thought of John Loving as a doctor who was becoming a psychoanalyst because of "'religious promptings and desire to understand self (unconsciously)'" (155). At seven, the age when Eugene was cast adrift at boarding school, John loses his idealized father, a doctor, "'who was not strict Catholic like mother,'" and when John is fourteen, the age at which Eugene learned of Ella's addiction, "[John's] mother became seriously ill." Remorse for an inner rebellion against religion "leads to 'a frenzy of piety—prayers for her—prayers to Lucifer—L's guilt about mother's death, his superstitions that *if* he had prayed she might have been saved.'"

As previously mentioned, according to psychoanalytic object relations theory, the premature loss of one's idealizations of one's parents constitutes a loss nearly as severe and difficult to mourn as the loss of parents to death. Premature loss of idealization is frequently noted in the childhood history of persons who are chronically depressed. As we know, about the time he learned of his mother's addiction, Eugene rejected the family Catholicism and insisted on going to a secular boarding school. His mother never set foot on the Betts Academy campus, perhaps because she disapproved of Eugene's defiance, and probably because she felt personally to blame. Ella is said to have wanted Eugene to be a priest, and she took his apostasy very hard, perhaps as a sign of retribution for her sinful addiction.

In notes dated May 12, 1932, O'Neill indicates that before he began to write, he had an idea for the "end of play." (No doubt the necessity to make the play conform to an abstractly conceived idea had much to do with the long struggle with composition). The ideas was that (as Floyd observes) his main character "has not been able to free himself from guilt and maternal domination." O'Neill analyzes his character as follows: "'Mother worship, repressed and turned morbid, ends by becoming Death love and longing.'" At the ending, in a church, Loving comes before "the altar of the Virgin [where] his longing for reunion [with his mother] "lures him to the point of suicide." At the same time, it is "his old resentment against mother, against Elsa [his wife] as mother substitute (infidelity) that keeps him from giving in to Catholicism—longing (confession)'" (Floyd 1981, 155–56).

The play, and the history of its composition, suggest that in writing the play, O'Neill was trying to engage the "work" of mourning his mother. Mourning led him regressively to relive struggles and fantasies associated with early adolescence.

Juxtaposing notes and details of various drafts of the play with the text of the final version suggests to a biographer some of the meanings that John Loving's final act of defiance or act of faith held for O'Neill. By creating such "biographical" meanings for John Loving, O'Neill reveals various ideas he has about himself.

The wife, undefined as a character, is explicitly a mother substitute. John has identified deeply with his mother, and a prominent aspect of his feelings about his wife is that he is often "her lost, despairing little boy" (Floyd 1981, 153). He has mostly been obedient and well behaved, but sometimes he is violently rebellious. He has felt the greatest pressure from his mother to accept the truth, confess, and merge with her: this aspect of his mother he equates with the Church itself. But the wish to merge is in conflict with the adolescent's burgeoning masculinity. Giving in to his mother's wish for her little boy to be pious, even to become a priest, seems to him an emasculation, which he feels he must resist by the most extreme defense (John Loving identifies with Lucifer or Mephistopheles or, in one version, Zarathustra). It seems that the adult John Loving must be unfaithful to his wife to "prove" that he has not been emasculated. As the creator of a plot, John the playwright or novelist has the power to cause the mother-substitute, his wife, to become mortally ill, and he can also make her well or kill her. As John Loving, the author within the play, uses his plot-devising to control the people and circumstances of his life, so O'Neill seems to do as the creator of the author.

At this point an explanation becomes discernible for O'Neill's long and tortuous labor of revising and changing the plot of *Days Without End*, now with one outcome, now another. As long as the play was in process, O'Neill could wield a power over the mother figure that he felt he did not have over the mother image within his psyche. By writing the play, he laid bare certain psychologically primitive fears and retaliatory impulses. He drew out for two years the process of exercising an imaginary control over the image that he feared controlled him from within. Guilt over his sadistic wishes toward his mother (and his wives) made him sick and depressed. To distance himself from the manipulations, he interposed John Loving, as author, and the dramatic abstractions of style and character. Elsa, the wife, he developed too little in any of the drafts to feel pain. Yet, like an analysand revealing his most shameful fantasies to the analyst, O'Neill could not himself escape either the pain of knowing the harm he intended in his thoughts and feelings or his suffering for it.

Eventually, five years in the future, it would be clear that writing *Days Without End* not only increased O'Neill's guilt and anxiety at the time but also furthered the self-analysis and the mourning that would allow him to write his finest work. For the present the act of composition carried him to the edge of a breakdown. For most of 1933 he was sick and depressed.

To escape the heat and mosquitoes of Sea Island, Eugene and Carlotta went to New York in early August 1933, on their way to spend several weeks in the Adirondacks. While in town, Eugene submitted *Ah, Wilderness!* to the Guild, which accepted it at once and decided to open the play in September. With George M. Cohan cast against type as the father, it made a great success. It has been translated into a musical and at least two movies and has very frequently been revived, once with Will Rogers. A 1988 performance won praise for Jason Robards and Colleen Dewhurst, who played the parents.

For weeks Eugene did nothing but fish, swim, and row. Back in New York at the end of August, he attended rehearsals of *Ah, Wilderness!* and worked with the Guild on the casting for *Days Without End,* while he simultaneously wrote another draft of the play. The O'Neills remained in New York, occasionally seeing friends and doctors. In the seventh draft John Loving once again became a lapsed Catholic, torn about returning to the faith. Back at Sea Island, O'Neill devoted late October and early November to finishing the draft and then spent a week fishing before returning to New York to work with rehearsals of *Days Without End* and to consult his doctors. Illness and depression had caused him to lose weight.

With an eye to book sales and in hopes of getting an "advance endorsement" from the Catholic hierarchy, Cerf asked O'Neill to make certain changes. O'Neill vehemently refused, replying that *Days Without End* was simply "a play about a Catholic." Such an endorsement "would throw my whole intention . . . into a misleading, false emphasis. . . . It is an attempt to express what I feel are the life-preserving depths in Catholic mysticism—to be fair to a side of life I have dismissed with scorn in other plays." Such an endorsement, O'Neill felt, would obscure the other aspect of the play, that it is a "psychological study" of a person undergoing a crisis of faith (SL, 426).

While the play was in rehearsal, O'Neill revised the conclusion yet again. The new ending (that of the published text) is most interesting as the culmination of the process of revision. It reveals what O'Neill was trying to achieve for himself psychologically by writing the play. In the church, John and Loving argue over the relationship between love and the Cross. John declares his faith; Loving mocks him for a self-deceiver and hypocrite. John begs God to let Elsa live and insists he believes, finally overriding Loving's scorn. At this point Loving slumps to the floor dead, while John Loving, now integrated, celebrates with the priest his triumph over death and the salvation of Elsa. The final ending of *Days Without End* expresses O'Neill's wish to annihilate the narcissistic isolation that has kept him from loving, or from being loved as he wished to be. The last version of the ending projects the achievement of a psychological integration that O'Neill now begins to feel he can claim.

For O'Neill, the great proof that he had grown more nearly whole and mature lay in the degree of constancy he felt in his relationship with Carlotta. In the first conception of the play in August 1927, while Eugene was still in Bermuda with Agnes, Elsa had represented not only Ella O'Neill but also Agnes. The act of adultery that in the play injured Elsa probably represented the adultery O'Neill contemplated (but had not yet acted on) with Carlotta. By the time he came to write the play, the wife Elsa not only was Ella but also came to be Carlotta. The increasing generality in his characterization of the wife allowed O'Neill to think of her in these several ways. Writing the play allowed him to work through some of his feelings about his mother so that he could begin to see the differences in his mental images of her and of Carlotta.

Carlotta proved daily that she chose to stay with him (because she always had the independence and the means to leave). She proved her love for him by devoting most of her waking thoughts and energies to making their home, to creating the conditions he needed to work. She was giving her life to him. More and more often he could see her not as his mother, but as the person herself. Moments of inconstancy continued, moments when he could feel nothing and when he turned on anyone within sight mistrust and even hatred that were outward reflections of his mistrust and hatred of himself. But he now seemed to know, even when mourning or depression dragged him into his past, that he would emerge and that Carlotta would be present and would still love him. It is the achievement of belief in his love of her and her love of him that he meant to celebrate by declaring the division between John and Loving healed. *Days Without End* does not win, aesthetically or emotionally, the victory over pessimism that it claims, and it certainly cannot convince anyone that its author is less the captive of his childhood narcissism than in the past. (O'Neill's psychological integration would proceed slowly, and it would only sometimes manifest itself in what he would write, or in occasional details of his life with Carlotta.) But during the time he struggled with *Days Without End,* O'Neill felt the progress he was making and used the play to proclaim it.

Days Without End was scheduled for a week's tryout in Boston on December 27, 1933, and was fairly well received there, reaping public praise in the Catholic and secular press. But nearly all New York critics hated it when it moved to the Henry Miller. To O'Neill's great pleasure, Yeats read and admired the play and personally wrote to the playwright to request permission for the Abbey Theatre to mount it, as it did, successfully, in April. (There were also successful productions in the Netherlands and Sweden.) O'Neill defended the play ever after, even knowing full well that critics he respected, including Nathan and Atkinson, disliked it.

The opening of *Days Without End* in Boston coincided with another loss for Eugene. He had heard that Terry Carlin was dying. For years he had helped support the old anarchist, who had kept him alive in the winter of 1915–1916 and had been a part-time member of his family when he and Agnes were in Provincetown. Terry, now seventy-nine, was living in a boardinghouse in Boston and was confined to a wheelchair. A friend told Sheaffer that Terry had been excited to hear that O'Neill's play was coming to Boston and had believed that he would surely see his old friend (LS, 427). For whatever reason, Eugene did not make the visit, and Terry died a few days later. O'Neill paid for his burial. Eugene nearly always mentions deaths of friends in his diary. That there is no reference to Terry or his death in the revised *Work Diary* may imply that O'Neill felt guilty for not having visited the old man.

The reason O'Neill did not pay a visit was probably that he was himself so depressed that he felt he could not bear to see Terry sick and dying or to acknowledge that yet another loss was imminent. When he and Carlotta returned to New York from Boston they got news that another old bohemian friend, Jack McGrath, had died a pauper at Bellevue. O'Neill arranged to pay for his burial, as well. Although O'Neill expected the critics to hate *Days Without End,* he fell into a deep depression when the reviews came out and, according to Carlotta's diary, he remained in it.

He caught a cold. He needed barbiturates to sleep, which caused a disturbed, restless slumber; he had had little appetite for some time and had become thinner than ever. Carlotta reported that he was "terribly nervous." On January 14, 1934, she wrote, he began "to sob horribly," seemed surprised to find her "still" with him, and then begged her, "For God's sake to hold me tight—I feel as if I'd burst through my skin" (CMD). (O'Neill in his diary mentions nothing of the episode, but at another times he writes of "flying out of skin.")

It seems likely that O'Neill was describing something more specific than simply being anxious, such as some neural malfunction as is associated with severe or chronic depression. Carlotta blamed "mix[ing] 'religion' up with his 'work'" for his state of mind and insisted *"He isn't well!"* (CMD, January 19, 1934). They postponed their planned return to Georgia for a week. When they got back to Sea Island in late January, his tremor was sufficiently worse than usual for Carlotta to mention it. It was probably about this time that the neurological changes that would gradually greatly intensify the tremor began to be evident.

Days Without End closed after seven weeks. O'Neill continued to be ill, now complaining of *"Nerves—liver—digestion all shot"* (WD, 183). The O'Neills went back in mid-March to New York, where he saw doctors and his dentist. A Dr. Whittemore "tells me," he noted on March 23, 1934, "on verge of nervous breakdown—also faint indication apex right lung—must rest for 6 mos—no work—or complete collapse." He now weighed 137 pounds "(minus coat & vest)"; the doctor prescribed a course of daily insulin injections to aid his appetite and help him gain weight. The insulin created a hypoglycemic effect that would make O'Neill hun-

gry and would cause such other neurological and psychiatric consequences as sweating, headache, tachycardia, irritability, apprehension,
nervousness, and in O'Neill's case a worsened tremor. Carlotta took on
the job of giving Eugene his insulin injections, which she hated doing.
Through the spring and early summer, he had three courses of insulin injections, and with the boost to his appetite, he gained about eighteen
pounds—which he lost as soon as he stopped the shots. While in New
York he underwent many medical tests, but nothing made his condition
clear.

They returned to Georgia. George Boll became increasingly close
to the O'Neills. Through the rest of their stay at Sea Island, he would be
a very frequent visitor, coming several nights a week for dinner, playing
cards until bedtime, staying over in bad weather. He sometimes accompanied them on trips to New York, and once on their summer holiday in
the Adirondacks. Given that Eugene was forbidden to work and Carlotta
had no major domestic projects, tension between the O'Neills was high.
An easy-going bachelor, Boll served as a buffer.

In August and September 1934, the O'Neills went again to the
Adirondacks. On the way home to Georgia in October, they stopped in
New York to see friends and doctors. Rumors were published that O'Neill
was to receive the Nobel Prize, rumors that proved premature. By the end
of 1934, O'Neill had resumed work on a play about a character, Bessie
Bowen, who was a pioneer in the auto industry. It was to be the final play
in the series that began with *Dynamo* and *Days Without End,* and although
O'Neill never finished so much as a draft of it, he worked at it fitfully over
several years. At this time he also began outlining the vast work known as
the Cycle.

His mood had been cheerier for several weeks. Carlotta worked hard
for weeks preparing for the Christmas holidays, then felt let down when
they arrived, and for days afterwards. She gave Eugene a fine Scott multi-
band radio that would receive European and New York stations. Eugene
had become very interested in symphonic music and had begun buying
gramophone records of classical music as well as jazz and blues. This year
his usual Christmas letdown was mild, but he caught a cold shortly thereafter.

Shane arrived on Carlotta's birthday for a week's visit, a visit both
he and Eugene enjoyed. But according to Carlotta's diary, both of them
were worried about the boy. On December 30, Eugene began work on the

Cycle, the work that would occupy him for the next four years and more. For several days both Carlotta and Eugene were edgy and depressed. Then on January 10, a beautiful day, he had a "bad nerves attack" (his phrase) and went into a "'slough of despond'" (hers). Carlotta often does not distinguish between Eugene's depressions and what he called "attacks of nerves," which seem to mean to O'Neill feeling anxious and jittery and having his tremor worsen. On this occasion, he seems to have experienced both "nerves" and depression. The next day she reported that "Gene is in a ghastly state of nerves." She was already depressed herself, and his state made her feel hopeless and "doubly nervous." In his dreadful state of agitated depression, she wrote, he kept trying to remind her that he loved her "*no matter what he does* or does *not* do!!?" In afterthoughts that must have arisen many years later, probably after O'Neill had died, Carlotta says she wonders if what disturbs him is inherent to creative people, or "is it part of the disease that is devouring him?" "This 'thing' called *nerves?*" she asks her reader, "What is it?"

At the time, and for decades after, no one, his wife, his physician, or O'Neill himself, had any idea what disease was "devouring" him. Nor is there any name today for a seemingly idiopathic disease of the sort vaguely grouped in textbooks with parkinsonism. Some process was killing certain nerve cells in particular parts of O'Neill's brain. The gradual extinction of the cells would increasingly affect fine motor coordination, making it difficult, often impossible, for O'Neill to walk or to swallow, or to coordinate the muscles required to speak clearly or do a thousand other things, including write; it would affect his balance, gait, posture—indeed anything requiring muscular coordination.

Much later, after O'Neill had died, a psychiatrist who had treated Carlotta, Dr. Harry Kozol, whom Sheaffer describes as an expert in forensic medicine (LS, 645), wrote an interpretation for Carlotta of the autopsy of the playwright's brain. He explained that O'Neill's cerebellar vermis, the brain center that coordinates muscle movement, which was once normal, had suffered an almost total extinction of the Purkinje cells, and that the atrophy of the olivelike structure of the medulla oblongata that controls swallowing was extensive. Gradually over the years, more and more Purkinje cells had died, causing spasmodic muscular movements over which O'Neill had little or no control. The effects appeared in the tremor. Although O'Neill's muscles did not atrophy and his reflexes remained intact, he could not coordinate the sequence of muscle contraction required to perform any action (Yale, paraphrased from a letter dated June 7, 1954).

The tremor began to worsen in 1934–1935, and it would grow much more severe over the next years, to the point that O'Neill would be repeatedly misdiagnosed as suffering from Parkinson's disease. The autopsy eventually made clear that the degeneration in O'Neill's brain in no way resembled that typical for sufferers of Parkinson's. Furthermore, O'Neill's tremor worked in the opposite way to the Parkinson's tremor (which lessens as one tries to do something); his increased as he tried to perform any action.

In a sense the diagnosis was unimportant, for there was no treatment at the time for O'Neill's condition, any more than there was a treatment for Parkinson's disease. But doctors, knowing that if it was Parkinson's, his case was atypical, must have felt uncomfortable both with their own inability to help and with the sense that they really had no idea what the playwright was experiencing. Among O'Neill's symptoms, one of the most troublesome was that the muscle control needed to swallow was severely affected. In the end, O'Neill died of pneumonia, which Dr. Kozol believed was caused by the difficulty in swallowing; pneumonia might well have begun when a tiny bit of food or drink entered the lung.

Doctors attempting to treat the complaints O'Neill presented in the mid-1930s, or even much later, faced formidable problems. Besides the degenerative neurological condition, for which they still have no explanation or treatment, a group of other conditions clouded the picture and made the patient's subjective description of his experience even harder to understand. He slept badly, had a poor appetite, had lost weight, and experienced episodes of low blood pressure, profuse sweating, severe intestinal cramps, gastritis, and heartburn.

Although the biochemical basis for depression was little known at the time, it was certainly understood that severe depression was typically accompanied by a preoccupation with physical ailments, which perhaps not only seemed worse but were actually made worse by one's mood. As for the tremor, O'Neill had had it since childhood, and it had always responded from day to day to varying circumstances. His kind of tremor, a "benign family tremor" or "intention tremor," generally does not deteriorate into major illness. Reports that the tremor seemed now to be worsening might reasonably have been taken as yet another indication of his pessimistic mood. At times he found it impossible to eat, but complaints that swallowing was difficult could reasonably be attributed to depression. No one would have guessed at so exotic a process as the focal atrophy of the brain centers that control swallowing, especially when the patient considered himself neurotic and depressed and would readily have agreed to the notion that most of his problems were probably "in his head." Medical tests led to no clear diagnosis, but the insulin injections were prescribed to improve his appetite, and thyroid medication was also administered. He was given barbiturates to sleep, for which he rapidly developed a tolerance. Physicians understandably felt frustrated that their patient's complaints made little sense according to available medical knowledge, and they and nurses gently advised the playwright to buck up and face his problems with better humor.

In retrospect, it seems clear that over and above the episodes of "nerves" and "jumpiness" to which he was subject, when the worsening tremor manifested itself, O'Neill was clinically depressed. In *Darkness Visible,* the novelist William Styron gives a moving account of a psychotic depression that laid him low at the age of sixty, the first such depression he had experienced, one that resisted medication or other treatment and nearly took his life. The only episode of extreme depression that O'Neill is known to have had was the one in late 1911–early 1912 that ended with his attempt to kill himself. O'Neill's depression was a chronic state, moderate to severe, but one that seldom reached psychotic depth.

It seems likely that O'Neill's episodes of melancholy arose from endogenous as well as intrapsychic or circumstantial sources. His own accounts to his wives and other people of his years in boarding schools, and accounts by others of his behavior with teachers and other students, all make it reasonable to infer that he was depressed for nearly all the time he was at St. Aloysius. Beyond this, he seems from childhood to have been inclined toward depression as a reaction to various incidents in life. Current psychiatric opinion tends to assume that depression that sets in as early as O'Neill's, lasts for days or weeks or months at a time, and is a frequent state of mind in adult life is probably, at least in part, the result of an inherent neurochemical dysfunction.

As depression seems to have occurred on both sides of O'Neill's family, circumstantial evidence would corroborate that his was a hereditary condition. It seems clear that his mother became depressed when her father died and remained depressed thereafter, and that her depression intensified with further losses. It is sensible to conclude that Ella O'Neill was especially vulnerable to morphine addiction because the drug (temporarily) alleviated her feelings of despair.

Depression seems to have affected James O'Neill also, expressing itself in his pessimism about money and his chronic expectation that he would end up in the poorhouse. According to Eugene, he treated his sons' childhood nightmares with doses of whiskey; he apparently regarded it as a specific against anxiety and depression and ministered to himself accordingly. Both sons adopted his belief in the treatment. If the family legend was correct, that James's father deserted his family because he anticipated his own coming death and that he died in circumstances that suggest suicide, it would imply that depression ran in the family. Eugene's two sons (by different mothers) suffered from depression, which they tried to alleviate with alcohol and street drugs, and both killed themselves.

O'Neill's melancholy was complex and took many forms. Regular episodes are mentioned in letters and diaries as occurring most years in August and around Christmastime. Guessing the cause of any particular episode is often difficult, especially in the aftermath of the deaths of his parents and brother, when he entered his prolonged mourning, because he had so many possible sources of melancholy. In earlier years he alleviated depression by drinking. In the 1930s, as his depression deepened, he suffered from various complaints, some of which were undoubtedly secondary effects of depression but some of which were probably caused by the cerebellar degeneration.

Neither the clinical depression nor, perhaps, the playwright's temperament allowed him to act on the advice to worry less, think less about his ailments, and avoid unhappy thoughts. But he did the thing he could do best. He resumed work, returned, as he put it, to the tragic view of life, the view syntonic with his temperament and gifts. He drove full speed into the largest project he would ever take on. On the last day of 1934 he started outlining the Cycle, a chronicle of American history eventually projecting to comprise nine (or sometimes eleven) connected plays. Of this work, which occupied O'Neill for much of the next four years, two plays survive.

Into the Summerhouse
1935–1939

THE LONG FORCED REST IN the first half of 1934 helped. O'Neill's general condition improved. With insulin treatment he gained about twenty pounds and felt well enough in late fall to resume writing. Wanting to work, casting about for something that seemed ready to write, O'Neill made notes on several play ideas.

Over the next nine years, fighting multiple illnesses and depression most of the time, O'Neill wrote a good deal. At the same time, his name was seldom in the public view; no new O'Neill play would be performed again until 1946. Later generations would remember the playwright for the five final plays, including *The Iceman Cometh* and *Long Day's Journey into Night*. In fact, he drafted as many as a dozen or more plays during the period, all but six of which he destroyed. From late fall, 1934, through early 1943, except for periods of extended illness, he wrote nearly every day.

Of O'Neill's work in the years 1934 to 1939 only *A Touch of the Poet* and *More Stately Mansions* survive, the latter against the playwright's wishes. They are all that remain of the vast work he called the Cycle, which was to give a psychological and economic account of American life. In its most extended form, he projected it to begin in 1755 and end in 1932. O'Neill conceived as many as eleven plays to tell his story of the successes and failures in commerce and politics of members of the Harford and Melody families. O'Neill's final working title for the Cycle was "A Tale of Possessors Self-Dispossessed."

O'Neill appears to have written "complete" (but not finished) drafts of perhaps six plays, all from the earlier stages of the narrative, 1755 to 1842. In 1944, when he decided he could not or would not finish even the drafted Cycle plays, O'Neill destroyed most of his notes, outlines, scenarios, and sketches for sets, along with some drafts. Again in 1951, knowing that he would not live much longer and not wishing to be judged on unfinished work, he destroyed Cycle material, and at that point he probably believed he had destroyed all of it except *A Touch of the Poet*. In the eleven-play schema, *Poet* would have been the fifth play (set in 1828) and *More Stately Mansions* the sixth (set in 1832 through 1842).

Some Cycle material was not destroyed, though. Combined with entries in the *Work Diary*, enough exists to permit speculation about the shape and character of the overall plan. The first ideas for the Cycle arose while O'Neill was thinking about a third play to complete the proposed trilogy that had begun inauspiciously with *Dynamo* and *Days Without End*. The unwritten third play, set in Michigan in the years 1893–1932, was to have been about a woman he called by several names, including Bessie Bowlan or Bowan or Bolan; she made a fortune in the automobile industry by mass producing her husband's invention, an engine-cooling device.

The thesis of the trilogy was to have been that, having lost God, twentieth-century Americans created a culture devoted to money. Late in 1934, O'Neill began to think of using the Bessie Bowlan idea as the conclusion to a much larger work that would study America's economic development. One surviving note acknowledges inspiration from Thoreau's chapter "Economy." The young Simon Harford, whom O'Neill eventually made a central figure in the Cycle, leaves his wealthy family's Boston home to live in a cabin by a pond, there to write a *Walden*-like utopian tract aimed at persuading humanity to renounce greed and possession. Having fallen ill, he is nursed by his future wife, Sara Melody. The Cycle plays on which O'Neill worked most, including the two that survive, show the rise and fall of Simon, his parents and ancestors, and Sara and her parents.

In the first conception, Simon barely existed. On New Year's Eve, 1935, O'Neill began making notes for a four-play series set in the years 1857 to 1893, each organized around one or more of the four sons of Simon and Sara. Simon died at the beginning of the first play, *The Calms of Capricorn*, which was set mostly on a clipper ship on a passage westward to San Francisco around Cape Horn. Sara was a passenger, and her son, Ethan, advanced from second mate to captain during the passage. O'Neill decided to conclude the series with a fifth play, the play of the woman he had been calling Bessie Bowlan, who would now be a descendant of the Harford and Melody families, and whose story would conclude the series in 1932. Of these five plays, only the first was ever developed beyond the stage of notes and a preliminary outline. O'Neill wrote a long scenario for *Calms* that was not destroyed. (It was transcribed and published in 1982, together with a play developed from it by Donald Gallup, former curator of American literature at the Beinecke Rare Book and Manuscript Library, Yale.)

Almost immediately after conceiving the four plays about the Harford brothers, driven by an autobiographer's instinct and a psychoanalyst's curiosity, O'Neill began exploring the origins of his characters. His question for them as for himself was, How did they reach their present state? Within the first month of work on the Cycle he was making notes for what he thought would be one or two plays about the parents of the Harford brothers. This idea led him to write *A Touch of the Poet* (set on July 27, 1828), the play about Sara and her parents that precedes his description of her marriage to Simon; and *More Stately Mansions,* set in 1832–1842, which is about Simon's rise and fall and his relations with his wife and his mother.

Poet (which will be discussed later) is the only Cycle play that O'Neill finished to his own satisfaction. In 1942–1943, realizing that he would not be able to finish the Cycle, he prepared *Poet* for performance and publication. He removed transitional scenes and other material that linked it to the plays that came before and after it in the Cycle. In the late 1940s, O'Neill wanted to have it performed, but his health, combined with postwar conditions in the theater, made a production impractical. In 1957, after O'Neill had died, Carlotta arranged for *Poet* to be premiered in Stockholm, and the same year O'Neill's text was published by Yale University Press.

More Stately Mansions is a difficult case. To a psychoanalytic biographer, the script seems so extremely and intensely personal and intimate that it is hard to imagine O'Neill's ever allowing it to be performed or published. There seems no question that he intended to destroy the play and believed that he had destroyed it. In fact, it was delivered to the Yale library along with other material given to Yale by O'Neill and packed by

Carlotta. O'Neill was apparently not told that the play had been spared from the fire.

The surviving draft is a single-spaced typescript of more than three hundred pages, typed by Carlotta in January 1939, with hundreds of corrections and changes in O'Neill's hand. It is longer by half than O'Neill's longest plays and would take an estimated nine hours or more to perform in full. The draft of *More Stately Mansions* did not become available to scholars until the early 1980s, when Martha Bower, who later prepared the text for the 1988 Oxford edition, arranged to obtain permission to read it. (The present author was permitted to read the text at Yale in 1985 by the then curator, David Schoonover.)

At the very beginning of his work on the Cycle, in January and February 1935, O'Neill made character sketches for Simon Harford, his mother, Deborah, and his wife, Sara, the three characters of *More Stately Mansions*. These characters and their stories were apparently fundamental to the thoughts that led the playwright from the clipper ship idea to the idea of the Cycle as he actually developed it. O'Neill wrote a long scenario for *More Stately Mansions* in March and April 1935.

The *Work Diary* shows that O'Neill worked on the Cycle nearly every day through the end of September 1935. Despite a few episodes of "nerves" and depression, he apparently felt fairly well. Occasional out-of-town visitors found their way to Sea Island, including the Van Vechtens, Cerf, Nathan, Sherwood Anderson, and Harry Weinberger. Carlotta's daughter, Cynthia, came to visit with her young husband, Augustus Barnett, whom she had married at seventeen, less than a year before. Cynthia was trying (as Sheaffer writes) to make a place for herself in a world where she felt unwelcome in the homes of her parents and grandmother (LS, 440).

When George Boll was on the island, he visited the O'Neills almost nightly for dinner and poker or rummy. Bored with Sea Island and increasingly impatient with the humid heat and mosquitoes, O'Neill began to think of moving to northern California, which he knew from childhood travels with his parents. Carlotta, who did not want to be near her mother and daughter, resisted for a time but eventually gave in.

Her diary shows that Carlotta was also bored and depressed much of the time in Georgia. Even when they had visitors, things did not always go well. She had gotten along with Nathan up to this point in the marriage, but some problem arose during his visit in late June, which had partly to do with Nathan and O'Neill's drinking beer together and with his defying Carlotta by promising to send Eugene some imported pilsener. About this same time, Carlotta's diary (for July 8 to 10, 1935) hints at a serious quarrel with her husband, having to do with her wish for him to revoke a trust and possibly involving his children's rights to royalties from his plays, or to inheritance of manuscripts. She wanted him to deed the rights to her and wired Harry Weinberger to visit them and make the deed of gift that she wanted. The dispute also had to do with the couple's making reciprocal wills. Evidently Weinberger advised O'Neill that he become Carlotta's attorney for the will, whereas Carlotta wanted O'Neill to make his will with her attorney, Morris Ernst. O'Neill apparently got drunk on August 23 and 24, when the quarrel again came to a head. He eventually gave in to her wishes. Otherwise, daily work on the Cycle during the first nine months of 1935 was seldom interrupted.

Through the spring and summer, O'Neill made notes and scene drawings, and outlined *More Stately Mansions, A Touch of the Poet,* and the four plays about the sons of Simon and Sara Harford. He also wrote scenarios for *More Stately Mansions* and *Poet.* For O'Neill at this time, outlines tended to be brief and sketchy preliminaries to the much more extensive writing of scenarios, which could be very long and virtually constituted first drafts of dialogue and action. (The published scenario of "The Calms of Capricorn" is fifty-five pages long.) Apparently, O'Neill never developed as far as the scenario stage any of the other plays about the brothers or the final play. Through late August, he conceived the Cycle as comprising seven plays and running from 1828 to 1932.

In September he reluctantly gave in to internal urgings to take the narrative back to 1806. He began notes for a play about the marriage of Simon's mother and father, "Greed of the Meek," which now made the Cycle eight plays long. By early October O'Neill was feeling the strain of nearly a year of arduous work. The sheer logistical problem of keeping story details consistent through eight interrelated plays was so formidable that O'Neill once joked he wouldn't wish a Cycle on his worst enemy.

Some abdominal pain had bothered him for a couple of months, and so, when he reached a stopping point, he and Carlotta went to New York for three weeks of medical examinations and visits with friends. He returned to Georgia knowing little more about his condition and fell into a deep depression. After a period of being unable to concentrate, he returned to "Greed of the Meek"; he then began to think of taking the story still further back, to the time of the French Revolution.

He stopped smoking again, probably on advice from a doctor who believed it might reduce the severity of his tremor, and he also resumed an old exercise routine. He struggled the rest of November trying to make himself concentrate on *A Touch of the Poet.* Many writers find it hard to concentrate on writing after they quit smoking; judging by the *Work Diary* this was the case for O'Neill each time he quit. Withdrawal from nicotine and the anxiety of resisting the urge to smoke may have been the causes of the uncharacteristic difficulty he experienced in losing himself in work. Until he resumed smoking at the end of December, he had to fight every day to make himself put in his daily stint at *Poet.* Still mentally sluggish, depressed, and irritable, he looked forward to a visit from Saxe Commins, who arrived January 5, 1936, for a two-week visit.

On January 10, O'Neill was back at work on *Poet,* and at first it seemed that this time nothing could impede his progress, even the loss of a cap on an eyetooth, which forced him to return to his dentist in New York. But the trip was prolonged when Carlotta became ill with ptomaine poisoning, and between one thing and another, O'Neill began drinking a little. Even so, for three weeks, he put in his daily shift on *Poet.* The stay in the city was extended into February because O'Neill himself became sick. There were frequent visits to the dentist and doctors, and then Carlotta became ill again. It isn't clear when or why O'Neill began a binge, but Carlotta complains about his mood, and the *Work Diary* shows no entries for February 18 to 20. On the 22nd he had a serious attack of gastritis with continuous vomiting. He spent several days in Doctors' Hospital.

He probably had the binge in mind when, back at Sea Island on February 28, he lamented in his diary that the trip to New York had been "one long siege of troubles & bad luck!" According to Carlotta's diary, they decided to sell Casa Genotta on March 12. That same day, O'Neill was able to resume work on *Poet,* and he labored steadily into mid-March, finishing his draft. He then shifted his attention back to "Greed of the Meek," which occupied him daily through early June. After finishing a scenario for the last act, he felt stuck and shifted to the outline of the new first play before starting to revise the scenario of "Greed of the Meek." He worked diligently through an intensely humid summer, despite attacks of illness and an episode of "extreme depression" (WD, June 25–26, 1936). In late June he resumed work on a scenario for the ending of *Poet*, then returned to "Greed of the Meek." By this time, possible buyers for the house were occasionally trooping through on inspection tours.

In late August, new friends from Seattle arrived for a visit, Sophus and Eline Winther. Sophus Keith Winther of the University of Washington had written a book on O'Neill that the playwright liked. In correspondence O'Neill had mentioned he wanted to move to the West Coast. The Winthers suggested a visit to Seattle, and Eugene agreed. Winther arranged for them to rent a secluded house high on a bluff in the Magnolia district with westward views of Puget Sound and the Olympic Peninsula. Even during the Winthers' visit, which went well, O'Neill kept working. Having finished for now his revisions of *Poet* and having become stuck again on "Greed of the Meek," he turned in September to *More Stately Mansions*, went over the scenario, and made further notes. Late in September, running a temperature and feeling generally ill, he drafted the first scene of *More Stately Mansions*. On October 4, the O'Neills left Sea Island for New York, the first step on their journey.

In New York, after several medical tests and consultations, Eugene noted on October 7 that his doctor's diagnosis had been, "Whole person sick but no definite organ to pin it on." In retrospect, it is easy to see how this assessment might describe an undefined systemic neurological pathology. O'Neill noted on October 24 that his doctor advised "absolute change—rest—forget work." After several consultations and the renewal of various prescriptions, after visits with Eugene Jr., Saxe and Dorothy Commins, the Van Vechtens, Nathan, and a few other friends, the O'Neills headed west. Eugene was afflicted with a cold, and then a bad attack of "nerves." On October 30, Shane's seventeenth birthday, Eugene and Carlotta left on the Twentieth Century Limited for Chicago, where they would change to the Great Northern Empire Builder.

The Winthers met them in Seattle, and that night they all listened to news of President Roosevelt's re-election. They had seven days for sightseeing before another public event engulfed them. On November 10, O'Neill learned that he had been awarded the Nobel Prize. The Winthers helped screen them from reporters. Carlotta's daughter, Cynthia, also assisted in the effort; she had come to Seattle to see them. Eugene and Carlotta answered congratulatory wires, and he was interviewed by Richard Neuberger, then a writer for the Portland *Oregonian*, on behalf of the *New*

York Times. Although reporters were respectful of O'Neill's obvious ill health, the strain of losing his privacy took a toll on him. "Nerves all shot—hell of a chance to rest cure & forget plays!—feel I am on edge of breakdown," he noted on November 15. Two days later, in expectation of going to Stockholm to accept the prize, he he wrote his acceptance speech. Ten days later, leaving the women, Sophus and Eugene went off on their own to drive around the Olympic Peninsula. Kenneth Macgowan, who had now worked in Hollywood for several years, flew up to Seattle, and Eugene met him at Boeing Field. Earl Stevens, with whom O'Neill had gone to Honduras in 1909–1910, came up from Portland to visit. Feeling more and more ill, O'Neill had to decide that his health would not permit a trip to Stockholm to accept the award. The wet and gloom of November and December in the Northwest oppressed the O'Neills, and they decided that they could stand no more of it. Carlotta asked Cynthia to drive them south, afraid that the publicity surrounding the Nobel would allow them no peace on the train. Cynthia, whose marriage to Gus Barnett had ended after a few months, was now engaged to Roy Stram (to whom she would remain married the rest of her life). Although she had returned to the Bay Area, she and Roy drove north again to take her mother and stepfather on the beautiful eight-hundred-mile drive south along the Cascades, through the Siskyous, past Mt. Shasta, and down to San Francisco. There the O'Neills moved into the Fairmont Hotel just in time for Christmas.

O'Neill enjoyed the drive but was sick when they arrived, with a "blinding headache" and severe abdominal cramps. Carlotta arranged for him to see her old friend Dr. Charles Dukes in Oakland, a man he immediately liked. Eugene complained in the diary that he was becoming "a god damned invalid!—it's revolting" (December 23, 1936). The day after Christmas, Dr. Dukes put him into the hospital with suspected appendicitis and prostatitis. Carlotta checked into the next room. She recorded in her diary that she was sick with the flu and depressed. On the basis of his interviews with her, Sheaffer concluded that she entered the hospital because she feared O'Neill might become romantically involved with a nurse or some other young woman (LS, 465).

On December 29, after having determined that O'Neill had acute appendicitis, Dr. Dukes operated. The surgery seemed to have gone well, but afterwards, other problems emerged, including kidney pain. Harry Weinberger, in Los Angeles on business, called several times and apparently was allowed to talk only to Carlotta. Fearing for O'Neill's life, he came and the two old friends had a good visit, even though Eugene was weak and shaky.

By January 11, 1937, O'Neill felt well enough to give a group interview to reporters in which he talked of plays and playwriting. Shortly after, however, as O'Neill recounted in a letter to a friend, an "interior abscess" flared up and burst, causing a peritoneal infection that nearly took his life (LS, 466). He was treated with morphine, atropine, codeine, adrenalin, and caffeine: "the works!" he noted (WD, 277). For a couple of days he was in danger, and when his temperature dropped, he underwent an episode of acute depression: "I feel too sick and ratty to give a damn whether I croak or not," he noted on January 12. There was another episode of high fever and delirium, and further opiate treatment. He remained in Merritt Hospital until March 12, and later he referred to the aftermath of surgery as his "crack-up." He had to undertake another enforced rest cure such as Dr. Draper had prescribed before the playwright left New York. From this point on, O'Neill made very few diary entries that did not include notes on his health and state of mind and record dosages of prescribed or other medicines.

While O'Neill was recovering in the hospital from the postoperative collapse, word came from George Boll that an offer had been made on Casa Genotta. The O'Neills agreed that Carlotta should go to Georgia to close the sale and supervise the packing and moving of their goods from the house. When Carlotta left, Eugene went into a deep depression and had an attack of nerves. On February 16 he slipped in the bathroom and sprained his back. He could hardly move the next day when the Swedish consul, Carl Wallerstedt, brought the Nobel Medal and certificate to his hospital room.

He passed his days with nurses who played cards with him, chatted, and walked with him around the hospital or the grounds as he tried to recover his strength. Finally on March 2, when Carlotta had returned from Georgia, he was released and could move back to the Fairmont. But after a few days, he had to return to the hospital for further treatment. Once he had recovered, he protested that Dr. Dukes's bill was too small, and when the doctor would take no more, Eugene bought him the best movie camera he could find as a gift. O'Neill and his nurses had become so attached to one another that they all wept at a parting dinner arranged by Carlotta. One of the nurses, Kathryne Radovan Albertoni, remained a friend of the O'Neills for the rest of their years in the Bay Area and helped them out from time to time as O'Neill's health continued to deteriorate.

The O'Neills were searching for a house to rent. Herbert Freeman, who had worked for the O'Neills in Georgia, had driven their car across the country, bringing their beloved dalmatian, Blemie. For the time being, Freeman and Blemie stayed in a hotel near the Fairmont that tolerated dogs, while the O'Neills redoubled their efforts to find a house. They found one they liked in Lafayette but could not move in until June 1. In early April they moved temporarily into a house in the Berkeley Hills where they planned to stay until June. Their Berkeley hosts remained friends during their California years. The O'Neills bought a hilltop site of nearly 160 acres east of Danville, and Carlotta began planning a white-brick U-shaped house with a blue tile roof, which they described as "California Gringo" in style. This would be Tao House, where the O'Neills would live until the end of February 1944.

On June 1 they moved into the Lafayette house, and once again Carlotta flourished, working with the architects and builders, planning the decor of Tao House, and shopping at Gumps for Asian furnishings that would include a carved mahogany couch supposed to have once graced an opium palace. O'Neill resumed thinking about the Cycle as a whole and making notes for the later plays as well as the earlier ones. In August he started to work his way into the new first play, one that would take the story back to the birth of Simon's paternal grandfather in 1755 on a farm. O'Neill bought drafting equipment so that he could draw up charts plotting family trees and showing all the connections between Cycle characters. He swam as often as he could because it seemed to help him ward off painful attacks of heartburn and bile. He had maddening episodes of hives that lasted off and on for days. At times he had trouble with his vision. Through the fall he felt generally rotten and was depressed, but he kept writing. He could not get into the new first play at once, though he worked at it every day. A painful neuritis, apparently caused by long hours of writing, afflicted his right shoulder and arm, and he suffered what he called sinking spells, episodes of low blood pressure, when he could barely stand or walk and felt on the verge of fainting.

Through it all, the O'Neills were less isolated than in Georgia. O'Neill resumed an old friendship with Felton Elkins, whom he had first known in Baker's class at Harvard. Occasionally Carlotta invited Cynthia and Roy Stram and her mother, Nellie. Nellie's mind was failing; she now lived with the Strams because she could not care for herself. The O'Neills sometimes saw Dr. Dukes and his wife or another of their doctors, George Reinle, and his wife, for tea or dinner. They saw a few other new or old friends. Through fall, O'Neill made gradual progress on the new first play in the Cycle, and he was able to finish the draft by working sometimes from morning until past ten at night. Finally, on December 21, as much from exhaustion as from satisfaction, he called it finished for now, with the comment that he knew it was only a draft. The next day he began making notes for the revision, but the soreness in his arm forced him to stop. At times the pain kept him awake at night. Still, he could not let go of the play, but persisted in rereading the draft, which was now longer than *Strange Interlude*. Reluctantly, he concluded that he would have to make two plays of it. The Cycle was now projected to contain nine plays. He consulted various specialists about the pain in his arm, which prevented him from assisting at all with the packing and hauling just before New Year's day, when they moved into Tao House.

O'Neill's arm hurt so that through January 1938, he still could not use it. Eugene and Carlotta loved the new house, with its fine views in all directions, but he could only rarely take pleasure in it because he could not work and because he was in so much pain. He went to the six-day bicycle races with Freeman to see if he could forget the pain, but he could not; he went to a football game with Carlotta and other friends but regretted it later because sitting in the stadium in the rain made his arm worse. Understandably, he became very depressed. Defying the neuritis, he began notes for the second play in the Cycle, in which his character would go to France, meet Robespierre, and become a Jacobin.

There were problems with the house that required the builders to make repeated visits. Eugene endured such a series of dental problems, including a broken front tooth, that he felt thankful that only a few natural teeth were left. Throughout February and March he could write little, but gradually his neuritis improved, and at the end of March he began studying the scenario written for *More Stately Mansions* three years before, when he had first conceived the Cycle. Through the rest of the year he worked nearly every day on *More Stately Mansions* and made steady progress despite his numerous ailments. He finished a first draft on September 8 and at once began rewriting. The neuritis returned with winter and slowed his work down. But on January 1, 1939, he started revising the typescript of *More Stately Mansions*. This is the revised typescript that survives.

Like the other late plays, *More Stately Mansions* is a work of considerable complexity and subtlety. Between *Poet* and *More Stately Mansions*, Simon Harford has become estranged from his father, who objected to his marrying Sara Melody, and has become a successful industrialist in a company that competes successfully with his father's. On his father's death, he acquires the family company, which he absorbs into his own. His mother, asking only that she be allowed to live in her garden and be with her grandsons, gives him and Sara the Harford mansion and estate and promises to seclude herself and not interfere in the lives of Sara and Simon. Simon becomes ever more grandiose in his corporate ambition: to assure his financial autonomy, he must own the Southern plantations that grow the cotton for his Northern mills; he must own the ships that bring cotton from South to North, that bring slaves to work his plantations, and that carry his goods to European markets; he must control the making of his cotton into clothing and other goods, and the retailers that sell the goods. As for his competitors, he drives them out of business or forces them to sell out to him.

Of all this, the audience hears much but is shown only a little. O'Neill dramatizes the interrelations of the play's three main characters, Simon, Sara, and his mother, Deborah. The playwright explores almost every conceivable variation on the theme of the triangle son-husband, mother, and wife. Each character is strongly developed. As in O'Neill's other late plays, action among the characters is almost never overt, in fact, almost never carried out. Action occurs in the possibilities the three characters suggest to each other regarding something that might be done and the consequences if it were.

Possibilities for action involving the three arise from their living together on the Harford estate. The proximity of his mother and wife leads to Simon's realization that his mental images of the two women merge, and that at times he hardly knows who he himself is. When this occurs, he feels that he is losing his *autonomy*—that is his word—and that he may go mad. In fact, he often has delusional moments, particularly in connection with obsessive thoughts about his childhood relationship with his mother. In his childhood, his mother entertained her son and herself with fantasies of romance and intrigue in the court of eighteenth-century France, fantasies that to Sara seem merely insane but that lead Simon back to feelings of an idyllic closeness that he once felt he shared with his mother. In his childhood, Deborah transformed the fantasies she derived from reading eighteenth-century memoirs into fairy tales of princes and wicked enchantresses. In Deborah's own fantasies, a summerhouse in the garden became a place of assignation where the king or the emperor met his mistress, a figure conjoined in the tales with the fairy enchantress and enacted by Deborah. Simon's youthful sexuality became focused on the gazebo, and later he half-believed it to be the place where his mother entertained regal lovers.

Simon's childhood oedipal conflicts fully reawaken, and at times his sexual desire for his wife wanes. Sara now seems to him "coarse," and he compares this impression of her unfavorably with the fineness of taste and feeling he believes he and his mother share. Such episodes alternate with periods of revulsion toward his mother and lust for Sara. And at times, his old feelings of love and friendship for Sara return, and he recognizes that he is approaching a state of desperation. To try to separate the images of his two women, he conceives a grand reorganization.

He decides that it will be dangerous for his sons to grow up as he did under the influence of what he calls his mother's madness. He decrees that Deborah will no longer be allowed to be with his sons except when he or Sara is present to protect them. In place of his sons, he offers his mother the daily company of himself. He will visit her for hours every day in her garden, from which Sara will also be excluded. In the garden, away from Sara's greed for possessions, he and his mother resume their old intimacy. They join in contempt for Sara's greed, as they formerly scorned the materialism of Simon's father. Sheltered by the garden walls, they can regard the world with Byronic aloofness, signified by a passage from *Childe Harold's Pilgrimage* (canto 3) quoted in both surviving Cycle plays:

> I have not loved the World, nor the World me;
> I have not flattered its rank breath, nor bowed
> To its idolatries a patient knee,
> Nor coined my cheek to smiles,—nor cried aloud
> In worship of an echo: in the crowd
> They could not deem me one of such—I stood
> Among them, but not of them. [quoted in CP3, 326–27]

Simon means to exclude Sara from his life only to a degree; he aims to separate his life with her from his life with his mother. He persuades Sara to become his business partner, at first as a confidential secretary who observes his negotiations with competitors and listens to him analyze situations and individuals. As her judgment of opponents and opportunities sharpens, Simon allows her to conduct negotiations and develop strategy; he encourages her to use her sexual power to overwhelm rivals in negotiations. At the same time he introduces a complicated sexual game between her and himself, in which Sara plays the whore with him, trading to him scandalous sexual adventures at his office for portions of the Harford business empire. In the game, Simon acts out as an adult the fantasies created in childhood and adolescence from his mother's tales of manipulating kings and emperors through sexual trysts in the summerhouse. He casts Sarah in the roles his mother played.

The long-term goal in the game leads to Sara's fully owning and controlling the corporation, so that Simon can gradually withdraw into dependency. In the end everything collapses because Simon, like his father, borrows so heavily that the entire financial structure becomes unstable. Simon's health breaks down, and Sara, who has finally had her fill of wealth, seizes an opportunity to destroy the corporation, believing that it will save her family. Ailing with that Victorian bugaboo, brain fever, Simon goes into a coma, and she takes him and their sons back to the one piece of property they retain besides Deborah's mansion, the cabin by the pond. There the boys can grow up in Thoreauvian simplicity, while she once again nurses Simon back to health. The play has come full cycle, back to its starting point.

Even a synopsis conveys at least some of the play's strength and subtlety. Its great length, and the seeming failure of attempts to abridge it, may make *More Stately Mansions* a work that will be usually read rather than seen onstage. From the mid-1920s on, O'Neill made no secret of his desire to write for readers as much as for theater audiences, and if he had any particular audience in mind besides himself while writing *More Stately Mansions,* it may have been readers. Even in its not-quite finished state, the play can seem quite fine to a reader. In its effects and its ways of achieving those effects, in combining action deferred or restrained with searching, detailed accounts of psychological processes, in its sense of purpose and of the tragic, it somewhat resembles a Wharton novel.

Like most other O'Neill plays, it is suffused with death, the deaths of parents. Act 1 begins with the wake for Sara's father; act 2 begins with Sara in mourning for her mother when news comes regarding the death of Simon's father. At the end, when Simon collapses with brain fever and the business is lost, Deborah dies.

From a psychoanalytic viewpoint, *More Stately Mansions* is a most interesting work because here, at long last, O'Neill let himself come face to face with his mourning for his mother, a task that required him to face his childhood and adult sexuality. O'Neill's illnesses of the mid-1930s were almost certainly exacerbated by unconscious or partly conscious conflicts that had festered because of mourning and mourning suppressed. As in a psychoanalysis, things got worse before they could become better. O'Neill's letters and diary notes suggest that he would surely be the first to agree that writing *More Stately Mansions* awakened or intensified irreconcilable inner conflicts that expressed themselves mostly in physical illness.

Working only from an abridged text published in 1964, Sheaffer concludes that Simon Harford's relationship with Deborah resembled Edmund Tyrone's with Mary, and O'Neill's with Ella. Perhaps if he had been able to read the corrected typescript (now available in the Bower edition and in the *Complete Plays*), he would have noticed that O'Neill was also representing his brother's relations with their mother. It seems accurate to say that O'Neill represented in Simon and Deborah's interactions some mixture of his own fantasies of a relationship with his mother and what he believed had been his brother's actual relationship with her. Writing *More Stately Mansions* seems to have given Eugene for the first time the freedom to explore his envy of Jamie, whom he thought his mother had preferred, his identification with Jamie, and his own fantasies of maternal seduction.

Deborah does not physically resemble other women characters assumed to derive from Ella O'Neill. She is described as small, thin, and "girlish." But the portrait of Deborah emphasizes the most prominent trait in other portraits of Ella, and the one that was apparently historically true of Ella, her immaturity. O'Neill twice uses the word "immaturity" in stage directions describing Deborah. The lurid fantasies that Deborah conjures from eighteenth-century memoirs of Versailles suggest a person who relishes regression. Deborah's rejection of disagreement and her snapping scorn for inferiors seems unlike most of Ella's reported behavior with servants, nurses, and friends, but it resembles the behavior of Mary Tyrone in *Long Day's Journey* when she is high on morphine. Deborah's walled garden calls to mind the convent to which both Mary Tyrone and Ella O'Neill longed to return, and also the isolated kingdom of Eugene's schoolboy fantasies.

By midway through act 4, scene 2, Simon has given virtually everything to Sara and wanders from moment to moment, often unaware of
where he is or what he sees. He goes to Deborah's garden, where he is
greatly shocked to find Sara talking to his mother. Deborah, who was still
youthful in her appearance in act 3, set a year earlier, now seems "a little,
skinny witch-like old woman, and evil godmother . . . from a fairy
tale. . . . [Her] face is haggard with innumerable wrinkles" (CP3, 503; all
remaining page references in this chapter are also to CP3, unless otherwise noted). The play's dramatic process is marked by constantly changing alliances among the three characters, now Sara and Simon against
Deborah, now Simon and Deborah against Sara, and so on. At this moment in act 4, the two women have passed from near-war to near-peace,
but the alliance weakens when Simon appears.

Simon sounds like a young Nietzsche as he tries to find a way to tolerate what he finds in himself and in the garden. He declares to the
women: "The true nature of man and woman, to which we have hitherto
given the bad name of evil because we were afraid of it, is, in a world of
facts dominated by our greed for power and possession, good because it
is true" (517). The wish to reduce the world to facts bespeaks a desperate
need to flee from impulses and emotions. O'Neill describes Simon's mood
as "tense, brittle, quiet" (516). His mood frightens both women when he
suddenly appears. They have just agreed that he seems on the verge of being torn apart by his inner conflicts, and he concurs.

Driven, compulsive, seeming about to snap from tension he barely
contains, he bursts out in a "violent accusation": "I have been forced
to the conclusion lately that in the end, if the conflicting selves within a
man are too evenly matched—if neither is strong enough to destroy the
other before the man himself, of which they are halves, is exhausted by
their struggle and in danger of being torn apart between them—then that
man is forced at last, in self-defense, to choose one or the other. . . . To
throw all his remaining strength to one and help it to destroy the other."
(517–18).

Consciously, Simon means to analyze the effect on him of intense
ambivalence. To the women characters and the audience Simon sounds
far less calmly rational than he means to be. If one bears in mind Simon's
voice, described in stage directions as "breaking" and "trembling," his
"brittle" state of mind, and his tenseness, the words seem to mean that he
is close to taking his own life, or perhaps to killing whichever of the

women he identifies with the weaker half of his ambivalence. The women attack him verbally, until he complains: "Is there no love or pity left in your hearts? Can't you see you are driving me insane? (*He begins to sob exhaustedly. . . . Their first reaction is victory. But there is no satisfaction or triumph.*)" (520). In pity, the women go to him where he has sunk down beside the pool. He becomes confused about who they are. In a "dreamy," peaceful daze, he thanks them gratefully "for life," turns to Sara and says "I love you my mother. (*He turns to Deborah.*) I love you, my—(*He stops guiltily—then springs to his feet.*)" (528).

In the horror of oedipal guilt, he tries to deny or explain his misperception. He cannot bear to be with both women at once and finds a way to send Sara into the house. Alone with her son, troubled by her own sexual feelings as much as by Simon's, Deborah coldly mocks him: "A Napoleon who believes in fairy tales and marches to Moscow in search of a magic door—the Emperor whose greatest ambition is to invade and conquer a summerhouse in his mother's garden." (523). Simon vows to discard Sara, perhaps by killing her, and Deborah asks him if he has gone mad. No, he insists, he now sees "the truth." "When finally the bride or the bridegroom cometh, we discover we are kissing Death" (528). The allusion to the bridegroom's finding death gives further expression to the oedipal horror he felt when he confused his wife and mother. Now he insists that he is not mad, that his horror comes from a "sane" but skeptical view of life. Deborah tries to stop him, but he talks on. "Obsessed by a fairy tale, we spend our lives searching for a magic door and a lost kingdom of peace from which we have been dispossessed by a greedy swindler." It is the murderer, Simon adds, who "possesses the true quality of mercy" (529).

Little by little, Simon seduces Deborah from her defenses, and gradually she acknowledges that she, too, thinks of murdering Sara, out of envy of her youth and her children and her power over Simon. She begins to drift into her fantasy world of court intrigue, and, as she does, Simon fixes his eye on the flimsy door to the summerhouse and insists that his mother save him from his lust for his wife. "I have waited since I was a little boy. All my life since then I have stood outside that door in my mind, begging you to let me re-enter that lost life of peace and trustful faith and happiness! I cannot wait any longer, Mother. And you cannot wait. You must choose between me and yourself. You once chose yourself and must either choose to repudiate that old choice, and give me back the faith you stole from me, or I will choose her!" (531).

Another motivation, besides the primal sexual longing, is evident in Simon's words, and in the memory of sexual rejection. If he chooses his wife, Simon explains, his mother will have no choice left. You can only "run and hide within yourself in [the summerhouse] again—and so be rid of me again," he tells her (531). Simon continues, demanding simultaneously that his mother gratify incestuous sexual longings and restore the childhood taken from him by her retreat from him and life: "I am waiting, Mother—for you to open that door, and give me back what was mine—my kingdom of the spirit's faith in life and love that your greed for yourself dispossessed me from!" (531–32). Deborah insists that he recognize that the door that obsesses him is merely a piece of flimsy wood, but he insists on clinging to the symbolic meanings he has given it. He tells his mother:

> The actual door there is a necessary concrete symbol. Your opening it and leading me inside will be the necessary physical act by which your mind wills to take me back into your love, to repudiate your treachery in driving me out of your heart, to deny the evil ruthless woman your dreams of freedom made you and become again your old true self, the mother who loved me alone, whom alone I loved! . . . . The kingdom of peace and happiness in your story is love. You dispossessed yourself when you dispossessed me. Since then we have both been condemned to an insatiable, unscrupulous greed for substitutes to fill the emptiness, the loss of love we had left within. (*He stares obsessedly at the door again.*) But you have only to open that door, Mother— which is really a door in your own mind. [533–34]

With a shudder, Deborah replies, "I know!—and I know only too well the escape it leads to." Simon, his eyes still fixed on the door, tells her seductively to forget her fears, to travel in her mind back to the garden as it seemed when he was a child. Then, with "bitter, vindictive condemnation," he tells of feeling betrayed and deserted by her: "By God, I hated you then! I wished you dead! I wished I had never been born!" (534). As Sheaffer (LS, 483) noticed, the words call to mind Edmund Tyrone's words to his mother in *Long Day's Journey* describing his feelings when he learned that she was a morphine addict, which "made everything in life seem rotten" (CP3, 787). In *More Stately Mansions* it seems clear that Ella

O'Neill's addiction was very much on the playwright's mind. Ella's morphine, like Deborah's summerhouse, offered her isolation from a child's curiosity. With the thinnest pretense of remorse but in fact with "cruel satisfaction," Deborah replies: "You were such a stubborn, greedy little boy, so inquisitive and pryishly possessive. I could feel your grasping fingers groping toward every secret, private corner of my soul. . . . At times I hated you and wished you had never been born. So I had to do something to warn you and I thought a fairy tale would be the most tactful way" (534). In "horror" at what she has found in herself, she denies what she has said, insists that he put the thought into her mind, and attacks him for saying he had wished her dead.

Simon "contritely" apologizes, but he continues to demand that she change the ending of the story: "Open the door and take me back" (535). Deborah begins to drift back into her romantic fantasy, describing herself to Simon in the third person: The woman Simon evokes "will not recognize you as her son! She never had a child." Deborah continues: "She has loved herself alone. . . . You will be no more than another man to her— that is, no more than a slave to her every whim and caprice—like the King before she discarded him to make a fool of Napoleon whom her poor weakling of a father confused with God and himself." (536).

Sara returns to the garden, suspicious of their long absence, and attacks Deborah for breaking their treaty. Deborah defies Sara and tells Simon, as if he were a character in her fantasy, "My love, you no longer remember this woman, do you? You will not permit a vulgar, common slut to intrude and delay our departure." Lost in regression, Simon obediently replies "No mother," and says to Sara, "Who are you? What do you want?" He continues: "It is true you remind me of a mistress I once bought to amuse myself observing her greedy attempts to swindle me of myself. But it was I who swindled her by paying her with counterfeit appearances. Then when her lust began to bore me, I deserted her and went off with another woman, an old lover of my childhood." (538). Deborah "exultantly" reaches behind her back to open the door, standing in the opening and confronting Sara who falls on her knees and pleads with Deborah to have pity on Simon. Deborah insists that she and Simon will cross the threshold, and Sara tries to warn Simon: "It's her madness in there! It's the asylum!" (539).

Exhausted, Sara is ready to go off, to leave Simon and Deborah to their madness, but at the last moment, she thanks Simon "for all the joy and love you gave me, and give you peace and happiness!" (542). In mad defiance, Deborah insists that she will show Sara that she loves Simon better than his wife can. When Simon tries to go into the summerhouse, Deborah catches him off balance and pushes him down the steps. He falls heavily beside the pond and lies half-conscious. Sara kneels by him, holding his head, while Deborah goes inside the gazebo and shuts the door.

Deborah dies soon afterward. Sara destroys the Harford company and takes Simon and her sons away from the mansion to the cabin beside the lake.

Of O'Neill's losses, it was undoubtedly the death of his mother that most disturbed him, because his relations with her had been the most disturbed. O'Neill believed as a child that his mother was intermittently mad. *More Stately Mansions* gives evidence that as an adult he decided that her drug addiction was secondary to her psychological immaturity. In writing *More Stately Mansions,* he seems to have set himself the task of trying to understand her by creating as accurate a picture of her disturbance as he could. He portrayed a person even more pitiable than Mary Tyrone in *Long Day's Journey*—deeply depressed and isolated, self-destructive, but harmless to others, except insofar as the others depend on her for love, attention, and affection that she cannot give.

For O'Neill, the greatest difficulty in mourning her must have been forcing himself to recognize that it was not any trait of his mother's which could be said to be within her control that prevented her from loving him—nothing that could be called willfulness or selfishness or even enslavement to morphine. He had to consider that she simply lacked the capacity to love anyone, including her own child, with any degree of selflessness. The recognition would end the lifelong search to understand how he had failed, what he might have done to win over the brilliant, hard-hearted lover he had been trying to woo (in his fantasies) since early childhood. To mourn her, he had to give up the child's idealization and let go of any notion that he once had lived in Eden with her, or might have, had it not been for the accident of her addiction. Mourning her required him to renounce the old images of her and himself and left the world a bleaker place, with fewer illusions of comfort than before.

21

Tragedy and Beyond
1939

FOURTEEN YEARS EARLIER, OBSESSED BY the recent
deaths of his mother and brother, O'Neill had written *Desire Under
the Elms.* The man and woman in *Desire* have a love affair that both
stepmother and son regard as nearly incestuous and that ends with the
lovers' destroying themselves and their child. For all the play's attention to the consequences of the lovers' crimes, the strongest and most
lasting impression left with the audience is of the lovers' passion and
their conviction, even at the end, that it has carried them beyond
earthly constraints, even beyond fear of the hangman. Psychoanalytically speaking, the play expresses the exultation of an oedipal lover
who triumphs in his fantasies and remains innocent of knowledge of
death, who escapes knowledge of mortal limits and expects to love
eternally.

Desire is the clearest antecedent in O'Neill's finished plays to
More Stately Mansions. To those who have considered both plays from
a psychoanalytic perspective, *Desire* may seem less complex and less developed, perhaps lacking the restraint and patience of the later work to
explore deeply fantasies of incest and their consequences. If *Desire*
shows O'Neill's attention to the social consequences of the crime and
the affair, its exploration of the psychological consequences to the
lovers is less subtle and more superficial.

In writing *More Stately Mansions,* after trying unsuccessfully for
a decade and a half to escape obsessive thoughts about his mother's relations with his brother and himself, the playwright set himself a far

more complex and more delicate task than he did in *Desire:* to create a mother and son who lose themselves in fantasies of incest that stop just short of becoming fully explicit or fully conscious. Stopping short is the difference between neurosis and such family crime as makes news. *More Stately Mansions* shows that the playwright has come far to understand the processes and dynamics of an oedipal neurosis in two adult characters. He imagines Deborah to be a woman who has spent most of her adult life isolating herself from the world by fantasizing love affairs with kings. Psychoanalytically speaking, her exalted lovers are screen figures that in part represent her son, Simon. For his part, Simon has spent his childhood playing audience to his mother's performances and rehearsing the role of suitor to her courtesan.

O'Neill shows the adult Simon placing himself in a position ever more dangerous to his own sanity. Simon often seems conscious, or nearly so, of the incestuous meaning of his mother's fantasies, and of his own fantasies that drive him to imagine storming the summerhouse, an act that to him as a child represented sexually possessing her. The arrogance and boredom that come with his worldly success lead him gradually to renounce the world in favor of the realm of his own fantasies; he arranges his life in a way that allows him to resume the game around which his childhood has developed. It seems, at times, that Simon has a half-conscious aim to overcome ambivalence and carry out in actuality the seduction or even the rape of his mother. As the game intensifies, Simon seems most of all to want a place of safety where he may fantasize his sexual longings, protected by his mother in the walled garden that excludes reality.

The garden serves Simon as the world of playwriting served O'Neill and as the analyst's consulting room has served many an analysand. *Desire* expressed oedipal fantasies as they might be enjoyed by a child or experienced by an adult in a dream or in such regression as accompanies mourning. *More Stately Mansions* expressed variations on oedipal themes as they were being created and analyzed by their author.

Writing *More Stately Mansions* allowed O'Neill to become conscious of differences between his relations with his mother and Jamie's. In certain respects, the interplay between Simon and Deborah in the garden and Simon's memories of his childhood courtship of his mother refer to Eugene's understanding of Jamie's relations with his mother before Eugene was born. Eugene fantasized about what it seemed to him his mother and Jamie had actually enjoyed. Historically speaking, the period in San

Francisco and the period until Jamie was five, when Edmund was born, must have been the happiest in both Ella's and Jamie's lives until after James O'Neill died and mother and son could be reunited. Such seems to be one of the meanings of Eugene showing Simon reuniting with his mother in the garden. By allowing such a fantasy to become conscious, Eugene could begin to view his oedipal feelings from new angles. One new point of view allowed him to see that his rival was his brother, as much as his father, a fact he has seemed not often aware of until that point. He further explored the new insight in the next play he wrote.

In January 1939, after finishing the draft of *More Stately Mansions,* O'Neill began rewriting *A Touch of the Poet;* but within the month he had been distracted by neuritis in his right shoulder, by attacks of prostatitis, and by fatigue, wooziness, and melancholia, symptoms that began in mid-January and that were diagnosed after several recurrences as episodes of dangerously low blood pressure. In early February, Carlotta began noticing problems with her vision and went to Stanford Hospital for extensive testing. She recorded in her diary for February 13 that her eye doctor had recommended surgery.

On February 16 Carlotta noted, "Am surprised to see Gene upset because I must have another operation on my eyes." Her surprise marked the state of the relationship between the O'Neills at the time. Each so closely identified with the other, each felt the other's thoughts and feelings so immediately, that either was likely to be uncertain whether a given feeling or thought arose in oneself or in the other. Carlotta was understandably preoccupied with worry about the eye surgery to the point that it surprised her to realize that Eugene worried in his own right. He, for his part, blamed himself for her eye problem, which he thought had come from her reading his microscopic script with a magnifying glass in order to type *More Stately Mansions.* Her surgery affected him as strongly as if it had been his eye, or perhaps more strongly, for he relied on her, when he was writing, to "see" for him—that is, to interpret the world for him and mediate between him and reality. While writing, he spent most of every day in a prolonged state of psychological regression into the world of the day's work, from which he might not emerge at all from day to day. Along with the regressions, which are part of most writers' working lives, there were his ailments. After O'Neill had an especially bad "sinking spell," Dr. Dukes ordered changes in his daily routine, including shorter work shifts and more exercise. Eugene began working in the garden several days a week and found he enjoyed it. Carlotta and Eugene got through her surgery, and she made a full recovery.

For more than two years, the O'Neills had been preoccupied with events in Europe. They listened daily to international broadcasts describing the Nazi occupation of Prague, which upset them greatly, as did Chamberlain's meeting with Mussolini in Rome. Through May Eugene revised *Poet,* finishing a third draft on May 19. The next day he got an idea for a play outside the Cycle about Napoleon's coronation, which undoubtedly arose from his preoccupation with Hitler's imperial designs. Unusually warm weather in late spring allowed him to start swimming in the pool, and he continued working in the garden.

He returned to *More Stately Mansions* and began work on a prologue; then he decided to introduce Deborah Harford into *A Touch of the Poet,* imagining a scene between her and Con Melody. This seems to have been the decisive moment in the transformation of *Poet* into a play that is almost entirely high comedy. On June 5 O'Neill became disgusted with the prologue for *More Stately Mansions* and destroyed it. That same day he wrote in his diary that he felt "fed up and stale on Cycle after 4½ years of not thinking of any other work" and had decided that it would do him good to lay it "on the shelf and forget it for a while—do a play that has nothing to do with it."

Reading over various play ideas on June 6, 1939, O'Neill felt a strong interest in two that he had had in mind for years but had hesitated to take on: one was set in a New York waterfront flophouse and bar like Jimmy the Priest's. He populated the bar with characters he had known at Jimmy's, at the Hell Hole, where he and Agnes had met, and at the Garden Hotel, where he had sometimes stayed with Jamie and where his father had liked to drink. The other idea was for a family play set in New London.

The next day the title for the saloon play came to him, *The Iceman Cometh,* a phrase alluding to an old joke that he and Jamie had apparently used to refer both to sexual betrayal and to death. (A salesman comes home early; finding no ice for the drink he wants, he yells upstairs to his wife, "Honey, has the iceman come yet?" She replies, "Not yet, but he's puffing pretty hard.") Scholars have noticed the echo of the biblical phrase about Christ the Bridegroom. But there was a more immediate, personal referent for O'Neill, both in the old joke he shared with Jamie, and in a later variation he had recently devised. In *More Stately Mansions* O'Neill had had Simon Harford tell his mother, when both are seemingly on the verge of incest, "When finally the bride or the bridegroom cometh, we discover we are kissing death" (CP3, 528).

Despite his preoccupation with the war in Europe and despite further debilitating episodes of low blood pressure, he finished an outline for *The Iceman Cometh* on June 24. The next day he began notes for *Long Day's Journey into Night,* which he outlined in eight days. As simply as this, O'Neill's long preoccupation with the Harfords and America's past came to a casual end.

Both new play ideas led O'Neill toward another complex set of thoughts and feelings for his mother, those which prevented him from adequately resolving adolescent oedipal conflicts. Oedipal deeds and wishes existed mainly in fantasy, and they could be partly resolved by being brought into consciousness and examined. But Ella O'Neill's addiction was real, and the guilt Eugene felt for it, while deeply entangled with oedipal wishes and fantasies, had some grounds in reality. Ella's death had reactivated both the oedipal guilt and other forms of guilt that had preoccupied Eugene since 1922. The exploration of complex forms of guilt became a central theme that led the playwright to *The Iceman Cometh.*

O'Neill organized *The Iceman Cometh* around two parallel stories that he told in carefully balanced counterpoint. He first introduced the eighteen-year-old Don Parritt, who has betrayed his anarchist mother to the police and caused her to be imprisoned. To Parritt, his mother's essential quality and ruling motivation was her need to be a "free woman," which meant to him that she took as many lovers as she wished, all the while ruling her son and her anarchist cell with an iron hand. Parritt felt as bitter about the lovers, and about his mother's refusal to tell him who his father was, as about his personal lack of freedom and enforced anarchist orthodoxy.

His rejection of the Movement and his betrayal of his mother express rebellion, the natural impulse to separate his self-image from his identification with his mother. Sick with guilt, Parritt believes he has sent his mother to a living death. Eventually he lets himself understand and acknowledge his ambivalent feelings toward her. The insight leads him to an ecstatic state that might, in other circumstances, mark growth toward autonomy. But his need for his mother remains primal. As he says, he never knows what to do or think until his mother tells him. Deprived of her guidance, he resolves his crisis of conscience by adopting a mystical certainty that he must die for betraying her. Near the end of the play, while the bums in the flophouse enjoy a raucous party, he jumps from an upper-story window, unnoticed by the revelers.

In rough outline, the story comes close enough to the playwright's own story of attempted suicide for one to see that throughout his long struggle to be free of his mother's ghost, O'Neill has focused on the guilt he feels for the living death of his mother's addiction. He makes of Parritt one more of his Orestean figures, men whose love and hatred of their mothers center on feelings of rejection, betrayal, and sexual jealousy that lead to a longing for vengeance. Like Orestes, like Eben Cabot, Reuben Light, Orin Mannon, and Edmund Tyrone, Parritt is made mad by his wishes and deeds. Unlike Orestes, Parritt is saved by neither a god nor a turn of chance.

O'Neill weaves Parritt's tale around the story of another doomed soul, the traveling salesman Hickey, a binge drinker like the playwright who created him. Hickey arrives every year just in time to celebrate Harry Hope's birthday and buy booze enough for all the regulars who get drunk with him. At last, someone sends him home to his constant wife, Evelyn. When he sobers up, he begs her forgiveness. She assures him that she knows this time will be different, that it's not his fault if women like him and if his pals tempt him to get drunk. He promises to reform, and every time he means it; Evelyn's faith convinces him that he can turn over a new leaf. Hickey has lived life according to this rhythm for years.

Hickey's sense of himself revolves around a romantic pipe dream that, as he says, no two people ever loved each other as much as he and Evelyn. He tells his friends that Evelyn, an offstage character, has lived by a pipe dream that seems to be nearly the mirror image of his: she is convinced that they love each other and that if she can love him perfectly enough and be constant and unwavering, it will eventually enable him to reform, as she knows he wants to do. He has tried since adolescence to become what she expects, but he invariably fails and goes on another drunk. His need for her is so great that away from her on the road, unable to drink while working, he'd get to "seeing things in the wall paper" of hotel rooms. He'd be "lonely and homesick. But at the same time sick of home." To escape his ennui and hallucinations, he would find a woman with whom he could be himself "without being ashamed" (CP3, 696).

He insists to himself and his saloon friends that the women "didn't mean anything." Saying he sees no meaning in the woman or his need for her is a way to deny the shame and self-loathing that he says being with Evelyn causes him. The statement also denies the difference between his pipe dream and Evelyn's. The difference could hardly be more important: he believes she loves him completely and forever, and feels her love makes him a better man than he would otherwise be; while (as he describes her) she loves the man she is sure he will become when improved by her perfect faith in the essential goodness she believes is within him. His need for Evelyn's love makes him identify with her dream and incorporate her dream into his own sense of himself while he's with her between business trips or binges. But the urge gradually builds to escape so that he can be himself. It is an urge to separate his image of himself from her image of him, which exists not only in her but in him when he is with her.

To an outsider, Evelyn's love seems to create in Hickey a constant sense of guilt that he struggles to avoid recognizing. He succeeds for longish times, until the strain of maintaining denial becomes too great. When the guilt he has denied resurfaces, life with Evelyn becomes as intolerable as the life he fled in Indiana, where his preacher father tried to whale virtue into him with a birch rod. Finally he gives up, goes on another selling trip, starts seeing things in the wallpaper, finds a woman, and begins to slide toward a binge that will go on until he hits bottom and can drink no more.

His love for Evelyn and his faith in the marriage depend on denying the difference between their pipe dreams, and on denying that his impulses to misbehave have meaning. When denial works, it conceals a world of resentment against her because he (half-consciously) believes she loves him not as he is but as she hopes he will become. Just before he has come to the saloon for Harry Hope's birthday binge, this year, he has killed Evelyn to "free her," as he tells his friends in act 4, from the humiliation of being married to a no-good, drunken cheater like himself. (Between act 3 and act 4 he has called the police to come and arrest him for the murder.)

To the men in the saloon, his motive for killing her seems simple. Shooting her allows Hickey to escape from the resentment he feels toward her expectations, her "pipe dream." He has escaped her gentle pressure to stray no more and feels at last free from the guilt, shame, and self-loathing he feels for himself, knowing he will again betray her. Killing her—killing her pipe dream, as he thinks of it—elevates Hickey into an ecstasy in which he believes that he has found the secret for permanent happiness, to renounce whatever "lying pipe dreams" poison and ruin a guy's life, as he tells the bums in act 1.

Hickey in his euphoria comes to the saloon on a mission, to convert the inmates to his new philosophy that happiness comes when one stops imagining that tomorrow will be better. To be happy, he says, a guy should admit he's a bum and not worry about it. Through most of the play Hickey attacks the regulars' pipe dreams, with which he is well acquainted because he has played his part up to now in supporting all the dreams. Without fully understanding what he intends, he does to his friends what he feels Evelyn has always done to him; he gets even with the world for things' being as they are. His psychological assaults at first deprive the men of whatever vestige of self-esteem they cling to and make them so anxious that alcohol depresses rather than elates them.

By act 4, when all the bums loathe him, when his jollity is strained and he desperately needs their friendship again, he tells them the story of his and Evelyn's undying love for each other. He has hinted throughout the play that his wife has died by some means. Finally, in act 4, he tells them that he shot her while she slept. It was "for her sake," so that "she'd never feel any pain, never wake up from her dream" of his improving. As he tells of killing her, he slips into a reverie and, without seeming to realize what his words mean, he describes chuckling after he shot her and saying, "Well you know what you can do with your pipe dream now, you damn bitch!" (CP3, 700). For an instant he realizes that he hated her as well as loved her. In the next moment, he disowns the knowledge, insisting to all that he was "insane" at the moment he spoke the slur. He has no tolerance for ambivalent emotion; having opposed feelings for someone leads him to believe he was mad.

In the instant of showing the audience why he shot his wife, he also shows why he has abused his friends at the bar: without fully knowing why, he treats them as he has felt treated by her, acting out his continuing rage against her. By making them feel as he thinks she has made him feel, he hopes to make them understand why he shot her. The psychoanalytic idea "acting out" means expressing an unconscious impulse through an action without bringing it to consciousness. Hickey remains unaware of what he has done to his friends or why, as we see at his final exit. As the police lead him off, he is still trying to save his friends from their pipe dreams. At the same time, it is clear that he still clings to his own pipe dream that he and Evelyn share a perfect love for each other—present tense. He cannot wait to go to the chair, he tells the bums and the police, because he needs to make Evelyn understand that he was crazy when he called her a bitch. Hickey shows why he has been able to assure the bums throughout that death is nothing to be feared. To him it has no reality.

As Manheim and others have noticed, there are many similarities between Hickey and Jamie O'Neill, a few of which will be mentioned here. Both grew up with churchly fathers in Indiana; both hated their fathers. Both have a gift of gab and make friends wherever they go. Both are greatly popular with women and with drinking companions; for both, sex is associated with prostitutes and is mostly separated from love of an idealized woman. The portrait of Jamie Tyrone in *Long Day's Journey* shows a man who, like Hickey, cannot tolerate ambivalence. The only ordinary job Jamie O'Neill ever seems to have found congenial was the one he held for several months in 1900 when he traveled through New England as a salesman for a lumber firm. Later he enjoyed his only theatrical success while playing the lead in a play called *The Travelling Salesman*. Jamie never came close to marrying, but in his fashion he was his mother's lifelong, devoted, and faithful cavalier, and Eugene's understanding of his brother's relationship with their mother is part of the model for the relationship between Hickey and Evelyn. Hickey's end, like Jamie's, came because he could not survive the death of his beloved.

Parritt, like Hickey, has come to Hope's bar on a mission; he is mad to understand why he betrayed his mother. Alienated from everyone else he has known by his act of betrayal, he is seeking Larry Slade, one of the regulars, a man who was his mother's lover for some time, ten years before. In his loneliness then and his desperation now, he has made of Larry a father figure whom he can ask for help. Notwithstanding his whining and lying, the audience must increasingly take Parritt seriously, and even see him as a tragic figure, because he makes a serious and determined effort to learn about himself. Larry loathes Parritt's crime and cannot bear to conjecture about the guilt that consumes the youth. Yet he cannot coldly reject Parritt as he would like to do and instead pities him now in his guilt, as he once pitied the "serious, lonely little shaver" the boy had seemed when Larry first knew him (CP3, 578).

Larry rebuffs every gesture of submission or dependency that the youth makes. But Parritt, in his attempts to explain his act or exculpate himself, repeatedly finds ways to nettle the old man by demanding from him any reaction at all. Through sheer persistence, Parritt forces Larry gradually to say enough things for the youth to sense how his act appears to another, and how weak his efforts to explain it to himself seem to other ears. To hold Larry's attention, Parritt must lie less and less, and finally he begins to see himself as the old man sees him. Late in act 4, just before Hickey explains that he killed his wife to give both Evelyn and himself "peace," Parritt makes the discovery that he betrayed his mother "because I hated her" (CP3, 700).

Of the major characters, Larry may seem particularly enigmatic because he is made to fulfill so many roles in the play. He was modeled outwardly on Terry Carlin, and O'Neill undoubtedly had in mind the winter of 1915–1916, when he was alienated from his father and gravitated toward Terry while scraping bottom in New York. Among other things, Larry participates in Parritt's struggle to discover why he has betrayed his mother and to validate the sentence the youth passes on himself. O'Neill makes Parritt's story a miniature Greek tragedy, which he sets in the context of the play as a whole. In relation to Parritt, Larry is chorus leader, the *choregos* who witnesses and feels the tragedy of Parritt's story; he is the only one among the regulars in the bar who can afford, emotionally, to notice it at all.

To a biographer, it may seem that Larry speaks the part of O'Neill himself, who believed that he was "born without a skin" and tried with almost no success to harden himself against knowing the thoughts and feelings of everyone he saw. Beyond this, O'Neill represents through Larry the difficulty he experienced in being with his own children. When with them or even when writing letters to them, he could seldom relax and enjoy their company. The presence of his children, in his home, or even in his mind, caused O'Neill's pessimism to emerge in its most extreme form, to the point that almost all he could see was the likelihood of disaster. Around that core of qualities he created the character of Larry.

As for Parritt, O'Neill made use of the youth to represent the parts of himself that denied or distorted his crimes against his mother and that refused to acknowledge what he truly felt and imagined. Parritt's story eventually suggests that the youth's real crime, greater even than that of betraying his mother, is the refusal to know that he hates her, which makes him vulnerable to an impulse to act against her. Perhaps neither crime is really a capital offense; nevertheless, the crime and punishment are piteous, terrible, and even credible. Parritt is as far from independence at eighteen as O'Neill was, and he has no tolerant and supportive father like James O'Neill to stand by a wayward son until he can straighten himself out.

Writing of Parritt, who hates his mother for putting the Movement before her son, for putting her right to be promiscuous ahead of her role as his mother, and for depriving him of a father—writing Parritt's story clarified for O'Neill important aspects of his anger and guilt toward his mother. It allowed him to see that beneath the primal guilt he felt for causing her addiction lay the ordinary and resolvable complications of a normal oedipal neurosis. Repressed in the normal way were hatred of his mother for preferring morphine to him, for neglecting him when he was ill, and for being so self-centered when high that she sometimes did not even know him.

One large matter had no direct relation to morphine: he resented her preferring Jamie to him. The representations of Parritt and Larry enabled O'Neill to begin to be conscious of an inhibition that had held him hostage for decades and prevented him from analyzing ordinary grievances against his mother. Growing up he had needed Jamie so much, to be the one from whom he could learn about his mother's behavior and family politics, the one on whom he could rely when he hated his father, that he had to conceal from himself the envy he felt toward Jamie because of his mother's bond with her first son. Parritt represents in part O'Neill's sense of his youthful self, and Larry represents the part of him that pretended to accept it all while sitting in dour, pessimistic judgment on himself and the world.

Writing Hickey's story took O'Neill deep into his mother's relations with Jamie. Because of her addiction, which had made it impossible for her to care for him in his childhood, Ella could not look at Eugene without feeling anxious, guilty, and ashamed. But no such complications affected her feelings about Jamie. She and the boy had adored each other from the start; she loved beguiling him, and he loved being her courtier.

Having written *More Stately Mansions* allowed Eugene to perceive that the intimacy between Jamie and his mother that he had long envied had come at a cost to both of emotional stultification. He must have grown up seeing hints of ambivalence in Jamie's feelings toward their mother, and even occasional outbursts against her, which Eugene had dismissed as the voice of liquor or the whim of the moment (and which he later represented as the slurs Jamie Tyrone makes against his mother in act 4 of *Long Day's Journey*). Jamie's behavior while Ella lay dying in Los Angeles, and on the train trip to New York, and the self-destructiveness of Jamie's last two years, must have convinced Eugene that intense hatred of Ella, concealed by Jamie's obvious regard for his mother, existed in Jamie as well as in himself. On reflection, Eugene evidently saw the inextricable attachment between Jamie and his mother as affecting Ella's marriage and Jamie's emotional development and leading to self-destructiveness in both. Such thoughts O'Neill expressed fairly directly in *More Stately Mansions* and less directly in *The Iceman Cometh;* they are most explicit in Hickey, in the murder of his maternal wife and his remark after he has killed her, "Well you know what you can do with your pipe dream now, you damn bitch!"

A great change took place in O'Neill's sensibility in response to his progress in understanding his and Jamie's lives. The gradual developments in O'Neill's awareness since the late 1920s allowed him to create a most surprising context for the tales of Parritt and Hickey. The playwright set his two tragic stories in a profoundly comic context.

As *The Iceman Cometh* opens, the bums in the bar are mostly asleep and painfully sober because Hope, the tavern keeper, worried about money, has refused to give out free drinks to his friends. Hope as much as the others needs Hickey's annual visit, when they expect that joy and wine will flow freely as from a god. The audience meets the inmates of Hope's No Chance Saloon through Larry, who describes to the outsider Parritt the pipe dreams that allow them to forget how impossibly difficult for them is the world outside Hope's saloon.

In introducing the inmates in act 1, O'Neill shows a group that works surprisingly well. Even in lean times, things are not unbearable. When Willie Oban, once a student at Harvard Law School, wakes up screaming from a nightmare about his dead father, Hope relents and tells the bartender to give him enough drink to shut him up and ease his pain. The others, awakened by Willie's scream, drift into their usual recital of tales of the glorious past; as part of the ritual, their fellows accept the tales with good humor. Revived by a few drinks, Willie sings a bawdy ditty he says he learned at Harvard. As Larry assures Parritt, pity is wasted on the bums because, having almost entirely rid their minds of the world of getting and fetching, "they have attained the true goal of their heart's desire" (CP3, 584).

Into a society that O'Neill shows as working well enough, Hickey comes, preaching a salvation that lies in confronting what he calls the truth about one's pipe dreams. Through acts 2, 3, and most of 4, the group becomes increasingly incoherent. Old friends quarrel with each other. Booze no longer brings peace and forgetfulness, but instead makes everyone unbearably anxious and irritable. To destroy the pipe dreams that he believes pernicious, Hickey aims to isolate each regular from his friends. Driven alone back into the world, each will have to confront old failures.

It is a painful test for the individuals, but the group survives intact. A few hours after Hickey has driven them out, the regulars trickle back to the bar, shaken and shaky from sobriety and their excursions. All sense of fellowship has disappeared from the bar. But when the intruding Hickey and Parritt excise themselves, the group regains its equilibrium almost at once. The play ends in raucous singing and uproarious laughter. O'Neill develops none of the bums as a character, or only enough to show the contributions each makes to the group's survival. His portraits of the bums are affectionate but not sentimental. He shows them as likable in their interactions with the group but never hints that any might have latent strengths or resources beyond what is apparent. O'Neill takes them seriously as members of the group, while taking Parritt and Hickey seriously as individuals.

O'Neill ends *The Iceman Cometh* with a spirit just the opposite of that which has marked his plays about individualists since *Beyond the Horizon:* Brutus Jones, Yank, Dion Anthony, and the rest live by the spirit expressed by the favorite Byronic stanza of Simon and Deborah Harford beginning: "I have not loved the World, nor the World me" (CP3, 326–27).

The group in Hope's bar has been forced to face no less a bugaboo than human mortality. As we see at the end, Parritt has come to the bar merely to put his thoughts in order so that he can die; and Hickey, as Larry repeatedly says, bears the stench of death, a stench that the salesman's denial of death's importance or permanence cannot efface. The regulars, their pipe dreams mocked and rejected, have been thrown out of their haven into the streets, where nothing protects them from the overwhelming anxiety that they have always faced in the world outside. They find nothing like the euphoria Hickey has predicted for them, nor do they find the denial that fuels the salesman's euphoria. Alone, they find death, dread of which has driven them back to their haven. The return of the regulars to Hope's bar is the emotional nadir of the play.

Yet, given no more help than the notion that Hickey must have been crazy to do and say the things he did, they soon reconstruct their mutual back-scratching society. The very thing about humanity that the young O'Neill was pleased to despise—the wishful thinking that denies unpleasant reality—he now celebrates. Being able to conclude that Hickey said those crazy things because he'd gone nuts and croaked his wife allows the barflies to dismiss the drummer, and also to ignore Parritt as a sap who never belonged. Once again they drink and sing and feel happy.

Perhaps no play by O'Neill is as complex as *The Iceman Cometh* and none has seemed to audiences, critics, and performers so pessimistic. Critics have been deeply divided in their interpretations of the play. Few critics (or directors) have given as much weight to Parritt as to Hickey, and when people speak of the "lead," they always mean Hickey. The view of the play proposed here is that Hickey and Parritt are taken by the author with about equal seriousness, and given no more weight than the group of men in the bar, taken as a whole. Indeed, the great individualist O'Neill gives the group the last word, a word he seems to endorse.

The problem that the play leaves with an audience is pessimism, a pessimism made unbearable by the absence of alternatives. O'Neill systematically rejects the various beliefs that modern people use to get through life. The examples of Larry and Parritt and Hugo seem to say that if religion is the opiate of the masses, then Marxism and political action are the opiate of the disaffected. As for religion itself, what could be more melancholy than Hickey trying to save souls by making the men in the group suicidally depressed? Hickey surely has no alternative to pessimism in his mad preaching, his evangelical popular psychology, his talk about facing up to the truth about oneself. Does O'Neill intend us to take seriously the idea that the bums with their pipe dreams have the right dope after all?

Perhaps, in a sense. From a psychoanalytic point of view, the bums' drinking and pipe dreams can be said to function in something like the way of the ego defenses that psychoanalysis considers to be the outcome of normal psychological development. People regarded as normal unconsciously use sublimation, repression, projection, regression, reaction formation, denial, and the other defenses to protect against thoughts and feelings that threaten their psychic equilibrium. The difference between the ego defenses and the pipe dreams and drinking is that the defenses are experienced as existing and functioning "internally" (or intrapsychically), while the drinking and pipe dreams are external and therefore more vulnerable: the supply of booze can be cut off; your friends can stop agreeing with your version of your life story.

From a psychoanalytic viewpoint, it is the development of the ego defenses that allows a person to live what is called ordinary life. To imagine life without defenses, recall a terrifying nightmare. Imagine being awake while the nightmare went on; imagine being unable to tell whether the terrifying thing is real or "only a dream," as we say; imagine being unable to awaken from the dream and have it go away. The ego functions to let us distinguish what is as we say *out there* from what is *in here,* and so we confine such terror to occasional dreams. But if psychoanalytic theory is correct about our need for intrapsychic defenses, then those of us (in the audience) who say we are normal may not have any very great claim to superiority over the bums who are dependent on alcohol and yea-saying friends to get through life's waking hours.

O'Neill seems to consider the pipe dreams of *The Iceman Cometh* as processes occurring on a continuum with normal intrapsychic defenses. There is the source of the play's overwhelming pessimism. The chief differences between Hope's regulars and those who count themselves normal lies in degrees of dependency. Those lucky enough not to be addicted to alcohol, who do not fear to go about a world full of strangers, may nevertheless find themselves in exactly the same situation as Hope's people when face to face with what Larry calls the stench of death. It makes sense to say that society works about the same way, no matter whose back one scratches. Any other differences are matters of personal preference.

The Iceman Cometh, like the Freudian idea that O'Neill invokes, seems to attack one of the basic premises of Western humanism, that human rationality and consciousness give us control over our selves, our lives, and our environment. O'Neill always wryly accepted that, as Freud eventually concluded, consciousness is an exceptional rather than a usual aspect of human mental life. When at the beginning and end of the play O'Neill reduces the importance of Hickey and Parritt and elevates the chorus of regulars, he makes the play as much comic as tragic, in the manner of Shakespeare's late plays or of *Oedipus at Colonos, The Bakkhai,* or the ending of the *Oresteia*. From the point of view of human narcissism, the affront is the same whether the play is comic or tragic or both. To a biographer, that O'Neill shows the group surviving, able to laugh and sing while ignoring tragedy, indicates progress, progress that does not negate the author's pessimism or his personal narcissism but moves beyond it.

Don Parritt is a striking characterization for several reasons, one of which is that he is the first male adolescent O'Neill has portrayed who seems more specific than generic. It seems likely that the playwright had in mind his son Shane, who was the same age as Parritt when the play was being written. Parritt's life story and personality partly derive from O'Neill himself. But there are also certain similarities between Parritt and Shane; both adolescents seem immature and dependent for their age. Considering Shane's expulsions from several schools, his prospects in the world did not seem promising. O'Neill seems to have had in mind a specific model for Parritt's syntax, tone of voice, and style of relating to others, and it was probably his troubled second son.

Indeed, O'Neill had reason to be worried about both his sons during the time he was writing *The Iceman Cometh*. Eugene Jr. had had a brilliant undergraduate career, which culminated in his election to Phi Beta Kappa. He was awarded the Winthrop Prize and the Berkeley Scholarship for travel and was Ivy Laureate. He traveled in Europe—the trip was a gift to him from his father. He knew six languages, including classical Latin and Attic Greek. He had wanted to take his doctorate in classics at the University of Freiburg and probably would have been accepted. But a visit to Freiburg and other cities, where he saw enough of the rise of Hitler to disgust him, led him to return to Yale, where he completed his doctorate in 1936, making swift passage through a most demanding program. Immediately after passing his final doctoral exams, he was appointed to the Yale classics faculty, and he gave promise of academic success by publishing articles in standard journals. In a project initiated by Saxe Commins, Eugene Jr. collaborated with Whitney Oates of Princeton on a two-volume collection of translations of *The Complete Greek Drama*, a work that was widely used and influential for nearly two decades. His father was delighted to receive an early copy of the volumes and could not have been more pleased. Increasingly, he considered his first son a friend with whom to discuss his own work, one of a very small circle.

Along with great success, however, came warnings of serious trouble. Eugene Jr.'s marriage of nearly six years to Elizabeth Green ended in divorce in 1937, and the young professor immediately remarried the daughter of a Yale mathematics professor. That marriage ended in divorce about a year later, and Eugene almost immediately made another marriage, which again did not last long. Like many an academic in the 1930s, he dabbled in populist politics and was briefly a member of the Communist Party. He grew increasingly impatient teaching the children of privilege and interested himself in bringing education to the masses. Unlike most academics of the time, he carried his politics and protest to the point of putting his career in jeopardy. He was not attracted to teaching in, say, the City Colleges of New York, which attracted brilliant students and charged low tuition. Instead he dreamed of reaching a vastly larger audience through radio broadcasting and, later, television. A large, strong-looking man with a black Vandyke beard, he was striking in appearance, taller than his father, and he is said to have had a wonderfully resonant voice, inherited, he believed, from his grandfather. He saw radio and television as a chance to make use of his education and voice in combination with the family tradition of acting.

Considering his own romantic history and the lifelong guilt he felt for abandoning Eugene Jr.'s mother, O'Neill neither could nor would criticize his son's marital behavior on moral grounds, and he had always sympathized with leftist political causes, however detached he had felt from them in practice. He paid the bills for Eugene's divorces and mostly refrained from criticism in his letters. Visits passed pleasantly, except for the growing tension between Eugene Jr. and Carlotta.

Carlotta felt outraged and probably said enough for two. Her diary records that when Eugene Jr. married his third wife, on July 3, 1939, his letter to his father did not even give the bride's last name, only Sally. Such carrying on affronted Carlotta, who through her four marriages had made herself socially prominent and financially independent. A man driven to marry by a need for love or sex seemed to her merely a weakling; nor was she interested in whatever psychological complexities drove feelings and behavior like her son-in-law's, especially when her husband felt obliged to pay the legal bills and settlements in the three divorces. She despised the self-indulgence that allowed a young man to waste a fine education and jeopardize his career, and she was angry that her husband gave him money that was needed to secure their own future, especially when it seemed uncertain whether the playwright would ever earn money again. (O'Neill refused to consider allowing any of the Cycle plays to be performed or published until the whole group was complete. The end of the project was far in the future, and much of the time he doubted that he could complete it.) Though she permitted herself no slurs, Carlotta went as far in her revised diary as allowing that she found the visits with Eugene Jr. and the new wives "thoroughly trying" and usually referred to them during the visits as merely "our guests."

During the 1939 visit by Eugene and Sally, O'Neill, who was finishing the first draft of *The Iceman Cometh,* stopped working long enough to swim each day with the couple and to drive with them and Carlotta to Palo Alto, where Eugene Jr. wanted to see the Stanford campus. O'Neill, who was almost always clear sighted about coming bad news, must have been greatly worried about Eugene, and indeed, the young man would soon begin to drink heavily and give up his academic career altogether. Through it all, O'Neill tried to be sympathetic toward his son and, against Carlotta's bitter protests, helped him from time to time financially.

Eugene's marital escapades surely expressed a troubled soul and probably one of their many meanings was that Eugene Jr. could tell his father of his emotional crisis only through action. Eugene Jr.'s behavior somewhat resembled that of his father in the days after he left the sanatorium, when he repeatedly fell in love with and wanted to marry different girls—but the son's case was more extreme. In retrospect, it seems clear that Eugene Jr. had inherited the family predisposition to melancholia, and his father, who was suffering frequent episodes of melancholy himself, had no better idea how to help his son than he had how to help himself. Certain letters between them suggest that depression was a topic they discussed. O'Neill, who still believed that love was worth anything, sympathized with the spirit, if not the results, of his son's attempts to find it. Going a step further, O'Neill must surely have identified with Eugene Jr. very strongly, so strongly that he lacked the objectivity necessary to be helpful.

A certain event just before Eugene and Sally were to end their visit appears to show indirectly O'Neill's concern for his first son. That August 15, O'Neill involved himself in the medical problems of Carlotta's son-in-law, an uncharacteristic thing for him to do. Roy Stram was dangerously ill with rheumatic fever. (He would survive but would be incapacitated for the rest of his life.) O'Neill had become very fond of Roy and

Cynthia, who were happy in their marriage; their daughter was just over a year old, and a son was on the way who would be named Gerald Eugene, after the playwright. O'Neill spent the afternoon talking to Roy and then took him to consult Dr. Dukes, who had performed the playwright's appendectomy.

Along with expressing his genuinely warm feelings, helping Roy must also have been an expression of a frustrated impulse to help Eugene Jr. O'Neill could probably guess that Eugene was seriously depressed. Perhaps the playwright had mentioned psychoanalysis to his son, and perhaps Eugene promised half-heartedly to consider the idea. (Psychoanalysis may well have been an unsuitable form of treatment in the case.) Knowing how different a person his son was, O'Neill could probably feel no confidence in any other idea. His solution for himself, to write plays, was so specific to him, worked so very slowly, and was so uniquely suited to his own gifts, temper, and circumstances, that it would probably not have worked for someone else. O'Neill undoubtedly felt helpless in the face of Eugene's circumstances.

With both Eugene Jr. and Roy facing serious problems, and help for Eugene seeming even more remote than help for Roy, O'Neill acted when he saw a course of action that might work: he could take Roy to a doctor he trusted. In the absence of a good idea for Eugene, O'Neill found a joke that allowed the two to stand on common ground in a shared sense of irony about the situation: "Tell Sally," he wrote his son, "to have you hog-tied and branded for life! I know she will agree with me that in future this marrying has simply got to cease!" (SL, 487). There would be no more marriages, but the marriage to Sally was short-lived and it left both bride and groom the worse for wear.

Although Eugene Jr. had not known his father until he was eleven, the two had gradually grown close since 1921 and had established a relationship based on occasional visits, infrequent but regular letters, and shared deep interests and values. O'Neill greatly respected his son's intelligence and learning, and the two shared a taste for sardonic wit and irony.

Forming a relationship with Shane had been a different matter, difficult for both, partly because Shane at seventeen or eighteen or later remained childlike and passively dependent. O'Neill did not know how to be with children. He had not been able to relate to children when he was a child himself, and he was no better at it now. He could fall back only on the sort of advice to work hard and learn the value of a dollar that he had hated to hear from his own father.

The relationship between O'Neill and Shane allowed for nothing so complex as the jokes and reflections that O'Neill and Eugene Jr. shared. If Don Parritt is indeed partly a portrait of Shane, the implication would be that O'Neill felt even worse about Shane than about Eugene, largely because he knew his older son much better and had more confidence in their relationship. Having seen Eugene succeed, his father sometimes hoped that his first son might right himself, even as he seemed to go out of control. But Shane still thought as a child thinks. Now, as then, planning for the future meant to Shane deciding whether he liked being around horses better than drawing pictures or fishing. Neither then nor later could he tolerate the boredom of swamping stables, caring for tack, maintaining a boat, or mastering the technical details of artistic materials and processes.

For some time, perhaps more than a year, O'Neill did not hear from either Shane or Oona. Although Shane later convinced his father that he had written, at the time O'Neill felt understandably irritated that he received no acknowledgment from either child of his receipt of the Nobel, and no expression of concern when he nearly died and was in hospital for three months, both events that made headlines in major newspapers. It appears that Carlotta intercepted and destroyed their letters, possibly in the belief that hearing from Agnes's children would impede her husband's recovery.

Once communications were restored, O'Neill learned that Shane had left the military school in Florida, in part because he was failing and was drinking heavily. He now attended a ranch school near Golden, Colorado. Letters between Shane and his father late the next spring show the difficulties the two faced in trying to get to know each other. From the ranch Shane wrote his father that he needed a horse immediately to replace his, which had died. The request came just before Shane returned to his mother in New Jersey for the summer. He would not see the horse for months, during which time someone else would have to care for it, and anything might happen to it. O'Neill suggested that it might be better to wait until Shane was back at school to look for a new horse. Sounding like his own father, Eugene mentioned that a horse would probably be cheaper at the end of the summer dude ranch season than at the beginning. Although O'Neill would not learn about it for some time, the ranch school had already decided that Shane would not be permitted to return.

O'Neill heard nothing more about the horse, but eventually he received a letter from Shane in New Jersey saying he had gotten a summer job on a sport fishing boat. O'Neill praised it as a sign of initiative. His first news of trouble in Colorado came when he heard that Agnes had somehow found a way to persuade Lawrenceville to allow Shane to return. By the time he learned of it, in October 1938, Shane was already in school and feeling, as before, miserably out of place amid the young sophisticates and achievers.

Given that it was already a month into the new term, O'Neill could only sympathize with a wish Shane expressed to switch to a public high school. Eugene agreed that a public school would offer a less trying experience; but changing in mid-term would be worse than staying, O'Neill wrote, and he urged the boy to make the best of the situation and work as hard as he could. Bowen (1959, 265) wrote that Shane passed only his art class and was dropped at the end of term. During this time Shane decided variously that he wanted to own a horse ranch, be an illustrator of horses like Frederic Remington, and become a veterinary doctor.

As O'Neill was beginning *The Iceman Cometh,* Shane drifted to Greenwich Village, where he took classes at the Art Students' League. As Bowen suggests, it was an even worse milieu for this very immature boy than Lawrenceville. Having no identity except as the son of a famous man, seeming to lack ordinary caution and common sense, he readily fell in with people who were taking drugs and soon became a heroin addict. He seemed sweet, wistful, and gentle, somewhat afflicted by shyness, and highly intelligent. Tall, thin, and handsome, strikingly like his father in looks, he easily attracted young women. He lived for a time with an art student whom Bowen calls Marjorie, who knew Shane for some time. She described to Bowen Shane's continuing dependent behavior: telling fellow students that he feared tuberculosis because his father had had it, he would ask them to nurse him when he caught a cold. She said she felt beneath Shane's sweetness, "a cruelty in him that was never apparent," which she said made him attractive to women (Bowen 1959, 278). Apparently the cruelty was usually turned against himself, as his drug addiction implies. Bowen (285–86) reports two suicide attempts in 1943, and there seem to have been others. Sheaffer recorded in his notes that in the early 1960s, while he was conducting frequent interviews with Agnes and often met Cathy Givens, Shane's wife, he saw bruises on both women that he believed Shane had caused.

People who knew Shane in his youth or later reported that he fanatically idolized his father. On Shane's visits, O'Neill and Carlotta went to lengths to find ways to divert and amuse the boy. Carlotta took him to movies or stage shows, or arranged for him to be driven on sight-seeing excursions. O'Neill swam or canoed or fished with him. But so slight a thing as an ordinary conversation between father and son could not take place when the father was usually taciturn and the son in such awe of his father that he felt he had nothing to say.

As with Eugene Jr., O'Neill must have seen himself all too clearly reflected in Shane, understanding both the boy's alienation from middle-class schoolmates and the attractions of alcohol: O'Neill identified so closely with Shane that he perhaps lost sight of the specific differences between himself at fourteen and Shane; as a consequence, he could think of no solutions or advice beyond what his father had given him. Creating a relationship during brief visits was beyond the resources of either, yet there is no doubting the love between father and son. Apart from paying the bills and passing on paternal advice, O'Neill tried to understand his son and their relationship in the best way he could, by seeking to capture his son's voice and his frailty in creating the doomed Don Parritt.

22

Celebrant of Loss
1939 – 1941

WHAT WITH THE VISIT FROM Eugene Jr. and Sally, and Roy Stram's nearly fatal illness, the summer of 1939 was "hectic," as O'Neill wrote Macgowan. What he called the bright spot came late in August when Oona, now fourteen, arrived for her first visit in five years. None of the O'Neills knew what to expect, but all were on their best behavior. Carlotta told Oona at once that she "loathed" children and had dreaded the visit, but when she found the girl "not covered in lip-stick and red nail polish," she decided to talk to her "woman to woman." Oona felt flattered and told Sheaffer that when she returned home, she had annoyed Agnes by alluding frequently to Carlotta's wisdom about the world (LS, 487). Carlotta found Oona well mannered, poised beyond her years, and reserved in expressing opinions. She gave the girl several expensive gifts of her own clothing.

O'Neill was working on *The Iceman Cometh* on the morning Oona arrived at Tao House, but he stopped and went swimming with his daughter. Although she later came to feel great bitterness toward her father, which lasted from the time of her marriage to Charlie Chaplin until shortly before she died, Oona remembered the 1939 visit with some fondness. In 1939 she barely remembered what her father looked like, and he must have seemed a complete stranger when she saw him, for he was now gaunt and frail, looked much older than his fifty years, and was obviously ill.

She told Sheaffer that she and her father had felt fairly comfortable with each other, even though neither talked very much. Like her father, Oona was basically shy, beneath the gracious manners, and was a determined person, with a capacity for inner growth. The two recognized and respected in each other the qualities that they shared. Photos from this visit show father and daughter by the pool, both beaming. Oona was a beautiful young woman, much more mature in appearance than her age would suggest, with long black hair, large dark eyes, and full lips and figure. She was immediately interested in the swimming pool bath house, which O'Neill had decorated with publicity posters of James O'Neill in *Monte Cristo* and other roles. Her interest in her grandfather won her father's approval. She told O'Neill that she thought the jazz and blues records he played in the evenings, while she and Carlotta were reading, were beautiful. As with all visitors, O'Neill kept working by day through her visit, but he paid attention to his daughter in the evenings and came to feel "exceedingly proud" of her, as he later told her (LS, 488). Oona, who attended Warrenton Country School in Virginia, was a good student. Her father and Carlotta strongly encouraged her to think of making a career for herself, rather than drifting into marriage. Oona remembered that Carlotta considered nursing suitable.

Even though Oona was more than five years younger than Shane, O'Neill's known letters to her over the next two years were written as to a young adult, whereas his letters to Shane were written as to a child. Oona told Sheaffer that her father discussed with her some of the problems he was having writing *The Iceman Cometh*, a high compliment, and one that made her feel very adult.

During the pleasant 1939 visit, Oona probably saw evidence of the extreme strain her father was under. When Germany invaded Poland, any sense of peace and content in Tao House must have vanished. O'Neill seldom showed anger, but a lifetime's accumulation poured out toward Hitler and the European war. He was equally outraged at the Russian invasion of Finland. Reversing an old sympathy, he wrote Harry Weinberger, another former leftist, that he supported the government's plan to outlaw the Communist party in America. The O'Neills usually slept late, but in those ominous times they rose at four to listen to short-wave broadcasts from Europe, and they listened in the evenings as well. Some of the playwright's letters at crucial points during the war years seem extreme in the rage they express about the war, even to one who well remembers the public mood of those years. At least some of O'Neill's anger at the world situation incorporated frustration over his illnesses, and old family grievances brought to the surface by the personal cost of writing *The Iceman Cometh* and the other play he had on his mind, *Long Day's Journey into Night*. For the next several years O'Neill's underlying anger would remain closer to the surface than in the past. Whatever Oona saw of her father's ire at the invasion of Poland may have been more than a little alarming and must have affected her understanding of her father, even though he assumed she shared his outrage at the European situation.

Carlotta's diary reports that during the fall and winter of 1939, while he was writing *The Iceman Cometh*, O'Neill suffered from depression, episodes of low blood pressure, insomnia, "nerves," and many other physical ailments. (His *Work Diary* makes fewer complaints about his health than Carlotta's diary.) By January, when he had finished cutting the third draft of *The Iceman Cometh*, he was exhausted. He planned to write *Long Day's Journey into Night* next, but he was too tired to begin at once. He tried working on a Cycle play but made little progress. Saxe Commins came for a working visit in January 1940, during which he typed a fresh copy of *The Iceman Cometh* to take to Random House for safekeeping. (O'Neill did not allow *The Iceman Cometh* to be published until 1946, after the war.) O'Neill stopped working often enough to chat, play cards, and take walks with his old friend. He got ideas for several new plays, including one that would deliberately use orchestral techniques with the "playwright as leader [of a] symphony" (WD, May 19, 1940). He also conceived "The Visit of Malatesta," a comedy he later worked on but never finished. After two months of what for him passed for rest, O'Neill began *Long Day's Journey*.

Through the first half of March, feeling terrible, physically and emotionally, he did preliminary work on the new play. At the beginning, he could concentrate only in fits and starts. The phrase *war obsession* appears regularly in the diary. When the German army skirted the Maginot Line, he noted that he felt his "second country" was being invaded (WD, 378). His doctors began giving him a series of shots intended to build up his resistance to infection. He had a prolonged case of flu. He sometimes worked in the garden and swam when the weather was warm.

In April, O'Neill got a letter from Shane, who wanted to marry a girl he knew in the Art Students' League. His father's reply does not survive, but O'Neill criticized himself in his diary for being "a bum at" playing the "heavy father" (WD, 375). On April 1 he began drafting act 1 of

Long Day's Journey and immediately fell ill. He worked intermittently on the act, weak with flu and suffering from the effects of the shots administered by his doctors. He finished the draft on April 30, and the same day he strained his lower back and had to stay in bed for more than a week. The O'Neills followed closely the British parliamentary calls for Chamberlain to stand down and tried to guess where the next invasion would strike. On May 10, when Hitler invaded Holland and Belgium simultaneously, O'Neill decided that work on his family play was "too insignificant in this madmen's world." President Roosevelt began to mobilize the armed forces and tried to persuade the country to enter the war.

Shane arrived for a visit, and Carlotta thought he look unwell, underweight and lacking energy. At twenty-one, he was taller than his father and even thinner. O'Neill made no mention of suspecting that his son was using drugs, but it seems impossible that he would have missed it, and it must have disturbed him very deeply. He swam with Shane most days and arranged for him to be entertained by Carlotta, who once spent a day showing him various sights in San Francisco. As always, Shane was sweet and agreeable and enjoyed everything that was done for him. On his day off, Herbert Freeman took Shane to San Francisco for drinks and to see the Ice Follies, and on another occasion he took the boy to dinner and to the Exposition. O'Neill tried to give fatherly advice. It now seemed clear that Shane would never complete secondary school, and O'Neill saw no signs that he could support himself, let alone support a wife. He wrote a letter to the father of Shane's fiancée explaining the boy's situation, and apparently the father persuaded his daughter to reconsider. Eugene talked at length with Shane and Carlotta about the importance of Shane's going to work, and he felt very pessimistic about his son's prospects when the youth returned to New York.

Dr. George Reinle, whom O'Neill had seen at least weekly since 1937 for complaints ranging from prostatitis to "nerves" to low blood pressure, had recommended a course of injections of Oreton, a preparation of testosterone, which was being tested at the time as a treatment for Parkinson's disease. The hormone was also used in cases of depression and low blood pressure, both of which were increasingly serious problems for O'Neill. Carlotta continued to loathe giving the shots, as she frequently noted in her diary; she found it more unpleasant to give them than the injections of insulin. O'Neill would sometimes give himself the shots, but he disliked the experience as much as Carlotta. Often they would take the longish drive to Dr. Reinle's office in Oakland for the injection. For a time the shots seemed to have little effect on any of O'Neill's symptoms. Dr. Dukes might come as often as once a week to give the injection at Tao House, and he and his wife might stay for dinner.

In mid-May, Dr. Dukes brought Edward Rynearson of the Mayo Clinic, who was visiting, to examine O'Neill. Rynearson recommended increasing the frequency of the injections, and for a time, things were better. O'Neill's blood pressure, which had been hovering around 100, rose to 120, and he seemed to come out of his depression. But on June 17, O'Neill noted that he felt "jazzed up & over stimulated" by the shots and discontinued the treatment; he saw his doctors again, who decreased the frequency of the injections. The treatment, continued off and on over the next several years, probably made O'Neill's mood more volatile.

Carlotta's diary makes it appear that she and Eugene might have little contact for much of the day during the spring of 1940. O'Neill was so constantly ill that Carlotta was likely to be up at night with him, and when his blood pressure was low, he might not get out of bed all day, while she rested or carried on the business of the house. The war brought them together; they were one in their preoccupation with Hitler's invasion of Belgium and Holland and continued to be appalled at Britain's policy of appeasement under Chamberlain. They listened to the war news off and on day and night. Churchill became prime minister and warned England to expect the worst.

On June 25 O'Neill decided that his obsession with the war was "becoming [a] neurosis." He continued in his diary: "Can't save even myself by not working and despairing about the future of individual freedom." The second subject of his despair, "the future of individual freedom," seems significant. Throughout the writing of *Long Day's Journey*, O'Neill was preoccupied by dread at the political repression of individual freedom in Nazi Germany and its conquests. At the same time, he was studying the conscious and unconscious compulsions and constraints on an individual's life that arise from being a member of a family.

He reluctantly read his draft of act 1 of *Long Day's Journey* and was surprised to find himself deeply interested by it. Within a day he was back in the world of the play, revising what he had written and feeling he could make it one of his best. He worked on the play daily through August 15, when he stopped to make notes on two new non-Cycle play ideas. In a low moment in May he had told Carlotta that he would never finish the

Cycle. As he continued work on *Long Day's Journey*, he found himself fascinated by a play idea arising from his preoccupation with the war, on the theme of the "duality of Man" in which the "Devil [is] a modern power realist" (WD, 386). This seems to have been his first conception of an unfinished play, "The Last Conquest" (he also called it "The Thirteenth Apostle"). By mid-August the air battle for Britain was fully engaged, and by late in the month, England and Germany were bombing each other's capitols. By the end of the month O'Neill was beginning act 4.

The Winthers drove to San Francisco, and the O'Neills saw them every day for a week. O'Neill let Sophus and Eline read *The Iceman Cometh*. In view of the war and war politics, *The Iceman Cometh*, and the deep skepticism the men shared, conversation between the two must have been gloomy indeed. Even before the visit, O'Neill was preoccupied with changes he saw coming in the world, which he thought would be greater than at any time in his life. To Oona he had written that the Cycle would "have little meaning for the sort of world we will probably be living in by the time I finish it. A period of universal unrest and change is a bad period for serious work which is not propaganda of some sort" (SL, 508).

At the mercy of his illness and of the drugs intended to alleviate it, pushed and pulled by uncontrollable swings of mood, and episodes of low blood pressure that left him almost helpless, O'Neill finished the first draft of *Long Day's Journey* by the end of September. On October 16, his fifty-second birthday, he wrote that he had finished the second draft of the play, and he went outside to prune a hedge. The next day he declared a holiday and took a drive with Carlotta. Bobby Jones came for a visit, and they talked all day about the theater. For the rest of the month and through November and early December, O'Neill thought of various schemes to revise the Cycle, perhaps by reducing it to seven or nine plays.

Blemie, the O'Neills' dalmatian, died December 17. It was a great blow to Eugene and Carlotta, who wrote that they had loved and trusted him more than any human friend for eleven years. The death threw O'Neill off the Cycle, and for weeks he wrote nothing except an elegy he called Blemie's "Last Will and Testament," an act of mourning without ambivalence that Carlotta had printed in 1956. For another two months he worked on plays he would not finish, "The Visit of Malatesta," "Blind Alley Guy" (about an American Hitler), and "The Last Conquest." In mid-March he began revising and cutting *Long Day's Journey into Night*, and he worked in the garden most days after he had finished his shift on the play. On March 30 he wrote in the diary: "Like this play better than any I have ever written—does most with the least—a quiet play!—and a great one, I believe."

Indeed, it is a quiet play. Voices are seldom raised, and there is almost no action or plot. Instead, the play begins with two simple questions of fact: Is Mama back on morphine? Does Edmund, the younger son, have consumption? By the end the four Tyrones know the answer to both questions. The play records the events of a single day in August 1912 when the younger son learns that he has consumption and when the mother reverts to taking morphine, an addiction from which she has been free for some time. In the morning the Tyrones seem sunny and happy, although they know that they are going to learn that day of Edmund's diagnosis.

Act 1 ends with the three men's recognition that Mary Tyrone has resumed taking morphine. A phone call from the doctor in act 2 tells James Tyrone that his younger son indeed has consumption, as they all have feared. Although Edmund guesses what has been said, he is not told immediately. Throughout the rest of the play the family quarrels almost constantly over such questions as the following: Has Edmund erred in leaving Mary upstairs alone for some time in act 1 when it is not clear whether she has already resumed using the drug? Is Edmund's current illness responsible for her relapse? Can Edmund be blamed as the original cause of her addiction, because it started just after his birth? Was Tyrone responsible because he hired a "cheap hotel doctor" to prescribe for her when she was in pain following Edmund's birth? Is it because Tyrone has never bought her the fine home she has wanted that she has had no incentive to remain free of the drug after her numerous cures? Is the addiction caused by Tyrone's general miserliness, one effect of which is to make her feel like a bird in an insufficiently gilded cage? Can Tyrone be blamed for his miserliness, given that it stems from the extreme poverty of his childhood and his father's abandonment of his family? Is Jamie responsible for the death of the baby Eugene, who died before Edmund was born and whose death caused the long depression that Mary experienced before Edmund's birth?

A common denominator links all the questions of the long day—the anxiety arising from loss and separation. Mary, who has never recovered from the loss of her father and her second son, now faces the possible loss of Edmund. She also grieves for the loss of her father's home and of the convent where she attended school, a time during which she was happy and felt safe and which ended with her father's sudden death. Mary's associations suggest that when her husband will not spend money to live as lavishly as she wishes, it reminds her of the loss of her father, his purse, and his home.

The playwright explores how separation anxiety affects each of the Tyrones. The threatened losses of his wife to morphine and of his son to tuberculosis exacerbates Tyrone's miserliness, which derives from the actor's loss of his father, and the loss of money and place suffered in childhood. To this cause is also traced a dread of returning to poverty by losing fortune through the spendthrift ways of his wife and sons. The immediate threats of loss are added to the old man's grief over the waste of his first son's promise in laziness and dissipation and the loss of his own artistic ideals and his potential to become one of the great Shakespearean actors of his time, which he feels he sacrificed to his fear of poverty.

For Jamie, the day is perhaps even worse than it is for his father, because he has never had anything in life that was important to him except his attachment to his mother and brother. Besides these attachments a powerful bond links him to his father, one expressed in fighting that arises from his lifelong dependency and from his blaming his father for the family's problems. The playwright shows Jamie as having fewer resources to withstand loss than does his father, because Jamie so loathes himself and has no work in which to lose himself. The only person more disgusted with him than his father is Jamie himself. He and his mother share a morbid bond of debased self-esteem. In part, Jamie's poor opinion of himself stems from the belief he shares with Mary that he deliberately infected the toddler Eugene with a fatal illness.

A complex, asymmetrical bond links Jamie and Edmund. Edmund has grown up idealizing Jamie, whom he has viewed, when estranged from Tyrone by adolescent rebelliousness, as a surrogate father. Even while idealizing Jamie, Edmund also maintains a faith that his father will not disown him, no matter how outrageous or unfair his acts of rebellion. A basic confidence in his father allows Edmund to idealize Jamie while privately retaining a more complex sense of the world than Jamie often has. Edmund tolerates occasional ambivalent feelings about his brother, while Jamie is more troubled by his own ambivalence toward Edmund. The playwright makes clear an important, subtle aspect of Jamie's character, that the first son has never developed the tolerance of ambivalence that ordinarily comes in the second or third year of life. One notices late in act 4 that Jamie envies Edmund his confident relationship with their father, and he resents the bond of guilt that links Edmund and Mary. Jamie tells Edmund, "I love your guts kid" (CP3, 818), and he tries to analyze the dilemma of both loving and hating someone, in a way that shows that instead of taking ambivalent feelings for granted, as Edmund does, Jamie is bothered by the conflict.

Edmund is of course more directly concerned with his illness than the others. He both shares and rejects the family opinion that he caused his mother's affliction and sometimes is convinced that he has no right to be alive. But he also believes that the loss of her mothering in infancy and childhood affected him more deeply than the loss of her, in their later lives, affected his father and brother. In Edmund's presence, Mary seems guilty and ashamed, awkward, and visibly ambivalent, whereas her relations with Jamie are more direct, as if taken for granted. O'Neill explores Edmund's relationship with Mary in two extended scenes when mother and son are alone. Edmund is more tolerant than his mother and brother of his father's miserliness and other quirks. A basic friendliness binds Edmund and his father, where no simple, basic confidence in the other's love seems to link Edmund and his mother. The closeness of Edmund and his father, of Jamie and his mother, and of Edmund and Jamie are relative constants throughout the play, although other alliances continually form and dissolve.

The Tyrones obsessively seek to understand sources of their unhappiness. Like human beings as a whole, they believe that if they understand something, they can control it. The crisis to be explained on this day is why Mary has resumed her morphine addiction. Time after time, after being freed from the addiction itself, she has returned to the drug. The Tyrones, Mary included, blame each other and themselves for her addiction and relapses. Indeed, most of the play consists of quasi-judicial proceedings in which accusations and denials are made, evidence is adduced and disputed, testimony is given, examined, and refuted, and conclusions are reached, rejected, and abandoned in the face of new accusation. The process repeats itself endlessly.

By the end of the play it seems clear that the process of constant accusation, denial, and cross-examination does not help. Any understanding it brings is apparently temporary, for the same matter must be argued again and again. In the end, it seems that the process that is supposed to bring understanding is itself a cause of the Tyrones' suffering. One assumes that what goes on this day is only a little more painful than events on any other day in the Tyrone household. It is obvious that if ever any increase in understanding occurs, it certainly gives no control over anything. Eventually the audience (if not the Tyrones) must wonder, Why do they persist in seeking to place blame?

Perhaps the question must be asked in a different way. Is anything worse, for the Tyrones, than the pain of blaming and being blamed for the family unhappiness? It seems that the dread of loss is worse.

For their various reasons, each of the Tyrones is acutely sensitive to losses, and each new loss seems to increase the sensitivity. As individuals the Tyrones cannot cope with losses except by denial. Like the bums in *The Iceman Cometh,* they have worked out a complex process that allows them to avoid feeling their losses. The process of *Long Day's Journey into Night* as a whole can be summarized as follows: Arguments transform grief into grievances, which prevent sadness from ever being directly felt and loss from being directly acknowledged. Thus, the sadness of loss is avoided, but at the price of constant pain, and at the further cost that loss can never be mourned, outgrown, and left behind.

The questions that open the play, about Mary's resumption of her morphine use and about Edmund's consumption, drop out of sight long before the end of the day. The characters become caught up in the courtroom debate, which supersedes more basic questions of fact. The same process goes on in audiences. Identifying now with this character, now with that, audience members can be heard at intermission repeating the accusations and refutations exchanged by the Tyrones; and like the Tyrones, the audience may lose sight of the family's—and humanity's—larger problem, how one can survive the loss or death of those on whom one depends.

The four Tyrones are bright, likable, attractive people, often charming, often funny, knowing about the world, deeply attached to each other. Yet they feud so constantly, and the warfare seems so deadly, that we may wonder how any of them will survive the long day's journey. They represent something essential to the spirit of the modern world. All passionately accept, or want to accept, the basic premise of Western humanism, that the human capacity for conscious understanding gives people control over themselves, their world, even the future. Circumstances have forced the Tyrones to become a family of philosophical skeptics. With them, guilt and innocence can never be proved but only argued and re-argued.

O'Neill revealed his intent to tell the O'Neill family's story in the *Work Diary*. The entry for March 31, 1941, alludes to "checking dates," which must refer to the sequence of real events in his parents' lives, for there seems to be almost nothing within the play to which the phrase could refer. On the next day, O'Neill adds to act 4 the long speech in which Tyrone tells of Booth's words of praise in 1874, and of sacrificing artistic ideals in favor of "the great money maker." Eugene refers to the latter as "father's M.C. speech." Whether he meant the father in the play or his own father, "M.C." seems clearly to refer to *Monte Cristo*. Tyrone's speech can in turn be traced to the letter of December 9, 1920, that O'Neill wrote to his father's friend George Tyler, four months after James O'Neill had died, in which Eugene spoke of James's "grudge" against *Monte Cristo* for leading him into artistic compromise (see Chapter 13).

To a psychoanalytic biographer, the facts of family life are no more interesting than the process in which they occur. The process itself ex-presses meanings more general than and different from anything explicit in things said. The purpose of the process of *Long Day's Journey* is to re-peat itself endlessly. Among its many effects, the process binds the four Tyrones together with almost unbreakable bonds, which ensure that no matter how unbearable matters become, the family will remain intact. An audience may leave a performance with the impression that the Tyrones endure endless dissension because it almost eliminates the risk of loss.

It is clear that one of the playwright's concerns in writing the play was to understand what made the O'Neill family behave as it did. He suc-ceeded in understanding the underlying family processes, obscured from the family members themselves by the constant need to participate. Mak-ing sense of the process, grasping it as a whole, made it possible for the playwright to understand with deep pity and forgive. The personal achievement brought O'Neill the conviction that he had written a quiet, beautiful play.

O'Neill finished the first draft of *Long Day's Journey* in September 1940 and, shortly after, began going over the typed copy and making re-visions. On July 22, 1941, his and Carlotta's twelfth anniversary, O'Neill gave the manuscript of *Long Day's Journey into Night* to Carlotta with a dedication that seems to make clear his intentions in writing the play. Acknowledging that it was a "play of old sorrow, written in tears and blood," he apologized that it seemed a "sadly inappropriate gift . . . for a day celebrating happiness." He continued, "But you will understand. I mean it as a tribute to your love and tenderness which gave me the faith in love that enabled me to write this play—write it with deep pity and understanding and forgiveness for all the four haunted Tyrones."

Pity, understanding, forgiveness: such is the stuff of mourning. Had O'Neill ceased to mourn? It seems he had made great progress, at least in his mourning for his father and mother. It is difficult or impossible to prove a negative, for we can never know every thought that passed through his mind in the dozen years of life left to him. But there is a marked change. In the new plays he would conceive or write after *Long Day's Journey*, including the unfinished plays and the many undeveloped play ideas, there appear to be no more characters resembling James or Ella. The long obsession appears to have ended. Further, O'Neill now shows himself able, for the first time, to imagine characters who suffer a loss, mourn, emerge from mourning, and pass beyond it.

By early 1941, O'Neill was ill and in discomfort or pain most days and nights. His tremor rapidly worsened, becoming so bad that at times he could not control the pencil with which he tried to write. Nevertheless, when he finished *Long Day's Journey*, he spent the next two months studying Cycle plays and his book of ideas, and another month going over the typescript of *Long Day's Journey*. On April 9 he began a new play, *Hughie*, which he finished in three weeks. After a few days of light revision, he called it done. When he had finished, he noted that he liked the play and had enjoyed writing it. A one-act play that is performed in about an hour, *Hughie* was not staged until 1958, in Stockholm. Yale published O'Neill's text the following year. There was no American performance until 1964, when Jason Robards and the late Jack Dodson played Erie Smith and the night clerk under the direction of José Quintero. Since then, the play has been given very frequently, including in numerous revivals with Robards and Dodson as the hustler and the night clerk.

Nearly the whole play consists of the story of Erie's friendship with Hughie, the former night clerk who has just died; Erie talks to the new night clerk who has taken Hughie's place. A small-fry Broadway wise guy who sometimes runs errands for bigger fish, Erie talks of big bets won and lost at the tracks, of games he has been in, cards and dice, and of the beautiful women he says have come to him when he has won—the stuff of stories he has told his dead friend Hughie and tries on the new clerk. Erie cannot stop talking, cannot force himself into the elevator that will take him to his fourth-floor room. As we gradually learn, Erie has lived the most important parts of his life in the hotel lobby, talking the nights away with his late friend.

The new night clerk's name, Charlie Hughes, shocks Erie by its similarity to his friend's name. Although the new clerk is present in the flesh behind the hotel desk, he carries on his emotional life outside the hotel; he creates scenarios of events of the night that are given in the manner of the thought asides of *Strange Interlude*. Preoccupied with grief for his friend, Erie is unaware of the new clerk's fantasy life until late in the play. Charlie constructs his outside life from such noises as the crash of trash cans, a distant El train, the echoing footsteps of a cop on the beat, an ambulance tearing down the street, the siren of a fire engine. Everyone in the city has a more interesting job than his, even the garbage collector, who has the joy of making enough din with his cans to rouse sleepers.

While the clerk fantasizes, Erie chatters to his vacant face and inattention. Gradually the audience learns details of his friendship with Hughie. Like the present night clerk, and like Erie himself, Hughie was a boob from the sticks. He had a wife and children, and a home with them in Brooklyn that to Erie seemed unbearably dull. Erie believed that Hughie's real life went on at night, with him in the hotel lobby. There Erie relieved the tedium of his friend's job with fanciful tales. According to Erie, his friend liked him to say that the women were from the Ziegfeld Follies; Erie, who suspected Hughie of living vicariously through his exaggerated stories, tried to give him what he wanted. The two would play at craps, using only Erie's money, which Erie divided between the two of them—"We'd play with real jack, just to make it look real" (CP3, 839). The idea was for Erie to win most of the time, often cheating but never getting caught by the unsuspecting Hughie. Hughie admired Erie's luck and skill, and he loved believing that his friend had connections with big-time gamblers and was a wise guy himself.

Twice the friends strayed outside the limits they implicitly set for their relationship. Once, carried away by the talk of racing, Erie took Hughie to Belmont to watch the thoroughbreds run. The track, the crowd, the beauty of the horses running: Erie feared his friend would "pass out with the excitement. And he wasn't doing no betting either" (CP3, 840).

The visit to the track went well but it had consequences. The next day Hughie took money from his wife's purse and tried to give it to Erie to bet for him on whatever horse Erie might hear was a sure thing. Erie sternly refused, saying he wanted no part of anything that might disrupt Hughie's home. The second transgression occurred when Hughie invited Erie to his home for dinner with his wife and children. Erie and Hughie's wife each immediately recognized the other as an enemy alien. After that the two friends ventured no more from the world of the lobby.

In telling his story, Erie shows that he knew his late friend, knew exactly how their friendship worked, and knew how to keep it working. That is, until the end. Hughie suddenly takes ill and soon goes to the hospital. Erie visits him there and encounters Hughie's wife, who sends him away on the grounds that Hughie must have no excitement. Erie visits again, just before Hughie dies, but is not allowed to see his friend.

The death stuns him. Erie loses his luck. He tells the new clerk he hasn't won a bet since Hughie died. Even worse, he has borrowed no less than a hundred dollars to buy a horseshoe of red roses for Hughie's funeral. He has gone up and down the street borrowing money from the wrong guys, and if he can't pay them back next Tuesday, he may have to "take it on the lam, or I'll get beat up and maybe sent to the hospital" (CP3, 849).

The night clerk hasn't heard a word. While Erie has been going on, the new night clerk's fantasies have become increasingly extreme. *"Will he die, Doctor, or isn't he lucky?"* he asks the doctor in his mind when he hears the ambulance. *"Is [the fire] a real good one this time? . . . Will it be big enough . . . to burn down the whole damn city?"* *"Sorry Brother, but there's no chance. There's too much stone and steel."* As the night clerk longs for an Armageddon, Erie thinks once again of going up to his room but can't make himself move. "Christ, it's lonely," he laments. If Hughie were here, Erie vows, with the greatest sadness, "I'd tell him a tale that'd make his eyes pop" (CP3, 844). Erie is above all things a talker, an entertainer, and Hughie was a wonderfully responsive audience. The new night clerk seems dead on his feet. As one critic has pointed out, O'Neill was known as a reticent man, but watching *Hughie* makes one realize that inside, he was full of talk.

A little of Erie's talk has finally penetrated the night clerk's fantasies—something about gambling. The night clerk imagines repeatedly beating Arnold Rothstein in a high-stakes card game, time after time cutting the higher card. *"Beatific vision swoons on the empty pools of the Night Clerk's eyes. He resembles a holy saint recently elected to Paradise"* (CP3, 848). O'Neill's narrative of the night clerk's beatitude shows that Luck means to him a connection with the infinite. The night clerk seems to be reacting, without much intervention of consciousness, to the intense sadness Erie expresses as he thinks of Hughie's death.

Erie envies his friend: "Hughie's better off at that, being dead. He's got all the luck. He needn't do no worryin' now. He's out of the racket. I mean the whole goddamned racket. I mean life." Erie's envy of the dead startles the new night clerk partly out of his gambling reverie and "with detached, pleasant acquiescence," he agrees: "Yes, it is a goddamned racket when you stop to think, isn't it, 492? But we might as well make the best of it, because—Well, you can't burn it all down, can you. There's too much steel and stone. There'd always be something left to start it going again" (CP3, 848).

Erie is bewildered and annoyed. "What the hell you talkin' about?" The clerk is at a loss to say. "Why, to be frank, I really don't—Just something that came into my head." For the first time in the play the two make contact in the realization that they've been ignoring each other. "Get it out of your head quick, Charlie," Erie advises, "or some guys in uniform will walk in here with a butterfly net and catch you" (CP3, 848). In the realization that he has an audience, Erie repeats some of his story, insisting that he really did spend a hundred dollars for the funeral flowers. Erie now pours out the sadness he feels about losing Hughie, his fear of being beaten up, and an even worse fear, that when he lost Hughie, Erie lost his luck: "I mean, I've lost the old confidence. He used to give me confidence" (849). At this point near the end of the play, Erie achieves his deepest recognition of the meaning of his friendship with Hughie. Hughie gave the con man confidence.

Erie is so buried in grief and self-pity that he doesn't recognize for a moment that things between him and the new clerk have changed. The new clerk is suddenly excited by the realization that much of Erie's talk, blather he has meant to ignore, has had to do with gambling, an activity that seems to him a link to the cosmos or Dame Fortune herself. Erie starts to get into the elevator again, but the night clerk insists on hearing about Arnold Rothstein. It is enough. Moments later, the two are playing craps with Erie's dice and money. When he makes a hard point on the first throw, Erie knows that he is in luck again. To the audience, it may also suggest that Erie has passed beyond his mourning for his friend. He has accepted the loss of his friend, grieved intensely, laid Hughie to rest, and eventually earned the peace of mind that lets him make a new friend, one who also inhabits an outer circle of Dame Fortune's world. *Hughie* is O'Neill's paradigm of mourning.

Critics, actors, and audiences have commonly made a connection between Erie and the salesman Hickey in *The Iceman Cometh,* and indeed they have much in common. In the present context it is useful to consider a couple of ways in which they are not similar.

In *The Iceman Cometh* Hickey seems to bring death to the saloon or even is himself the Iceman of death, and at the end, Larry remarks, enigmatically, that he is the only "convert to death Hickey made" (CP3, 710). Larry apparently means that he believes Hickey's frequent insistence that he doesn't fear death, and that other people should not be afraid of it, either. To an outsider, it seems clear that Hickey is a poor one to teach about death. He does not fear it because he denies its reality. To him, his wife Evelyn is not dead at all. One difference between Hickey and Erie is that after the funeral, Erie knows that Hughie is dead.

Erie's ability to mourn grows out of a capacity we never see in Hickey, one that Michael Manheim has called kinship. Erie's relationship with Hughie has been based on mutuality and reciprocity. In all his long narrative of his life with Evelyn, Hickey tells us almost nothing about the woman herself or his relationship with her. Like Hickey, Erie speaks in clichés about marriage—indeed he sneers at Hughie and the new night clerk for having that "married look"—and he regards children as the consequence of being "careless." Despite the rough words, though, he respects his friend's marriage in a way one might not have predicted. When Hughie has taken money from his wife's purse, with the intention of asking Erie to bet it for him, Erie refuses: "If you're going to start playin' sucker and bettin on horse races, you don't get no assist from me" (CP3, 840). He thinks it's a joke on him that he would foolishly turn down a chance to cheat a sucker. Instead he persuades Hughie to sneak the money back and avoid a falling out with his wife. Erie preserves the conditions necessary to maintaining the friendship.

Later, when he meets Hughie's family, a meeting that is uncomfortable all around, he sees beyond his own clichés. Despite his expectations, he confides, he found that Hughie's plain wife has made a pleasant home and raised civilized children instead of the "gorillas" Erie expected (CP3, 843). The orderliness of the home makes him understand its importance to Hughie, as we know from a surprising and selfless moment of introspection.

After the awkward visit, Hughie has apologized for his wife's strict upbringing, which has caused her to show her disapproval of Erie's low-life ways. But Erie has "shut him up quick" (CP3, 843). Immediately after, he tells a sordid story against himself, about his cheating a hooker. He tells it in a way that shows the shame he feels and suggests that he judges himself about as Hughie's wife—and not only she—judges him. When his friends learn that he cheated the woman, they will drop him, he fears. It is an admission that Hickey could not have made. Erie has more tolerance for shame and guilt, and consequently sees himself more clearly than Hickey can. Rather than face up to his misbehavior, Hickey would simply have gone off on a drunk.

The achievement of *Hughie*—its clarity and seeming simplicity, and its convincing account of mourning—shows how far O'Neill had come as a result of writing *Long Day's Journey into Night*. From this point on his ideas for plays would usually be as much comic as tragic. When he had finished *Hughie*, O'Neill felt optimistic enough about his work that he resumed thinking about the first Cycle play. In June and July he worked on "The Thirteenth Apostle," and when he "went dead on it," he turned to "Blind Alley Guy." Oona, who had not seen her father for nearly two years, came for a visit in July, and the O'Neills found her changed. She had transferred from the Country School in Virginia to Brearley School in New York City, where she had been invited into Gloria Vanderbilt's circle. Oona told Carlotta that she had decided to go to Hollywood and marry "a really rich man," and Carlotta, who had married a really rich man in her own youth, gave the girl a long, emphatic lecture on folly (LS, 525). Again, when Oona mentioned thoughts of acting in the movies, she elicited a lecture on Hollywood corruption. That Oona at sixteen seemed hardly aware of the war in Europe outraged the senior O'Neills. Everything that could have gone wrong with the visit did. Through some deterministic web, O'Neill seemed to re-enact *"Anna Christie,"* in which he had shown a father and daughter, reunited after a long estrangement, nearly lose each other merely for being the people they were. He noted, on the day she left: "Damned N.Y. school—or maybe she's just at the silly age."

Even before Oona's visit, O'Neill had been losing patience with his children. Probably borrowing an idea from his sister, Shane had written to say that he was considering a career in the movies and asked for "an introduction" to Kenneth Macgowan, an obviously disingenuous request, for almost from birth Shane had seen Macgowan as almost a member of the family. The letter infuriated O'Neill, who scolded Shane for being frivolous when the country was about to go to war and all young men would surely be drafted (SL, 516).

Despite his worsening tremor, the injections of testosterone and attendant mood swings, daily bouts with other illnesses, and his obsession with the war, O'Neill worked through the summer of 1941 on "Blind Alley Guy" and an idea he called "Time Grandfather Was Dead." Dr. Dukes occasionally made the long drive to visit and give O'Neill his injections, which sometimes seemed to help the tremor. Otherwise, O'Neill had himself driven to Oakland to Dr. Reinle. Dr. Dukes, who was actively seeking out any remedies reported to be helpful, tried injections of vitamins, which were supposed to alleviate symptoms of Parkinson's disease. The side effects of the various medications sometimes caused O'Neill to become lethargic, disoriented, confused, and forgetful.

The young Ingrid Bergman played Anna Christie in San Francisco, and O'Neill, who said he could not stand to see the play again, nevertheless sent Carlotta to see it. When she reported favorably, he invited the young actor for lunch, and they had a pleasant meeting on August 14, 1941. O'Neill was sufficiently impressed with Bergman to tell her about the Cycle and invite her to become a member of a permanent repertory company he hoped to organize to perform the whole work.

According to Bergman's account, a certain amount of mutual flirtation went on between her and the playwright (see her memoir in Floyd 1979, 293–95). The flirtation is worth mentioning because it suggests that despite his numerous illnesses and the ordeal of having written *The Iceman Cometh* and *Long Day's Journey into Night* in about two years, O'Neill felt cheerier than he had for years.

About this time, relations between the O'Neills began to change. Arthritis in her hands and eye problems made it difficult for Carlotta to continue typing her husband's manuscripts, and she hired her daughter,

Cynthia, to take her place. Carlotta may also have wanted Cynthia in the house as a buffer between her and O'Neill; in any case, Eugene seemed happy when Cynthia was around.

In addition, Carlotta took to inviting her old school friend, Myrtle Caldwell, and Myrtle's daughter Jane to the house, also to diffuse tensions between the O'Neills. A hearty, cheery soul with a salty sense of humor, Myrt amused Eugene. They took to each other at once, discovering that they both loved to sing old bawdy songs and that both had terrible voices. Eugene hit it off immediately with Jane, too. Sheaffer reports that during one of their first meetings, Carlotta dramatically told Myrt and Jane that she would be happy with O'Neill even if they "lived in a tent," at which Jane replied, "What woman wouldn't?" Sheaffer reported that O'Neill "blushed" at this and shortly after gave Jane a book of his plays inscribed "from one about to order a tent" (LS, 525). From that point on, O'Neill mentioned in his diary frequent occasions when Myrt or Jane or both came to visit. Carlotta's revised diary for the summer did not mention the visits, but it conveyed her sense of almost palpable tension.

In early September Eugene Jr. came to visit, this time without a wife. He and his father enjoyed the visit, and after a few days O'Neill decided he wanted his son to read *Long Day's Journey* and *The Iceman Cometh*, which he began doing at once. As his son read, the playwright revised *Hughie* lightly, and he decided he wanted Eugene to read it as well. How remarkable an experience it must have been for a young man of Eugene's literary sophistication to read in a week's time these three new plays written by his father! A *Work Diary* remark that Eugene Jr. was "greatly moved" by *Long Day's Journey*—"pleases me a lot"—must have been understated in all respects. When Eugene's visit was over, his father noted, "A son who is also a friend!—hate to see him leave."

O'Neill returned to "Blind Alley Guy" but in late September became overwhelmed by a profusion of new ideas for it and had to set it aside. He began rereading the early Cycle plays and was impressed with their potential, but he felt the job too tough "to tackle now." The O'Neills passed Eugene's fifty-third birthday peacefully with friends in Berkeley. He spent a day making notes in preparation for another one-act play for the projected series "By Way of Obit," this one about an elderly Irish chambermaid in a New York hotel. Then on October 28, he conceived a "S[haughnessy] play idea, based on story told by E[dmund] in 'L.D.I.N.'—except here Jamie principal character & story of play otherwise entirely imaginary, except for J's revelation of self." The play was *A Moon for the Misbegotten,* and the entry in the revised *Work Diary* assures future scholars and biographers that Josie and Phil Hogan are imaginary characters and that there was no love affair near the end of his brother's life. He began his notes for the play at once and became enthusiastic as he explored the possibilities for combining comic and tragic ideas. He worked on the play every day through November and up to December 6, 1941. The next day Pearl Harbor was bombed.

23

Beyond Mourning
1942–1943

IMMEDIATELY AFTER PEARL HARBOR, SHANE qualified for seaman's papers. He told friends that he was an "able-bodied seaman just like my father was" (LS, 538). For the next year and a half Shane served on ships sailing the dangerous waters patrolled by the German submarine "wolf pack" that aimed to prevent American relief supplies and munitions from reaching England or France.

Eugene Jr., now thirty-two, expected that with knowledge of five modern languages he would be welcome in the Intelligence Corps. But when he tried to enlist, he was rejected, apparently because of a record of leftist political sympathy. He resigned from Yale because he expected to be drafted, but when he was called up, the army rejected him because in childhood he had suffered a fractured skull and because, like his father, he had inherited the family tremor. Shocked by the unexpected rejection, Eugene went to work in a New Haven cable factory, where he continued throughout the war. At this time he began drinking heavily. It seems clear that he experienced rejection by the services as a decisive alienation. His shame was such that he couldn't tell his father of his rejection for some time, during which his father assumed he was in the army and could not write even to give an address. At some point Eugene began to think of himself as a reincarnation of his uncle Jamie and predicted that he would not live past forty. From the early 1940s his visible depression deepened.

After war was declared, nearly everyone in the United States suffered hardships. The senior O'Neills were most affected because of the isolation of Tao House. Until that point, they had managed logistically because Herbert Freeman, who had now worked for them for nearly ten years, drove them for daily shopping trips and medical appointments. They also had cooks, gardeners, and housekeepers who helped Carlotta. But soon after the war started, Freeman went into the Marines. Gasoline became scarce, and few household workers wanted to live in so isolated a spot. O'Neill had to go to Oakland several times a week for medical treatment intended to alleviate his worsening tremor and other illnesses, and Carlotta, too, was frequently ill.

With the United States in the war, O'Neill's "war obsession" became more nearly managable. He tried to adopt what he called the Archimedes viewpoint: if one is physically unfit for military service, one should "stick to one's job" (WD, 424). He determined to finish at least a first draft of *A Moon for the Misbegotten*. His interest in the play was deflected by Pearl Harbor but remained sufficiently strong that he finished a very rough draft in late January 1942. Nevertheless, he confessed, "Had to drag myself through it since Pearl Harbor," and he noted that the play seemed to "wander" (427). Writing about his brother's last days, especially Jamie's self-revelation in act 3, meant reawakening memories of the family and personal problems Eugene had confronted in writing *Long Day's Journey*. At this time he reported that his tremor was very bad.

He put the new play aside in late January, when Saxe Commins came for a welcome visit. Saxe arrived in a heavy rain, which went on throughout his stay, as he wrote to his wife (Commins 1986, 201–2). He told Dorothy that he and O'Neill were virtually inseparable for the two weeks, except when he read *Long Day's Journey*. O'Neill put *A Moon* out of his mind and immediately conceived ideas for four companion one-act plays for *Hughie* for the series "By Way of Obit." It would be nearly a year before he would return to *A Moon*.

He reread *A Touch of the Poet*, which he had drafted in 1938, the Cycle play that was to precede *More Stately Mansions*. Having decided that he wanted to finish at least one Cycle play, he revised *Poet* to exclude most of what tied it to the rest of the Cycle. He leaves in a long and bizarre speech in which Deborah tells Sara in detail of the Harford madness and, in so doing, summarizes some of the action of the first four plays (in the eleven-play version) of the Cycle. Perhaps O'Neill left the passage in as a deliberately obscure and private joke, or as a hint at what he had meant to do in the Cycle. Work on *Poet* was soon interrupted by a worsening of the tremor, which put a stop to his writing for a while. Between one illness and another, weeks passed before he could resume work. When he did, he had lost his momentum on *Poet* and set to work instead on notes for "The Thirteenth Apostle."

This work too stopped in mid-March, when the O'Neills' physician and friend Dr. Dukes, suddenly went into a diabetic coma, a complication of flu, and died the next day in the hospital. He had become close to both O'Neills, whom he had often seen socially as well as professionally. Both O'Neills felt the loss keenly, Carlotta possibly even more than Eugene. She was already in mourning for her mentor and benefactor, James Speyer, who had died during the winter. Carlotta experienced distress not only because of her personal attachment to Speyer. His death threatened to expose the secret trust that he had settled on her in 1927, for Speyer's heirs warned her that they planned to sue to abolish the trust. She concealed the threat from Eugene and was greatly concerned how he might react if and when he found out her old secret, that she had been Speyer's mistress; she also worried about losing the income that had always provided at least half the funds needed to keep the couple living in both privacy and style. Eventually the heirs decided not to sue (LS, 532).

Soon after Dr. Dukes died, O'Neill was shocked to learn that Oona had been voted "Debutante of the Year" in a publicity stunt for the Stork Club. The West Coast was on alert and expecting attack from the air or by submarine, and the military outlook in general was very bad. Oona's act seemed to her father too frivolous to bear and made him feel shamed. He tried to preserve his former image of Oona by blaming the affair on bad advice from Agnes.

The reversal of his fond pride in Oona reawakened the old fury Eugene felt about the divorce, a fury kept alive by the alimony he still paid every month, which he believed Agnes used to support various lovers. But he was angry at Oona as a person as well, however little he knew her. His attachment to her had come late but had been strong and idealizing, and ultimately was as fragile as any new love. In his fondness he had judged her more adult than her years could have allowed, and capable of wisdom and self-control that few adults possess. He was silent for a time, but months later his anger at her erupted in a severe letter.

Oona was driving to California with a girlfriend and, just before his birthday, asked her father to be allowed to visit and perhaps to explain the Stork Club publicity, some of which had come against her wishes. Infuriated, O'Neill refused, sarcastically informing her that the country was at war and adding that both he and Carlotta were unwell. Both the rage and several details of the letter remind one of a lovers' quarrel—she should have guessed that he was sick!—but he was too angry to have any insight into his love for her or his fury.

The scolding brought correspondence between them to an end. Soon he heard that Oona was on her way to Hollywood. He was told she was trying out for a part in a Charlie Chaplin movie. In fact Oona was already in Hollywood and, at seventeen, began dating Chaplin, who was fifty-four, two months younger than her father. Oona was soon joined in Hollywood by Agnes, who brought with her a journalist she had been living with, Morris Kaufman. She arranged for Kaufman to get work as a screenwriter. The following spring, Oona decided to marry Chaplin.

Although O'Neill seems to have had no personal animus against Chaplin, the comedian's seeming cultivation of publicity about his scandalous love life represented everything O'Neill detested about Hollywood and public life in general. In any case, the bare facts were sufficiently outrageous to a father-in-law. Three times married and divorced, Chaplin was defending a paternity suit brought by a woman who had briefly lived with him and, as he described in *My Autobiography*, he was using the publicity of the trial to his own ends (Chaplin 1964, 427). Chaplin wrote that he wanted to delay the wedding to Oona until he had been vindicated in court, to spare her from becoming involved in the scandal, but the trial was delayed, and Oona insisted on marrying at once, wanting the right to stand by him in court. In the hills east of San Francisco Bay, Eugene daily read gossipy accounts of his daughter's adventures. In Beverly Hills, Agnes gave her blessing when Oona and Chaplin eloped to Carpinteria. A few months after the wedding, when publicity concerning the elopement and the trial had abated somewhat, Oona wrote to her father saying that she was very much in love with her husband and that she greatly hoped for a reconciliation with her father. But O'Neill refused to answer and never wrote her again, despite further attempts on her part to make peace. (The Chaplins remained married until Sir Charles's death in 1977 and had eight children. Their marriage survived further scandal when Chaplin was accused of Communist leanings during the McCarthy era and had his U.S. residency permit withdrawn while he was out of the country. The Chaplins moved to Switzerland, where they lived from then on in a seclusion that increasingly resembled O'Neill's. All evidence suggests that their marriage was a strong one. Oona died of cancer in September 1991.)

By early June 1942, the tremor had eased sufficiently for Eugene to resume work. Still unable to face *A Moon,* he turned back to "The Thirteenth Apostle," the long play about God versus Satan, which O'Neill had first projected in August 1940 and which he now renamed "The Last Conquest." But he felt too ill to do much. He prepared a group of manuscripts to send to the Yale library for safekeeping, and he made final revisions on *Hughie.*

At the end of June he resumed work on *A Touch of the Poet* and wrote a new act 2. With the world, his body, and his family in tatters, he created one of his lightest comic scenes. He brings Deborah Harford into Con Melody's tavern just in time to catch Con posing in uniform in front of his mirror and reciting Byron to himself: "I have not loved the world. . . ." The scene is as funny as Schnitzler and more subtle. Showing no shame, perhaps in revenge for shame he conceals, Con makes a crude pass at the patrician Deborah, which stirs her more than she wishes to be stirred.

Another prolonged and severe episode of the shakes and low blood pressure with attendant depression made work impossible through most of July and August. In answer to a request, O'Neill wrote a letter on behalf of the U.S. Maritime Commission to be sent to next of kin of merchant mariners who perished in the war.

His interest in finishing *A Touch of the Poet* persisted, and in September the tremor and other ailments eased enough for him to resume work. He took much longer than he thought he should to write the new act 2, not because of lack of interest, he noted, but because the tremor made the act of writing so difficult. The comment suggests that the act was fully conceived in his mind. When act 2 was finished, he moved immediately into act 3 and revised it to make it fit with the new act 2. He carried on into act 4 in October and November. He felt satisfied with the play when he finished it, considering the state of his health. He admitted that although he knew it had minor faults, he had decided to let it go for the time being and make final revisions when he felt better.

Despite the difficult circumstances in which it was written, *A Touch of the Poet,* revised and detached from the Cycle, is a delightful and absorbing play. Its characters and action are deeply thought out, but the touch is usually light. It is tightly structured and conventional, taking place in a single day and night. During the day, young lovers, having overcome family complications, decide to marry. It is also a play about the marriage of the bride's parents. The father, a narcissistic, bullying former major in Wellington's Seventh Dragoons, is made to face some of his pretensions and renounce them. The wife, self-effacing in the extreme and wholly devoted to her husband and daughter, glories in the selflessness of her love and eventually triumphs to emerge as the strongest character of the three in the depth of her feeling.

The three chief characters are Con Melody, his wife Nora, and their daughter, Sara, who is to marry Simon Harford—they are the Sara and Simon of *More Stately Mansions*. Simon, who has been living in a cabin by a pond, becomes ill, and Sara brings him to her father's inn to nurse him. Simon never appears, but his mother, Deborah, has a prominent brief part. In *Poet*, O'Neill permits Deborah to show almost no hint of the madness of *Mansions*, nor any development beyond the stock character her scenes require.

Con Melody, born in Ireland on a fine estate to wealthy peasants and educated with the gentry, has let spendthrift ways, a scandal with a woman, and a duel ruin him, and he has had to resign his commission. Having brought his peasant wife and their daughter to Massachusetts, he is tricked by the Yankees into buying a dilapidated roadhouse on a disused highway where the family daily sinks further into poverty. While Con lords it over the local Irish, his wife and daughter scrape to make ends meet. Con bullies his wife and daughter, drinks up all the profits, and makes his wife borrow to buy feed for his expensive blooded mare.

On this day in 1828 he prepares to celebrate the anniversary of his greatest day—irony within irony. The Irishman who fought with the English glories in having been commended for valor at Talavera. O'Neill delights in the details of his character. Con is a large, imposing man with a "ruined face . . . once extraordinarily handsome . . . an embittered Byronic hero." He puts on the manner of a "polished gentleman. Too much so" (CP3, 197). In each act we see him preen ritualistically in front of a full-length mirror while quoting from *Childe Harold* "as if it were an incantation by which he summons pride to justify his life to himself" (203). It is something Con apparently does whenever he believes himself to be alone. He quotes the same stanza that Deborah and Simon quote in *Mansions;* having decided he would not finish the Cycle, O'Neill could not quite throw away the delicious irony of having vanity reveal itself so heroically.

In act 1, Con's rebellious daughter catches the end of one of these performances and asks her father if he saw anything in the mirror to admire. In act 2, Deborah also catches Con reciting, having come to the inn looking for her son. To escape the shame he feels at being caught, he imposes on her all his considerable physical presence. In spite of herself she is "frightened," and O'Neill makes clear that it is as much her response to Con as his presence that frightens her. When she smells the reek of whiskey on his breath, it allows her to decide that he is merely a drunken bumpkin; it saves her from herself. Nora and Sara, who witness part of the scene, do not know whether to be angrier at Con's perfidy or at Deborah's snobbish rejection of their man.

Michael Manheim points out many biographical echoes in the characterizations and sensibly writes that O'Neill himself is the primary model for Con. There is anecdotal corroboration of the point, unavailable to Manheim at the time he wrote: as previously mentioned, during an interview Agnes once told Sheaffer that if the biographer wanted to know what O'Neill sounded like he should study the scenes in which Con talks to the mirror (LS papers). It is also the case that Con has some traits in common with James O'Neill.

At the same time, Con is so fully realized a character that he seems to a biographer finally and simply himself—rather as Don Quixote and Falstaff seem to transcend the necessity of plot or idea, or the demands of an author's private demons; such characters develop within their own terms until they finally seem simply themselves. The point is emphasized because the revised version of *A Touch of the Poet* marks a change in O'Neill's ability to develop a character, a change that started with *Long Day's Journey*. Not only are Con, Nora, and Sara all well developed, but their relationships with each other are explored much more fully than in O'Neill's plays of the 1920s. An especially interesting quality of the play is the detailed attention to the characters' interactions with each other. O'Neill develops each possible relationship among the Melodys nearly as fully as he does with the Tyrones.

Above all the play is a comedy. Not that it is set in a world different from that of *The Iceman Cometh* or *Long Day's Journey*. When Con kills his mare at the end, it assures us that O'Neill has not forgotten what the world is like. That has been the case with great comedy since *The Winter's Tale* and other late Shakespeare plays and, indeed, since the *Oedipus at Colonos* of Sophocles. Great comedy often expresses a view of the world almost identical to that expressed by tragedy. The difference seems to be that in comedy individuals are not taken so seriously. Comedy deflates a heroic figure and claims that he or she is full of nothing but hot methane. Comedy shows perfect awareness of the alienation and self-deceptions of people and their institutions, but it expects less perfection from the world than tragedy does. Comedy exhorts us to be glad of an opportunity to celebrate a marriage, no matter what we know about marriage: not simply in cynical irony, but from a sense that despite all its problems, society should go on, because any alternative is unimaginable and marriage remains the basic institution of human society.

A Touch of the Poet hints at the possibility that O'Neill can sometimes take even himself not so seriously. It is the first O'Neill play since the early 1920s in which there is no human death, and where no hint of mourning is detectable to anyone but a biographer. Although *A Touch of the Poet* may tell a biographer something important about the playwright, no reader or watcher of the play needs to know anything of O'Neill's life to understand the play. Here finally is an O'Neill play that one can fully understand and appreciate without regard for O'Neill's self-psychoanalysis.

The writing of *Long Day's Journey into Night* implies that two decades of mourning were coming to an end, and O'Neill's completion of the comedy *A Touch of the Poet* confirms the implication, for it suggests a turning away from a preoccupation with the self that had prevailed for so many years. O'Neill had further mourning to face, however, in the unfinished play of Jamie's ending that he had set aside the previous winter. Still feeling an urge to assist the war effort, O'Neill tried to work on "The Last Conquest," which he conceived as an act of faith in the ethos of the Allied nations opposing Hitler, "propaganda for the spirit," as he put it. Yet, as with *Days Without End,* he kept sensing "some inner struggle about it that has held it up," as he noted on November 19, 1942. He never went further than compiling several sets of extensive notes. The conflict, he decided, arose from the paradox of the attempt at "a declaration of faith by one who is faithless." It was "a hope for faith instead of faith" itself and was undermined by "a futile feeling that no one will see the truth, not even the author." He tried to persevere, telling himself "to be the objective dramatist—after all, many a thief sincerely admires honesty" (WD, 451).

O'Neill's health continued to deteriorate, to the point that he "faded out" nearly every day after working no more than three hours. His tremor was now bad almost every day, and he often slept little at night. His ailments were probably compounded by the large amounts of various drugs he was taking and especially by the testosterone.

To counteract the hormone, he took bromide almost daily to sleep, a sedative no longer in use because it gradually and subtly builds up, until serious side effects become apparent, ranging from persistent lethargy and somnolence to psychotic symptoms, including hallucinations, paranoia, and profound depression. Bromide toxicity may also cause seizure-like episodes. O'Neill woke up very early one morning in January 1943 in what he called a "fit . . . when I thought I'd hop right out of my skin" (WD, 455). He experienced a number of such episodes. The side effects of prescription drugs played a part in the increasing strains on the marriage in the last ten years of O'Neill's life.

While recovering from the January episode, he felt his original enthusiasm for *A Moon for the Misbegotten* returning and began making notes in preparation for revising the draft. The first draft, later destroyed, had apparently been quite sketchy in the early scenes: most of O'Neill's attention had gone to laying out the self-revelation of Jamie, as he then called the character representing his brother.

The *Work Diary* shows that by January 3, 1943, O'Neill was once again enthusiastic about *A Moon,* which inspired in him a "real affection." As he continued working slowly through the month, he felt increasingly certain that this was the last play he would write. On January 28 he destroyed notes for at least "seven plays . . . dating back to Sea Island or to France." The tremor had slowed him down to about a page a day, not because he could not think but because of the "constant strain" of trying to form legible letters and words. On March 10 he noted that he felt "eager" to work but got "little done" because "nerves jumping out of hands, arms—can't control." At this time he experimented with trying to type or dictate to a secretary or to a dictating machine that Lawrence Langner had given him. But like many writers, he had a particular way of composing and could not change it. He also began destroying old files of letters. He destroyed all that he had done on "The Life of Bessie Bowen," the partially drafted play that formed the basis for the last phase of the Cycle.

A Moon for the Misbegotten continues the theme of mourning that had pervaded his plays since the early 1920s and merges it with the most common theme of his early plays, that of the struggle of young people like Robert Mayo and Anna Christie to become autonomous. Set on Phil Hogan's run-down Connecticut farm, the play begins with Josie Hogan's helping her youngest brother escape his father's tyranny and flee to the city to join other brothers whom Josie has also helped to leave. The brothers, too intimidated to cope with Hogan's tricks and threats and left with nothing but their righteous indignation, flee to the city to join the police. Larger and stronger than her brothers or father, Josie is an O'Neill original. Her talk of carrying on with all the men in the neighborhood scandalizes her brothers but is a subject of kidding between her and her father. On the whole, she gets along very well with her father, taking the place of her mother, who died giving birth to Josie's youngest brother. The Hogans, like the Melodys of *Poet*, seem mainly imaginary characters, without obvious models in the O'Neill family.

It is undoubtedly the relationship of father and daughter that sparked much of O'Neill's enthusiasm for the play, for he made them very likable. Since coming to know his own daughter and since writing *Long Day's Journey*, O'Neill had seemed to understand better than before how family relationships might work, at least in his imagination, and he can dramatize his understanding if not put it into practice. Josie is nearly a match for Hogan, both in physical combat with him and as a fellow trickster. The two scheme against each other in ways that keep the peace and get the work done. When the chance arises to embarrass a wealthy neighbor—who comes to complain that they have broken down his fence to allow their pigs to wallow in his ice pond—they team up perfectly to humiliate the snob. O'Neill has borrowed the very funny scene from Edmund's anecdote in act 1 of *Long Day's Journey into Night*. He apparently thought it was too good to waste and believed that *Long Day's Journey* would never be performed or read until twenty-five years after his death (see "A Word to the Reader").

The Hogans on their ramshackle farm get along together and get on in the world. They, and especially Josie, are the people O'Neill has chosen to hear and understand his brother's self-revelation. O'Neill has Jim Tyrone come to the farm from his haunts on Broadway to try to collect overdue rent—he has inherited the farm as part of his parents' estate. The play is set in September 1923, at which time Jamie O'Neill was in reality already in the sanatorium and barely conscious after a stroke he would survive only a few weeks.

In *A Moon*, Jim is not so ill physically as Jamie. The Hogans know him as a Broadway sport, the son of a famous father who has been their landlord and Phil's sometime drinking companion. To the Hogans Jim seems witty and charming, and they like his company; he is glad to be with unpretentious friends, whom he likes better than small-town sophisticates. Josie has had a crush on Jim since she was a child, a crush she considers safe because she thinks of herself as much too large and plain for Jim even to notice as a woman. In one of the subplots of the play Hogan, hoping his trick may lead to marriage, and wishing a better life for her than he can provide on the farm, tries to beguile his daughter into intimacy with Jim, perhaps even into going to bed with him.

O'Neill is particularly interested in what the Hogans see in Jim. When Jim first appears in act 1, still at some distance, walking toward them from the town, Josie tells her father, "Look at him when he thinks no one is watching, with his eyes on the ground. Like a dead man walking slow behind his own coffin" (CP3, 874). In the context of a teasing conversation with Hogan, she seems merely to mean that Jim looks like he has the blues or a hangover. But as the play progresses, the idea and word recur—Jim is "dead." Later in act 1, Josie kisses Jim on the lips and afterwards looks "startled and confused, stirred and . . . frightened." "Och," she says. "It's like kissing a corpse" (882). After she and her father have had their game with the rich neighbor, she hears Jim laughing offstage and muses "It's good to hear him laugh as if he meant it," and at the end of the act, she urges him to eat, saying, "You're killing yourself" (891).

The allusions to Jim being or seeming dead, which appear at first to be unthinking hyperbole, come frequently throughout the play and eventually build to a question that can't be ignored: What does it mean, wondering if he is dead? It reminds a biographer that the same word is on Jamie Tyrone's lips in the last-act quarrel between the brothers in *Long Day's Journey*. There Jamie tells Edmund that part of him is dead, the part that hopes Edmund will fail and even hopes that "the game has got Mama again!" He advises Edmund to tell people, if he survives consumption, "I had a brother, but he's dead" (CP3, 821).

At the end of act 1 and through act 2, Josie has little thought of the state of Jim's soul or body but only self-consciousness about her own size and plainness. She has invited Jim to come visit her that night while Phil is drinking at the inn. She dresses in her best but waits for him in vain. Hogan returns, less drunk than he seems, with the news that Jim has agreed to sell the farm to the neighbor Harder, who will pay well to rid himself of insufferable neighbors. Josie is furious at having waited in vain for Jim, furious to think Jim would sell the farm out from under them, and furious with her father for seeing her in a vulnerable state. Phil exploits her weakness to persuade her to trick Jim into going to bed with her; they hope it will provide a pretext for blackmailing him into selling the farm to them cheaply. She will have to take the lead, he says, because Jim in his cups is sure Josie's a virgin, for all her rough talk, and it will be "a sin on his conscience" to seduce her (902). Jim finally arrives in a distant mood, quoting Keats's "Ode to a Nightingale":

> Now more than ever seems it rich to die,
> To cease upon the midnight with no pain,
> In such an ecstasy! [CP3, 909]

Midway through act 3 Jim launches into the self-revelation that O'Neill wrote the play to understand. The story largely follows what is known historically about the circumstances surrounding Ella O'Neill's death in Los Angeles, although many sordid details are omitted, including the attempt to exclude Eugene from inheriting the New York City property, and the nomination of Jamie's woman friend as Ella's executrix. Tyrone tells Josie about resuming drinking before his mother died, unable even to wait for the end, in spite of his belief that even in her sickness she knew of his fall and was disappointed. Seeing her in her coffin before her body was put on the train for the trip to New York, he could hardly recognize her: she seemed almost a stranger, and he felt almost nothing. "I seemed dead too." He faked some sobs. Then, on the train, drunk all the time, he spent every night with a fifty-dollar woman in his compartment, loathing himself every moment and somehow satisfied that he was fulfilling some inner "plot I had to carry out" (CP3, 931–32), as if his destiny were endlessly to repeat acts of self-abasement.

Throughout Jim Tyrone's confession, O'Neill makes Josie's attention to it as important, dramatically, as the confession itself. From this point on, two well-defined and diverging points of view exist, Jim's and Josie's. Josie's idealization of Jim at first makes it easy for her to be sympathetic and to identify with his suffering and self-hatred, and she tries to offer him comfort. But her sympathy is strained further and further by his revelations until, when he relates that he was "too drunk to go to her funeral," she withdraws in revulsion, a reaction that Jim already feels toward himself (932). At this point it becomes obvious to her that her identification with Jim, like her crush on him, is related to her idealization, rather than to the man he is. It is what he has tried to tell her throughout the play—that she doesn't know him—and the audience sees a certain decency in his refusal to take advantage of her crush on him.

She sees that her image of him as a charming drunk whom she might reform through deep and constant love does him a disservice, however sincere and well-intentioned the belief. The disservice stems from the refusal to know Jim as he is, from her insistence that he be a different man than he is capable of being. As Jim has revealed himself, he is as "dead" as she thinks he is; the "deadness" she has detected and denied becomes so apparent that she can no longer disown her knowledge of it. Josie begins to detach herself from the crush and the identification with Jim, and to offer him a different kind of attention than she had intended or had known herself capable of. At this moment, the world changes for Josie. The insight that she does not know Jim is the beginning of insight into herself that will lead to change. Seeing herself as a separate person from Jim allows her to begin to see herself as a person.

A Moon for the Misbegotten provides a cumulative gloss on Jamie's word "dead": it refers to the part of him that hates, that cannot love, and especially, the part that cannot tolerate being loved by someone else. After her moment of revulsion, when he has recognized the change of feeling and is prepared to leave, Josie physically draws him back, saying "I won't let you [go] . . . . I understand now, Jim darling, and I'm proud you came to me as the one in the world you know loves you enough to understand and forgive" (CP3, 933). She continues to hold Jim, who is now silent, and she understands the words previously spoken by a man whom she now realizes she barely knows. He immediately feels the change and is grateful for it, and he sleeps in her arms through the night. She holds him protectively all night, thinking of what she has learned, and finally she sees the world's joke on her, "sitting here with the dead hugged to my breast, and the silly mug of the moon grinning down, enjoying the joke" (934).

Act 4 begins with the same scene, Jim still asleep, neither of them having moved. Hogan, thinking Josie is asleep, sneaks up on them, and she startles him by proclaiming cryptically that Jim is dead. It's a "great miracle," she says; "a virgin bears a dead child in the night and the dawn finds her still a virgin" (934). Josie has long since figured out her father's scheme to trick her into marriage with Jim, and in a gesture of independence, tells Phil that she is leaving him and the farm. The conversation that follows marks a new beginning to life on the Hogan farm.

For three decades, O'Neill tried to understand, in writing his plays, how the young can grow to independence and leave home, and usually he imagined separation to be the most violent wrenching. When his own children were having the same problem he had, he was able to imagine that change as it might affect a person like Josie. Josie has had a full and happy relationship with her father and has grown up into part wife, part pal. When she is forced to mourn the death of her unknown beloved, she learns that she has not known the real Jim at all. The act of grieving pushes her past whatever barriers have kept her obscurely dependent on her father. She declares her independence, announces that she is leaving, but then decides to stay, for she has no visible prospects for life away from the farm, and life there is tolerable enough. As for romantic love, she seems to have passed beyond its attractions, at least for the moment, in her recognition that she has not known Jim in the least. When he awakes in act 4 and prepares to go, Josie still knows what she learned beneath the moon. Seeing that she does not despise him, Jim too lets himself remember what he learned the night before, though he learned much less than Josie. He is very grateful to her for the great gift she gave him, after she ceased to be in love, a gift of empathy that asked nothing of him. It is the only form of love he can accept.

The play marks the great gradual changes its author passed through in three decades of playwriting. He began as a young man driven to write again and again of young people trying to break the ties of dependency. His own ties made mourning nearly impossible when it came time to mourn, and he lingered with his ghosts for two decades, making only the most gradual progress. In his last play, he creates a woman who is first an objective witness to his own last act of mourning. Gradually the playwright's point of view merges with Josie's. Through her, he wishes his brother peace and lets him go quietly to his death with the recognition of having been loved selflessly. The playwright had passed beyond mourning and tragedy.

24

San Francisco and New York
1943–1947

WE DO NOT KNOW EXACTLY when O'Neill finished *A Moon for the Misbegotten,* because existing diary entries cease after May 4, 1943. Jane Caldwell, who typed O'Neill's letters and manuscripts from 1944 to 1946, told Sheaffer she remembered retyping a script of *A Moon* with penciled revisions (LS papers). Probably O'Neill finished the play in the early summer of 1943 and made the penciled revisions in the fall. In a prefatory note to the published text dated August 1952, O'Neill wrote that he had made no changes in the play after 1943.

Although the O'Neills continued to live at Tao House in 1943, the war made it inevitable that they would have to move. Neither could drive, and both were increasingly infirm. Gasoline was rationed, and they had to beg rides to town with neighbors to shop or visit their doctors. In the fall of 1943 they reluctantly decided to move to a hotel in San Francisco, the Huntington.

Relations between Eugene and Carlotta were increasingly strained for reasons that are very complex. The most important change in their lives was that both knew that Eugene's writing life was ending. As Travis Bogard has pointed out, the center—almost the whole—of their life together had been their absolute devotion to Eugene's creative work (see Commins 1986, xvii). In most other respects they had little in common, including literary taste, politics, and impressions of people. Each had made compromises, learned to let the other be different, and learned something of the other's world. He had learned from her a little about money, and the two had worked out ways to remain financially independent of each other. Their home was large and the design of it complex enough for them to live fairly separate lives within it, coming together by choice rather than jostling by constant necessity. For two such strong-willed people to live together with anything resembling harmony, there had to be separation. But the changes coming changed everything.

In important ways, the loss of his physical ability to write was probably easier for him to tolerate than for her. He still was getting ideas for new work as often as ever. There is no reason to doubt that if he could have finished the Cycle and "By Way of Obit," he would have produced more plays of the quality of *Hughie, More Stately Mansions,* and *A Touch of the Poet.* He had the consolation of knowing that in his last years of work he had written his best plays and had achieved the emotional and artistic maturity he had so long sought. If the Cycle could not be finished, and many other ideas could not be developed, he had still done very well with his life and talents and could face death with the knowledge that all in all his life had not been badly lived.

The changes Carlotta faced may have been the more difficult. In a private communication, Margaret Loftus Ranald once compared Carlotta to Alma Mahler and Cosima Wagner, each of whom was a woman who greatly needed to be the wife and muse of genius. Carlotta needed to make a home for a man she could and did call "the master"—pronounced "mah-ster"—in which what she called "masterworks" could be created, and so play her part in the work of creativity. She believed she had found her life's calling in being Mrs. Eugene O'Neill. She had seen O'Neill at his worst and had lived daily with a man as preoccupied and self-absorbed as only a writer can be. While the two made their peace with their differences and their demons, she found great satisfaction in the work of making their various homes, and in helping O'Neill fulfill his gifts.

Although both O'Neills deeply needed each other, a subtle shift in the balance of dependency was occurring, one that would have been hard to predict. As we shall see, the satisfaction O'Neill felt with his late work, and the personal development that his long labor had brought with it, made him a little less dependent than in the past on Carlotta and even seemed occasionally to lighten a little his view of the world. At the same time, the loss of O'Neill's physical ability to write marked the end of what seemed to her the reason for her life with him. Although she took exquisite care with grooming to the end of her life, and although her face looked much younger than her years, her body had inevitably changed, and her aches and pains made her feel her age.

Above all, the O'Neills were affected by their illnesses. Carlotta suffered from mild arthritis, and her vision continued to give her problems. Like her husband, she apparently suffered from some chronic depressive condition. Beyond whatever endogenous neurochemical processes may have been at work, she and her husband both were subject to emotional ups and downs that resulted in part from the medications they took. Carlotta took bromide daily for arthritic pain and almost every night to sleep, and Eugene often took it at night. The drug tended to cause depressive and psychotic symptoms, which might become full-blown before the user realized that too much had been taken. Although Ella O'Neill was clearly the primary model for Mary Tyrone in *Long Day's Journey into Night,* O'Neill cannot have failed to notice that much of what he wrote about the character based on his mother described his wife as well. When he had Mary explain she took morphine to ease rheumatic pain in her hands, it must have crossed his mind that his wife's behavior was often dramatically affected by the bromide she took to control pain from arthritis.

Both O'Neills took many drugs prescribed or recommended by their physicians. In addition, both used calomel to counteract the anticholinergic effects of various medicines. Calomel also was known commonly to cause serious depression, an effect that eventually caused the drug to fall into disuse. The depressive effects of bromide and calomel in two depressed, volatile people like Eugene and Carlotta must have been considerable.

In addition, as has been previously mentioned, O'Neill's tremor was itself related to the biochemical sources of depression, as his doctors described to him. He passed on his understanding of the condition in a letter to Eugene Jr. (written in July 1944):

> [The tremor] customarily follows a rhythm, no one knows
> why, of ups and downs, the downs being accompanied by
> acute mental depression as well as increased shakes. The
> other day my hands without warning jerked a cup of coffee
> all over the surrounding landscape, and suddenly I burst
> into weeping, not because I'd spilt the coffee but impelled

by the same nervous impulse, as it were. As I've never been
addicted to nervous weeps, no matter what the strain or (in
the old days) how much booze was in me—I am terribly
upset by such exuberant blues, and if the docs didn't say
these things were all part of the game, I would feel more
than slightly nuts. As it is, I try to be merely disgusted with
myself. [SL, 562]

The natural volatility of both O'Neills led so often to all-out war
that Myrtle Caldwell frequently found herself implored to make the long
drive to Tao House, where, as she told Sheaffer, her presence eased the
tensions between Eugene and Carlotta. Ever since the O'Neills had returned to the States from France, they had brought other people to their
home to dissipate the rancor that built up between them if they were by
themselves for long. The realtor George Boll had served that purpose
when they were in Georgia, and Herbert Freeman had done likewise after they moved to California.

Things between the O'Neills came to a head in the fall when, as
Sheaffer reports, O'Neill found Carlotta and her female masseuse in a sexual embrace (SL, 543–46). During the uproar that followed, Carlotta
summoned Myrtle to come out and help restore order. Myrtle told Sheaffer that she tried to convince Eugene that he had not seen what he believed he had seen, and although in time things gradually calmed down,
relations between the O'Neills were never again the same. At certain
times, especially around anniversaries, O'Neill would feel a deep need for
her and even an ardent love, but the steady day-to-day trust and affection
he had usually felt toward Carlotta for more than a decade was now largely
replaced by misgivings and wariness.

O'Neill could not have been unaware of rumors, widespread among
show people in the 1920s, that Carlotta preferred women to men sexually;
and undoubtedly he had understood the implications of Carlotta's being
Elizabeth Marbury's special friend when he met her in Maine in 1926. Evidently by the time their affair began a year later, he had denied or repressed whatever he knew of Carlotta's reputation, for when he saw her
with the masseuse, he could not extend to his wife the tolerance he had
always shown for homosexual friends. Carlotta later told various people
that O'Neill was impotent from 1943 until his death, a claim not consistent with others of Carlotta's own statements and actions. The assertion

appears to mean that he was not so often strongly attracted to her as in the past. Assuming that whatever caused his tremor and depression also affected his sexual energy, it might partly explain his fury at discovering Carlotta with the masseuse. With his mood and body increasingly out of control, he would probably have been greatly upset over any sort of infidelity by Carlotta with anyone, and the element of homosexuality gave him a particular reason to blame her for making him feel useless. At the same time, it is easy to sympathize with Carlotta's need for relief from the daily tensions of their life.

The year 1943 had been difficult. On the day of the last existing diary entry, O'Neill lamented that he didn't know Eugene Jr.'s army address and so, "for 1st time," could not send his son a birthday gift. Evidently Eugene Jr. could not bear to write his father with the news that the services had rejected him, and for some time the two were out of touch. This was about the time Oona married Charlie Chaplin.

By late 1943, the time had come for the O'Neills to move. Sheaffer learned that they sold Tao House to an Oakland lawyer who paid sixty thousand dollars for the house and acreage that had cost the O'Neills a hundred thousand. Most of the fine Oriental furnishings that Carlotta had bought from Gump's she sold back to the store. Remaining possessions went into storage, including a hundred cartons of Eugene's books and the player piano, "Rosie," that Carlotta had given Eugene in a happier time.

In place of the hilltop estate with its complex of corridors and twenty rooms and its walled garden, they arranged for a tenth-floor suite of four rooms in the Huntington Hotel with a view of Grace Cathedral, then under construction. The suite gave the O'Neills the separate bedrooms they always required, a sitting room, and a kitchen-dinette. Here they would remain until the fall of 1946. Tension between them, already high, increased greatly in the confinement of their new quarters.

No sooner had they settled in San Francisco than Carlotta became seriously ill with a kidney and bladder infection accompanied by a high fever. She was sick for some time and was eventually cured by the new wonder drug, penicillin. The infection was considered dangerous, and O'Neill was very worried. Just as she started to recover, O'Neill was shocked by news that Harry Weinberger had died suddenly in New York. He mentioned it in letters several times over the next months. He had met Harry early in 1916 while hanging around left-wing groups, and Harry had been his lawyer, friend, and confidant for more than a quarter-century. Carlotta told Sheaffer that Eugene had sat next to her bed all one night while she was recovering from the infection, to keep her company and partly because his sorrow was so great over his old friend's death.

While Carlotta was ill, the O'Neills hired Kathryne Radovan Albertoni, who had been one of Eugene's nurses during his nearly fatal illness of 1937, to care for the two of them; for the rest of the time that they were in California, Kaye was with them five days a week. She gave daily injections to both of them, but later she told Sheaffer that she felt her main service was to be "a buffer, a mediator between them" (LS, 549). In early May, when she had recovered, Carlotta brought in two other buffers as well—Myrtle Caldwell and her daughter Jane (called Janie). Janie became Eugene's secretary in the spring of 1944.

Since mid-1942, O'Neill's typist had been Cynthia Stram. Carlotta had hired her daughter for secretarial work when her own eye problems made it impossible for her to continue typing. Cynthia had typed *Long Day's Journey into Night*, *Hughie*, *A Touch of the Poet* and *A Moon for the Misbegotten*. In the spring of 1944, however, a crisis developed over the condition of Nellie Tharsing, who could no longer care for herself and was living with the Strams. After Nellie gave her a nasty bite, Cynthia called her mother to insist she make other arrangements for Nellie's care. Cynthia and Carlotta quarreled bitterly, and Carlotta denounced her daughter. Carlotta eventually arranged for Nellie to go to a nursing home; she then fired Cynthia from her job working for Eugene and refused to see her daughter again.

The job had been a serious matter to Cynthia, who needed the money to support her son and her husband. (Rheumatic fever had made Roy Stram a permanent invalid). Cynthia had survived emotional warfare with her mother and grandmother by being feisty; but she remained emotionally open, and consequently vulnerable. So the potential for hot conflict was always present when mother and daughter were together. That is how things stood in May 1944 when Janie was hired to do secretarial work for O'Neill.

Photos show Janie Caldwell to have been a dramatically good-looking young woman at twenty-one, with long hair and an oval face. It was she who had impulsively asked, at their first meeting, what woman wouldn't live with O'Neill, even in a tent. She quit another secretarial job to work for the playwright. She typed for him for the year and a half the O'Neills remained at the Huntington and was at the apartment five days a week from ten until five.

In fact, there was less typing to do than in the past. She typed a revised text of *A Moon for the Misbegotten* and incorporated penciled corrections made the previous fall, and she remembered typing an almost complete draft of "The Thirteenth Apostle," which lacked an ending. There were letters to answer, which she typed, and O'Neill wrote an occasional poem. But on the whole, it seems that the reason Carlotta hired her was to serve as a buffer. Sheaffer believed that Carlotta meant Jane to replace her as the playwright's muse and hoped that her husband's creative spirit might catch fire again. In fact, O'Neill occasionally drifted into a kind of creative musing during which Janie believed that he wasn't aware of her presence. If this is so, he must have been very comfortable in her company. But O'Neill was too ill, and the internal pressure that had driven him to confront his demons each day throughout his long writing life had been partly eased by his work on the late plays. By this time, writing was so difficult that it sometimes took him several minutes to sign his name to a letter Janie had typed.

The relationship between Eugene and Janie was marked by affectionate teasing from the start, and the affection was enhanced rather than concealed by the rough, antisentimental style of the time. O'Neill kidded her about her youth and his antiquity. (He looked much older than his years.) Jane told Sheaffer that during the first June she worked for him, O'Neill warned her that if she got him a Father's Day gift, he would bite her ear off. He gave her several gifts of books, inscribed to her, and also what he called an "enchanted mirror," accompanied by a card that explained the charm: that if she looked past her image in just the right way she might see the face of her friend admiring her in a certain way.

O'Neill knew that Janie often had dates after work with a man (whom she would later marry). Perhaps the combination of safety and the hint of a chase inspired him. According to Kathryne Albertoni, O'Neill would kiss Janie on the lips when she came or went each day, in Carlotta's presence if she happened to be there. Neither Kathryne nor Carlotta approved of the display, nor of the noise of hot jazz that often came from Eugene's room during working hours. Besides working, Eugene and Janie would listen to records and frequently dance together. Janie told Sheaffer that although O'Neill was not a very good dancer, he liked fast numbers like the Bunny Hug and the Turkey Trot. She never saw any hint of O'Neill's dark side. "He was the kindest human being I've ever known," she told Sheaffer (LS, 535).

The relationship between the frail, aging playwright and the twenty-one-year-old Janie was lighthearted, and yet an emotional attachment developed on both sides that lasted even after the playwright returned to the East. Her mother believed that Jane might have won O'Neill away from Carlotta if she had been more aggressive and had followed the O'Neills to New York. Jane told Sheaffer that O'Neill seldom seemed to her very ill—testimony to the healing power of affectionate attention, and perhaps to her idealization of her friend.

O'Neill liked to daydream aloud with her about the two of them being reincarnated as seagulls: she would rest on a piling, and he would bring her a fresh fish. Or they would go to Russia together and spend the rubles he was owed in royalties but which could not leave the country. He fantasized about a production of *A Moon for the Misbegotten* and encouraged Jane to gain weight and muscle so that she could play Josie. But O'Neill knew all too well how sick he was and probably never seriously contemplated leaving Carlotta, not at that point, despite the change in his feelings toward his wife and his affection for Janie.

Carlotta tolerated the situation for more than a year with no more than grumbling. Then, about late August 1945, shortly after the bombing of Hiroshima and Nagasaki ended the war, there was some sort of confrontation. Carlotta exploded at both Myrtle and Janie and banished them. They went to Los Angeles to see *Mourning Becomes Electra* at the Pasadena Playhouse. Janie sent O'Neill a picture postcard from their hotel, in which she referred to herself as "your atomic bombshell." Since, as Janie knew, Carlotta usually saw the mail first, the message must have been intended for her as much as for Eugene. Following Hiroshima, the phrase "atomic bombshell" came into the widest usage almost instantly, as in "Betty Grable, Hollywood's atomic bombshell," and would seem to refer to some sexual talk between the correspondents. O'Neill raised Cain over the expulsion of the Caldwells, and Carlotta called them several times in their L.A. hotel to beg them to return. They relented, and things resumed their former course.

According to Jane, Carlotta frequently threatened suicide during the next months, and O'Neill took to calling her Hazel when he thought she had become too dramatic. Carlotta would rage at O'Neill for days on end, Jane, Myrtle, and Kathryne Albertoni told Sheaffer, calling him, among other things, "a nasty, dirty, senile old man" (LS, 556). For Kathryne and Jane the atmosphere at the suite was Strindbergian. Carlotta stopped confiding in Myrtle, who, she decided, was now in the enemy camp.

However justified Carlotta's anger, it seems likely that bromide poisoning had contributed to the extremity of some of her thoughts and feelings, and perhaps to some of Eugene's as well. He told Myrtle that "if a millionaire came along who wanted her," Carlotta would "drop me in a minute." Apparently he had in mind Carlotta's old friendship with James Speyer, the nature of which he had guessed or learned of. Carlotta "loves being Mrs. Eugene O'Neill, she loves the name," he told Myrtle, but he insisted that she didn't care about him otherwise (LS, 556).

Kathryne Albertoni told Sheaffer that late in September, she was ordered by Carlotta to pack for her so that she could leave at once for New York. Kathryne ignored the order and walked out, but she could hear the battle continue behind her. The next morning, Sheaffer reports, Carlotta told Kathryne that she wanted to kill Eugene; then, a day or so later, she claimed that Eugene had threatened her with a gun and that she had gotten a butcher's knife. The only signs of battle were her slightly swollen jaw and his slightly swollen hand. When Carlotta threatened to kill herself by overdosing on bromide, Kathryne, deciding that things were beyond her control, called the doctor. Both O'Neills blamed the confining hotel suite for making them crazy, and, forgetting their former discomfort in the muggy southern heat, decided to return to Georgia. They went so far as to buy several seaside lots from their old friend George Boll. The fight that Kathryne described to Sheaffer made them realize their situation was too volatile for them to try to live in isolation. The idea of going back to Georgia seems so unrealistic that one can infer the desperation they felt. They eventually decided to go to New York and decide later about Georgia.

Not long before the O'Neills left, the Winthers drove down from Seattle for a visit. Perhaps the O'Neills were able to conceal their problems from Sophus and Eline during the brief visit. The Winthers later told Sheaffer that they had not noticed any particular tensions between the spouses. Two melancholy men of mordant wit talked of tombstones. O'Neill told Winther that on his he wanted:

EUGENE O'NEILL
There is Something
to be said
For Being Dead

Eugene no doubt had many reasons for becoming involved with Jane, including his continuing resentment that Carlotta had betrayed him with the masseuse. Heated accusations of infidelity issued from both sides during the battles of the Huntington. Nevertheless, Eugene's attachment to Jane Caldwell probably represented a response to the great change taking place in his life. He was losing the thing that had been at the center of his attention for more than thirty years. What is interesting is his response to the loss. For decades a loss or change had driven him inside, where he would spin out of himself something he could put into the world to restore what was damaged or missing. The response to contemplated retirement—having a fling with an attractive young girl—was more ordinary and less artistically creative than had been usual for him for several decades. To this point in his adult life, in spite of many temptations, O'Neill had apparently remained faithful to Agnes and Carlotta, except that he had been unfaithful to Agnes in his affair with Carlotta in 1927. But now he looked outward, rather than within, for an answer to loss, and he found Jane. Eugene may not have decided to leave Carlotta, but his whirl with Jane had permanent consequences for the marriage, which deteriorated further and would never recover.

Just before the O'Neills boarded their train to New York, Eugene invited Cynthia to lunch. They had a pleasant meal together, neither mentioning Carlotta, whom Cynthia assumed was out. But a noise in the apartment shortly before she left let her know that her mother was there and did not want to see her daughter. Cynthia and O'Neill grinned at each other in recognition and friendship.

Near the end of a half-century's reflections on the human condition, Freud noted without irony that at the end of a successful psychoanalysis neurotic misery might give way to the ordinary unhappiness that is the lot of every life. Nothing in Freud's remark suggests that analysis allows one to escape one's destiny or the influence of the early physical and psychic determinants around which one forms one's self. The same must have been true of O'Neill in his later years. Writing *Long Day's Journey* and *A Moon for the Misbegotten* seems to have allowed him to bring to a close his two decades of mourning. The comedy in the latter, in the revised version of *A Touch of the Poet,* and in *Hughie* show O'Neill writing as he almost never had before and provides evidence of growth comparable to the development that might occur in successful psychoanalysis.

Freud's remark could apply to the last decade of O'Neill's life. O'Neill's self-analysis could alleviate his depression only to the extent that the relaxation of neurotic conflicts meant that they contributed less than before to his condition, which was apparently the result of a primarily neurochemical process. Indeed, the playwright's depression generally worsened as his tremor increasingly incapacitated him, and not just because it was demoralizing to lose control of his body and to be unable to write. The worsening tremor was one response to the neurological deterioration; depression was apparently another. The gain from laying his dead to rest and from the psychological development that accompanied mourning was offset by the neurological anomaly.

During the three years that the O'Neills lived in New York, the problems in the marriage increased, in part because the relative anonymity and isolation that the couple had enjoyed in California ended as soon as they disembarked at Grand Central Station. O'Neill found himself surrounded by old friends, most of whom believed that Carlotta kept her husband separated from others who cared about him. To a biographer it seems clear that whatever Carlotta did in guarding her husband's privacy was what he wanted, in substance if not in every detail or in style. (As Jamie says of the playwright's alter ego Edmund in *Long Day's Journey,* "he's stubborn as hell inside and what he does is what he wants to do" [CP3, 733].) Now Eugene found himself being treated like royalty by old and new friends who regarded Carlotta as the dragon of the moat, and he did nothing to dissuade them.

As if things were not already bad enough between the O'Neills, a postwar housing shortage forced them into a two-room suite at the Hotel Barclay. For the first time in their married life, they had to share a bedroom. They remained there, on East Forty-eighth Street, for a tense seven months.

Saxe Commins had loved O'Neill like a brother for nearly thirty years and had shared enough tough times with the O'Neills to suppose that he could not be surprised. With the O'Neills' return to Manhattan, Saxe saw them as often as he could and, like others before him, was drawn into the family as a buffer. Soon he found himself more deeply engulfed in battle than he wanted to be. From the earliest days, the time of the couple's elopement, Saxe had cultivated an attitude of friendly neutrality toward Carlotta in the face of her volatility, condescension, and unconcealed anti-Semitism.

A few days after the O'Neills checked into the Barclay, Saxe witnessed an incident that, from a publisher's point of view, had important legal implications and that seemed to him an example of "wantonly calculated cruelty," as he wrote in an extended account (Commins 1986, 218–25). A group of manuscripts that O'Neill had brought from San Francisco had somehow vanished. Saxe wrote: "Gene had brought with him from California . . . finished plays, notes in long hand running to 125,000 words, tentative drafts, character sketches, scene divisions, snatches of dialogue, stage directions and the like for the nine plays of the cycle in progress. . . . Our dinner was a dismal affair; eaten in silence and gloom. It was all too apparent from Gene's nervous anxiety and Carlotta's angry gibes that something serious had occurred. When the table was cleared I learned the cause of the tension; the manuscripts were lost. They had disappeared mysteriously during the day and there was no clue to their whereabouts" (218).

With Saxe's help, Eugene tried to recall every act and event since the last time he had he had seen the manuscripts. He had not taken them with him to the Theatre Guild offices that morning. The hotel room had been locked when he had left and the key deposited at the desk. He could describe packing the trunk and recalled checking on the manuscripts when they first arrived at the Barclay.

Carlotta ridiculed Eugene's and Saxe's concern. Eugene was senile, she said; his memory was failing him, and he seldom knew what he was doing. Saxe suggested searching the apartment to see if, "like Poe's purloined letter," they might be "in the most obvious of places" (219).

> Whereupon we went through every trunk, closet, cupboard
> and bureau drawer in the apartment, all to no avail. Carlotta
> taunted us while we explored likely and unlikely places of
> concealment, omitting only an examination of the drawers

in which she kept her lingerie and other items of a personal nature. When we stopped there, she insisted with growing resentment that we should not let delicacy deter us and she flung open the bureau in which she kept her underwear. Gingerly and embarrassedly we removed every garment, but still no manuscript came into view.

As the search continued, Gene's nervousness manifested itself in an uncontrollable tremor of his hands and a quivering of his lips. He was trying desperately to prod his memory and thus solve the mystery of the missing manuscripts, but he was completely blocked. Our systematic examination of the apartment convinced us that they had disappeared without a trace. We gave up the search and I went home.

Two days later when Gene and I were alone for a moment, he whispered to me that the manuscript had been found and begged me to forget the entire unhappy episode. He explained, as if he were trying to condone a sick child's perverse behavior, that Carlotta had taken them out of the apartment and hidden them to punish him for reasons totally obscure to him. [Saxe apparently never learned about Jane Caldwell.] She knew where the manuscripts were during all the time of his torment and of the vain search. Only Strindberg, he observed grimly, would understand his predicament and know the motivations for such wantonly calculated cruelty. [Commins 1986, 219]

Strindberg, that is, would have understood domestic warfare in which all passion, intimacy, and intensity expressed themselves in acts of cruelty instead of affection.

O'Neill's insistence that Saxe never mention the incident is interesting, for it suggests several things, most obviously that O'Neill urgently wished to conceal an act in which he would have appeared to most contemporaries an innocent victim. Undoubtedly, he did not feel innocent at all but assumed he was being paid back for flaunting his friendship with Jane. Beyond this, he seems now to have made a decision like the one he had had to make about his mother in order to mourn her, that she was not "evil" (Saxe's word for Carlotta) but ill and that she really could not help herself. Somewhat later, after another such incident, O'Neill would explicitly tell Saxe of his belief and beg Saxe to understand that Carlotta could not help herself.

Trying to look at the incident from her point of view, one might suggest that, apart from whatever else drove her, Carlotta might have been asserting a claim she felt she had on the manuscripts. She believed she had helped create the plays by giving her husband the conditions he needed in order to write, including young women, her daughter Cynthia and then Jane Caldwell, whom she hoped might inspire him.

Aware now of the risks of his situation, Eugene sent a sealed copy of *Long Day's Journey into Night* to Bennett Cerf at Random House, together with a note dated November 29 instructing that the play could not be published until "twenty-five (25) years after my death," that no advance should be paid before "the said publication date," that the publisher should hold the copyright in its name, and that payment should be made to his "Executors or Administrators" (SL, 575). In addition to guaranteeing the safety of the play, the clause forbidding advance payment gave him a hold over Carlotta that would work as long as he lived, even if he should be declared incompetent, by making it hard to capitalize on the play, a work they both believed would sell very widely if published.

When Harry Weinberger had died, his practice had been taken over by his associate, Winfield Aronberg, called Bill. After meeting on matters of business, Bill Aronberg accompanied Eugene on jaunts around Manhattan, to football and hockey games, six-day bicycle races, and prize fights. A jazz buff like the playwright, he toured the Fifty-second Street jazz clubs with Eugene, where they heard the great players of the day. "Gene was the politest man I ever knew," Aronberg told Sheaffer, "a helluva guy" (LS, 561). O'Neill resumed his friendship with George Jean Nathan, who also went with him to sporting events and jazz clubs.

At first, O'Neill saw his first son frequently. Eugene Jr. was now thirty-five, divorced from his third wife and self-estranged from Yale. He lived in Greenwich Village with an artist's agent, Ruth Lander, with whom he had a stormy relationship (both had frequent affairs with others). Since the war he had worked briefly as a radio announcer in a small station and sometimes taught a course in drama at the New School. He hoped to use his voice, which sounded rather like Orson Welles's, according to one of Sheaffer's informants, and his striking appearance to make a career in television or perhaps the theater, but training and experience did not seem to improve on his basic gifts. O'Neill worried that Eugene was drinking too heavily. Carlotta hated his beard and squabbled with him over it and over his leftist politics. After several increasingly difficult episodes, he became reluctant to visit them because of the upset that his presence indirectly caused for his father.

Eugene Jr. told Shane that their father had returned to New York. Although Shane received money through his father's lawyer from time to time, there had been no contact between him and O'Neill for some time. Shane's life, like Eugene Jr.'s, had been affected by the war. Following a year and a half of maritime service, during which he saw ships torpedoed and sailors drowned and burned alive in flaming, oil-covered waters, Shane had a serious breakdown and was hospitalized. He was now very frequently drunk. Back in Greenwich Village, he was using marijuana heavily, and also heroin. At least twice he was found, unconscious and with the gas jets open, by a friend, Margaret Stark. Both times she saved his life. One friend from that time described Shane to Sheaffer as an innocent resembling Prince Myshkin, Dostoyevsky's Idiot (LS, 563). He seems seldom to have had work, even in a time of almost full employment, and he lived on whatever food and lodging friends gave him and whatever funds his mother and father sent him through their lawyers, most of which must have gone for drugs or booze.

On July 31, 1944, Shane had married Catherine Givens. A year and some months later, Shane learned that his father was in New York, and he saw him several times. On November 16, 1945, Cathy gave birth to a son that she and Shane named Eugene Gladstone O'Neill III. O'Neill was pleased and proud, and Carlotta visited Cathy at the hospital several times with gifts for the baby.

Soon after, Carlotta invited Shane and Cathy to dinner. Cathy later told Croswell Bowen that she expected the playwright to be an "old sailor, the saloon guy I had read about." Instead, he seemed to her "very elegant" and "very shy." O'Neill broke the ice immediately by looking directly into Cathy's eyes, smiling, and telling her, "Why, you look just like Agnes!" a remark she took as a high compliment (Bowen 1959, 303). If Bowen reported accurately, it is interesting that this comparison sounded friendly to Cathy. It suggests that O'Neill's feelings toward Agnes had finally thawed a little. O'Neill made both of them comfortable, she told Bowen, and they spent the evening talking eagerly about jazz, about which all except Carlotta were knowledgeable.

On February 10, 1946, the infant Eugene III died, probably a victim of Sudden Infant Death Syndrome, a phenomenon not established at the time. The death certificate listed the probable cause of death as "postural asphyxia from bed-clothes, accidental" (Gelbs, 869). The doctor who filed the death report wrote that "the infant showed evidence of neglect . . . with maceration of scrotal tissue and lower abdomen, probably from unchanged diapers" (Gelbs, 868–69). Apart from diaper rash, the doctor found no abnormalities.

Shane himself told the doctor that he and his wife had gone to bed about 4 A.M., that he had gotten up early to go to work, and that neither had looked in on the baby after they went to bed. Cathy slept until noon and then awoke to find the baby dead. Eugene and Carlotta were greatly upset. Enraged, Carlotta denounced Shane and Cathy, refused to see them again, and at least once blamed the young couple for the child's death, an accusation that was almost certainly unfounded.

O'Neill was deeply saddened, and Shane and Cathy were naturally filled with guilt, even before Carlotta's accusation. Agnes, in Los Angeles, where Oona was about to deliver her second child, arranged for Shane and Cathy to go to Bermuda and stay in the old house, Spithead. Eugene had Shane and Cathy over to the apartment for dinner in late February, the night before they were to leave for Bermuda, and Cathy told Bowen that it was a relaxed and pleasant evening, with Eugene reminiscing about Shane's boyhood at Spithead.

Although Agnes had arranged for one of her support payments from Eugene to go directly to Shane and Cathy, the couple soon ran out of money in Bermuda. Perhaps feeling justified because Shane and Oona would eventually inherit the house and its contents, Shane and Cathy systematically stripped it of its furnishings: Sheaffer reports that they sold almost everything portable: linens, furniture, barrels of dishes that included some of Ella's fine china, and James O'Neill's costumes; even plumbing and electrical fixtures they stripped from the walls. Eugene apparently heard of the ravages and continued to brood about the death of his infant namesake, but he remained tentatively open to his son and daughter-in-law for a time. Having exhausted their source of money for drugs, Shane and Cathy returned to New York.

Several months later, Eugene lost patience. The last straw, a trivial thing in itself, came sometime in the spring or summer of 1946. When Shane seemed to have the flu, Cathy, pleading poverty, called her father-in-law and asked for medical help. Eugene agreed and sent Bill Aronberg with a doctor, in what turned out to be a comedy of errors. Before help arrived, Shane suddenly felt better, so he and Cathy went out for a steak dinner at a friend's house. A drunken friend of Shane's named Seymour dropped by after Shane and Cathy had left and fell asleep. Assuming that Seymour was Shane, the doctor gave Seymour a medical injection against the flu. When the mistake was explained, Eugene and Bill Aronberg were both annoyed at having their feelings aroused for an emergency that did not seem to have been serious, and O'Neill was less amused at the case of mistaken identity than he might have been. Carlotta was enraged and unforgiving.

In mid-March of 1946 Eugene entertained his old acquaintance and biographer Barrett Clark. Clark wrote that he was "shocked" by the change in O'Neill's appearance. In the ten years since they had met, Eugene had come to appear "painfully thin and shrunken"—he now weighed about 130 pounds, his fine French suits hung on him, and his face was deeply lined. His tremor was so severe that he had trouble with almost everything he tried to do. It was especially apparent when he was lighting a cigarette. He told Clark that he could no longer write with a pen or use a typewriter. He looked a decade older than his age, fifty-seven. As always, he spoke very slowly, pausing for seconds as his sentences formed themselves. "He spoke to the point, with complete clarity, with good humor and graciousness, and with an almost complete lack of self-consciousness," Clark wrote (1967, 150). They talked about *The Iceman Cometh,* which the Theatre Guild had begun to prepare, and about the Cycle. O'Neill told Clark that he had decided to "detach" *A Touch of the Poet* from the rest of the Cycle and allow the Guild to produce it after *The Iceman Cometh.* If all went well, *A Moon for the Misbegotten* would follow. As they talked, they heard the sounds of the St. Patrick's Day parade. Clark "wondered why a man who called himself O'Neill was not marching," and O'Neill grinned broadly.

By this time, the O'Neills knew that they would not return to Georgia, and they decided to look for a permanent residence in Manhattan, where they were close to their doctors. Shortly after the Clark interview, a penthouse apartment at 35 East Eighty-fourth Street became available when the playwright Edward Sheldon died; the O'Neills leased it. While her husband worked with the Theatre Guild on the *Iceman* production, Carlotta at once set about redecorating their apartment with bright colors and fine Chinese furniture. The Gelbs report that she got a canary, which she named Jeremiah (863). Perhaps Jeremiah prophesied doom for *The Iceman Cometh.*

In discussions with Lawrence Langner, O'Neill had asked that Eddie Dowling, whom Nathan had recommended, be hired to direct. Bobby Jones, O'Neill's old friend from the Provincetown, was already at work transforming O'Neill's sketches and drawings into sets and costumes. The playwright became involved in casting and other chores, and the Guild assigned a young production assistant, Sherlee Weingarten, to follow him around and help in any way she could.

Sherlee told Sheaffer that either she had been warned about Carlotta's jealousy or she intuitively sensed a problem. In any case she found ways to attend warmly and unobtrusively to O'Neill without arousing Carlotta's ire. Sherlee made notes of Eugene's comments on rehearsal, carried messages to people, and even became "a cigarette fiend." She took to lighting one of her own whenever she saw Eugene take one out, so that she could offer him a light without seeming to notice that his tremor made him struggle to light his own. Later Eugene gave her an inscribed copy of *The Iceman Cometh,* in which he wrote, "I have a guilty feeling I have not been sufficiently appreciative at times . . . taking it for granted you should light cigarettes for playwrights!" (LS, 573).

Working closely with the playwright, Sherlee was impressed with O'Neill's attention to the actors as individuals, regardless of what he thought of their work in the play. Tom Pedi, who played Rocky the bartender, and E. G. Marshall, who played the failed lawyer, Willie, both remembered O'Neill as friendly; and Marcella Markham, who played the hooker Cora, told Sheaffer that she and the playwright had carried on a mild flirtation, discreetly concealed from Carlotta (LS, 573). Also concealed from Carlotta were the frequent visits to rehearsals of Eugene Jr. He was now so alienated from Carlotta and so alarmed by some fights he had seen between her and his father that, to keep out of sight of his stepmother, he lurked in obscure corners of the theater for fear his father might suffer in the repercussions.

Unfortunately, there was little to please anyone in the rehearsals.

The somber text greatly affected the actors. One cast member began having nightmares, and another gave up liquor for months and became impeccably fastidious about his appearance. Several complained to each other that they could not maintain the usual professional distance from the part they played. Jeanne Cagney, who played Margie and who was devoutly, quietly Catholic, began wearing a conspicuous crucifix. James Barton, miscast as Hickey, felt that the atmosphere at rehearsals was "as bad as being in church"; meanwhile the playwright sat in the theater and dictated notes about things he thought did not work. Sheaffer's interviews with cast members give no hint that the comedy in the play was apparent to anyone during the original production. Eddie Dowling, the director, was the most troubled of all. Cast members said he seemed "cowed," "like a whipped child," and "afraid to suggest anything" in O'Neill's presence (LS, 574). Although O'Neill was always courteous to Dowling, he was thoroughly dissatisfied with the directing and with the progress of the production. Before the opening O'Neill signed copies of the newly printed Random House edition of the play with personal notes for each of the eighteen actors and many production people. By this time it often took him as long as ten minutes simply to write the letters of his name.

When it opened October 9, *The Iceman Cometh* was very widely reviewed, and most reviewers found it disappointing. On the whole, a reviewer who might grasp one aspect of the play saw little else, and no one came close to understanding how much O'Neill had done and how intricately he had interwoven it all. In fairness to the critics of 1946, no one except possibly Nathan had the least inkling of how much O'Neill had developed artistically in the dozen years since his last new play had been performed. *The Iceman Cometh* remains by far the most complex and difficult to perform or interpret of O'Neill's later plays, its difficulties enhanced by the very qualities that give it beauty: by its fugal interweaving of (musical and ideational) themes and (vocal and characterological) voices.

Neither "realistic" nor surreal, not impressionistic, not an imitation of the Greeks, not an obvious response to a political idea or to Nietzschean philosophy or Freudian psychology, it seemed, most of all, a work wildly out of harmony with its time. Like the actors, almost none of the critics seemed to notice how often the play was funny. Just the opposite: all the best critics could do was to say that it resembled Gorky's *Lower Depths* and hope that the analogy would somehow help the reader know what they had been through.

The critics simply reflected the spirit of the time. Consider how few music critics in 1946 were ready to accept the symphonies of Mahler and Shostakovich, the works which *The Iceman Cometh* perhaps most nearly resembles. The times were optimistic, for a great war had just been won. The economy was booming, and the United States had newly emerged as leader of the "free" world. The country was more unified and homogenous than ever before or since. The time could not have been worse for O'Neill's deep questions about the universal human belief that we control our destinies and that we progress and improve. Whatever in the text might seem comic, including the cheery ending, simply bewildered critics and producers alike. It was asking too much to require cheerful people who had just won a war to sit for more than four hours in a theater watching a bunch of hopeless derelicts drinking themselves to death. To expect an audience to try to figure out some connection between themselves and the bums onstage—it was all too complicated. It would be years later, in 1954, that *The Iceman Cometh* would receive the production it deserved (under the direction of José Quintero and with Jason Robards as Hickey) and begin to have a public aesthetic existence.

Reviewers (like the actors and the director) found the play overly long, repetitive, simplistic in its ideas, yet also confusing; they charged it with being too much given to revealing essentially simple characters but also lacking in development of character or thought. O'Neill himself was held in such esteem that a few critics hedged their opinions. Hostile reviewers like Mary McCarthy and Eric Bentley, caught up in the coolly intellectual existentialist spirit of the 1940s and 1950s, ridiculed the play. In the time of Sartre and Beckett, of hipsters, beats, and cool jazz, O'Neill—with his heat and passion, his looking back to Nietzsche and Spengler, his turn-of-the-century slang, and his affinity for hot jazz—was no longer shockingly new, as he had been in the 1920s; and his late plays constituted a new continent, barely discerned, not yet discovered.

Despite *The Iceman Cometh*'s unpopularity with reviewers and a spotty production, the play ran for 136 performances. Nevertheless, it would be the last new O'Neill play to reach Broadway for eight years.

The paradox of O'Neill's situation after he had ceased to write was evident, even while his great saloon play was being viewed and criticized. O'Neill himself was an object of respectful national interest, his picture widely featured in major newspapers and on magazine covers—twice on *Time*. He was too frail to stand many interviews, but when, mumbling and hesitating as always, his speech made less articulate by the tremor, he spoke to a group of reporters, his thought was firm and clear. The interview was very widely published. Yes he knew he had gone against the grain in *The Iceman Cometh*. Instead of believing that the United States had achieved the most, he said, he thought it had achieved the least, because it had started out with more and better natural and human resources than any nation in history. That is what he had meant to work out in the rumored cycle of historical plays he had had to put aside and that came out in plays like *The Iceman Cometh,* written before the United States entered the war in Europe.

O'Neill was less bothered than might be expected by criticism and haphazard misunderstanding of *The Iceman Cometh*. He and Carlotta went to a few parties, and several anecdotes exist of the playwright's singing old bawdy songs into the late hours, and other anecdotes about him surrounded by admiring younger women. At such times he seemed hardly self-conscious at all about his tremor. Biographers seize upon such anecdotes because they are evidence of a few light moments during an increasingly gloomy time.

An old friend, the playwright Russel Crouse, and his wife Anna, became close to the O'Neills for a time and enjoyed the friendship greatly. O'Neill's tremor would sometimes abate enough to allow him to eat dinner with the Crouses, who would serve stew, a dish not too hard to handle. One such night Crouse invited Irving Berlin, who told Sheaffer that O'Neill remembered the words to old Berlin songs that even the composer had forgotten (LS, 588). Another occasion ended less happily. At a party given by the Bennett Cerfs, who also invited the Comminses, Burl Ives came to sing, and to O'Neill's delight, his songs got raunchier and raunchier. As usual Eugene remembered all the words. Finding herself alone in her disgust, Carlotta went home.

Not long after, following an old pattern, O'Neill composed a dedicatory Christmas note for Carlotta, full of guilt and apology.

25

The Long Voyage Home
1947–1953

DESPITE THE FAILURE OF *The Iceman Cometh* with critics and O'Neill's dissatisfaction with the performance, the Theatre Guild decided to open its next season with one of the other late plays. O'Neill would have preferred that it be *A Touch of the Poet*, but the Guild members believed *A Moon for the Misbegotten* had a better chance with the public.

Early in 1947, while *The Iceman Cometh* was still playing, the Theatre Guild began searching for a woman large in person and spirit, capable of ranging "from Greek tragedy to farce" and experienced enough to carry *A Moon for the Misbegotten*. No one having been found after some time, O'Neill himself interviewed a young, not very experienced actress of average size, Mary Welch, and gave her the part simply because her parents were from County Cork and because she convinced him (as she describes in a memoir) that she intuitively understood Josie's combination of "bluff and hurt and discovery" (Cargill, 87).

O'Neill must not have attended many rehearsals, for it became apparent that the director, the Guild, and the leading male actor had no idea how the play was meant to work. O'Neill was satisfied with Mary Welch but dissatisfied with James Dunn, who did not want to be in the play and who played Jim Tyrone as if he were a bum from Harry Hope's saloon.

O'Neill's complaints about the style and tone made no sense to Dunn or Arthur Shields, who directed, or to Lawrence Langner, any more than his urging that they play the first two acts for broad comedy and not let the tragic sense show itself much until act 3. Later, when it was discovered that Jim Tyrone was a portrait of the author's brother, the autobiographical nature of the play became an excuse for the Guild's failure. In his memoir, Langner remarked, "I felt that [O'Neill] idealized his brother, and would never accept any actor in the part" (Gelbs, 882).

The problems faced by the Guild and its actors were hardly minor. The O'Neill they had known in the 1920s was a different playwright from the one who had written the later plays. The later plays are deeper, subtler, and more complex in ways that are still hard to describe or explain, and so different from the plays of the earlier years that they seem to reduce in magnitude even the largest of the earlier achievements. During his dozen years of solitary writing, O'Neill had matured, and the artist had become more coherent and integrated with the man. At the same time, his plays had ceased to make any concessions at all to public mood or current values.

Too ill to do enough to change the production, and knowing that the Guild had had trouble finding enough plays to fill its season, O'Neill resigned himself to the inevitable. The play opened in Columbus, where censors roasted it for offensive language and "obscenity" and for alleged insults to the Irish. Eliot Norton of the Boston *Post* thought the play "profoundly beautiful," but he was almost alone in seeing its beauty. O'Neill sent Mary Welch a dozen red roses and a vote of confidence. From Columbus, the play moved to Pittsburgh, where it was declared shocking, and from there to Detroit, where it was closed by police not only for "profanity," the police censor said, but for "slander on American motherhood"—this because the words *mother* and *prostitute* occur once in the same sentence. Eight words were deleted, and the play went on for two weeks in Detroit, followed by a week in St. Louis. The Guild decided to recast the play with O'Neill's help and postpone it until the next season. The revised production did not materialize, and O'Neill would never see the opening of another of his unperformed plays, though he kept hoping to see *A Touch of the Poet* onstage.

Through the Langners, he met Patricia Neal and decided immediately to cast her as the daughter, Sara Melody, in *Poet,* if the Guild did the play. She told Sheaffer that she and O'Neill became friends, meeting occasionally in the Guild offices, and once, when his tremor was not too bad, they walked to an ice cream shop a few steps away. They talked about the theater, Hollywood, and books they both liked. Like his father before him, O'Neill gave career advice to a young actor. For years, Neal confided to Sheaffer, she had a clause in all her movie contracts that allowed her to take a leave of absence if she were wanted to do *Poet*. When Carlotta eventually found out about the friendship, she was furious and never forgave it, even though there seems never to have been an opportunity for anything but conversation between Patricia Neal and the playwright. (Years later, when Neal was about to be signed to play Abbie in *Desire Under the Elms*, negotiations were broken off without explanation immediately after Carlotta learned of them.) Through 1947–1948, relations between the O'Neills were almost constantly inflamed.

That fall O'Neill agreed to talk at length with Hamilton Basso, who planned a three-part profile for the *New Yorker*. Most of O'Neill's friends declined to be interviewed, either because they planned to write about the playwright themselves or because they feared that Carlotta would cut them off from Eugene. As Sheaffer reports, O'Neill himself proved unexpectedly cooperative. Basso told Sheaffer that he found O'Neill "the most incorrigibly honest man about himself I've ever met," and the playwright evidently showed the biographer more of himself than he had Basso's predecessors (LS, 599). Unable to corroborate facts and details with other witnesses, and under the spell of O'Neill's magnetism, Basso inevitably made numerous factual errors, some possibly planted by the playwright. Nevertheless, Basso gave a psychologically more complex and more credible portrait than any before. It is therefore particularly striking that when Sheaffer interviewed Basso, he learned that the *New Yorker* writer had not the least awareness that relations between the O'Neills were strained. Guarding their privacy as always, they apparently maintained a smooth front when the journalist was in their apartment, and he never guessed how difficult things were.

Carlotta now began to turn against Sherlee Weingarten, who had so far been immune to suspicions. In declining an invitation to a wedding party for Sherlee and her groom, Carlotta announced that she would instead have them to dinner after the wedding (which she did). Sherlee told Sheaffer that to everyone's surprise, O'Neill came alone to the party, his tremor barely visible, and he was soon surrounded by admiring young people who wanted to talk to him about the theater and about politics.

Mostly he listened, smiling, but it was obvious that he greatly enjoyed himself. One woman guest later declared to Sheaffer, "He was the warmest, friendliest person I ever met. He liked people . . . but he was shy—that's all." Sherlee herself took O'Neill home and kissed him on the cheek before he went into his building. O'Neill murmured to her that he was "going to catch hell" (LS, 603). O'Neill gave the couple, as a wedding present, a check representing a week's royalties for a production of *The Iceman Cometh* in Prague.

The Winthers arrived for a visit in November, and although the O'Neills appeared to get along when together, Carlotta took Eline aside to recite a litany of complaints about Eugene, including a detailed description of a near-murderous fight; Eline later wrote her narrative down in detail (it is in the Sheaffer papers) but said she found the complaints increasingly incredible and Carlotta's behavior inexplicable. The Winthers sensed a strain and somehow connected the tension with Freeman, who remained out of sight throughout the visit. Sheaffer hints that O'Neill suspected or discovered some sexual impropriety between Carlotta and Freeman. He fired Freeman a few weeks later.

At Christmas in 1947 O'Neill neglected to write his annual holiday greeting to Carlotta, and in making up for it three days later on her fifty-ninth birthday, he apologized and noted that he had "paid for [his neglect] in tears"; he acknowledged in writing "great need for your love, which is my life" (SL, 579). These autograph testimonials to his need for her and his gratitude were of the greatest importance to Carlotta, who later had them published in a volume she called *Inscriptions*. Apparently she believed that they would help secure a claim against his estate if the need ever arose.

The problems came to a head in mid-January 1948, while Saxe Commins happened to be visiting. Eleanor "Fitzi" Fitzgerald, who had held everything together for the Provincetown Players nearly thirty years before, was sick and broke, and afraid she had cancer. She needed money for advance payment for diagnostic tests at Mt. Sinai Hospital, which Eugene immediately agreed to send. Possibly transported back to what she considered an old insult, when Fitzi had failed to congratulate Eugene upon his marriage to her, Carlotta became enraged and, as Saxe reports, would not be pacified. He left in embarrassment. Eugene later went to his bedroom to escape her fury, but, as he later described the scene to Saxe, she followed him, smashed a thick glass top on his bureau that covered some pictures, seized one of him as an infant with his mother, and tore it to shreds, screaming, "Your mother was a whore." O'Neill slapped her, and she packed some clothes and left (Commins 1986, 220–23).

From Saxe's account we know that the next morning O'Neill took full blame for the fight and for Carlotta's departure. Eugene tried to make Saxe understand that there were reasons for Carlotta's explosion which he could not give, perhaps thinking of her bromide consumption or his fling with Jane Caldwell, perhaps of his belief that Carlotta was mentally ill and could not help herself. Saxe reported seeing detectives watching the O'Neills' apartment. On O'Neill's orders, Bill Aronberg hired his own detective to find Carlotta, who had gone to the New Weston Hotel. O'Neill sent her a letter pleading with her to return, which she ignored.

She would not speak to Eugene, but she made calls to several friends, including the Crouses. Her telephone monologues detailing her husband's sins and omissions had a ritualized quality. The pattern of such lists of complaints was compulsively repeated during the last ten years of Eugene's life and tended to elicit sympathy for Eugene and mistrust of Carlotta. These angry litanies may have been a feature of some neurological process, possibly a consequence of her many years of excessive use of bromide.

Alarmed by the severity of Eugene's tremor and distressed at his friend's mood, Saxe called Eugene's physician, Dr. Shirley C. Fisk, who found that his patient's tremor was at its worst, greatly impairing O'Neill's gait and balance. Dr. Fisk feared for the playwright's safety and warned Saxe and Eugene that the playwright should not be left alone. Saxe called in a New London friend of Eugene, Walter Casey, who lived in Manhattan. Casey came to the penthouse prepared to stay with his old friend as long as he was needed.

Late the night of January 28, Saxe left O'Neill with Casey, who had had several drinks. O'Neill may have drunk something also after Saxe left, although probably not very much, because the large doses of bromide he took for the tremor would have greatly magnified the effect of alcohol. Later, on his way to the bathroom, Eugene fell and broke his left shoulder. He could not rise. His voice impaired by the tremor, he could not cry out loudly enough to waken Casey from his sleep or to rouse a neighbor. Cold and faint with excruciating pain, he rolled himself in a rug and passed out. Casey, when he awoke and found his friend, called Dr. Fisk, who had Eugene taken to Doctors' Hospital in an ambulance.

Eugene Jr. came to the hospital almost every day, and at first he tried to persuade his father to leave Carlotta. But his father said only, "I can't live without her" (LS, 607). On February 10 O'Neill sent Carlotta a note for the anniversary of their elopement to Europe. She called Dr. Fisk to check on Eugene's condition but then launched into a tirade about his cruelty and his affairs with actresses. She checked herself into Doctors' Hospital, ostensibly because of arthritis, and stationed Freeman outside O'Neill's room with instructions to ask the name of every person he did not recognize who visited the playwright and to inform her who visited. O'Neill suddenly became worried about his manuscripts at the penthouse and had Casey take them to Saxe at Random House. Saxe made an inventory of the manuscripts and other papers and put them into the safe.

Carlotta guessed what Eugene had done and demanded that Saxe give the papers to her, but he refused. As Sheaffer describes it, "she screamed that Hitler had not killed enough of 'your kind,' called him 'a crook, a Jew bastard,'" and other names and slammed down the phone (LS, 609). She visited Eugene in his hospital bed and, as O'Neill told Russel Crouse, she deliberately moved his left arm to cause great pain to his broken shoulder (LS, 610).

Yet both O'Neills wanted a reconciliation, and for weeks negotiations went on. Both agreed that they could not return to the penthouse without being constantly reminded of dreadful events that had taken place there. They agreed to move to Boston and left Manhattan in April 1948.

After a month of searching the coastal areas around Boston, they bought a cottage situated at the tip of Marblehead Neck, almost surrounded by the waters of the harbor and open sea. O'Neill liked it because it reminded him of Monte Cristo Cottage and because it received the full brunt of wind and waves, almost like a ship at sea. Carlotta told the wife of the architect they hired to rebuild the cottage that it seemed like a "birdcage" (LS, 613). Carlotta cashed in the last of her stock investments, realizing about forty-eight thousand dollars, and bought the cottage for twenty thousand, believing that the rest of the money would be sufficient to cover remodeling. She hired Philip Horton Smith, who considered the purchase disastrously unwise. The birdcage was open underneath except for latticework, with no real kitchen, no heat, and minimal electric wiring. In the end, the cottage would cost nearly as much as they had spent building Tao House from scratch. The O'Neills found in the Smiths another buffer whose presence brought out the best in their relationship. The Smiths, for their part, liked both O'Neills, and Mrs. Smith told Sheaffer that at first they did not sense that the marriage was troubled.

In August, while the cottage was being winterized and modernized, came the latest turn in Shane's sad life. Shane was arrested for heroin possession on August 10, and he and Cathy frantically asked his father for five hundred dollars for bail. O'Neill reviewed the situation with Bill Aronberg. Shane could contest the charge, would probably be found guilty, and would be sent to prison; meanwhile he would in all likelihood resume using heroin while he was out of jail awaiting trial. Or he could remain in jail, plead guilty, and be sent to the federal treatment program at Lexington, a program that had a good reputation for rehabilitation at the time. Given the choices, and feeling guilty about whatever he did, O'Neill declined to pay his son's bail.

As we can infer from Sheaffer's conversation with a friend of Shane, Marc Brandel, being in jail or in treatment probably made Shane feel as if he had lost the meaning of his life, the meaning given by the need to obtain each day's supply (LS, 615). Yet he defended his father's refusal to pay his bail, even while resenting it. In any case, the Lexington treatment worked only for a while, and for the rest of his life, off and on, Shane was addicted to various drugs. About 1960, while Sheaffer was interviewing Agnes and seeing her frequently, he once found her bruised and confused, having apparently been attacked the night before by an intruder who she believed was probably Shane, looking for something he could pawn for drug money (LS papers).

In 1948, Shane's father must have been reminded not only of his mother and her addiction but also of his friend Louis Holladay, who had killed himself with heroin in January 1918, after a year of successful rehabilitation in Oregon. When Shane's story appeared in newspapers in August 1948, Carlotta urged her husband to tell the Smiths about his son. Hearing the story sent Carlotta off on a diatribe against children, her own ungrateful daughter included, during which she made the unfounded accusation to the Smiths that Shane and Cathy had "smothered" their first child.

The Smiths told Sheaffer that they began to wonder about Carlotta as they saw her moods and view of life change wildly from moment to moment and situation to situation. One morning Carlotta told Elinor at great length of her compassion for her husband in his inability to write; then, a few minutes later, breaking forth in a denunciation to Philip of Eugene, Carlotta recited her list of grievances. It seems likely that Carlotta's mood was affected by the unexpected cost she faced in remodeling the cottage, among other things (LS, 618).

The friendship with the Smiths ended abruptly, soon after the O'Neills moved into the cottage in September. Carlotta had invited Elinor to drop in whenever she felt the impulse. But when Elinor did drop in once, the O'Neills were apparently in the midst of a terrible fight. Elinor told Sheaffer that they looked like "two murderers, with the body still on the premises, who were being visited by the police. He was at one end of the porch looking fearful, and she was at the other end glowering. A great smile spread over his face when he saw me, but she stormed off upstairs" (LS, 618–19).

As if she were living their life of a decade before, Carlotta sent Elinor Smith a note informing her that the O'Neills never saw anyone without an appointment. "Gene spends a certain time in his study & is *never* disturbed," Carlotta wrote. "I have all his secretarial work to do—& . . . must have a rest period" (LS, 619). Carlotta had hated the house since they moved in and had been shocked at the cost of remodeling. Perhaps she turned against the Smiths for their connection to the house, or perhaps she began to doubt that they unreservedly believed all she said to them and therefore decided that they would no longer serve as buffers.

Mrs. Smith found the change in Carlotta as shocking as others had. Nearly everyone Sheaffer interviewed about the O'Neills during the years after they returned to New York reported similar impressions: that he was nice, sweet, shy, considerate, and that she seemed to range unpredictably in her behavior from great charm to frightening savagery and cruelty. Sherlee Weingarten's last encounter with Carlotta occurred when she answered a phone in the Theatre Guild offices during the time Carlotta and Eugene were separated. Sherlee told Sheaffer that when she had identified herself, Carlotta demanded: "'I want to speak to Miss Marshall. Get off the phone!' Her voice was so full of hate that I dropped the phone, and while I'm not the fainting kind, I almost blacked out" (LS, 607).

O'Neill had still not given up hope of resuming writing. In early December, on a day when his hands were quiet enough for him to write legibly, he told Nathan of his intention to get back to work. "God knows

I have plenty of ideas" (LS, 619). His Christmas greeting to Carlotta was also written in a fairly steady hand. His physician, Dr. Frederick B. Mayo, suggested that he try an experimental course of treatment, and he agreed, going to Boston Hospital for each treatment. But the cure did not help. Instead, it coincided with a worsening of the tremor and of O'Neill's condition in general. He had now mostly lost control of his legs and gait, and in a letter to Dr. Lyman of the Gaylord Sanatorium, he blamed the treatment for making him worse. Nevertheless, his condition, according to Dr. Mayo, was not as severe as people in late stages of Parkinson's disease might experience, and O'Neill was not affected with the Parkinson's dementia. He spent a good deal of time listening to his jazz records, and Carlotta came to loathe the sound, which she could not escape in the small, thin-walled house.

The O'Neills now saw very few people. The neck was a crowded tourist spot in the summer but almost deserted the rest of the year. Their doctor called frequently, and a policeman checked the house from time to time at Carlotta's request, perhaps four or five times over the winter, he told Sheaffer. A barber, who came every other week to trim their hair, said to Sheaffer that he considered O'Neill as great a man as Verdi and the players for the Boston Braves who had just been in the World Series. A Japanese-American houseman lived with them, and a woman came out daily from Marblehead to cook. In late summer 1949, the Winthers visited from Seattle. Eugene told Sophus he believed that his life had "come full circle," the meaning of which he did not elaborate (LS, 621). The Winthers said that O'Neill did not seem to them much changed from their last visit with him two years before (622).

Carlotta increasingly detested the house, but O'Neill resisted her pleas to move to some more convenient place. Sheaffer turned up a bill for repair work suggesting to him that sometime in the year 1950 a violent episode occurred. Someone, presumably Carlotta, tried to break down the door to Eugene's room from the outside. Probably she could stand the music no more, nor bear her husband's isolating himself from her.

As sequestered as they were, the world could still intrude. On September 25, 1950, Eugene Jr., whose tempestuous life had spun further and further out of control, killed himself at his cottage at Woodstock. A classicist to the end, he had chosen the Roman way, filling a tub with warm water and then slitting the arteries in his left wrist and ankle with a straight razor. Someone called Saxe with the news and asked that Eugene's father be told. Saxe, hating to deliver the news and reasoning that Carlotta would probably hang up on hearing his voice, called Bill Aronberg. Aronberg subsequently told Saxe that Carlotta's only response to the news was to rage, "How dare you invade our privacy!" and slam down the receiver (Commins 1986, 231). Carlotta, who gave the Gelbs and Sheaffer a somewhat different account of the phone call, claimed that when she hung up, she broke the news to her husband that his son was "very ill." O'Neill immediately guessed the truth and asked when Eugene had died (LS, 632). He paid for the funeral and sent a blanket of white chrysanthemums that almost concealed the coffin, a gesture that calls to mind Erie Smith's flowers for Hughie's funeral. No impression in words survives to indicate O'Neill's state of mind on his learning of his first son's death, but strong evidence nevertheless demonstrates the effect on him of his grief. He withdrew even further into himself, answering few letters and seldom talking. More ominously, he almost stopped eating and by the following February weighed less than a hundred pounds, having lost more than thirty pounds, about a quarter of his weight. The dramatist of mourning, who had spent two decades mourning for his parents, was dying of grief over his son's death.

After Eugene Jr. died, O'Neill agreed to let Carlotta sell the house. But there were no buyers, and the couple remained there through the next winter. The barber told Sheaffer that twice that winter Carlotta appeared to him with her breasts exposed and seemed to extend a sexual invitation, which he eluded by seeming not to notice it (LS, 637). Sheaffer suggests that her behavior was a further sign that a bromide psychosis was developing. It was certainly also a reaction to her husband's isolating himself from her.

On the night of February 5, 1951, escaping a fight, O'Neill fled outside into the snow, without a coat or the cane he used to help his balance. Dr. Mayo gave Sheaffer his impression that O'Neill may have gone outside that bitter night intending to die in the icy waters that nearly surrounded the house (LS, 637). If so, aside from the immediate battle with Carlotta, Eugene's suicide must have been much on O'Neill's mind. Saxe talked to Dr. Mayo and other witnesses and wrote a detailed account of his findings and impressions. Saxe's narrative is the main source of information about what happened that night.

O'Neill fell and broke his right leg at the knee. Fearing that he would freeze to death, O'Neill called out, and later he told Saxe that Carlotta appeared at the door when he had called, looked down on him, and said: "How the mighty have fallen! The master is lying low. Now where is all your greatness?" She then closed the door, leaving him in the snow, and shortly after, he blacked out (Commins 1986, 232).

After some time, Dr. Mayo arrived. Someone had called his office but had not suggested that there was an emergency. Probably it was the houseman, Mr. Narazaki. Dr. Mayo heard a moaning sound when he approached the house and found O'Neill lying in the snow. O'Neill weighed so little that Dr. Mayo could half-carry him into the house. O'Neill was taken to Salem Hospital. At the time Dr. Mayo was so occupied with Eugene that he paid little attention to Carlotta, but he noticed that she was not making sense.

The next night, the Marblehead Neck patrolman found Carlotta wandering in the snow and talking incoherently. Maintaining, "The air is full of people," she refused to go back into her house, so he went inside to call for help (LS, 639). Dr. Mayo drove out and followed a police car back to Salem Hospital, where Carlotta was admitted without a diagnosis, pending examination by a psychiatrist. She was considered disoriented and mentally confused, and her remark to the patrolman that the air was full of people suggests hallucinations as well. After O'Neill was informed, she was transferred to McLean Hospital, which had psychiatric facilities. There she was diagnosed with bromide psychosis. Years later, when interviewed by Sheaffer, Carlotta gave an account of O'Neill's accident and of their both being taken to hospital that is notably incoherent and internally inconsistent (LS, 637–38, and LS papers).

As usual, O'Neill immediately became a favorite of his doctors and nurses at the hospital: he tolerated pain and procedures without much complaint and asked for no special treatment. To his medication for the tremor, bromide and chloral hydrate, was now added a narcotic for pain, and the combination caused hallucinations. Once while Saxe sat on his bed chatting, Eugene thought he saw Carlotta climbing in the window and shrank back in terror; at other times, he saw people from his family, long dead. He did not, however, show signs of the disorientation and extreme confusion that Carlotta experienced in her bromide psychosis.

A prominent Boston psychiatrist, Dr. Merrill Moore, was now called into the case by Lawrence Langner in New York, who believed that the O'Neills should be separated from each other. As Sheaffer points out, Dr. Moore was anything but a disinterested party, for he was a cousin of

Ralph Barton, Carlotta's third husband (who had killed himself). No other doctor then or later questioned O'Neill's sanity; but Dr. Moore, ignoring the medical chart with its record of prescribed bromide, chloral hydrate, and narcotic, pronounced O'Neill unfit to care for himself and recommended an asylum or a legal guardian. His recommendation was ignored by O'Neill's physicians. Dr. Moore then visited Carlotta, who was by now recovering from her bromide psychosis. He condescendingly kissed her hand, she later told Sheaffer, said she was young and beautiful, and informed her that she must never see her husband again. "I could have slapped him for treating me like a fool," Carlotta said (LS, 644).

O'Neill refused to see her, and she became convinced that Moore was part of a plot devised by O'Neill to have her committed (as she related to Sophus Winther in a letter.) Indeed, there was a sort of conspiracy, although O'Neill had almost no part in it. Heavily sedated, and under pressure from Dr. Moore, O'Neill signed a petition alleging that Carlotta was insane and unable to care for herself and that the court should appoint a guardian for her.

In the meantime, Carlotta had been withdrawn from bromide, released from McLean Hospital with a prognosis of "good," and advised to consult a young psychiatrist, Dr. Harry Kozol. Shortly after checking out of the hospital, she learned of the guardianship petition and immediately got in touch with lawyers who filed a petition for separate maintenance. The petition initiated by Dr. Moore alleging her insanity was almost certainly the chief cause of the separation that followed.

At the urging of friends, O'Neill had gone to New York by train, and an ambulance drove him from Grand Central to a nursing home. Hating the place on sight, he immediately had himself transferred to Doctors' Hospital, where Dr. Shirley Fisk resumed his care of O'Neill. Dr. Fisk was dismayed at the deterioration in the playwright, whose weight had continued to drop and who seemed simply "skin and bones," as a nurse put it (LS, 646). O'Neill developed pneumonia after a week at Doctors' Hospital, lost another ten pounds, and seemed on the verge of dying. But he seemed to decide to live, and, with the help of penicillin, he recovered. Dr. Fisk eliminated his bromide treatment, and O'Neill's hallucinations ceased. But he was deeply depressed and passively uncooperative with rehabilitation efforts; he would go all day without speaking, even when spoken to by nurses.

Most of O'Neill's friends assumed that the marriage was over, and

O'Neill did not argue the point. Probably his own feelings changed from moment to moment in response to his thoughts or to whomever he was with. Sherlee Weingarten visited O'Neill frequently and at his request took care of his mail. He was so indifferent to the world that he did not even ask who his correspondents were or what they said, and he left it to her to devise answers. Sherlee feared that he would "become like a vegetable" (LS, 651).

Both lawsuits were dropped in April, and by the end of the month O'Neill had decided he wanted a reunion. At once, his spirits improved and he could occasionally make a joke. Knowing that his friends would disapprove, he kept his plans secret, but he told the Comminses.

On May 15 Saxe brought Eugene a large envelope from Oona. Dudley Nichols, who had visited O'Neill at Marblehead Neck, had tried to arrange a reconciliation with Oona and had urged her to fly to New York to see her father. But she could not, for she was in the final month of pregnancy with her fourth child. Instead, she had written her father and enclosed pictures of herself and the children (LS, 654). Oona received no response.

Saxe and Dorothy had invited Eugene to come and live with them in Princeton for the rest of his life and let them care for him, and it would surely have been an easier life than any he would face going back to Carlotta. Yet as he told the Comminses, he could "not even hold a cup of water." He could not bear for anyone except Carlotta to see him as he was or to look after things for him, and he felt he owed her everything, for she had sacrificed her life for him and his work. O'Neill put his arms around Saxe when they parted and called him "my brother." The Comminses left the hospital knowing that they would not see him again (LS, 654–55).

Sherlee visited him the day before he left for Boston to rejoin Carlotta and chatted as brightly as she could, knowing it was their last visit. By now he had regained twenty pounds. A nurse accompanied him on the train ride to Boston. Dr. Kozol met him at Back Bay Station with a wheelchair to take him to the Shelton.

The nurse who had accompanied O'Neill to Boston witnessed the reunion with Carlotta. Carlotta hugged and kissed him, and he seemed to the nurse to be relieved and happy to be home (LS, 657). Carlotta paid Eugene's hospital bills and repaid money he had borrowed from Lawrence Langner, after which she immediately cut off contact with nearly all O'Neill's friends. The cottage at Marblehead Neck finally sold for about fifty thousand dollars, Carlotta clearing about thirty thousand after paying off a mortgage made necessary by the cost of renovation.

The hotel overlooked the Charles, and O'Neill spent much of his time watching sailboats and sculls; or he read or listened to baseball games on the radio. He was now being given the sedative Nembutal for his tremor, and accounts describing his reaction to it conflict. Carlotta convinced Sheaffer that her husband became addicted to the drug and would demand it constantly. Dr. W. Richard Ohler, an internist who became O'Neill's general physician, believed that his patient was being oversedated by Carlotta to make him more passive (LS, 662).

Even so, the O'Neills would fight. Neighbors and hotel staff told Sheaffer of hearing a ferocious battle in Suite 401. Impatient with his helplessness, O'Neill was quick to take offense with Carlotta, and she became even more explosive than ever. They fought when O'Neill decided to publish *A Moon for the Misbegotten*. Carlotta, concerned for his declining reputation on Broadway, wanted the play revised to eliminate the description of Jim Tyrone sleeping with the "blonde pig" on the train. O'Neill refused, and the text appeared unrevised. Publication of the play had no immediate effect one way or the other on O'Neill's reputation. Most critics who still took O'Neill seriously considered the play slight; it sold very few copies and did nothing to improve the couple's financial situation. Revivals of *"Anna Christie"* and *Desire Under the Elms* received good reviews but had short runs.

In the winter of 1952–1953, O'Neill destroyed all the drafts and scenarios from the Cycle that he could find, other material already having gone to Yale. He was now nearly helpless, but because he had gained weight, he appeared healthier than a year or two before. In the summer of 1953, Oona, now living in Switzerland, gave birth to her second son, whom she named Eugene. It is not known whether her father ever learned of this namesake.

Carlotta said that in the final months O'Neill talked of suicide, but he seems not to have made any attempt, and if there was such talk, it may simply have expressed his extreme frustration at remaining sentient while imprisoned in a body he could not control. Indeed it would be hard to imagine not thinking of ending one's life, in such circumstances. In September O'Neill seemed to have given up and remained in bed most of the time. He lived on past his sixty-fifth birthday on October 16 but in late November developed an infection that turned into pneumonia. Carlotta told Sheaffer and others that near the end, O'Neill "suddenly struggled up to a half-sitting position and, staring wildly around the room, cried 'I knew it, I knew it! Born in a goddam hotel room and dying in a hotel room'" (LS, 670). He lost consciousness on November 26 and died the next day. In a letter to Oona, Saxe described his friend as the "gentlest and noblest man I ever knew" (LS, 672).

Carlotta told Sheaffer that she was determined to carry out her husband's wish for an entirely private funeral (LS, 671–73). She managed to outwit the press. O'Neill was buried at Forest Hills Cemetery at 9:30 A.M. on December 1, 1953, in a service that took but a few minutes, with no one present except Carlotta, Dr. Kozol, and a nurse who had helped Carlotta care for him. And two others who had guessed what Carlotta would do followed her car to the cemetery and watched from a distance. One was the barber who had cut O'Neill's hair at Marblehead Neck, and the other an English instructor from Brandeis who loved O'Neill's plays.

Notes

ONE

James and Ella

1. Eugene's design for his own tombstone gives a birth date for Bridget of 1829 (SL, 475 and note). Shaughnessy (1991) found Bridget's death certificate, giving her age as sixty, from which a birth date in the first seven months of 1827 can be inferred. Her husband's age was given as forty when he died in May 1874. If parish records are correct, Thomas must have been born about 1834. The Quinlan son, whose name is given by Alexander as William Joseph, seems to have been Joseph Dominick Quinlan, born in 1858, who died in Buffalo on June 10, 1911; Joseph Dominick Quinlan is buried in Lakeview Cemetery in Cleveland, where (I am told) "the social leaders and elite of Cleveland are buried" (letter from Chris Krosel, archivist of the Diocese of Cleveland).

2. In any discussion of Mary Tyrone's behavior the question of how morphine affects her thinking must arise. Judging by the difficulty the other Tyrones have in knowing whether she is back on the drug or not, its effect must be simply to heighten qualities she ordinarily has, to make her feel euphoric, to lower her inhibitions (especially those concerning the expression of anger), to help her fight more vociferously than usual against things she considers inconvenient or uncomfortable. As for her abrupt shifts from one psychic reality to another, the drug may make the shifts more fluid and labile than when she is not high, but it probably does not cause the shifts.

THREE

The Sons of Monte Cristo

1. Tyler described the incident in his autobiography written in old age, George C. Tyler and J. C. Furnas, *Whatever Goes Up* (Indianapolis: Bobbs, Merrill, 1934), 91–92. He gives a date for the incident as 1891, when Eugene would have recently passed his third birthday. There is reason to doubt Tyler's memory of the date. In 1891 Ella had the experienced and competent Sarah Sandy traveling with her to care for Eugene. It seems unlikely that two women used to the ways of young children would have become so frightened over a routine case of colic in a three-year-old. It is possible that the event instead occurred during Eugene's first win-

ter, when his mother had not yet recovered from childbirth and the nanny, if there was one, would have been a woman Ella barely knew.

SIX
Eugene Adrift

1. "Crimping," as explained by the Gelbs, involved coercing a drunken sailor into signing over his future pay to a boardinghouse operator in return for release of his sea bag, whereas a shanghaied sailor was usually unconscious when he was dumped on board an undermanned ship that would be at sea when the man awoke.

SEVEN
A Stroll on the Bottom of the Sea

1. Eugene glossed over the whole episode so successfully that as late as 1962 the Gelbs had to guess at when it happened—they concluded that it was sometime in May. Sheaffer makes a convincing circumstantial case for January.

NINE
Among God's Fools

1. My comments on the O'Neill-Ashe letters often parallel and sometimes diverge from those of James W. Hamilton (1979), whose discussion I discovered after I had studied the letters.

Annotated Bibliography

Writings of Eugene O'Neill
PLAYS

"The Ancient Mariner." Donald C. Gallup, ed. *Yale University Library Journal* 35 (1960).

The Calms of Capricorn: A Play Developed from O'Neill's Scenario by Donald Gallup, with a Transcription of the Scenario. New Haven and New York: Ticknor and Fields, 1982.

Complete Plays, 1913–1920; Complete Plays, 1920–1931; Complete Plays, 1932–1943. New York: Library of America, 1988. Texts selected and annotated by Travis Bogard. The standard edition. The third volume includes O'Neill's only published short story, "Tomorrow."

Eugene O'Neill, the Unfinished Plays: Notes for "The Visit of Malatesta," "The Last Conquest," "Blind Alley Guy." Virginia Floyd, ed. New York: Ungar / Continuum, 1988.

The Unknown O'Neill: Unpublished or Unfamiliar Writings of Eugene O'Neill. Travis Bogard, ed. New Haven, Conn.: Yale University Press, 1988.

Work Diary, 1924–1943. Preliminary edition. Transcribed by Donald C. Gallup. New Haven, Conn.: Yale University Library, 1981.

CORRESPONDENCE

Commins, Dorothy Berliner, ed. *"Love and Admiration and Respect": The O'Neill-Commins Correspondence.* Durham, N.C.: Duke University Press, 1986. Introduction by Travis Bogard. Correspondence of Eugene O'Neill and his editor Saxe Commins, with narrative continuity and commentary provided by Dorothy Commins.

Bogard, Travis, and Jackson R. Bryer, eds. *Selected Letters of Eugene O'Neill.* New Haven, Conn.: Yale University Press, 1988. An important collection with few duplications of letters in other collections.

Bryer, Jackson R., and Ruth M. Alvarez, eds. *The Theatre We Worked For: Letters of Eugene O'Neill to Kenneth Macgowan.* New Haven, Conn.: Yale University Press, 1982.

Roberts, Nancy L., and Arthur W. Roberts, eds. *As Ever, Gene: The Correspon-*

dence of Eugene O'Neill and George Jean Nathan. Rutherford, N.J.: Fairleigh-Dickinson University Press, 1987.

PERSONAL DOCUMENTS

The following holographs can be found in the Eugene O'Neill Collection Beinecke Rare book and Manuscript Library, Yale University.

[Autobiographical Narrative.] Untitled private account of the lives of the playwright's parents and his own early life, ca. 1926.
"Cycles." O'Neill's arrangement of events in his life into seven-year cycles, ca. 1946.
Untitled diagram depicting O'Neill's understanding of various trends and lines of psychological development in his life from birth through adolescence, ca. 1926.

MISCELLANEOUS PUBLISHED WRITINGS

"A Letter from O'Neill." *New York Times* (April 11, 1920). Reprinted in Oscar Cargill, N. Bryllion Fagin, William J. Fisher, eds., *O'Neill and His Plays: Four Decades of Criticism.* New York University Press, 1961. On *Beyond the Horizon.*
"Eugene O'Neill's Credo and His Reason for His Faith." *New York Tribune* (February 13, 1921). Reprinted in Oscar Cargill, N. Bryllion Fagin, William J. Fisher, eds., *O'Neill and His Plays: Four Decades of Criticism.* New York University Press, 1961. On *Diff'rent.*
New York Times (December 18, 1921). Letter on *"Anna Christie."*
"Strindberg and Our Theatre." *Provincetown Playbill* 1 (1923–24): 1, 3. Reprinted in Oscar Cargill, N. Bryllion Fagin, William J. Fisher, eds., *O'Neill and His Plays: Four Decades of Criticism.* New York University Press, 1961. Note on "The Spook Sonata."
"All God's Chillun." New York Times (March 19, 1924).
"Playwright and Critic: The Record of a Stimulating Correspondence." *Boston Transcript* (October 31, 1925). Correspondence with George Jean Nathan.
"Are the Actors to Blame?" *Provincetown Playbill* 1 (1925–26). Calls for a repertory theater.
"The Fountain." Greenwich Playbill 3 (1925–26).
"The Playwright Explains." *New York Times* (February 14, 1926). On *The Great God Brown.*
New York Times (March 7, 1926). Letter on *Goat Song* by Franz Werfel.
"Letter to George Jean Nathan." *American Mercury* (January 16, 1929): 119.
"O'Neill's Own Story of Electra in the Making." *New York Herald Tribune* (November 8, 1931).

"O'Neill Says Soviet Stage Has Realized His Dream." *New York Herald Tribune* (June 19, 1932). Reprinted in Oscar Cargill, N. Bryllion Fagin, William J. Fisher, eds., *O'Neill and His Plays: Four Decades of Criticism.* New York University Press, 1961. Letter to Kamerny Theatre concerning its productions of *Desire Under the Elms* and *All God's Chillun,* which he saw in Paris.

"Memoranda on Masks." *American Spectator* (November 1932): 3. Reprinted in Oscar Cargill, N. Bryllion Fagin, William J. Fisher, eds., *O'Neill and His Plays: Four Decades of Criticism.* New York University Press, 1961. Ideals for the theater.

"Second Thoughts." *American Spectator* (January 1933): 2. Reprinted in Oscar Cargill, N. Bryllion Fagin, William J. Fisher, eds., *O'Neill and His Plays: Four Decades of Criticism.* New York University Press, 1961. Continuation of the above.

"A Dramatist's Notebook." *American Spectator* (January 1933): 2. Further continuation.

"Professor George Pierce Baker." *New York Times* (January 13, 1935). Eulogy for his late teacher.

"Gustav Presents Nobel Prize to 3." *New York Times* (December 11, 1936). Gives text of acceptance speech written by O'Neill but not read in person because of illness.

Last Will and Testament of Silverdene Emblem O'Neill. Privately printed "for Carlotta." New Haven, Conn.: Yale University Press, 1956. Elegy for the O'Neills' dalmatian Blemie.

Inscriptions: Eugene O'Neill to Carlotta Monterey O'Neill. Privately printed. New Haven, Conn.: Yale University Press, 1960. Notes from Eugene to Carlotta on her birthdays, holidays, and occasions of gift-giving.

Poems, 1912–1944. New York: Ticknor and Fields, 1980. Reprints seventy-two of O'Neill's poems.

Bibliographies

Atkinson, Jennifer McCabe. *Eugene O'Neill: A Descriptive Bibliography.* Pittsburgh: University of Pittsburgh Press, 1974. Indispensable. Includes reproductions of covers and title pages.

Bryer, Jackson R. *Checklist of Eugene O'Neill.* Columbus, Ohio: Charles F. Merrill, 1971.

Frenz, Horst. "A List of Foreign Editions and Translations of Eugene O'Neill's Dramas." *Bulletin of Bibliography* 18 (1943): 33–34.

Miller, Jordan Y. *Eugene O'Neill and the American Critic: A Bibliographical Checklist,* 2d rev. ed. Hamden, Conn.: Archon Press, 1973.

Smith, Madeline, and Richard Eaton. *Eugene O'Neill: An Annotated Bibliography.* New York: Garland, 1988. Supplements Miller bibliography.

General Works

Alexander, Doris. *The Tempering of Eugene O'Neill.* New York: Harcourt, Brace, 1962. A biography to 1920. Particularly useful for newspaper accounts of the career of James O'Neill.

―――. *Eugene O'Neill's Creative Struggle: The Decisive Decade, 1924–1933.* University Park: Pennsylvania State University Press, 1992.

Baker, George Pierce. *Dramatic Technique.* Boston: Houghton Mifflin, 1919.

Barlow, Judith E. *Final Acts: The Creation of Three Late O'Neill Plays.* Athens: University of Georgia Press, 1985.

Basso, Hamilton. "The Tragic Sense." *New Yorker,* February 28, March 6, and March 13, 1948. Profile of O'Neill's life and work.

Bateson, Gregory, Don D. Jackson, Jay Haley, and John H. Weakland. "Towards a Theory of Schizophrenia." *Behavioral Science* 1 (1956): 251–64. Reprinted in Gregory Bateson, *Steps to an Ecology of Mind.* New York: Ballantine, 1972, 201–27. Defines the concept of the "double bind."

Berlin, Normand. *O'Neill's Shakespeare.* Ann Arbor: University of Michigan Press, 1993.

Black, Stephen A. "America's First Tragedy." *English Studies in Canada* 8 (June 1987): 195–203. On *Beyond the Horizon* as a "Greek" tragedy.

―――. "Ella O'Neill's Addiction." *Eugene O'Neill Newsletter* 9 (Spring 1985): 24–26.

―――. "Eugene O'Neill in Mourning." *Biography* 11 (Winter 1988): 16–34. States part of the thesis of the present biography.

―――. "Letting the Dead Be Dead: A Reinterpretation of *A Moon for the Misbegotten.*" *Modern Drama* 29 (December 1986): 544–55.

―――. "O'Neill's Dramatic Process." *American Literature* 59 (March 1987): 58–70. On *Long Day's Journey into Night.*

―――. "Reality and Its Vicissitudes: The Problem of Understanding in *Long Day's Journey into Night.*" *Eugene O'Neill Review* 16 (Fall 1992): 57–72.

―――. "The War Among the Tyrones." *Eugene O'Neill Newsletter* 11 (Summer–Fall 1987): 29–31.

Bogard, Travis. *Contour in Time: The Plays of Eugene O'Neill.* New York: Oxford University Press, 1972.

―――, ed. *The Eugene O'Neill Songbook.* Berkeley, Calif.: East Bay Books, 1993.

Boulton, Agnes. *Part of a Long Story: Eugene O'Neill as a Young Man in Love.* London: Peter Davis, 1958.

―――. *The Road Is Before Us.* Philadelphia: Lippincott, 1944. A novel.

Bowen, Croswell, assisted by Shane O'Neill. *Curse of the Misbegotten: A Tale of the House of O'Neill.* New York: Ballantine, 1959.

Brink, Andrew. *Creativity as Repair: Bipolarity and Its Closure.* Hamilton, Ontario: Cromlech Press, 1982. This and Brink (1977) are most important works for the study of the creative process. They argue that creativity serves to repair psychic wounds caused by the too-early loss of people on whom the (future) writer is dependent.

———. *Loss and Symbolic Repair.* Hamilton: Cromlech Press, 1977.

Cargill, Oscar, N. Bryllion Fagin, William J. Fisher, eds. *O'Neill and His Plays: Four Decades of Criticism.* New York University Press, 1961. An important collection of essays by and about O'Neill and his plays.

Carpenter, Frederick I. *Eugene O'Neill.* Boston: Twayne, 1979.

Cavell, Stanley. *Disowning Knowledge in Six Plays of Shakespeare.* Cambridge: Cambridge University Press, 1987.

———. *Must We Mean What We Say?* Cambridge: Cambridge University Press, [1969] 1976.

———. *The Senses of Walden.* San Francisco: North Point Press, 1981.

Chabrowe, Leonard. *Ritual and Pathos: The Theater of Eugene O'Neill.* Lewisburg, Pa.: Bucknell University Press, 1976.

Chaplin, Charles. *My Autobiography.* New York: Simon and Schuster, 1964.

Chase, Ilka. *Past Imperfect.* Garden City, N.Y.: Doubleday, 1942.

Chothia, Jean. *Forging a Language: A Study of the Plays of Eugene O'Neill.* Cambridge: Cambridge University Press, 1979.

Clark, Barrett H. *Eugene O'Neill: The Man and His Plays.* New York: Dover, 1967. Fifth revision and expansion of work first published in 1926; first edition contained revisions by O'Neill.

Commins, Dorothy Berliner, ed. *What Is an Editor? Saxe Commins at Work.* Chicago: University of Chicago Press, 1978. Biography of her husband, Saxe Commins, with emphasis on his long friendship with O'Neill.

Commins, Saxe, and Lloyd Coleman. *Psychology, A Simplification.* New York: Liveright, 1927.

Cowley, Malcolm. "A Weekend with Eugene O'Neill." *Reporter* (September 5, 1957): 33–36. Reprinted in Oscar Cargill, N. Bryllion Fagin, William J. Fisher, eds., *O'Neill and His Plays: Four Decades of Criticism.* New York University Press, 1961.

Crichton, Kyle. "Mr. O'Neill and the Iceman." In Kyle Crichton, *Total Recoil.* Garden City, N.Y.: Doubleday, 1960, 113–31. Reprinted in Mark Estrin, ed., *Conversations with O'Neill.* Jackson: University of Mississippi Press, 1990, 188–202.

Deutch, Helen, and Stella Hanau. *The Provincetown: A Story of the Theatre.* New York: Liveright, 1931.

Eldridge, Florence. "First Curtain Call for Mary Tyrone." In Virginia Floyd, ed., *Eugene O'Neill, A World View.* New York: Ungar, 1979.

Estrin, Mark, ed. *Conversations with Eugene O'Neill.* Jackson: University of Mississippi Press, 1990. Reprints interviews.

Falk, Doris V. *Eugene O'Neill and the Tragic Tension.* New Brunswick, N.J.: Rutgers University Press, 1958.

Floyd, Virginia. *Eugene O'Neill at Work: Newly Released Ideas for Plays.* New York: Ungar, 1981.

———. *Eugene O'Neill: A World View.* New York: Ungar, 1979. Essays and reminiscences, including presentations from the 1978 Modern Language Association conference.

Freedman, Albert M. "Opiate Dependence." In Harold Kaplan, et al., *Comprehensive Textbook of Psychiatry III,* vol. 2, 3d ed. Baltimore: Williams and Wilkins, 1980, 1591–1614.

Freud, Sigmund, 1912. "Recommendations to Physicians Practising Psycho-Analysis." In James Strachey, ed., *The Standard Edition of the Complete Psychological Works of Sigmund Freud,* vol. 12, 111–19. Joan Riviere, trans. London: Hogarth Press, 1958.

Gassner, John, ed. *O'Neill: A Collection of Critical Essays.* Englewood Cliffs, N.J.: Prentice Hall, 1964.

Gelb, Arthur, and Barbara Gelb. *O'Neill.* New York: Harper & Row. [1962] 1973. Enlarged ed. with a new epilogue (concerning Carlotta Monterey O'Neill).

Gelb, Barbara. *So Short a Time: A Biography of John Reed and Louise Bryant.* New York: Norton, 1973.

Hicks, Granville. *John Reed: The Making of a Revolutionary.* New York: Macmillan, 1936.

Glaspell, Susan. *The Road to the Temple.* New York: Stokes, 1927.

Hamilton, Gilbert V. *A Research on Marriage.* New York: Lear, 1929.

Hamilton, Gilbert V., and Kenneth Macgowan. *What Is Wrong with Marriage.* New York: Boni, 1929.

Hamilton, James W. "Early Trauma, Dreaming and Creativity: The Works of Eugene O'Neill." *International Journal of Psychoanalysis* 3 (1976): 341–64.

———. "Transitional Fantasies and the Creative Process." *Psychoanalytic Studies of Society* 6 (1975): 53–70.

———. "Transitional Phenomena and the Early Writings of Eugene O'Neill." *International Review of Psychoanalysis* 6 (1979): 49–60. Studies O'Neill's letters to Beatrice Ashe, as well as *The Personal Equation* and "The Sniper."

Hapgood, Hutchins. *An Anarchist Woman.* New York: Duffield, 1909. Gives an account of Terry Carlin's life.

———. *A Victorian in the Modern Age.* New York: Harcourt, Brace, 1939.

Jones, Robert Edmond. *The Dramatic Imagination.* New York: Duell, Sloan and Pearce, 1941.

Kantor, Louis [Kalonyme]. "O'Neill Lifts the Curtain on His Early Days." *New*

York Times (December 21, 1924). Reprinted in Mark Estrin, ed., *Conversations with O'Neill*. Jackson: University of Mississippi Press, 1990, 64–69.

Kellner, Bruce. *The Last Dandy: The Life of Ralph Barton*. Columbia: University of Missouri Press, 1991. Gives a vivid portrait of Barton's marriage to Carlotta Monterey.

Kenton, Edna. "The Provincetown Players and the Playwrights' Theatre, 1915–1922." Travis Bogard and Jackson R. Bryer, eds. *Eugene O'Neill Review* 21, nos. 1 and 2 (Spring/Fall 1997): 1–160.

Lewisohn, Lewis. "*All God's Chillun*." *Nation* 118 (June 4, 1924): 664. Reprinted in Jordan Miller, *Playwright's Progress: O'Neill and the Critics*. Chicago: Scott, Foresman, 1965.

Long, Chester Clayton. *The Role of Nemesis in the Structure of Selected Plays of Eugene O'Neill*. The Hague: Mouton, 1968.

McDonough, Edwin J. *Quintero Directs O'Neill*. Pennington, N.J.: A Capella Books, 1991.

Mandl, Bette. "Absence as Presence: The Second Sex in *The Iceman Cometh*." *Eugene O'Neill Newsletter* 6 (Summer–Fall, 1982): 10–15.

Manheim, Michael. *Eugene O'Neill's New Language of Kinship*. Syracuse, N.Y.: Syracuse University Press, 1982.

———, ed. *The Cambridge Companion to Eugene O'Neill*. Cambridge: 1998.

Martine, James J. *Critical Essays on Eugene O'Neill*. Boston: G. K. Hall, 1984.

Miller, Jordan Y. *Playwright's Progress: O'Neill and the Critics*. Chicago: Scott, Foresman, 1965. An important collection of reviews and criticism.

Miller, William D. *Dorothy Day: A Biography*. New York: Harper & Row, 1982.

Mollan, Malcolm. "Making Plays with a Tragic End." Philadelphia *Public Ledger Sunday Magazine* (January 22, 1922).

Nietzsche, Friedrich. *The Philosophy of Nietzsche*. Thomas Common et al., trans. New York: Modern Library, 1927. The translation O'Neill read. Includes *Thus Spake Zarathustra* and *The Birth of Tragedy*.

Pendleton, Ralph. *The Theatre of Robert Edmond Jones*. Middletown, Conn.: Wesleyan University Press, 1958.

Quintero, José. *If You Don't Dance They Beat You*. Boston: Little, Brown, 1974. On the director's life in the theater, with extensive commentary on his pioneering productions of O'Neill's late plays.

Raleigh, John Henry. *The Plays of Eugene O'Neill*. Carbondale: Southern Illinois University Press, 1965.

———. *Twentieth Century Interpretations of* The Iceman Cometh: *A Collection of Essays*. Englewood Cliffs, N.J.: Prentice Hall, 1968.

Ranald, Margaret Loftus. *The Eugene O'Neill Companion*. Westport, Conn.: Greenwood Press, 1984.

Reaver, J. Russell, comp. *An O'Neill Concordance*, 3 vols. Detroit: Gale Research Press, 1969.

Reed, John. *Ten Days that Shook the World.* New York: Boni and Liveright, 1919.

Robeson, Paul. *Here I Stand.* New York: Beacon Press, 1958.

Robinson, James A. *Eugene O'Neill and Oriental Thought.* Carbondale: Southern Illinois University Press, 1982.

Rycroft, Charles. *A Critical Dictionary of Psychoanalyis.* New York: Basic Books, 1968.

Sárlos, Robert Károly. *Jig Cook and the Provincetown Players: Theatre in Ferment.* Amherst: University of Massachusetts Press, 1982.

Sergeant, Elizabeth Shipley. "Eugene O'Neill: Man with a Mask." In Elizabeth Shipley Sergeant, *Fire Under the Andes: A Group of Literary Portraits.* Port Washington, N.Y.: Kennikat Press, 1927, 81–104.

Shaughnessy, Edward L. *Down the Nights and Down the Days: Eugene O'Neill's Catholic Sensibility.* Notre Dame, Ind.: Notre Dame University Press, 1996.

———. "Ella, James, and Jamie O'Neill." *Eugene O'Neill Review* 15 (Fall 1991), 5–92.

———. *Eugene O'Neill in Ireland: The Critical Reception.* New York: Greenwood Press, 1988.

Sheaffer, Louis. "Correcting Some Errors in Annals of O'Neill." *Comparative Drama* 17 (Fall 1983): 201–32.

———. *O'Neill, Son and Artist.* Boston: Little, Brown, 1973.

———. *O'Neill, Son and Playwright.* Boston: Little, Brown, 1968.

Simon, Bennett. "Poetry, Tragic Dialogue, and the Killing of Children in Eugene O'Neill's *Long Day's Journey into Night.*" *Hebrew University Studies in Literature and the Arts* 14 (Autumn 1986): 66–105.

Skinner, Richard Dana. *Eugene O'Neill: A Poet's Quest.* New York: Longmans, Green, 1935.

Timberlake, Craig. *The Life and Work of David Belasco.* New York: Library Publishers, 1954.

Tiusanen, Timo. *O'Neill's Scenic Images.* Princeton: Princeton University Press, 1968.

Tornqvist, Egil. *A Drama of Souls: Studies in O'Neill's Super-Naturalistic Technique.* Uppsala, Sweden: Universitatis Upsaliensis, 1968.

Vena, Gary. *O'Neill's* The Iceman Cometh: *Reconstructing the Premiere.* Ann Arbor: UMI Research, 1988.

Weissman, Philip. "Conscious and Unconscious Autobiographical Dramas of Eugene O'Neill." *Journal of the American Psychoanalytic Association* 5 (July 1957): 432–60.

———. *Creativity in the Theater.* New York: Basic Books, 1965.

Welch, Mary. "Softer Tones for Mr. O'Neill's Portrait." *Theatre Arts* (May 1957).

Reprinted in Oscar Cargill, N. Bryllion Fagin, William J. Fisher, eds., *O'Neill and His Plays: Four Decades of Criticism*. New York University Press, 1961.

Wilkins, Frederick C., ed. *The Eugene O'Neill Newsletter*, triannual, vols. 1–12 (1977–1988). Succeeded by *The Eugene O'Neill Review*, biannual, commencing 1989, in progress. A major source of current scholarship on all aspects of the playwright's life and work; international reviews of major performances; and current bibliography of research.

Winnicott, D. W. "Transitional Objects and Transitional Phenomena." In D. W. Winnicott, *Through Paediatrics to Psycho-Analysis*. Introduction by M. Masud R. Khan. New York: Basic Books, 1975, 229–42.

Winther, Sophus Keith. *O'Neill, a Critical Study*. 2d rev. ed. New York: Russell and Russell, 1961.

Acknowledgments

AMONG THE MANY INSTITUTIONS AND individuals that helped make possible the writing of this biography, I take pleasure in mentioning first the Canada Council and the Killam Program. A Leave Fellowship from the Canada Council in 1975–76 allowed me to take a year away from my home university, Simon Fraser University in Burnaby, British Columbia, and spend it in Seattle, where I was a research candidate at the Seattle Psychoanalytic Institute (now called the Seattle Institute for Psychoanalysis). It was there, in 1974–75, that I began planning biographical work on Eugene O'Neill (whose plays I had been reading with the greatest interest since about 1953). Twenty years later, the Canada Council, as administrators of the Killam Trust, awarded me a Killam Research Fellowship that allowed Simon Fraser to hire replacement teachers for my classes and permitted me to work full-time on the biography from late fall 1994 to fall 1996. For a writer, there can be no greater gift than the gift of time.

A substantial and generous grant from the Social Sciences and Humanities Research Council (SSHRC) of Canada allowed me to examine and photocopy documents and other material on O'Neill in the collections of the Beinecke Rare Book and Manuscript Library at Yale University, the Louis Sheaffer–Eugene O'Neill Collection at the Charles E. Shain Library at Connecticut College, the Performance Library of the New York Public Library at Lincoln Center, and the Berkeley home of the late Travis Bogard. A most important benefit of the grant was that it afforded me the painstaking and accurate research assistance of Susan McFarlane.

Simon Fraser University gave me various kinds of assistance, including several sabbatical leaves, which have enabled me to work on the biography. The university also provided financial assistance in the form of several small grants from the President's Research Grant fund that enabled me to do archival work in 1984, 1985, and 1986 at the Yale, Princeton, Harvard, and Columbia University libraries and at the New York Public Library at Lincoln Center. Simon Fraser University also allowed me to spend part of each week between 1974 and 1983 in Seattle, where, after teaching my classes for the week, I studied psychoanalytic theory and clinical process.

Perhaps even more important than the gifts of money has been the opportunity to talk with hundreds of Simon Fraser students since the mid-1960s about O'Neill and his plays. Listening to students read aloud parts in the plays sometimes gave me a sense of a character's voice that I had not been able to hear before; and talking with them about the characters and dramatic situation, hearing their reactions to my notions of O'Neill and his life—all these things and more allowed me to constantly refine and redefine my ideas and understandings. Indeed, it is hard to imagine a more satisfying way for a literary person to live than to have the opportunity to talk regularly in searching ways with bright people about works ranging from the Homeric narratives and Attic tragedy to Shakespeare and to the novelists, poets, and playwrights of the nineteenth and twentieth centuries.

My nearly nine years of involvement with the Seattle Institute were immensely interesting and stimulating for many reasons, the greatest being the opportunity to read, in the company of other committed people, and discuss, with the greatest engagement, nearly all of Freud's writings, as well as the writings of successive generations of psychoanalysts who have followed Freud and added new dimensions to psychoanalysis in their various ways. George M. Allison, then director of the institute and later president of the American Psychoanalytic Association, arranged for a nonmedical candidate to participate fully in three years of seminars, as well as case conferences and the other didactic meetings attended by the medical candidates. I particularly want to thank certain individuals for their help and instruction, beginning with Edith Buxbaum, who in 1929, along with Anna Freud, began studying child psychoanalysis with Miss Freud's father. Dr. Buxbaum eventually made her way to Seattle, where she established psychoanalytic education in the Pacific Northwest; in the 1970s she taught me about child development and child therapy and supervised a couple of my (adult) therapy cases. Theodore Dorpat demonstrated that Freud's work, read almost in full, and with close, critical, skeptical attention, remains of the greatest interest, though it may in some ways be an interest different from that which swayed Freud's original cohort. Charles Mangham taught memorable courses on child development and supervised observational studies of individual children. Werner Schimmelbusch provided a model for theoretical and clinical thinking.

The late Travis Bogard, the leading O'Neill scholar of his time, allowed me to come into his home every day for a week in September 1993, to study his photocopies of O'Neill's letters in the files he and Jackson R. Bryer compiled while preparing O'Neill's *Selected Letters*. Travis and Jackson also answered various questions from time to time. Edward Shaughnessy has been an inspiration in his friendship, in his courage in the face of adversity, and in his dedication to research on Irish-American affairs in general and O'Neill in particular. John Cody, a psychoanalytically trained psychiatrist, author of psychoanalytic work about Emily Dickinson and Richard Wagner, and a painter of genius, kindly read a draft of the first four chapters and commented helpfully. Sylvia A. Thorpe gave me the benefit of her expert knowledge of diagnosis and neurophysiology and also offered advice on early drafts of several articles on Eugene O'Neill. (These and other articles in which my biographical ideas on O'Neill and his plays were first published are listed in the bibliography.)

No work like this can be carried on without research archives and the people who make their use possible. I immediately think of numerous telephone conversations with librarians at the Vancouver Public Library who chased down many pieces of information and who are not allowed, by policy, to give their names to those they help. I can mention the "team" at the library's Newspaper and Magazine Division. I was similarly helped by librarians at the University of British Columbia medical library who found information, or gave their time to try to find it, and who were similarly anonymous. I would thank them all by name if I could. To them and to anyone I am not now able to remember, I give my thanks.

O'Neill gave a great store of his papers to the Yale University library in various installments during the 1940s and 1950s. The person most associated with this material is Donald C. Gallup, curator of the American Literature Collection and protector of its holdings and interests. Dr. Gallup gradually made O'Neill's manuscripts and personal material available to scholars with sensitivity to the interest of still-living persons. He took time in his retirement to answer various questions of mine. His successor, David Schoonover, went out of his way to make my trips to the Beinecke in 1985 and 1986 useful and fulfilling. I especially thank David for allowing me in 1985 to read and photocopy the typescript of *More*

Stately Mansions. It was at this time that I knew I had confirming evidence for my thesis interpreting O'Neill's psychological development. David's successor, Patricia Willis, has also helped in many ways, including arranging permission for me to quote from published and unpublished O'Neill material and helping me plan a research trip in 1995. Others at the Beinecke have been helpful over the years, especially Mary Angelotti, Stephen Jones, and recently Miriam B. Spectre, the archivist who has reorganized the O'Neill collections, and Ellen Cordes, who is in charge of Public Services for the Beinecke.

Over the years, several librarians at the W. A. C. Bennett Library at Simon Fraser University have helped in various ways as I have worked on O'Neill, including Aleksandra Zielinski, Gene Bridwell, the late Charles Watts of Special Collections, Heather Ann Tingley, Marjorie Nelles, and Percilla Groves. Ann Margret Malinski, former director of our media resources services, went out of her way time after time to help obtain filmed and taped versions of O'Neill performances for the benefit of my students and their teacher.

I take pleasure also in mentioning several other librarians: Chris Krosel, archivist of the Catholic Diocese of Cleveland, helped me track down information about Ella O'Neill's brother. At the Houghton Library, Harvard University, Marjorie Pepe assisted me during a research visit in 1986; and Fredric Woodbridge Wilson, curator of the Harvard Theater Collection, arranged for permission to quote from unpublished letters of Eugene and Agnes Boulton O'Neill. At the Boston University Library, Sean Noel, public services administrator, Department of Special Collections, arranged for permission to quote from unpublished notes by O'Neill to Jessica and Dolly (Grace) Rippin. At the Princeton University Library, Margaret M. Sherry arranged for permission to quote from O'Neill's letters to George Tyler. And at the Berg Collection of the New York Public Library, Rodney Phillips arranged permission for me to quote from O'Neill's unpublished letters to Beatrice Ashe and offered friendly encouragement.

Mimi Muray Levitt not only gave permission to use three portraits of Eugene and Agnes by her father, Nikolas Muray, but also recalled to me her mother's memories of her father's friendship with the O'Neills. Maura O'Neill Jones generously allowed the use of a snapshot of her father, Shane O'Neill, as a teenager. Raymond Wemmling of the Hampton-Booth Library at the Players kindly gave me the use of a 1915 photo of James

O'Neill Sr. Anne Easterling of the Museum of the City of New York, Vivian Gonzalez of the New York Public Library Theatre Collection at Lincoln Center, and Kevin Rettig, representing the Bettman Archives, also helped obtain permission to reproduce pictures. Barbara Burton or Maura Jones confirmed the unusual spelling of Barbara's grandmother's name, Cecil.

After the Beinecke, the archives of the late Louis Sheaffer constitute the richest storehouse of information about O'Neill. Brian Rogers, curator of the Sheaffer-O'Neill Collection, obtained the collection for Connecticut College and has spent the past seven years organizing it and helping O'Neill scholars who have dropped in for a look. He has helped in numerous ways to guide me through the material that had been organized and to help find things not yet fully classified. He helped me photocopy documents, and later, when I was trying to obtain copies of photos to use in the biography, he personally printed the copies and sent them to Yale University Press. He has become a good friend as well as a trusted and valued professional colleague.

Margaret Loftus Ranald read an early draft of the first four chapters and later read the entire manuscript, as expert reader for the Yale University Press. She wrote more than twenty pages of greatly helpful comments on substantive matters in the manuscript, and then, as I revised, discussed these matters and many others related to the book and the revisions, via E-mail that crossed the continent sometimes more than once a day. Professor Ranald, John Cody, Travis Bogard, Jackson Bryer, Michael Manheim, Judith Barlow, and Frederick Wilkins allowed themselves to be nominated as evaluators for my Killam Research Fellowship and my SSHRC Research Grant applications. All these people, and particularly Professor Ranald, saved me (and the reader) from various errors of fact and style.

Jonathan Brent, the editorial director of Yale University Press, arranged in 1993 for the press to publish the book. Jonathan and his assistant Sally Anne Brown were helpful during the subsequent five years of writing and revising. Joanne Richardson read page proofs and prepared the manuscript.

My son and friend Gordon Black provided lodging, logistical support, and good company during a 1993 research trip. Beyond the specific help, he has been a source of hope, encouragement, and good cheer.

At every step since 1991 in the writing of this book, my wife, Georgina, has given the fullest support it is possible for me to imagine, the least of which was helping me photocopy seemingly endless amounts of archival material. She has also helped he read the proofs, every word, every comma. More importantly, she constantly encouraged my work by reading the drafts of each chapter as they emerged. She tolerated without complaint the preoccupation and absentmindedness of one who was spending most of his time in another world—a world complex and troubling for an outsider to enter, as O'Neill's world is. She has made these years rich and memorable and full.

S. A. B.

Index

Fontanne, Lynn, 350
Ford, Colin, 175
Fordham University (St. John's College), 58, 68
Forest Hills Cemetery (Boston), 505
Forrest, Edwin, 3, 61
Fountain, The: composition of, 268, 270–71, 274, 293; production, 331–32; mentioned, 274, 291, 368
France, Anatole, 64, 322
Francis, John A., 191, 197, 201, 214, 223, 225, 235
Francis's Flats (Provincetown), 223
Frank, Waldo, 198
Frazer, Mrs. (character in *Servitude*), 171
Frazer, Sir James, 268
Freeman, Herbert, 403, 404, 439, 457, 473, 494, 496
French Revolution, 16, 399, 404
Freud, Sigmund, 28, 89, 122, 143, 190, 199, 203, 224, 300, 321, 322, 327, 336, 428, 479–80, 488

Gallup, Donald C., 396
Ganey, Dr. Joseph, 124, 332
Garbo, Greta, 262
Garden Hotel (New York City), 186, 187, 196, 210, 417
Gaylord Farm Sanatorium, 131, 132, 133, 134, 135, 154, 499
Gelb, Arthur and Barbara, xv, 3, 8, 12, 14, 16, 18, 21, 23, 62, 64, 65, 66, 68, 82, 83, 84, 99, 102, 105, 106, 112, 114, 115, 118, 126, 127, 131, 137, 138, 139, 154, 155, 157, 162, 163, 165, 175, 177, 181, 182, 188, 192, 203, 209, 228, 276, 299, 301, 302, 336, 349, 357, 485, 486, 492, 500, 507n
Gelb, Barbara, 222
Ghost Sonata, The (Strindberg), 306, 308
Gilpin, Charles, 265–66, 269, 273, 316
Gilpin, Rev. William, 101
Gish, Lillian, 371
Givens, Catherine. *See* O'Neill, Mrs. Shane
Glaspell, Susan (Mrs. George Cram Cook), 189–93; 224–25, 232, 234, 235, 238, 239, 244, 248, 310; and Provincetown Players, 189–93, 195; on O'Neill; 189; trip to Greece, 276, 290, 309

Glendale (Calif.), 274, 277, 282, 284, 285, 296, 297
Gold: composition of, 224, 239, 256, 258, 264; production, 266, 270
Golden Bough, The (Frazer), 286
Golden Swan (bar). *See* Hell Hole
Goldman, Emma, 89
Gorky, Maxim, 87, 175, 488
Grace Cathedral (San Francisco), 474
Great God Brown, The: composition of, 313, 319, 322–27, 329; discussion, 287, 323–28; production, 266, 270; mentioned, 187, 306, 328, 331, 368, 380
Greece, 190, 276, 290, 309, 380
Greek mythology, 90, 369, 381
Green, Elizabeth (first wife of Eugene O'Neill, Jr.), 371, 430
Greenwich Village: Eugene O'Neill in, 91, 113, 181, 194, 203, 215; Eugene Jr. in, 483; Shane in, 434, 484
Greenwich Village Theater, 313
Gregory, Lady, 116, 124
Group Psychology and the Analysis of the Ego (Freud), 321, 322
Guéthary, France, 359, 361, 362
Guilty One, The (play by Elinor Rand, pseud. of Agnes Boulton O'Neill), 316

Hairy Ape, The (short story), 186, 204
Hairy Ape, The (play): composition of, 273; production, 274, 275–76, 289–90; opening, 278–79; Carlotta Monterey in, 343; Louis Wolheim in, 273, 276, 279, 289, 316; mentioned, 57, 113, 186, 203
Hamilton, Bermuda, 329
Hamilton, Clayton, 159, 162, 181
Hamilton, Dr. Gilbert V., 300, 332, 335, 336–37, 340, 318
Hamilton, Dr. James, xv, 63, 183, 507n
Hammond, Edward Crowninshield, 128, 163
Hardy, Doc (character), 128, 131
Hardy, Thomas, 249
Harlem, 331
Hartford, 86
Harvard University, 159, 162, 163, 164, 167, 175, 181, 183, 199, 222, 235, 238, 239, 242, 244, 245, 246, 247, 248, 249, 250, 251, 252, 270, 348, 403, 425

treatment, 319, 330–31, 332; consults Dr. Wilkinson about alcoholism, 321; reads Freud, Nietzsche, 321–22; stops drinking, 333, 343; treatment with Dr. Gilbert V. Hamilton, 332–38; reads Greek dramatists, sociology, psychologies, ancient religions, 340; receives honorary doctorate from Yale, 341; reputation grows, 341–42; meets Carlotta Monterey, 342–43; and theme of mourning in *Strange Interlude*, 344–48; writes *Dynamo*, 360, 361, 362; takes cruise to Asian ports, 363–66; gets Saxe Commins a job as editor at Boni and Liveright, 382; leases and remodels Le Plessis, 366–67; divorced by Agnes, 367; and death of Fifine Clark, 367; and marriage to Carlotta, 367; and theme of mourning in *Dynamo*, 368–69; writes *Mourning Becomes Electra*, 368–72; returns to U.S. with Carlotta, 371; has idea for play about dead O'Neills, 372–73; O'Neills lease Park Avenue apartment, 374; and Shane and Oona's visit, 375; and Cynthia and Nellie Tharsing's visit to Carlotta, 375–76; begins *Days Without End*, 376; and purchase of building lots in Georgia, construction, 375; sells Park Avenue lease at loss, 375; moves into Casa Genotta, 378; writes *Ah, Wilderness!*, 378–80; finishes *Days Without End*, 386; goes to New York because of tremor and other illnesses, 388–93; begins work on Cycle, 394–400; moves to Seattle, 400; awarded Nobel Prize, 400; moves to San Francisco, 401; nearly dies after emergency appendectomy, 401–402; builds Tao House, 403–404; finishes draft of *More Stately Mansions*, 404; writes *The Iceman Cometh*, 418; and Eugene Jr.'s problems, 429–32; and Shane's problems, 432–35; gets to know Oona, 436; as health deteriorates, begins *Long Day's Journey*, 438; finishes revisions, 441; writes *Hughie*, 447; begins *A Moon for the Misbegotten*, 455; and bombing of Pearl Harbor, 455; when Shane joins Merchant Marines, Eugene Jr. is rejected for service, 456; begins revising Cycle play *A Touch of the Poet*, 457; break with Oona, 457–58; Oona marries Chaplin, 459; finishes revising *Poet*, 460; resumes work on *A Moon*, 463; move from Tao House to San Francisco, 470; marriage deteriorates, 470–79; return to New York, 480; when Shane marries, 484; when grandson, Eugene III, dies of SIDS, 485; and Theatre Guild production of *The Iceman Cometh*, 487–90; when guild produces *A Moon*, which fails in tryouts, 491–92; Carlotta leaves him, 495; breaks shoulder, 495; marriage resumes, 496; buys and remodels cottage on Marblehead Neck, 496–98; and Shane's arrest for heroin, 497; when Eugene Jr. kills himself, 499–500; after fight, breaks leg in snow, 500; and Carlotta's hospitalization in bromide psychosis, 501–502; when O'Neills again separate, reconcile, 502–503; dies, 505. See also *Long Day's Journey into Night*: Edmund Tyrone; Autobiographical narrative (O'Neill's); "Cycles" (O'Neill's life chronology); Diagram, life; *individual titles of plays and names of family members, friends, and places*

O'Neill, Eugene Gladstone, Jr., 102, 139, 314, 375, 433; birth, 105; and mother, 139; and step-father, 271; and grandmother, 271; renamed, 271; military school, 271; reunion with father, 272; resumes birth name, 272; visits father, 291, 322, 329, 371, 378, 400, 454; and Barbara Burton, 291, 314; sees Strindberg's *Ghost Sonata*, 306; marriage to Elizabeth Greene, 371; divorce, 430; graduation from Yale, appointment to Yale Classics faculty, 429; co-edits *Complete Greek Drama*, 429; and Carlotta, 430, second and third marriages, 430; alcoholism and depression, 431–32; reads *Long Day's Journey* and *The Iceman Cometh*, 454; rejected by military services, 456; father confides about tremor, 472; out of touch with father, 474; and Ruth Lander, 483; in Greenwich Village, 483; and Shane, 484; and

O'Neill, Eugene Gladstone, Jr.
(*continued*)
father, 484, 487, 496; death of, 499–
500
O'Neill, Eugene Gladstone III (grandson): birth, 105; death, 499–500
O'Neill, James, Jr. (brother): birth, 23; nursing, 40; childhood oedipal conflicts, 28; and death of Edmund Burke O'Neill, 38; at Notre Dame School, 37, 41–42, 43, 44, 53–58; intolerance for ambivalence, 47, 50; as mother's ally, 52–53; oedipal conflicts, 52–53, 287–88; symbiosis with mother, 53; as rival to father, 53; discover's mother's addiction, 58; leaves Notre Dame, goes to Georgetown, 58; at St. John Prep School, 58, 68–71; expulsion from St. John's, 71; and Eugene, 44, 62, 64, 65, 69–71, 73–74, 287–88; and death of father, 252, 258; after father died, 267, 270, 274; and death of mother, 274–75, 277–80, 282–86; and Marion Reed, 277, 283–86; and mother's will, 283–87; and Agnes Boulton, 206, 297, 291; death of, 296–98; relationship with mother represented in *More Stately Mansions*, 408, 415, 416, 424–25; partial model for Hickey in *The Iceman Cometh*, 422, 424–25. See also *Long Day's Journey into Night:* James Tyrone, Jr.; *A Moon for the Misbegotten*
O'Neill, James, Sr. (father): birth and family, early life, education, 1–2; early career, 3–6; acted with Edwin Booth, 4; affair with Nettie Walsh, 3–5, 6, 8, 14–15, 19–22, 65, 69, 101; paternity suit, 19–22, 69; affair with Louise Hawthorne, 5–6, 14, 15, 22; meets Ella Quinlan, 4, 7, 8, 9, 14–15; marries Ella, 15–17, 18–20; devotion to Ella, 18, 23, 36, 129, 265, 305; and Passion Play and arrest for blasphemy, 25–26; devoutness, 25; loss of artistic ideals, 26–27; 266; behavior with money and property, 23–24, 26, 30, 32, 34, 35, 36, 127, 130–32, 136, 163, 182, 237, 240, 277, 282, 393; and Kathleen Jenkins, 101–102, 105–106; decline of career, 95–97,

123–24, 127, 246; and Agnes Boulton, 226–27, 233; death of, 252, 259–60. See also *The Count of Monte Cristo; Long Day's Journey:* James Tyrone
O'Neill, Oona (Lady Chaplin): and mother (Agnes Boulton), 315; birth of, 318, 328, 329, 330; infancy of, 335, 339, 348; loss of father, 348, 358; and Mrs. Clark, 339, 367; visits father, 375–76, 436–437, 452–53; and father, 433, 441; break with father, 458–59; meets and marries Charlie Chaplin, 459–60; inheritance of Spithead, 485; writes to father, 503; names second son Eugene, 504; and Saxe Commins on death of her father, 505
O'Neill, Shane Rudraighe: birth, 235–36; colic, 239, 246; and mother (Agnes Boulton), 213, 239–43, 246, 247, 250, 258, 292, 316, 328, 330, 358, 435; and grandparents, 237; and Fifine Clark ("Gaga"), 237, 274, 314, 328, 335, 358; loss of, 358; death of Mrs. Clark, 367; fear of tuberculosis, 434; and father, 213, 348, 371, 375, 389, 438, 439, 453, 484; break with father, 486; and education, 375, 433, 439 (*see* Lawrenceville; Art Students' League); maritime service, 456; suicide attempt, 484; and addiction, 434, 484; marries Catherine Givens, 484; and birth of Eugene O'Neill III, 484; and death of baby, 485; in Bermuda, 485; arrested for heroin possession, 497; treatment at Lexington, 497; and Carlotta, 371, 435, 439; and Eugene Jr., 291, 378, 484; and Oona, 330, 453; as model for Don Parritt (in *The Iceman Cometh*), 429; mentioned, 100, 102, 238, 245, 249, 270, 292, 339, 376, 400
O'Neill, Mrs. Shane (Catherine Givens), 484–85
Oresteia (Aeschylus), 340, 368, 369, 429
Orestes (character), 90, 369, 419
Othello, 4, 19, 21, 22, 147, 248; and *Recklessness,* 347–48

Pabst's Cafe, 88
Palmer, A. H., 5, 6, 14, 19, 21, 22, 23
Pan (god), 97, 322, 327